*Second Edition*



# Ancient Civilizations

**Christopher Scarre**
*McDonald Institute for Archaeological Research*
*Cambridge University*

**Brian M. Fagan**
*University of California, Santa Barbara*

Prentice Hall

Upper Saddle River, New Jersey 07458

Library of Congress Cataloging-in-Publication Data

Scarre, Christopher.
Ancient civilizations / Christopher Scarre, Brian M. Fagan.—2nd ed.
p. cm.
Includes bibliographical references and index.
ISBN 0-13-048484-9
1. Civilization, Ancient. I. Fagan, Brian M. II. Title.

CB311 .S33 2003
930—dc21

2002070382

AVP, Publisher: Nancy Roberts
Project Manager: Joan Stone
Cover Director: Jayne Conte
Cover Designer: Bruce Kenselaar
Director, Image Resource Center: Melinda Reo
Manager, Rights and Permissions: Zina Arabia
Interior Image Specialist: Beth Boyd-Brenzel
Photo Researcher: Elaine Soares
Cover Image Specialist: Karen Sanatar
Cover Photo: British Museum, London/SuperStock, Inc.
Cover Image: an ancient Archaemenid gold statue of two human figures in a chariot drawn by a team of horses. 5th-4th century B.C.
Prepress and Manufacturing Buyer: Ben Smith
Senior Marketing Manager: Amy Speckman
Marketing Assistant: Anne Marie Fritzky

This book was set in 10/12 Palatino by TSI Graphics
and was printed and bound by Hamilton Printing Company.
The cover was printed by Phoenix Color Corp.

Prentice Hall


Pearson Education, Inc.
Upper Saddle River, New Jersey 07458



Printed in the United States of America

10 9 8 7 6 5

ISBN 0-13-048484-9

Pearson Education LTD., London
Pearson Education Australia PTY, Limited, Sydney
Pearson Education Singapore, Pte. Ltd
Pearson Education North Asia Ltd, Hong Kong
Pearson Education Canada, Ltd., Toronto
Pearson Educación de Mexico, S.A. de C.V.
Pearson Education—Japan, Tokyo
Pearson Education Malaysia, Pte. Ltd
Pearson Education, Upper Saddle River, New Jersey

# Contents

# Part V: Northeast Africa and Asia

## Part VI: Early States in the Americas

# Preface

> Three thousand, four thousand years maybe, have passed and gone since human feet last trod the floor on which you stand, and yet, as you note the recent signs of life around you—the half-filled bowl of mortar for the door, the darkened lamp, the fingermark on the freshly painted surface, the farewell garland dropped on the threshold. . . . Time is annihilated by little intimate details such as these, and you feel an intruder.
>
> Egyptologist Howard Carter, notebook entry on Tutankhamun's tomb, November 26, 1922

Ancient civilizations tempt romantic visions of the past: golden pharaohs, great cities and temple mounds, lost palaces mantled in swirling mists. The discovery of the Assyrians, Homeric Troy, and the Maya civilization of Central America was one of the nineteenth century's great adventure stories. Archaeologists like Englishman Austen Henry Layard, who dug biblical Nineveh, and New Yorker John Lloyd Stephens, who revealed the ancient Maya to an astonished world, became celebrities and bestselling authors. They and other early excavators are the prototypes of the swashbuckling Indiana Jones of late twentieth-century movie fame. The romance continued into the 1920s, culminating in Howard Carter and Lord Carnarvon's dramatic discovery of the undisturbed tomb of the pharaoh Tutankhamun and Sir Leonard Woolley's spectacular excavation of the Royal Tombs at Ur in Iraq. Even today, the occasional spectacular find, like the terracotta regiment of the first Chinese emperor Qin Shihuangdi or the Lords of Sipán in coastal Peru, reminds us that archaeology can be a profoundly exciting endeavor.

The nineteenth century was the century of archaeological adventure. The twentieth saw archaeology turn from a casual pursuit into a complex, highly specialized academic discipline. *Ancient Civilizations* describes what we know about the world's early civilizations today, 150 years after John Lloyd Stephens and artist Frederick Catherwood stumbled through the ruins of Maya Copán and Paul-Emile Botta and Austen Henry Layard electrified London and Paris with spectacular bas-reliefs from Assyrian palaces. This book is about science and multidisciplinary research, not about adventure and romance, an attempt to summarize state-of-the-art knowledge about preindustrial civilizations in every corner of the world. We draw on many avenues of inquiry: on archaeological excavations, surveys, and laboratory work; on highly specialized scientific investigations into such topics as the sources of volcanic glass and metals; and on both historical and ethnohistorical records. In the final analysis, this book is a synthesis of science and ancient voices, for in many cases the latter add telling detail to a story reconstructed from purely material remains.

*Ancient Civilizations* is divided into six parts that lead logically from one to the other. Part I gives essential background, some key definitions, and historical information. It also describes some of the major theories concerning the development of civilizations, one of the key controversies of archaeology for more than a century. Part II focuses on the very first civilizations: Sumer, Egypt, the Indus Valley, and the earliest Chinese states. Parts III and IV build on earlier foundations and trace later civilizations in the Near East and the Mediterranean. This book is unique in that it describes Classical Greek and Roman civilizations, whose roots lie much deeper in the past than many authorities would have one believe. Part V links the Mediterranean and Asian worlds with the discovery of the monsoon winds of the Indian Ocean about 2,000 years ago. Finally, the last four chapters, Part VI, describe the remarkable states of Mesoamerica and the Andean region of the Americas. An epilogue rounds off the narrative.

This book provides the reader with a straightforward narrative account of the ancient civilizations from their first appearance in the Near East some 5,000 years ago to the Spanish Conquest of Mexico and Peru in the early sixteenth century A.D. As such, it is written from a global perspective and without forcing it into a particular theoretical framework—this results both from the variability in the ancient societies themselves and from the diversity of the ways that they have been researched in recent decades. Chapter 2 summarizes major theoretical viewpoints and makes the point that the development of state-organized societies was a complex, multifaceted process, which took hold in many parts of the world. It also stresses that there were no overall principles or rules that governed this process. Rather, each civilization is a reflection of local conditions and of the distinctive worldview that shaped its institutions. Divine kingship is characteristic of Egyptian civilization, the Khmer, the Maya, and the Inka. But that does not mean that divine monarchy originated in one place and spread to all parts of the world thereafter. If there is a theoretical bias to this book, it is that each early civilization was a unique society, an attempt by human beings (as individuals and groups) who subsisted in very different environments to deal with problems of rising populations; increasingly cheek-by-jowl living conditions; and ever greater economic, political, and social complexity. We know that each instructor will use this book in a different way, each bringing his or her theoretical emphases to the narrative in these pages, so this approach seems appropriate.

We have elected to provide Guides to Further Reading at the end of each chapter rather than a comprehensive bibliography because the individual literatures for each area are now so complex that they are confusing, even for specialists. The works cited in the chapter-by-chapter guides will give readers access to the more specialized literature through widely quoted standard works and some guidance through a myriad of specialized monographs and periodical articles.

Inevitably, a book of this nature is a compromise, both in geographical coverage and in topics selected for more detailed discussion. We are also limited in our ability to illustrate the complex archaeological record of these societies. Perceptive readers will notice, for example, that we do not describe sub-Saharan African kingdoms in this book. Although they have sometime been described as "civilizations" or "states," they did not qualify for those terms until relatively recent centuries, so we made a conscious decision to omit them here. Readers who wish to delve into early African kingdoms should consult Graham Connah's admirable *African Civilizations, Second Edition*. By the same token, our coverage of many aspects of Egyptian and Mesopotamian civilization is inevitably sketchy, especially in the areas of religion, philosophical beliefs, and literature. The Guides to Further Reading refer the reader to works that cover these subjects in detail. Our primary concerns are to achieve balanced geographical coverage and to place the world's ancient civilizations in as broad an archaeological and historical context as possible. We believe that one can understand these societies only by seeking their roots deep in the past, by understanding their local environments, and by placing them in both an indigenous and a broader perspective. We hope we have succeeded.

## Highlights of the Second Edition

The second edition of *Ancient Civilizations* has been revised throughout to reflect the latest advances in the field, and it includes suggestions by both instructors and students who have taken the trouble to contact us after reading the first edition. There is new coverage throughout the book, specifically of new discoveries and the latest theoretical advances.

### *Updating and Rewriting*

- *New perceptions of the origins and collapse of states.* Chapter 2 reviews the issue of sustainability. A new generation of research into climate change is revising perceptions of the vulnerability of early states to environmental and climatic shifts.
- *The first civilizations.* New discoveries, surveyed in Chapters 3 and 4, are changing long-established ideas on the origins of Sumerian and Egyptian civilization.
- *South Asian and Southeast Asian Civilization.* Chapters 5 and 13 describe entirely new understandings of these civilizations derived from recent fieldwork.
- *Revision and updating throughout.* The entire text and Guides to Further Reading have been revised and updated on a page-by-page basis.

### *Boxes*

Three types of in-text boxes enhance the book, designed to amplify the narrative:

- *Discovery.* These boxes describe important finds that changed our perceptions of an early civilization.
- *Sites.* Important sites of unusual interest and significance receive special coverage.
- *Voices.* Some chapters include special boxes that quote from writings of ancient times, giving an unusual "voice" to the text.

### *New and Revised Art Program*

The second edition's art program has been expanded with new photographs and fresh or revised line art. These illustrations provide additional background on recent discoveries, amplify the narrative, or replace older art with new pictures. Some expanded captions serve to integrate the illustrations more closely into the text.

### *Complete Redesign*

The entire book has been completely redesigned to make it more user-friendly.

## Acknowledgments

This book results from years of experience, visiting sites in all parts of the world, and from many hours of discussion with colleagues. It is impossible to name all these individuals personally. We hope they will take this collective acknowledgment as an inadequate reflection of our gratitude for their advice and intellectual insights.

A number of scholars reviewed the manuscript while it was in preparation. We are grateful to Gina Barnes, Joan Oates, Nicholas Postgate, Jane McIntosh, Christine Morris, and Charles Higham for reviewing the Chinese, Mesopotamian, South Asian, Aegean Bronze Age, and Southeast Asian chapters, respectively.

Detailed criticisms also came from the following reviewers: Thomas H. Charlton, University of Iowa; Jeffrey T. Clark, North Dakota State University; and Michael Kolb, Northern Illinois University.

We are deeply grateful to Nancy Roberts of Prentice Hall for her encouragement and support at every turn, to her assistant Lee Peterson for many kindnesses, and to the production team in-house, who made the process of turning a complex manuscript into a book a (comparative) pleasure.

Chris Scarre
Brian M. Fagan

# About the Authors

Chris Scarre is an archaeologist specializing in the prehistory of Europe and the Mediterranean, with a particular interest in the archaeology of Atlantic façade (Iberia, France, Britain, and Ireland). He took his MA and PhD at Cambridge, the latter a study of landscape change and archaeological sites in western France. He has participated in fieldwork projects in Britain, France, and Greece and has directed excavations at Neolithic settlement and mortuary sites in western France. His early work was published in *Ancient France*. He is currently Deputy Director of the McDonald Institute for Archaeological Research, University of Cambridge, and editor of the twice-yearly *Cambridge Archaeological Journal*. As a Fellow of Girton College, Cambridge, he teaches a wide range of archaeological subjects from early stone use in the Paleolithic to the expansion of the Roman Empire.

His research interests include the relationship of prehistoric monuments to their landscape setting, the use of color in prehistoric societies, and the development and character of early state societies. Recent papers have considered the meanings which prehistoric societies may have attached to natural landscape features in Brittany, and the manner in which those meanings were given material expression through the construction of burial mounds or settings of standing stones. The nature of early farming societies along the Atlantic façade in relation to theories of demographic displacement is reviewed in a number of articles published since 1992. His latest field project is the excavation (together with French colleagues) of a prehistoric burial mound at Prissé-la-Charrière in western France.

As Deputy Director of the McDonald Institute he is involved with the wider research programs of the Institute that include field projects in Europe and the Middle East and laboratories specializing in the analysis of faunal and botanical remains.

Brian Fagan is one of the leading archaeological writers in the world and an internationally recognized authority on world prehistory. He studied archaeology and anthropology at Pembroke College, Cambridge University, and then spent seven years in sub-Saharan Africa working in museums and in monument conservation and excavating early farming sites in Zambia and East Africa. He was one of the pioneers of multidisciplinary African history in the 1960s. Since 1967, he has been Professor of Anthropology at the University of California, Santa Barbara, where he has specialized in lecturing and writing about archaeology to wide audiences.

Professor Fagan has written seven best-selling textbooks: *Ancient Lives: An Introduction to Archaeology; In the Beginning; Archaeology: A Brief Introduction; People of the Earth; World Prehistory; Historical Archaeology* (with Charles E. Orser)—all published by Prentice Hall—that are used around the world. His general books include *The Rape of the Nile,* a classic history of Egyptology; *The Adventure of Archaeology; Time Detectives; Floods, Famines, and Emperors: El Niño and the Fate of Civilizations; Ancient North America;* and *The Little Ice Age.* He is General Editor of the *Oxford Companion to Archaeology.* In addition, he has published several scholarly monographs on African archaeology and numerous specialized articles in national and international journals. He is also an expert on multimedia teaching and has received the Society for American Archaeology's first Public Education Award for his indefatigable efforts on behalf of archaeology and education.

Brian Fagan's other interests include bicycling, sailing, kayaking, and good food. He is married and lives in Santa Barbara with his wife and daughter, four cats (who supervise his writing), and, last but not least, four rabbits.

# PART I

# Background

Between them Sennacherib and his hosts had gone forth in all their might and glory to the conquest of distant lands, and had returned rich with spoil and captives, amongst whom may have been the handmaidens and wealth of Israel. . . . Through them, too, the Assyrian monarch had entered his capital in shame, after his last and fatal defeat.

Austen Henry Layard (1853: 212) on the human-headed bulls that guarded Assyrian King Sennacherib's palace at Nineveh.

*Chapter 1*

# The Study of Civilization

King Assurbanipal's lion hunt. (© Copyright The British Museum.)

*The chariot rattles over the plains as the driver clutches the reins, steadying the horses so the king can take better aim. Bowstring pulled taut, Assurbanipal, supreme ruler of the mighty Assyrian empire, stands ready to fire a volley of arrows against the fleeing lions. Already he has had good sport in the royal park, killing or wounding several of them in a show of kingly skill. Suddenly king and driver hear a roar behind them. An injured lion breaks cover and charges the chariot, seeking to kill its tormentors, but the royal attendants are too quick. Stationed on the back of the chariot for just such an emergency, they thrust their long-handled spears into the lion's chest. The great beast falls dead in the dust. . . .*

The modern visitor can see this scene, carved in stone, in the Assyrian gallery of the British Museum. It is one of the many monuments of "civilization" that fill great Western museums, be it the Louvre in Paris or the Metropolitan in New York. Wander into adjacent galleries and you will find mummiform coffins from ancient Egypt and intricate bronze ritual vessels from early China. Just around the corner will be red-figured vases from classical Athens or marble busts of Roman emperors. Many enthusiastic and intrepid tourists venture further afield and visit the places from which these priceless relics originated. They wonder at the sheer size of the pyramids in Egypt or at the desolation that now surrounds many of the ancient cities of Mesopotamia. They sail the Aegean, tracing the routes taken by ancient Greek mariners 2,500 years ago. Or they wander over the Maya ball courts of lowland Mexico, pondering just how the game was played, or climb the steep hill to the "lost" Inka city of Machu Picchu in Peru.

All these are remains of what today we call "ancient civilizations" (Figure 1.1; Table 1.1). Their study has attracted both archaeologists and the general public since at least the rebirth of Western learning in the sixteenth century. *Ancient Civilizations* describes these extraordinary early societies, using archaeological evidence and historical records, oral traditions, and scientific evidence from many academic disciplines. Thus, our story comes not only from modern science but from the voices of those who created the early civilizations as well.

In space and time, the societies we will describe span five thousand years and cover most regions of the world: from the first cities of the ancient Near East, around 3500 B.C.; through Egypt and China, classical Greece and Rome; to the New World civilizations of the Maya and Olmec; ending with the Aztec and Inka empires, which were flourishing at the time of the Spanish conquest in the sixteenth century A.D.

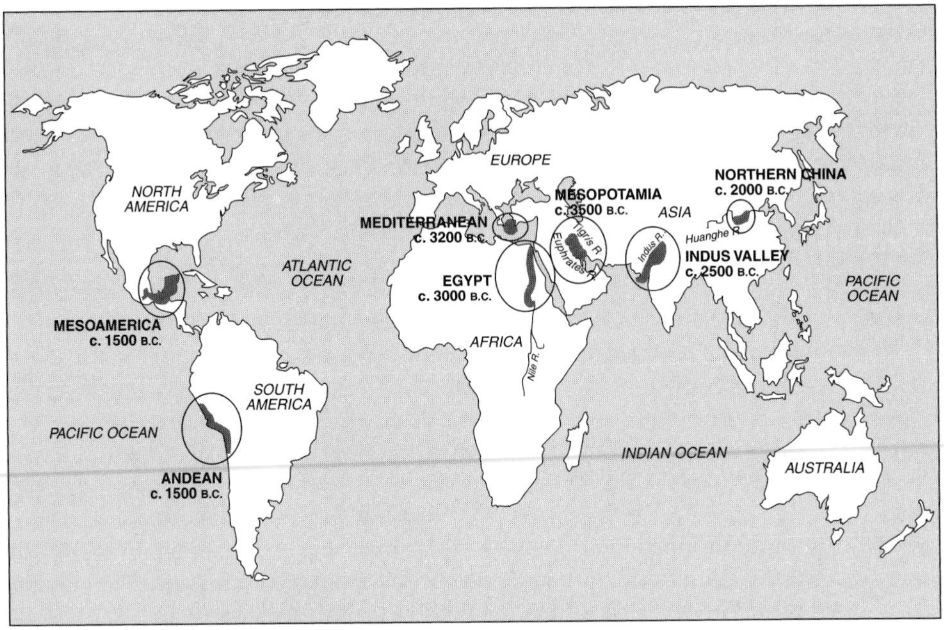


**Figure 1.1** The distribution of early world civilizations.

## What Is a "Civilization"?

The proper definition of civilization has occupied the minds of archaeologists, anthropologists, and historians for generations. An enormous scholarly literature surrounds this complex subject, but for the purposes of this volume we must content ourselves with a simple, if possible all-embracing, working definition that covers a great multitude of complex, early civilizations.

According to that ultimate arbiter of the English language, the *Oxford English Dictionary,* "to civilize" is "to bring out of a state of barbarism, to instruct in the arts of life; to enlighten and refine." The notion that "civilization" is a condition superior to "barbarism" underlay Victorian doctrines of racial superiority of more than a century ago and lives on today in the popular understanding of the word. But it has no place in archaeology. Archaeologists do not regard civilizations as better than hunter-gatherer societies or those of small-scale farmers, only different. It is perhaps only natural to admire the grandiose monuments, the powerful artworks, and the evocative literature left by the ancient Romans or Egyptians. These give us a vivid picture of complex societies, in some senses comparable to our own. But they are not "better" than earlier or contemporary less complex societies.

Politically minded commentators might well draw the opposite conclusion: that the ancient civilizations, with their privileged elites and centralized governments, were worse places to live for the ordinary peasants or the urban populace.

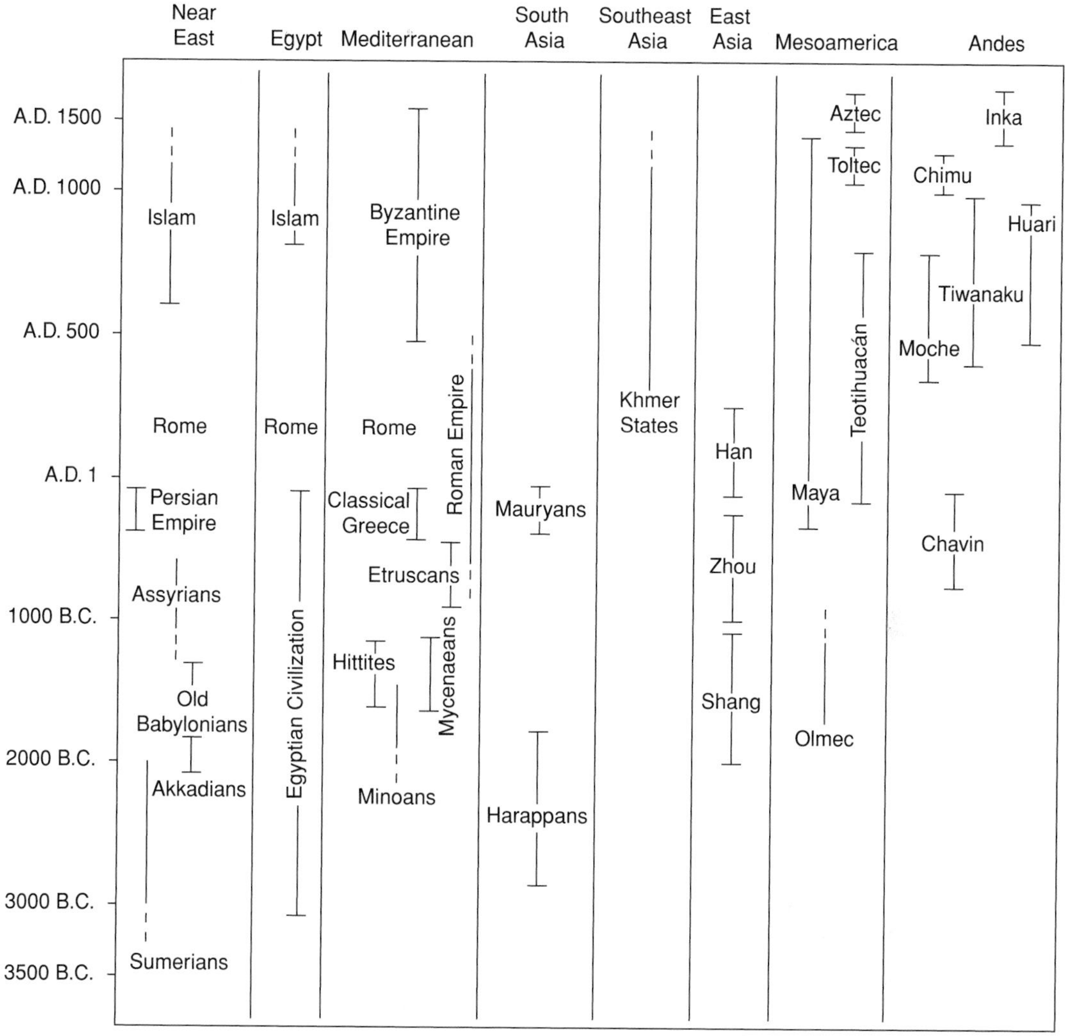


**Table 1.1** Chronological Table of the World's Early Civilizations.

There is certainly ample evidence of the cruelty that so-called civilized societies could inflict on their enemies, or even on their own subjects, through warfare, slavery, coercion, and punishment. Even in Classical Athens, home of the philosophers Socrates and Plato, there were probably as many slaves condemned to working the lead and silver mines as there were male Athenians who were citizens. Furthermore, many of the artworks we so much admire today were produced for an elite and were seen by only a privileged few. Yet the achievements of the early civilizations are undeniable, and we must not underestimate their significance to world history.

It is really only in the twentieth century, and particularly during the past half century, that archaeologists have finally abandoned the idea of civilization as a condition superior to other types of human society. A hundred years ago, the climate of scholarly opinion was very different. Nineteenth-century archaeologists and anthropologists were heavily influenced by theories of biological and social evolution developed by the biologist Charles Darwin and the social scientist Herbert Spencer. In his *Origin of Species*, published in 1859, Darwin had shown that in the natural world, it was only the fittest plants and animals that survived and that "natural selection" was the guiding force in making others extinct. Early social scientists attempted to apply the same reasoning to human societies. They saw well enough that urban literate societies (civilizations) were replacing less complex societies throughout the world, and they considered this to be proof that civilizations were in an evolutionary sense "superior." French archaeologist Gabriel de Mortillet summarized this thinking and the achievements of nineteenth-century archaeologists in a guidebook to the archaeology exhibits at the Paris Exposition of 1867: "A Law of Human Progress, a Law of Similar Human Development, and a High Antiquity for Humanity."

English anthropologist Sir Edward Tylor was one of the fathers of Victorian anthropology and a fervent believer in human progress. He surveyed human development in all of its forms, from crude Stone Age axes found in France to Maya temples in Central America and finally to Victorian civilization. Tylor reemphasized a three-level sequence of human development popular with eighteenth- and early-nineteenth-century scholars: from simple hunting "savagery" through a stage of simple farming to "barbarism," and then to "civilization," the most complex of human conditions. Tylor's contemporary, American anthropologist Lewis Henry Morgan, went even further. In his *Ancient Society* (1877) he proposed no fewer than seven distinct periods of human progress, starting with simple savagery and culminating in a "state of civilization."

Such doctrines of unilinear (single-line) cultural evolution remained popular well into the twentieth century. In the 1930s and 1940s, Australian-born archaeologist V. Gordon Childe refined this general approach in *What Happened in History* (1942). He equated "Savagery" with the hunter-gatherers of the Palaeolithic and Mesolithic, "Barbarism" with the farmers of the Neolithic and Copper Age, and "Civilization" with the Bronze Age communities of the Near East. As "barbarism" was superior to "savagery," so was "civilization" to "barbarism." Childe believed that progression from one condition to the next needed little explanation, only the opportunity to be presented for societies to make the change. These emotive terms are no longer acceptable in modern archaeological thinking.

Today, archaeologists use the term *civilization* as a shorthand for urbanized, state-level societies. These are sometimes called "preindustrial civilizations" because they relied on manual labor rather than fossil fuels such as coal. Not everybody accepts the definition in such simple terms. Some scholars have even drawn up long lists of features that they feel societies must possess to qualify as civilizations. Such lists often include writing and metallurgy. The limitations of this approach are obvious. For example, the Inka of the Andes did not use writing, yet they had centralized government, substantial cities, an ordered and hierarchical society, specialized craft skills, metallurgy, and an elaborate network of roads and rest houses. Few would deny them the status of a civilization.

How, then, do archaeologists recognize and define a civilization? This is a difficult area of discussion. We have already referred to two of the primary characteristics: urbanization (the presence of cities) and the state (a centralized political unit). These features in turn need to be defined:

- A city is a large and relatively dense settlement, with a population numbered in at least the thousands. Small cities of the ancient world had 2,000 or 3,000 inhabitants; the largest, such as Rome or Changan (China), may have had over a million.
- Cities are also characterized by specialization and interdependence between the city and its rural hinterland and between specialist craftspeople and other groups within the city. The city is what is termed a "central place" in its region, providing services for the villages of the surrounding area while at the same time depending on those villages for food. Most cities, for example, would have had a marketplace where agricultural produce could be exchanged.
- Cities also have a degree of organizational complexity well beyond that of small farming communities. There are centralized institutions to regulate internal affairs and ensure security. These usually find expression in monumental architecture such as temples or palaces or sometimes a city wall. Here we must recognize an overlap between the concept of the city and the concept of the state. States, too, are characterized by centralized institutions. It may be possible to have states without cities; but it is hard to envisage a city that is not embedded within a state.

An ancient city site will usually be obvious to archaeologists, both from its size and from the scale of its remains. The state is more difficult to define. It is essentially a political unit, governed by a central authority whose power crosscuts bonds of kinship. Kin groups do not disappear, of course, but their power is reduced, and a new axis of control emerges that is based on allegiance to a ruling elite.

Cities and states are not the only factors that have been cited in historical attempts to define civilization. One of the most famous attempts was made by V. Gordon Childe, whom we have already mentioned. In 1950, he drew up a list of traits that he considered to be the common characteristics of early civilizations throughout the world. More recently, archaeologist Charles Redman has divided Childe's list into "primary" and "secondary." The primary characteristics include cities and states, together with full-time specialization of labor, concentration of surplus, and a class-structured society. The five secondary characteristics are symptoms or by-products of these major economic and organizational changes: monumental public works, long-distance trade, standardized monumental artworks, writing, and the sciences (arithmetic, geometry, and astronomy).

We have already noted the shortcomings of such lists of shared traits. Whether they can ever be considered an adequate "definition" of a civilization is open to question. Furthermore, as we have seen, not all civilizations possess all of Childe's ten traits, although they nonetheless provide a handy checklist of items we might expect to find.

This is a book about preindustrial civilizations drawn on a very wide canvas. Many surveys of early civilization confine themselves to the first states and to the controversies surrounding the origins of civilization, one of the great issues in archaeology. We have chosen instead to describe early civilizations on a global basis and their development over long periods of time. For instance, in the Near East, we cover not only the first city-states but also the empires of Assyria and Babylon. In the Mediterranean region, where many surveys of early civilization stop with the fall of Late Bronze Age Mycenae in about 1200 B.C., we have included chapters on the Greeks, Carthaginians, Etruscans, and Romans. In East Asia, coverage of the earliest Chinese civilization, that of the Shang, is followed through in a later chapter on the Han empire, where the emergence of states in Korea and Japan is also outlined. Similarly, in the Americas, we cover the entire 3,500-year trajectory of state-organized societies in Central and South America.

## Comparing Civilizations

The world's early civilizations developed along many different lines while at the same time sharing some fundamental core features, such as social complexity, that define them as civilizations. Cities are characteristic of both Sumerian and Mayan civilizations on different sides of the world. The Egyptians buried their monarchs under pyramids; so did the Maya. Social inequality is common to all early civilizations, as is a strongly centralized government headed by a minority who controlled all valuable resources and the loyalty and labor of thousands of commoners. Force, or the threat of force, was all-important as a means of coercing rivals and rebellious citizens. The Egyptians, the Khmer of Cambodia, and the Aztecs of Mexico all had forms of divine kingship, but there the resemblances end. Comparison is helpful at a different level, however, one that does not seek to establish grand theories but merely to describe or review similarities and differences. This is the approach taken by Canadian archaeologist Bruce Trigger, who in a recent book has endeavored to situate ancient Egypt (the focus of his own research) by comparing it with other civilizations in such features as population density, technology, religious beliefs and practices, legal systems, and family and community organization.

Trigger emphasizes an important distinction between civilizations based on city-states (such as those of Mesopotamia, the Maya, or Greece) and those (such as Egypt, the Inka, and Shang China) that were territorial states. He points out that in city-states the city's populace made up the whole spectrum of society, with craftspeople, farmers, and the elite. The cities themselves were hubs of commercial activity, with flourishing markets. By contrast, in territorial states the earliest cities were principally political centers. Farmers lived in the rural hinterland in small settlements, secure without walls (since territorial states were less afflicted by internecine strife). Trigger argues that in territorial states the interaction between rural farmers and urban centers was largely in the form of taxes paid by the farmers to the city-based bureaucracies. The farmers were less reliant on urban craftspeople and markets than they were in city-state societies.

Contrasts and parallels such as those proposed by Trigger are thought provoking and provide valuable new insights. They do not explain everything—why in China, for instance, the cities of the Shang civilization (which he classifies as a territorial state) were elite centers whereas those of the succeeding Zhou period (also territorial states) were true cities. But they do invite us to address general questions and to consider why human societies in very different contexts in widely separated parts of the world chose to adopt such strikingly similar solutions, a point we return to shortly.

## Civilizations and Their Neighbors

One fundamental feature shared by every civilization is a dense concentration of people. This is the basis of both city-dwelling and state formation. Small bands of hunter-gatherers or subsistence farmers do not build cities, nor do they create territorial states. It is large concentrations of people that make these achievements possible or perhaps even make them necessary. Small-scale societies manage to survive quite successfully without the burdensome economic and political organization necessary to support and regulate city life. Once several hundred people are living in a single settlement—whether we would call it a large village or a small city—it becomes essential to have some centralized authority to give direction to the community and resolve disputes. Gradually, as a result of this process, these large populations become qualitatively as well as quantitatively different from other societies around them. It is not just that there are more people crowded into a small space (be it a single city or a limited area of fertile farmland). Rather, they begin to organize themselves differently, to have distinct ideologies and social institutions. It is these innovations that identify them as civilizations.

High population densities were a feature of all early civilizations. Organizing this rich human resource made possible the pyramids of Egypt and the Shang tombs at Anyang. But large populations also had a major impact on surrounding areas. Early civilizations were not hermetically sealed units. They generated a new level of need for raw materials, and those that were not found within their own territories had to be imported from abroad. Consider Mesopotamia as a typical example. The famous early cities such as Ur, Uruk, and Babylon were in the south of the country, a fertile plain fed with water by the twin rivers Tigris and Euphrates. This was a land rich in crops and clay but hardly the place to find hard stone for tools, still less the copper, tin, and gold that were increasingly in demand by urban elites. To obtain these raw materials, Mesopotamian traders had to travel far afield, to the Zagros Mountains, the Taurus range of southern Turkey, across the Iranian plateau, or by ship to Oman or India. Here they came into contact with communities at a very different level of social organization. They traded Mesopotamian manufactures in exchange for raw materials, winning the favor of local leaders by gifts of textiles and other products of foreign craftsmanship.

Such contacts were not always peaceful. The enormous human resources and centralized organization of early civilizations made it possible for them to dispense with the protocols of commerce and simply to raid, invade, or annex neighboring areas and appropriate their valuables. Mesopotamian records contain frequent references to military campaigns against troublesome mountain tribes. The converse was also true. Mountain tribes and desert nomads found rich pickings on settled lands. One object of state-organized military campaigns therefore was to dissuade people on the fringes from attacking the cities of the plain. But the main aim was to appropriate timber, metal, and valuables or to extort tribute, which dispensed with the requirement for the "civilized" to give anything—other than the threat of violence—in exchange.

Thus, being a close neighbor to an early state was often an uncomfortable experience. By means such as these the impact of early civilizations spread far beyond the confines of the states themselves. The peoples with whom they came into contact could hardly have remained unaffected by their presence. We may imagine that local peoples were both impressed and mystified by the traders, with their exotic trade goods and stories of faraway places—still more so when a sizable army arrived on their doorstep, equipped with bronze weapons and armor and led by a king dressed in priceless regalia the like of which they had never seen before. The prestige of civilizations among neighboring peoples should not be underestimated. It held true not only in the early Near East, Shang China, or Toltec Mesoamerica but also in relations between Greeks and Romans and the "barbarian" peoples beyond their frontiers.[1]

## "Primary" and "Secondary" Civilizations

We have discussed relations between civilizations and less complex societies. What about contacts between the civilizations themselves? That such contacts existed is shown both by finds of traded items and by documentary evidence. Distinctive Mesopotamian cylinder seals, for example, turn up in the Indus Valley and tie in with the boast of King Sargon of Agade (a Mesopotamian ruler) that Indus ships docked at his capital. Similarly, finds of Chinese silk at Roman sites in the Mediterranean are supported by written references to the visit of a Chinese emissary to Antioch in the first century A.D.

The vexing question is whether contacts from one civilization actually gave rise to another. This is where the terms *primary* (or *pristine*) and *secondary* come in. Primary is usually reserved for those civilizations that are thought to have come into being independently. They are sometimes called simply the "first civilizations." The list includes Mesopotamia and Egypt, the Indus Valley, Shang China, the Maya, and the early civilizations of Peru. In none of these cases is stimulus from another center of civilization thought to have played a decisive role. The secondary civilizations are those of later date: notably the Minoans and Mycenaeans in the Aegean or the early civilizations of Nubia and Southeast Asia. Here it is held that influences from long-established civilizations had a crucial formative impact.

1. Archaeologists conventionally use the term *Andean* to describe the culture area encompassing highland and lowland Peru and adjacent areas where civilization developed in South America. *Mesoamerica* refers to that area of highland and lowland Central America from Mexico to Guatemala where civilization developed.

Many archaeologists (including us) would now question the usefulness of this division. Evidence of contact between civilizations is neither surprising nor rare. As we have seen, the need for raw materials and the prestige and power of these societies of unprecedented scale sent ripples far afield. They provided new sets of ideas about how to organize life and held out for all to see the wealth that might be available to elites in this new and complex type of society. But availability does not lead immediately or inevitably to adoption. One of the most striking features of the early civilizations we describe in these pages is their individuality and distinctiveness. So, contact between civilizations, yes, but no simple connection between the rise of one and the birth of another.

The once popular, and still sometimes proposed, idea that the early civilizations of the world share some common point of origin may easily be disproved by considering the global pattern. Contacts between Mesopotamia, Egypt, the Indus Valley, and the Aegean are clearly documented and come as no surprise. This does not lead us to regard any of them as simply an imitation of the others. Shang China, too, may have had some links with western Asia; at any rate the war chariots found in Shang graves at Anyang were a western Asian invention and must have reached China via the steppes of central Asia. But no archaeologist today would suggest that Shang civilization owes its origin to western contact.

The case for independent development of civilizations becomes fully incontrovertible when we turn to the Americas. American civilizations may (to a greater or lesser extent) have been in contact with one another or certainly became so as the centuries passed. But there is no evidence for significant contact with the Old World until the arrival of the Norse in Newfoundland in the late tenth century A.D. and Spanish conquistadors in Mexico five centuries later. Yet both Old World and New World civilizations share such features as agriculture, writing, metallurgy, urbanism, and state-level organization. The appearance of these parallel innovations in separate parts of the world at approximately the same time is one of the most striking features of human history. It suggests, in effect, that humans under certain conditions are preprogrammed to develop along similar paths. But when they develop complex societies, they do so in the context of their own religious and philosophical beliefs, their own social traditions and conventions, and their own economies and technologies.

There is no need, then, to lay undue stress on contacts and borrowings in describing the rise of civilizations. In this book, we treat each as a separate, independent development, though at the same time noting the evidence for contact and trade between them.

## The Rediscovery of Ancient Civilizations

A century ago, a journey by boat up the Nile River took you through the heart of rural Egypt. Victorian travelers like the British writer Amelia Edwards described a kaleidoscope of village life unfolding along the banks, little changed from the days of the pharaohs. The ruined temples and burial places of Egypt's ancient god-kings lay among mud-brick villages. Egyptian *fellahin* (peasants) have always known of the existence of one of the world's most ancient civilizations. They are well aware of their illustrious ancestors, as the modern-day Maya of the Yucatán lowlands have always remembered their roots among great kingdoms of the past. In some cases, Maya groups have carefully preserved oral histories and traditional learning handed down from generation to generation, which now provide invaluable information on the remote past. Thus, it is misleading to write of the "discovery" of the early civilizations. However, the "rediscovery" of the world's first state-organized societies over the past two centuries ranks among the greatest achievements of Western science.

Archaeologists have brought a refined and disciplined methodology to the study of ancient civilizations, which has produced often astonishingly detailed information about preindustrial states. Today's knowledge of the early civilizations results from a powerful synthesis of archaeology and data from historical and traditional sources. Thus, on many occasions, we are able to combine the data of science with actual "voices" from the remote past preserved in contemporary documents or even in oral traditions.

The archaeology of the ancient civilizations began five centuries ago, in the hands of adventurers, antiquarians, and some remarkable pioneering archaeologists. For clarity, we describe the rediscovery of early civilizations in the order in which they were found.

## *Classical Civilizations: Greece and Rome*

Our story begins during the Renaissance, in the fifteenth and sixteenth centuries. This was when European scholars, first in Italy, and then in northern Europe, took a new interest in the writings of the classical authors of Greece and Rome. Italian architects compared Greek and Roman art and architectural works with the remains of surviving Roman buildings to gain a new appreciation of classical architectural principles. The interest in Greek and Roman art and literature was soon followed by an interest in the countries from which they came. Wealthy Europeans soon began to make their own collections of portable classical antiquities, at first mainly from Italy. In the early seventeenth century, King Charles I of England was one of the greatest of these collectors. So were the popes at Rome, whose collections of Etruscan, Greek, Roman, and Egyptian antiquities form a significant part of the holdings of the Vatican museums.

Italy was relatively accessible, and Italian rulers and noblemen were among the first excavators of Roman archaeological sites. These excavations fell well short of the standards acceptable today, and their primary aim was often the recovery of collectable objects. But some excavators did at least begin to record the provenance of artifacts such as vases in their original settings, be it a tomb or a residence, making scholars aware of the wealth of information that could be obtained from buried remains. The cities of Pompeii and Herculaneum, entombed in ash since the great eruption of Vesuvius in A.D. 79, provided some of the most spectacular results: sculptures, bronzes, and precious metal objects were ripped from the ruins in the 1740s and 1750s on the orders of the king and queen of Naples. It

**Figure 1.2** The cast of a beggar smothered by falling ash outside the Nucerian Gate at Pompeii, Italy.

was only in the 1860s that more sensitive methods were applied, and Pompeii began to yield evidence of splendid wall paintings and the gruesome plaster casts of those who died while fleeing from the ash-fall (Figure 1.2).

The connoisseurs of ancient art and literature had less easy access to the other main classical civilization of the Mediterranean since Greece remained under the control of the Ottoman (Turkish) Empire. Some Western scholars and collectors nonetheless made visits to Greece, where they found the local people consigning many priceless antiquities to lime kilns or otherwise destroying them. A major turning point was the expedition of British architects James Stuart and Nicholas Revett in 1751–1753. They spent several months in Athens, drawing with meticulous accuracy the ruins of the great classical buildings they found there, and published the results in a handsome three-volume illustrated set on their return. Fifty years later the British diplomat Lord Elgin shipped the famous frieze of the Parthenon from Athens to Britain. The Elgin Marbles went on display in the British Museum and remain in London to this day. The removal of Greek antiquities continued during much of the nineteenth century, though a sense of scholarly interest gradually replaced the love of collecting. By the end of the century the archaeology of classical Greece was at last put on a more secure basis by large-scale excavations, both foreign and Greek-led, at Athens, Delos, Delphi, Corinth, and Olympia.

## *Egypt*

Greece and Rome were in one sense accessible to Western scholars even before archaeology: their writings—histories, literature, and plays—were in Greek and Latin, which could still be read. For other civilizations, however, access was more difficult since knowledge of both the languages and the scripts in which they had been written was lost. Decipherment, breaking the code of these forgotten writings, was a critical first step.

Nowhere has decipherment played a more significant role than in the exploration of the Near Eastern civilizations of Egypt, Mesopotamia, and Persia. The Greeks and Romans always considered Egypt as the cradle of human civilization. Roman tourists visited the Nile Valley, pausing to admire the pyramids of Giza (see Box 4.1) and the temples of Thebes (Luxor). But few later travelers ventured to Egypt until the nineteenth century since it was an obscure province of the Ottoman Empire and effectively off-limits to Christians. The occasional traveler drew the pyramids or purchased powdery remains of Egyptian mummies, which were said to be a powerful medicine and aphrodisiac. Egyptian hieroglyphs and mummies caused intense interest in European scholarly circles because of the close association between the Land of the Pharaohs and the Old Testament. But it was not until Egypt assumed strategic importance during the Napoleonic Wars that Westerners finally became familiar with Egyptian civilization.

The immediate cause was the military expedition by Napoleon Bonaparte of France, who thought that control of Egypt would give him access to Britain's possessions in India. So he invaded the Nile Delta in 1798, wresting control of Egypt from its Ottoman governor. With characteristic thoroughness, Napoleon took with him a scientific team of 40 scientists, "Napoleon's Donkeys," whose job was to record the geography, culture, and archaeology of the country. The scholars fanned out over the Nile Valley with pen and pencil—collecting, recording inscriptions, and sketching. They published their results in a magnificent multivolume work, *Description de l'Egypte* (1799–1813), which caused a sensation throughout Europe, influencing art and architecture and setting off a craze for Egyptian antiquities in the Western world. But the greatest discovery of all came at the hands of some soldiers building a fortification at Rosetta in the Egyptian delta. They uncovered a stone slab bearing parallel texts in Greek and in two versions of Egyptian, one hieroglyphic, which provided the key for the eventual decipherment of ancient Egyptian writing by French scholar Jean François Champollion in 1822.

The *Description de l'Egypte* set the stage for more than a century of spectacular archaeological discoveries, culminating in the finding of the tomb of the New Kingdom pharaoh Tutankhamun by Howard Carter and Lord Carnarvon in 1922. Tutankhamun's tomb unleashed an epidemic of "Egyptomania," which has convulsed the world at intervals ever since. This mania takes many forms: a preoccupation with golden pharaohs, with the mystical, with the alleged properties of pyramid power and ancient Egyptian religion, or with the curses of royal mummies immortalized in several Hollywood movies. Ancient Egypt has a popular appeal that few other civilizations can equal.

## *Mesopotamian Civilizations: Assyrians and Sumerians*

Among the greatest archaeological discoveries of the nineteenth century were those at Nimrud, Nineveh, and other ancient Mesopotamian cities. Until Frenchman Paul-Emile Botta and Englishman Austen Henry Layard dug into Nineveh in the 1840s, however, the Assyrians of II Kings were only a shadowy presence on the historical stage. Layard, a young man with a taste for adventure and a hunger for fame and fortune, dreamed of romantic discoveries: "Visions of palaces underground, of gigantic monsters, of sculptured figures, and endless inscriptions, floated before me. After forming plan after plan for removing the earth, and extricating these treasures, I fancied myself wandering in a maze of chambers from which I could find no outlet. Then again, all was reburied, and I was standing on the grass-covered mound" (Layard, 1849: 111). He wrote these words while on the dusty mounds of Nineveh in northern Iraq in 1845.

Layard worked first at Nimrud and later, from 1849, at Nineveh (Figure 1.3). Meanwhile Botta had been appointed French consul to the obscure town of Mosul in northern Iraq in 1840 specifically so he could dig at Nineveh, directly across the Tigris River, and acquire antiquities for the Louvre in Paris. He was also the first to unearth an Assyrian palace at nearby Khorsabad. Both men uncovered spectacular bas-reliefs of great kings and their courtiers, of armies marching out to conquest, of slaves laboring on great palaces, even of scenes from a royal lion hunt (already described) and the siege of Lachish in Israel, mentioned in II Kings 18:3. When a team of scholars, among them cavalry officer-turned linguist Henry Creswicke Rawlinson, deciphered cuneiform, the wedge-shaped Mesopotamian script, Layard could read King Sennacherib's boast before Lachish: "Sennacherib, mighty king, king of the country of Assyria, sitting on the throne of judgement, before the

**Figure 1.3** Englishman Austen Henry Layard floated his Assyrian finds from Nineveh down the Tigris River on wooden rafts supported by inflated goatskins. Once the rafts reached the Persian Gulf, the skins were deflated, loaded on donkeys, and packed upstream. The wood was sold for a handsome profit. The Assyrians themselves used similar river vessels.

city of Lachish. I gave orders for its slaughter." Layard's discoveries also included the royal archives of the Assyrian monarch Assurbanipal, which were to throw light on the origins of creation legends in the first chapter of Genesis.

The clay tablets from Assurbanipal's library revealed the existence of a much earlier civilization in southern Mesopotamia, between the Tigris and Euphrates rivers. But it was not until French diplomat Ernest de Sarzec excavated the Telloh mounds in 1877 that the existence of such an earlier urban society was confirmed. And the Sumerian civilization did not catch the popular imagination until 1922, the year of the Tutankhamun discovery, when British archaeologist Leonard Woolley began digging at biblical Ur. These were large-scale excavations, directed by an archaeologist with a brilliant imagination and the ability to share his discoveries with a wide audience. In 1926, he unearthed a huge Sumerian cemetery containing 16 "royal" tombs and thousands of commoners' graves. Working with shoestring budgets, Woolley excavated a great death pit, where, he claimed, an entire royal court took poison and lay down to die with their master (Figure 1.4). The Royal Graves at Ur caused almost as great a sensation as Tutankhamun's tomb and stimulated a new level of interest in the first city dwellers of southern Mesopotamia.

Decades of persistent and dedicated work by archaeologists of many nationalities have assembled the rich picture of ancient Near Eastern society that we possess today. Much still remains to be done, especially in less well studied areas such as Anatolia. It is salutary to reflect that the Hittites, one of the major peoples of the ancient Near East, were hardly known until German excavations at Boghazköy,

**Figure 1.4** A reconstruction of the royal burial pit at Ur. (© Copyright The British Museum.)

their capital, in 1906–1908. More recently, French discoveries at Mari on the Euphrates (from 1933); Italian excavations at Ebla (from 1964); American investigations at Tell Leilan, Tell al-Raqa'i, and neighboring sites (from 1978); and British excavations at Tell Brak (1937–1938, resumed in 1976) have thrown new light on important early developments in northern Mesopotamia and Syria, away from the south Mesopotamian heartland.

## *Greece and Crete: Minoans and Mycenaeans*

The late nineteenth century also saw the first exploration of the Bronze Age civilizations of Greece and Crete, at the hands of some remarkable archaeologists. "I am fatigued and have an immense desire to withdraw from excavations and to pass the rest of my life quietly. I feel I cannot stand any longer this tremendous work. Besides, wherever I hitherto put the spade into the ground, I always discovered new worlds for archaeology at Troy, Mycenae, Orchomenos, Tiryns—each of them has brought to light new wonders," wrote German millionaire businessman Heinrich Schliemann in March 1885 (Schliemann, 1885: 22). Obsessed since childhood with Greek legend, Schliemann retired from business in his 40s and devoted the rest of his life to archaeology and to proving that Homer's poems, the *Iliad* and the *Odyssey*, were the literal historical truth.

Schliemann's main accomplishment lies in his excavations at the Hissarlik mound on the Dardanelles in modern Turkey, which both he and a local British resident named Frank Calvert identified as Homeric Troy. The aim was nothing less than the verification of Homeric legend, which told of a ten-year war led by the Bronze Age Greeks against the city of Troy at the mouth of the Dardanelles in modern Turkey. The story forms the background to the great epic poem the *Iliad*, written by Homer in the eighth century B.C. Schliemann and his Greek wife, Sophia, excavated Hissarlik on an enormous scale in the early 1870s and uncovered no fewer than seven superimposed cities. He claimed that a thick layer of burnt masonry and ashes, the second city from the base, was the Homeric Troy destroyed by the Greeks. At first Schliemann scarcely understood the significance of what he had found at Troy, but most people were convinced (and remain so today) that he had indeed discovered the city described in the legend.

The Greek leader who had led the expedition to Troy was Agamemnon, king of Mycenae in southern Greece. Buoyed up by his successes at Hissarlik and convinced that Agamemnon was a real historical figure, Schliemann turned his attention across the Aegean to the site of Mycenae itself in 1874. There he discovered the spectacular Shaft Graves and the skeletons of 19 gold-adorned men and women, some wearing golden masks (Figure 9.3). Schliemann proclaimed to the world that he had found Agamemnon's grave. In fact, he had uncovered Bronze Age Mycenaean civilization.

Greek legend also told of a shadowy early civilization on Crete, associated with a king named Minos. This had to wait longer than Mycenae for its rediscovery. The principal site was the palace of Knossos, its remains buried beneath a great mound of debris. English archaeologist Sir Arthur Evans was attracted to the site in the 1890s by carved Cretan sealstones bearing a curious script, which he had purchased from antiquities dealers in the Athens flea market. Evans tracked down the source of these sealstones to Knossos, and in 1900 began excavations there that were to continue at intervals for more than 30 years. He was not the first person to excavate at Knossos—a local Cretan enthusiast had worked there some years before—but he was the first to realize the significance of what he had found. The palace was a confusing huddle of courtyard, staircases, storerooms, and small chambers, with residential areas and public rooms, often decorated with vivid friezes. Evans saw this as the residence of King Minos himself and named the civilization that it represented Minoan.

The Minoans traded with the Egyptians, with the Greek mainland, and with eastern Mediterranean states. They developed a new script, known as Linear A, inscribed on clay tablets to record economic and administrative information, but although the contents of the clay tablets can be guessed from the layout and form of the symbols, this script has never been deciphered. However, Knossos yielded many more tablets in a different script, Linear B. To his eternal regret, Arthur Evans never deciphered Linear B either. It was only in 1953, 12 years after Evans's death, that Michael Ventris announced his discovery that some of the tablets represented an early form of Greek. The reading of the Linear B tablets has thrown considerable light on the administration of the palace of Knossos in its latter days, as well as on Mycenaean palaces on the Greek mainland, which also used the script.

## *The Indus and Eastern Asia*

The archaeological discovery of early civilizations in South Asia and the Far East is the work of the present century. Excavations by British and Indian archaeologists at the cities of Harappa and Mohenjodaro in 1921 first revealed the existence of a hitherto unsuspected Bronze Age civilization in the Indus Valley of what is now Pakistan. Harappa and Mohenjodaro have remained the best-known sites, but they are now recognized to be only two among over a dozen large settlements of the Indus civilization. Unfortunately, no one has yet succeeded in deciphering the enigmatic Indus script, which appears on square sealstones and copper plates.

The 1920s were a key period in the investigation of early Chinese civilization, too. Chinese historical records of later periods spoke of a Shang dynasty, which had ruled northern China during the second millennium B.C. Little more was known of it, however, until 1899, when a collection of cattle shoulder blades bearing an early form of Chinese script was traced to the site of Anyang in the Huanghe valley. To that extent the story of the discovery parallels that of the Minoan civilization of Crete. In the Chinese case, however, the first excavations at Anyang had to wait until 1928. Once begun, under the direction of Chinese archaeologist Li Chi, they revealed an amazing record of wealthy royal graves and palace platforms, giving archaeological substance to the shadowy historical Shang. Work has continued at Anyang and other Shang centers up to the present day, confirming the essential accuracy of Chinese legends. Recent discoveries have also thrown light on developments in other regions of China, where distinctive regional traditions emerged in parallel with the Shang.

## *The Americas: Mesoamerica*

Even as Paul-Emile Botta and Austen Henry Layard labored on Assyrian cities, Boston historian William Prescott was studying ancient American civilizations. He started with the accounts of Spanish conquistadors, who were astounded by the sophistication of Aztec civilization in the Mexican highlands.

> When we saw so many cities and villages built in the water and other great towns on dry land and that straight and level causeway going towards Mexico [Tenochtitlán], we were amazed and said that it was like the enchantments they tell of in the legends of Aamadis, on account of the great towers . . . and buildings rising from the water, and all built of masonry. And some of our soldiers even asked whether the things we saw were not a dream [Diaz, 1963: 118].

So wrote conquistador Bernal Diaz of the Spaniards' first sight of the Aztec capital, Tenochtitlán. When Hernán Cortés and his soldiers arrived before Tenochtitlán in 1519, they were met with the sight not of an archaeological ruin but of a great preindustrial city in full vitality. Here was a native American empire with architecture, writing, and metallurgy and with great temple-pyramids and organized systems of warfare, government, and taxation.

Unfortunately, Cortés and his men embarked on an orgy of destruction, which effectively banished Aztec civilization into historical oblivion. A colonial capital, Mexico City, rose on the ruins of Tenochtitlán, burying the great pre-Columbian city under urban sprawl. Only a few Spanish friars bothered to learn the native dialect and to record oral traditions of the once-great civilization. Their researches have preserved a priceless, but alas incomplete, archive of Aztec culture for modern scholars.

The conquistadors were colonists and conquerors, people who came to the Americas to "serve God and get rich." Catholic friars destroyed Aztec cult objects and priceless written codices (illustrated documents) to obliterate all traces of "pagan" beliefs. Sympathetic study of the traditions and history of the conquered peoples was not encouraged. It was not until the nineteenth century that both American and Mexican scholars probed historical and native sources and began to write not only about the Aztecs but also about much earlier Mesoamerican civilizations. William Prescott's romanticized masterpiece *The Conquest of Mexico* (1843) became a best-seller, the first account of early Mesoamerican civilizations based both on archival and archaeological sources. That he could use archaeology at all was because of two remarkable travelers, American lawyer John Lloyd Stephens and English artist Frederick Catherwood. Together they made two difficult journeys (1839–1840 and 1841–1842) into the jungles of lowland Mexico and Guatemala, visiting and drawing the ruins of Maya centers like Copán, Palenque, Chichen Itzá, and Uxmal. Catherwood was a brilliant artist, capable of producing pictures as accurate as photographs (Figure 1.5). Stephens was a vivid writer. Together, they published their discoveries in two disarmingly entitled volumes: *Incidents of Travel in Central America, Chiapas and Yucatán* (1841) and *Incidents of Travel in Yucatán* (1843). These best-sellers revealed the spectacular Maya civilization to an astonished world.

**Figure 1.5** John Lloyd Stephens examines a temple at Palenque in the Maya lowlands. Drawing by Frederick Catherwood.

Forty years were to pass before any serious work was done on the Maya. British archaeologist Sir Alfred P. Maudsley produced the first general study of Maya archaeology in four volumes between 1889 and 1902. Part of this publication was a long appendix on Maya inscriptions. Excavation and interpretation of Maya sites have been major areas of archaeological research in the century since Maudsley, but the greatest breakthrough has been made only recently, with the decipherment of Maya glyphs in the 1980s. Forty years ago, the ancient Maya were thought to have been a peaceful people, interested in mathematics and astronomy, living in splendid ceremonial centers in the midst of the lowland jungle. The texts have now forced a complete reassessment of this view, with accounts of fierce warfare between rulers and cities, not unlike those of Mesopotamia or, indeed, many other parts of the ancient world.

## *Peru*

The Aztec civilization was a decade in ruins when another Spanish adventurer, Francisco Pizarro, encountered the Inka ruler Atahuallpa high in the Andes foothills in 1532. Pizarro and his small band of soldiers succeeded in capturing Atahuallpa, then held him for ransom against a roomful of gold. The Inka empire soon collapsed. Within ten years, the Spaniards were the masters of Peru. The Inka capital, Cuzco, lay in the highlands, connected to all parts of the royal domains by a network of roads and couriers. The conquistadors stripped Cuzco's temples of their gold and set out to obliterate all traces of a "pagan" civilization, just as their predecessors had done in Mexico. Only a handful of Spanish and native scholars preserved some memories of Inka civilization, but nothing like the rich material saved in Mesoamerica.

Four centuries passed before scientists began to explore the spectacular Inka ruins of the Andes and even earlier monuments on the arid Peruvian coast. Two names stand out in particular: German scholar Max Uhle, who first revealed the time depth of South American civilization in his excavations at Pachacamac on the southern Peruvian coast in 1896–1897; and the more famous Indiana Jones–like figure of the American scholar Hiram Bingham, archaeologist and historian. Bingham set off from Cuzco in July 1911 in search of the "lost city of Vilcabamba," the citadel where the Inka made their last stand against the Spanish. Instead, what he visited (a mere five days later!) was the ruins of Machu Picchu, a small but spectacularly preserved Inka hilltop town (Figure 18.10). What had saved it from destruction was its remote setting. Only 97 kilometers (60 miles) from Cuzco, it had never been found by the Spanish and had never suffered destruction at their hands. Nor was it obvious when Bingham visited the area; it was only when a local farmer led him to the place that the ruins of Machu Picchu were revealed to Western scholarship. "It seemed like an incredible dream. . . . What could this place be?" wrote Bingham, whose extravagant claims of lost cities have not stood up to later scientific scrutiny.

The discovery of Machu Picchu stands as one of the last pioneer explorations of the ancient civilizations. Much still remains to be discovered, however—witness the spectacular finds of recent years, among them the Bronze Age shipwreck at Uluburun off the coast of southern Turkey, which contained artifacts from nine areas of the Near East (Chapter 9). And when archaeologists working at Sipán in the Lambayeque Valley of northern coastal Peru unearthed a series of gold-laden Moche warrior-priest burials in 1989, they recovered the richest unlooted tombs ever excavated in the Americas (see Box 18.1).

Discoveries like those at Sipán and Uluburun are dramatic; they make the headlines and grab the popular imagination. But less spectacular discoveries can be just as, if not more, informative. Royal burials and richly adorned palaces illuminate the lives of kings and queens, the privileged elites who ruled different civilizations. But sometimes the most telling clues come from the commonplace find, from an obscure ancient inscription or a well-preserved hut floor. It is then that we learn about the commoners, the slaves, the humble artisans who lived out their lives in quiet anonymity, in the shadow of great rulers and sometimes world-changing events. The ancient civilizations were built on the labors of thousands of faceless people who tilled the land, built temples, created artistic masterpieces, and traveled long distances in the service of the state. Their lives come down to us in silent, dispassionate artifacts and food remains; in the foundations of small dwellings; and from the fills of storage pits. With such finds, archaeology presents a more balanced view of the societies that built the Pyramids of Giza, created the great Mexican city of Teotihuacán, and laid out royal mausolea in Southeast Asia that replicated the mythic Hindu world.

Such architectural masterpieces, built by long-dead hands, are the common cultural heritage of us all. But they are under threat from unscrupulous looters and industrial development, from the ravages of civil war and air pollution, and from the busy feet of package tourists. The ancient civilizations are under siege from modern society in ways that we may sometimes be powerless to control. Tragically, much of the damage is deliberate—for example, the stripping of sites and burials of fine artworks and inscriptions by professional looters to feed the insatiable maw of the international antiquities market. As long as wealthy individuals in the industrialized nations are prepared to pay high prices for ancient artworks, there will continue to be those prepared to dig into unrecorded sites, to burgle museums, and to cut away fragments of standing monuments in order to sell them on in the antiquities markets of Europe, North America, and Japan. The loss to archaeology—and to world heritage in general—is incalculable.

## Summary

In this chapter we have considered alternative meanings of the term *civilization* and have seen how it must be divorced from ideas of cultural progress or superiority. Early civilizations share many important features, including urbanization and state-level sociopolitical organization. Other features, such as writing and metallurgy, are common but not universal to early civilizations. The rediscovery of early civilizations has been a gradual process, beginning in the sixteenth century with the European Renaissance and the arrival of Spanish conquistadors in the New World. Discoveries such as the tomb of Tutankhamun, the Royal Graves at Ur, and the Moche Lords of Sipán kept civilizations in the headlines throughout the twentieth century, but looting and destruction cast a shadow of concern over the future fate of many of the major sites and monuments.

## Guide to Further Reading

General works on ancient civilizations include Charles K. Maisels, *The Emergence of Civilizations* (London: Routledge, 1990) and the same author's *Early Civilizations of the Old World* (London: Routledge, 1999); Charles Redman, *The Rise of Civilization* (San Francisco: Freeman, 1978); Jeremy A. Sabloff and C. C. Lamberg-Karlovsky, *Ancient Civilizations of the Near East and Mesoamerica*, 2nd ed. (Prospect Heights, IL: Waveland Press, 1995); and Bruce G. Trigger, *Early Civilizations: Ancient Egypt in Context* (Cairo: American University in Cairo, 1993). The same author's monumental and definitive *Early Civilizations and the Logic of Human Behavior* (Cambridge: Cambridge University Press, 2003) is essential reading for all serious students. A popular account of the discovery of the ancient civilizations will be found in C. W. Ceram's classic, *Gods, Graves and Scholars* (New York: Knopf, 1953). Ceram's work can be amplified by Brian Fagan, *The Adventure of Archaeology* (Washington, DC: National Geographic Society, 1984); Glyn Daniel, *The First Civilizations: The Archaeology of Their Origins* (London: Thames and Hudson, 1968); and William H. Steibing, Jr., *Uncovering the Past: A History of Archaeology* (New York: Oxford University Press, 1993). For more regional historical studies, see, for Greece, R. Etienne and F. Etienne, *The Search for Ancient Greece* (London: Thames and Hudson, 1992); for Egypt, Nicholas Reeves, *Ancient Egypt: The Great Discoveries* (London: Thames and Hudson, 2000); for Mesopotamia, Seton Lloyd, *Foundations in the Dust: The Story of Mesopotamian Exploration*, rev. ed. (London: Thames and Hudson, 1980); for the Maya, Michael Coe, *Breaking the Maya Code* (London: Thames and Hudson, 1992). For early scripts, see also Andrew Robinson, *The Story of Writing* (London: Thames and Hudson, 1995).

*Chapter 2*

# Theories of States

Bas–relief of the the Egyptian goddess Maat, goddess of rightness. (Painted stone relief. Egypt, 19th dynasty. Museo Archeologico, Florence Italy. © Scala/Art Resource, NY)

*A.D. 1487: The long line of brightly adorned prisoners of war ascends the steep stairway step by step, toward the twin shrines on the summit atop the great pyramid in the heart of the Aztec capital, Tenochtitlán. The captured warriors look neither to left nor right, some walking boldly upright, others going unwillingly to their sacrificial death. The noise of the vast crowd below envelops them and masks the beating of drums atop the pyramid. As each victim steps on the summit platform, four masked priests spreadeagle him across a convex sacrificial stone. Before he can cry out, a lightning blow of a razor-sharp obsidian knife breaks open his chest. A priest tears the still-beating heart out of the bleeding cavity and dashes the bloody mess against the image of the sun god, Huitzilopochtli, close by. As a new victim steps to his death, the still-warm corpse tumbles down the side of the pyramid to waiting priests below. A few minutes later, the victim's head joins hundreds of others on the skull rack within the sacred precincts. Such was the Flowery Death of the Aztec warrior, which allowed the slain victim to join the sun god in his daily journey across the heavens.*

In A.D. 1519, Spanish conquistador Hernán Cortés and a small band of soldiers and adventurers fought and bluffed their way from the Gulf of Mexico into the distant Mexican highlands. Finally, they gazed spellbound at the great capital of the Aztecs, Tenochtitlán, the "Place of the Prickly Pear Cactus." High pyramids and temples gleamed white in the sunlight, dwarfing human figures on the plazas beneath. Tenochtitlán lay on an island in the shallow waters of a lake in the valley of Mexico, joined to the mainland by earthen causeways. A quarter of a million people lived in or around the Aztec capital. Twenty thousand people a day, many more on formal market days, visited its vast market, larger than that of Seville or Constantinople. The Spaniards marveled at the well-ordered city. They persuaded the Aztec ruler Moctezuma to let them climb to the summit of the highest pyramid, where the shrines of Huitzilopochtli, the sun god, and Tlaloc, the deity of rain, lay side by side. Here they found the great figures of the gods hung with precious ornaments. Braziers smoked with copal incense and the hearts of three human victims sacrificed that very day. "All the walls of that shrine were so splashed and caked with blood that they and the floor too were black," wrote conquistador Bernal Diaz. He recalled how the eyes of the figures glinted with semiprecious stones. Human sacrifice lay at the very core of the Aztecs' religion, for they believed that the souls of those who died on the sacrificial altar rode with the sun god on his daily journey across the heavens. The nourishment of their blood assured the continuity of Aztec life (Figure 2.1).

**Figure 2.1** Aztec Eagle Warrior, detail, an elite warrior class with their own regalia. Many Aztec soldiers died on temple altars as captives in the "Flowery Death," which, they believed, assured them immortality, riding across the heavens with the sun-god. (Museo del Templo Mayor, Mexico City, D.F., Mexico. © John Bigelow Taylor/Art Resource, NY)

Cortés and his followers were almost the last Westerners to witness a preindustrial civilization at the height of its powers. The Aztecs lived under the rule of a remote leader, Moctezuma, who was considered a living god. Divided into rigid social classes, the Aztecs were taught from birth that conformity was expected of them. Most wealth and all economic, political, and religious power flowed to the ruler, to his benefit and that of a tiny class of nobles, priests, and high officials. Everyone was taught that they were on earth to serve the state and the divine Huitzilopochtli, whose soul was nourished by human hearts. Like many other ancient civilizations, the Aztecs believed there was a continuum between the realm of the living and that of the spiritual world. Their worldview was totally different from that of the Christians who encountered them—which makes it very hard for us to study and understand their society or that of other early civilizations, for that matter. This chapter surveys some of the theories of the origin of states and the major factors that may have contributed to the rise of civilization.

## Historical and Anthropological Perspectives

### *Civilizationists and World Systems*

In Chapter 1, we described some of the common attributes of early civilizations. But why did civilizations, complex human societies, appear in the first place and why did they collapse with often bewildering rapidity? Both historians and anthropologists have contributed to an enormous literature on these topics.

Scholars of world civilization, often called "civilizationists," are comparative historians who conceptualize cyclical patterns in the history of civilization. A survey of their changing ideas lies outside the scope of this book, but we should mention the British historian Arnold Toynbee, who developed famous theories of cyclical change in his monumental (12 volumes) *A Study of History* (1934–1961). He likened civilizations to dynamic organisms, with distinctive life cycles of genesis, growth, breakdown, and disintegration. Toynbee's work was much criticized for its generalizations, among others by his contemporary Pitirim Sorokin, a Harvard historian who focused on cultural diversity, the central ideas behind different civilizations. However, like Toynbee, Sorokin believed in cycles, that is, that his "central ideas" went through distinctive cycles as civilizations developed. In 1961, another historian, Carol Quigley, theorized in *The Evolution of Civilization* that civilizations did indeed go through cycles, but she focused on the frontiers of such states. State-organized societies arose, she said, on the periphery of earlier states through a mixing of cultures and societies, and then expanded through population growth, the accumulation of economic surplus, and trade. The civilizationist literature continues to proliferate, with some consensus that civilizations are more dynamic than less complex societies and that they support higher population densities. Each is considered unique, with its own basic "essence," as the famous German historian Oswald Spengler once called it. But most of them share certain basic patterns, among them centralized government and usually writing and cities.

However, new generations of anthropological and historical thinking, drawing on research in many parts of the world, have resulted in new perspectives. The often myopic views of civilization of earlier generations, based on intense study of Western history, have given way to more multidisciplinary, global syntheses, which view civilizations against a background of fluctuating growth, shifting centers of civilization, and their multiplicity of peoples and cultures.

## *Evolutionary Schemes*

While historians think in terms of civilizations, archaeologists and anthropologists use a different approach and a terminology that emphasizes a significant increase in social complexity as a conspicuous feature of preindustrial civilization. Thus, they tend to stress social and political organization, to speak of "states" and "complex societies" and to look at the development of civilization in the context of many other forms of simpler human societies and through an evolutionary perspective. Archaeology is the only scientific way of studying cultural change over far longer periods of time than the mere five thousand years of civilization in the Near East. Thus, the excavator's spade combined with sophisticated archaeological theory play a fundamental role in the debate over the origin of civilization. Such research focuses on both description of the past and reconstruction of ancient lifeways but, most important, seeks to explain the dynamics of how the world's first states came into being—what archaeologists commonly call "cultural process." With its emphasis on the study of culture change and with its long-time perspective, archaeology lies at the very core of the study of early civilization.

The pages that follow describe some of the major anthropological approaches to the origins of the state and some of the factors that contributed to their subsequent growth.

## *Prestate and State-Organized Societies*

Anthropologists and archaeologists have long been interested in the origins of civilization, believing that human societies have evolved along many branchlike tracks. Such "multilinear evolution" at a general level is a fundamental tenet of most anthropological theorizing about the origin of states, and it rests on the assumption that the roots of all preindustrial civilizations lie in earlier and simpler tribal societies, which in many respects resembled the "traditional" tribal societies of recent times. This assumption led to a widely used classification of human societies into prestate (bands, tribes, and chiefdoms) and state-organized societies (civilizations).

*Prestate societies* are societies on a small scale, based on the community, band, or village. They vary greatly in their degree of political integration and can be divided into three categories:

- *Bands* are autonomous and self-sufficient groups that usually consist of only a few families. They are egalitarian, with leadership coming from the experience and personal qualities of particular individuals rather than from political power.
- *Tribes* are egalitarianlike bands but with a greater level of social and cultural complexity. They have developed kin-based mechanisms to accommodate more sedentary living, to redistribute food, and to organize some communal services. In egalitarian societies, public opinion plays a major role in decision making. While some of the more complex societies like the Pacific Northwest groups were hunter-gatherers, most were associated with village farming.
- *Chiefdoms* are societies headed by individuals with unusual ritual, political, or entrepreneurial skills and are often hard to distinguish from tribes. Society is still kin-based but more hierarchical, with control concentrated in the hands of powerful kin leaders responsible for the redistribution of food, luxury goods, and other resources. Chiefdoms tend to have high population densities and to display the first signs of social ranking, reflected in more elaborate material possessions. They vary greatly in their elaboration depending on many factors, including the distribution of population over the landscape. Classic examples include the Tahitian and Hawaiian chiefdoms of the Pacific and the elaborate Mississippian chiefdoms of the American Midwest and South, which flourished about one thousand years ago, maintaining trade networks and ritual contacts over long distances.

*State-organized societies (civilizations)* operate on a large scale, with centralized social and political organization, class stratification, and intensive agriculture. They have complex political structures, many permanent government institutions, and they are based on social inequality, with a small ruling class presiding over the state.

Inevitably this loosely defined taxonomy of human societies led to assumptions that chiefdoms, the most elaborate prestate societies, had evolved into states in some parts of the world. For more than 30 years, this "stepladder" model has prevailed as a general assumption, almost without challenge. Now the stepladder, with its emphasis on chiefdoms, is under attack.

## Chiefdoms

The label *chiefdom* has been widely used to describe the somewhat less than egalitarian societies that immediately preceded states all over the world. Such a label allowed for comparative studies, but the definition of what constitutes a chiefdom has changed markedly since it was first proposed. Chiefdoms are kin-based societies headed by hereditary chiefs, often priest chiefs who have a title but little authority except as a master of ceremonies and as a redistributor of goods. They listen carefully to public opinion when wielding their limited powers.

Archaeologists have made wide use of chiefdoms because of a chief's perceived importance in the redistribution of trade goods, food, and other resources throughout society. But many archaeologists disagree and minimize the importance of redistribution; as archaeologist Timothy Earle found with Hawaiian chiefdoms, the chief's major role was as a landowner and supervisor of the labor of the commoners who worked his acreage as dependents. In short, the chiefdom is a political unit, not a mechanism for redistribution. Under this rubric, the chiefdom was a political breakthrough, the moment when the local autonomy characteristic of bands and tribal societies gave way to a new form of authority in which a single important individual controls a number of communities. Thus, the chiefdom was an early stage in the rise of states, a society headed by an individual who ruled over a regional population of thousands and controlled the production of staples and the acquisition of exotic objects.

In recent years, the chiefdom has received further refinement with a subdivision into simple chiefdoms, which rely on kin lines, and complex chiefdoms, in which there is a regional hierarchy of a paramount chief and lesser chieftains. The former have centralized decision making for mobilizing resources, whereas the latter enjoy considerable autonomy over their own subordinate communities. Thus, argue proponents of complex chiefdoms, the paramount chief has external authority to organize the acquisition of resources, but internally there is no complex bureaucracy to administer food surpluses and the distribution and storage of resources. Thus, society is divided into nobles and commoners, with the nobility competing with one another for leadership, prestige, and religious authority. But without a bureaucracy, a standing army, and other means to enforce control of goods on a long-term basis, the chiefdom is a volatile, ever-changing form of society in a condition of constant rebellion, breakdown, and flux. Nevertheless, chiefdoms are important since they apparently provide a political stepping-stone toward the centralized state, with its much denser population, infinitely larger food surpluses, and new systems for administering society.

This political view of the chiefdom has been criticized for diverting attention from the trends toward economic and social differentiation, which were a vital part of the early stages of development of the state. These developments can be clearly seen in Mesopotamia (Chapter 3), predynastic Egypt (Chapter 4), and lowland Mesoamerica (Chapter 15). Norman Yoffee, himself an authority on ancient Mesopotamia, believes the ladderlike chiefdom stage as a predecessor to the state is meaningless. For example, Yoffee points out that nothing in the archaeological and historical record suggests that pre-Sumerian cultures in the region were organized as chiefdoms in the sense suggested by the evolutionists. Rather, records speak of ongoing competition for power between kin groups and centralized institutions, as a rapid, large-scale process of urbanization took place just before 3000 B.C. This process brought profound changes in the division of labor, in the organization of the countryside for intensive agriculture, and in unparalleled opportunities for acquiring wealth for a few at the expense of most members of society. Early archives refer to councils of elders, who played a vital role in city-state affairs, for power was vested in communities, not in chiefs. The evolving relationship between the growing power of priests and rulers and the community-based structures of earlier times is a major theme in state formation in this area. Yoffee believes that the emergence of non-kin-based relationships between the rulers and the ruled was the critical departure point for the state. This, not chiefdoms, was the power that provided the ingredients of enforceable authority and more than short-term stability.

### *Settlement Hierarchy*

A defining feature of state-level societies is their hierarchical social structure, and many archaeologists have sought to find a parallel hierarchy on the ground, in terms of settlement organization. These approaches start by dividing settlements into four types: cities, towns, large villages, and small villages. In direct analogy with theories of social evolution, so proponents of the settlement hierarchy approach hold that complex prestate societies may display three types of settlements—towns, large villages, and small villages—while the transition to statehood is marked by the appearance of cities. In such a hierarchy, the city will be the focus of centralized government, possessing a palace, administrative buildings, and major temples; whereas towns and large villages would have the offices of delegated authority, such as regional governors or village elders. Small villages might be expected to have no public buildings of any kind.

Four-tiered hierarchies of these kinds can be documented among the remains of early state societies by careful field survey, such as those carried out by Robert McC. Adams and his team in southern Mesopotamia. When textual information is added in, however, the historical reality is rarely as simple as the four-tier scheme would suggest. Thus as Kent Flannery has observed for one particular polity in Mesopotamia, the state of Lagash, archaeology reveals that it contained not one but three cities, along with more than 20 towns and at least 40 villages. The degree of variability in settlement types and sizes, and their spatial arrangement, can nonetheless be a useful pointer to the scale and complexity of the social unit concerned and to the presence or absence of a state.

## Six Classic Theories for the Emergence of State Societies

Everyone who has studied the early human past agrees that the emergence of civilization in different parts of the world was a major development in our history. From 2.5 million to about ten thousand years ago, all humankind lived by foraging for animals and plant foods. As the Ice Age ended about ten thousand years ago, global warming caused major changes in the world's environments, as glaciers shrank, sea levels rose, and forests spread to cover open tundra. Humanity adapted by developing increasingly specialized ways of gathering and hunting and, in some areas, by deliberately planting wild grasses to supplement existing food resources. By 10,000 B.C., wheat and barley were being cultivated in the Near East and goats and sheep were being domesticated from wild forms. The new farming economies spread rapidly, as contacts between far-flung, now permanent agricultural villages increased rapidly. By 5000 B.C., agricultural communities flourished throughout the Near East, in South and East Asia, and in Europe. Village agriculture began independently in northern China by 7000 B.C., in Southeast Asia by 3000 B.C., and in Mesoamerica by 2600 B.C. This dramatic transformation from foraging to farming set the stage for the development of the first preindustrial civilizations in widely separate areas of the world.

In Chapter 1, we defined civilization as a shorthand for urbanized, state-level societies. But what common attributes separate civilizations from other ancient societies? There are many variations among the preindustrial civilizations, but the following features are characteristic of all of them:

- Urbanized societies, based on cities, with large, highly complex social organizations. The preindustrial civilization was invariably associated with a substantial geographical territory, such as the Nile Valley.
- Economies based on the centralized accumulation of capital and social status through tribute and taxation. For instance, Sumerian kings monopolized trading activity in the name of the state. This type of economy allows the support of hundreds, often thousands, of nonfood producers such as smiths and priests. Long-distance trade and the division of labor, as well as craft specialization, are often characteristic of early civilizations.
- Advances toward formal record keeping, science, and mathematics and some form of written script. This took many forms, from Egyptian hieroglyphs to the knotted strings used by the Inka of the Andes.
- Impressive public buildings and monumental architecture, like Maya ceremonial centers and Roman temples.
- Some form of all-embracing state religion in which the ruler plays a leading role. The Khmer of Cambodia considered their leaders to be living gods. These kings lived in great palaces built as depictions of the symbolic Hindu world.

How, then, did such societies develop? We will now survey six widely discussed theories, which identify some of the key factors involved.

## *Childe and the Urban Revolution*

The Victorians believed passionately in the notion of human progress, in hierarchical forms of cultural evolution that placed modern industrial civilization at the pinnacle of human achievement. Humanity, they believed, had evolved at different rates in various parts of the world, progressing from simple hunting and gathering toward the full realization of human potential. Like the Greeks and Romans before them, they assumed that civilization had originated along the Nile, in the Land of the Pharaohs, in spite of the discovery of the Sumerian civilization in Mesopotamia in the 1870s. Eventually, early theorizing took in a broader canvas, embracing all of Southwest Asia and the Near East. In the 1920s, American archaeologist James Breasted coined the enduring phrase "the Fertile Crescent," a curve of territory that encompassed the Judean Hills, the Zagros Mountains, and lower Mesopotamia. The Fertile Crescent was the cradle of early civilization, the place of origin of the first complex societies in the world.

The first relatively sophisticated theories about the origins of civilization were formulated by Australian-born archaeologist V. Gordon Childe (1892–1957). Childe claimed that a "Neolithic Revolution," which witnessed the beginnings of farming, was followed by an "Urban Revolution." (Neolithic is a widely used, general label in the Old World that refers to early—Stone Age—farmers who did not have metal tools.) He theorized that this second revolution saw the development of metallurgy and the appearance of a new social class of full-time artisans and specialists who lived in much larger settlements, that is, cities. Among the Sumerians of Mesopotamia, for example, Childe believed that the new specialists were fed by food surpluses raised by peasant farmers. But the artisans' products had to be distributed and raw materials obtained, often from great distances. Both needs reduced the self-sufficiency of peasant communities, Childe argued. Agricultural techniques became more sophisticated as a higher yield of food per capita was needed to support a growing nonagricultural population. Irrigation increased productivity, leading to the centralization of food supplies, production, and distribution. Taxation and tribute led to the accumulation of capital. Ultimately, said Childe, a new class-stratified society came into being, based on economic classes rather than traditional ties of kin. Writing was essential for keeping records and for developing exact and predictive sciences. Transportation by land and water was part of the new order. A unifying religious force dominated urban life as priest-kings and despots rose to power. Monumental architecture testified to their activities.

Childe considered technology and the development of craft specialization in the hands of full-time artisans a cornerstone of the Urban Revolution. A half century later, most archaeologists associate craft specialization with cultural complexity, to the point that they equate the appearance of specialist artisans with the formation of states. Thus, goes the argument, evidence of increased levels of craft specialization thereafter indicates even further cultural complexity. This perspective has been challenged by scholars who point out that craft specialization is a feature of many more-egalitarian societies. Many chiefs, ruling over chiefdoms large and small, patronized specialists who produced prestige goods and artifacts, like canoes, that needed unusual skills. Another theory considers craft specialization to be the fate of peasant farmers disenfranchised from their lands as states expanded and cities grew.

Archaeologists John Clark and William Perry tested these theories against a sample of data from societies in widely contrasting environments and with very different cultural institutions. They found that craft specialization was common in both chiefdoms and states, but they doubt from their studies that it was a major factor in the development of civilization, although there was a strong correlation between full-time craft specialization and civilization. They are intrigued by the possibility that patronized craft specialization was crucial to the emergence of states, for it is associated with rank and may have been a major factor in the acquisition of economic power outside the confines of the kin system. They believe that patronizing artisans was one way to acquire social prestige and status, as well as wealth, through production and exchange with other communities, as may have occurred along the Nile. Craft specialization was not, in itself, a major cause of civilization, but it may have laid a foundation for more permanent investments in what eventually became inheritable wealth, a major feature of civilizations.

Childe's Urban Revolution theory enjoyed widespread popularity between the 1930s and 1950s. It was a logical synthesis of complex events at a time when relatively little was known about early Near Eastern civilization and even less about complex states in China, South Asia, and the Americas. But the revolution hypothesis has serious flaws. For example, craft specialization is more a symptom than a cause of state formation and is not unique to civilizations. Furthermore, predicating state and city formation on surplus production does not explain why surpluses came about in the first place.

Robert Adams and other Mesopotamian archaeologists argued in the 1960s that the term Urban Revolution puts undue emphasis on the city at the expense of social change, that is, the development of social classes and political institutions. Adams pointed out that both early Mesopotamian and American civilizations followed a basically similar course of development in which kin groups, who controlled land communally, were replaced by the growth of private estates owned by noble families. The eventual result was a stratified form of social organization rigidly divided along class lines.

## *Ecology and Irrigation*

Most scholars now agree that three elements of Childe's Urban Revolution were of great importance in the development of all the world's early civilizations: large food surpluses, diversified farming economies, and irrigation agriculture. Early ecological theories revolved around these three broad themes.

- River floodplains, with their rich, fertile soils, contained great ecological potential.

Breasted's Fertile Crescent hypothesis assumed that the exceptional fertility of the Mesopotamian floodplain and the Nile Valley was the primary cause for the appearance of cities and states in these regions. Larger grain surpluses over and above basic subsistence and storage needs resulted from increased agricultural efficiency, as did social and cultural changes. The extra food supported nonfood producers such as artisans, priests, and traders, who made up new classes of society that were the backbone of state-organized societies.

Some scholars, among them the economist Esther Boserup, take the opposite tack. They believe that population growth, not food surplus, was the incentive for intensified agriculture and eventually more complex societies. Following Boserup, others have argued that agricultural systems such as those in early Mesopotamia or along the banks of the Nile River (where annual floods inundated the fields), tended to be more intensive and to exploit the environment in a more ordered and systematic way. They created conditions in which more settlements per square mile could exist on foods whose annual yields were at least roughly predictable. The more specialized ecosystems created by these efforts supported more concentrated, rapidly growing populations, and thus civilization. But, though important, dense populations did not characterize all state-organized societies, as the Mycenaean or Inka civilizations show.

- Because of the ecological diversity of other environments, differences in altitude, access to food and other resources, and soil fertility varied greatly from one area to another. The resulting diversity of food resources protected the people against famine and stimulated trade and exchange for food and other products, as did the growth of distributive organizations that encouraged centralized authority.

Diversified agricultural economies tended to focus on fewer, more productive crops, but the ultimate subsistence base remained wide. The Egyptians farmed wheat and barley on a large scale but also raised large herds of cattle and goats, for example. The earliest civilizations in the Old World and the New were certainly based on complex subsistence patterns, which integrated several ecological zones. For instance, the highland Andean states relied heavily on their lowland neighbors for fish meal, cotton, and other resources. The Harappans of the Indus Valley may have exchanged cotton for semiprecious stones, while highland and lowland Mesoamerican civilizations depended on one another for all manner of commodities, foodstuffs, and artifacts. In these circumstances, a local center might control products from several nearby ecological zones, giving it a hedge against crop failure and famine that was vital for managing and controlling food surpluses.

- The adoption of irrigation agriculture was a major factor in the rise of civilization, as it supported far higher population densities.

Early ecological theories were closely tied to the apparent widespread use of irrigation agriculture by early states to enhance agricultural output. The intensification of agriculture implies major modification of the environment, which usually means irrigation—the development of canals and other works for storing water and watering fields during dry months. Irrigation theories were popular a generation ago, when anthropologist Julian Steward and historian Karl Wittfogel argued during the 1950s that irrigation lay behind the development of socially stratified societies in Egypt, Mesopotamia, and elsewhere, which Wittfogel famously called "hydraulic civilizations." In areas where irrigation was practiced, both scholars argued, the relationship among the environment, food production, and social institutions was identical. Wittfogel was a Chinese specialist, who believed that early Asian civilizations became "mighty hydraulic bureaucracies," which owed their despotic control over densely populated areas like China, Egypt, and India to the technological and environmental demands of large-scale water control projects in areas of scant rainfall. The state bureaucracy controlled the labor forces that built hydraulic works and maintained them. Thus, the social requirements of irrigation led to the development of states and urban societies in several parts of the Old World, and the same requirements led to remarkable similarities in their economic and social structure.

Wittfogel's arguments were originally formulated in the 1920s and refined over more than 30 years, during which time a mass of new data, including large-scale landscape surveys, sharpened our perceptions of early irrigation. For example, archaeologist Robert McC. Adams carried out major field surveys of ancient irrigation works in Mesopotamia in the 1960s. Adams found that early Mesopotamian irrigation consisted of cleaning natural river channels and building a few smaller feeder canals. Most settlements lay near major rivers and made the most of the natural hydrology of the waterways. Each community controlled its own small-scale irrigation works. Only centuries later did a highly centralized state government organize irrigation schemes on a massive scale. The same was true of Egypt, where the greatest irrigation works were undertaken during the New Kingdom, using thousands of laborers who were fulfilling tax obligations to the state. In contrast, early Egyptian agriculture relied on natural basins to hold back Nile water—a village-level, small-scale operation that needed no official supervision (Figure 2.2). Large-scale irrigation requires constant maintenance and supervision, to say nothing of political stability and control of water sources. For

**Figure 2.2** Egyptian Dynasty XI, egyptian estate workers labor in a granary. A Funeral Model from the Thomb a Middle Kingdom official named Meket-Re, Thebes. (Metropolitan Museum of Art, New York/Museum Excavation, 1919–1920. Rogers Fund, supplemented by contributions of Edward S. Harkness [20.3.11].)

example, the Chimor state on the Peruvian coast was overthrown by the expanding Inka empire, partly because the latter acquired control of the watersheds that fed coastal irrigation schemes (Chapter 18).

While some form of irrigation was a necessary precondition for the settlement of the southern Mesopotamian plains, where the world's first cities arose, large-scale irrigation does not everywhere appear to have been a factor in the rise of early civilization. By the same token, modern studies have shown that ecology was only one component in a mosaic of many changes that led to state-organized societies. But climate may have been of particular significance in some areas in view of the major environmental changes, especially shifts in rainfall patterns and rising sea levels, that affected the world during post-Ice Age global warming.

## *Technology and Trade*

The origins and evolution of complex societies have long been linked to technological innovation and to growing trade in raw materials like obsidian (volcanic glass used for stone tools, mirrors, and ornaments), copper, and luxury products of all kinds. V. Gordon Childe considered metallurgy an important component in the urban revolution, but in fact, copper and other exotic materials were at first used in the Near East for small-scale production of cult objects and jewelry. In many cases the technological innovations that did appear, like the wheel in Mesopotamia and the sailing ship in Egypt, were of more benefit in transportation than in production. Not until several centuries after civilization started did copper and bronze become more abundant as demands for transportation and military needs burgeoned. Technology did evolve, but only in response to developing markets, new demands, and the expanded needs of a tiny segment of the population—the elite.

Any form of trade involves two elements, both the goods and commodities being exchanged and the people doing the exchanging. People make trade connections and create exchange systems that handle trade goods, for instance, gold dust or copper ore, when they need to acquire goods and services that are not available to them within their own local area. This trade (more conventionally called "exchange") can involve gift giving, that is, the exchange of gifts that reinforces a social relationship between both individuals and groups as a whole. The gifts serve as gestures that place obligations on both parties. This kind of exchange is commonplace in New Guinea and the Pacific and was widespread in Africa during the past two thousand years. Bartering was a basic trading mechanism for many thousands of years; often sporadic and usually based on notions of reciprocity, it involved the mutual exchange of commodities or objects between individuals or groups. Redistribution of these goods through society lay in the hands of chiefs, religious leaders, or kin groups. As we have seen, such redistribution was a basic element in chiefdoms. The change from redistribution to formal trade—often based on regulated commerce that perhaps involved fixed prices and even currency—was closely tied to growing political and social complexity and hence to the development of the state.

In the 1970s, a number of archaeologists gave trade a primary role in the rise of states. British archaeologist Colin Renfrew attributed the dramatic flowering of Minoan civilization on Crete and through the Aegean to intensified trading contacts and to the impact of olive and vine cultivation on local communities. As agricultural economies became more diversified and local food supplies could be purchased both locally and over longer distances, a far-reaching economic interdependence resulted. Eventually, this led to redistribution systems for luxuries and basic commodities, systems that were organized and controlled by Minoan palaces and elsewhere in the Aegean where there were major centers of olive production. As time went on, the self-sufficiency of communities was replaced by mutual interdependence. Interest in long-distance trade brought about some cultural homogeneity from commerce, gift exchange, and perhaps piracy. Thus, intensified trade and interaction and the flowering of specialist crafts, in a complex process of positive feedback, led to much more complex societies based on palaces, which were the economic hubs of a new Minoan civilization. Renfrew's model made some assumptions that are now discounted (see Chapter 9). For example, he argued that the introduction of domesticated vines and olives in the Early Bronze Age allowed a substantial expansion in the amounts of land under cultivation and helped to power the emergence of a complex society. Many archaeologists and paleobotanists now question this view, pointing out that available evidence for cultivated vines and olives suggests that they were present only in the later Bronze Age. Trade, nevertheless, was probably one of many variables that led to the emergence of palace economies in Minoan Crete.

American archaeologist William Rathje developed a hypothesis that considered an explosion in long-distance exchange to be a fundamental cause of Maya civilization. He suggested that the lowland Maya environment was deficient in many vital resources, among them obsidian, salt, stone for grinding maize, and many luxury materials. All these could be obtained from the nearby highlands, from the Valley of Mexico, and from other regions, if the necessary trading networks came into being. Such connections, and the trading expeditions to maintain them, could not be organized by individual villages alone. The Maya lived in a relatively uniform environment, where every community suffered from the same resource deficiencies. Thus, argued Rathje, long-distance trade networks were organized through local ceremonial centers and their leaders. In time, this organization became a state, and knowledge of its functioning was exportable, as were pottery, tropical bird feathers, specialized stone materials, and other local commodities. Rathje's hypothesis probably explains part of the complex process of Maya state formation, but it suffers from the objection that suitable alternative raw materials can be found in the lowlands. It could be, too, that warfare became a competitive response to population growth and the increasing scarcity of prime agricultural land, and thus played an important role in the emergence of Maya states.

Now that we know much more about ancient exchange and commerce, we know that trade can never be looked on as a unifying factor or as a primary agent of ancient civilization simply because no one aspect of it was an overriding cause of cultural change or evolution in trading practices. Many ever-changing variables affected ancient trade, among them the demand for goods. This demand prompted a search for supplies, themselves a product of production above local needs, created to satisfy external requirements. Then there were the logistics of transportation, the extent of the trading network, and the social and political environment. Intricate market networks channeled supplies along well-defined routes. Authorities at both ends might regulate the profits fed back to the source, providing the incentive for further transactions. There may or may not have been a market organization. Extensive long-distance trade, like large-scale irrigation, was a consequence rather than a cause of civilization.

## *Warfare*

In a classic paper published in 1970, Robert Carneiro used the archaeology of coastal valleys in Peru to propose that warfare played a key role in state formation. His "coercive theory" of state origins argued that the amount of agricultural land in these valleys was limited and surrounded by desert. So a series of predictable events led to the development of states. At first, autonomous farming villages flourished in the valley landscape. But as the population grew and more land was taken up, the communities started raiding each others' fields as they competed for limited acreage. Some of the village leaders emerged as successful warlords, became chieftains, and presided over large tribal polities. The valley population continued to grow, and warfare intensified until the entire region fell under the sway of a single successful warrior, who presided over a single state centered on the valley. Then this ambitious ruler and his successors started to raid neighboring valleys. Eventually a multivalley state developed, creating a much larger civilization.

Carneiro's theory is hard to test in the field, although an attempt to do so in Peru's Santa Valley showed no sign of autonomous villages but rather indicated a much more complex, evolving settlement pattern over many centuries. Archaeologist David Wilson points out that the only "coercive" processes occurred around A.D. 400, when the Moche people carved out a multivalley state by military conquest of neighboring valleys (Chapter 18). The conquest took place long after complex irrigation-based societies flourished in the Santa Valley. As with irrigation hypotheses, reality is more complex than the straightforward Carneiro scenario.

Warfare can be rejected as a primary cause of civilization on other grounds, also. In earlier times, the diffuse social organization of village communities had not yet led to the institutional warfare that resulted from the concentration of wealth and power in a few hands. Only when absolute and despotic monarchs came into power did warfare become endemic, with standing armies to control important resources, solve political questions, and ensure social inequality. This type of warfare presupposes authority and is a consequence of civilization.

## *Coercive versus Voluntaristic Theories*

Several of the theories that we have reviewed would fall within the category of coercive: that individuals and communities were forced to participate in the process of state formation. The pressures leading to such an outcome include:

- hostile external coercion (as in Carneiro's model of military conquest)
- oppressive internal coercion (where an elite group gains control over some crucial element such as irrigation water in Wittfogel's hydraulic despotism scenario)
- self-preservation in a context of military threat, as where individuals are obliged to concede increased central control in order to withstand the threat posed by a more powerful neighbour

It is important to recognise, however, that in some circumstances, societies voluntarily coalesce into states under the impluse of other factors. Thus the city of Uruk in southern Mesopotamia was clearly an important cult center and may have attracted settlers through its sanctity and religious prestige. The same may have been true of Teotihuacán, where the cave below the Pyramid of the Sun was reputed to be the locus where creation took place. Thus whatever its military and political power, Teotihuacán may also have drawn upon religious authority. There are many more recent examples, including Jerusalem and Mecca, of cities which grew great as centers of pilgrimage.

One category of theories which combine both coercive and voluntaristic elements in charting the development of state societies are those which employ the concept of the cultural system.

## Cultural Systems and Civilization

Most archaeologists agree that urban life and preindustrial civilization came into existence gradually, during a period of major social and economic change. Everyone agrees, also, that linear explanations that invoke irrigation, trade, or warfare are inadequate. Recent theories of the rise of states invoke multiple and often intricate causes and are frequently based on systems models.

In the 1960s, Robert McC. Adams, an expert on ancient Mesopotamia, introduced a new generation of complex theories when he argued that irrigation agriculture, increased warfare, and "local resource variability" were three factors vital in newly appearing urban civilizations. Each affected society and the other factors with positive feedback, thus each helping to reinforce change. The creation of food surpluses and the emergence of a stratified society were critical developments. Irrigation agriculture could feed a bigger population. Larger populations and an increase in permanent settlement, as well as trade with regular centers for redistributing goods, were all pressures for greater production and increased surpluses, actively fostered by dominant groups in society. The greatly enlarged surpluses enabled those who controlled them to employ larger numbers of artisans and other specialists who did not themselves grow crops.

Adams argued that some societies were better able to transform themselves into states because of the favorable variety of resources on which they could draw. Increased populations led to monopolies over strategic resources. These communities eventually were more powerful than their neighbors, expanding their territories by military campaigns and efficiently exploiting their advantages over other peoples. Such cities became early centers of major religious activities, of technological and artistic innovations, and of writing. And literacy, a skill confined to a few people, became an important source of power (see Box 3.1).

During the 1960s, archaeologists began to think of human cultures as "cultural systems," made up of many interacting parts, among them, for example, technology, social organization, and religious beliefs. The cultural system itself was part of a much larger, ever-changing ecological system and varied in response to constant environmental modification. The notion of cultures as systems led to more elaborate models of the origins of states.

Archaeologists like Kent Flannery, who works in Mesoamerica, saw the state as a very complicated "living" system, the complexity of which could be measured by the internal differentiation and intricacy of its subsystems, such as those for agriculture, technology, religious beliefs, and so on. The way in which these subsystems were linked and the controls that society imposed on the system as a whole were vital. This model seemed to work well with Mesoamerican states, where pervasive religious beliefs formed close links among public architecture, the economy, and other "subsystems" of civilization. Colin Renfrew used a form of systems approach when studying the origins of Minoan civilization, a model in which trade and agricultural intensification played a leading role (see p. 36).

Systems approaches to the origins of civilization tend to be somewhat abstract and to make a distinction between the processes of culture change (the succession of changes by which early states acquired their new complexity), the mechanisms by which these processes occurred, and the socioenvironmental stresses that select for these mechanisms. Thus, an explanation of the development of states centers on the ways in which the processes took place.

The subsystems within a cultural system are regulated by a control apparatus that keeps all the variables in a system within bounds so that the survival of a system is not threatened. This apparatus of social control is vital, for it balances subsistence needs with religious, political, social, and other ideological values. There is a well-defined hierarchy of regulation and policy, ranging from those decisions under the control of individuals, to institutions within society with specialized functions, such as the priesthood, to the basic highest-order propositions, those of societal policy. These abstract standards, or values, lie at the heart of any society's regulation of its cultural system.

The management and regulation of a state is a far more elaborate and central undertaking than that of a small chiefdom. Indeed, the most striking difference between states and less complicated societies is the degree of complexity in their ways of reaching decisions and their hierarchic organization, not necessarily in their subsistence activities. Any living system is subjected to stress when one of its many variables exceeds the range of deviation that the system allows. The stress may make the system evolve new institutions or policies. Such coping mechanisms may be triggered by warfare, population pressure, trade, environmental change, or other variables. These variables create what Mesoamerican specialist Kent Flannery calls an "adaptive milieu" for evolutionary change.

Systems models of early states are bound to be complex, for they have to distinguish between mechanisms and processes and the socioenvironmental pressures by which we have sought to explain the origins of civilization. Religion and control of information now appear to be key elements in the regulation of environmental and economic variables in early civilizations and, indeed, in any human society.

## Ecological Theories

Ecologically based theories, which also rely heavily on systems approaches, have enjoyed a relatively long life compared with many other hypotheses, but they face the objection that testing such models is very difficult. For example, in a classic study of the Valley of Mexico, William Sanders and a group of archaeologists showed how the Aztec state created and organized huge agricultural systems that spread over the shallow waters of the lakes that once filled the valley. The variability of the local environment meant that the Aztecs had to exploit every environmental opportunity afforded them. Thus, Sanders argues, the state organized large-scale agriculture to support a population of up to 250,000 just in and around the Aztec capital, Tenochtitlán. Environmental factors were decisive in each area where civilization began, he believes. Another important factor was centralized leadership.

Some support for this perspective comes from Mesopotamia, where recent studies of rising sea levels have thrown new light on the changing geography of the low-lying Mesopotamian delta between the Tigris and Euphrates. During the late Ice Age, world sea levels were about 90 meters (300 feet) below modern shorelines. The Persian Gulf was dry land 20,000 years ago, with rising sea waters only entering the basin about 10,000 B.C. At the time, the ancestral Tigris and Euphrates river system flowed through the deepest part of the gulf, down a deep canyon caused by the rivers' erosion effect to the low sea level of the Indian Ocean. Today's Mesopotamian delta did not exist and the entire region was very arid. Between 10,000 and 4000 B.C., shorelines rose rapidly in the Persian Gulf, sometimes at a rate of 11 meters (36 feet) a century, at a time when rainfall increased slightly throughout the Near East. By 6500 B.C., the sea had flooded the old river system and reached the northern shore of the Gulf. The rise in sea level slowed in about 5000 B.C. as river estuaries reached their northern limits, extending as far inland as the ancient city of Ur. The vast estuaries filled with wind-blown sand from the Arabian Desert. But the water table remained high, creating large swampy areas in the silt-choked river mouths.

Unfortunately, the archaeological record of these millennia lies buried under deep layers of silt and today's high sea levels. But James and Douglas Kennett, geologist and archaeologist, have suggested a hypothetical environmental and cultural scenario, as follows. After 7000 B.C., and for about fifteen hundred years, southern Mesopotamia enjoyed an unusually favorable climate, with greater and more reliable rainfall. This may have been a period when people hunted and gathered along the rapidly changing sea coast, using temporary settlements now buried under

Gulf waters. Some of these communities may have begun cereal farming. As the climate became drier and the floodplain expanded, some groups may have turned to simple irrigation farming, which provided higher crop yields. Population densities rose proportionately to the yields, increasing competition for agricultural land and other food resources just when the rising Gulf was moving inland at as much as a kilometer (0.6 mile) a decade. In such circumstances, communities living near the water's edge may have moved at regular intervals, eventually coalescing into larger villages. At first, small communities dug their own watercourses, diverting river meadows and side streams. Kin leaders, men and women with unusual supernatural powers, may have been those who organized canal digging, perhaps even allocating land, as they do in many village communities. In time, these individuals became the spiritual and political leaders of a farming village in transition, on its way to becoming a settlement and society of far greater complexity. Small villages became towns and then bustling cities, central places with political and economic tentacles that extended into settlements near and far. Thus was born the city and, ultimately, Mesopotamian civilization.

The Kennett scenario is based on new and highly sophisticated climatic data but remains entirely hypothetical in archaeological terms. It contrasts with the traditional view that farming spread into southern Mesopotamia from the north and east (see Chapter 3). But it does highlight the great importance of local environmental change to the origins of all preindustrial civilizations. Declining Nile floods may have been a factor in the formation of the Egyptian state, for example. It also suggests that a centralized organization was of significant importance. A powerful leader has the information about state-held resources at his or her disposal, along with the ability to command peoples' labor and to collect and redistribute its results. Thus, goes the argument, states arise in social and environmental contexts in which centralized management solves problems effectively.

The ecological approach has serious problems. How, for example, does one tell which environments would foster state formation? Fertile floodplains like those in Mesopotamia and Egypt? Coastal river valleys like those in Peru? Highland plateaux like those of Mesoamerica? Or areas where land is in short supply (also coastal Peru)? States have arisen in regions where there are few geographical constraints, like the Maya lowlands of Mesoamerica. Further, preindustrial civilizations have developed without any sign of rapid population growth in Iran and parts of the Near East. But there can be no doubt that environmental change and environmental factors were major players in a very complex process of cultural change and response.

## Social Theories

In recent years, archaeology has shifted away from systems-ecological approaches toward a greater concern with individuals and groups. These theories have often tended to be somewhat impersonal, treating states as rather anonymous, even mechanical entities, which operated according to complex processes of cultural change. A new generation of researchers is carrying social approaches in new directions, arguing that all human societies consist, ultimately, of individuals and groups interacting with one another and all pursuing their own agendas. Their hypotheses revolve around such phenomena as power, ideology, factionalism, and the role of the individual.

## *Power in Three Domains*

Archaeologically, one can look at power in three domains: economic power, social and ideological power, and political power. The combination of economic productivity, the control over sources and distribution of food and wealth, the segregation and maintenance of the stratified social system and its ideology, and the ability to maintain control by force were the vital ingredients of early states. Each of these domains was closely linked to the others, but they can be studied separately in the archaeological record.

Economic power depends on the ability to create more specialized production and to organize the diverse tasks of storage and food distribution. In time, stored wealth in food and goods develops into relationships of dependency between those who produce or acquire the wealth and those who control and distribute it. A state comprises elites (the noble class), officials (the managers), and dependents (the commoners). The landowning class and the estate—whether owned by a temple, the ruler, or a private individual—provide security for its dependents. All early states developed from foundations in which agricultural production became more intensified and diverse while at the same time moving away from purely kin-based organization into centralized structures, which cross-cut or overrode kinship ties.

Economic power also rested in trade and exchange, in long-distance networks that provided access to commodities not available locally. Sumer obtained its metal from Anatolia, Iran, and the Persian Gulf. Egypt acquired gold and ivory from Nubia, and highland Andean civilizations imported fishmeal from the Pacific coast. The acquisition of exotic commodities or goods on any scale required organization, record keeping, and supervision. The archaeological record shows that the extent of state supervision of trade and traders varied considerably from civilization to civilization.

Social power means ideological power, and it comes from the creation or modification of certain symbols of cultural and political commonality. Such common ideology, expressed in public and private ceremonials, in art and architecture, and in literature, serves to link individuals and communities with common ties that transcend those of kin. Those who create and perpetuate these ideologies are held in high honor and enjoy considerable prestige, for they are often perceived as interceding with the spiritual world and the gods, and they are sometimes even seen as living deities themselves. The guardians of ideology are privileged individuals, for their spiritual powers give them special social status and allow them to perpetuate social inequality. So important is ideology that one can speak of the Mesopotamian or Maya areas not in a political sense, for they were made up of patchworks of city-states, but in an ideological one.

Many great cities of the past, like Teotihuacán in the Valley of Mexico or Angkor Thom in Cambodia, were a combination of the spiritual and the secular. They all boasted of powerful priesthoods and religious institutions, which owed their wealth to their ability to manage the spiritual affairs of the state, to legitimize rulers as upholders of the cosmic order. And temples, pyramids, and plazas provided imposing settings for elaborate public ceremonies, which ensured the continuity of human life and the universe.

Political power rests in the ruler's ability to impose authority throughout society by both administrative and military means. Those who held positions of authority within either the bureaucracy or the army did not come from within the kin system but were recruited outside of it. This political power lay in foreign relations and in defense and waging war. It also operated at a statewide level, dealing with the resolution of major disputes between different factions. But a great deal of power lay outside the political estate, in the hands of community and kin leaders who handled many legal matters that revolved around such issues as land ownership and family law.

Norman Yoffee believes that the interplay between these three sources of power led to the development of new, society-wide institutions, to supreme rulers and the state. There was, he says, no one moment when civilization came into being, for social evolution did not end with the rise of the state. Preindustrial states functioned in an atmosphere of continual change and constant disputation. Some collapsed; others survived for many centuries.

This approach to the origin of states argues not for neoevolutionary ladders but for a much greater diversity of social evolution, which saw many trajectories for the development of social complexity. Many societies operated under significant constraints; they may have lacked, say, dependable crops or domesticated animals or the ability to store large amounts of food. Constraints like these took human societies along very different evolutionary paths than those of the state. That some societies did not become civilizations does not mean that they were stuck in a backward "stage" but simply that constraints on growth prevented the interplay of the major factors that led to state formation elsewhere. Thus, the chiefdom where social inequality came from within the kin system—where inequality was based on access to resources and the power this control provides—is an alternative trajectory to the state. This approach to the origin of states will require sophisticated research that combines archaeological and historical records in a new synthesis, seldom attempted in the past.

## *Ideology and Factionalism*

Every early civilization had a pervasive set of religious beliefs and philosophies, which reached out to every corner of society. These ideologies shaped society and ensured the conformity of its members, but to study such intangibles is a formidable task. Ideologies come down to us in distinctive art styles, like those of the Egyptians or the Chavín art style of the Andes, serving as visual reminders of a state's ideology, reinforcing the power of supreme rulers and their special relationships to the gods and the spiritual world. In societies where only an elite minority are literate (or have scribes in their employ), art has a powerful role to play in shaping society and reinforcing ideology.

Public architecture also reinforces ideology. The first Mesopotamian cities grew rapidly, turning from loose agglomerations of villages to sizable, closely packed urban precincts clustered around a central complex of public buildings. The ancient ziggurats, the temple pyramids of Sumerian city states like Ur, towered high over their surroundings, artificial mountains that rose toward the heavens (Figure 3.10). The Maya lived in cities like Copán and El Mirador, which were depictions in stone, wood, and stucco of a symbolic landscape of sacred hills, caves, and forests (Figure 15.8). It was here that great lords appeared before the people in elaborate public ceremonies. Through ritual bloodletting and shamanistic trance, they entered the realm of the Otherworld, the world of the deities and ancestors. These sacred rituals validated the world of the Maya and linked noble and commoner, ruler and humble village farmer, in a complex social contract. The leaders were the intermediaries, the people who guaranteed plentiful crops and interceded with the gods to ensure the continued existence of human life. The ceremonial centers, with their pyramids, plazas, and temples, were reassuring settings where the dramas of life and death, of planting and harvest, were played out against a backdrop of ever-changing seasons and of passing time. These ceremonies justified social inequality, the great distinctions between the ruler and the ruled.

The ceremonial center ensured the continuity of cultural traditions and was an instrument of religious power. Here the religious and moral models of society provided a sacred canon that circumscribed political institutions and delineated the social order. The words of the gods rang out in reassuring chants passed down from generation to generation, often in the name of divine rulers, themselves deities on earth. Pyramids and temples, public buildings, were tangible expressions and instruments of religious power. Many early civilizations, like those of the Maya, Mesopotamians, and Harappans, were founded with powerful religious beliefs at their very core. Eventually, the ceremonial centers were taken over by rising secular rulers, who were sometimes installed by force. As the power of kingship grew, the political power of the ceremonial center declined, although its religious functions were carefully maintained. The king assumed the secular, and often militaristic, leadership of the state. Inevitably, the king's residence, the royal palace, became an important part of public architecture and ceremonial centers, even if the ruler's powers were entirely secular, and all the more if he assumed a divine role himself. Royal tombs achieved great elaboration, standing as garish and splendid monuments to the awesome political and social power behind them.

In every part of the world where early civilizations appeared, ceremonial centers were preceded by inconspicuous prototypes tended by priests or cult leaders and often honoring revered ancestors. These people must have been among the first to be freed of the burden of producing food, supported by the communities they served. Thus it was no coincidence that the ceremonial center was the initial focus of power, exchange, and authority, an authority vested in religious symbolism and organized priesthoods. Very often, those who served these divine beings became the people of authority, the individuals who controlled economic surpluses, offerings, and the redistribution of goods. The temples became a new instrument for organizing fresh political, social, and religious structures. Soon symbolic statements describing society served as models not only for behavior and belief but also for the ceremonial centers that perpetuated and formulated them. Khmer and Maya cities were reproductions of symbolic worlds in clay and stone. Egyptian pyramids symbolized the close relationship between the pharaoh and the sun god in heaven. The plazas and pyramids of Mesoamerican cities such as Teotihuacán and Tikal provided imposing settings in which the elaborate theater of religious ceremonies was played out before enormous audiences. At such occasions, the ruler, as intermediary to the gods and the spiritual world, would appear before the people in a theatrical reinforcement of the beliefs that caused society to run on smooth rails and ensured the continuity of human life and of civilization.

Ancient ideologies were as complex as our own, and they defy ready archaeological analysis by their very complexity and nonmaterial nature. To understand the true complexity of ancient ideologies really requires texts written by people of the time, such as exist for Sumerian, Egyptian, and other civilizations. The recent decipherment of Maya script has shown just how important and pervasive ideologies were in ancient civilizations. Until decipherment, most authorities assumed Maya rulers were peaceful priest-kings, who used their power as astronomers to preside over small city-states. But Maya glyphs reveal an intricate and complex pantheon of deities and religious beliefs that often defy modern analysis. Each day in the Maya calendar possessed a combination of qualities; every compass direction, colors and characteristics; each deity, many roles and moods. Nothing in Maya society occurred without acquiring symbolic and often ideological meaning. In Egypt, too, the ancient precedents of the pharaohs' rule and the teachings of the gods permeated all society and governed even the collection of taxes and the distribution of rations. As we see in Chapter 4, the development of the distinctive ideology of Egyptian kingship played a vital role in shaping more than two thousand years of civilization along the Nile.

With ideology comes factionalism. As we have seen, ancient societies were as diverse as modern ones, especially when their leaders traded with neighbors near and far. The state functioned for the benefit of a minority, privileged rulers and nobles to whom all wealth and power flowed. A ruler governed his domains by deputing governance to relatives and loyal followers, who became provincial governors. The Inka lords colonized newly subjected lands with loyal nobility who ruled in their name. They often resettled thousands of farmers in lands far from their homeland to protect themselves against rebellion. But, inevitably, some individuals were more ambitious than others, rebelling against authority and plotting to gain supreme power. Competing factions within local groups and in different regions triggered social inequality and changing patterns of leadership, increased specialization, and the development of states. And once civilizations came into being, they would challenge royal successions and even lead to civil war when a ruler was perceived as weak or indecisive.

The study of factionalism relies on a combination of archaeology, anthropological observations, and historical records. For example, the recent decipherment of Maya glyphs has revealed dynasties of ambitious, warlike lords obsessed with genealogy and with legitimizing their succession, living by their wits and military skills in a world of ever-shifting diplomatic alliances and factional disputes. Maya stelae and inscriptions show how two large states, Calakmul and Tikal, dominated the Maya world for centuries, locked in bitter rivalry, each riven by factionalism and constant rebellion. As Chapters 4 and 16 show, competition and emerging factionalism were powerful catalysts in the development of many early states.

## *Individuals and Gender*

Studies of gender relations and the roles of small groups in early civilizations are still in their infancy but promise to be of great importance. For example, Aztec women learned how to weave in childhood, for skillful weaving was considered an important attribute of Aztec womanhood. "The good middle-aged woman [is] a skilled weaver, a weaver of designs, an artisan, a good cook, a preparer of good food." Thus did sixteenth-century Franciscan friar Bernardino de Sahagun's Aztec informants describe a noblewoman's role in Mexican civilization before the Spanish conquest. But this description is grossly misleading and simplistic because it ignores the links between weaving, cooking, child rearing, and other tasks and the wider society in which the women lived. Women wove textiles and the capes that were the badges of social status in Aztec society. Their woven products were vital to the enormous tribute system on which Aztec civilization depended. Cotton mantles were a form of currency, and cloth became a primary way of organizing the ebb and flow of goods and services that sustained the state.

Archaeologist Elizabeth Brumfiel has shown that the women living in the Aztec capital turned away from weaving to the cultivation of nearby swamp gardens and the salting of fish. In contrast, women living at some distance outside the capital spent most of their time weaving to satisfy the tribute demands of the capital. Thanks to Brumfiel's work, we know that the Aztec household and the roles of women were much more varied than Sahagun's informants suggested. Cooking and weaving were important ways of maintaining social and political control. Women were makers of both valuable goods and of people. It was they who ensured the continuity of Aztec kin groups. Women played a dynamic and highly adaptive role in this remarkable civilization.

Another archaeologist, Christine Hastorf, has studied changing gender relations among ancient Sausa maize and potato farmers in highland Peru. Before the Inka conquest of A.D. 1460, the Sausa lived in local population groups of several thousand people. The Inka dispersed the Sausa into small village settlements and forced them to increase maize production. Hastorf used the distribution of food remains from ancient and modern dwellings and stable isotope analyses of male and female skeletons from archaeological sites to study the resulting changes in gender relations. Under the Inka regime, each male had to perform agricultural and military service. They were fed meat, maize, and corn beer. Unlike earlier times, the tasks of men and women were separated physically, politically, and symbolically. The men farmed and were often absent, while the women intensified their food-producing and beer-making activities in support of the males. Hastorf found that in pre-Inka times, males and females ate quinoa, potatoes, and some maize. But after the Inka conquest, many of the male diets were much richer in maize than those of women, which may reflect a higher rate of beer consumption by the men. The political climate had changed. Men were involved in many more activities outside the household, while the women worked harder and had a more restricted role in the new society.

Similar processes of change have been documented in early Mesopotamia, where one of the main craft products (as in Aztec Mexico) was textiles. Weaving began as a domestic occupation carried out by women in their own households. During the 3rd millennium B.C., however, as the Mesopotamian cities grew, conditions changed and textile production became connected to the large estates. Documents record thousands of people, including many women and children, working in these establishments as forced laborers who had effectively lost control of the products of their work. Archaeologist Joy McCorriston argues that such changes in textile production played an essential role in the transformation of ancient Mesopotamia from a predominantly kin-based to a predominantly class-based society.

Relatively small, often anonymous groups within ancient societies can sometimes be identified by their distinctive artifacts. A case in point comes from the great Mexican city of Teotihuacán in the Valley of Mexico, where a special quarter was home to a flourishing community of artisans and merchants from the Valley of Oaxaca. Archaeologist René Millon was able to identify this minority group from their distinctive pottery, which was confined to their barrio within the city. Many early civilizations were far more diverse than conventional wisdom has allowed—witness the polyglot population of Babylon recorded in the Old Testament and the known diversity of imperial Rome's teeming urban populace.

Only recently have archaeologists begun to use artifacts and other material remains to study the many groups within early civilizations. This research shows us that archaeology has the potential to probe the ways in which men and women adapt to changing circumstances and allows us to move beyond the deeds of kings and divine rulers and study the ever-changing interactions among the many groups that made up the societies over which they presided. And in complex, state-organized societies, this kind of meticulous inquiry will tell us much about the intricate and ever-changing dynamics of societies very different to our own.

In an era when archaeological research has become increasingly specialized, it is probably futile to search for a theory of state formation that can be applied to all civilizations. Some common questions, however, revolve around the implications of ecological variables for the political orders of societies about to become states: How is ecological opportunity or necessity translated into political change? What were the goals of the political actors, who were pursuing their individual goals while states were being formed? Which ecological variables were obstacles? Which were opportunities? The answers to these questions will come from sophisticated studies that combine systems-ecological approaches with careful research into what British archaeologist Colin Renfrew once called "the archaeology of mind," the elusive intangibles behind the material record of the past.

## Cycling Chiefdoms: Processes and Agents

The world's first states, politically centralized and socially stratified societies, developed in only a few locations—in Egypt and Mesopotamia by 3000 B.C., and in Mexico and the Andean region by 200 B.C. Invariably, they were formed in a distinctive political environment, in what Kent Flannery calls "the dynamic crucible of cycling chiefdoms." He and others believe that states arise in situations where a group of chiefdoms are competing with one another, as they did along the Nile River in the fourth millennium B.C., for example. Eventually, one of the competitors succeeded in achieving political dominance over its neighbors, so that they become provinces of a larger political unit. This competition can arise from many causes: rivalry between chiefly families, factionalism, endemic warfare and raiding, dramatic differences in population densities from one area to the next, crop failure, or just plain weak leadership or outright conquest.

Henry Wright has described this process among chiefdoms as "cycling," a constant fluctuation between simple and more complex chiefdoms. Each chief presides over a single village and some lesser hamlets nearby. Then one leader usurps the power of his once egalitarian neighbors and forms a much larger political unit, where the former village chiefs become subchiefs. The newly powerful kingdom expands, then breaks down into smaller chiefdoms again, or simply collapses in a recurrent process of emergence, expansion, and fragmentation.

Ancient chiefdoms had the hereditary inequality and hierarchical social structure from which a state could arise, but this rarely happened. Robert Carneiro, an expert on chiefdoms, has suggested no less than six processes for creating one. You defeat neighboring communities in war, then incorporate them into a larger political unit. At the same time you take prisoners and force them to work for you as slaves. Once you have established control, you appoint close supporters to administer the conquered areas, unless the defeated chiefs are cooperative. Your subjects pay you tribute at regular intervals and are expected to provide fighting men in times of war. States were much larger and more centralized than chiefdoms, as well as being much more stratified socially and politically. Invariably, however, they shared the processes which Carneiro lays out.

Under this argument, state formation began with Carneiro's six processes, with the addition of chiefly cycling. Centuries might pass with the usual cycles of simplicity and complexity without any quantum jump in social and political complexity. Then, suddenly, three processes come together:

- A standoff of some kind between neighboring and constantly warring chiefdoms develops, reflected in the dispersal of population and the development of "buffer zones" between neighbors.
- One center rapidly acquires additional population, perhaps at the expense of its neighbors. Sometimes highly organized warfare comes into play, as campaigns of conquest

replace the constant raiding of earlier times. Conquered areas are incorporated into the new, much larger kingdom.

- A large capital settlement, usually a city, develops as the ultimate level in a four-level settlement hierarchy: city, regional centers, subcenters, and villages.

Carneiro and Wright believe that the formation of states required some form of territorial expansion. But there are limits to the amount of resources that chiefs and their elites can extract from their followers. When that moment comes, they have several options: increase their demands on their subjects, which raises the specter of rebellion, intensify agricultural production with technological innovation, or expand their territory by subjugating their neighbors. If the third alternative is chosen, the kingdom rapidly comes to a point where it becomes larger than the chief himself can administer, so he has to restructure the way he administers his domains and probably make ideological changes to reflect the new political system—a state. This process is reasonably well documented in Mesopotamia and Egypt, also in Mesoamerica and the Andes.

These are, however, generalized, anonymous processes, like those criticized by postprocessualists. As scholars of the latter school have often pointed out, it is people, individuals and groups, who are responsible for political and other cultural change. They are the "agents" as opposed to the "processes." To study ancient agents requires very rich historical records, which enable us to identify individuals and describe their deeds. In some case, like Egypt, we know the names of seminal rulers like the first pharaoh Horus Aha, but they are little more than shadowy personages on the stage of history. No question, however, that people of great ability and charisma were responsible for the rise of many powerful states known from historical times. Flannery cites the example of the remarkable King Shaka, who set up the Zulu state in South Africa in the early nineteenth century, King Kamehameha of Hawaii, and others (Figure 2.3). All of them were individuals who were products of their times, whose personal abilities made the most of unusual circumstances, accidental situations, and other moments where they could further their political and military goals. The result was, invariably, a process of historical change.

Flannery lists ten qualities that marked Shaka and other agents and argues that they were shared by the chiefs of unusual ability who created the first civilizations. They were members of an elite, people with aggressive and authoritarian personalities, with outstanding military abilities that gave them upward social mobility. They usurped the position of chief by fair means or foul, then conquered their immediate neighbors, while seeking a competitive advantage over more distant rivals (this could be technological, a matter of military strategy, and so on). They used this advantage to expand into more distant lands, while using forced labor to intensify agricultural production, as a means of keeping subjects content and of provisioning armies. If they could not intensify their food production, they acquired additional resources by raiding. Finally, they solidified their position by power-sharing, even if it was nothing more than a nominal gesture. This was definitely not democracy, for the earliest states were ruled by strong, able rulers, who governed autocratically, even if they had nominal councils of advisers.

**Figure 2.3** The Zulu ruler Shaka.

Much depends on ideology, too, for invariably the pre-industrial states were held together by a powerful and distinctive ideology. The famous Epic of Gilgamesh gives us a flavor of Mesopotamian ideology. The pharaohs ruled as the living personification of the sun god. Maya lords were shamans and intermediaries between the people and the ancestors. These ideologies were reflected in sacred places, where lavish ceremonies and public appearances by the ruler were important symbols of continuity and stability, where the ruler's subjects directed their loyalty to the central figure at the pinnacle of the state. Ideology never caused states to come into being, but was an invariable and important part of their fabric once they had come into being.

Both processes and individual agents played vital roles in the formation of states. Aggressive individuals of great ambition have been members of human societies since the beginning, but, until about six thousand years ago, they never lived at a time when conditions of social inequality and chiefly competition were endemic in areas like Mesopotamia and the Nile Valley, or later in Mesoamerica and the Andes. Then these circumstances, competitive advantage, military prowess, and other factors turned a very few of them from powerful chiefs into authoritarian kings, soon supported by compelling new ideologies developed from earlier and less complex worldviews.

## The Collapse of Civilizations

Many historians, most recently the Yale University scholar Paul Kennedy, have written about cycles of history, the rise of civilizations, their brilliant apogees, and their sudden declines. Eventually one civilization falls and another rises to take its place, which in turn goes through the same cycle of rise and fall. The record of early civilizations could easily be written in cyclical terms, for states have risen and then collapsed with bewildering rapidity in all parts of the world within the past 5,000 years. In the Mexican highlands, for example, the great city of Teotihuacán flourished between about 200 B.C. and A.D. 700. In A.D. 600, it had a population of more than 125,000 people. For 600 years, more than 85 percent of the population of the Valley of Mexico lived in or close to Teotihuacán. Then the city collapsed in the eighth century A.D. Within half a century, the population shrank to a quarter of its former size. A series of lesser states competed to fill the political vacuum left by the great city's fall, until the Toltecs, and later the Aztecs, rose to supremacy.

Archaeologist Joyce Marcus has referred to the repetitive cycles of consolidation, expansion, and dissolution that were a feature of so many early civilizations as the "Dynamic Model." Initially developed through study of the growth and decline of Maya states such as Tikal and Calakmul, the same framework can be applied to Central Mexico, the Andean region, Mesopotamia, and the Aegean. She has argued that in each of these cases, an initial unitary state endured for about two hundred centuries before breaking down into smaller units (often city-states), which then underwent further cycles of expansion, unification, and fragmentation as political and economic fortunes rose and fell. The reason for these cycles lies, in her view, in the difficulty of maintaining large-scale inegalitarian structures over the long term: the "peaks" of consolidation inevitably give way to the "valleys" of dissolution.

When a complex society collapses, it suddenly becomes smaller, simpler, and much more egalitarian. Population densities fall, trade and economic activity dries up, information flow declines, and the known world shrinks for the survivors. Joseph Tainter, one of the few archaeologists to have made a comparative study of collapse, points out that an initial investment by a society in a growing complexity is a rational way of trying to solve the needs of the moment. At first the strategy works. Agricultural production increases through more intensive farming methods; an emerging bureaucracy works well; expanding trade networks bring wealth to a new elite, who use their authority and economic clout to undertake great public works such as pyramids and temples that validate their spiritual authority and divine associations. Maya civilization is an excellent example of these processes in action. It prospered greatly for centuries in the Mesoamerican lowlands until a point of diminishing return was reached.

As the most costly solutions to society's needs are exhausted, it becomes imperative that new organizational and economic answers be found, which may have much lower yields and cost a great deal more. As these stresses develop, argues Tainter, a complex society such as that of the Maya is increasingly vulnerable to collapse. There are few reserves to carry society through droughts, famines, floods, or other natural disasters. Eventually, collapse ensues, especially when important segments of society perceive that centralization and social complexity simply do not work any more and that they are better off on their own. The trend toward decentralization, toward collapse, becomes compelling. Tainter calls collapse not a catastrophe but a rational process that occurs when increasing stress requires some organizational change. The population decline and other catastrophic effects that just preceded, accompanied, or followed collapse may have been traumatic at the time, but they can be looked at as part of what one might call an economizing process.

There is, of course, more to collapse than merely an economizing process. Complete collapse can only occur in circumstances where there is a power vacuum. In many cases, there may be a powerful neighbor waiting in the wings. In early times, numerous city-states traded and competed with one another within a small area. Sumerian cities, Minoan and Mycenaean palace-kingdoms in Greece and the Aegean, the Maya in Mesoamerica—all lived in close interdependence, in a state of constant peer polity interaction. They traded, fought, and engaged in constant diplomacy. Under these circumstances, to collapse is an invitation to be dominated by one's competitors. There is only loss of complexity when every polity in the interacting cluster collapses at the same time.

The collapse of early civilizations, then, may be closely connected to declining returns from social complexity and the normal political processes of factionalism, social unrest, succession disputes, and even civil war.

## Civilization and Sustainability

Sustainability is a key question when considering the formation, growth, and collapse of states. These societies were characterised by populations unprecedented both in their size and in their density. It was not just the number of people that lived in the Maya area or in ancient Mesopotamia, but the relatively small area into which they were concentrated. To support such populations, various intensive agricultural methods were developed, including large-scale irrigation and the terracing of hillslopes. These were designed both to increase yields from a given area and to increase the absolute amount of land under cultivation. These strategies were in essence very successful: They made it possible to feed larger populations than ever before and supported the growth of cities. But they also placed considerable strains on the environment and rendered them increasingly fragile and vulnerable to unexpected climatic events, and even to the short-term fluctuations with which these societies must already have been familiar. Thus, the argument is that ancient state societies were fundamentally unsustainable owing to their size and the demands that they generated for ever more intensive agriculture.

The evidence is often, however, very difficult to read. Thus in Egypt, it has long been argued that the rise and fall of successive dynasties was a direct consequence of environmental impacts manifest in the heights of the Nile flood. The annual Nile flood was vital to the agricultural system of ancient Egypt, bringing both water and fertile silt to the fields. A good year was one which watered the fields and filled the irrigation basins; a bad year, one where the flood was either too low or too high, bringing drought or washing away field systems and villages. A period of low Niles ushered in the First Intermediate Period c. 2180 B.C. Contemporary texts tell of widespread famine, but in such graphic terms that hyperbole must be suspected. The background is, after all, the collapse of centralized royal rule and all the certainties that went with it. Evidence from Birket Qarun demonstrates that the low Niles of the period were a reality, but the extent of famine recorded belongs to a literary genre of lamentation that cannot be relied upon as eyewitness accounts of actual conditions. Furthermore, it is clear that famine was already known from earlier centuries, as depicted in the pyramid complex of Unas around 150 years before. We need to distinguish carefully here between exceptional events and the regular pattern of fluctuation that characterizes every climatic regime. Furthermore, we should note that the human response is always crucial: Paradoxically, whereas low Nile floods may have disrupted the Egyptian state around 2200 B.C., a similar pattern of declining Nile floods has been claimed by some as a primary cause behind the initial foundation of the unified Egyptian state a thousand years earlier.

Intensification is nonetheless a risky business, and the idea that these societies were nourishing the seeds of their own demise—a disaster waiting to happen—does deserve serious attention. Can we assume that the agricultural technologies designed to provide the high yields needed to support the growing urban populations necessarily had an adverse impact on the local environment? That might at first seem to be an inevitable conclusion: The early city sites of Mesopotamia, for example, stand today surrounded by an arid landscape. Yet it would be a mistake to attribute this automatically to overexploitation by early farmers.

The city of Uruk was one of the largest in southern Mesopotamia, and by around 3000 B.C. had grown into an enormous metropolis covering no less than 400 hectares (1,000 acres). Intensive irrigation agriculture supported this high population level, which must have placed a strain on the carrying capacity of the immediate environment. Uruk continued to be occupied for a further 3,000 years, however, which suggests that some stable accommodation with its local environment must have been reached. Furthermore, its desertlike setting today is the result not of overexploitation of the land but of a westward shift in the branch of the Euphrates that flowed past the western edge of the city and provided water for irrigation agriculture of the surrounding fields.

It is well recognized today that one of the damaging consequences of irrigation in climates with high evaporation rates is salination: the increased salt content of the ground water, or in extreme cases the formation of a salt crust on the surface of the fields. The effects are visible in parts of Mesopotamia today, as for instance in the area around Mari on the Middle Euphrates. In the 1950s, it was argued that salination had been a problem in southern Mesopotamia in the third millennium B.C., during the period of the early cities. In around 2450 B.C., the ruler of the city of Lagash built a canal to draw water from the River Tigris; 15 years later, clay tablets record salinity problems in the Lagash area. Salination became an element in curse formulae; it was what you wished upon your enemies or upon would-be transgressors: In the frontier war between the cities of Lagash and Umma, the boundary was protected by the curse "May [the god] Enlil make salt surface in his furrows" should the ruler of Umma attempt to infringe it.

It is quite clear from this that South Mesopotamian farmers in the third millennium B.C. were familiar with the problem of salination, albeit the process may have been more localized than some have tried to suggest. The long occupation of city sites like Uruk, however, show that it did not lead to dramatic societal collapse. Furthermore, documentary evidence suggests that fields that had been recorded as damaged by salination in one year reappear under cultivation a few years later: Mesopotamian farmers understood methods of remedial action to counter the effects.

Claims for environmental degradation have figured prominently in discussions of the "collapse" of the Maya city-states of lowland Mesoamerica. When explorers Stephens and Catherwood "rediscovered" the Maya cities in the 1830s, they were struck by the setting of tall pyramids and elaborately carved stelae among luxuriant forest growth. Here was the archetypal picture of a great "lost" civilization, abandoned cities submerged by vegetation. Theories of catastrophic or apocalyptic overthrow came naturally to mind to explain these dramatic scenes.

Recent studies of the Maya collapse have emphasised the gradual and progressive nature of the process, beginning earliest in the south and advancing northward. It was not a single, sudden event, as had once been thought. Warfare and social unrest are thought to have played a part, but these may well have arisen through pressure from other causes. The Maya cities had after all flourished for over five hundred years, and had frequently been at war with each other.

But what about the possibility of food shortages? These could have come about either through natural or through humanly induced changes in the environment. Increasingly fierce competition between Maya cities led to an upsurge of monument construction during the eighth and ninth centuries A.D., which would have placed added strain on agricultural production and expansion. Interstate rivalry may hence have pushed the Maya toward overexploitation of their fragile ecosystem. Deforestation and soil erosion might ultimately have destroyed the capacity of the land to support the high population levels of the Maya cities, leading to famine, social unrest, and the collapse of the major Maya centers.

Yet it may be incorrect to lay the blame entirely on human action. Several of the lowland cities, such as Tikal, appear to have depended heavily on the cultivation of raised fields set in the marshy depressions known as *bajos,* which today flood intermittently in the rainy season but may originally have been permanent lakes. The raised field system of intensive cultivation allows year-round food production through the constant supply of soil nutrients from the drainage ditches dug around the raised fields. Stable water levels were essential to this subsistence system, but evidence from Lake Chichancanab in Yucatán shows that between the years A.D. 800 and 1000 this region suffered its driest period of climate for the last several thousand years. We may expect that as a result water levels fell and the raised fields in many areas became unusable. But the human response must be viewed through the lens of the social, political, and cultural circumstances. These exerted a powerful mediating effect on the way in which the Maya endeavoured to cope with their difficulties. Had population levels been lower, the impact of the drought may not have been catastrophic; as it was, the Maya were already reaching the limits of the available subsistence capacity, and Maya elites had espoused certain social and political agendas (including expensive intercity warfare and competition). It was against this specific background that a period of drought led quickly to crisis and collapse.

Environmental impacts may have been much more directly responsible for the decline of the Moche state of northern Peru. This is a much more fragile setting for dense human settlement. The coastal zone is exceptionally arid, with significant rainfall only once every few years. As a result, settlements rely almost entirely on the water brought from the Andes by the rivers that flow through this coastal desert to the sea, such as the Lambayeque, Chicama, and Moche rivers. From the fourth to the sixth century A.D. the major Moche center was the capital Cerro Blanco with its two mud-brick pyramids in the broad lower reaches of the Moche valley. Then, some time during the sixth century, Cerro Blanco was abandoned and new centers appeared further up the valley—at Galindo in the Moche Valley, and above all at Pampa Grande in the Lambayeque Valley. These were located at the point where the rivers emerge from the highlands into the lowland plains, at locations that are ideal for maximizing the irrigation potential of those water flows.

Ice cores from the Quelccaya glacier in the north Peruvian highlands have shown that this relocation coincided with a massive 30-year drought, from A.D. 563 to 594. Sand dunes encroached on the former Moche capital, while massive deposits of alluvium indicate that the long drought was punctuated by a series of powerful El Niño events, bringing devastating floods. The shift of settlement upstream and to the north was an attempt to move away from the drought-prone areas to parts of the valleys where a more reliable irrigation system could be established. They indicate an understanding of the predicament and an attempt to cope, and to anticipate future droughts. But they were still vulnerable to floods, and a century later a massive El Niño flood destroyed the irrigation systems around Galindo and Pampa Grande, leading to the destruction of both settlements.

The Moche relocation indicates that this society sought to learn from its traumatic sixth-century experience and adapt to it by a modified irrigation strategy. A few centuries later, the Chimu state in the same coastal valleys of Peru attempted to resolve the drought problem by even more extensive canal systems, a process that reached its height with the construction of the 84 kilometers (52 miles) Chicama-Moche intervalley canal in the twelfth century. This and similar ventures sought to even out flow differences between the different valleys and above all to bring water to the fields around Chan Chan, the Chimu capital. Within a century, however, this large intervalley canal had fallen out of use, as slight tectonic tilting or erosion of the canal walls impeded the water flow. In this case it seems that the limits of the available technology were reached, but that technology was simply not adequate to cope with erratic water flows coupled with urban population growth.

A parallel example is provided by the Marib dam in southern Yemen. Here again an urban society in an effectively desert setting depended entirely on the control of river water for irrigation purposes. This was achieved by constructing an enormous dam, some 580 meters (635 yards) in length, with massive masonry sluice-towers at either end. As sediments accumulated behind the dam, the structure itself was raised and repaired, growing taller but more vulnerable to floods. Eventually, in the late sixth century A.D., it broke for the last time and was abandoned, probably because it was no longer within the technical competence of the inhabitants of Marib to maintain it.

The examples given above illustrate the interaction between population, social organization, technology, and environmental impacts among early state societies. The unprecedented size and food requirements of growing urban populations placed very heavy demands on agricultural systems. These in turn were often in fragile environmental settings—vulnerable either to overexploitation by the farmers themselves or to climatic irregularities. Some climatic events were on such a scale that they would have overwhelmed even low-density farming communities, but it is clearly the case that the scope for human catastrophe was made all the greater by the dependence on fragile irrigation systems.

This may well lead one to ask to what extent these societies were aware of their vulnerability, or of the way in which population size and agricultural intensification were increasing that vulnerability. Famine was certainly not unknown, as we have seen even in the relatively stable environment of the Nile valley. Likewise, some societies were aware of irrigation-related problems such as long-term salination, but appear to have devised measures to cope. Here the traditional knowledge of farmers themselves—the experience built up over centuries—must have been a major factor in achieving a high level of sustainability lasting several millennia. We may suspect, nonetheless, that early state societies had the same problem as modern societies in implementing effective policies to deal with long-term risks; phenomena, like global warming today, which appear to threaten not today or tomorrow but with consequences for the future, are simply too remote in time for the normal span of a human lifetime. However clear the threat, effective action is very difficult to mobilize. Yet in very fragile circumstances, early societies did go to extraordinary lengths to strive for some security, as exemplified by the construction of the Peruvian intervalley canals. This may be interpreted not as a response to immediate need but as a measure to anticipate and to counter future droughts such as that which so severely damaged the Moche state.

What is evident above all is the fragility of the relationship between state societies and their environments. This relationship, and the human response to crisis when it has occurred, must, however, always be viewed in the context of social, political, and cultural factors. Mechanistic interpretations in which drought, flood, volcano, or cometary impact lead directly to societal collapse must always be judged inadequate, however important those factors may have been in placing immense pressures on society. On the other hand, the needs of the elites in early states for wealth and tribute—to support their high-status lifestyles or to fuel territorial expansion—compounded the problems of population growth and led in many cases to an intensification of agriculture that was close to the limit of sustainability given the technology available. In some cases, these pressures will have driven processes of change and collapse over which human agents—whether rulers or ruled—had little effective control. In a few instances, changes arising from natural causes were so overwhelming that it would be hard for any society to cope adequately. But in all cases, the outcome owed much to human factors—the high density and distribution of population, the agricultural technology, and particular social strategies. Several societies appear to have been responsible for environmental degradation and, in that sense, may be held to have contributed to their own demise. But then again, we must note the long-term sustainability demonstrated by Dynastic Egypt or Mesopotamia, albeit with fluctuating fortunes. Thus there is no simple answer, and we must resist invoking extraneous factors with proper reference to the specific social, cultural, and political setting. What is true of early state societies is also of course the case in the modern world, where human attitudes as much as scientific evidence drive the contemporary debates over chlorofluorocarbons (CFCs), greenhouse gases, and genetically engineered crops.

In the chapters that follow, we turn from theory to analytical narrative, tracing the key developments that shaped distinctive and highly complex early civilizations in many parts of the world.

## Summary

Chapter 2 contrasts historical and anthropological approaches to the origins of states and summarizes the main theories developed by archaeologists as a background to later chapters. We summarize six classic theories for the origin of states, starting with Childe's Urban Revolution theory on the development of the city. Another group of theories invokes intensification of agriculture and irrigation. Exchange networks and warfare have also been espoused as potential causes of civilization. Many modern theories revolve around systems-evolutionary hypotheses and explanations involving environmental change. A new generation of social approaches, in contrast, argue that religious and informational factors, epitomized by centralized authority, appear to have been key elements in the regulation of environmental and economic variables in early civilization. Such theories also stress that the social structure of a society ultimately determined its transformation, so the search for the causes of civilization means focusing on ecological variables and the opportunities they presented to individuals who pursued political goals in different societies. In other words, how is ecological opportunity or necessity translated into political change? Recent studies are now focusing on factionalism, ideology, gender, and charismatic leadership as promising areas of inquiry. The issue of sustainability is seen as critical to the formation, growth, and collapse of civilizations.

## Guide to Further Reading

An enormous literature surrounds the origins of civilization. For historical and anthropological perspectives, see the essays in Stephen K. Sanderson, ed., *Civilizations and World Systems* (Walnut Creek, CA: Altamira Press, 1995). Charles L. Redman, *The Rise of Civilization: From Early Farmers to Urban Society in the Ancient Near East* (San Francisco: W. H. Freeman, 1978) summarizes different theoretical approaches and takes a systems approach. *Archaic States*, eds. Gary M. Feinman and Joyce Marcus (Santa Fe: School of American Research Press, 1998) provides a provocative and up-to-date series of case studies of individual early state societies, plus several broad overviews: Among the latter, Kent Flannery's "The Ground Plans of Archaic States" (pp. 16–57) is particularly to be noted. A broad developmental perspective of the development of human societies, focusing on economic issues in anthropological context, is provided by Allen W. Johnson and Timothy Earle, *The Evolution of Human Societies: From Foraging Group to Agrarian State* (Stanford: Stanford University Press, 2001). Timothy Earle, *How Chiefs Come to Power: The Political Economy in Prehistory* (Stanford, CA: Stanford University Press, 1997) discusses chiefdoms on a broad canvas. Now somewhat outdated, it remains a useful source. V. Gordon Childe, *Man Makes Himself* (London: Watts, 1936), and *New Light on the Most Ancient East*, 2nd ed. (London: Routledge and Kegan Paul, 1956) presents the "revolution" theories. Robert McC. Adams, *The Evolution of States* (Chicago: Aldine, 1966) is still an authoritative statement, as is Kent V. Flannery's "The Cultural Evolution of Civilizations," *Annual Review of Ecology and Systematics* 4 (1972): 399–426, which is a classic statement of the systems perspective. William T. Sanders, Jeffrey R. Parsons, and Robert S. Santley, *The Basin of Mexico: Ecological Processes in the Evolution of a Civilization* (Orlando, FL: Academic Press, 1979) is an exemplary regional study of highland Mesoamerican civilization with strong ecological undertones. For writing, see Andrew Robinson, *The Story of Writing* (New York: Thames and Hudson, 1995). Norman Yoffee's "Too Many Chiefs? Or Safe Texts for the 90s," in Andrew Sherratt and Norman Yoffee, eds., *Archaeological Theory—Who Sets the Agenda?* (Cambridge: Cambridge University Press, 1990) reflects much current thinking. For social approaches, see Elizabeth Brumfiel, "Aztec State Making: Ecology, Structure, and the Origin of the State," *American Anthropologist* 85, no. 2 (1992): 261–284; Elizabeth Brumfiel and John Fox, eds., *Factional Competition and Political Development in the New World* (Cambridge: Cambridge University Press, 1994) offers some trend-setting case studies on the role of competing factions in the development of states. Kent Flannery's influential essay "Process and Agency in Early State Formation," *Cambridge Archaeological Journal* 9 (1999): 3–21, discusses chiefly cycling and charismatic leadership. For the view from the countryside, see Glenn M. Schwartz and Steven E. Falconer, eds., *Archaeological Views from the Countryside* (Washington, DC: Smithsonian Institution Press, 1994). For the center and periphery, see Michael Rowlands, Mogens Larsen, and Kristian Kristiansen, eds., *Centre and Periphery in the Ancient World* (Cambridge: Cambridge University Press, 1987). Joseph Tainter, ed., *The Collapse of Civilizations* (Cambridge: Cambridge University Press, 1988), and Norman Yoffee and George Cowgill, eds., *The Collapse of Ancient States and Civilizations* (Tucson: University of Arizona Press, 1988) are important discussions of the decline of early civilizations. Roderick J. McIntosh, Joseph A Tainter, and Susan Keech McIntosh, *The Way the Wind Blows: Climate, History, and Human Action* (New York: Columbia University Press, 2000), and Charles L. Redman, *Human Impact on Ancient Environments* (Tucson: University of Arizona Press, 1999) explore the role of climate change in culture change. For the cycles of recent civilizations, see Paul Kennedy, *The Rise and Fall of the Great Powers* (New York: Random House, 1987); for cycles of early civilizations, Joyce Marcus, "The Peaks and Valleys of Ancient States," in Gary M. Feinman and Joyce Marcus, eds., *Archaic States* (Santa Fe: School of American Research Press, 1998), pp. 60–94.

# PART II

# The First Civilizations

> Rock-tomb, pyramid, and temple succeed in the endlessly similar, endlessly changing landscape. . . . For many centuries they were removed from human lives and emotions. No one living understood their significance or the civilization which built them. Even today, measured, restored, visited, they are difficult to comprehend. How should the twentieth century know the heart of Sekhmet the lion-goddess, or fear, like Herodotus, even to pen the name of Osiris?
>
> Robin Feddon, *Egypt: Land of the Valley* (London: John Murray, 1977), p. 72.

## Prelude to Civilization: First Villages in the Fertile Crescent

The study of agricultural origins is an enormous subject and is not the focus of this book, but farming provided the basic underpinning for the development and success of Near Eastern civilization, and a brief account is included here to set the scene. Without farming, cities and states would have been impossible.

For tens of thousands of years, the Near East was populated by nomadic bands of hunters and gatherers, surviving by hunting deer and gazelle and gathering wild seeds, nuts, and berries. Just over twelve thousand years ago, some of these bands began to change their lifestyle, taking advantage of the expanding grasslands and the nutritional potential of the wild cereals, wheat and barley. By 9000 B.C., they were no longer simply gathering wild cereals but planting and harvesting them; agriculture had begun.

Most explanations for the development of agriculture in the Near East have invoked environmental change, or a disequilibrium between populations and resources. One view holds that the switch to colder and drier conditions in the Younger Dryas period (c. 10,500–9200 B.C.) caused a shrinkage in the stands of wild cereals on which the expanding hunter-gatherer communities had come to depend; the first evidence for the cultivation of einkorn falls at exactly this time, suggesting that the introduction of farming was a direct response to environmental scarcity. An alternative view, championed in particular by French archaeologist Jacques Cauvin, places more emphasis on symbolic and cognitive developments, arguing that the crucial change is represented by the appearance of bull images and female figurines in the southern Levant during the tenth millennium B.C., indicating fundamental changes in outlook and sociocultural organization among hunter-gatherer communities.

Whatever the cause, the consequences of agriculture were enormous. One of the most significant was that it allowed the growth of larger settlements. Strictly speaking, the first villages in the Near East were those of hunter-gatherers. A good example is Ain Mallaha in modern Israel, a group of circular huts occupied perhaps on a permanent, year-round basis. Still more recently, similar villages have been excavated at Hallan Çemi in southern Turkey and Nemrik in northern Iraq. Once farming was established, sedentary settlements such as these multiplied in size and numbers, laying the foundations of all that was to follow in the Near East and leading ultimately to the formation of the first cities.

These earliest farming settlements grew up in the band of territory known as the Fertile Crescent (see Chapter 2). Much of the Near East, including most of central and lowland Mesopotamia, is arid and dry with insufficient rainfall to allow farming without irrigation. The exception is the hilly flanks, which do catch the rain at certain limited seasons and where farming is possible. These hilly flanks form a great arc extending from the Judaean hills of the southern Levant, swinging eastward across the upper reaches of the Euphrates and Tigris, and then running southeast again down the Zagros Mountains toward the Persian Gulf. This, then, is the Fertile Crescent. An extension to the zone runs westward into the mountainous uplands of southern Turkey. All the early farming settlements of the Near East lie within this zone, which also corresponds roughly with the natural distribution of wild wheat and barley, the early farmers' staple crops.

Three of the key settlements of the early farming phase are Jericho, Tell Abu Hureyra, and Çatalhöyük. Neither at Jericho nor at Tell Abu Hureyra, however, are the earliest levels those of a full farming society. They nonetheless show the beginning of something that is larger than a simple village, as communities grew and prospered and became more populous.

## *Jericho*

Jericho, in the Jordan valley, has claims to be the oldest town on earth. The earliest structure here was small, interpreted by some as a shrine, and lay beside the perennial "Spring of Moses" (Ain Musa). Nomadic bands of hunters and gatherers built this first structure, but within a thousand years their descendants were living in a permanent settlement on the site. This early permanent settlement, belonging to the so-called Pre-Pottery Neolithic A (PPNA) phase (8500–7300 B.C.), was relatively small—covering a mere 2.4 hectares (6 acres)—a cluster of modest circular houses beside the well-watered farmland around the spring. The inhabitants may already have begun to dig channels to take the spring water to their fields; although the area in which this can be done is very limited, cereal remains found by archaeologists show that their crops were flourishing. Within a few hundred years early Jericho was a walled community.

In the famous Old Testament story the walls of Jericho fell when the Israelite leader, Joshua, ordered the trumpets to be blown. That event (if based on historical reality) took place around 1000 B.C., and the wall of Jericho seen by the Israelites was a late successor in a lengthy sequence. The wall built by the earliest farmers of Jericho dates back to before 8000 B.C. It is a substantial dry-stone structure incorporating no less than 10,000 tons of building material, reinforced at one point by a circular tower over 9 meters (30 feet) high and solid in construction except for an internal stairway that gives access to the roof. In front of the wall runs a ditch cut into the rock, 8 meters (26 feet) wide.

When British archaeologist Kathleen Kenyon discovered this wall in the 1950s, she at once interpreted it as defensive. The farmers of Jericho, the argument ran, had accumulated wealth, perhaps in the form of grain stores, which they wished to protect from their still-nomadic neighbors. So they surrounded themselves with a substantial wall and ditch, complete with towers. It is a neat hypothesis, but Israeli archaeologist Ofer Bar-Yosef has reexamined the evidence and suggests an alternative explanation. He points out that the wall was found only on the western side of the settlement, facing a wadi mouth, and suggests it was built to protect early Jericho not from human enemies but from flash floods. Furthermore, he argues that the famous tower is not designed as a defensive structure and may instead have been used for ritual ceremonies, such as the exposure of corpses (a practice attested by the human remains from Jericho). Whichever explanation—defensive or ritual—is correct, it does not detract from the unprecedented scale of the Jericho wall, one of the oldest surviving achievements of communal village labor.

One further discovery at Jericho must be mentioned here: the plastered human skulls. These belong to the PPNB phase (7300–6500 B.C.). Defleshed skulls had been covered in plaster and modeled to portray living individuals, with cowrie shells inserted for the eyes. A number of these plastered skulls were found during Kenyon's excavations. They testify to a cult of the human head or, more likely, a cult of ancestors whose skulls were preserved and modified in this fashion. Plastered skulls have been found at other Levantine sites of the period, including a bitumen-covered example from Nahal Hemar cave in Israel, showing that this was a fairly generalized custom at this period. Further north, at the foot of the Taurus Mountains in southern Turkey, excavators in Çayönü, another prepottery village, have found an eighth-millennium building with small cellars piled high with human skulls. Once again, a special mortuary cult seems to be indicated.

## *Abu Hureyra*

Jericho's lifeblood is a perennial spring, but other early village sites took advantage of the natural fertility and water supplies of the major rivers. One such is Tell Abu Hureyra on the Euphrates. This has been the subject of a recent excavation project specifically directed to the question of early farming and the transition from hunting and gathering. Like Jericho, it is a settlement mound containing the superimposed remains of several successive occupations. The earliest occupants of the site, in the tenth millennium B.C., were gatherers rather than farmers, who hunted local gazelle and collected wild grasses and cereals. Thus Abu Hureyra like Ain Mallaha was a hunter-gatherer village, occupied for perhaps a large part of the year, if not year-round. The secret here lay in the local resources: The site lay on the path of seasonal gazelle migrations, and the inhabitants were also able to exploit local stands of wild cereals and other steppe and valley bottom plants. They continued to rely on gazelle hunting even after they had begun to grow cultivated cereals around 8700 B.C. It was only later, during the eighth millennium, that gazelles were replaced by domestic sheep and goats. The site is interesting in other ways, too. The evidence for ritual is less spectacular than at Jericho, but a number of human skulls from Tell Abu Hureyra had traces of red paint, as if they, too, had been prepared for ritual display.

## *Çatalhöyük*

This settlement, near Konya in southern Turkey, covers over 12 hectares (30 acres), an area far larger than its Near Eastern predecessors. It represents a large village or town. It is also notable for its curious agglomerated architecture, with houses built back-to-back without intervening streets. Access seems to have been across the flat rooftops, with ladders leading down into the houses themselves. When British archaeologist James Mellaart excavated the site between 1961 and 1965, he found a still greater surprise: About a third of the houses were decorated with elaborate wall paintings, plaster relief of sculptures, or benches incorporating bulls' horns. He called these decorated buildings "shrines," but whether they were indeed special religion structures or simply richly decorated houses remains uncertain. Radiocarbon dates from Mellaart's excavations show that Çatalhöyük was occupied from 6500 to 5400 B.C., though recent work at the site suggests that the occupation may have been established as early as 7200 B.C. Either way, it is a little later than the other settlements we have just discussed.

The chief significance of Jericho, Çatalhöyük, Çayönü, and to a lesser extent Tell Abu Hureyra is that they show the degree of symbolic and ritual complexity attained by some of the earliest village communities in the Near East. They form part of a growing body of evidence for cultural sophistication among early farming communities in the Near East: wall paintings at ninth-millennium Ba'ja in southern Jordan and eighth-millennium Jerf-el-Ahmar, Halula, and Mureybit in Syria; lime plaster human figurines from Ain Ghazal in Jordan; engraved stones with symbols from Jerf-el-Ahmar. None of these settlements, however, can compare in size with the earliest cities that became established in southern Mesopotamia some three or four thousand years later. It is the development of those cities that is the subject of Chapter 3.

## Guide to Further Reading

The origin of farming in the Near East is covered by Charles Redman, *The Rise of Civilization* (San Francisco: Freeman, 1978) and Trevor Watkins, *Origins of Agriculture in the Near East* (London: Routledge, 2001). A shorter account is A. M. T. Moore, "The Development of Neolithic Societies in the Near East," *Advances in World Archaeology* 4 (1985): 1–69. Jacques Cauvin's views on the cognitive background to farming in the Near East are set out in *The Birth of the Gods and the Origins of Agriculture* (Cambridge: Cambridge University Press, 2000). Kathleen Kenyon provides an accessible account of her excavations at Jericho in *Digging Up Jericho* (London: Benn, 1957). The plastered skulls and their significance are discussed by Yosef Garfinkel, "Ritual Burial of Cultic Objects: The Earliest Evidence," *Cambridge Archaeological Journal* 4 (1994): 159–188. Results from Tell Abu Hureyra are presented by A. M. T. Moore, G. C. Hillman, and A. J. Legge, *Village on the Euphrates: The Excavation of Abu Hureyra* (New York: Oxford University Press, 2001). For Nemrik and Çayönü, see articles in *World Archaeology* 21, no. 3 (1990). For Çatalhöyük there is the popular account by James Mellaart, *Çatal Hüyük: A Neolithic Town in Anatolia* (London: Thames and Hudson, 1967); see also Ian A. Todd, *Çatal Hüyük in Perspective* (Menlo Park, CA: Cummings, 1976); for the most recent fieldwork at the site, see Ian Hodder, ed., *Çatalhöyük 1993–5: On the Surface of Things* (Cambridge and London: McDonald Institute for Archaeological Research/British Institute of Archaeology at Ankara, 1996) and *Towards Reflexive Method in Archaeology: The Example at Çatalhöyük* (2000). (Note the revised spelling of the site name.) Paul K. Wason has used Çatalhöyük as a case study in social inequality in *The Archaeology of Rank* (Cambridge: Cambridge University Press, 1994).

*Chapter 3*

# Mesopotamia: The First Cities

## (3500–2000 B.C.)

Statute of Gudea, ruler of the Mesopotamian city of Lagash.

*The scribe smiled as the herd of livestock approached. Gripping the soft clay tablet in his left hand, with the reed stylus poised in his right, he stood ready to record the numbers of cattle as they passed. The beasts lowed gently as they made their way into the shelter of the temple wall: first, a group of grass-fed oxen from the pastures beyond the Euphrates; then six, fed on barley, from the neighboring villages to the west; finally, three, long overdue in payment of a debt by the temple of the god Enlil. Each group of animals was escorted by two young men, who plied long switches of alder to keep their charges moving. Bowing to the scribe, they turn by turn declared the number of cattle they had brought in tribute or debt payment to the great temple of Uruk, sacred to Anu, god of the firmament. They were looking forward to a jar of beer after their thirsty day's walk from the fields. The scribe deftly recorded the number of cattle each had brought, carefully incising marks into the clay tablets. The herdsmen were familiar with the clay tablets but had no knowledge of the mysterious wedge-shaped signs he used. Writing, that revolutionary invention of early Mesopotamia, was as yet the preserve of a shaven-headed elite, the Sumerian scribes in their flounced woolen skirts who administered the world's first cities.*

The city of Uruk and the invention of writing together stand at the heart of early Mesopotamian civilization. People had lived in village settlements for several thousand years, farming the fields around them, producing their pottery and food, and perhaps coming together from time to time for seasonal feasts and festivals. But never before had they lived permanently together in such numbers—a concentration of several thousand people clustered cheek-by-jowl. Such a community was not simply larger than anything that had gone before. It involved a wholly different way of life, a society divided into craftspeople, farmers, and priests. Among these were scribes, the trained specialists who alone understood the wedge-shaped cuneiform signs used to record the multifarious commercial transactions of temple and city. At the base of the whole majestic edifice was the natural fertility of the Mesopotamian plain, the essential prerequisite for the emergence of civilization in this dry and dusty lowland.

In this chapter, we review the development of Mesopotamian civilization, from its origins among the early farming societies of the region to the first empires of the later third millennium B.C. (Table 3.1). Key themes are the development of cities, the adoption of irrigation farming, and the invention of writing. Attention is also drawn to other aspects of urban life: monumental temples, elite graves, and large-scale warfare. And we seek to assess the contribution that early historical records can make to the study of Mesopotamian society during this key period.

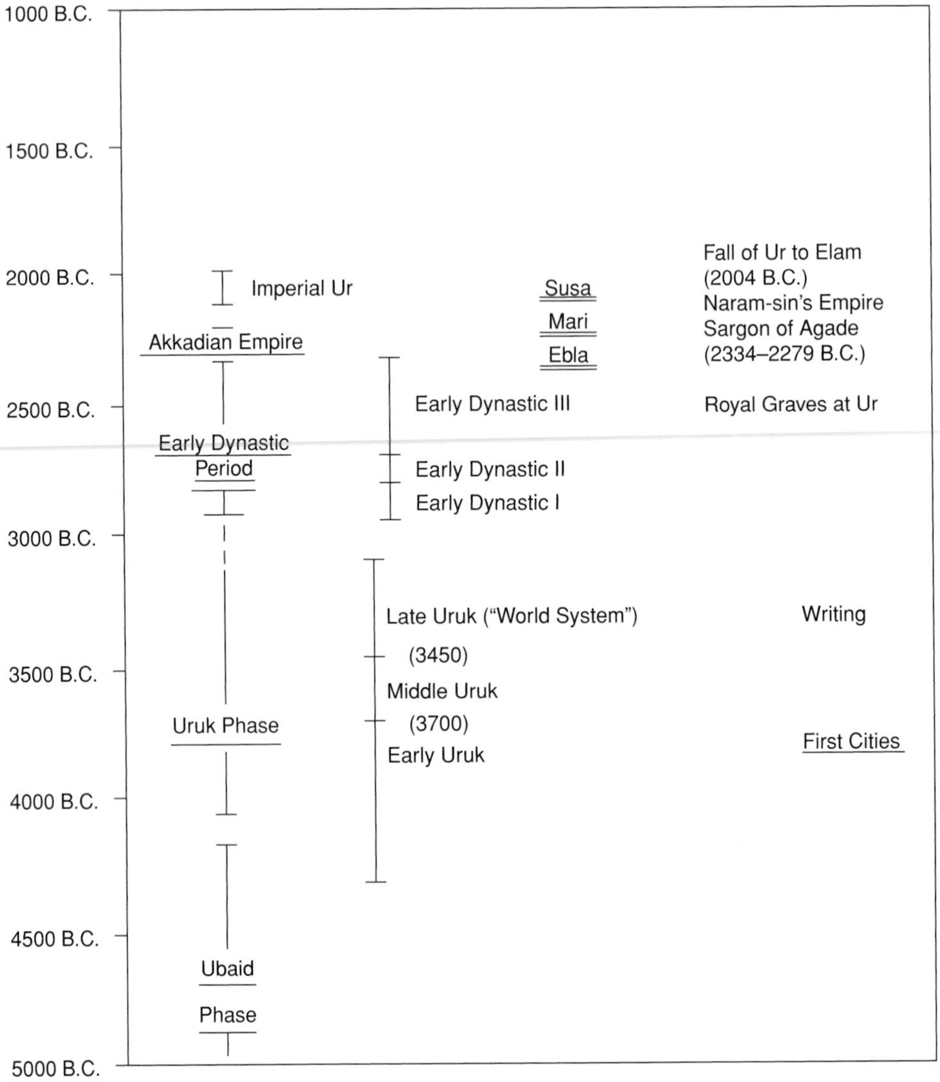


**Table 3.1** Chronological table of early Mesopotamian civilization.

Another major theme is trade, for Mesopotamia was not a country turned in on itself but an active producer of manufactured goods and an avid consumer of raw materials, including metals and other minerals from the surrounding uplands.

## The Setting

Mesopotamia, "the land between the rivers," is a band of territory sandwiched between the mountains and uplands of Iran to the east and the arid deserts of Arabia and Syria to the west (Figure 3.1). Most of it would be desert itself were it not for

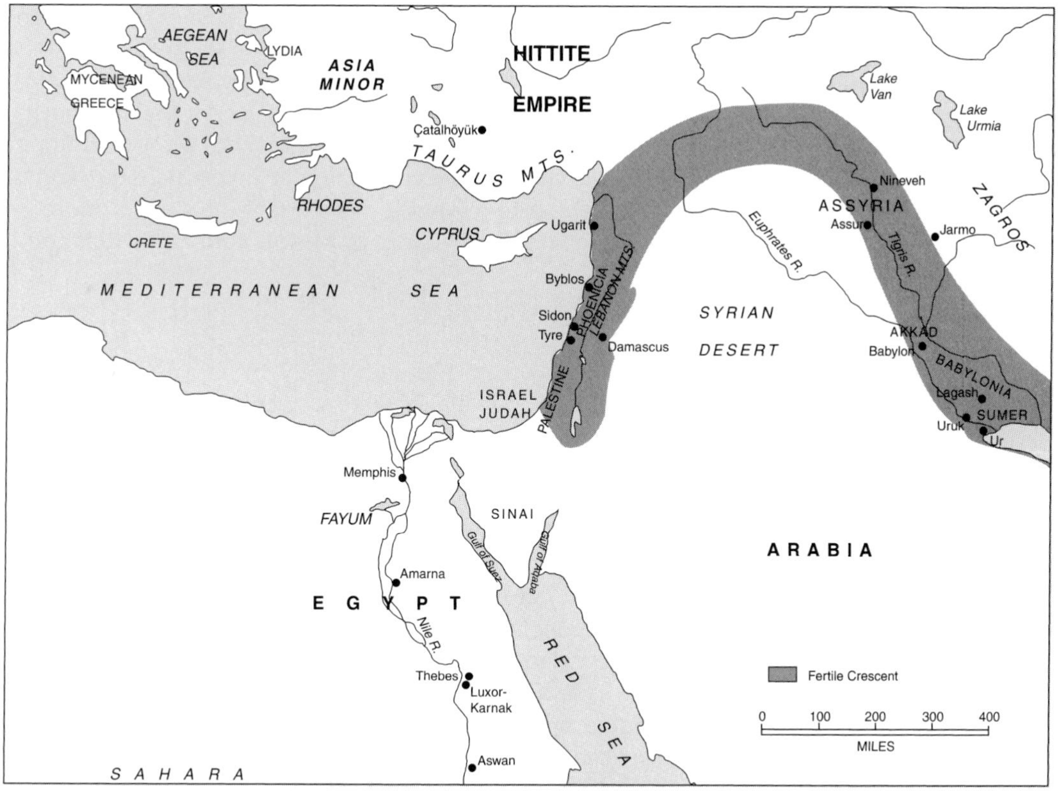


**Figure 3.1** Map of the ancient Near East.

the two great rivers, the Tigris and Euphrates, which water it. The rivers rise in the mountainous terrain of eastern Turkey, where they are fed by winter rains and spring meltwater.

Mesopotamia is divided into an upper and lower plain. In the north, the upper plain becomes parched and brown during the hot, dry summers. But in the autumn, cooler temperatures and light rains turn northern Mesopotamia into a green and verdant plain. Downstream, by contrast, aridity gains the upper hand, even in the cooler months. Rainfall here is slight and undependable, averaging less than 200 millimeters per year, and is insufficient for growing crops. How, then, to live in such a hostile landscape? The answer is river water and irrigation. With irrigation, the alluvial soils of the lower plain can be farmed and their natural fertility unlocked. The result is high primary productivity—the ability to obtain high crop yields from relatively limited areas of land, sufficient to feed relatively dense populations.

In the 1950s, anthropologists such as Karl Wittfogel and Julian Steward put forward the theory that irrigation and control of water resources lay behind the development of riverine civilizations, such as that of Mesopotamia. Their argument was that the digging of canals required cooperative labor and some degree of central control. Furthermore, once the canals were dug, farmers became entirely dependent on irrigation water for their survival. This gave an enormous opportunity for community leaders to expand their power by exploiting control over the irrigation system, cutting off any who refused to accept their authority. We now know the picture is not so simple, but even in northern Mesopotamia irrigation would have been essential for cereal cultivation on any scale. The digging of canals and sluices to bring water to the fields, whether at the state or more localized level, provided the crucial infrastructure of Mesopotamian civilization.

## Irrigation and Alluvium: Hassuna, Samarra, Halaf, and Ubaid (6500–4200 B.C.)

By the seventh millennium B.C. farming villages were scattered throughout the Fertile Crescent, that arc of cultivable land stretching from the southern Levant across the broad sweep of the north Mesopotamian plain and down toward the Persian Gulf, skirting the edges of the arid zone. These villages were clusters of mud-brick houses whose occupants grew wheat, barley, and pulses and herded sheep, goats, cattle, and pigs. They also made pottery and had begun to experiment with copper metallurgy, exploiting veins and natural outcrops in the uplands of Anatolia and Iran. They were far from being isolated communities but rather were joined together in networks that are revealed by the spread of obsidian, a glassy stone used for sharp-edged tools that was brought by exchange from Anatolian sources in the far north to Jordan and southern Iran. Archaeologists are able to trace the path of obsidian supplies because each volcanic source has its own special chemical signature. Even small pieces can be identified in this way as coming from Çiftlik, Açigöl, or one of the other Anatolian sources. Community links are also made evident by the pottery styles, which are shared across different parts of the region and which allow these sites to be assigned to particular ages, or phases. For Mesopotamian developments, the most important of these phases are Hassuna, Samarra, Halaf, and Ubaid.

These phases or styles overlap somewhat in both space and time but can be considered to represent a succession of stages, or periods. The proto-Hassuna style is the earliest, represented at sites such as Umm Dabaghiyah, Tell Sotto, and Kashkashok (early seventh millennium B.C.). It is followed by Hassuna (6500–6000 B.C.) in the north of Mesopotamia, running parallel with Samarra (6500–5900 B.C.) further south. Hassuna in turn was replaced by Halaf (6000–5400 B.C.), characterized by elegant painted pottery and in its later stage by the "beehive" houses excavated at Arpachiyah near Nineveh. Further to the south, Samarra gave rise to the Ubaid style (5900–4200 B.C.). At first confined to the southern plains, Ubaid spread north to replace first the Samarra style and then, around 5400 B.C., the Halaf style of the north.

The villages of the Hassuna area, from around 6500 B.C., were clustered on the fertile, rain-fed plain of northern Mesopotamia. Farmers of the Samarra culture (6500–5900 B.C.), however, began to move out of the rain-fed zone southward and westward into the heart of Mesopotamia. To survive there they would have needed to divert river water through irrigation canals to nourish their fields, and this indeed is what we find evidence for at Choga Mami, a Samarran site on the edge of the Mesopotamian plain, dating to around 6000 B.C. Archaeologists who excavated this site found remains of disused canal systems and types of wheat and barley that could only have been grown under irrigation. Another Samarran settlement, Tell es-Sawwan, consisted of multiroomed, mud-brick houses, with an inner group of buildings surrounded in its middle phase by a buttressed fortification wall. The buildings within the enclosed area were T-shaped and may have been grain stores. This suggests a high level of community organization. The burials at the site are richly furnished, suggesting that it was also a particularly wealthy community. The grave goods include materials that had been obtained through trade and exchange from distant sources: copper, obsidian, carnelian, and turquoise. Tell es-Sawwan is an early expression of the developments seen in more pronounced form in the late Ubaid and Uruk periods.

Samarran villages are confined to the central area of the Mesopotamian plain. It is a partly contemporary group, represented by material of the Ubaid period (6000–4200 B.C.) that first settled the southern plains. One of the earliest Ubaid sites is Oueili, a small farming village dated to around 6000 B.C. Oueili is assigned to an initial Ubaid 0 phase. Like its successors in this zone, it must have depended on irrigation agriculture. The success of the new economy became increasingly apparent as the Ubaid period progressed. At Eridu in southern Iraq, the occupation begins in the next Ubaid phase, labeled Ubaid 1. Here the excavators discovered a long sequence of mud-brick buildings. By the middle of the Ubaid period, these were elaborate structures with niches, buttresses, and altars, raised on mud-brick platforms—the ancestors in style and layout of the temples we find in the early historic period.

The Eridu temples underline the key role of religion in the formation of the first cities. Temples dedicated to patron deities formed a focus of community attention and identity and also became powerful economic institutions, owning large areas of land. The end result was a kind of state religion, where the temple establishment was one of the major centralized institutions of the early Mesopotamian cities.

Ubaid people needed raw materials such as stone and metal, and other exotic or luxury materials that the alluvial plain could not provide. They soon established trading networks extending into the uplands to north and east of Mesopotamia and along the coast of the Persian Gulf to the south. In northern Mesopotamia, Ubaid pottery replaces regional types in the middle of the sixth millennium and coincides with a growth in the size of settlements there. There is even a possible Ubaid "colony" at Degirmentepe in eastern Anatolia. To the south, Ubaid pottery was carried by seaborne fishermen, or perhaps traders, down the coast of the Persian Gulf as far as the Straits of Hormuz. These extensions to north and south suggest that the Ubaid zone had some of the qualities of an "interaction sphere." By settling the southern plains, the Ubaid communities were able to draw north Mesopotamia and the Persian Gulf (temporarily at least) into a single circuit of exchange.

American archaeologist Norman Yoffee has described the Ubaid culture as laying the foundation of Mesopotamian cultural identity. Leaving aside excursions into Anatolia and the Persian Gulf, the distribution of Ubaid material roughly conforms to the cultural boundaries of later Mesopotamia. It would be wrong to overstate the case, however, since there was significant variation between the different regions of Mesopotamia even during the Ubaid period. And even this degree of cultural uniformity broke down during the fourth millennium, when northern and southern Mesopotamia went their own separate ways in the early Uruk period.

The Ubaid settlement of the southern plains of Mesopotamia transformed the earlier pattern of transitory hunters and gatherers and established villages of farmers instead. Once the strategy and technology of irrigation agriculture had been developed, there was scope for tremendous expansion, both in population size and in social and cultural complexity. Farmed in the right way, the Mesopotamian alluvial plains could yield amazing harvests. Such abundant crop yields formed the economic foundations of the first cities.

## The Uruk Revolution

Cities, states, and writing are three of the key features of civilizations or complex societies. In the Near East they appeared together around the middle of the Uruk period, c. 3500 B.C. This marks the beginning of Mesopotamian civilization and was accompanied by a number of other significant developments: increasing craft specialization, the growth of centralized religious and secular control (temple and palace), and an expansion in trade between the south Mesopotamian plain and neighboring regions rich in raw materials.

The Uruk period lasted over a thousand years (4200–3100 B.C.) and saw the greatest transformation of Mesopotamia: the rise of complex societies and the foundation of the first cities. It was accompanied by other changes of equal significance, notably the invention of writing systems to record and control the complex activities of urban populations (Box 3.1). Furthermore, these urban societies were not simply large agglomerations of villages but also a new kind of settlement with special political, religious, and economic institutions. The Mesopotamian cities were in fact city-states, political centers controlling their surrounding territory.

### *Cities and States*

The concept of the city was an important innovation, not only in fourth-millennium Mesopotamia but also in all the other regions of the world where urban societies developed. At a basic level, it implies a concentration of population, often too large to be supported simply by the produce of the fields in its immediate vicinity. This means that a city will usually need to draw on a network of villages in the surrounding area to feed its population. The city in turn serves as a political, religious, and ceremonial center for this surrounding territory. In return for food, cities supply goods and services to the dependent villages, but they are often the dominant partners in an unequal relationship, able to impose their will on smaller settlements by sheer size of population. However, cities themselves grow out of the coalescence of smaller rural communities.

## Box 3.1 *The Birth of Cuneiform*

The Mesopotamians were the first people in the world to devise a system of writing, using symbols inscribed on slabs of clay known as writing tablets. Its origins lie in the earlier use (from the early fourth millennium) of three-dimensional clay tokens that represented livestock or objects. A number of such tokens were sometimes enclosed in a clay sphere, or *bulla* (plural *bullae*), which was then marked with a seal impression. Denise Schmandt-Besserat, following suggestions of earlier specialists, has argued that these were records of commercial transactions and that it was the growing tendency to inscribe marks on the outside of the *bullae* to indicate their contents that led to the development of the earliest Mesopotamian writing system. Why not simply dispense with the tokens and rely on the symbols inscribed in the clay?

The motivation for the development of writing lay in the need of the growing urban communities for new ways of recording and storing information to assist their accounting procedures. The temple economy—receiving goods and distributing rations—may have been one stimulus behind the invention. Temple scribes needed to know how much they had received, what was due to them and what was in store, and how much they should pay out in wages or rations. The first writing is very rudimentary in form: a series of symbols and numbers. These appear during the Late Uruk period (later fourth millennium) in various parts of Mesopotamia, from Uruk itself in the south to Tell Brak in the north. These earliest symbols need not be recording any particular language. They used clearly recognizable signs (pictographs) such as the head of a bull for cattle or an ear of barley for that particular cereal. Indeed, one reason for the invention of writing may have been the need for a common recording system that could be understood by people

**Figure 3.2** Accounts table with cuneiform script, c. 2400 B.C. (terracotta).

(Cont.)

who spoke different languages. We know that in the early cities of Mesopotamia a number of different ethnic groups lived side by side, and the very earliest writing may have been designed to overcome language differences.

By 2800 B.C. this early use of symbols had developed into a system of regular cuneiform script used to record Sumerian (and later Akkadian) (Figure 3.2). The name derives from the Latin *cuneus* (a wedge) and refers to the wedge-shaped nature of the marks made by the wooden or bone stylus in the soft clay. The cuneiform signs were derived from the earlier pictographic script but were abstract and were no longer recognizable as actual objects. Each sign represented a sound or syllable.

Knowledge of cuneiform was restricted to a small group of trained professionals (scribes). Some were in the employ of a temple or palace, but writing was also used by merchants. Accountancy remained an important function of writing, but scribes soon realized the enormous potential of the new tool they had in their possession. Within a matter of centuries writing was being used for law codes, religious texts, mathematics, and astrology. Cuneiform was widely replaced by the less cumbersome alphabetic scripts during the fifth century B.C., but it survived until the first century A.D.

Cities are thus larger in both area and population than smaller rural settlements. They number their inhabitants in thousands rather than tens or hundreds. They are more complex than smaller settlements, with markets, manufacturing zones, and administrative machinery. Early cities both in Mesopotamia and Mesoamerica were often divided internally into separate zones based on kinship or occupation. Some may have been centrally planned, with a regular layout of streets and buildings, but many (including those of early Mesopotamia) developed in a more haphazard manner. Cities have a special sense of identity, one based not on kinship but on a city-based allegiance. This may be highlighted by the construction of a city wall, marking a clear division between the residents of a city and the rural population beyond. The city wall is a communal work of civil defense, built and maintained by the city dwellers for their own protection, though of course controlled to a degree by central authority. The same is true for the temple, a focus of civic pride and identity in many urban communities, with the citizens considering themselves under the protection of a particular patron deity.

Alongside the city is the concept of the state. The greater complexity of urban living will by itself have accelerated the growth of central authorities. There will have been a greater need for organization and control to ensure the smooth flow of goods and services and to impose peace and security on the more numerous city dwellers. One aspect of this in Mesopotamia was the invention of writing as a tool of administration. Writing was developed by secular and religious authorities and by private individuals to document economic transactions that became too complicated to be handled conveniently by more traditional methods. The key feature of state formation, however, was the decline of kinship as the organizing principle of Mesopotamian societies and its subordination to central control, which cut across kinship lines. Yoffee has said that the emergence of states can be defined by the appearance of certain socioeconomic or government roles that are emancipated from real or fictive kinship. Our first evidence of this—the presence of palace and temple officials—in a Mesopotamian context arrived with the appearance of written records in the Late Uruk period. It is clear that by the last quarter of the fourth millennium, a number of city-states had developed in southern Mesopotamia. They were to increase in numbers in the centuries that followed.

The Ubaid period had seen the farming settlement of the south Mesopotamian plain. The processes leading to the formation of the first cities and states become apparent during the Early and Middle Uruk periods (4200–3450 B.C.), when settlements on the southern plain increased both in size and in number. This shows that population levels were rising rapidly, taking advantage of the vast potential of the soil that was made available through irrigation systems. Larger and larger areas of land were taken into cultivation by this means. The villagers farming these lands may already have had ties of religious allegiance or kinship, which bound them together into a larger political unit, a kind of protostate. This development culminated in the middle of the fourth millennium, when in each protostate one settlement assumed a size and importance far outstripping any ordinary village. It became, in effect, a small urban center.

The most important of these early urban centers was Uruk (modern Warka). This large and long-occupied site is dominated by two temple areas: the later shrine of Kullaba, dedicated to Anu, god of the firmament, and the early Eanna precinct, which later contained the shrine of Inanna, goddess of love and war (Figure 3.3). The city may have owed its initial importance to its religious cults, which made it a focus for a wide surrounding area. Early texts reveal that other Sumerian cities were in the practice of sending ritual offerings to Uruk for the shrine of Inanna. The city may in fact have originated as two separate villages, each with its own cult center. Excavations in the Eanna precinct have revealed a whole series of temples and other public buildings stretching back into the fourth millennium B.C. These include the important columned hall in Level IVb, decorated with colored "cone mosaics." These were large and impressive buildings, the work of an established elite, intended to instill awe and respect in the subject populace.

The Eanna precinct at Uruk is justly famous for one other major find: the earliest clay writing tablets from southern Mesopotamia. Writing was at first an elite activity, in the hands of a tiny group of trained scribes, but along with the extensive use of cylinder seals it indicates the new needs generated by the complexity of Mesopotamian urban societies (Box 3.2; Figure 3.5 on pages 75, 77).

The formation and the rapid growth of the city of Uruk must have come about through a flow of population from the surrounding countryside. This process and its dramatic effects have been termed the "urban implosion" of Uruk. It was paralleled on a lesser scale at other sites throughout the southern plains, leading to the formation of competing centers that are the world's first cities.

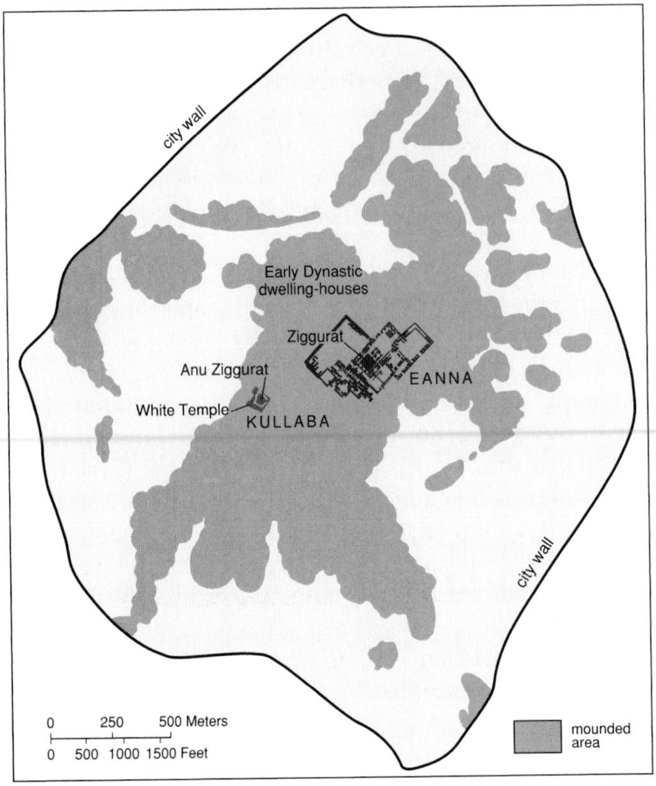


**Figure 3.3** Plan of Uruk, showing Kullaba and Eanna precincts.

## *Landscape and Cityscape*

The impact of city formation on the rural settlement of southern Mesopotamia has been documented by the careful surveys conducted by archaeologist Robert McC. Adams (Box 3.2 and Figure 3.4). These show that the landscape has changed in significant respects since the Uruk period. Satellite images have shown that the courses of the Tigris and Euphrates were not separate streams but ran much closer to each other than at the present day, and they joined, parted, and rejoined to form a braided river pattern as they crossed the southern Mesopotamian plain. The coastline, too, has altered; the head of the Persian Gulf was in places up to 200 kilometers (125 miles) north of its present position in the fourth millennium B.C. This meant that early cities such as Eridu, Ur, and Uruk were much closer to the sea and would have been able much more readily to exploit marine, marsh, and estuarine resources.

One of the surveys conducted by Adams focused on the area around Uruk. He concluded that in the Late Uruk period, Uruk itself was the only true urban settlement in the area, covering an area of up to 250 hectares (600 acres). One hundred and seven smaller settlements of the same period were located, but none of these was larger than 15 hectares (37 acres), and most were smaller than 6 hectares

(15 acres). This Late Uruk pattern may then be contrasted with the position 500 years later, during the Early Dynastic period. By this stage Uruk had grown into an enormous metropolis, covering no less than 400 hectares (1,000 acres), and was surrounded not only by rural villages but also by a network of towns and smaller urban centers. Uruk now stood at the center of a mature hierarchical settlement system, with dependent towns within its territory, each in turn surrounded by a cluster of smaller villages.

## Box 3.2 Anatomy of Settlement I: The Regional Level

Robert McC. Adams of the University of Chicago's Oriental Institute surveyed ancient settlement and irrigation systems on the Mesopotamian plain between 1956 and 1971 (Figure 3.4). This work has provided a wealth of information on the changing size and location of early Mesopotamian sites. Adams combined three approaches. First, he and his team patiently walked the landscape, recording details of even the smallest sites visible, such as low tells or pottery scatters. Second, he assessed the date and size of each site by studying the pottery that littered the surface. Third, he made full use of aerial photographs, including the Landsat satellite images that were just then becoming available. The aerial photographs were especially valuable in allowing Adams and his team to trace the courses of rivers and canals on which the cities of southern Mesopotamia depended for their existence.

Adams's surveys give a thorough archaeological picture of the landscape of ancient Mesopotamia and its development from the appearance of the first cities to the arrival of Islam. They have enabled us to chart how rural village settlements were affected as populations became concentrated in cities. They have also thrown light on the shifting courses of the major rivers, especially the Euphrates. This appears to have been a braided river in ancient times, flowing in a number of parallel channels through the southern floodplain. Changes—probably natural—in the relative importance of the channels had major, and sometimes disastrous, impact on the settlements along their banks. If one channel stopped flowing, irrigation water for the fields around the city would no longer be available and people would have to move elsewhere. The great city of Uruk suffered a serious, if temporary, decline at the beginning of the Akkadian period, a reversal that may have owed much to the growing importance of the eastern Euphrates channel that ran through Adab and Umma (Figure 3.4). The western branch, through Nippur and Shuruppak, may have been hit by water shortages. This reflects and perhaps helps to explain the fall in Uruk's political fortunes as the third millennium drew to a close.

In recent years, surveys have increasingly been undertaken on the rain-fed plains of northern Mesopotamia, balancing Adams's work in the south. These surveys show that in the Ubaid period, site densities were much higher in the rain-fed plains than on the southern alluvium, highlighting once again that the path to urban growth in southern Mesopotamia must have been extremely rapid.

*(Cont.)*

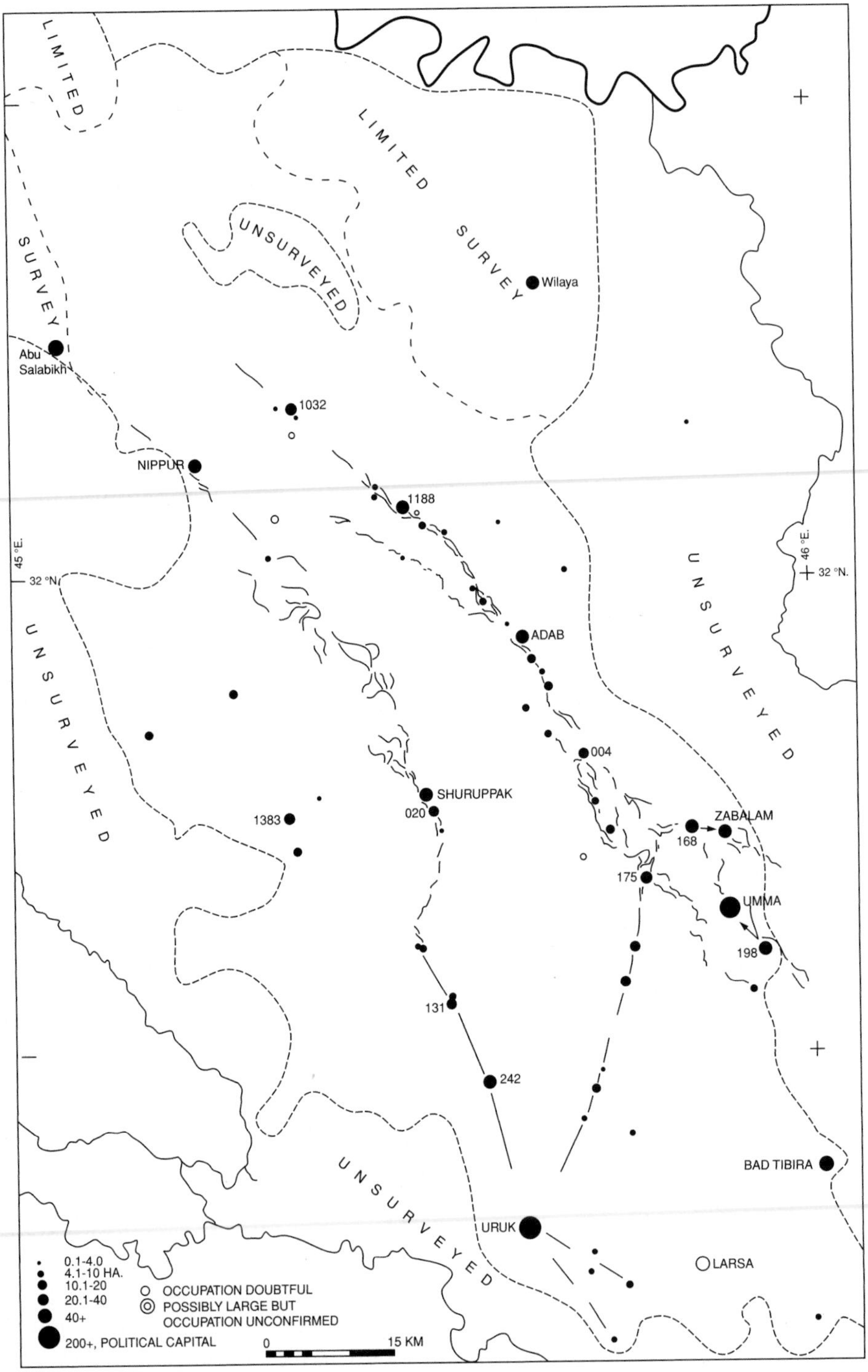


**Figure 3.4** Settlement patterns of the Akkadian period in southern Mesopotamia, from the survey by Robert McC. Adams and his team.

This hierarchical settlement pattern is one hallmark of a state, and it had become common throughout southern Mesopotamia by the early third millennium. The core of each state was an important city, with its ruling dynasty and protective patron deities. The state gathered taxes from its subjects and demanded conscripts in time of war. Some of the taxes were levied in the form of labor, which might have been used to farm state lands or to repair or expand the all-important irrigation system. The temples were the most impressive public buildings and were decorated in the Late Uruk period with cone mosaics. One of the main types was the temple raised on a high mud-brick platform for maximum visual and symbolic impact. A significant proportion of a city's territory belonged to the temple or the palace, and large numbers of people were employed as their servants. Clay tablets were used extensively to record the dues and produce of the temple and palace economy, to allocate rations, and a little later to record religious myths (Figure 3.5).

Writing was the preserve of a tiny percentage of the population in early Mesopotamian cities, mainly scribes in the service of the temple or palace. Control over writing and record keeping strengthened the control of these central institutions over the workings of the city-state. Hans Nissen has suggested that this in itself helped promote the development of the state, allowing tasks to be broken up into a larger number of component parts, creating greater interdependence among the separate sections of the community and requiring centralized bureaucratic organization. Another indication of Late Uruk centralization that is

**Figure 3.5** Cylinder seal and rolled-out seal impression. Cylinder seals first appeared in the Late Uruk period; these are distinctively Mesopotamian artifacts that consist of a small cylinder of stone carved with the reverse impression of a miniature figurative scene and often the name of an owner or official. The seal was designed to be rolled out on the surface of soft clay in order to leave a clear "signature." Along with writing, they show the concern for administration and control in the early cities of Mesopotamia. Cylinder seal impressions marked clay writing tablets (as evidence of their authenticity) and sealed jars, chests, or doorways. The carving of the miniature scenes was an intricate and sophisticated process; but the scenes themselves are a useful source of information, including as they do gods and heroes, episodes from myths and legends, and everyday items like livestock or buildings. Cylinder seals remained in use throughout a wide area of the Near East from the fourth millennium to the first millennium B.C. They also occur in foreign lands visited by Mesopotamian merchants, such as Egypt and the Indus.

very prominent in the archaeological record is a particular kind of pottery vessel known from its form as the beveled-rim bowl. These are so numerous that they constitute over 50 percent of the pottery assemblage on some sites. They have been interpreted as bowls for the distribution of rations to temple or palace workers. If this is correct, these vessels provide graphic illustration of the scale of centralized labor organization in the Late Uruk period.

Temple and palace were the twin centralized institutions of the early Mesopotamian cities. In certain respects, they were interdependent. Most rulers, for example, needed ritual sanction to confirm their legitimacy. At the same time, temple priesthoods could be direct competitors for political control. We know of at least one historical instance in which the temple priesthood mounted a successful coup against royal power.

Yet temple and palace were not the only forces in the early Mesopotamian city. There were also the leading families, who controlled extensive private property. It is possible, indeed, that at the outset all that did not belong to the king or temple was the communal property of a clan and was effectively in the control of clan elders. The cities no doubt drew their kings and rulers from these leading clans. At the time when written information became available, however, a major transformation was underway, with leading families acquiring and disposing of land as if it were privately owned. The buying and selling of land became a normal and accepted activity in Mesopotamia from this time on, though people continued to live in extended family units, as is shown by the large houses of Abu Salabikh and other excavated cities.

Early texts emphasize the importance of community power in the Mesopotamian cities. This is demonstrated by references to councils of elders in writings such as the *Epic of Gilgamesh*. Although the earliest surviving version of the Gilgamesh text is of a later date, Gilgamesh is a known historical king of Uruk, and the text may well reflect the situation prevailing in Uruk and other cities in the fourth and early third millennia B.C. The presence of the councils suggests that these cities were still in some sense in a transitional stage, where overall control was in the hands of an individual ruler but traditional law and settlement of legal disputes were usually left to community elders.

Most of the ancient cities of southern Mesopotamia survive today as tells—settlement mounds consisting of layer upon layer of collapsed mud-brick. As houses decayed, they were simply leveled to make way for new ones since the material for construction was so readily at hand (Box 3.3). We have already mentioned the temple platforms as being the most conspicuous feature of these city sites. Over succeeding generations they were extended and rebuilt, and many of them eventually took the form of the towering step-like ziggurat (temple platform) first seen at Ur (see Figure 3.10 on page 98). Palaces, too, have been excavated at a number of sites, including Ur and Kish. As public works, however, they are less impressive today than the city walls built during the early third millennium to defend these cities from attack by their neighbors. It was the walls of Uruk that drew praise from the author of the *Epic of Gilgamesh*, who remarked on their solid core of baked (rather than mud) brick. This substantial defensive circuit, which may indeed have been built by the historical Gilgamesh, measured no less than 9.5 kilometers (6 miles) in length (Box 3.4).

Today, the ruins of ziggurats loom over the level dusty plains—dusty because in most cases the rivers and canals no longer run near the ancient city sites, which now stand in arid desert. Centuries of intensive agriculture completed the work, laying a salt crust on the fields as the irrigation water evaporated.

## *The Uruk World System (3450–3100 B.C.)*

The first cities were founded in the south and had their greatest impact there. The size of their populations, however, sent ripples of influence far afield. This is the tale revealed by remarkable evidence from sites in northern Mesopotamia, in southeast Anatolia, and on the eastern fringes of the Mesopotamian lowlands. These key areas adopted a range of Uruk features and were basically enclaves of Uruk influence some distance from the Uruk heartland. The most famous site is Habuba Kabira, on the banks of the Euphrates in Syria. This was a substantial settlement, stretching for almost a mile along the bank of the river and defended by a stout brick wall. Its temples were built on a plan familiar from southern Mesopotamia. Even minor artifacts conform to typical southern styles.

Three separate theories have been proposed to account for these enclaves. The first sees them as colonies established by Uruk traders and settlers. Thus Habuba Kabira has been interpreted as a colony of south Mesopotamian merchants,

### *Box 3.3 Anatomy of Settlement II: The Early City*

Most early Mesopotamian cities were continuously occupied for several thousand years, which means that all too often the third-millennium layers are hidden beneath the accumulated building debris of later centuries. This makes it very difficult to gain any idea of the plan of an Early Dynastic city. Furthermore, since archaeologists have usually concentrated their efforts on the major public buildings, very little indeed is known of the ordinary houses and residential areas. An exception is the site of Abu Salabikh, which was excavated by British archaeologist Nicholas Postgate from 1975 to 1990. Here erosion has conveniently removed the later deposits. The mud-brick walls of the third-millennium buildings can be revealed simply by scraping the surface of the mound with shovels, thereby exposing the plan of large areas of the city. Analysis of floor deposits has been used to distinguish streets, roofed spaces (rooms), and open courtyards (plus a residual "uncertain" category) (Figure 3.6).

The houses of ancient Abu Salabikh were crowded together, with few clear thoroughfares; that remained true of many Near Eastern cities until the advent of motorized transport. Many houses were of substantial size, consisting of six or more good-sized rooms grouped around a courtyard, and may have housed as many as 20 people. Of these, some may have been servants and retainers, but textual sources suggest that early Mesopotamian households sometimes took the form of an extended family or kin group, and this may explain the large size of the house compounds at Abu Salabikh.

*(Cont.)*

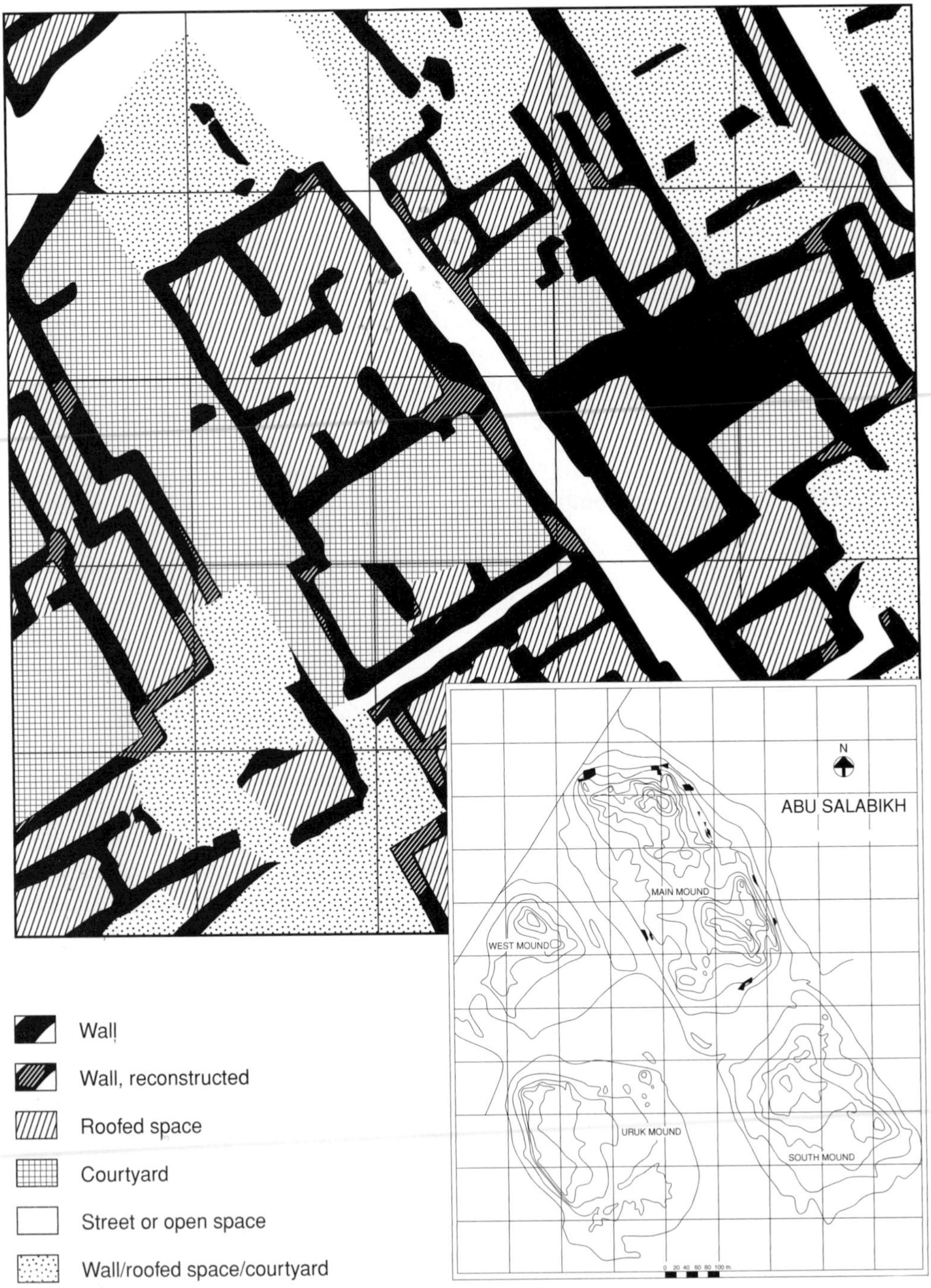


**Figure 3.6** Plan of a 50-meter by 50-meter (164-foot by 164-foot) square excavated at Tell Abu Salabikh in southern Iraq, showing the division into streets, courtyards, and roofed spaces.

## Box 3.4 Gilgamesh, King of Uruk

> In Uruk he built walls, a great rampart, and the temple of blessed Eanna for the god of the firmament Anu, and for Ishtar the goddess of love. Look at it still today: The outer wall where the cornice runs, it shines with the brilliance of copper; and the inner wall, it has no equal. Touch the threshold, it is ancient. Approach Eanna the dwelling of Ishtar, our lady of love and war, the like of which no latter-day king, no man alive can equal. Climb upon the wall of Uruk; walk along it, I say; regard the foundation terrace and examine the masonry: Is it not burned brick and good? The seven sages laid the foundations. . . . One third of the whole is city, one third is garden, and one third is field, with the precinct of the goddess Ishtar. These parts and the precinct are all Uruk.*

Gilgamesh, a semilegendary king who sought the secret of immortality, was king of Uruk in c. 2600 B.C. and is credited in the famous *Epic of Gilgamesh* with having built many of Uruk's most famous monuments. Among these are the city walls, remains of which still survive today. The description given here is of particular interest for its account of the city's layout. The walls of Uruk extend for no less than 9.6 kilometers (6 miles), but it is clear that only part of the enclosed area was built up, the rest being given to fields and gardens.

*From Nancy K. Sanders, ed. *The Epic of Gilgamesh* (Harmondsworth, England: Penguin, 1960), pp. 59, 114.

established far from the homeland in an attempt to secure vital raw materials from the less-developed margins of the Near East. The problem for the early cities of the south was access to raw materials such as metals, hard stone, and timber. The south Mesopotamian plains were rich in agricultural potential but had no resources of these kinds, which were largely the product of more mountainous regions. Once the south Mesopotamian centers had grown to urban proportions, the need for raw materials would have become acute. This need was satisfied, during the Uruk period of the fourth millennium, by the establishment of long-distance trade routes secured by Uruk-influenced centers at crucial points. Habuba Kabira is one example. Uruk influence is also strong at Susa, on the eastern plains of south Mesopotamia; at Nineveh, on the Tigris; and at Tell Brak, in the north. It is argued that in each zone colonies of Uruk merchants tapped into existing localized exchange networks.

Not all of these were new settlements like Habuba. Nineveh and Tell Brak had been important regional centers for many centuries. Around the middle of the fourth millennium, however, both were drawn into the Uruk sphere of influence, with beveled-rim ration bowls and other Uruk pottery, Uruk-type clay sealings, and at Tell Brak clay writing tablets even slightly earlier than those from Uruk itself. But these do not seem to have been locally inspired developments. They reflect a massive increase in commercial and cultural influence as merchants of south Mesopotamia sought to secure their supplies of vital raw materials from the uplands of Anatolia and Iran.

American archaeologist Guillermo Algaze has labeled this sphere of Uruk influence a "world system." This term is meant to indicate that the cities of south Mesopotamia and the surrounding less-developed regions were integrated into a single economic unit in which the southern cities played the dominant role, with the rest acting as a supporting or supply area. There is no suggestion that this was a unified empire. Eventually, however, the peripheries themselves developed under Uruk influence to the point where they reasserted their own political and economic personality (Figure 3.7).

Others have argued for a rather different view of these Uruk-influenced enclaves. They reject the world system hypothesis on the grounds that there is a near-complete absence of any of the supposedly traded materials at these supposed trading centers. Even if the bulk of the materials were being passed on to the cities of south Mesopotamia, we would still expect to find some trace of their passage in the trading centers set up to obtain them.

In place of Algaze's model, two alternative theories have been proposed to account for the wide dispersal and localized concentration of Uruk features. The first is that these peripheral "colonies" were in fact indigenous regional centers that chose to adopt Uruk styles and artifacts to give them an advantage in prestige competition with their neighbors. This interpretation reverses the dynamic of the world system model, suggesting that it was not Uruk populations that sought trade goods around the peripheries of Mesopotamia but peripheral centers that were seeking Uruk artifacts from the south Mesopotamian heartland.

A second theory accepts the presence of Uruk colonists at the peripheral centers but proposes that they were refugees fleeing some late Uruk collapse in the Uruk heartland. There is at present no clear means of deciding among these three hypotheses, but the world system model continues to be preferred by many regional specialists. It has the further advantage of fitting into a broad-scale pattern of cyclical changes in Mesopotamian history, with phases of expansion alternating with phases of contraction or retrenchment. Seen in that light, Ubaid represents an expansive phase, followed by contraction in Early Uruk, the expansion of the Late Uruk world system, contraction in the Early Dynastic period, and then a further expansive phase represented by the Akkadian empire of the late third millennium B.C. This alternating pattern is easy to discern but very difficult to explain.

Recent excavations at Hacinebi in eastern Turkey have thrown new light on the nature and chronology of Uruk influence in northern Mesopotamia. This was not an Uruk colony like Habuba Kabira, but an Uruk quarter established within an existing local settlement. It also begins earlier than Habuba Kabira, with Middle Uruk as well as Late Uruk pottery. Thus Uruk expansion to the north may have begun as small enclaves within local settlements before developing pristine colony foundations. Particularly significant at Hacinebi was the presence of Uruk-style administrative equipment, shown by clay *bullae* with seal impressions, alongside stamp seals of local Anatolian type. Thus we have here a center of interaction between south Mesopotamian and north Mesopotamian and Anatolian traditions.

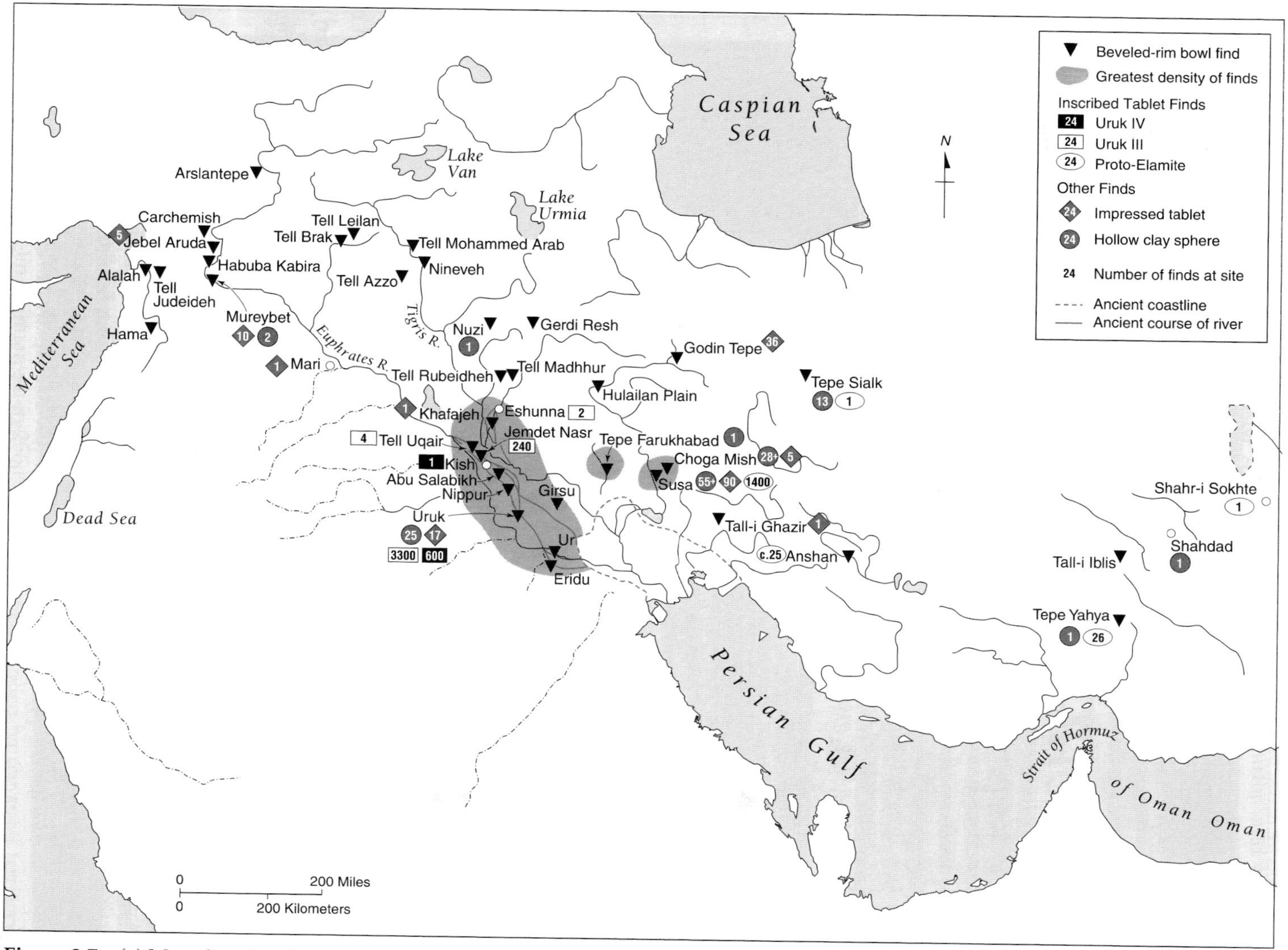


**Figure 3.7** (a) Map showing the extent of Uruk influence in the Near East.

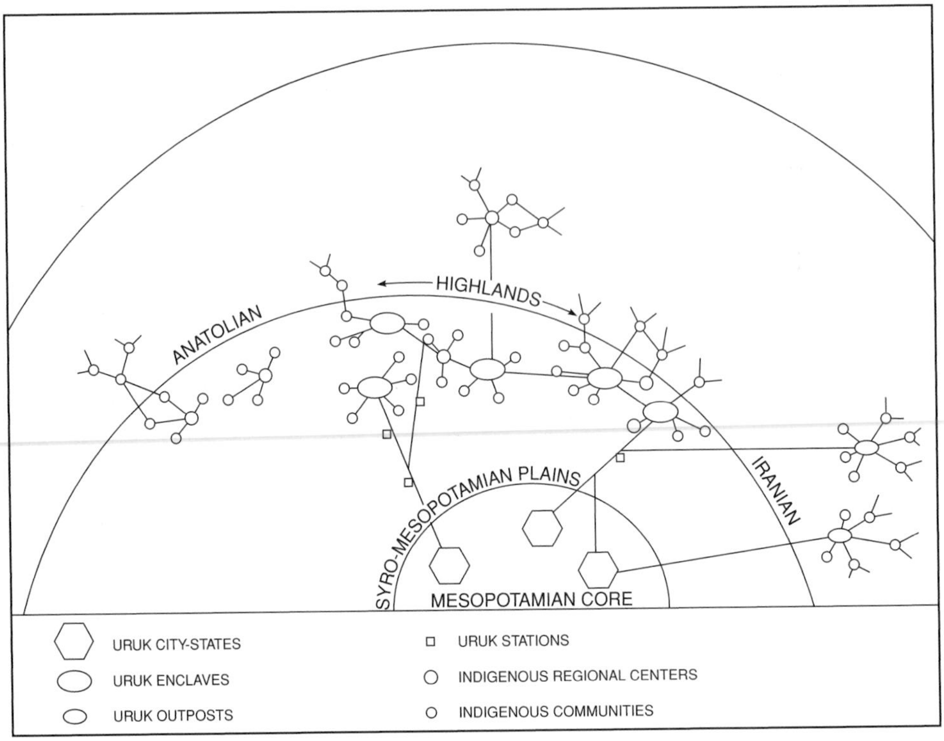


**Figure 3.7** (b) Diagram of the Uruk "world system."

Whatever the impact of the Uruk expansion, it is increasingly clear that cities had developed in the north by the middle of the fourth millennium, and may have been an indigenous development. Thus Uruk enclaves were sometimes established in existing cities. Tell Hamoukar and Tell Brak in northern Syria may both have been urban in scale by the beginning of the Late Uruk period, as suggested by stamp seals used by administrators found in early layers at Tell Hamoukar. It may thus be that we should envisage series of parallel developments in the fourth millennium, leading to cities, states, and writing in both northern and southern Mesopotamia and on the lowland Susiana plain of southwestern Iran.

By the end of the Uruk period around 3100 B.C. we are tantalizingly close to the beginnings of history. There are written records, but these are economic or administrative in character and tell us little about the political developments of the time. Late Uruk was followed by the Jemdet Nasr period (3100–2900 B.C.), named after another site in southern Mesopotamia. By then, the important early cities of the Mesopotamian lowlands were growing and flourishing, and the framework of Mesopotamian civilization had been established. The historical background only becomes clear, however, during the Early Dynastic period (2900–2350 B.C.), the age that witnessed the apogee of the Sumerian city-state.

## The Early Dynastic Period (2900–2350 B.C.)

The Early Dynastic period marks the beginning of historical records in ancient Mesopotamia. Around 2900 B.C. early writing became standardized into the cuneiform script that was to be used in the Near East for the next three millennia. The Early Dynastic period was also the first great age of the southern city-states, a time when the Sumerians were the dominant force in Mesopotamian culture and politics. It ends with the conquests of Sargon, king of Agade (2334–2279 B.C.), and the establishment of the Akkadian empire.[1]

### *The Sumerians*

Mesopotamia at the dawn of history was remarkable in one major respect. It had a common culture—a single system of writing and a single pantheon of major gods—but in population it was multiethnic and polyglot. Furthermore, it was far from being a unified state, as, say, was ancient Egypt (see Chapter 4). Instead, it was divided into a pattern of city-states, each notionally independent of its neighbors. There were at least two dozen major cities on the alluvial plains of southern Mesopotamia, each with a major temple to its principal or patron god and each surrounded by a stout brick wall to defend it from its neighbors.

Southern Mesopotamia was itself divided into Sumer in the south and Akkad in the north. Sumer extended from the mouth of the Persian Gulf in the south; Akkad was the territory north of this to the "narrows," where today the Tigris and Euphrates converge, in the neighborhood of modern Baghdad. Near the junction of Sumer and Akkad, thus centrally placed within the urban landscape, lay the city of Nippur, the most important religious center of the region. Control of Nippur was a vital element in Mesopotamian politics; the ruler of any city who was seeking preeminence over his neighbors had first to secure this sacred city. Those who were successful built shrines at Nippur to signal their devotion to the preeminent god, Enlil, whose main temple was there, and to proclaim their authority. In the Mesopotamian scheme of things, where the hierarchy of kings on earth mirrored the hierarchy of gods in heaven, it was only right that the dominant ruler of southern Mesopotamia should associate himself publicly with Enlil, the god who at that time was head of the Mesopotamian pantheon.

Nippur was a Sumerian city and Enlil a Sumerian god. To call them "Sumerian," however, is to say more than that they came from Sumer, the southernmost part of the Mesopotamian plain. The Sumerians were a people, one of the major ethnic groups of early Mesopotamia, with their own language and cultural identity. Sumerians were the dominant force in the cities of Ur and Uruk; they provided the first historical ruling dynasties, and their influence spread far afield to Mari in the north and onto the Iranian plateau in the east.

[1] The Early Dynastic (ED) period is itself subdivided. Early Dynastic I is dated approximately to 2900–2700 B.C., the period of the kings who reigned "before the Flood"; Early Dynastic II, 2700–2600 B.C.; and Early Dynastic III, 2600–2350 B.C.

Who exactly the Sumerians were has been much disputed. Many earlier writers thought they were originally from outside Mesopotamia itself and had migrated onto the fertile plain where they founded the first cities. It is more likely, however, that they were the indigenous inhabitants of the region, possibly the ancestors of the modern Marsh Arabs who live among the extensive reed beds and lagoons of the southern fringe of Mesopotamia. Sumerian sealstones show elaborate buildings (probably houses or cattle byres) built of bundles of reeds, very similar to those of the Marsh Arabs in recent times.

For generations, archaeologists assumed that the Sumerians were the sole founders of Mesopotamian civilization. This has changed with new discoveries in northern Mesopotamia, which show that cities were developing there, too, even before the spread of Uruk culture and the establishment of the proposed Uruk world system. The role of the Sumerians has had to be reassessed. They were in fact merely one of several peoples involved in the formation of the first Mesopotamian cities. But they were still enormously influential, and it was they who invented writing and many other key features of general Mesopotamian culture.

## *The Flood and the King-List*

The earliest Mesopotamian writing was used only for accountancy and inventories; we must wait until the third millennium for the first historical records. These are encapsulated largely in a single document, the king-list, which in its final version was compiled by Mesopotamian scribes around 1800 B.C. It consists of a long series of terse statements, each beginning with a city name and announcing a new dynasty; then the various rulers of that dynasty (on the lines of "A reigned *x* years, B reigned *y* years"); then at the end of each dynasty, the phrase "that city was smitten with arms, the kingship was taken to its successor."

This is not promising material from which to construct a detailed history of Mesopotamia during the third millennium, but it does provide a basic skeleton of rulers, which can be related to finds of inscriptions and sealings that bear their names. We can also relate the individuals to the cities from which they came.

The King-list does in fact begin long before this, with a legendary series of kings who ruled "before the Flood." The flood in question is the Mesopotamian equivalent of the biblical flood associated with Noah, and it is clear that both legends belong to a body of material widespread in the Near East during the third to second millennia B.C. In tablet XI of the *Epic of Gilgamesh*, Utnapishtim, the Sumerian Noah, tells Gilgamesh the story of the Flood, which he alone of humans had survived:

> Just as dawn began to glow there arose from the horizon a black cloud.
> Adad rumbled inside of it,
> before him went Shullat and Hanish, heralds going over mountain and land.
> Erragal pulled out the mooring poles,
> forth went Ninurta and made the dikes overflow. The Anunnaki lifted up the torches,
> setting the land ablaze with their flare.

Stunned shock over Adad's deeds overtook the heavens, and turned to blackness all that had been light.
The land shattered like a pot.
All day long the South Wind blew, blowing fast, submerging the mountain in water, overwhelming the people like an attack.
No one could see his fellow, they could not recognize each other in the torrent.
The gods were frightened by the Flood, and retreated, ascending to the heaven of Anu [Kovak, 1989, tablet XI, lines 96–114].[2]

In Mesopotamian (as in biblical) legend, the Flood was an event that had befallen many centuries before. Whether it refers to any real environmental catastrophe has long been debated. The issue was given special prominence by the British archaeologist Sir Leonard Woolley. In 1929, during his excavations at Ur, Woolley found 3.4 meters (11 feet) of clean, water-laid (or even windborne) silt in a deep sounding. His immediate thought was that these must be sediments laid down by the biblical Flood. The claim was soon dismissed—the silt proved to have come not from *the* Flood but simply from *a* flood, one of the many that have periodically afflicted the low-lying plains of southern Iraq. Archaeology provides no evidence of a single widespread catastrophe on the scale suggested by the Flood legend. Recent attempts to locate it in the Black Sea area are no more convincing than many earlier theories. Most scholars today regard it as simply a legend. Whatever its reality, however, it assumed great importance for the Mesopotamian scribes, who used it as a crucial event in dividing their list of kings into two parts—the hazy rulers before the Flood and the historical personages who came after it.

## The Early History of Sumer

When the waters subsided and the gods restored kingship to the earth, it came to rest at the city of Kish. This first dynasty of Kish consists of otherwise unknown rulers with impossibly long reigns, that is, until we arrive at the twenty-second king of Kish, Enmebaragesi. He, too, has an improbable tally of years—900 according to the king-list—but at this point the mists of uncertainty begin to clear since Enmebaragesi is known not only from the king-list but also from an inscription made during his lifetime and found at the city of Tutub (modern Khafaje). This provides a crucial link between the king-list and archaeology and forms the starting point of Mesopotamian history.

The reign of Enmebaragesi is now dated to around 2600 B.C. Although from this point onward we are on firmer ground, the evidence of the king-list is brief and gives only occasional details of historical events. The king-list is most valuable in giving an insight into the political structure of early Mesopotamia. The archaeology presents a pattern of city sites scattered over the Mesopotamian plains. Some are larger,

[2] Adad was the storm god; Shullat and Hanish, minor weather gods, heralds of Adad. The Anunnaki were a group of 50 gods, sons of Anu, god of the firmament. The god Erragal ruled the Netherworld, and Ninurta was the god of war. This is a truly terrifying array of menacing deities!

some smaller, but there is nothing in the archaeology itself to tell us whether we are dealing with a single state ruled by one dynasty of kings from a major capital or, conversely, a series of totally autonomous city-states, each with its own rulers and territory. The king-list reveals two crucial facts: on the one hand, that the cities had grown up as politically independent centers (city-states) and, on the other, that there was the concept of a unified kingship, whereby one city and one dynasty were overlords of the others.

The first overlords after the Flood were the kings of Kish, as we have seen. But not all cities were content simply to accept this situation. Shortly after 2600 B.C. the ruler of Kish—Agga, son of Enmebaragesi—was faced with a rebellion by one of his most powerful subjects, Gilgamesh, king of Uruk. Gilgamesh refused to recognize Agga as overlord, but when the king of Kish advanced to besiege Uruk it was Gilgamesh who gained the upper hand, and Agga became his vassal. Thus the kingship passed from Kish to Uruk.

Struggles for supremacy among the major cities of southern Mesopotamia continued throughout the middle centuries of the third millennium. Kings of Kish, Uruk, Ur, and other cities successively held sway and then were obliged to cede overall supremacy to one of their rivals. The pattern of shifting hegemonies and alliances gives the history of the period a kaleidoscopic quality.

## *The Royal Graves at Ur (2600–2350 B.C.)*

When Sir Leonard Woolley arrived at the site of Ur in southern Mesopotamia in 1922 he can hardly have anticipated the remarkable discoveries that were to follow. The city, famous in biblical terms as the supposed home of Abraham, was marked by the remains of a ziggurat. Woolley began his investigations by digging a cautious series of exploratory trenches to define the edges of the sacred area around the ziggurat. Soon, gold beads began to appear in one of these trenches, and Woolley became aware that he was on the verge of a major find. He judged that his local workmen were not yet sufficiently experienced, and with commendable patience he waited five years more before returning to the "gold trench" to renew his excavations. When he did so, he was confronted by a staggering array of graves, some of them richly furnished. The contents remain to this day the masterworks of early Mesopotamian craftsmanship.

The Royal Graves at Ur formed part of a large cemetery of the middle to late third millennium (c. 2600–2100 B.C.) located just outside the Sacred Precinct, to the south of the great ziggurat. Woolley divided the graves into two groups: those that were poorly furnished, which he ascribed to the "common folk" of Ur (at least 2,000 in number, perhaps as many as 8,000 altogether), and the 16 spectacular Royal Graves that he attributed to the ruling dynasty of Ur. Whereas the ordinary graves were simple pits, containing a body wrapped in matting or placed in a coffin of wood or clay, the Royal Graves had elaborate burial chambers of brick or stone. They were also distinguished by the wealth of accompanying offerings and by a more grisly feature: an array of human sacrifices. One grave held the remains of as many as 74 attendants, who may have been drugged or poisoned before burial (Box 3.5).

## Box 3.5 *The Grave of Pu-abi*

The most spectacular of the 16 Royal Graves discovered by Sir Leonard Woolley at Ur was that of Pu-abi, a woman who must have been a member of the ruling dynasty or a high court official. (Note that Woolley called her Shub-ad, through a mistaken reading of the cuneiform characters.) Pu-abi's stone-built tomb chamber lay at the bottom of a deep shaft and was sealed by a stone vault. Within it on a wooden bier lay the body of Pu-abi herself, dressed in a cloak of lapis, gold, and carnelian beads. She also wore a wig, with an elaborate decoration of gold bands, and was accompanied by three female attendants. Adjacent to this chamber was the "death pit," which contained the bulkier grave goods of the deceased, notably a huge clothes chest and a sledge chariot, decorated in red, white, and blue mosaic and pulled by a pair of oxen (represented by their skeletons). There were many smaller treasures, including an inlaid gaming board and two richly ornamented lyres. The entrance to the death pit took the form of a sloping ramp, guarded at the foot by the bodies of 5 men with copper daggers at their waists—the tomb sentries. Immediately inside the entrance stood the chariot and clothes chest and the bodies of the 4 grooms responsible for attending the oxen (Figure 3.8b). The largest group of bodies lay in the annex to the left, where 13 female attendants were carefully laid out in two rows. These people were buried to accompany their mistress to the Otherworld. There were no marks of violence on the skeletons, but whether they died voluntarily or were executed by poison or strangulation is unclear.

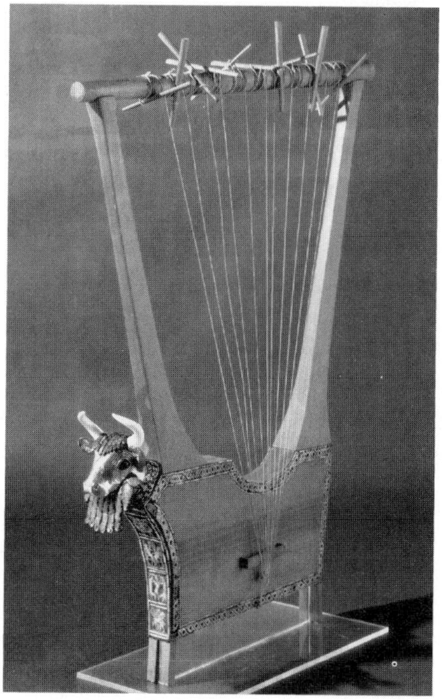

**Figure 3.8** (a) Gold and lapis cow-head lyre from Pu-abi's tomb.

*(Cont.)*

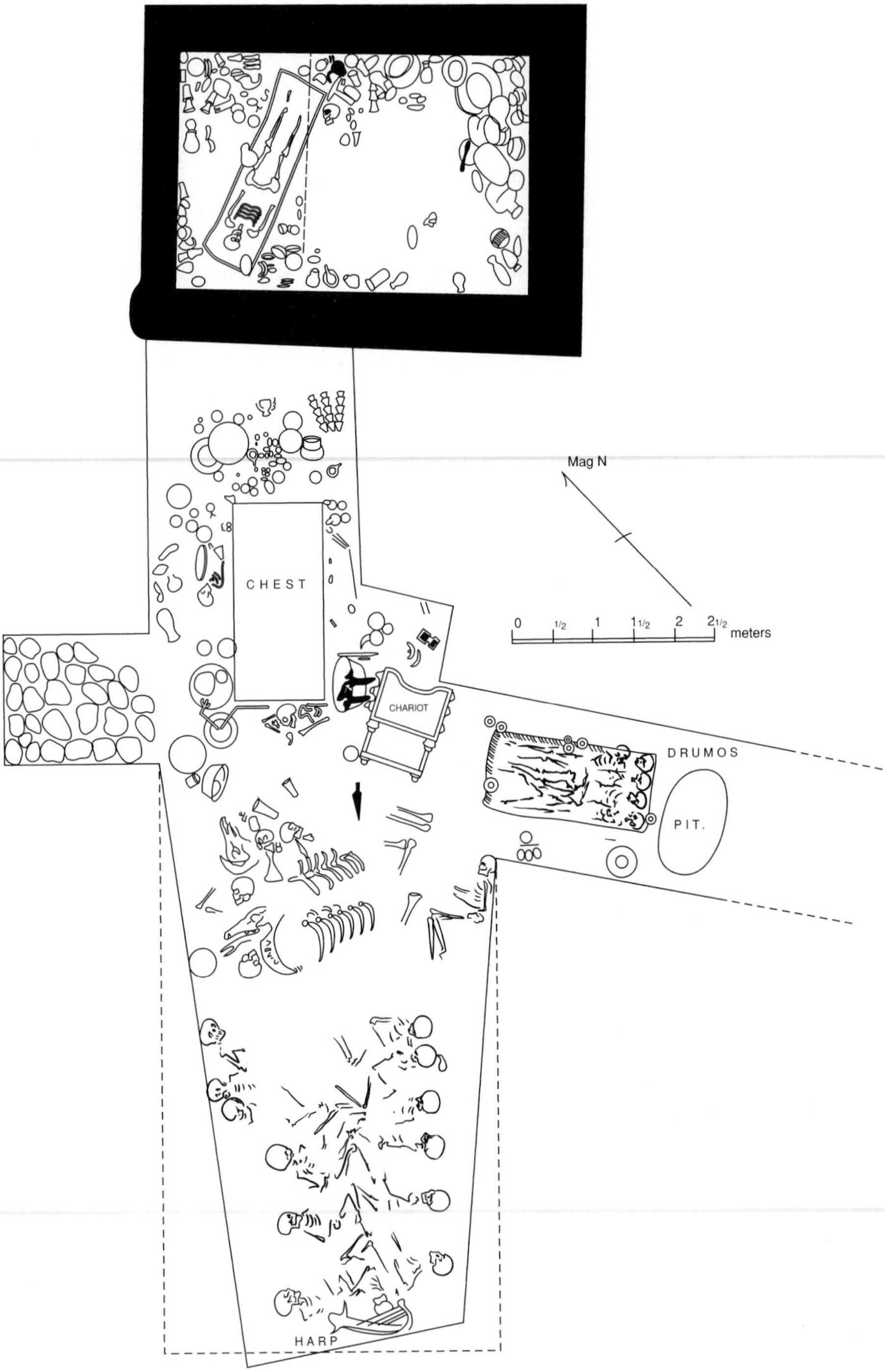


**Figure 3.8** (b) Plan of Pu-abi's tomb and death pit.

The objects recovered from the Royal Graves give us crucial insights into courtly life in third-millennium Mesopotamia. Inlaid panels depict scenes of feasting or four-wheeled battle wagons in action against the enemy. The feasting scene shows a stringed lyre decorated with an ornamental bull's head being played before an audience of courtiers, and remains of several such lyres were found in the graves themselves (Figure 3.8a). The wood of the lyres had long decayed, and we owe their recovery to a special technique used by Woolley in these graves. He soon realized that there were small voids in the fill of the chambers left by the decay of wooden objects. He carefully poured hot wax into the voids, which made it possible to reconstruct the form of the wooden objects and to restore their original decoration of inlay panels or precious metals.

One of the most striking features of the Royal Graves is the exotic provenance of many of the materials used in the creation of these priceless objects. The people buried in the Royal Graves could call on silver from Anatolia, gold from Egypt or Persia, and lapis lazuli from Afghanistan.

Who were the people who could command such wealth and could demand human sacrifice of their retainers? Woolley argued that they must be the rulers of Ur since some of the artifacts from the graves bore the title of king or queen, but others have questioned this theory. We cannot say that they were not royalty, but equally they may have been leading courtiers or priests and priestesses. Their wealth is apparent, but their identity remains shrouded in mystery.

## *New Developments in Northern Mesopotamia*

The historical record for third-millennium Mesopotamia is richest in the south, but we should not ignore important developments in the north Mesopotamian plain, especially in the neighborhood of Nineveh and the region of the Khabur River, between the Tigris and Euphrates.

In the fourth millennium, the Khabur region had formed part of the broad Uruk culture area. One of the principal Khabur sites, Tell Brak, had already attained urban proportions by that period. Indeed, if we include the outlying mounds in the reckoning, Tell Brak in the mid-fourth millennium was larger in simple areal terms than at any later period, possibly even as large as fourth-millennium Uruk.

Archaeologists have now shown that there are in fact two distinct phases of urbanization in this region of Mesopotamia: the first, in the mid-fourth millennium B.C., is represented by only a few sites like Tell Brak, and the second phase, in the early third millennium B.C., for which one key site is Tell Leilan, currently under excavation by Harvey Weiss and a team from Yale University. Leilan began the twenty-seventh century as a modest center some 15 hectares (6 acres) in area. Within 200 years it had mushroomed to a major urban site, ringed by defenses that enclosed an area of 90 hectares (222 acres).

## City Neighborhoods in the Third Millennium

Mesopotamian cities of the Early Dynastic period and later had a number of standard elements, though they were far from rigid in their overall plan and configuration. We have already mentioned the defensive wall and the temple or temples. There were palaces, too. Temple and palace together formed the joint poles of economic and administrative activity. All important cities and many lesser settlements stood on gradually accumulating tells, artificial mounds composed of mud-brick debris from previous building phases. Within the city limits there were often a main tell and a number of smaller tells, which correspond to suburbs inside the occupied area.

Archaeologists have found evidence that the cities were divided into neighborhoods, some of them associated with particular crafts or callings. One area at Nippur seems to have been a scribal quarter; another, at Abu Salabikh, may have been occupied by bakers. At Ur and Mari there were public spaces fronting onto the Euphrates River, and many cities had riverside harbors. Our knowledge of residential areas is limited, however, since relatively few excavations have concentrated on uncovering the dwellings of ordinary people.

A prime exception is Ur, where Woolley excavated an area of housing dating mainly from the early second millennium B.C., though some of the buildings were older. They may not be far different from urban housing in third-millennium Mesopotamia: mud-brick courtyard houses arranged along streets and lanes, with shops and chapels mixed in among the dwellings. Woolley thought they were of two stories, with stairs leading to the upper floors. At Tepe Gawra in northern Iraq, the third-millennium houses had stone footings and small ground-floor rooms, which may have been the basis for mud-brick dwellings of several stories. Upper floors would have been an entirely logical feature where city space was restricted, especially if the city stood on top of a tell.

In addition to temples and houses, these early cities must have had markets where agricultural produce, manufactures, and raw materials could be bought and sold. Where these were located remains a mystery, though they may have been near the city gates, as in Near Eastern cities in recent times. Two sites in northern Iraq—Tell Taya and Tell Brak—have third-millennium buildings that have been interpreted as caravanserais, where merchants could find lodging and could store their goods and pack animals. Texts from Ebla in northwest Syria show that Brak was noted at the time as a place to buy an expensive variety of mule.

## Urban Centers and Rural Complexity

With the arrival of cities on the archaeological scene, the rural hinterland can too easily be seen as merely the support system of the cities, providing the food that kept the urban populations alive but offering little of interest on its own account. As American archaeologists Glenn Schwartz and Steve Falconer have observed, "In regions and time periods that provide ancient written records, this prejudice tends to be reinforced by the urban preoccupations of those texts and the world views of their authors, typically city-dwelling elites and the scribes in their employ."

We saw earlier how intensive surveys of the Mesopotamian plain by Robert McC. Adams and his colleagues identified a whole range of smaller settlements—hamlets, villages, and towns. Recent work has considered the question of rural sites in much greater detail, through the excavation of selected examples. What the excavators have found is that these are not the simple, undifferentiated agricultural villages they had expected. This work has raised the whole issue of rural complexity, as a counterpart to urban complexity, in early civilizations generally and in Mesopotamia in particular.

A particularly interesting site is Tell al-Raqa'i in the middle reaches of the Khabur River, a tributary of the Euphrates in northeast Syria. This was a small settlement of only a third of a hectare (as compared with the 50 to 100 hectares of nearby urban sites). Tell al-Raqa'i was founded around the beginning of the third millennium B.C. The lowest well-preserved levels, dated to around 2800 B.C. or a little earlier, reveal a settlement of rectangular mud-brick buildings clustered around a massive Rounded Building, an irregular ovoid enclosure with substantial mud-brick walls. Within the Rounded Building are a series of platforms and walls, but most notable of all is a number of deep silo-type rooms, entered from above. Schwartz interpreted this building as a specialized installation for grain storage and processing. Mud-brick platforms were used to dry the grain, ovens and cooking pots to parch it (to ensure its long-term preservation), and silos for storage. Tell al-Raqa'i is far from the only site of this type in the immediate vicinity. On the contrary, it is one of a series of contemporary sites on the banks of the middle Khabur that seem to have been centrally planned grain-collection facilities. Canadian excavators found remains of grain-storage facilities at Atij, 2 kilometers (1 mile) downstream from Tell al-Raqa'i. They also identified a possible riverside quay, underlining the crucial role of water transport at these sites.

Schwartz calculated that the storage facilities at Tell al-Raqa'i were capable of holding 75,000 kilograms (34,000 pounds) of grain, sufficient to feed around 500 people for a year. Yet the size of the site suggests a resident population of only 30 to 60 people. Schwartz concludes that the surplus was intended to feed some nearby urban center and that Tell al-Raqa'i and the other riverside sites on the middle Khabur were intentionally founded as units in a specialized system of state-organized grain supply. These were not the villages of self-sufficient peasant farmers but parts of a centralized plan. The Rounded Building and similar defensive structures at the other sites suggest that the grain store itself had to be secured against theft or hostile attack, and the scale of these structures again suggests central control.

Thus the cities were not the only new feature on the Mesopotamian scene in the fourth and early third millennia B.C.; they were accompanied, in some regions at least, by a radical reorganization of the rural settlement pattern.

## The Akkadian Empire (2334–2230 B.C.)

A notable feature of many complex societies throughout the world is the creation of a propaganda machine that legitimizes the ruling elite and glorifies their achievements. The ultimate expression of such propaganda is the creation of public monuments and inscriptions, conveying an impression of power and control even where most of the populace cannot read. Rulers may also adopt grandiose titles and may even claim to be divine. In Mesopotamia, these tendencies found their first full development in the Akkadian period, when a new ideology of kingship and imperial power was created.

We have already seen how the alluvial plain of southern Mesopotamia was divided into two regions: Sumer, land of the Sumerians, in the south, and Akkad, land of the Akkadians, in the north. The distinction between the two peoples is best seen in terms of language. The Sumerian language has no living descendants, whereas Akkadian belongs to the broad family of Semitic languages represented today by Arabic and Hebrew.

We have also seen how Sumer and Akkad together consisted of a patchwork of some two dozen major city-states, each surrounded by its own territory and dependencies (which could include other towns). Although for much of the time one city or dynasty was considered dominant over the others and had control of the sacred center, Nippur, each city retained its own rulers and constituted a separate political unit.

Around 2334 B.C., all this suddenly changed. A new ruler, an Akkadian official at Kish, seized power in his home city and then marched against and overthrew Lugalzagesi, king of Uruk, the High King of the time. The new ruler took the name Sargon (Sharru-ken), a name that means "legitimate ruler" and ties in with historical evidence that shows just the opposite—that he was a usurper (Figure 3.9). The name was pure propaganda. The victory over Lugalzagesi made Sargon overlord of Sumer and Akkad. There had been earlier Semitic rulers of Kish, but what distinguished Sargon from his predecessors was his ambition and a new ideology. He was not content to remain merely overlord of Mesopotamia.

**Figure 3.9** Copper head of an Akkadian ruler, the supposed Sargon of Agade (Baghdad Museum). Imperial ideology and charismatic leadership were two of the most striking features of the Akkadian empire and had a profound effect on later Mesopotamian dynasties. From this time on, ambitious Mesopotamian rulers sought to have themselves portrayed in public monuments as heroic and godlike individuals, deserving reverence from their subjects. (Head of Sargon of Arkkad, 3rd mill. B.C. Bronze Iraq Museum, Baghdad, Iraq. © Snark/Art Resource, NY.)

He wished to extend his power north, east, and west. From this arose the Akkadian empire, the first supranational state.

Sargon established a new capital at a place called Agade, not far from Baghdad. Its site has not been identified, but it was no doubt a splendid place, its harbors frequented by ships from distant countries such as Meluhha (the Indus Valley), Magan (Oman), and Dilmun (Bahrain, an important trading entrepôt even at this early date). It is from Agade (sometimes written Akkade) that the land of Akkad and the language Akkadian take their name. Sargon himself is known as Sargon of Agade, and the empire he founded is called Akkadian. Such was its prestige and influence that the Akkadian language became the lingua franca throughout the Near East for almost two thousand years.

Much of what we know about Sargon's exploits comes from later tradition, in which history is embroidered by legend. He became a figure of mythical proportions, a great warrior king whose onslaught no enemy could withstand. This makes it difficult to assess the real nature of Sargon's achievement. What is clear, however, is that during a long reign of perhaps half a century (2334–2279 B.C.) he used his dominance over the cities of southern Mesopotamia to launch a sustained series of campaigns against neighboring lands.

The two main axes of expansion were east, against the peoples of Elam on the edge of Mesopotamia, and northwest, toward the upper Euphrates and the Mediterranean. What we know of these campaigns comes either from Sargon's own grandiose claims, contained in his inscriptions, or from later Assyrian records in which Sargon and his successors are regarded as heroes of the distant past. Neither source of evidence is entirely reliable, and they both contain a significant admixture of boastfulness and legend. Nonetheless, for what they are worth, they tell us that there was hard fighting in the east, and only after a struggle did Sargon force the local rulers there to become his vassals. In the northwest, Sargon claimed that even rulers in western Syria were soon acknowledging him as overlord. If so, they were probably as much cowed into submission by Akkadian military expeditions as conquered in systematic campaigns.

What Sargon's campaigns achieved was access to many of the sources of raw materials on which southern Mesopotamia depended: silver, copper, and timber. His own inscriptions claim that he reached the cedar forest and the silver mountains, referring probably to the Amanus Mountains of Syria and the Taurus range of southern Turkey, respectively. But whether this or mere territorial aggrandizement was his aim is open to doubt. So is the reality of his imperial control: Neighboring kings may have offered their submission out of political or military convenience, but it was a different matter when Sargon was preoccupied elsewhere or stamping out the general revolt that troubled his later years.

Sargon's son and successor, Rimush (2278–2270 B.C.), also had to suppress rebellions, both at home in Sumer and Akkad and among his dependencies. He in turn was succeeded by another of Sargon's sons, Manishtushu (2269–2255 B.C.), who launched a famous campaign across the "Lower Sea" (the Persian Gulf) and may have raided parts of Oman. The greatest of Sargon's successors was not these, however, but his grandson Naram-Sin, who succeeded Manishtushu in 2254 B.C. and ruled over the Akkadian empire for 37 years.

It was Naram-Sin who completed the task of turning a collection of territories into a true empire. He appointed Akkadian governors to rule the major cities and destroyed those that resisted him. The scale of his power is illustrated by a number of monumental buildings at Tell Brak, one of which is protected by brick walls 10 meters (33 feet) thick and may have been a citadel or fortified administrative center. To underline his power Naram-Sin took a step that the rulers of Egypt had taken long before: He proclaimed himself not the agent of a god, like his predecessors, but a god himself (though very much a lesser god) and took the grandiloquent title "king of the four quarters, king of the universe."

One of the key elements in the imperial program was the use of state propaganda. For Sargon and Naram-Sin it was part of a concerted imperial policy. The concept of charismatic kings and the notion of empire are both ascribed to the rulers of Akkad by later Mesopotamian tradition. People had only to look around them in the cities of southern Mesopotamia to see the evidence of Akkadian greatness with their own eyes. The lands of Sumer and Akkad were virtually inundated with public monuments that extolled royal achievements and the power of these charismatic Akkadian kings. The reality was probably less impressive.

How far real Akkadian rule extended is difficult to say. There is incontestable evidence of Akkadian control at Tell Brak and elsewhere in the Khabur region of northern Mesopotamia, and probably also (though less certainly) at Nineveh and Assur. Further west, the layers of destruction found by Italian archaeologists at Ebla in Syria may have been the work of either Sargon's or Naram-Sin's armies, but there is no evidence that this region became a regular part of the Akkadian empire. Still further afield, the rock inscription of Naram-Sin at Pir Hussein, near Diyarbekir in southern Turkey, testifies to the long reach of the Akkadian armies but does not imply political control.

In the Khabur region, investigations by American archaeologist Harvey Weiss and his colleagues at Tell Leilan have suggested that Akkadian conquest was followed by significant economic changes. Agricultural production seems to have been intensified by the new rulers, and watercourse channels were deepened and straightened. Then, around 2200 B.C., Akkadian control disintegrated. Some archaeologists argue that the Khabur region experienced a massive population decline at this time and that the main regional centers became deserted. They put forward environmental change as one of the causes—a period of drier climate that persisted for several centuries. Corings taken from the seabed in the Gulf of Oman provide evidence for a three-century period of drought in the region beginning around 2100 B.C., which may indeed have been one of the factors behind the fall of the Akkadian empire. Epigraphic and other archaeological evidence, however, shows that some of the Khabur sites, such as Tell Brak and Tell Mozan, continued to flourish in the post-Akkadian period as centers of independent kingdoms.

Naram-Sin's empire, great as it was, did not long survive his death. His son Shar-kali-sharri held on for 25 years against foreign attack and internal revolt, but when he died around 2230 B.C. the Akkadian realm collapsed into anarchy; city-states and tributary peoples were once more independent, as they had been before the advent of Sargon. The Akkadian empire had lasted a mere century, but it was a presage of things to come.

## Imperial Ur (2112–2004 B.C.)

The habit of empire, once formed, died hard. What one ruler had achieved, others sought to emulate. Yet not all of them chose, or needed to choose, the route of military conquest to achieve their ends. A remarkable example of the diplomatic route to empire is provided by Ur-Nammu, who in 2112 B.C. founded the Third Dynasty of Ur.

Ur had always been one of the leading cities of southern Mesopotamia and a major port (perhaps the leading port) for the Indian Ocean trade, which brought copper from Oman and gold from India to the head of the Persian Gulf. Two previous dynasties of Ur had held sway over large tracts of Sumer and Akkad, and the wealth of the city is amply attested to by the discoveries from the famous Royal Graves. But the Third Dynasty took Ur to new heights of fame and influence.

Unlike Sargon and Naram-Sin, Ur-Nammu does not seem to have been a ruthless military man but used diplomacy as well as warfare to extend his influence over neighboring cities. There was also a religious element in this expansion, since Ur-Nammu embarked on an ambitious building program at his capital and elsewhere, rebuilding and enlarging the great ziggurat of Nanna, the moon god and principal deity of Ur (Figure 3.10). This was a building without precedent in terms of scale and gave a great boost to the dynasty's prestige. Ur-Nammu built ziggurats at other cities, too. He is also credited with one of the oldest extant codes of law, preserved in fragmentary form on clay tablets found at Nippur, an important administrative center of the Ur dynasty.

Ur-Nammu ruled almost the whole of Sumer and Akkad, but it was his son and successor, Shulgi (2094–2047 B.C.), who in a long reign of almost 50 years made Ur the capital of an extensive empire. He appointed governors to rule the cities of Sumer and Akkad on his behalf (though many came from ruling families of those cities) and introduced a system of monthly taxation (known as *bala*, meaning "rotation") for this core territory. Shulgi also conquered the lowland region to the north and east of Sumer and Akkad, stretching up into the foothills of the Zagros Mountains, and appointed military commanders to govern these realms and pay tribute known as *gun mada*. *Gun mada* was annual and was paid in the form of livestock to special administrative centers such as Puzrish-Dagan near Nippur, which processed 350,000 sheep in a single year. Sheep were the source of wool used in textile manufacture, which was one of the major economic activities of third-millennium southern Mesopotamia. Some archaeologists even refer to a "fiber revolution" following the specialized husbandry of the wool-bearing sheep in the early third millennium, and it is clear that textiles were one of the leading exports. One text of the period refers to a Mesopotamian textile production center in which over 4,000 adults and 1,800 children worked as weavers. Weavers were overwhelmingly women and had poor wages and low social status. Large-scale production centers owned by major landholders or by the state alienated textile laborers from both agricultural production and their kin-groups, leading to a major transformation in the political economy during the Ur III period.

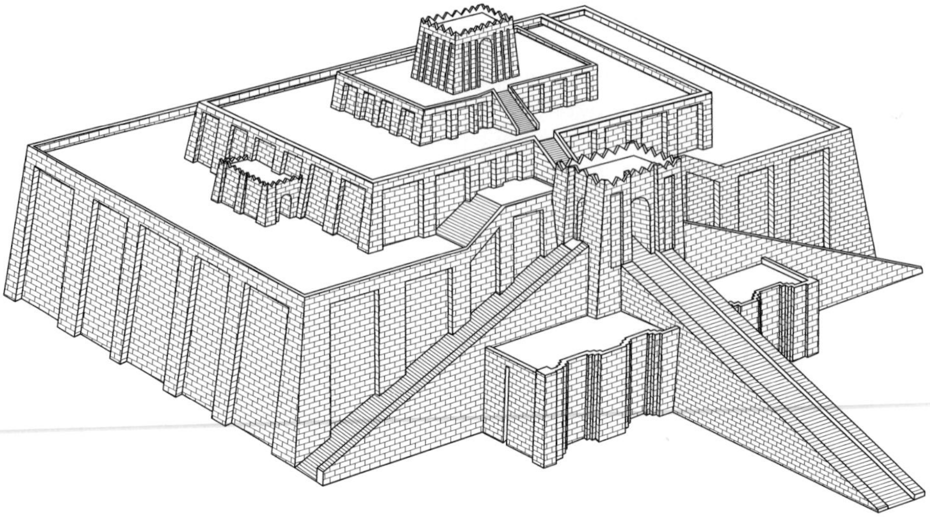

**Figure 3.10** Reconstruction of the Ur ziggurat. The most impressive remains at Ur today are those of the great ziggurat, the massive stepped pyramid dedicated to the moon god Nanna. It was built by Ur-Nammu (2112–2094 B.C.), founder of the powerful Third Dynasty of Ur. Ur-Nammu's ziggurat proved to be the first in a long tradition, stretching into the Neo-Babylonian period (605–539 B.C.). Its origin lay in a brick platform built to raise temples above the surrounding city houses. Such platforms are seen at Eridu as early as the Ubaid period, but as time went by they became grander and more impressive. The ziggurat was a logical culmination, consisting not merely of a single platform but also of a whole series of superimposed platforms, with a temple on the summit. The idea may have been to raise the temple closer to the sky, where the gods were thought to live. This is reflected in the biblical story of the tower of Babel, which is clearly a reference to the famous ziggurat of Babylon. It also placed the scene of the ceremonies far above the ordinary populace, who could only watch and wonder from a distance.

One further feature of the Third Dynasty of Ur deserves mention: the emphasis placed on traditional Sumerian culture, even though the royal family itself used a mixture of Semitic and Sumerian names. Many scholars argue that the religious buildings of Ur-Nammu and Shulgi were one part of a conscious strategy of Sumerian cultural revival. Building temples and dispensing justice were, however, the duty of every legitimate Mesopotamian ruler (Figure 3.10).

## Wider Horizons (2500–2000 B.C.)

The historical record during the Early Dynastic period is focused on southern Mesopotamia, the land of Sumer and Akkad, and so it remains during the empires of Agade and Ur. This richness of historical evidence must not, however, be allowed to obscure important and contemporary developments in adjacent parts of the Near East, notably in Syria and Anatolia to the west and in Susiana (the plain lying at the foot of the Iranian highlands) in the east.

## *Mari and Ebla*

In the west, two of the most important sites are Mari and Ebla. These were cities founded in the third millennium B.C.—a little later than the earliest cities of Sumer and Akkad. Both lay on key trade routes leading from Mesopotamia to the west: Mari on the Euphrates itself, Ebla on one of the routes leading from the Euphrates valley to the Mediterranean coast. Both developed into important cities and, by the later centuries of the third millennium, were governed from large and luxurious palaces. Both lay within the orbit of Mesopotamian traditions. At Mari, the temples and gods were Sumerian, and its rulers (depicted on statuary) wore the distinctive Sumerian fleece skirts, even though they had Semitic personal names. Furthermore, Mari depended, like the cities of southern Mesopotamia, on irrigation agriculture for its food. Over the course of centuries constant irrigation has sadly damaged the fertility of the floodplain; as irrigation water evaporates under the strong Near Eastern sun, it leaves a crust of salt. Mari today is flanked by extensive reaches of salt flat on the edge of the Euphrates River.

Ebla, by contrast, was located in higher terrain to the west and practiced rain-fed agriculture. Like Mari, it used the Sumerian script with a Semitic language (akin to Akkadian) for its official records. Sumerian gods featured in its religious affairs, but the Eblaite religion was not purely Mesopotamian since it also included divinities of western origin. It was thus a link between Mesopotamia and the west, a city sitting at the junction of two separate worlds. It was not far enough away to escape the attentions of the Akkadian kings. When Italian archaeologists were excavating the royal palace (Palace G) in 1974, they came across a scene of devastation. Two adjacent rooms of the palace had held an official archive on clay tablets. These had been carefully stored on shelves fixed to the walls, but when found they were scattered across the floor and showed traces of fierce burning. The whole palace evidently perished in a massive conflagration. The excavators were quick to attribute this destruction to Naram-Sin, who boasted how he had put the city of Ebla "to sword and flame" sometime in the twenty-third century B.C. Whether or not this attribution is correct, the fire had baked the clay tablets in the palace and had thus accidentally helped to preserve them.

Ebla's archive gives us a vital insight into the life of a Near Eastern city in the late third millennium. The clay tablets cover a variety of subjects, including trade, taxation, and military affairs. One document records receipts of over 7 tons of silver in a single year. Others reveal that the king of Ebla owned 80,000 sheep. Many of the texts concern textiles, some received as tribute from surrounding territories. A more violent background is revealed by references to "the year of the taking of Darasum" (a rival city) and "3,600 dead in the city of Darasum." This is evidence of local warfare; texts from Mesopotamia itself speak of armies of over 10,000 men, and carvings such as the *Stele of the Vultures* from Lagash depict serried ranks of soldiers who are marching menacingly into battle with helmets, shields, and lowered spears.

## *The Southern Levant*

Southwest of Ebla lay the coastal strip of the southern Levant, backed by the hinterland of the central hills and the Jordan valley. Here the course of urbanization followed a very different pattern from that seen in Syria or Mesopotamia.

Cities first appeared in the southern Levant in the Early Bronze II period, beginning around 3100 B.C. They were found only in the coastal plain and were much smaller than those of Mesopotamia, attaining a maximum size of only 25 hectares (62 acres), as compared with the 400 hectares (988 acres) of Early Dynastic Uruk. Rural settlement, meanwhile, steadily declined throughout Early Bronze II and III (3100–2300 B.C.), until the Levantine cities themselves were abandoned in the Early Bronze IV period (2300–2100 B.C.). This strange development pattern suggests that, unlike Mesopotamia, the early cities of the southern Levant failed to integrate the smaller communities of the rural hinterland into a single settlement system. The cities flourished for several centuries, and those on the coast enjoyed trade links with Old Kingdom Egypt, but rural decline ultimately undermined their viability and led to their abandonment.

Cities did not appear again in the southern Levant until the Middle Bronze II period, around 2000 B.C. Thus, as in the Khabur region of northern Syria, there appear in this region to have been two distinct phases of urbanization. (The Middle Bronze Age cities of the Levant will be discussed in Chapter 7.)

## *Susa and Elam*

On the eastern flank of Mesopotamia lived a series of peoples with whom the city-states of the plain were often at war. Some were confederations of tribesmen from the Zagros hills, such as the Lullubi defeated by Naram-Sin or the Gutians who attacked his successors. These were inhabitants of the central Zagros, but to the south a more centralized state emerged in the late fourth millennium, straddling the hill country and the fertile plain at its foot. This was the kingdom of Elam, centered on Anshan in the mountains but expanding to absorb Susa on the plains.

The development of the Elamite kingdom owed much to contacts with the Mesopotamian heartland. Susa, as we have seen, was one of the enclaves of Uruk culture in the late fourth millennium B.C., a key element in the proposed Uruk world system. During that period of close contact it shared many Uruk features, including beveled-rim ration bowls and hollow clay spheres, or *bullae*, which may lie at the origins of clay writing tablets. These features are also found far to the east of Uruk, at important centers such as Tepe Sialk and Tepe Yahya on the Iranian plateau. The spread of this material illustrates the operation of ancient trade routes that linked the Mesopotamian plain with sources of raw materials on the uplands to the east.

A significant political change seems to have occurred shortly before 3000 B.C., at the end of the Uruk period in Mesopotamia. This is the point when on the Iranian plateau and the plains around Susa we enter what is known as the

Proto-Elamite period (3200–2900 B.C.). Its most distinctive feature is the use of clay tablets, inscribed in a pictographic script, as were those of Late Uruk Mesopotamia, but with a completely different language: Proto-Elamite. This language has no living descendants, though it may be related to the Dravidian languages spoken in southern India today.

The Proto-Elamite script is linked in its basic conception to Sumerian writing, but experts argue that it developed largely independently. If so, it is a curious parallel, though we must recall that both the Susa region and the Iranian plateau had fallen under heavy Mesopotamian cultural influence in the Late Uruk period. But the appearance of the script is not the only change at the beginning of the Proto-Elamite period. At the same time we see evidence of the emergence of a centralized state in southwestern Iran, named Proto-Elamite after the script. The core area of this state was probably Anshan, in the Fars province of modern Iran. The Anshan state expanded to absorb the city of Susa on the lowlands to the west, taking it out of the Sumerian orbit. Distant sites on the Iranian plateau such as Yahya and Sialk shared in these developments—they, too, for instance, have yielded small numbers of Proto-Elamite tablets—but they are interpreted as colonies, absorbed in a different way into the Proto-Elamite realm.

This Proto-Elamite state was a relatively short-lived phenomenon. It lost control of its "colonies" and collapsed around 2800 B.C. The Iranian plateau then fragmented politically into a number of smaller units, which were less centralized in nature and hence had no need for writing. They were nonetheless powerful in their own way and sat astride major axes of trade and communication, controlling the flow of raw materials, such as metals and fine stone, that made their way to the lowland cities of Mesopotamia. Tepe Yahya became an important center for the production of elaborate chlorite bowls, while the people of Shahr-i Sokhta engaged in the transport of the much prized lapis lazuli from Badakhshan in modern Afghanistan.

In the southwest, meanwhile, the city of Susa continued as the capital of a much-reduced Elamite kingdom. Historical records show that it came regularly into conflict with the cities of the Sumerian heartland. In the Akkadian period Susa was conquered by Sargon and after a brief period of independence fell under the control of Shulgi, of the Third Dynasty of Ur. These conquests pulled it back within the Mesopotamian orbit. The Elamite princes of the highland zone around and beyond Susa remained unsubdued, however, and when the empire of Ur weakened they took revenge on their once-powerful neighbors. In 2004 B.C. Kindattu, king of Elam, invaded Mesopotamia and captured the imperial capital of Ur. Susa once again became the capital of a powerful Elamite kingdom extending onto the Iranian plateau.

The fall of Ur may at the time have seemed just another vicissitude in the fluctuating fortunes of southern Mesopotamia. But the political geography was changing, as new states on the fringes of Mesopotamia became increasingly powerful and important. The continued development of the Near East during the second millennium is the subject of Chapter 7.

## Summary

This chapter has described the emergence of the key features of Mesopotamian civilization: cities, writing, and state-level political organization. We began with the growth of farming villages and the settlement of the dry Mesopotamian plain. The successful development of irrigation farming provided the economic basis for the cities that appeared in the fourth millennium B.C. Bureaucracy and writing were essential tools of government in the new urban centers. Competition among city-states led eventually to the formation of the empires of Akkad and Ur. The cities themselves form the most striking archaeological sites of the period, large tells rising above the Mesopotamian plain. Yet we must not forget that it was successful exploitation of the landscape by peasant farmers that made the whole phenomenon possible; nor must we ignore the importance of long-distance economic links, which supplied the cities with essential raw materials and in turn carried their influence far beyond the confines of Mesopotamia.

## Guide to Further Reading

Good accounts of the development of Mesopotamian civilization are provided by Charles Redman, *The Rise of Civilization* (San Francisco: Freeman, 1978); by David Oates and Joan Oates, *The Rise of Civilization* (Oxford: Phaidon, 1976); and more recently by Susan Pollock, *Ancient Mesopotamia* (Cambridge: Cambridge University Press, 2000). A more geographically based perspective is given in the early sections of Michael Roaf's *Cultural Atlas of Mesopotamia and Ancient Near East* (New York: Facts on File, 1990).

The role of irrigation in early Mesopotamian civilization is discussed by Robert McC. Adams, *The Evolution of Urban Society* (Chicago: Aldine, 1966); Karl A. Wittfogel, *Oriental Despotism: A Comparative Study of Total Power* (New Haven, CT: Yale University Press, 1957); and Julian Steward, ed., *Irrigation Civilizations: A Comparative Study* (Washington, DC: Pan-American Union, 1955). The earliest archaeological evidence for irrigation canals in Mesopotamia is described by David Oates and Joan Oates, "Early Irrigation Agriculture in Mesopotamia," in G. de G. Sieveking, I. H. Longworth, and K. E. Wilson, eds., *Problems in Economic and Social Archaeology* (London: Duckworth, 1976), pp. 109–135. For Adams's famous settlement surveys, see *Heartland of Cities* (Chicago: University of Chicago Press, 1981); more recent survey work is reviewed by T. J. Wilkinson "Regional Approaches to Mesopotamian Archaeology: The Contribution of Archaeological Surveys," *Journal of Archaeological Research* 8 (2000): 219–267. For the impact of cities and complex societies on rural settlement, see the studies in Glenn M. Schwartz and Steven E. Falconer, eds., *Archaeological Views from the Countryside: Village Communities in Early Complex Societies* (Washington, DC: Smithsonian Institution Press, 1994). The Tell al-Raqa'i excavations are described by Glenn Schwartz in Chapter 3, "Rural Economic Specialization and Early Urbanization in the Khabur Valley, Syria," pp. 19–36.

Competing theories for the formation of states in the Uruk period are reviewed by Susan Pollock, "Bureaucrats and Managers, Peasants and Pastoralists, Imperialists and Traders: Research on the Uruk and Jemdet Nasr Periods in Mesopotamia," *Journal of World Prehistory* 6 (1992): 297–336. See also G. Stein and M. S. Rothman, eds., *Chiefdoms and Early States in the Near East* (Madison, WI: Prehistory Press, 1994). Evolutionary theories of the rise of the Mesopotamian state are critiqued by Norman Yoffee, "The Decline and Rise of Mesopotamian Civilization," *American Antiquity* 44 (1979): 5–35. See also his chapter, "Too Many Chiefs?" in N. Yoffee and A. Sherratt, eds., *Archaeological Theory: Who Sets the Agenda?* (Cambridge: Cambridge University Press, 1993). For a summary of recent work at Uruk itself, see Rainer Michael Boehmer, "Uruk 1980–1990: A Progress Report," *Antiquity* 65 (1991): 465–478. The classic account of the Uruk world system is by Guillermo Algaze, *The Uruk World System: The Dynamics of Expansion of Early Mesopotamian Civilization* (Chicago: University of Chicago Press, 1993), recently revised and updated in his article "Initial Social Complexity in Southwestern Asia: The Mesopotamian Advantage," *Current Anthropology* 42 (2001): 199–233. Excavations at Hacinebi and a review of the Uruk "colonies" is provided by Gil Stein and co-authors in "Uruk Colonies and Anatolian Communities: An Interim Report on the 1992–1993 Excavations at Hacinebi, Turkey," *American Journal of Archaeology* 1000 (1996): 205–260. For recent work at Tell Hamoukar, see McGuire Gibson and Muhammam Maktash, "Tell Hamoukar: Early City in Northeastern Syria," *Antiquity* 74 (2000): 477–478. Uruk period urbanization in Susiana is described by Henry T. Wright, "Uruk States in Southwestern Iran," in Gary M. Feinman and Joyce Marcus, eds., *Archaic States* (Santa Fe: School of American Research Press, 1998), pp. 173–197.

For the theory of clay tokens as the precursors of writing, Denise Schmandt-Besserat's two-volume *Before Writing* (Austin: University of Texas Press, 1992) has now been revised and abridged in *How Writing Came About* (Austin: University of Texas Press, 1996). Early writing is also discussed in Hans J. Nissen, Peter Damerow, and Robert K. Englund, *Archaic Bookkeeping: Early Writing and Techniques of Economic Administration in the Ancient Near East* (Chicago: University of Chicago Press, 1993). Several useful articles on Mesopotamia and the Near East are contained in the special number of *World Archaeology* 17, no. 3 (1986) devoted to "Early Writing Systems."

For Mesopotamian raw materials, see P. R. S. Moorey, *Ancient Mesopotamian Materials and Industries: The Archaeological Evidence* (Oxford: Clarendon Press, 1994).

The third millennium in southern Mesopotamia receives thorough treatment from Nicholas Postgate, *Early Mesopotamia: Society and Economy at the Dawn of History* (London: Kegan Paul, 1992). House sizes at Tell Abu Salabikh are discussed by the same author in relation to city population estimates in "How Many Sumerians per Hectare?—Probing the Anatomy of an Early City," *Cambridge Archaeological Journal* 4 (1994): 47–65. The Royal Graves and ziggurat at Ur are described and illustrated by the excavator himself in Sir Leonard Woolley, *Ur of the Chaldees,* revised and updated by P. R. S. Moorey (New York: Barnes & Noble, 1982). Sumerian life and religious beliefs are vividly described by Samuel Noel Kramer, *The Sumerians: Their History, Character and Culture* (Chicago: University of Chicago Press, 1963) and Thorkild Jacobsen, *The Treasures of Darkness* (New Haven, CT: Yale University Press, 1972).

Standard general accounts of early Mesopotamian history are provided by the relevant chapters in I. E. S. Edwards et al., eds., *The Cambridge Ancient History,* 3rd ed. (Cambridge: Cambridge University Press, 1980). For the history and ideology of the Akkadian empire, there are now the specialist studies in M. Liverani, ed., *Akkad: The First World Empire* (Padua: Sargon srl, 1993), in particular the chapters by Piotr Michalowski ("Memory and Deed: The Historiography of the Political Expansion of the Akkadian State," pp. 69–90) and Harvey Weiss and Marie-Agnès Courty ("The Genesis and Collapse of the Akkadian Empire," pp. 131–155).

Evidence supporting the climatic explanation for the fall of the Akkadian empire is reviewed by Peter deMenocal, "Cultural Responses to Climate Change during the Late Holocene," *Science* 292 (2001): 667–673. The development of fiber technology and the role of women in textile production is discussed by Joy McCorriston, "The Fiber Revolution: Textile Extensification, Alienation, and Social Stratification in Ancient Mesopotamia," *Current Anthropology* 38 (1997): 517–549.

For discoveries at Ebla, see Paolo Matthiae, *Ebla: An Empire Rediscovered* (London: Hodder and Stoughton, 1980). Urban development in the southern Levant and Mesopotamia are compared by S. E. Falconer and S. H. Savage, "Heartlands and Hinterlands: Alternative Trajectories of Early Urbanization in Mesopotamia and the Southern Levant," *American Antiquity* 60 (1995): 37–58.

On the Elamites and the Iranian plateau, see Elizabeth F. Carter and Matthew W. Stolper, *Elam: Surveys of Political History and Archaeology* (Berkeley: University of California Press, 1984) and John Curtis, ed., *Early Mesopotamia and Iran: Contact and Conflict 3500–1600 B.C.* (London: British Museum Press, 1993). The argument for Proto-Elamite colonies is presented by C. C. Lamberg-Karlovsky, "The Proto-Elamites on the Iranian Plateau," *Antiquity* 52 (1978): 114–120. Evidence for specialized craft production at Shahr-i Sokhta and other third-millennium centers on the Iranian plateau is discussed from a Marxist standpoint by Maurizio Tosi, "The Notion of Craft Specialization and Its Representation in the Archaeological Record of Early States in the Turanian Basin," in Matthew Spriggs, ed., *Marxist Perspectives in Archaeology* (Cambridge: Cambridge University Press, 1984), pp. 22–52.

# Chapter 4

# Egyptian Civilization

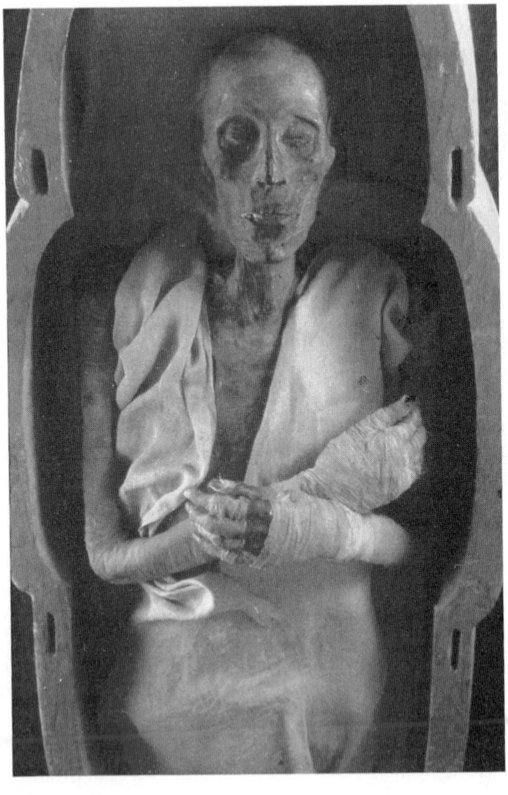

The mummy of pharaoh Ramesses II.

*The crowd has gathered since dawn, courtiers and high officials dressed in fine linen robes. Men and women stand on low earthen mounds, gazing at the brightly painted pavilion by the T-shaped lake in the desert sand. Sailing ships still crowd the Nile, bringing people from nearby Thebes to Amenhotep's Sed festival, his ceremony of renewal. The year is 1360 B.C., the thirtieth year of King Amenhotep's reign. Excitement runs high on this festive day. A trumpet sounds. The great double doors of the House of Rejoicing open. Amenhotep appears suddenly, dressed in ceremonial finery, surrounded by his family and chamberlains of the court. The crowd falls silent as the king stands still, in his role as sun god on earth. His vizier and the high priests lead forward a line of courtiers and high officials. The pharaoh hands out rewards for distinguished service, gifts of green linen and ornaments of gold. Each person honored accepts a gift of food from the king's table and eats in the king's presence. They walk to the lake and grasp the tow ropes of the Morning or Evening Barges with their precious cargoes of sun god statues. In a symbolic reenactment of the sun god's daily journey, they haul the barges to the very foot of the royal throne, celebrating the stability of the state and the longevity of the king.*

The Sed festival was one of the oldest ceremonies of Egyptian kingship, an institution that endured for more than 25 centuries. Chapter 4 describes the origins and development of Egyptian civilization from its beginnings among simple farming communities more than 6,000 years ago (Table 4.1).

## Kmt: "The Black Land"

"Egypt is the gift of the river," wrote the Greek writer Hecataeus of Miletus, who visited the Nile around 500 B.C. He saw that Egyptian civilization depended on the annual flood that coursed down the greatest of Africa's rivers. The Nile slashes like a green arrow through the arid landscape of extreme northeast Africa (Figure 4.1). The slash is more than 4,800 kilometers (3,000 miles) long, from high in the Ethiopian highlands and Lake Victoria in Uganda northward to the Mediterranean Sea. For most of the last 1,127 kilometers (700 miles), the Nile cuts a deep gorge through some of the driest landscape on earth, then fills it with layer after layer of deep, fertile river silt. The floodplain was bountiful, for the Nile waters overflowed their channel every year, bringing life-saving moisture to parched fields. Perhaps half a million people lived in Kmt, the "black land," when Egyptian civilization began around 3100 B.C. in a valley where land was abundant, where there was plenty of wilderness, and in good flood years lush marshland teemed with fish and fowl.

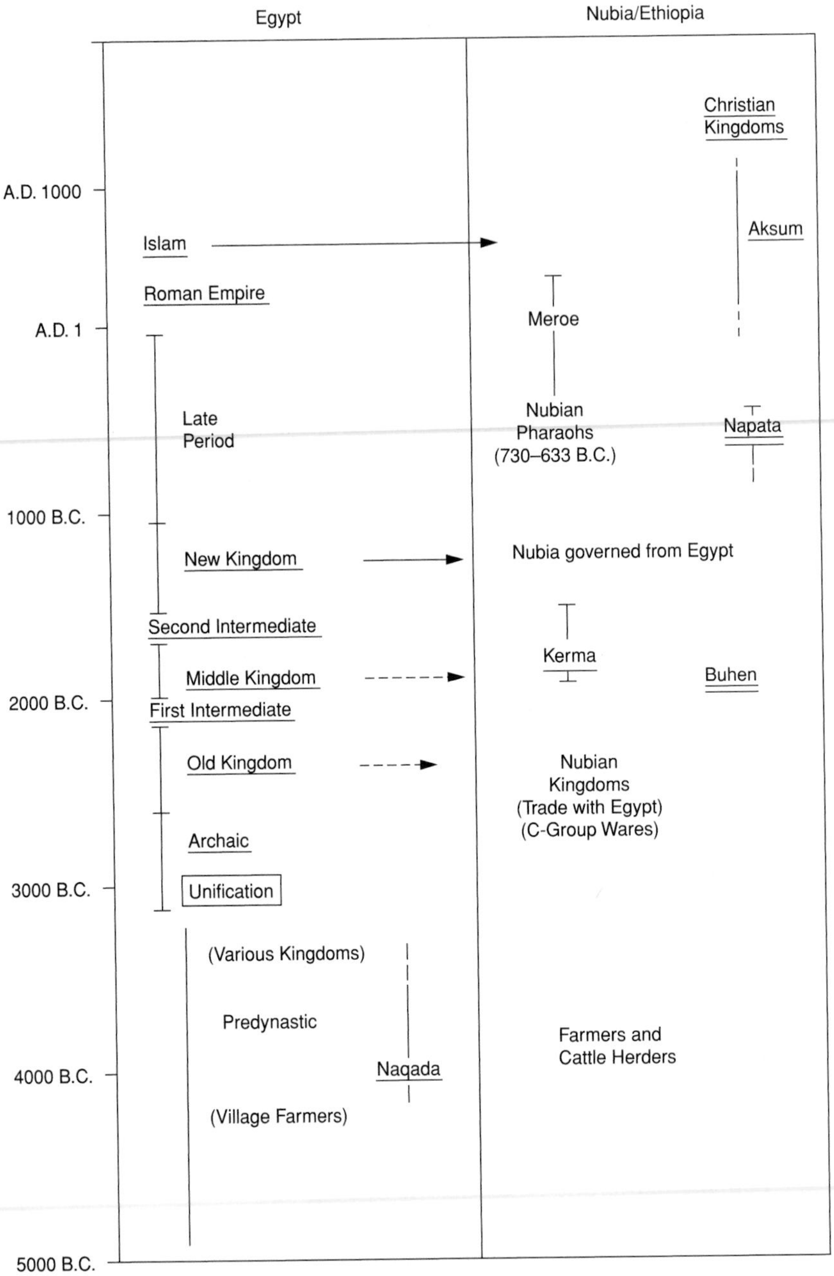


**Table 4.1** Egyptian and Nubian civilization. There are almost as many chronologies of Egypt as there are Egyptologists! The widely accepted chronology used here is that of John Baines and Jaromir Malek, *Atlas of Ancient Egypt* (New York: Facts on File, 1980). Manetho's King-lists are still the subject of debate, for both the priest's calculations and assumptions that kings ruled in order have been challenged. Pharaohs' names are spelled in their Egyptian forms here.

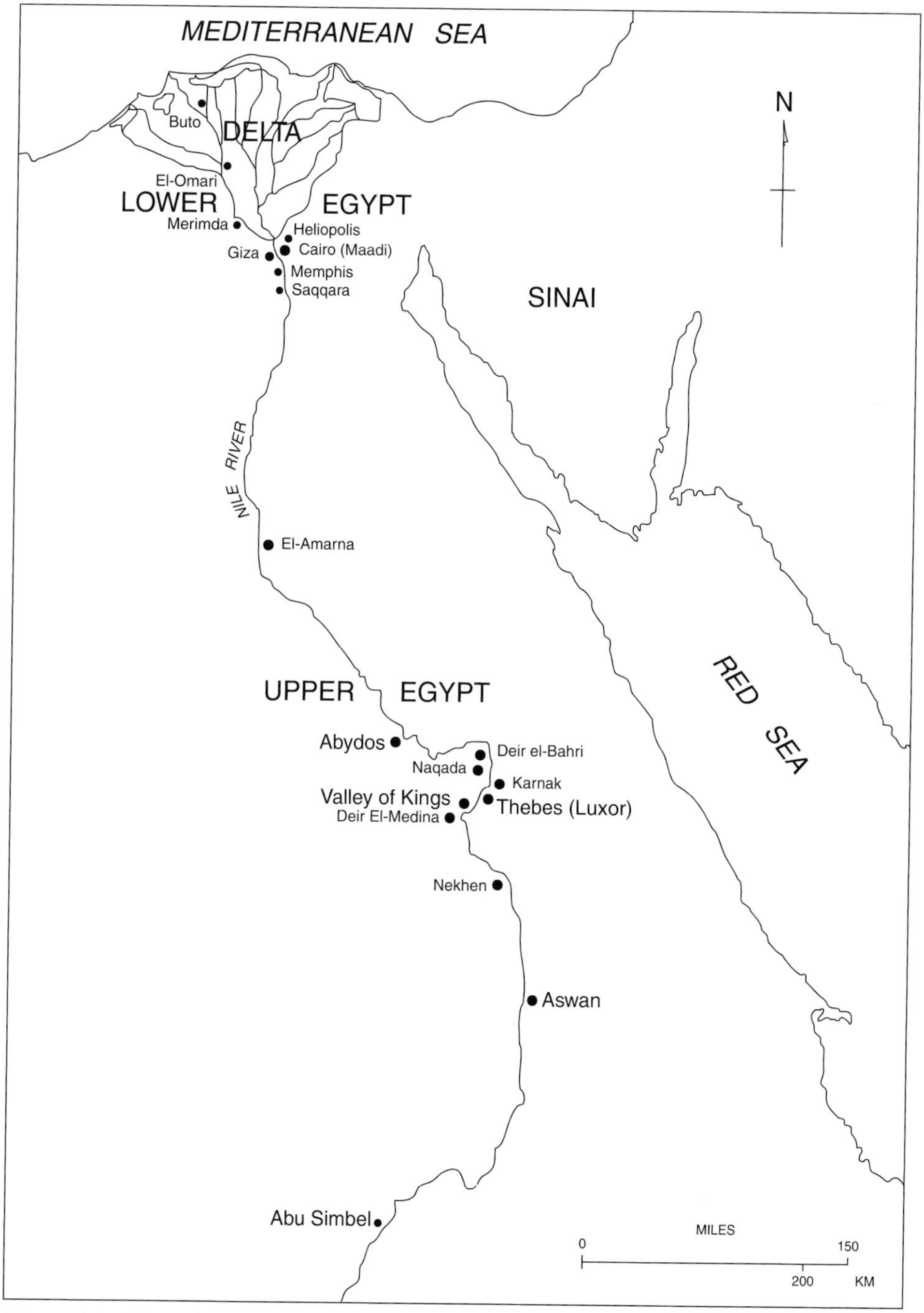


**Figure 4.1** Map of sites and geographical features mentioned in Chapter 4.

Food was plentiful if the annual flood rose high enough to fertilize the land and if the waters were not so high and fast-moving as to sweep everything away in their path.

The Nile's tributaries, the Atbara and the Blue Nile, both rise in the mountainous Ethiopian plateau. Each year, they carry the runoff from heavy summer rains in the tropics. The water surge flows downstream, swelling the Nile in summer. Before the days of modern hydroelectric schemes, the river would rise above its banks, turning the countryside into a vast, shallow lake, its towns and villages like islands on low mounds above the floodwaters. This was *akhet*, the season of inundation. As the current slowed, the river dropped its silt on the flooded lands, then receded as the farmers planted their crops on the muddy ground. Then came *peret*, the season of growing, when crops of wheat and barley would ripen slowly in the late summer and autumn sunlight without the need for watering. After the harvest in March or April, the early summer sun would harden and crack the ground, aerating the soil and preventing the accumulation of harmful salts in the earth. *Shemu*, the season of drought, ended with the onset of the new inundation.

Compared with turbulent rivers like the Tigris of Mesopotamia and the Indus of Pakistan, with their violent floods and wild fluctuations, the Nile was relatively predictable. There were occasional extreme highs and lows, but in most years government officials could forecast the crest within a few meters and calculate tax levies from it. The Egyptians dreaded high flood years, when the river swept everything before it, and drought cycles, when the floodplain was a dust bowl. In such circumstances, Egypt was a vulnerable kingdom, a state held hostage by a great river. But its kings ruled, not always decisively, for 3,000 years. Much depended on the efficiency of their administration.

The Egyptians knew the Nile's floods and fluctuations intimately and lived their lives according to its rhythms. Symbolically, the great river was the source of life, personified by the god Hapi, the manifestation of the annual inundation. Hapi was depicted as a man with full breasts, which symbolized the rich fertility of the river. He flowed with the waters of Nun, the dark ocean in the realm of the gods, where the primordial earthen mound emerged, in turn to give rise to Re, the sun. The divine Nile was part of the Egyptians' cosmic order.

The modern Egyptian landscape bears no resemblance to the riverine environment of 3000 B.C. We know little of the narrow floodplain's original appearance. We can only draw analogies from other large rivers like the Mississippi and African rivers such as the Zambezi, which flood each year. The Nile must have had a well-defined channel, which meandered between natural banks. Shallow basins and swamps retained receding floodwater, capturing fertile silt. Small farming villages flourished on higher ground or on the river banks, in strategic locations near good soil. As the floodwaters receded, the farmers would plant their crops in the fresh silt, grazing their cattle in nearby meadows and scrublands. By the time the waters rose again, the harvest was over. The villagers' herds grazed on dry lands at the margins of the flood. The Egyptian farmer of 5,000 years ago had no need for elaborate irrigation technology, just the ability to exploit flood basins and a varied environment that teemed with edible plants, fish, and game animals.

The harsh desert pressed in on the floodplain from both sides, difficult of access and hard to traverse except in organized caravans. The Sahara and Sinai isolated Egypt both from tropical Africa and from the Near East. Its distinctive civilization developed and flourished in relative isolation, but from the earliest times it obtained gold from the eastern desert, ivory and semiprecious stones from far upstream, and timber from the Levant. For all this trading, Egypt was a conservative land set apart by virtue of its geography but united within by easy communication through river travel. Most people settled and traded along the river, for the Nile is navigable all the way from the Mediterranean to the First Cataract at Aswan. When sailing boats came into use before 3500 B.C., the prevailing north winds allowed people to sail upstream; they then used the current to return to home port. Throughout its long history, Egypt was a linear kingdom of considerable size, held together by powerful theological beliefs and centralized government and by the realities of communication and geography.

## Origins (5000–2920 B.C.)

How did the Egyptian state arise? Was it an indigenous civilization, or did it originate elsewhere in the Near East or downstream in tropical Africa? The Egyptians themselves had a straightforward view of their history. The past was a model of order, king succeeding king in peaceful succession in an uninterrupted line back to the moment when time met the cosmos. Civilization was built on continuity, on meticulous record keeping, and above all on divine and royal precedent. Egyptian scribes maintained king-lists with scrupulous care. Luckily for science, Manetho, the High Priest of Heliopolis, wrote a history of Egypt in the third century B.C. Only fragments of his book survive, among them king-lists from Menes, the first pharaoh, to the conquest of the Nile by Alexander the Great in 332 B.C. Manetho divided his list into 31 dynasties, a subdivision used to this day. Modern Egyptologists have further separated Manetho's dynasties into larger time spans that coincide with distinct episodes in Egyptian history (Table 4.2 on page 118). The actual chronologies of individual reigns and dynasties still generate controversy.

All Egyptian kings considered themselves rulers of Upper Egypt (the valley) and Lower Egypt (the delta), the boundary between the two lying somewhere near modern Cairo. Their ceremonial title was symbolic of all important unity, the reconciliation of the conflicting powers of Horus, the god of Upper Egypt, with Seth, the deity of Lower Egypt. This reconciliation was the source of political order and stability for Egyptian society and, in symbolic terms, marks the beginning of Egyptian civilization. The Egyptians themselves cloaked the origins of their state in a complex ideology and symbolism of which Horus and Seth were a part. But they had no doubt that theirs was a society born and bred along the Nile.

In contrast, some modern-day Afrocentrist scholars believe that Egyptian civilization was a creation of black Africa. In the 1950s, the Senegalese scholar Chiekh Anta Diop asserted that all ancient Egyptians were black. "When we scientifically clean the skin of mummies, the epidermis appears pigmented in the same way as that of all other African Negroes," he wrote. The skin color of Egyptians in tomb paintings is dark red, but Diop claimed it was the "natural color of the Negro." Diop marshaled descriptions by classical authors, isolated language traits from all over Africa, and collected such cultural features as earthen mounds ("pyramids") in West Africa's Niger delta to support his belief that black Africans were "the first to invent mathematics, astronomy, the calendar, science and the arts, religion, agriculture, social organization, medicine, writing, technology, architecture." To Diop, Egypt was a purely African civilization, founded by Africans from Ethiopia, who migrated from the south. As such, it was a fountainhead of all human civilization.

Diop's *Nations Nègres et Culture* first appeared in 1955 and was largely ignored by Egyptologists, who saw few signs of African influence in Egyptian art, artifacts, and architecture. Then linguist Martin Bernal formulated his now-famous "Black Athena" hypothesis in the late 1980s. Using a patchwork of widely scattered archaeological, historical, and linguistic clues, he claimed that Egyptian civilization was "fundamentally African," that many of its most powerful royal dynasties in Upper Egypt were those of "pharaohs whom one can usefully call black." Bernal also argued that Egypt was a major contributor to early Greek civilization.

Bernal's theory has drawn heavy fire from classicists and archaeologists but gained an enthusiastic and uncritical following from Afrocentrists. The association seems to be a simplistic one—that because Egypt was in Africa, its citizens were automatically black. In fact, evidence from tomb paintings, papyri, and well-preserved Egyptian mummies and burials shows that the Nile Valley population was fairly cosmopolitan, especially in later times when it traded over wide areas. Even the Egyptians made a clear distinction between themselves and the black Nubians, as tomb portraits show. Egyptian civilization is simply Egyptian, and only African to the extent that Egypt is geographically part of Africa.

Archaeology provides overwhelming evidence that Egyptian civilization developed from entirely indigenous roots without any direct influences from tropical Africa upstream (see Chapter 12). How this complex process of indigenous development took hold can only be guessed at, with telling insights from archaeology and traditional myths—and analogies with the modern game of Monopoly.

## *Predynastic Chiefdoms*

Archaeological evidence tells us that by 5000 B.C. simple farming based on cattle herding and cereal agriculture had replaced a combination of foraging and cultivation along the Nile as far south as what is now the Sudan, ushering in the predynastic period of Egyptian history. Two thousand years later, a patchwork of small kingdoms and villages had become a unified state with a distinctive, common ideology.

Most explanations for the origin of the state focus on population growth and competition for land and natural resources. In Egypt's case, state formation took place in an environment where population densities were still relatively low and there was plenty of vacant land, so neither of these factors played a significant role. Egyptologist Barry Kemp believes that the village farmers of 4000 B.C. had strong ties to their ancestral lands, expressed in deeply symbolic terms. At first dozens of small communities, each with their own patchwork of farming land, competed and traded with their neighbors. Kemp compares their behavior and its long-term effects to those in a game of Monopoly. In Monopoly, each player maximizes the opportunities afforded by the dice. In Egypt, both individuals and entire villages took full advantage of favorable locations, of their access to desirable resources like potting clay, and to chance breaks that came their way. At first the communities, like Monopoly players, were basically equal, but inevitably someone or some hamlet gained an unforeseen advantage, perhaps from trading expertise or unusually high crop yields. Equilibrium gave way to a seemingly inevitable momentum, in which some communities acquired more wealth and more power than their neighbors—the prehistoric equivalent of building hotels on Park Place. Their victory was inevitable, as they established a monopoly over local trade, food surpluses, and so on, which overrode any threat posed by other political or economic players.

In predynastic times, there were probably hundreds of such "games" in progress. As time went on, the number of players grew fewer, but the stakes were higher as increasingly large chiefdoms vied for economic power and political dominance. Just as in Monopoly, players changed over time, some acquiring great power and then losing it as charismatic individuals died or trading opportunities changed. Kemp points out that Egypt had more than enough fertile land and resources to enable such changes, such a game, to play out over many generations. Surplus resources like grain or tool-making stone were the foundation of power. But he believes the Egyptians also had a genius for weaving a distinctive ideology that imbued leadership and authority with elaborate symbols and rituals. These ideologies became a powerful factor in promoting unification.

The elaborate processes of state formation leave few signals in the archaeological record. In Egypt, such changes triggered the formation of larger settlements, small towns with all their potential for intensive interaction among individuals. Their leaders were buried with elaborate grave goods and with symbols that denoted an emerging ideology of power.

Major changes in human settlement can be seen at Naqada in Upper Egypt, 25 kilometers (15.5 miles) south of Thebes, where small hamlets were spaced about 1 kilometer (0.6 mile) apart in 4000 B.C. Demographic archaeologist Fekri Hassan has calculated that these small settlements grew enough grain at the edge of the floodplain to support 76 to 114 persons per square kilometer (0.386 square mile). By clearing trees, removing dense grass, building dikes, and digging drainage canals to clear still-inundated acreage, the farmers soon opened up much larger tracts of agricultural land. By the time the farmers had put four or even eight times more ground under cultivation, they could support as many as 760 to 1,520 people per square kilometer, many of them nonfarmers such as officials, traders, and artisans who lived in permanent towns. A walled town with cemeteries stood in the heart of the Naqada area by 3600 B.C., with new forms of housing, rectangular mud-brick dwellings that were typical of later Egyptian villages. In some settlements, larger, more palatial residences housed a prosperous elite who enjoyed contacts with other communities up- and downstream. Naqada may have been the capital of a major chiefdom.

Another important chiefdom flourished downstream at Nekhen (Hierakonpolis), "the City of the Falcon" in Upper Egypt. In 3800 B.C., Nekhen was a small community inhabited by a few hundred people. During the next three centuries the population mushroomed to as many as 10,500 townsfolk, who lived in closely packed mud-brick houses. The ancient city was originally a small community of several hundred people living in sprawling villages along a stretch of well-wooded river bank. The villagers were famous for their distinctive, red plum-colored pots, which were much in demand as funerary offerings up- and downstream. One potter lived in a small house of stout wooden posts and mud-coated reeds, his kiln only about 5 meters (16 feet) from his flimsy dwelling. One day, the wind shifted suddenly as he fired some pots. Within moments, the potter's house was ablaze. Wisely, he rebuilt in stone.

Nekhen prospered, the population rose steadily, and the demand for clay pots mushroomed, not only for grave furniture, but also for standardized jars of several sizes used to brew wheat beer, a nutritious and mildly alcoholic beverage. A brewery just north of the growing city could produce as much as 300 gallons of beer a day, enough for more than 200 people. The smell of fermenting beer must have permeated much of the city. Pottery and beer were but two industries in a city that was rapidly becoming a dominant economic and spiritual power in Upper Egypt, thanks, also, to shrewd investment in agriculture, in simple canals and reservoirs to conserve the waters of the receding inundation.

Much of this power came from the close associations between the city's rulers and the local falcon god, probably an early form of Horus. In the center of Nekhen rose Egypt's earliest known temple. An image of the god stood atop a pole in the center of an oval court in front of the shrine. At its foot, makeshift platforms displayed sacrificial offerings: cattle and crocodiles, newborn goats, and river fish, some weighing as much as 175 kilograms (385 pounds). Four massive wooden posts, at least 6 meters (20 feet) high, supported the facade of the three-room shrine and its walls of brightly colored mats. The posts can only have come from coniferous forests in far-away Lebanon and been floated laboriously up the river. The brilliantly colored temple towered over the huddled buildings of the town, a potent symbol of the patron god of its charismatic rulers. Horus was to become the symbol of Egyptian kingship for over 3,000 years.

Curving rows of the sand-filled burial places of Nekhen's ruling families lie on the banks of a dry gully named Abu Suffian located outside the town. The sepulchers are humble by the standards of later royal burial places, but impressive for their day. Looters ravaged the cemetery in ancient times, leaving behind them an archaeological jigsaw puzzle—a jumble of finely made black-topped jars, flint arrowheads, and wooden furniture fragments. Egyptologists Barbara Adams and Michael Hoffman undertook a complex salvage operation, using brushes, trowels, and sophisticated recording equipment. They discovered the cemetery was a symbolic map of Upper and Lower Egypt, with the dry gully serving as the boundary between the two. They also found the earliest known royal sepulcher in Egypt.

A cemetery of working class people has yielded over 150 graves, including womens' bodies with their hands and arms padded, then wrapped in resin soaked linen, the earliest evidence of any form of mummification yet found in Egypt. One matting-covered woman was buried with six loaves, mostly comprised of chaff. Two others still had full heads of hair, one elaborately styled and dyed with henna. Their heads were wrapped and padded, again anticipating the mummification of the dead that was to become commonplace in later times.

"Tomb 100" is a mud-brick sepulcher with painted walls. A symbolic universe is a line of boats, which represent perpetual movement through time. One carries the anonymous ruler, standing under a simple awning protected by female guardian figures. The forces of evil surround the boats on every side, wild beasts and human enemies, but the leader prevails. Below, he holds apart two facing lions and smites his bound foes with a royal mace. The style is simple compared with later Egyptian art, but the message of an elemental struggle between the forces of order and chaos waged during the voyage through time is unmistakable. The same scenario appears in more sophisticated forms in much later New Kingdom royal tombs in the Valley of the Kings. Even before unification, Egyptian rulers were seen as upholders of order, justice, and piety, and vanquishers of chaos. Nekhen was an important cult center for Horus, the falcon-headed god.

Nekhen was the cradle of Egyptian kingship, but the names of its earliest kings are lost to history. We glimpse them only from occasional scenes on decorated artifacts. A magnificent mace head of polished green and white porphyry is one of the earliest symbols of leadership known from the Nile Valley. Its owner may have been one of the "Divine Souls of Nekhen," the primordial rulers of legendary Egypt. Another mace head shows a ruler in full ceremonial dress, with a ritual bull's tail, a symbol of kingly authority hanging from the back of his belt. He wears the white crown of Upper Egypt and wields a mattock, as if he is about to breach the wall of an irrigation canal to release flood water. A scorpion dangles before his face, presumably a depiction of his name. Fan and standard bearers participate in the ceremony as an official prepares to receive the first sod in a basket. Below, the state barge waits to carry the ruler into the flooded basin once it is filled. He wears only the crown of Upper Egypt, so he probably ruled before the climactic event of unification.

## *Unification*

As late as the fifth millennium B.C., much of the Delta was still near-desert. Then the Mediterranean finally rose to modern levels, causing the Nile to back up and overflow its banks. By 3500 B.C., growing towns flourished by the watercourses that dissected the plain, each with their own gods and local rulers. Deep layers of silt mantle these towns, so we know little about them. Egyptian legends speak of the "Souls of Pe," legendary predynastic kings who ruled from a town of that name, now known as Buto. Buto, now under a sand dune, was first occupied in the fourth millennium B.C. and remained an important center for more than five centuries.

Potsherds are among the least glamorous of all archaeological finds, but at Buto they tell a remarkable story. The first inhabitants used highly distinctive, beautifully made pots adorned with white painted bands that bear a close resemblance to wares made in the Negev Desert, far to the east. Apparently, they soon left or gave up potting, for their distinctive wares vanish, to be replaced by much cruder local pots. These were no match for the elegant Upper Egyptian ceramics, which soon began to appear in the town by 3200 B.C. as contacts with the north accelerated and the pressures for unification intensified.

Upper and Lower Egypt were different lands with diverse cultures, the one influenced by the desert, the other by regular contacts with Asia. Even before unification, the Delta was host to a cosmopolitan world. Every year, small caravans of donkeys would arrive in the Delta towns from the east carrying saddle bags laden with exotic seashells, semiprecious stones, or lumps of copper ore from the Palestinian mines in the Sinai Desert.

A poorly defined Maadi culture flourished over much of the delta, comprising small towns and farming villages. The Maadi site itself, on the outskirts of Cairo, was an important center for the overland trade with the Levant and even Mesopotamia. Weatherbeaten ships from the Levant tied up at Buto's wharves, their bilges lined with clay pots filled with olive oil and wine, long cedar logs stacked on deck. Their crews rolled the precious timber into the river, where waiting boats towed the logs laboriously upstream to towns as far away as Nekhen. But for all its cosmopolitan ways, Lower Egypt eventually succumbed to more powerful kingdoms upstream.

Egypt 3200 B.C. Chieftain vies with chieftain. Opportunists all, they fight and trade with one another. They control a supply of potting clay or a source of building stone or have access to desirable commodities like gold. Inevitably, one chieftain or community gains an unforeseen advantage for a while, from trading expertise, high crop yields, or victory in a small war, then fades just as rapidly into obscurity. In the end, some communities acquire more wealth and power than others. The victor secures valuable monopolies over local trade, food surpluses, and other commodities, which make it easier to overcome threats posed by potential opponents. A scatter of ornamented palettes from Nekhen, Abydos, and elsewhere depict chieftains at war, vultures and crows attacking the dead. A king as a bull gores a bearded enemy. Another palette depicts the tribute exacted by conquerors—asses, cattle, rams, and incense trees.

The surviving kingdoms grow larger and larger. Nekhen overcomes Naqada. Then the chiefdom of This near Abydos downstream achieves dominance over Nekhen by conquest or dynastic marriage (Figure 4.2). The ruler of This becomes a king, powerful in war, an expert trader, and a living Horus on earth. He controls lucrative trade routes with Lower Egypt and develops his own contacts for wine and other luxuries along the eastern Mediterranean coast. He and his successors wage war on the Delta cities for control of trade routes. Eventually, one of them conquers the Two Lands and becomes the first pharaoh of a unified Egypt.

Who was this first pharaoh? Was he Menes or some earlier, still undiscovered king? The answers are coming from Abydos, a holy place from the earliest days of Egyptian civilization. Five thousand years ago, this was the realm of the jackal-god Khenti-amentiu, "Foremost amongst the Westerners," close to a dramatic canyon

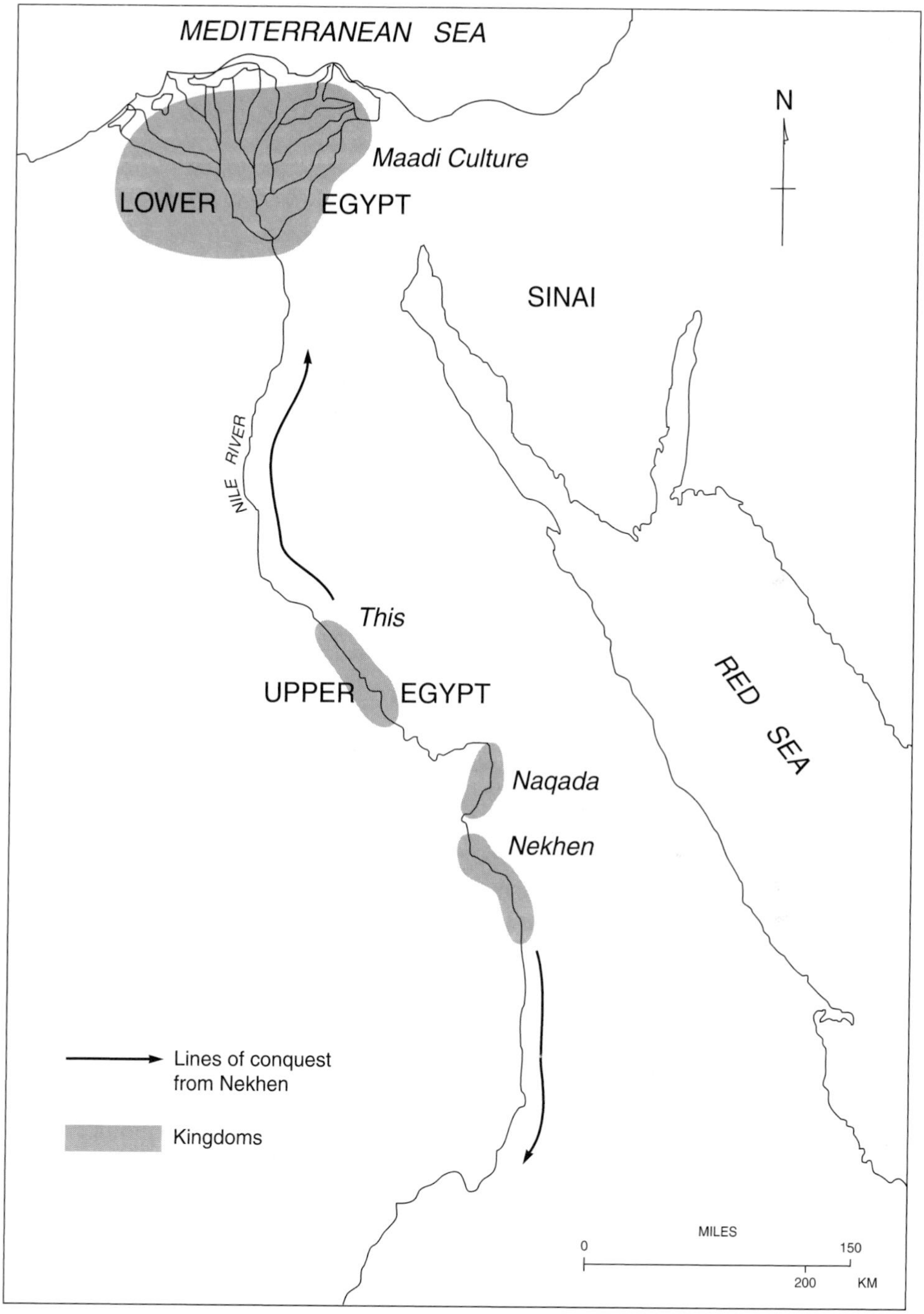


**Figure 4.2** Approximate positions of known chiefdoms in predynastic Egypt, c. 3300 B.C. This is a gross simplification of a very complex and ever changing political situation.

that served as a symbolic entrance to the underworld. The first two dynasties of pharaohs chose to be buried here, almost midway between the First Cataract and the Delta and close to their immediate ancestors at This.

The royal cemetery became a magnet for nineteenth-century archaeologists, who dug with abandon through tombs that had already been pillaged in ancient times. Günter Dreyer of the German Archaeological Institute thought otherwise. He suspected that the very latest excavation methods might yield unexpected dividends when used around abandoned excavations. In 1988, he excavated a neglected area east of the royal cemetery, where he made a surprising discovery: a brick lined royal tomb with 12 rooms designed as a house for the otherworld, complete with windows and doors, built for a king who reigned in about 3250 B.C.

The unknown monarch had gone to eternity with lavish possessions and ample food supplies. His burial chamber contained a shrine and an ivory scepter. Three storerooms held about 700 tightly stacked wine jars, amounting to about 1,200 gallons of wine. Using infrared spectrometry, Patrick McGovern of the University of Pennsylvania found high levels of tartaric acid associated with wine in the crusty residues inside the bottle shaped jars, also traces of terebinth resin, a commonly used preservative. He knew the wine was imported, because vines were not cultivated in the Delta until centuries later. Another high-tech method, neutron activation analysis, identified the trace elements in the clay and sourced them to an area of early vine cultivation in the southern Levant. Interestingly, the wine was checked and restoppered, probably at Abydos itself: the clay plugs are of Nile clay. The wine stash was a real eye opener as to the volume of trade between Egypt and Asia 5,000 years ago. One can understand why an ambitious ruler would seek to control such a lucrative commerce.

Another chamber yielded 150 small bone and ivory labels, once attached to bolts of linen. They bear numbers indicating amounts, even size, but many are readable hieroglyphic signs, which spell out the phonetic names of the places where the goods came from. Some of the places, like Buto, are towns in the Delta, as if the labels were attached to tribute offerings from as far away as Lower Egypt. Some of these tags have been radiocarbon dated to 3200 B.C., making them the oldest examples of Egyptian writing. The unknown ruler's scribes were also using a fully developed writing system to inventory the yields, fully 150 years earlier than hitherto suspected. Some seal impressions from the Abydos tombs date to as early as 3400 B.C.

Who was the mysterious king who collected tribute from the Delta and traded with the Levant? Dreyer noticed that many of the clay vessels have the name Scorpion painted on them and believes this was the king's name. But there are other names as well, written as animal signs of dogs, lions, elephants, and even seashells, which may be those of earlier rulers in the dynasty. We still do not know.

The Narmer palette, found at Nekhen in 1898 (Figure 4.3), shows the king smiting Delta enemies, with two mythical beasts entwined harmoniously on the other side. No one knew whether the palette commemorated an actual historical event of unification until recently, when Günter Dreyer recovered a tiny ivory label close to Narmer's long plundered Abydos tomb. The sliver bears a sketch of the king smiting an enemy from the Delta, depicted as a human head sprouting papyrus

(a) (b)

**Figure 4.3** The Narmer palette, a slab of slate carved on both sides with scenes that commemorate King Narmer, who lived just before the First Dynasty. (a) Narmer is wearing the white crown of Upper Egypt. He carries a pear-shaped mace head in his right hand and is about to smite a captive, perhaps from the delta in Lower Egypt. A falcon head (the southern Horus) emerges from papyrus reeds, carrying a human head above the victim. A sandal bearer follows the king, who stands on two dead enemies. (b) Narmer is wearing the red crown of Lower Egypt (top), as he inspects rows of decapitated enemies from the town of Buto in the Delta, accompanied by two high officials. The central design of intertwined animals symbolizes harmony, balancing images of conquest in the upper and lower registers. At the bottom, a bull destroys a city wall and tramples on its enemies. Height: 63 centimeters (29 inches).

reeds.The labels once marked the dates of oil shipments, the years being identified by major events such as Narmer's victory in the Delta. This is obviously the same event as that shown on the famous Narmer palette, proving that this was an actual historical conflict.

Who, then, unified Egypt? Almost certainly a series of able, and still unknown, rulers from Upper Egypt. They, Scorpion, and Narmer belong to a shadowy Dynasty 0, made up of capable kings who may be the Spirits of Nekhen of Egyptian legend. Narmer's famous victory may have been the final moment of conquest, but it was his successor, King Horus Aha, who became the first ruler of a truly unified Egypt in about 3100 B.C.

By 3100 B.C., a semblance of political unity, commemorated by the Narmer palette, joined Upper and Lower Egypt in the symbolic linking of Horus and Seth, depicted in later Egyptian art. As these events unfolded, a new state came into

| Years B.C. | Period | Characteristics |
|---|---|---|
| 30 B.C. | Roman occupation | Egypt an imperial province of Rome |
| 322 to 30 B.C. | Ptolemaic period | The Ptolemies bring Greek influence to Egypt, beginning with conquest of Egypt by Alexander the Great in 322 B.C. |
| 1070 to 332 B.C. | Late period | Gradual decline in pharaonic authority, culminating in Persian rule (525 to 404 and 343 to 332 B.C.) |
| 1550 to 1070 B.C. | New Kingdom | Great imperial period of Egyptian history, with pharaohs buried in Valley of Kings; pharaohs include Ramesses II, Seti I, and Tutankhamun, as well as Akhenaten, the heretic ruler |
| 1640 to 1550 B.C. | Second Intermediate period | Hyksos rulers in the delta |
| 2040 to 1640 B.C. | Middle Kingdom | Thebes achieves prominence, also the priesthood of Amun |
| 2134 to 2040 B.C. | First Intermediate period | Political chaos and disunity |
| 2580 to 2134 B.C. | Old Kingdom | Despotic pharaohs build the pyramids and favor conspicuous funerary monuments; institutions, economic strategies, and artistic traditions of Egypt established |
| 2920 to 2580 B.C. | Archaic period | Consolidation of state |
| 3100 B.C. | Unification of Egypt under Horus-Aha | |

**Table 4.2** Subdivisions of Egyptian history with major cultural and historical developments.

being, founded not only on physical but also on symbolic geography, a harmony achieved by balanced opposites, of which Horus and Seth are only one manifestation. For thousands of years, the Egyptians were concerned with a world torn between potential chaos and order. They believed that disorder, disequilibrium, could be contained by the rule of kings and by the benign force of the power of the sun. Thus, the Egyptians' intellectual view of the nature of the universe coincided with the structure of political power.

## The Archaic Period (2920–2680 B.C.): Kingship, Writing, and Bureaucracy

The first two and a half centuries of Egyptian civilization were a long period of consolidation, of subordinating powerful local chiefdoms into a unified whole.

Aha and his successors came from Upper Egypt, where desert traditions of leaders as strong bulls and herdsmen ran deep. They were the remote descendants of leaders who had been tribal shamans or medicine men. They had supernatural power over the Nile and its lifegiving waters, which nourished their people. Their

Nekhen ancestors had mediated between the forces of order and chaos, and the new kings followed in the same tradition. Like gods, they kept the forces of evil at bay—the Nubians and Asiatics, the animals and diseases which preyed on herds and ripening crops. Good rulers hunted lions and wild cattle and pursued hippopotamus, the evil god Seth personified, in the marshes. Human beings were the primary cause of unrest in the Egyptian world. The ideal order was *ma'at*, "order" or "right," social justice and moral righteousness, which always existed in opposition to, and in conflict with, *Isfet*, the forces of disorder. The Egyptian world was never static, but one of a constant struggle to maintain or enforce order against chaos, personified by the evil snake god Apophis in heaven and Egypt's enemies on earth.

The rising of the sun each day established order out of the dark chaos of night. For the king, *ma'at* meant keeping order and holding enemies at bay. For people generally, living according to *ma'at* was living in harmony with others and with the gods. The world was made for the benefit of humans by the Creator, who had instituted *ma'at* at the beginning. An ancient wisdom text advises a later ruler: "Well tended is humankind—god's cattle. He made sky and earth for their sake." *Ma'at* governed the deeds of every Egyptian pharaoh in an ancient style of leadership that passed from Nekhen to This, from Scorpion to Narmer, and then to Aha and his dynastic successors. The kings were Creators incarnate, who returned to him at death.

The royal cemetery remained at Abydos, where the kings lay in subterranean, mud-brick tomb complexes in full regalia with their grave goods, close to a major wadi leading to the desert mountains. The sepulcher was unmarked, except, perhaps, for a low mound and a simple stela. A divine king was immortal, so many of his wives and retainers died with him, to lie in small pit graves around the grave of their lord. The practice of human sacrifice survived into the Second Dynasty (about 2700 B.C.) before it died out. A separate mud-brick ceremonial enclosure lay above ground, closer to the cultivated land, with a niched facade—called *shunet* in Arabic. The facades were paneled with ornamented recesses that replicated those of the royal palace, as if to create a mansion for eternity. The enclosure served as a form of mortuary temple for the deceased king and had structures and a mound symbolizing the primordial mound of creation inside. Fourteen wooden Nile boats, averaging 23 meters (75 feet) long, lie entombed in whitewashed mud-brick structures close to the desert cemetery. Whether they were boats designed to carry the king through the solar cosmos is unknown.

The practice of mummification had roots deep in Egyptian history, dating back to predynastic times. The natural aridity of the Nile climate helped preserve the dead, but preservation of corpses for eternity achieved great elaboration in later times. The Egyptians believed that the tomb was a place of transfiguration, where the spirit of the deceased emerged from the body and soared into the heavens to ride among the stars with the goddess Nut. (See chapter opener for a picture of the pharaoh Ramesses II's mummy.) At the same time, they believed that the body should be preserved to allow the dead person's spiritual essence, or *ka*, to visit it. Mummification for the wealthy began with ritual washing and purifying of the body. The priests then removed the brains and internal organs, except the heart, often storing them in separate containers. Next, they soaked the corpse in natron (sodium salt) for 40 days to dry it out. The desiccated body was stuffed and padded, coated with milk and aromatic resins, and then covered with molten resin. After cosmetic treatment, the corpse was bandaged in a complex ritual that lasted two weeks, a process that could require as much as 368 square meters (440 square yards) of linen, with many amulets and semiprecious stones within the wrappings. An elaborate mask was sometimes placed on the completed mummy. The entire process took between 70 and 90 days, after which the body was placed in its coffin and the funerary rituals began. On the other hand, poor Egyptians were often stacked in dry caves without elaborate ceremony.

For 400 years, the earliest pharaohs grappled with the task of consolidating a mosaic of towns and villages scattered along 975 kilometers (600 miles) of river into a centralized state. The task would challenge even a modern-day government with sophisticated communications. They succeeded by turning their kingdom into a glorified family business, which flourished on personal loyalty and kin ties, and by assuming the mantle of the falcon god Horus. Gods are remote, seldom seen. So were the pharaohs. They dwelt in magnificent palaces surrounded by the trappings of power, their every movement circumscribed by strict protocol. Their rare public appearances at important festivals were occasions of great importance, symbolizing the rising of the sun at dawn, moments to celebrate a god, give thanks for a victory, or reward high officials. The pharaoh's official entourage formed the "followers of Horus," loyal officials who surrounded the king in the palace and on his royal progresses through the land. They transmitted his commands to the world outside the palace audience chamber. (The word "pharaoh" actually came into use much later, during the New Kingdom, derived from the word *per aa*, the "great house," after the royal palace.)

Over a million people lived in Egypt at unification, most of them in the Delta. Most villages and towns lay along the river, separated one from another by cropland and pasture, untouched marshes and thickets. Village headmen brought together the farmers to work on dikes and canals, to dredge natural flood basins. They, in turn, owed allegiance to chieftains, who presided over *nomes*, or tribal provinces, that coincided, in large part, with the natural configurations of the valley. Competition between these *nomes* had been the crucible for unification. Now the *nomes* were provinces of a 600-mile-long state, but the ancient network of headmen and chiefly families still survived. The pharaohs created a system of government that built on these old foundations, placing members of their own family and trusted relatives in positions of high authority, rewarding loyal chieftains by making them governors of their *nomes*. A small elite governed Egypt for the king, rewarded with titles and emblems of rank and with estates.

The "followers of Horus" ran the king's household and helped him administer the kingdom. Two high officials were in charge of the Red and White Treasuries, the storehouses of Lower and Upper Egypt. They were ancient equivalents to secretaries of the treasury. Two controllers of the granaries collected and distributed commodities of all kinds—the corn, oil, wine, and other rations paid to everyone who worked for the state, whether official, scribe, or laborer. The "Overseer of the King's Bounty" handed out perks to privileged courtiers and officials. From Memphis, the tentacles of administration reached out into towns and villages, through governors, mayors, and headmen, counting, inventorying, taxing, and making decisions. How high will the flood be? When is the right moment to heighten dikes or dredge canals? When shall we plant or harvest? How many rations are due the men working on the new temple? From the beginning, Egypt depended not only on a strong king and competent officials, but on large numbers of literate scribes.

Today, in a world of universal literacy, we tend to look down upon lower-level government bureaucrats. Egyptian society could not afford this luxury, where scribes formed a minority and held the key to power—information. Theirs was an honored profession, writing an invention of the scribe god Thoth, a deity with an ibis (bird) head. Thus, words had a magical power, the scribe a special role in the kingdom. Literacy passed from father to son, starting with hesitant glyphs brushed on potsherds and small stones, then on papyrus reed, the paper of Ancient Egypt. (The modern word "paper" derives from the Greek and Latin "papyrus," a reference to Egyptian papyrus.) A schoolbook from later times adjures reluctant pupils: "Be a scribe, your body will be sleek, your hand will be soft. . . . Set your sight on being a scribe; a fine profession that suits you. You call for one; a thousand answer you." Limitless horizons greeted the conscientious scribe. "You stride about inspecting. . . . You have a powerful office, given you by the king. Male and female slaves are about you. Those who are in the fields grasp your hand." Ubiquitous scribes were the gear cogs of Ancient Egypt, the mechanism that made an increasingly complex bureaucracy run on oiled wheels. You see them everywhere with pens, palettes, and papyrus rolls: in tomb paintings measuring and supervising the harvest, sitting in rows counting baskets of grain loaded into bins, inventorying storerooms. Even the humble seals that once closed granaries and temple stores bear their imprint.

Writing was power, the key to controlling the labor of hundreds, if not thousands, of people. Egyptian scribes developed their own script, which was easier to produce with papyrus reed paper and ink than on the clay tablets used in Mesopotamia. Hieroglyphs (Greek for "sacred signs") are commonly thought to be a form of picture writing. In fact they are a combination of pictographic (picture) and phonetic (representing vocal sounds) script and were set down on paper, carved on buildings, or painted on clay or wood (Figure 4.4). Ultimately, the scribes developed a cursive hieroglyphic script that was a form of handwriting. Only the consonants were written in all forms of hieroglyphs, although vowels were pronounced as *ths smpl xmpl shws*. This intricate script typified the symbolic nature of Egyptian thought.

As the state matured, so did the arts of writing and mathematics. The cumbersome glyphs of Aha's time soon developed into a more informal cursive script, written in pen on papyrus. Now the scribes could send rapid instructions afar and receive replies, record the heights of Nile floods and send them to Memphis, count the numbers of families and oxen in remote villages. But they needed to make calculations as well—the dimensions of temple floor plans, the size of corn fields, the

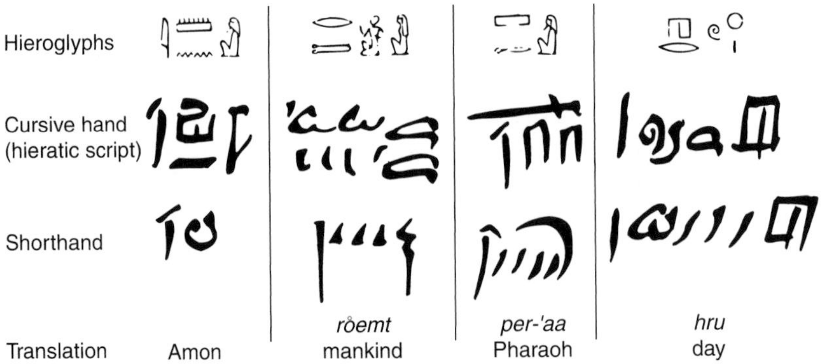


**Figure 4.4** Egyptian writing is referred to as hieroglyphs, the familiar symbols that appear in formal inscriptions and on tomb walls. In fact, Egyptian scribes developed cursive hands used in everyday life. These examples show formal hieroglyphic script (top line) and below it both the cursive script and the scribe's shorthand, which was used for rapid writing.

number of loaves issued to a ship's crew, the quantities of bricks needed for a royal burial chamber. Scribes had to calculate dimensions and volumes, compute fractions, survey land, all with a simple linear measure based on the dimensions of the human body and standard units of cubic measurement.

For four centuries, the pharaohs wrestled with competing religious agendas. Each nome, each community, had its own deities, despite the divine figure of the king towering over the state. Each ruler juggled loyalties, favored strategic *nomes*, made diplomatic marriages to cement relationships with potential rivals. They also forged a new religious ideology that was to endure for 3,000 years. A standardized canon of Egyptian art came into use, replacing the diverse regional traditions of earlier times.

From the beginning, the First and Second Dynasty pharaohs identified themselves with Horus, "the One on High," a divine force. Their scribes wrote the ruler's name inside a panel or *serekh* depicting the paneled facade of his palace with the falcon-headed god perched above, denoting the king as Horus: present, alive, and in residence. Aha also assumed the title *Nebti*, "He of the two Ladies," the cobra of Lower Egypt, the vulture of Upper. By 2500 B.C., the king's name appeared within an oval cartouche signifying the circuit of the sun around the universe. The sign, derived from the circular *shen* glyph, also symbolized eternity, thus protecting the king's name, and the king, forever. A second cartouche named the pharaoh "Son of Re," identifying his even closer relationship with the sun god.

Supreme rulers thrive on propaganda. So the early pharaohs proclaimed that they maintained order in the presence of a supreme divine force, the power of the sun. The pharaoh's clothing and regalia became a mantle of divinity—of potency in creation. He was herdsman and protector of the people. Each king wore the regalia of a pastoral chief, a *shemset* apron at his waist, his back guarded by a bull's tail hanging from a belt. He carried the crook and incense gum collecting flail of a shepherd, a goat-hair beard on his chin. By the pharaoh Den's time (about 2900 B.C.), the ruler wore a double crown that combined the red headdress of Lower Egypt and the white of Upper Egypt.

The propaganda of divine kingship rang out in chants and recitations, in elaborate public ceremonies, as hieroglyphic inscriptions on temple and palace walls, in art and architecture. In art, inscription, and regalia, the king became a warrior and a builder. He passed the goodness of humankind to heaven and received the blessing of the creator and the other gods for earth. The king is seen making offerings to gods, proffering the produce of the land, or standing face to face with the falcon-headed Horus. The god clasps the king's forearm with his left hand, while his right arm encircles the royal shoulders as a sign of protection.

To tour an Egyptian temple is to be bombarded with a constant recitation of divine kingship: the king in the presence of the god Osiris, the king making offerings to the sun god Amun-Re, the king offering a figure of the goddess Ma'at, "rightness," to Amun, Re, and Ptah. The litany soon becomes monotonous but is overwhelming in its repetition. Always the pharaoh triumphs.

For all the propaganda, rivalries between north and south bubbled below the surface constantly. The age-old conflict between Horus and Seth broke out again amidst savage fighting between north and south. The last pharaoh of the Second Dynasty, Khasekhem, suppressed rebellious armies from Lower Egypt after savage fighting, commemorated by piled corpses around the bases of two seated statues of the pharaoh found at Nekhen. Khasekhem changed his name to Khasekhemwy, "Appearance of Two Powers." He married a northern princess named Nemathap as a gesture toward better relations. A surviving clay jar seal records her title as "The King-Bearing Mother." She was the ancestral figure of the Third Dynasty, when the Egyptian state came of age.

## The Old Kingdom (c. 2680–2134 B.C.): Territorial and Divine Kingship

Around 2680 B.C., the Third Dynasty ushered in the four-and-one-half centuries of the Old Kingdom, the first great flowering of Egyptian civilization. By this time, Egyptian society was shaped in the image of a state where the well-being of the common people depended on their ruler, who was supported by their labors. According to the Greek traveler and writer Herodotus, who visited Egypt in the fifth century B.C., long after the heyday of the Egyptian state, some Old Kingdom pharaohs, notably Khufu and Khafre, went too far. They became harsh tyrants who ignored the wishes of the gods and the people alike. Their enormous pyramid tombs stretched the state to the limit. Menkaure, who built a third and much smaller pyramid nearby, may have made a timely adjustment, for Herodotus records him as a generous ruler. Many scholars dismiss Herodotus's account as mere hearsay, but it might reflect historical reality.

## *Saqqara: The King as Supreme Territorial Claimant*

The Old Kingdom pharaohs, like their predecessors, used dramatic settings for their public appearances. A large open space; an elevated place shaded with a canopy, where the king would be glimpsed; a small palace for donning formal attire and resting—these were the ingredients for a setting for the pageantry that accompanied the eternity of death and for the ever-important Sed festival, the jubilee ceremony after 30 years of royal rule. The Third Dynasty pharaoh Djoser considered himself the supreme territorial claimant, a role he celebrated in a large enclosure dominated by a unique structure: the Step Pyramid at Saqqara, opposite the royal capital at Memphis.

Djoser's vizier, Imhotep (c. 2680 B.C.), high priest of the sun god, devised the architecture of the Step Pyramid (Figure 4.5). By this time, all manner of local beliefs had fused into the familiar pantheon of Egyptian gods, headed by the sun god Re or Re-Harakhty. Each day, Re-Herakhty sailed in his barque over the waters of heaven, bringing light and life to a world that otherwise would be moribund as it was before Creation. At sunset, Re changed barques and became inert in the form of a ram-headed manifestation of the Creator, passing over the waters under earth. There he battled with the demonic forces of *Isfet* led by the snake god Apophis. Triumphant, the sun god emerged on the sun barque at the beginning of a new, young day as a new cycle of Creation began.

Under the new doctrines, Djoser was more than a personification of Horus, he ruled on earth as the son of Re, or even as the sun god himself. He and Imhotep boldly changed the superstructure of his tomb to reflect their innovative theology.

**Figure 4.5** Step Pyramid of Djoser I at Saqqara. The stepped pyramid was part of an elaborate setting for public ceremonies that symbolized the king's role as supreme territorial ruler and claimant.

The primordial mound now became a stepped pyramid, a stairway whereby the deceased pharaoh could ascend to the sky to join Re in his sun barque at the moment when the rising sun illuminated the summit. At the same time, the king ordered his pyramid built, not alongside his ancestors at Abydos, but far downstream at Saqqara, in the desert west of Memphis.

The great architect drew his inspiration from earlier royal tombs, rectangular structures like those at Abydos, which were eternal mansions for dead monarchs. Such tumuli had associations with the primordial earthen mound that formed an important part of the Egyptian legend of the creation. Using small armies of workers from every village in the realm, Imhotep erected a stepped pyramid instead of a mound. At one stroke, the state broke down the isolation of hundreds of village communities, by mingling them with their fellow countrymen in what must have been seen as a common act of piety, a gesture toward a sacred cosmos—somewhat similar to the building of a medieval cathedral. The social consequences were enormous. The Saqqara pyramid rose in six diminishing steps to over 60 meters (372 feet) above the desert, the faces oriented to the cardinal points. The effect is like a giant double staircase rising toward heaven. A wall with a palacelike facade over 1.6 kilometers (1 mile) in perimeter surrounded the entire mortuary complex. The court in front of the pyramid was a setting for royal appearances, complete with ceremonial territorial markers, a throne platform, and a token palace. The entire complex was an arena for the eternal pageantry of kingship on earth.

## *Pyramids: Mountains of Re*

Djoser and his predecessors were terrestrial monarchs, supreme rulers who epitomized the triumph of order over chaos. But a new image of kingship emerged some time after his death in 2649 B.C. The ruler was now absorbed into the mystic symbol of the sun. An increasingly powerful priesthood fused sun worship with the cult of the pharaoh. The sun god became a heavenly monarch, the pharaoh no longer a territorial conqueror but the deity's representative on earth. After death, the king assumed the identity of Osiris, the Lord of the Dead. According to Egyptian beliefs, the stars were divine beings and the ruler was destined to take his place among them. "The king goes to his double . . . a ladder is set up for him that he may ascend on it," says a spell in a royal pyramid text. Thus it was that the Old Kingdom pharaohs lavished enormous resources on building their sepulchers, at first earthen mounds, then pyramids that became symbolic ladders to heaven.

The pyramids were symbolic depictions in stone of the sun's rays bursting through the clouds, a permanent stone stairway with the king's mortuary temple on the east side, the side of the rising sun (Box 4.1).

The court cemeteries and pyramid complexes of the Old Kingdom pharaohs extend over a 35-kilometer (22-mile) stretch of the western desert's edge, mostly slightly north of the royal capital at Memphis. Snofru was the first Fourth Dynasty pharaoh. He built no less than three pyramids, which bridged a transition from a stepped to true pyramid design. In about 2528 B.C., Snofru's son and successor, Khufu, built the Great Pyramid of Giza, one of the spectacular wonders of ancient

## Box 4.1 The Pyramids of Giza

The Pyramids of Giza are one of the marvels of the ancient world (see Figure 4.6). How did the Egyptians, armed with only simple technology, build such enormous structures, apparently within a relatively short period of time? The pyramids would be a stupendous undertaking, even for twenty-first century contractors with elaborate, heavy machinery and unlimited construction budgets. Egyptian construction methods were simple but highly effective. Their tools were little more than stone and copper hammers, mallets, grinders, and saws. The Egyptians' expertise lay in their ability to organize, feed, and deploy large numbers of artisans and unskilled laborers to quarry, haul, and dress stone. Much of the stone for the pyramids came from quarries nearby, while a rock-cut harbor close to the Giza plateau brought rubble and finished blocks to the heart of the site. Every flood season, when agriculture was at a standstill, the government organized thousands of villagers into construction teams, who quarried stone and transported rubble and finished blocks up the earthen ramps that rose round the pyramid. First the plateau was leveled, then masons cut a grid of channels into the rock, filling them with water to level the base. Next the architects built a circular mud-brick enclosure, the top of which formed a level horizon. Then they sighted key stars with a notched stick, marking the points where they rose and set on the wall. This enabled them to lay out north-south lines—the base of the pyramid. Meanwhile, a canal and causeway were built to bring supplies to the site.

Course by course, the pyramid rose from the plateau, the passages and burial chamber constructed and covered with ever-rising boulders. Long beforehand, the architects had calculated the correct dimensions for a massive mud-brick ramp that spiraled up the side of the growing pyramid. Hundreds of men hauled blocks on sledges up the long ramp. Dozens of laborers ran ahead of them, throwing down bucketfuls of water to lubricate the surface. (Experiments by French scientists have shown that Nile mud is a wonderful lubricant for moving heavy weights on sleds.) After years of hauling, the king's priests supervised the placing of a gilded pyramidion atop the pyramid. Then expert masons smoothed the slant-faced and polished casing stones, working downward as the ramp was removed brick by brick and literally melted in the Nile. When Khufu was buried in his pyramid, his funerary barge was buried in a special chamber close to his sepulcher, ready to assemble for a journey in the afterworld. Even today, lapped by the suburbs of Cairo, the Pyramids of Giza are an awe-inspiring tribute to the ruthless genius and precision of those who built them. They were harsh taskmasters. The skeletons of workers in cemeteries by the pyramids show many signs of malnutrition and disease. From carrying heavy loads, their spines are bent over, the bones inflamed, which caused great discomfort. Egyptian anthropologist Azza Sarry el-Din has studied 162 skeletons of the haves and have-nots of the Old Kingdom from these cemeteries. The overworked commoners lived to between 18 and 40 years of age. Privilege brought better food, fewer diseases, and a life expectancy between 50 and 75.

By the time King Khafre built his slightly smaller pyramid and temple complex immediately to the southwest in 2494 B.C., the Giza plateau was an elaborate mortuary complex. It was Khafre who commissioned the carving of the Sphinx from a convenient outcrop (Figure 4.7); 73 meters (240 feet) long, the vast image was plastered and painted brightly in its heyday. The recumbent lion with Khafre's head served as guardian of the sacred precincts, as keeper of the threshold. Khafre wore the royal beard and headdress with its symbolic cobra of Lower Egypt.

(a)

(b)

**Figure 4.6** (a) The Pyramids of Giza; (b) stepped boulders now form the sides. Originally smooth casing stones covered the sides.

*(Cont.)*

Khafre's successor, Menkaure, built a third and smaller pyramid, again to the southwest, in 2472 B.C. This was hastily completed, perhaps because the king died unexpectedly, but by this time the tempo of pyramid building was slowing. The last of the Giza pyramids is about a third of the size of its predecessor. By the end of the Fourth Dynasty (2465 B.C.), royal pretensions had scaled down, perhaps because it was simply too expensive to erect such large sepulchers. It may simply have been a matter of economic exhaustion, for the sheer effort of the organization and feeding of so many people must have been staggering, especially in poor flood years.

Africa and one of the Seven Wonders of the Ancient World. It covers 5.3 hectares (13.1 acres) and is 146 meters (481 feet) high. Well over two million limestone blocks, some weighing 15 tons apiece, went into its construction. A long causeway linked each pyramid in the Giza complex to a royal mortuary temple. These were austere buildings that housed statues of the king, best shown in the complex of Khafre, who built the second pyramid of Giza. Khafre's temple was crafted in limestone and granite. Ceiling-height louvers let in a diffused glow that shone on the royal figures within. Khafre himself sat on a royal throne, protected by the god Horus, who wrapped his wings around the nape of the pharaoh's neck. The nearby sepulchers vested these temples with great authority, for they associated the ruler with what was, in effect, a powerful ancestor cult that linked them to their predecessors and to the gods.

**Figure 4.7** The Sphinx at Giza.

We do not know why the pharaohs suddenly embarked on this orgy of pyramid construction, with all the accompanying demands that it made on the fledgling state. Their construction, like other major public works in Egypt, was a triumph of bureaucratic organization—transporting food and building materials and then the skilled artisans and workers to quarry, dig, and drag stone into place. What is staggering is the efficient management overview, achieved without computers and deploying and supporting thousands of villagers for short periods of time as they fulfilled their annual tax-by-labor obligations to the state.

The supervision of construction consumed many hours of scribal time, scrutinizing and measuring precise quantities of raw materials, even ensuring that each laborer carried, transported, or dug his proper day's work for the rations he received. For example, ten cubic cubits (a cubit is 52 centimeters [20.6 inches]) was the daily norm for a man transporting raw materials. The scribe's pen was as much a driving force behind construction as the ingenuity of the king's engineers or the supervisors who drove on the labor gangs.

Quite apart from the construction of the pyramid complexes, small armies of priests and workers labored to fulfill the dead pharaoh's needs in the afterlife. New villages and estates were founded near Giza to service the needs of the royal cults and feed their servants. A large worker settlement lies south-southeast of the pyramids. A massive stone wall 10 meters (33 feet) high, with a 7-meter (23-foot) gateway, separates the sacred precincts around the pyramid complex from the secular activities without. Mark Lehner has excavated a large bakery in the settlement, which turned out thousands of standard-sized loaves, and a fish processing facility—rations for pyramid workers.

After the pyramids were completed, the village area became a cemetery for the people who supported the pyramid cults. Well-built stone sepulchers housed prosperous supervisors, such as the director of the draughtsmen and the overseer of masonry. Egyptian archaeologist Zahi Hawass excavated the tomb of a man named Nefer-thieth, who had two wives and 18 children. His senior wife, Neferhetepes, was a weaver. His occupation is unknown, but he may have been a bakery supervisor, for many scenes in the tomb depict bread and beer making. Fourteen different types of beer and cakes are listed in his wife's funerary offerings! Hawass has excavated more than 600 pyramid workers' tombs, most less than a few feet square. None of the workers were mummified, at that time still a privilege reserved for the elite, but their bones tell of harsh lives of unremitting toil. Arthritis and degenerative back ailments from backbreaking labor were commonplace. Most of the laborers died young.

The pharaohs started a great engine of growth by commissioning massive, labor-intensive public works. The state became the great provider. Perhaps, as Kurt Mendelssohn has argued, the pyramids were built as a means of linking the people to their guardian, the king, and to the sun god, the source of human life and of bountiful harvests. The relationship between the king and his subjects was both reciprocal and spiritual. The pharaoh was a divine king, a tangible divinity, whose person was served by annual labor. In short, pyramid building created public works that helped define the authority of the ruler and make his subjects dependent on him.

## *"The Herdsman of This Land"*

The capital of Old Kingdom Egypt was at Memphis, where the royal court resided. Here both the pharaoh and the chief vizier lived. The king ruled by his own word, following no written laws, only the precedents set by kings before him. The political and religious powers of the pharaohs changed somewhat through time, but essential continuity was maintained through many dynasties of supreme rulers. The king was the holder of a divine office. He was the "good god," a specific incarnation of Horus, the sky and falcon deity, who was in turn closely associated with the sun cult of Re, the sun god. The king's was an intensely political existence, hemmed in by elaborate protocol and ritual observance. "There was a set time not only for his holding audience or rendering judgement, but even for his taking a walk, bathing, and sleeping with his wife," reported one Greek writer in later times.

We know little of royal routines or of town life, but we know even high officials had strong roots in the countryside where they were born. Lively paintings and reliefs on the walls of the nobility's rock-cut tombs create an idyllic dream of what life was supposed to be like after death. We see the benevolent owner and his wife, living at ease on their estate. They supervise the sowing and harvesting of the grain, the winnowing of the seed, the baking of the bread, the brewing of the beer, and the trampling of the grapes. Cattle are raised and butchered, birds trapped, and poultry fattened. Artisans are hard at work making furniture, building funerary boats, and preparing possessions for the afterlife. The owner spears fish, hunts waterfowl, and goes after hippopotamus (Figure 4.8). The estate servants work hard, their trials and tribulations carefully recorded as they argue with a tax collector or wrestle with a stubborn donkey. The tomb scenes give an impression of a lively, colorful society, where the continuity of life between the world of the living and that of eternity was all important. But, in reality, most commoners lived lives of grinding poverty and hard work.

Old Kingdom Egypt was a time of powerful, confident rulers, of a virile state governed by a privileged class of royal relatives and high officials. Their talents created a civilization that was for the benefit of a tiny minority. It was for this

**Figure 4.8** The noble Meketre inspecting his livestock. (From the Tomb of Meketre, West Thebes. Painted wood. H. 55cm. 11th dynasty, reign of Mentuhotep I. Inv. 6080. Egyptian Museum, Cairo, Egypt. Photograph Copyright Scala/Art Resource, NY.)

privileged elite, headed by a divine king, that Egyptian merchants traded for the famed cedars of Lebanon; mined turquoise and copper in Sinai; and sought ivory, semiprecious stones, and mercenaries for Egypt's armies from Nubia.

## The First Intermediate Period (2134–2040 B.C.)

The prosperity did not last long. The last great Old Kingdom pharaoh was Pepi II (2246–2152 B.C.), who reigned for 94 years, having ascended the throne as a 6-year-old. His successors never matched his authority. As the central power of the state declined, so local leaders (nomarchs) became more or less independent rulers within their own provinces. This decline in the monarchy coincided with a prolonged drought cycle, which settled over northern Africa after 2250 B.C. The droughts of early dynastic times had taught the pharaohs the importance of centrally controlled agriculture. They had responded to new economic realities by expanding irrigation works, canals, and the agricultural development of the Delta. In the short term, they were so successful that Egypt's population had risen to more than a million by 2250 B.C. But the intensification of agriculture made the Egyptians even more vulnerable, for when another lean cycle struck in that year, there were many more mouths to feed. There were repeated famines for more than 300 years. Contemporary writers refer to widespread plundering and anarchy, to drinking water shortages and corpses rotting in the fields. "The Nile was empty and men crossed over on foot," laments a chronicler of the day, as the magical powers of short-lived pharaohs fell into disrepute.

The leaders who profited from the disaster were not the pharaohs but the local nomarchs (provincial governors), who were able to maintain their irrigation works in good order and maintain basic food supplies. Egypt became a land in turmoil, a patchwork of competing kingdoms, as long-distance trade with the Levant dried up and the exploitation of mines in the Sinai Desert ceased. The strongest leaders were those who managed to feed their people and ward off marauders from the desert. When Egyptologist Herbert Winlock excavated an Eleventh Dynasty tomb at Deir el-Bahri near Thebes, he found graphic evidence for the vicious warfare of the day. The sepulcher contained the desiccated bodies of 60 young Theban soldiers. They were war casualties, men who fell attacking a fortress and were showered with ebony-tipped arrows and slingshots from high above. As they tried to sap the defenses, deadly arrows pierced their exposed shoulders. The attack was beaten off. The defenders searched for the enemy casualties, grabbed them by their hair, and clubbed or stabbed them to death. Some of the corpses bore the telltale tear wounds of vultures and ravens. A later attack must have been successful, for someone gathered up the corpses and buried them.

## The Middle Kingdom (2040–1640 B.C.): The Organized Oasis

The soldiers Winlock described may have died when a Theban prince named Mentuhotep II defeated his rivals in the delta and reunited Egypt under his rule around 2040 B.C. Mentuhotep was a southerner who made his capital at Thebes. He reigned until 2010 B.C., bequeathing a peaceful and prosperous kingdom to his son. But unity was superficial, for ambitious officials vied for supreme power. It was not until Amenemhet I seized the throne in 1991 B.C. and moved the capital downstream to Lisht at the border between Upper and Lower Egypt that political stability once again came to Egypt.

By this time, the pharaohs were concerned both with internal security and with expanding or consolidating their borders. Amenemhet and his successors made a determined effort to subjugate Nubia and established fortified towns as far south as Kerma, above the Third Cataract (see Chapter 12). They also consolidated the northeastern boundary of the kingdom with the "Walls of the Prince," fortified strongholds set up at strategic points to guard the main routes from the Sinai Desert into Egypt. At the same time, trade relations with the Levant expanded dramatically. The pharaohs mined copper and gold in the Sinai and traded cedar from Lebanon. Objects bearing their inscriptions have been found as far afield as Byblos and the port of Ugarit on the northern Syrian coast. It was from such centers that items from the Aegean Islands and Minoan towns on Crete reached the Nile (Chapter 8).

The government also tried to increase agricultural production. At the height of the Middle Kingdom, the pharaoh Senusret II began the development of the Fayyum oasis about 80 kilometers (50 miles) southwest of Memphis. He and his successors turned the marshy oasis into a vast network of fields and irrigation canals protected by large dikes, an unprecedented agricultural project that provided high crop yields for the state, even in droughts. This kind of organized irrigation was very different from the informal, village-based canals and drainage ditches that marked most earlier Egyptian agriculture. The Fayyum project was only one manifestation of a state concerned with remodeling a society with strong local roots into a closely regimented and centralized one, which established planned towns even in sparsely populated areas. The pharaohs strove for an organized oasis, a state run by prosperous officials.

Enormous public works and royal mortuaries required small armies of workers, sometimes housed in special communities some distance from their place of work. The Middle Kingdom town at Kahun (known to the Egyptians as Hetep-Senusret, "King Senusret is at peace") stood close to the entrance to the Fayyum, near the pyramid of Senusret II. Here lived the priests and workers responsible for the king's mortuary cult, as well as people engaged in other construction works and agriculture. Kahun lay inside mud-brick walls, the interior laid out on a strict grid pattern of small houses and streets. Egyptologist Flinders Petrie uncovered intricately designed, fairly large houses with substantial granaries, in which household activities revolved around an inner court and walled garden. Much smaller houses outnumbered these residences by about 20 to 1, with an estimated 3,000 people living within the tightly packed community. The town plan reflects a society with well-defined social classes, reflected in house design as well as occupation.

Papyri found during Petrie's excavations reveal the existence of a mayor, legal offices, and a prison. They also contain census data, for example, the household of a mortuary priest with only one son and daughter but many "serfs," some of them a product of his office, others domestic servants, "field laborers," cooks, tutors, and women who were "clothmakers" and gardeners. These groups of workers depended on the granaries of larger houses for their rations, thereby forming the economic teams that were so much a part of Egyptian society. Kahun's population also included scribes and soldiers and numerous small households of half a dozen people or more, many of them relatives and widows with dependent children.

Kahun represents the ultimate in Egyptian bureaucracy—a town laid out by noble officials with little conception of the realities of society. They organized Kahun at two levels: top officials and others. In fact, the papyri reveal a more complex reality, that of individuals and households who were wrestling with debts and children, sudden inheritances, and care for the elderly. After the Middle Kingdom, the state gave up planning any form of community other than small workers' camps. (In contrast, the New Kingdom pharaoh Akhenaten's capital at el-Amarna was much more loosely organized.)

Unfortunately, we know little of Middle Kingdom religious buildings, many of which were remodeled during the New Kingdom. But the tomb and mortuary temple of Mentuhotep II on the west bank of the Nile at Thebes give some impression of their magnificence. Mentuhotep's imposing resting place lay in a bay of cliffs, a double-colonnaded temple complex surmounted by a pyramid, thought to be a depiction of the primeval mound of Egyptian legend. A 950-meter (3,100-foot) causeway lined with statues of Osiris led to a temple close to the river.

The Middle Kingdom has been described as the classic period of Egyptian civilization, when the pharaohs became more human and more approachable than their Old Kingdom predecessors, who cast themselves in the role of gods. During these centuries, Egypt's rulers strove to create a kingdom in the image of a bureaucratic Utopia, a realm where there were logical, often mathematical solutions to every economic problem. The experiment was successful for a while but faltered when Egypt's human and natural resources proved unequal to the task.

The last great Middle Kingdom pharaoh was Amenemhet III (1844–1797 B.C.), who reigned for 47 years and used his wealth to build colossal temples and to commission magnificent statuary. Amenemhet died in 1797 B.C., just as another cycle of irregular floods descended on the Nile. A succession of weak pharaohs followed rapidly one after the other as political power passed to provincial governors with the organized food supplies to tide the country over hungry years. Once again, Egypt split into local kingdoms. Nobles in Thebes competed with powerful rivals downstream and with new rulers in the delta.

## The Second Intermediate Period (1640–1550 B.C.)

By the Thirteenth Dynasty (1783–c. 1640 B.C.), large numbers of Asiatics lived in Egypt. They were cooks and brewers, seamstresses, and merchants. Many of the finest Egyptian winemakers came from Syria. Some foreigners assumed positions of influence and trust in noble households. Others were nomadic herders who moved into the delta to seek sanctuary from drought or to buy corn. Their chiefs were called *Hikau khasut,* "Princes of Desert Uplands," a term that the industrious Manetho translated as "Hyksos," referring not only to chiefs but also to all their people.

By the seventeenth century B.C., the delta had come under the political control of a line of Hyksos kings, who had taken advantage of the weakness of the Thirteenth Dynasty pharaohs to seize power over Lower Egypt, ruling it from the town of Avaris. They assumed the titles, traditions, and religious beliefs of the pharaohs, acquiring such prestige that the princes of Thebes paid them tribute, perhaps linking the royal houses through intermarriage.

The Second Intermediate Period was a turning point in Egyptian history. The Hyksos brought new ideas to a conservative civilization that was slowly stagnating away from the mainstream of the Near Eastern world. They introduced more sophisticated bronze technology and traded silver from Asian mines. Friezes in the palace at Avaris in the delta are painted in the Minoan style, as if Cretan merchants and artisans lived in their capital (Chapter 9). In their battles with the Thebans, the Hyksos brought new weaponry to the Nile—stronger bows, new forms of swords and daggers, and the horse-drawn chariot. All these innovations kept Egypt current and ensured that subsequent pharaohs played a leading role in the wider eastern Mediterranean world.

## The New Kingdom (1550–1070 B.C.): Imperial Kings

The relationship between the Hyksos and the Theban state was never comfortable but often a matter of angry diplomatic exchanges and sometimes fighting. Around 1550 B.C., a Theban prince named Kamose sailed downstream and attacked Hyksos strongholds along the river. His son Ahmose (1550–1525 B.C.) continued the offensive and took Avaris after a long and bloody siege. Ahmose was determined to secure his Asian frontier, so he chased the Hyksos as far as the town of Sharuhen in southwestern Palestine and into Syria. From this moment, Egypt became an imperial power, a major political force in the fragile balance of power in the eastern Mediterranean (Box 4.2).

At the same time, Ahmose turned Egypt into an efficiently run military state, tolerating no rivals, rewarding his soldiers and mercenaries with grants of land, but retaining economic power and wealth in his own hands. Like Mentuhotep in the Middle Kingdom, Ahmose set the tone for an entire era, the greatest in Egyptian history. The pharaoh became a national hero, a military leader who sat on a throne midway between the Asiatic world in the north and the black Nubian kingdoms of the south. He was an imperial ruler and a skilled general, the leader of a great power. Egypt became a major player in the shifting sands of eastern Mediterranean politics, competing with two great states: Mitanni, to the east of the Euphrates, and Hatti, the kingdom of the Hittites in Anatolia. Each wanted to control the lucrative gold, copper, and pottery trade of the eastern Mediterranean for itself.

The pharaohs financed their state and empire with Nubian gold, turning the lands upstream of the First Cataract into a lucrative colony (see Chapter 12). At the same time, the Egyptians expanded their trade routes down the Red Sea to the mysterious "Land of Punt," which probably lay between the Red Sea and the Middle Nile, on the north and northwest flanks of the Ethiopian highlands in the modern

## *Box 4.2 Discovery: Avaris*

Ahmose took no chances in the strategically vulnerable Delta. He rebuilt the Hyksos town of Avaris as a heavily defended fortress. The new town rose on the ruins of the Hyksos citadel. A huge mud-brick platform with a riverside gate gave a magnificent view over the Pelusiac branch of the Nile, at that time a deep water channel to the ocean. Military barracks, several temples, storerooms, and a palace for the pharaoh once lay behind the walls of the citadel. Unfortunately, ancient builders quarried away the abandoned structures many centuries ago, leaving a gigantic archaeological jigsaw behind them. Instead of excavating buildings, Austrian Egyptologist Manfred Bietak and his colleagues have spent years dissecting huge piles of mud-brick and wall plaster—with astounding results.

Bietak unearthed hundreds of lime wall-plaster fragments adorned with paintings executed by Minoan artists from Crete. The Cretan motifs and style of the wall paintings are unmistakable—a bearded priest, performing acrobats, river landscapes and craggy mountains like those in Crete, unknown in Egypt. Such scenes are not unique. Cretan wall paintings occur at other Bronze Age cities in the Levant, as Cretan kings sent artists abroad as tokens of favor to important trading partners. But only the Avaris palace boasts of bull-leaping scenes. One frieze scene shows bulls, bull-leapers, and others cavorting against a labyrinthine background, characteristic of Cretan palace art. A bull charges, his face turned toward the artist. The bull leaper grasps the beast around the neck, his legs in the air. Another bull lunges nearby, but this time the acrobat has fallen off the animal.

Why would Cretan artists paint friezes on the walls of an Egyptian palace? The explanation may lie not in Egypt, but in Crete. A century ago, the great archaeologist Arthur Evans excavated the Palace of Minos at Knossos in northern Crete and revealed the hitherto unknown Minoan civilization to an astonished scholarly world. The Palace was a labyrinth of courts and small rooms, many adorned with magnificent wall paintings of people and bulls. Evans reconstructed some of the friezes, somewhat imaginatively according to his critics. Goddesses and priestesses, processions, bulls, mythic animals, and lions, even waving grass and flowers: Knossos art is lively and highly distinctive. The most famous scenes depict acrobats jumping over fierce bulls, twisting and turning in the air as they cavort with the charging animal. Despite extended search, no one had ever found bull-leapers anywhere else, until they turned up at Avaris. They were unique to the Western Court at Knossos, the greatest Minoan palace ever built.

Manfred Bietak believes the Avaris friezes depict the distant Western Court. Avaris and Knossos share other royal art and symbolism, too—depictions of mythical griffins and felines, animals at the summit of nature's hierarchy. At Knossos, griffins protected goddesses and queens. Maybe they did at Avaris as well. Bietak wonders if a diplomatic marriage between the Egyptian and Knossos royal families might not be involved. Ahmose is known to have married two of his sisters, but may have had a Cretan wife as well: We do not yet know. Perhaps Ahmose, having ousted the Hyksos, feared a surprise attack by land and sea. The Minoans were the best seafarers of the day, so

*(Cont.)*

the pharaoh may have cut a deal with the lord of Knossos—protection of sea lanes in exchange for access to Egyptian ports and her abundant gold. We know that Minoan trade delegations were soon familiar sights at the Egyptian court. They appear on the walls of Theban nobles' tombs.

Avaris was a fortress and palace compound for the victorious pharaoh, a base for his campaigns in southern Palestine. Here troops could rest while their officers kept a close eye on Egypt's northeastern frontier. Here, too, Ahmose could embark his invading armies for a quick coastal passage to the strategic ports of the Levant. For centuries, Avaris remained a meeting place between Egypt and the eastern Mediterranean world. Polyglot crowds of artisans, seamen, and traders from the world without thronged her quays and streets. Perhaps the dockyard was *Penu-nefer* (Happy Journey), the famed harbor in Lower Egypt once thought to lie at Memphis upstream. Just under three centuries later, the city became the port for Ramesses II's royal residence at nearby Pi-Ramses and thrived as a vital link to the outside world.

Ahmose was well aware of the economic and strategic importance of his fortress. He realized only too well that the key to his power lay in consolidated, expanded frontiers, close political ties with potential rivals, and complete control of Nubian trade. Whether the pharaoh's officials liked it or not, Egypt had become part of what today we would call a "global economy." A vast web of economic and political interconnectedness linked the Nile with the Levant, with copper-rich Cyprus, with Turkey, Mesopotamia, and the Aegean islands. The ancient world was linked together economically and politically as never before—and Egypt was an important part of it. Her products and raw materials, her ideas, knowledge, and religious beliefs were carried far and wide, by ship, on the backs of donkeys and people, in the hands of her armies. Soon New Kingdom Egypt achieved a wealth, sophistication, and power undreamed of in earlier times.

eastern Sudan. A Punt expedition was a major undertaking—first an overland journey from Koptos on the Nile to the Red Sea coast, then by ship southward through windy, often treacherous waters. In 1472 B.C., Queen Hatshepsut sent a royal trading party to Punt. Spectacular reliefs on her mortuary temple chronicle the successful voyage. Separate scenes depict the ships under sail, the arrival at Punt, "very heavily with the marvels of the land of Punt: with . . . good herbs of God's Land and heaps of nodules of myrrh." The story ends with the triumphant return to the sun god Amun's sacred city: Thebes.

## *"The Estate of Amun"*

Thebes, the home of Amun, was known to the Egyptians as "The City" or the "Estate of Amun." The Temple of Amun at Karnak, mostly built during the Eighteenth Dynasty (1550–1307 B.C.), was the heart of the sacred capital, a great shrine built on the foundations of a much older town, which was leveled to create Amun's home (Figure 4.9). The temple lay on the old city mound, surrounded by the buildings of the New Kingdom city. Karnak represented a major shift in public architecture.

**Figure 4.9** The Temple of Amun at Karnak.

Earlier kings had built their most imposing monuments on the edges of the Western Desert, and local temples were usually modest mud-brick structures in the heart of a community. In contrast, Karnak and its lesser equivalents were settings for important public ceremonies and processions, when the boatlike shrine of Amun was paraded along carefully prepared routes. Religion now became public spectacle, a psychological way of influencing public opinion that was more subtle and probably more effective than the bureaucratic regulation of earlier times.

Karnak and its equivalents were surrounded by mud-brick walls, painted white and modeled like turreted battlements, which kept out most of the populace. The great pylons that marked the entrance bore brightly colored scenes of the king conquering his enemies in the presence of the gods. Karnak was a statement of raw imperial power but also the place where the gods found shelter and were nurtured by food offerings. In short, as Barry Kemp points out, the gods were landed gentry, fed from vast temple estates cultivated by smallholders who paid their rent in produce. Amun's temples owned cattle and mineral rights and maintained enormous grain stores. The mortuary temple of Ramesses II near Thebes had storerooms capable (theoretically) of feeding as many as 20,000 people. The wealth of the large temples and the authority of their gods was such that they were not only a major element in the New Kingdom economy but also an important factor in the affairs of state.

Amun-Re was the "king of the gods," a solar deity portrayed in human form and the source of fecundity. He was the divine father figure who conceived, then protected, the kings in life and in death. The great pageants at Thebes, the processions between the temples at Karnak and Luxor during the annual Opet festival, proclaimed to the populace that the king had renewed his divine *ka,* or spiritual essence, in the innermost shrine of Amun himself. The myths, rituals, and great temples all served to guarantee the continuity of proper rule, a concept absolutely central to Egyptian thinking. At the same time, the priesthood had little political power, for the ultimate authority lay in the hands of the king and his army of carefully trained scribes.

"The Estate of Amun" extended across the Nile to the western bank. Here the pharaohs erected an elaborate city of the dead. Soon after the beginning of the Eighteenth Dynasty, around 1505 B.C., Pharaoh Amenhotep and his illustrious successors elected to be buried in secret, rock-cut tombs in the arid Valley of Kings on the west bank of the river opposite Thebes. The underground tombs evolved over the centuries to become models of the caverns of the underworld, traversed by the night sun until it was transformed in the burial chamber each dawn. The royal mortuary temples lay on the plain nearby, surrounded by the tombs of queens, princes, and court officials.

Generations of necropolis workers—masons, painters, and skilled artisans—lived in a compact laborers' community at Deir el-Medina nearby. The most expert among them were known as "Servitors of the Place of Truth," the Royal Necropolis. They aped the burial customs of their royal masters, constructing for themselves elaborate tombs, sometimes with small brick pyramids and fine wall paintings. But most laborers lived under harsh conditions. Contemporary records tell of strikes and absenteeism, sparse rations, and occasional violence.

## *Akhenaten and Amarna*

Amun's power came through the age-old cult of Re Herakhty, the primordial sun god. His Great Disk, Aten, illuminated the worlds of the living and the dead. Amun was all-powerful until Pharaoh Akhenaten came to the throne in 1353 B.C. The new ruler departed from religious orthodoxy by placing a greater emphasis on Aten alone, excluding all the old gods of the pantheon from their association with Re Herakhty. Akhenaten in effect made Aten a divine pharaoh, the equivalent in heaven of the living king on earth. We do not know why Akhenaten altered the sacred canon, but the art of his day suggests that he regarded himself and his family as the sole intermediaries between the people and the sun god. Akhenaten expected to be adored like a god (Figure 4.10).

In the fifth year of his reign, the heretic pharaoh founded a new capital at Amarna downstream of Thebes, on land not associated with any established deity. Amarna was occupied for little more than a quarter of a century before it was abandoned, leaving an Egyptian city of more than 20,000 inhabitants for archaeologists to investigate. The ceremonial precincts of Amarna centered on a processional way that linked the North (royal) City to the Central City. The fortified royal palace at the north end was isolated from the rest of Amarna. Here Akhenaten and his court resided in a self-sufficient, well-guarded community with its own warehouses. The pharaoh rode down the processional way on festival days, protected by his bodyguard as his subjects adulated him. The road ended at the Great Palace, a huge structure by the waterfront with a central courtyard, where the king received emissaries and conducted many ceremonies, sometimes rewarding high

**Figure 4.10** The pharaoh Akhenaten with his wife and child. His reign bred an entirely new, representational art style—realistic, with an emphasis on intimate family life. The royal art style of these years is strong evidence that Akhenaten was engaged in a vigorous attempt to reduce the power of the Theban priesthood of Amun and to strengthen his own secular and spiritual power. (The Royal Family [Akhenaten]. Egyptian relief. 1345 B.C. Aegyptisches Museum, Staatliche Museen, Berlin, Germany. Copyright Vanni/Art Resource, NY.)

officials who were dependent on his largesse. The administrative functions of state were performed in offices attached to the palace. It was here that the Bureau for the Correspondence of the Pharaoh lay, the archive that housed the now-famous Amarna diplomatic tablets (Chapter 7). The Great Temple of Aten stood nearby.

But Amarna's greatest significance lies in its unique archaeological evidence for New Kingdom Egyptian society. Most Amarna residents lived in two large housing tracts north and south of the central city, huddled in small houses along streets parallel to the river that were intersected by smaller alleys. Each flat-roofed dwelling stood in a small, walled compound among a maze of alleyways and garbage heaps. Each had a central living room with a low brick dais for receiving guests. Around the central space were reception rooms, bedrooms, and storage rooms. Wealthier people had larger houses, built to the same general design. We know the names of only a few individual owners, among them Re-nefer, a chief charioteer, who lived in a modest house; Thutmose was a sculptor who carried out his work in small courtyards near his house in an area devoted to sculptors. In the teeming city neighborhoods, papyri tell us how some prominent officials struggled to maintain a prosperous lifestyle, using income from their small country estates and donations from

(a)

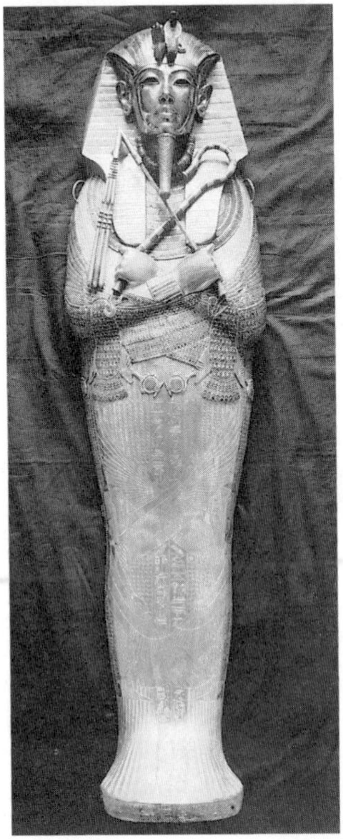

(b)

**Figure 4.11** Tutankhamun's tomb. (a) The antechamber with its jumble of furnishings ; (b) the golden sarcophagus of the king. Tutankhamun's jumbled possessions were so opulent that it has taken generations for us to appreciate their wealth and significance. The dead pharaoh traveled through the heavens in the sun god's barque. His many gold leaf and inlaid figures and amulets ensured his well-being during the eternal journey. At the same time, his tomb provided for his material needs—clothing, perfume and cosmetics, personal jewelry, and chests to keep them in. There were chairs, stools, beds, headrests, weapons, and hunting gear. Baskets and vases contained food and wine. Even the pharaoh's chariots lay in pieces inside the tomb. The tomb provides a fleeting portrait of the fabulous wealth of Egypt's court. (Egyptian Dynasty XVIII, Thebes: Valley of the Kings, Tomb of Tut-ankh-amun: Antechamber south end. Photography by Egyptian Expedition, The Metropolitan Museun of Art)

the king. Minor officials, domestic servants, merchants, fisherfolk, sailors, and farmers huddled in the crowded, smaller houses. Everyone had close ties to the countryside, to their home villages, often many miles away. Few Egyptians were true city dwellers. Egyptian cities were little more than large agglomerations of villages. Their inhabitants lived their lives in another world from that of the pharaoh, who dwelt in splendid isolation surrounded by his relatives and bodyguards, appearing at regular intervals to receive the adoration of his subjects.

### *The Imperial Power*

Religious fanatic, indolent madman, benevolent pacifist, or heretic, history's judgments on Akhenaten have rarely been favorable. He died in the seventeenth year of his reign, leaving behind a corrupt and chaotic kingdom. His successor, Smenkhkare, a son of Amenhotep III, reigned for a mere three years and was succeeded in turn by 8-year-old Tutankhamun (1333–1323 B.C.), who achieved in death an immortality that transcends that of all other pharaohs, simply because Howard Carter and Lord Carnarvon discovered his intact tomb in the Valley of Kings (Figure 4.11).

Tutankhamun presided over a troubled country, abandoned to chaos by the alienated gods. The young king's powerful and experienced advisers took the obvious course of someone reared in the deeply religious Egyptian world. They propitiated the gods by restoring the old spiritual order, rebuilding temples and reverting to the dynastic traditions of early pharaohs. The cult of Amun was revived at Thebes and Amarna was abandoned. An able general named Horemhab campaigned in Syria, while Tutankhamun himself may have led a raiding party into Nubia in 1323 B.C., which resulted in a fatal arrow wound by his left ear. (The cause of his death is much debated.) His unexpected death caught the court by surprise. It was not until Horemhab assumed the throne in 1319 B.C. that the old ways were fully restored.

The Ramesside pharaohs of the Nineteenth Dynasty (1307–1196 B.C.) who followed labored hard to elevate the kingdom to its former glory as an imperial power. Their wealth came from Nubian gold and far-flung trade, for Nubia was now an Egyptian dependency (Figure 4.12). (See Chapter 12.) Ramesses II (1290–1224 B.C.) campaigned far into Syria until he met his match at the battle of Kadesh, where the Hittites fought his army to a standstill. From that moment on, Egypt steadily lost political influence in the Near East and began a slow, at first barely perceptible, decline.

## The Decline of Egypt (after 1100 B.C.)

The Egyptian state was built around a powerful ideology for the glory of kings and gods. The pharaohs developed a system of government that maintained food surpluses and stable grain prices by intervening massively in the agricultural economy (Figure 4.13). The state deployed labor on public works of all kinds, feeding the workers with allocations of grain carefully rationed by achievement and rank.

**Figure 4.12** Abu Simbel temple, built by Ramesses II on the banks of the Nile in Lower Nubia as a statement of political power. The temple was moved to higher ground by UNESCO during the building of the Aswan Dam, which created Lake Nasser during the 1960s.

**Figure 4.13** Estate workers working in the fields of Menna, scribe of the fields and estate inspector under Pharaoh Tuthmosis III of the Eighteenth Dynasty. Tomb painting from Deir el-Medina, Thebes.

For more than 2,000 years, the "Egyptian Solution," as Barry Kemp calls it, was a crude form of provider state, which defined the way in which people and a civilization should relate to each other. Broadly similar solutions developed in other parts of the world—along the Indus River and in Mesoamerica, for example.

During the Old and Middle Kingdoms, Egypt achieved much, its people living passively under a society in which their rulers controlled every aspect of daily life by bureaucratic regulation. But as excavations at the city of Amarna show us, the New Kingdom Egyptians lived under a more loosely structured state in which the interests of the pharaoh and individual assertiveness and initiative coexisted uncomfortably. The great king, surrounded by his courtiers and commemorated by art and festival, had held together Egyptian civilization for many centuries. But after Ramesses II, the shackles of royal authority were loosened as a series of weak kings presided over a faltering society.

By 1200 B.C., the delicate balance of power in the eastern Mediterranean dissolved as the Hittite empire disintegrated (Chapter 7). With the death of Ramesses III in 1163 B.C., Egypt entered a period of slow decline. Setbacks in Asia and a retreat from Nubia helped turn the vision of the Egyptians inward once again, to the confines of their lush homeland. The prestige of the throne dwindled, there was chronic corruption within the bureaucracy, and bands of hungry soldiers periodically terrorized the population. Organized gangs of tomb robbers pillaged the royal graves in the Valley of Kings, greedy for the fabulous gold that lay beneath the ground (Box 4.3). Pharaohs who had once been gods on earth were now targets of blatant robbery.

## *Box 4.3 Voices: A Tomb-Robbing Scandal at Thebes*

We can imagine the careful plotting beforehand, the secret rendezvous in a desolate ravine, quiet figures moving stealthily through the pitch-black Egyptian night. Frantic digging in the dark: Candles in hand, the robbers grab as much portable treasure as they can and slip away before the sun rises. Such robbery was unavoidable. Every Egyptian knew the rich and powerful took treasure with them to eternity. Even one ornament from a pharaoh's sepulcher could keep a poor villager in food for years. The tomb robbers' nefarious trade was a silent war between loyal royal cemetery guards and those who preyed on the dead. No pharaoh was safe in his tomb, even Khufu, who built the Great Pyramid of Giza in 2550 B.C. Bold predators drugged or bribed guards and tunneled into the most inaccessible burial chambers.

A spectacular discovery in 1881 dramatizes the desperate struggle. Rumors reached the authorities in Thebes of exceptionally fine antiquities coming onto the market. They could only have come from a royal tomb. Suspicion fell on known grave robbers, the Rasoul brothers. They were hauled in for questioning, but to no avail. Eventually, the brothers quarrelled and one of them went to the police. He led archaeologist Emil Brugsch to an inconspicuous, rocky cleft in the desolate cliffs on the west bank opposite Thebes.

*(Cont.)*

Brugsch descended by rope into a tiny chamber crammed with priceless artifacts and royal mummies, including the bodies of some of Egypt's most powerful pharaohs, among them Ramesses II and Seti I. The cache was a chaotic jumble of tomb furniture and mummies gathered together by desperate royal priests, who managed to stay one step ahead of rapacious looters. Finally success, until modern-day robbers made the discovery of a lifetime. Unfortunately, most royal treasure vanished forever long before archaeologists came to the Nile.

The royal tombs in the Valley of Kings near Thebes were comparatively sacrosanct during the reigns of the great pharaohs of the Eighteenth and Nineteenth Dynasties, when Egypt was prosperous and a large force of guards supervised the royal sepulchers. By 1200 B.C., her kings were much weaker. The custodians of royal tombs were lax, even corrupt. A wave of grave robbing enveloped Thebes. We know of this because a spectacular law case involving tomb robbing was heard during the twelfth century B.C.

The case involved Paser, the mayor of eastern Thebes, an honest but rather officious local bureaucrat, who became alarmed at the constant rumors of tomb robbing that came from the cemeteries on the west bank of the Nile. Perhaps he was anxious to ingratiate himself with higher authority, or to discredit his hated rival Pawero, mayor of Thebes of the Dead. Whatever his motive, Paser started an official investigation into tomb robbing, something that technically lay outside his jurisdiction. He soon uncovered all manner of disturbing testimony from actual eyewitnesses of grave robberies. Paser laid his case before the local vizier, who sent an official commission to inspect the tombs. A quick cover-up ensured they found little out of order. To Paser's embarrassment, his witnesses now denied their earlier testimony. He had underestimated the degree to which his rival controlled the looting.

Paser was a determined man. He continued to bombard the vizier with evidence of tomb robbing. A year later, even the highest officials could not deny that something was wrong. The vizier convened a new inquiry. Forty-five tomb robbers were brought before the court and beaten on the soles of their feet to extract confessions. Their testimony survives, ironically on papyri looted and sold to nineteenth-century tourists. One witness testified: "There we found the august mummy of the king. There were numerous amulets and golden ornaments at his throat, his head had a mask of gold upon it." He had watched as robbers stripped the ruler of his finery. The incense roaster of the temple of the sun god Amun recounted how a group of robbers approached him. "Come out," they said, "We are going to take plunder for bread to eat." The priest described how the robbers broke into a royal tomb and divided the spoil in baskets. "The scribe of the Necropolis was examined with the stick [until] he said: 'Stop, I will tell.'" He confessed to the stealing of silver vases from a single tomb. When his memory faded, he was examined again "with the birch and the screw," but to no avail. The case ended with savage punishments for the offenders, which probably included death by impalement. Some of the accused were acquitted when it became obvious that beatings produced false testimony. Not that the cases did much to stem the flood of robberies, for there are isolated mentions of later trials. The epidemic of looting was inevitable in a poverty-stricken country where wealth was for the few, more of it buried below ground than in the land of the living.

As had happened before when royal authority declined, Egypt fell apart into its constituent parts. Eventually, military leaders seized control of Thebes and the priesthood of Amun, while a dynasty of merchants took control of the delta. With their ascendance, the "Egyptian Solution" passed into history, as the Nile became part of a much wider Near Eastern world (Chapters 9 and 12).

# Summary

The roots of Egyptian civilization lie in the Nile Valley itself, for the institutions of the pharaohs' state developed along the river after 4000 B.C. as competing kingdoms vied for control of trade routes and political power. The unification of Egypt around 2920 B.C. at the hands of Pharaoh Horus Aha was followed by the Archaic period (2920–2680 B.C.), when the basic institutions of kingship and bureaucracy were established and writing appeared. In the Old Kingdom (c. 2680–2134 B.C.) the king was the supreme territorial claimant and the pyramids were built under despotic rule. After a short period of political unrest, Middle Kingdom pharaohs (2040–2016 B.C.) created a bureaucratic state with a strongly centralized organization, which gave way to the New Kingdom (1550–1070 B.C.), after another interval of unrest, when Hyksos kings from the Near East ruled Egypt. The New Kingdom was the period in which Egypt became an imperial power in the Near East, competing with the Hittites and other neighbors in the Levant. Egyptian civilization gradually declined after 1070 B.C. and became a province of the Roman Empire in 30 B.C.

# Guide to Further Reading

An enormous literature surrounds Egyptian civilization, much of it the preserve of specialist Egyptologists. General accounts also abound, but the best stand out from the crowd. Barry Kemp, *Ancient Egypt: Anatomy of a Civilization* (London and New York: Routledge, 1989) is a perceptive synthesis. Cyril Aldred, *The Egyptians*, 3rd ed. (London and New York: Thames and Hudson, 1998) offers an excellent popular summary. Ian Shaw, ed., *The Oxford History of Ancient Egypt* (Oxford: Oxford University Press, 2000) contains authoritative essays and an excellent bibliography. For a chronicle of archaeological discoveries, see Nicholas Reeves, *Ancient Egypt: The Great Discoveries* (London and New York: Thames and Hudson, 2000).

The literature on Afrocentrism is extensive: Chiekh Anta Diop, *Nations Nègres et Culture* (Paris: Présence Africaine, 1955) and Tarharka Sundiata, *Black Manhood: The Building of Civilization by the Black Man of the Nile* (Washington, DC: University Press of America, 1979) are often quoted. Ivan van Sertima, *The African Presence in Early America* (New Brunswick, NJ: Transaction Press, 1987) lies firmly in the Afrocentrism camp, while Martin Bernal, *The Afroasiatic Roots of Classical Civilization* (New Brunswick, NJ: Rutgers University Press, 1987 and 1992) assesses Egypt's contribution to Western civilization. G. T. Martin, *The Hidden Tombs of Memphis* (London: Thames and Hudson, 1991) contains wonderfully realistic depictions of Nubians.

Works on specific topics abound, among them Salima Ikram and Aidan Dodson, *The Mummy in Ancient Egypt* (London and New York: Thames and Hudson, 1998). For predynastic Egypt and origins, see Michael A. Hoffman, *Egypt before the Pharaohs* (Austin: University of Texas Press, 1991) and *The Predynastic of Hierakonpolis* (Cairo: Egyptian Studies Association, 1982). The archaeology of the predynastic is well covered by Kathryn A. Bard, "The Egyptian Predynastic: A Review of the Evidence," *Journal of Field Archaeology* 21, no. 3 (1994): 265–288; and Robert J. Wenke, "The Evolution of Early Egyptian Civilization: Issues and Evidence," *Journal of World Prehistory* 5 (1991): 279–329. A. H. Wilkinson, *Early Dynastic Egypt* (London: Routledge, 1999) covers much valuable ground. For the pyramids,

Mark Lehner, *The Complete Pyramids* (London and New York: Thames and Hudson, 1997) is authoritative. Kurt Mendelssohn, *The Riddle of the Pyramids* (New York: Praeger, 1974) offers a provocative hypothesis. Peter James, *Centuries of Darkness* (New Brunswick, NJ: Rutgers University Press, 1993) discusses Manetho's King-lists. For Akhenaten, see Donald B. Redford, *Akhenaten: The Heretic King* (Princeton, NJ: Princeton University Press, 1984). For a more sympathetic treatment, see Cyril Aldred, *Akhenaten: King of Egypt* (New York: Thames and Hudson, 1991), also Nicholas Reeves, *Akhenaten* (London: Thames and Hudson, 2001). For Tutankhamun, see Nicholas Reeves, *The Complete Tutankhamun* (London and New York: Thames and Hudson, 1990). For ancient Egyptian writing and religious beliefs, see Richard H. Wilkinson, *Reading Egyptian Art: A Hieroglyphic Guide to Ancient Egyptian Painting and Sculpture* (London and New York: Thames and Hudson, 1992). The voices of the Egyptians themselves appear in Miriam Lichtheim, ed., *Ancient Egyptian Literature: A Book of Readings* (Berkeley: University of California Press, 1973–1980). For Late Period Egypt, see Alan Bowman, *Egypt after the Pharaohs* (Berkeley: University of California Press, 1996).

*Chapter 5*

# South Asia: Harappan and Later Civilizations

Terracotta figurine from Mohenjodaro, Pakistan: Third millennium B.C.

*The yellow Baluchistan shoreline recedes into the far distance, shimmering in the intense haze of late afternoon. The weathered sailing vessel heels slightly as a gust of land breeze reaches the ship from the depths of an arid canyon ashore, bringing a scent of dust and dry undergrowth. The white breakers are only 100 yards away, but the skipper has sailed the desert coast many times, progressing for hundreds of miles on the fickle winds from the shore. His eyes search the smooth, blue water, looking for the telltale ripples of a strengthening gust. The mast creaks as a puff fills the much-patched cotton sail. A waft of smells from the hold assaults the captain's nose: heady marjoram, dry cotton, aromatic timber. His ship carries a full cargo from the land of Meluhha far behind him to the east.*

South Asia lies within vast geographical barriers (Figure 5.1). To the north stand the Himalayas, a huge mountain chain extending more than 2,000 kilometers (1,200 miles) from the Hindu Kush in the west to Assam in the east. High passes traverse the mountains into Afghanistan, central Asia, and Tibet, but the most accessible routes are the northwestern defiles into western Afghanistan, Iran, and Baluchistan. The Arabian Sea, the Indian Ocean, and the Bay of Bengal surround the Indian subcontinent, while tropical rainforests restrict access to the east. With such geographical frontiers, one might expect South Asia to have become a cultural backwater. In fact, as this chapter shows, it has assimilated people and ideas for thousands of years, developing highly complex societies of considerable diversity.

A rim of mountainous terrain rings the north and northwest of South Asia, giving way in the west to the alluvial plains of the Indus River, which merge with the Thar Desert in the east, 150 meters (500 feet) above the floodplain. The desert in turn yields to the central tableland, the Deccan plateau, more fertile and once densely forested. North and east of the central tableland lies the Gangetic basin, which extends into Bihar, Bengal, and Bangladesh. This vast alluvial corridor enjoys greater rainfall as one moves east and gives way to the dense tropical forests that continue into Southeast Asia. The Deccan peninsula lies south of the higher terrain of the central tableland, higher on the west than in the east, which means rivers flow eastward and the coastal plain is wider on the Bay of Bengal side.

Like the rest of the world, South Asia underwent a major environmental change at the end of the Ice Age, as Himalayan glaciers retreated and sea levels rose. By about 8000 B.C., climatic conditions throughout the subcontinent were more or less the same as they are today, but local environments were very different, for humans had not yet deforested and modified the landscape for their own purposes. For example, the Ganges valley of Uttar Pradesh was once marshy

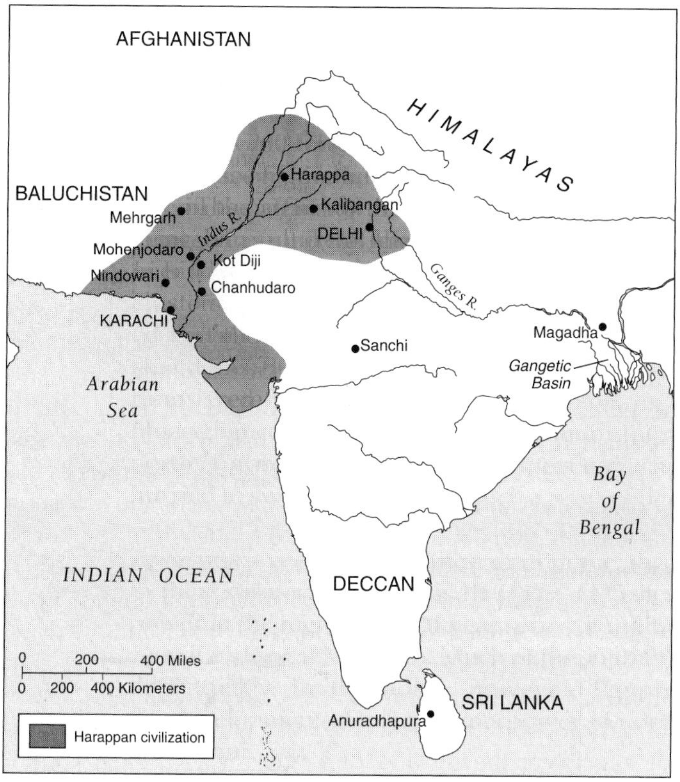


**Figure 5.1** Map of archaeological sites mentioned in Chapter 5.

and densely forested, the legendary Mahavaṇa ("great forest") of the early epic poems. But when Iron Age farmers settled the area in the first millennium B.C., deforested it, and drained the swamps, the character of the landscape changed fundamentally.

A key feature of Indian climate that had become firmly established by the end of the last Ice Age was the monsoon. From May to September, monsoon winds blow northeastwards across the Indian Ocean bringing torrential rains first to Sri Lanka, then to peninsular India and the north. The annual cycle in South Asia is governed by the strong seasonality of the monsoon cycle, which brings life-giving rains or, when occasionally the monsoon fails, drought and famine. These were the conditions in which agriculture and early states became established in the northwest of the subcontinent during the third millennium B.C.

Hemmed in by mountains, oceans, and tropical rainforest, South Asia developed its own distinctive civilizations, marked by their ability to assimilate ideas from outside. The subcontinent itself always had, and still has, a distinctive cultural identity, as well as great local diversity created by the isolation caused by east-west flowing rivers, different ethnic origins, and linguistic differences. In later times, certain South Asian empires, like that of the Mauryans in the third century B.C., did impose some political and cultural unity. So did the Hindu region and culture, with its four pilgrimage centers located in the extreme corners of South Asia.

## The Origins of Village Life and the Rise of the Harappan Civilization (before 3000 B.C.)

South Asian civilization began in the west, on the banks of the Indus River (Table 5.1). The Indus rises in southern Tibet and descends 1,609 kilometers (1,000 miles) through Kashmir before flowing through the semiarid Indus plains. There, deep silt deposits provide soft, easily turned soils, which can be cultivated on a large scale without metal tools. The Indus plains border on Baluchistan and eastern Afghanistan, forming a region with some environmental resemblances to that of the southern Mesopotamian plains and the neighboring Iranian plateau. Like Mesopotamia, this is an area of climatic extremes: searingly hot summers and sometimes very cold winters. Both the higher borderlands and the Indus plains are outside the monsoon belt. Farmers living in this harsh region obtain their water supplies from rivers and streams that rise in the mountains.

Twelve thousand years ago, both borderland and plains were home to Stone Age hunter-gatherer groups, who continued to flourish for many thousands of years. Despite now-refuted claims to the contrary, there is little evidence for agricultural communities in South Asia before the third millennium B.C., except in the northwest, where farming was probably introduced from the west. And even when agriculture took hold, as it did over wide areas between the fifth and third millennia, hunting and gathering remained a viable lifeway for many South Asians, as it did into modern times.

### *Mehrgarh*

The Mehrgarh site, 200 kilometers (125 miles) west of the Indus River, was occupied by village farmers before 6000 B.C. The people grew western Asiatic wheat and used domesticated goats from the same region, as if the new economies were introduced from the west, for Mehrgarh had cultural links with western and central Asia (Turkmenia). A thousand years later, the local people lived in sizable, permanent, mudbrick houses. Their village lay astride a centuries-old trade route from the Indus Valley to the Iranian highlands. The Mehrgarh graves contain copper artifacts and imported turquoise from Iran and shells from the distant Arabian coast, obtained, perhaps, by exporting cotton. The centralized organization of the Mehrgarh settlement is shown by the arrangement of the houses, which from the earliest phase followed a defined orientation and prefigure in that respect the planned Indus settlements of later periods such as Mohenjodaro.

A surprising feature of Mehrgarh is the reliance on domesticated plants and animals of west Asian origin: wheat and barley, sheep, goats, and cattle. There is no suggestion that this settlement was in any sense a colony, but it indicates the transfer of the new farming economy into South Asia across the Iranian plateaux. Only later were indigenous local crops such as cotton and rice brought into regular cultivation.

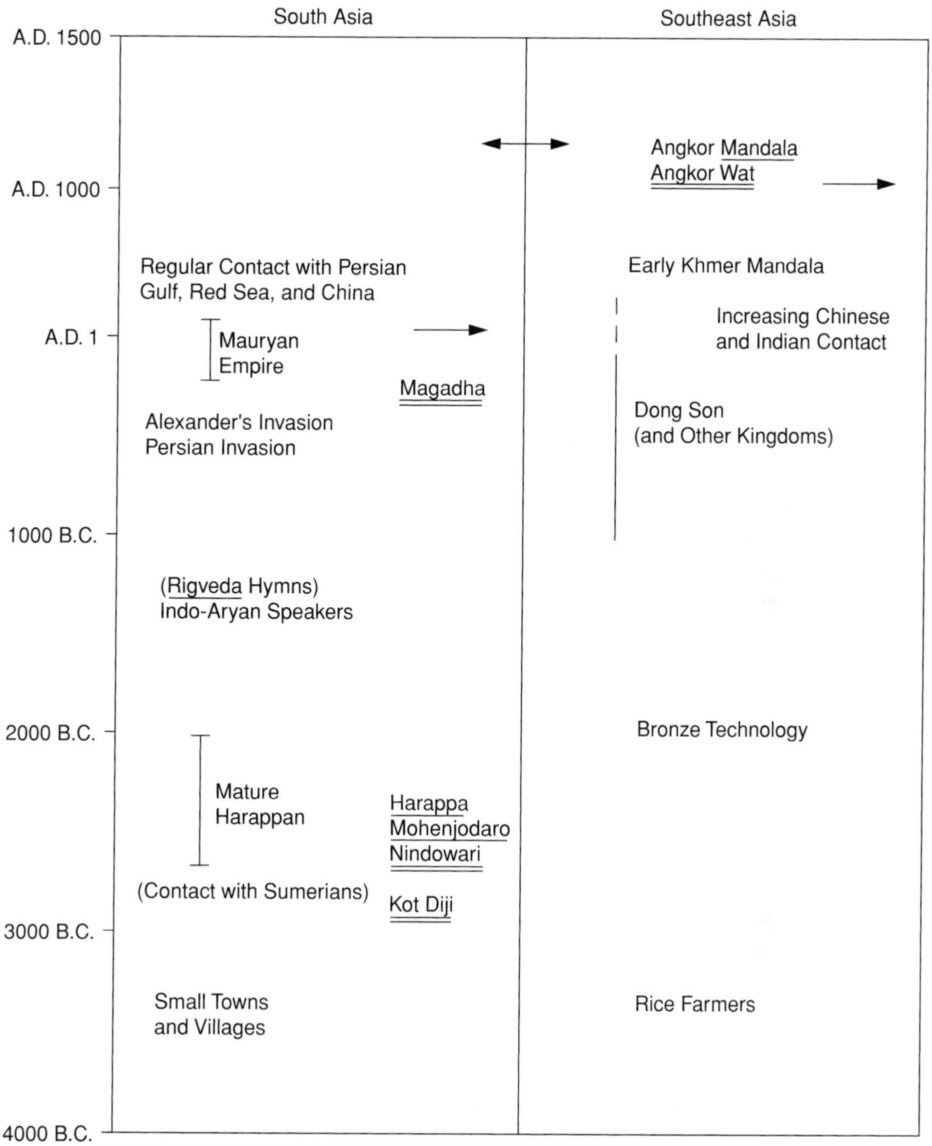


**Table 5.1** Chronological table of Harappan civilization and later states in South and Southeast Asia.

## *Early Harappan (Late Fourth and Early Third Millennia B.C.)*

During the fourth millennium B.C. the alluvial plains of the Indus and its tributaries were densely settled by dozens of small towns and villages, each perhaps with its own irrigation systems, often grouped under the label Early Harappan. The Indus floods each year between June and September. The farmers planted their wheat and barley as the floods receded and then harvested them the following spring, using the flood-borne silts as a natural fertilizer. Over many centuries, the Indus Valley became an artificial environment, a maze of irrigation canals and flood works with human settlements built above the highest flood level but as close to the river as possible. Indus floods are sometimes violent and always unpredictable, so massive flood works were sometimes needed. The Kot Diji settlement, occupied in the early third millennium B.C., lies 33 kilometers (20 miles) from the river. Yet the inhabitants were forced to pile up boulders to protect themselves against high inundations. The flood works soon became defensive walls as well, the stone and mud-brick houses of the inhabitants clustered inside the perimeter fortifications. Kot Diji was attacked and burned at least twice, perhaps as a result of factional disputes between ambitious local leaders competing for agricultural land, water rights, and other resources.

The Indus, like the Nile, the Tigris, and the Euphrates, is essentially a river flowing through the desert, and without the water and silt which it carries, settlement of the region would be extremely limited. The major difference between the Indus and the Nile, however, is the much greater extent of the Indus river system, with its numerous tributaries and channels. Thus the cities of the Harappan complex do not lie along a single river channel but along a series of stream courses. Furthermore, a second major river once flowed across the southern edge of the plain; this, the "lost" Saraswati, has become extinct during the intervening millennia. Thus the Indus cities depended on two major river systems and their annual flood regime. The impact of the major floods is graphically revealed by the depth of flood deposits at sites such as Mohenjodaro, a major Harappan city with a population estimated at perhaps 35,000. The high raised podium of the "citadel" at this and other sites, and the substantial perimeter wall traced around parts of the Lower City, may have been intended as a protection against these floods as much as against hostile neighbors.

The principal crops were wheat and barley, sown in autumn on the alluvial plains as the flood waters receded. They were supplemented in certain areas by summer-sown crops grown on higher-lying and drier land to take advantage of the summer monsoon rains: These included cotton, mustard, dates, and peas, and by 2600 B.C. may also have included rice and sorghum in Gujarat, on the southern edge of the Harappan cultural area. The support of major Harappan centers such as Mohenjodaro is thought to have depended on the transport of foodstuffs grown in complementary ecological zones. This changed during the later years of the Indus cities when there was an increase in the variety of locally cultivated crop species, suggesting that the earlier system of specialization and exchange—in which particular areas concentrated on specified crops, which were then distributed throughout the regional settlement system—was supplanted by greater reliance on local produce as the regional distribution system weakened or collapsed. The regional system also allowed the effects of occasional low floods and famines to have been buffered by the movement of crops from less affected areas. Its existence is shown in the adoption of standardized brick sizes and standardized weights and measures throughout the Harappan area, and by the exchange of raw materials and manufactures. Once these regional integration mechanisms broke down, around 2000 B.C., the major Harappan cities were abandoned. Other theories for the demise of the Harappan cities will be discussed later in this chapter.

The formative phases of the Harappan civilization are made difficult to understand by centuries of accumulated Indus alluvium; the fertile silts that made the cities possible have also hidden their origins from archaeological enquiry. Many early sites are covered and lost, while at others, the early phases lie deeply buried beneath the water table. At first sight, the Harappan civilization appears to burst upon the world fully formed, and the lengthy process of state formation remains wrapped in mystery. According to one theory, the formative approach began in the low hills fringing the plain, where prosperous village communities had developed over the previous millennia. These communities may have recognized the huge potential offered by the Indus lowlands and steadily expanded settlement into the area, using the agricultural strategies that have just been described. The reward was enormous agricultural productivity, leading rapidly to the formation of cities. From modest fourth millennium centers such as Kot Diji it may hence have been only a small step to major cities of 30,000 to 40,000 inhabitants at Mohenjodaro and Harappa.

The obvious leaders of these new communal efforts were the chieftains, priests, and kin leaders, who acted as intermediaries between the people and the gods. By 2700 B.C., the most successful leaders of larger settlements presided over hierarchies of cities, towns, and villages. This hypothetical scenario fits the few archaeological facts available from the Indus plains. Later we will discuss the nature of Harappan political organization.

## *Trade and Exchange*

Long before the rise of Harappan civilization, the ancestors of the Indus peoples interacted constantly with their neighbors to the north and west. Over many centuries, the relationship between lowlands and highlands was fostered by both regular exchange of food and other commodities and by seasonal population movements that brought enormous herds of cattle down from summer mountain pastures in Baluchistan to the lowlands during the harsh winter months. Economic and social development in both regions proceeded along parallel if somewhat diverse tracks, each region dependent on its neighbors.

The Nindowari site in Baluchistan was occupied between 2600 and 2200 B.C., the largest of a hierarchy of large and small centers known as the Kulli complex, contemporary with the mature Harappan civilization in the lowlands. Harappan artifacts occur at Nindowari, and there are signs that this and many other Kulli communities were engaged in trade with Iran to the west and the Indus lowlands to the east. The ongoing trading relationships between the highlands and the valley may have been a major factor in the rise of complex societies in both areas. One major commodity was cotton cloth. A South Asian–domesticated crop, cotton was probably first used as fodder for cattle before people discovered that its white, fluffy flower could be woven into cloth both for domestic use in a hot climate and as a hard-wearing fabric ideal for export. Such cloth first appears at the Harappan city of Mohenjodaro in the third millennium B.C.

The transition from egalitarian to ranked society took place before 2700 B.C., in what archaeologist Gregory Possehl has called "a veritable paroxysm of change." In contrast with Egypt and Mesopotamia, where economic, political, and social complexity developed over many centuries, a short period of explosive growth along the Indus lasted only one or two centuries. Possehl believes this growth may have coincided with a major shift in trading patterns. As we saw in Chapter 3, the Sumerians obtained many exotic objects and basic raw materials from the Iranian plateau before 2600 B.C. Their contacts, if any, with the Indus were overland and very indirect. Judging from written records, they experienced considerable frustration in their transactions with these trade networks. After 2600 B.C., the Sumerians reorganized their trade in luxuries and raw materials. They now acquired many of them by sea, from three foreign states—Dilmun, on the island of Bahrain in the Persian Gulf; Magan, an area on either side of the Persian Gulf (Oman and the Makran coast of Iran and Pakistan); and Meluhha, even further away, where ivory, oils, furniture, gold, and carnelian, among other commodities, could be obtained. The Mesopotamians exchanged these goods for wool, cloth, leather, oils, and other exotic goods. Most experts believe that Meluhha was the Indus Valley region.

This seaborne trade, involving vessels that sailed along the coast from the Persian Gulf to South Asia, grew rapidly and persists to this day. In about 2350 B.C., King Sargon of Agade in southern Mesopotamia boasted that ships from all these locations were moored at his capital. There are even records of villages of Meluhhans near Lagash and elsewhere in Mesopotamia. The maritime trade, recorded with clay seals and involving not casual exchange but specialized merchants, increased the volume of Sumerian exports and imports dramatically. One shipment of 5,900 kilograms (13,000 pounds) of copper is recorded. According to Possehl, the trade was under Mesopotamian control, much of it conducted through Dilmun. Interestingly, its beginnings coincided with the development of large urban centers in both Mesopotamia and the Indus Valley.

A dramatic increase in seaborne trade may well have been the context in which Harappan civilization developed, trade that amplified the centuries-old symbiosis between highlands and lowlands to the northwest. With the development of these coastal trading routes between the Persian Gulf and the South Asian peninsula, South Asia became part of what some archaeologists call an early world system, which linked the eastern Mediterranean, parts of Eurasia, and western and southern Asia with loose and ever-changing economic ties. It is only fair to point out, however, that many scholars believe that overseas trade was less important than sometimes claimed.

## Mature Harappan Civilization (c. 2500–2050 B.C.)

By 2600 B.C., the Indus people had mastered the basic problems of irrigation and flood control, partly by using millions of fired bricks made of river alluvium and baked with firewood from riverine forests. Mature Harappan civilization developed and flourished over a vast area of just under 1,295,000 square kilometers (500,000 square miles), a region considerably larger than modern Pakistan. The

Indus and Saraswati valleys were the cultural focus of the Harappan civilization, but they were only one part of a much larger, varied civilization whose influences and ties extended over the lowlands of Punjab and Sind, from the highlands of Baluchistan to the deserts of Rajastan, and from the Himalayan foothills to near Bombay. The age-old relationship between highland Baluchistan and the Indus plains placed the Harappans within a larger cultural system, as did their maritime links with the Persian Gulf. A similar kind of relationship may have flourished between the Indus Valley and Gujerat to the south. But Gregory Possehl calls the Harappan civilization "an experiment in sociocultural organization which failed." It was a large system, he says, but one that did not fully mature.

The Harappan civilization was different from that of the predominantly urban Sumerians in Mesopotamia. Possehl makes an analogy with Egypt, where the Upper and Lower Nile were part of the same civilization, but there were always administrative, cultural, and social differences between the two regions. The same may have been true of the Harappan, with Mohenjodaro in Sind and Harappa in the Punjab, Ganweriwala on the Saraswati, and Dholavira (or a similar site) in Gujerat and Saurashtra. These were major regional subdivisions of the Harappan civilization.

## *Cities and Artisans*

Mohenjodaro is by far the largest of the Harappan cities at 120 hectares (296 acres), roughly twice the size of Harappa, 70 hectares (173 acres), and was rebuilt at least nine times, sometimes as a result of disastrous inundations. Widely accepted population estimates, based on densities of modern, somewhat similar settlements, place 35,000 to 40,000 people at Mohenjodaro. Ganweriwala and Dholavira were also major centers, and there were important second-order settlements, among them Kalibangan, Chanhudaro, Dhoraji, and the port community of Lothal.

In each large city, the builders followed an irregular, netlike plan that evolved over many generations. One of Mohenjodaro's excavators, Mortimer Wheeler, described both Mohenjodaro and Harappa as giving an impression of "middle-class prosperity with zealous municipal supervision." A high citadel lies at the west end of each city, protected by great fortifications and flood works (Figure 5.2). Harappa's is 414 meters (460 yards) long and 194 meters (215 yards) wide, surrounded by a forbidding brick wall at least 13.5 meters (45 feet) high. Mohenjodaro's citadel rises 12 meters (40 feet) above the plain, protected by huge flood embankments and a perimeter wall with towers. The public buildings on the summit include a pillared hall almost 27 meters (90 feet) square, perhaps the precinct where rulers appeared in public and gave audiences. There are no spectacular temples or richly adorned shrines. Religious life was centered on a great lustral bath made of bitumen-sealed brickwork and fed by a well (Figure 5.3). An imposing colonnade surrounded the pool, which was approached by sets of steps at both ends. We cannot be sure of the exact use of the bath nor of the rituals that unfolded there, but lustration was an important part of later Indian religions.

**Figure 5.2** The massive walls of the Citadel at Harappa.

**Figure 5.3** The Great Bath on the Citadel, Mohenjodaro.

The rulers of each city looked down on a complex network of at least partially planned streets. The widest thoroughfares at Mohenjodaro were 9 meters (30 feet) wide, the cross streets only half as wide and unpaved (Figure 5.4). Hundreds of standardized houses built to at least five basic designs presented a blind brick facade to the streets and alleys they lined. The more spacious dwellings, perhaps those of the nobility and merchants, were laid out around a central courtyard, where guests may have been received, where food was prepared, and where servants probably worked. Stairways and thick ground walls indicate that some houses had one or even three stories. The larger residences had wells, and they also had bathrooms and toilets that may have been joined to an elaborate public drainage system. There were also groups of single-roomed tenements or workshops at both Harappa and Mohenjodaro where the poorest people lived, many of them presumably laborers.

Recent excavations at Harappa have revealed an urban pattern somewhat different in character from that known at Mohenjodaro and Kalibangan. The city did not consist simply of a citadel and a lower town, but took the form of a cluster of walled mounds within a loosely built-up area. This contrasts with the single lower town area of grid-plan streets and houses found at Mohenjodaro and indicates that toward the edge of the Harappan area the uniformity that is such a striking feature of the Harappan as a whole may have been less pronounced. The radiocarbon dates available from Harappa also suggest that this city lay outside the area of the original Harappan zone and may only have been founded in the late third millennium B.C. As we have seen, settlements further south in Sind, the core Harappan area, go back at least to 2700 B.C.

**Figure 5.4** A street in Mohenjodaro.

## *Technology and Trade*

Some areas of Harappa may have served as bazaars or artisans' quarters, where beadmakers, coppersmiths, cotton weavers, and other specialists plied their trades. The potters' workshops were filled with painted pots decorated with animal figures and everyday, plain, wheel-made vessels manufactured in all Harappan settlements. There were water jars and cooking bowls, storage pots and drinking vessels. Metalworkers cast simple axes in open molds and manufactured chisels, knives, razors, and other utilitarian artifacts. Only a few expert craftspeople made more elaborate objects, such as small figurines. They would make a wax model of the figurine and encase it in clay, which was fired to melt the wax. Then molten copper or bronze was poured into the mold. This lost-wax method is still used by South Asian metalworkers to this day (Figure 5.5).

The technologies developed in Harappan cities were developed centuries earlier in small villages and transferred to urban settings without change. One of the most developed manufactures was the stamp seal, made from steatite or other types of soft rock. Seal workshops have yielded both finished specimens,

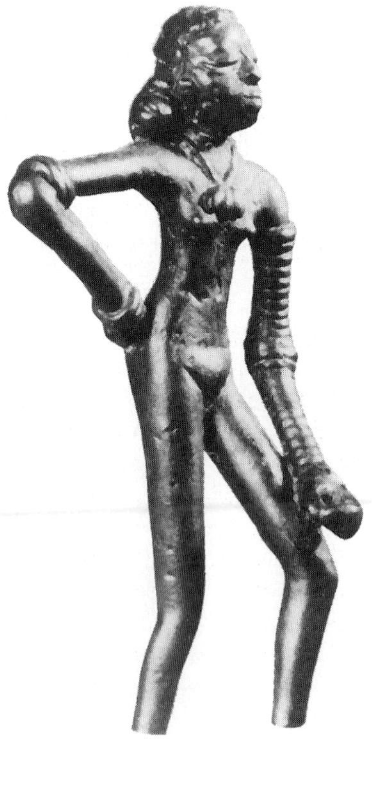

**Figure 5.5** A bronze figurine of a dancing girl from Mohenjodaro. Height: 10.2 centimeters (4 inches).

hardened in a furnace, and blocks of steatite from which the seals were cut as intaglios. For hours, the seal workers would crouch over the tiny squares, expertly cutting representations of animals in profile. They reserved some of their best efforts for religious scenes. Archaeologists at Chanhudaro, south of Mohenjodaro, found a complete beadmaker's shop that gave some idea of the labor needed to produce small ornaments. The beadmakers would prepare agate and carnelian bars about 7.6 centimeters (3 inches) long, which were then ground and polished into shorter, perforated cylinders and hung in necklaces. To experience the beadmaking process, the archaeologists took a Harappan stone-tipped drill and some abrasive pounder from the same workshop and attempted to drill through one of the bead blanks. It took them 20 minutes to drill a small pit in the end of the bead. At that rate, it would have taken 24 hours to drill a single bead!

Some Harappan crafts were organized on the basis of what may have been the earliest manifestation of the Indian caste system. Others, involving more exotic materials such as metals or semiprecious stones, revolved around long-distance trade and may have required some degree of centralized control. But the very uniformity of artifact designs and decorative styles over the Indus Valley region is testimony not to imposed cultural uniformity but to a high level of intercommunity trade among settlements, large and small, over extensive areas of the lowlands. Trade was so important that the Harappan authorities developed a standard weight system to reinforce their trading monopolies. Their standard weight was close to one-half of a modern ounce. Most stone weights found at Mohenjodaro were made of chert in cubic form and organized in series; the smallest were found in jewelers' shops, presumably for weighing precious materials. The weights double from 1 to 2 units, then on to 64, and thereafter to 160 and multiples of 160. Later South Asian societies used a unit known as the *karsa* for the same purpose. This weighed the equivalent of 32 *rattis,* seeds of the Gunja creeper, a measure that would fluctuate slightly from year to year. Four *karsas* weighed almost exactly the same as the basic Harappan unit of a half ounce. Similar devices were used in nineteenth-century South Asian bazaars.

In its heyday, the Harappan civilization formed part of a much wider economic world. Regular caravan routes linked highlands and lowlands. The Harappans even maintained small colonies in Afghanistan, near strategic sources of raw materials. There was extensive trade in gold, copper, and carnelian with central and southern India. But the burgeoning maritime trade routes of the Indian Ocean were of far greater importance. Vessels hugging the coast linked the Indus with the Persian Gulf, where Arabian and African products were to be obtained. The ships that plied these routes never ventured far from shore, but they forged economic ties that were to wax and wane as the fortunes of individual civilizations and societies ebbed and flowed. Centuries later, these same maritime highways and the discovery of the monsoon winds of the open sea brought China, Southeast Asia, South and West Asia, and the Mediterranean world into a vast, ever-changing web of interconnections.

## Political and Social Organization

Harappan political organization remains a mystery. We do not know whether the Indus Valley was ruled by a series of city-states or whether great rulers presided over a territorial state that covered many thousands of square miles. Harappan script is still undeciphered, which makes it impossible to reconstruct historical events or the ebb and flow of political power from one city to another.

We also know little of Harappan social organization and religious beliefs. Those who ruled Harappa and Mohenjodaro remain anonymous, for they never commemorated their deeds on grandiose palace walls and left almost no portraits. One exception is a limestone figure from Mohenjodaro that depicts a thick-lipped, bearded man staring at the world through slitted eyes. He seems to be withdrawn in meditation, perhaps detached from worldly affairs (Figure 5.6). The man wears an embroidered robe that was once inlaid with metal. The only clue to his status is that one shoulder is uncovered, a sign of reverence during the Buddha's lifetime more than 1,500 years later. Conceivably, this is a clue that he was a priest or a priest-ruler. So far, archaeology reveals leadership by rulers, perhaps merchants, ritual specialists, or people who controlled key resources or large areas of land. They seem to have led unostentatious lives marked by a complete lack of priestly pomp or lavish public display. There is nothing of the ardent militarism of the Assyrians or the slavish glorification of the pharaohs.

**Figure 5.6** Limestone sculpture of a bearded man, perhaps a priest or ruler, Mohenjodaro. Height: 19 centimeters (7.4 inches). The rarity of such portrayals underlines the nonrepresentational nature of the Harappan political ideology.

One reason we know so little about Harappan leaders is because their script is still undeciphered. Almost 400 different pictographic symbols have been identified from seals and other short inscriptions, but linguists do not even agree on the language in the script, let alone on the ultimate identity of the Harappans. Some success has been achieved with computer-aided decipherment techniques, which have established the script as logosyllabic, that is, a mixture of sounds and concepts just like Egyptian hieroglyphs, perhaps an early form of Dravidian. The bulk of Indus inscriptions are dated to the Mature Harappan period, c. 2500–2050 B.C. Excavations at Harappa itself have however recovered examples of the script, inscribed on pottery sherds, from earlier layers dated to 2800–2600 B.C. This makes it less likely that the adoption of the script was influenced by contacts with Mesopotamia, since such contacts are not well attested before the middle of the third millennium B.C. There are indeed claims for even earlier examples of Indus script dating back to 3500 B.C.

Some authorities believe that the seals served both as religious symbols and as tags or labels for bundles of merchandise sent to distant Sumer. Enough of the script has been understood to show how many of the short seal inscriptions designate individuals and their titles. Some may describe major figures in the Harappan cosmos, as well as identify scribes and major artisans. Most everyday writing will have been on perishable materials such as ola leaves, traditionally used in South Asia until recent times. Soaked, pounded, and smoothed, these provide a smooth surface into which symbols can be scratched, then made more visible by rubbing across the surface with an ink-soaked cloth. The restricted nature of the surviving Indus inscriptions makes it very difficult to be sure what range of information the script was used to record: whether it was comparable, for example, to the Mesopotamian cuneiform, with important administrative and economic functions, or was employed for a more restricted range of purposes such as ritual or ownership. This is a question to which we shall return in the next chapter when considering the earliest Chinese writing.

Everything points to a centralized government and a stratified Harappan society, with the focus on agriculture and trade. Irrigation produced large surpluses of barley and wheat close to the cities, but many villagers away from the valley and river still practiced dry agriculture. Cotton and dates were also important crops in a society where the state may have controlled many acres of land and where every farmer turned over much of the household crop to the government. The entire agricultural enterprise was a much larger version of the communal village farming that originally had made colonization of the Indus Valley possible, but one that supported a hierarchical, ranked society.

This reconstruction has, however, been challenged by scholars such as Michael Jansen and Gregory Possehl, who argue that the Harappan cities did not form city-states or focal points within a larger territorial state. They argue that the formation of the Mature Harappan system was a relatively rapid process taking place around 2600 B.C., preceded by severe disruption and the burning of many Early Harappan settlements such as Kot Diji. Warfare may have been the cause. What followed, however, was not the result of the military unification of previously independent cities, but another kind of social formation altogether. For a start, there are no structures which can clearly be identified as temples or palaces. Both Harappa and Mohenjodaro housed a comfortable and unpretentious middle class of merchants and officials who lived in standardized brick houses along the cities' narrow streets. The absence of elite dwellings is coupled with an absence of monumental sculpture and elite graves. We have seen how early rulers in Mesopotamia and Egypt understood the importance of royal propaganda—in terms of major buildings and statues—to support their status and their separation from the rest of society. Egyptian royal graves and the rich elite graves from Ur in Mesopotamia provide further indications of social hierarchy and social distance. There is no comparable evidence from the Harappan civilization, and this has led scholars to question whether indeed it was a state at all.

Some have argued that the Harappan centers of Mohenjodaro and Harappa itself were not truly urban, but merely religious centers at which people from the surrounding regions congregated for certain ceremonies. This view is hard to square with the evidence of streets and houses from so many of these sites; it is difficult to argue with the notion that they were indeed cities. Furthermore, though writing does not in itself indicate the existence of a state, the standardization of weights and measures, the standardization of brick sizes, and the similarities in material culture throughout the Harappan realm all argue that there was a strong common bond which held these settlements together. It may indeed prove to be the case that Harappan society was politically decentralized and lacked the kings and rulers of other early urban societies. It is also quite possible that the rulers of the Harappan polity or polities used different devices to promote their authority, which did not depend on monumental display or richly furnished graves. The debate illustrates the difficulty of identifying the state in circumstances where the written evidence—the script—has yet to be deciphered, or where there is no later historical tradition. It also reminds us that early states were not identical, and that there was no tightly defined blueprint to which they must all have adhered.

## *Religious Beliefs*

Like the Sumerians, the Harappans lived in an environment that they modified for their own protection, one in which the annual floods meant a renewal of life and food for the coming year. We can speculate that the primordial roots of South Asian religion may have been age-old fertility cults that served the same function as the goddess Inanna among the Sumerians and mother deities in many other early civilizations. Such cults provided an assurance that life would continue, that the endless cycle of planting and harvest would be renewed. The only clues we have to the origins of Harappan religion come from minute seal impressions and small clay figurines from Harappan villages and cities that depict a female deity with conspicuous breasts and sexual organs. We do not know her name, but she probably embodied earth and life-giving nature for the Indus people.

A seal from Mohenjodaro bears a three-headed figure who sits in the yogic posture and wears a horned headdress. He is surrounded by a tiger, an elephant, a rhinoceros, a water buffalo, and a deer. Some Harappan experts think that the seal represents a forerunner of the great Hindu god Shiva in his role as Lord of the Beasts. Many Harappan seals depict cattle, which may be symbols of Shiva, who was worshiped in several forms. To judge from later beliefs, he may have had a dual role, serving as a fertility god as well as a tamer or destroyer of wild beasts. Shiva gave life by planting the seed but could also destroy any creature, including human beings, at a flick of a finger. In part he may have symbolized the unpredictable dangers of flood and famine that could threaten a village or city. Harappa and Mohenjodaro have yielded dozens of carved phallic symbols and circular stones with round holes, which may represent the teeming womb of Devi, Shiva's consort. Perhaps these are simple prototypes of the Hindu *lingam* and *yoni* symbols, which are found in the temples of Shiva and Devi to this day. If the evidence of the figurines and seals is to be believed, the symbolism of early Indus religion bears remarkable similarities to that of modern Hinduism. Many other elements of more modern South Asian religion may have flourished in Harappan society, among them the use of fire altars in homes, worship with fruit and flowers, meditation, and well-developed astronomical knowledge. These similarities highlight the deeply ingrained conservatism of South Asian society from the earliest moments of Harappan civilization and even further in the past.

## *Collapse (c. 2000 B.C.)*

Harappan civilization reached its peak around 2300 B.C. Three centuries later, Harappa and Mohenjodaro were in decline and were soon abandoned. Their urban populations dispersed into smaller settlements over an enormous area as the volume of long-distance trade declined dramatically, except perhaps in metals (Figure 5.7). The reasons for this change are still little understood, although theories abound.

One of the earliest explanations for this collapse was the invocation of invading Aryans, as set out in the *Rigveda*, a Hindu sacred text which some claimed to be a memory of the battles fought between the newcomers and the indigenous Harappans. British archaeologist Mortimer Wheeler found a few skeletons in the upper levels of Mohenjodaro and speculated that the Harappan cities were overthrown by foreign, Indo-Aryan-speaking invaders, but his evidence is simply too inadequate for such an explanation. Yet the chronology of the Aryan invasions (if indeed they ever occurred) is far from clear, and the *Rigveda* was codified only in around 1000 B.C., a thousand years after the abandonment of Mohenjodaro. Furthermore, recent research has shown that the skeletons concerned seem to have been the victims of disease, hastily buried in abandoned buildings.

Other theories invoke environmental change. Robert Raikes and George Dales argued that the demise of the Indus cities was caused by tectonic movements that raised a natural dam on the source of the Indus River in the area of Sehwan. The waters of the Indus, no longer able to reach the sea, spread out behind this natural dam to create a vast lake which flooded the area around Mohenjodaro and certain other major cities, causing their abandonment. An alternative theory seeks the cause for the demise in the drying up of the Saraswati and Drishadvati rivers, important foci of Indus period settlement, once again owing to tectonic change that caused the

(a) (b)

**Figure 5.7** Rojdi, Pakistan, a Harappan town dating to the period immediately following the abandonment of cities. (a) Excavation of house walls; (b) artist's reconstruction of the same dwellings.

waters flowing from the Himalayas to be progressively caught by streams and rivers flowing eastward into the Ganges floodplain. Yet a third environmental theory proposes that climatic change in the form of greater aridity was to blame. Some of these hypotheses are more plausible than others: Neither the damming of the Indus nor the reduction in rainfall are well supported by the evidence, but the drying-up of the Saraswati is now generally accepted. Whether the resulting disruption was entirely responsible for the demise of the entire Harappan civilization, however, is still open to question. It is important to note that the post-Harappan phase sees a substantial increase in the number of settlements on the margins of the Indus zone, though these are smaller in size than those of Harappan times. This may correspond to a phenomenon of de-urbanization, but it indicates continuity of prosperous agricultural settlement as contrasted with the pattern in Sindh, Cholistan, and Baluchistan, where there is a severe decline in site numbers. Since the latter was the heartland of the Harappan civilization, its failure, operating through a kind of "domino effect," may have caused the changes seen elsewhere in the decline of urbanization and the abandonment of the Harappan script. Thus changes in the natural environment may have struck the major blow, but the way in which this affected the entire area of the Harappan civilization owed much to sociocultural factors.

Botanists have chronicled major ecological changes by using pollen grains from the Indus alluvium. They found that natural tree and grass cover on the floodplain increased between 2400 and 1000 B.C. This thicker tree cover became established just as the farming population was taking advantage of good rains and expanding agricultural production. The pollen counts show both more tree cover and dramatic rises in the proportions of cereal grains and cultivated weeds at the expense of the natural vegetation. A complex multiplier effect seems to have occurred, as rapidly rising village populations became linked to higher crop yields, leading to drastic consequences for the environment. As village populations rose, so did pressure on the land. The farmers cleared and burned off more and more riverside forest and grazed ever-larger herds of cattle on watershed meadows. Pastoral groups grazed their herds seasonally in the empty lands between agricultural communities; they may have played an important role in internal trade networks, for which their animals served as beasts of burden. Acres of forest were burned to bake bricks for the houses of growing villages and expanding towns. Mile after mile of the plains were denuded of their natural vegetation, with drastic consequences for erosion control and the floodplain environment. Deprived of natural controls, the rising floodwaters of summer swept over the plains, carrying everything with them. Confronted with what may have seemed to be the wrath of the gods, the people had only one defense—cooperative flood works and irrigation agriculture that fed more mouths and provided at least a degree of security from the vagaries of the environment.

## Rural Interlude (2000–600 B.C.)

No cities developed in South Asia east of the Indus region until long after the Harappan civilization went into decline. As the highly developed socioeconomic system of the Indus broke down, so urban life vanished, to emerge once again far to the east in the Ganges valley many centuries later. At the same time, many well-developed, but still little known, regional farming cultures flourished both inside the Indus region and beyond. The second millennium B.C. was a period of vital importance in South Asian history. By 1500 B.C., rice cultivation had taken hold in the Ganges basin, opening up a new environment for farming where conditions were unsuitable for wheat and barley cultivation. At the same time, millets, some of them of African origin, became important in the Gujerat region, and were especially suited to the more humid parts of southern India. The effect of these new crops may have been to widen the area where agriculture was practiced, thereby reducing the environmental circumscription that may have been one of the bases of Harappan civilization.

During the second millennium B.C., flourishing village settlements existed through northern South Asia, from the Indus plains and foothills in the west to the Ganges zone in the east. Historically, this is also the so-called Vedic period, when according to tradition, Indo-Aryan-speaking people spread into the subcontinent, an event described in the *Samhita*, a compilation of the hymns (Vedas) of the *Rigveda*. Many of the hymns were composed centuries earlier, then passed from generation to generation by word of mouth.

The Indo-Iranian languages are one of the branches of the vast Indo-European family of languages, which originated on the Eurasian steppes. The development and spread of Indo-European tongues is one of the great controversies of both linguistics and archaeology. Archaeologists have tried in vain to associate different prehistoric cultures with the arrival of Indo-European languages, but there is still no consensus. Much of the controversy centers on Europe, but Iran and South Asia were also deeply affected by these changes. Many scholars argue that Indo-European-speaking peoples spread across the Iranian plateau into South Asia during the second millennium B.C., where they intermarried with indigenous groups. Thus were born the Indo-Aryan languages spoken throughout South Asia today. But another school of thought believes there was no invasion, that Indo-Aryan developed indigenously in South Asia and was present there from a much earlier period. They point to features of the Harappan civilization which appear to prefigure later Indian features, such as the importance of bathing and purification (prefigured in the Great Bath of Mohenjodaro), and the yoga position of a figure represented on Indus seals who appears to adopt the pose of the Hindu god Shiva.

Whatever the historical reality behind the *Rigveda*, archaeology shows clearly that by the early first millennium B.C., agricultural villages were proliferating on the Ganges plain, aided by the adoption of iron metallurgy. Iron tools accelerated rice cultivation on the Ganges plain. What had previously been numerous small tribal territories had by 600 B.C. coalesced or been incorporated into 16 major kingdoms or republics concentrated around the urban centers of the Ganges plain. By 550 B.C., at least five of the Ganges cities are known to have had massive stone or mud-brick fortifications. The mud-brick fortifications of Ujjain measured 75 meters (246 feet) wide at the base, were 14 meters (46 feet) high, and extended over 5 kilometers (3 miles). By the third century, some of the cities were very large indeed. Ahicchatra, for example, covered an area of nearly 180 hectares (450 acres). Pataliputra, the capital of Magadha, may have been even bigger, and it eventually became the capital of the Mauryan empire.

## Early Historic Cities (600–150 B.C.)

City life in the Ganges valley marked the beginning of the classic period of South Asian civilization. The new cities became economic powerhouses and centers of great intellectual and religious ferment. Brahmanism was the dominant religion during the early first millennium, a form of Hinduism that placed great emphasis on ritual and sacrifice. The Brahmin class exercised priestly authority over all aspects of life through their responsibility for the transmission of the sacred tradition and the performance of sacrificial rituals. But revolutionary philosophers of the sixth century B.C. like Buddha and Makhali Gosala challenged Brahmanism with revolutionary doctrines that militated against sacrifice. Buddhism, with its teachings of personal spiritual development, spread rapidly, becoming the dominant religion in the north within five centuries.

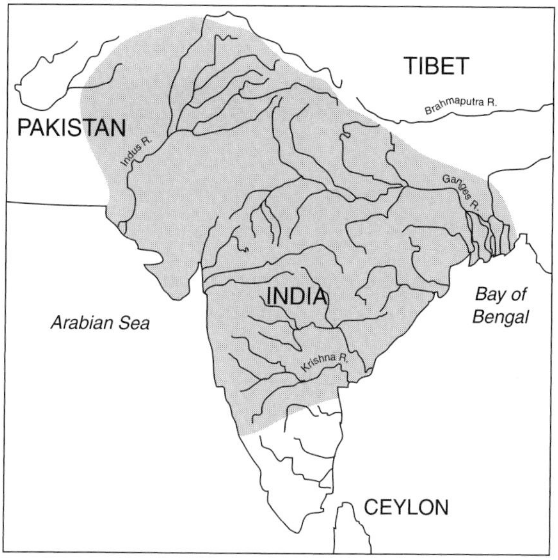


**Figure 5.8** Map of the extent of the Mauryan empire.

Meanwhile, outside powers eyed the fabled riches of the subcontinent. King Darius of Persia invaded the northwest in 516 B.C. and incorporated the Indus Valley into the Persian Empire. Two centuries later, Alexander the Great ventured to the Indus River and brought Greek culture to the area. In the northeast, the leaders of the Ganges kingdoms had fought constantly until the sixth century B.C., when the kingdom of Magadha began to grow at the expense of its neighbors. The great ruler Chandragupta Maurya of Magadha benefited from the power vacuum following Alexander the Great's conquests and carved out a huge empire (the Mauryan empire), which extended from Nepal and the northwest deep into the Deccan (Figure 5.8). His grandson Asoka presided over the empire at its height, between 269 and 232 B.C., seeking to unify its diverse people by a well-defined moral and ethical code based on Buddhist principles, which he promulgated with inscriptions throughout the empire. His capital at Pataliputra (Patna) in Magadha extended nearly 14 kilometers (9 miles) along the Ganges. Great Buddhist monuments like the *stupas* (temples) at Sarnath and Sanchi were built at this time.

Magadha and other northern cities in Asoka's empire prospered greatly from overland trade routes that led northwest to Charsada, Taxila, and other frontier cities. Far to the east, the port of Tamluk at the mouth of the Ganges gave access to new and expanding marine trade routes to Southeast Asia. And as the Mauryan empire came to an end in 185 B.C., the newly discovered monsoon winds of the Indian Ocean linked the South Asian coast with the Roman world and its insatiable demands for ivory, spices, and fine textiles from South Asian markets. Roman coins have come from ancient ports in the south, as well as from Arikamedu, a trading station on the east coast of the Deccan.

By Roman times, South Asia was part of a vast trading network that linked the Mediterranean world to all parts of the Indian Ocean and, indirectly, to new sources of raw materials many sea miles to the east. New South Asian connections were a significant factor in the development of indigenous civilizations in Southeast Asia (described in Chapter 13).

## Summary

Food production and animal domestication began in the northwest before the third millennium B.C. The new economies were probably introduced from the west. Many of these communities maintained close trading and herding relationships with villages in highland Baluchistan. A hierarchy of larger communities developed in the Indus Valley during the fourth millennium B.C., culminating in the mature Harappan civilization of c. 2700 to 2000 B.C. The Harappan civilization was based on a number of large cities, including Harappa and Mohenjodaro, that produced large agricultural surpluses. Its prosperity came from the intensive cultivation of wheat, barley, and cotton, combined with maritime trade with Mesopotamia. We know little of Harappan social organization or of the society's religious beliefs, which may in part have foreshadowed some of the principles of Hinduism. Harappan civilization collapsed just after 2000 B.C. Harappa and Mohenjodaro were abandoned, and their inhabitants were dispersed into village communities. The ensuing centuries saw the center of gravity shift east to the Ganges valley with the growth of rice cultivation. By 600 B.C., 16 kingdoms flourished on the Ganges plains, eventually united into the Mauryan empire in the fourth century B.C. Buddhism became the dominant religion of the Mauryan empire, replacing earlier Brahmanic teachings of ritual and sacrifice. These developments took hold as South Asia became part of the enormous trade network that developed out of the discovery of the monsoon winds of the Indian Ocean.

## Guide to Further Reading

A general summary of early South Asian civilization can be found in Bridget and Raymond Allchin, *The Rise of Civilization in India and Pakistan* (Cambridge: Cambridge University Press, 1982). Urban development in both the Harappan and Early Historic periods is described by D. K. Chakrabarti, *The Archaeology of Ancient Indian Cities* (Delhi: Oxford University Press, 1998). Raymond Allchin, *The Archaeology of Early Historic South Asia* (Cambridge: Cambridge University Press, 1995) covers later periods.

The Indus civilization has spawned a proliferating literature. The classic but much outdated source is Mortimer Wheeler, *The Indus Civilization*, 3rd ed. (Cambridge: Cambridge University Press, 1968). Gregory Possehl, ed., *Harappan Civilization*, 2nd ed. (New Delhi: Oxford and IBH Publishing, 1993) contains a series of valuable essays. A recent overview is J. M. Kenoyer, *Ancient Cities of the Indus Valley Civilization* (Karachi: Oxford University Press, 1998). See also Jane McIntosh, *A Peaceful Realm: The Rise and Fall of the Indus Civilization* (Boulder, CO: Westview Press, 2001). For Harappan script, see Asko Parpola, *Deciphering the Indus Script* (Cambridge: Cambridge University Press, 1994). Harappan overseas trade is covered by S. Ratnagar, *Encounters: The Westerly Trade of the Indus Civilization* (Delhi: Oxford University Press, 1981) and, more recently, "The Bronze Age: Unique Instance of a Pre-Industrial World System?" *Current Anthropology* 43 (2001): 351–379. The political organization of the Harappan cities is discussed in Gregory L. Possehl, "Sociocultural Complexity without the State," in *Archaic States*, eds. Gary M. Heinemann and Joyce Marcus (Santa Fe: School of American Research Press, 1998), pp. 261–291.

For Indo-Aryan languages, see J. P. Mallory, *In Search of the Indo-Europeans* (London and New York: Thames and Hudson, 1991). For later archaeology, see Anna King, "Some Archaeological Problems Regarding Gangetic Cultures in Early Historical India," and James Heitzman, "Early Buddhism, Trade and Empire," in Kenneth A. R. Kennedy and Gregory L. Possehl, eds., *Studies in the Archaeology and Palaeoanthropology of South Asia* (New Delhi: Oxford and IBH Publishing, 1984), pp. 109–119 and 121–137.

*Chapter 6*

# The First Chinese Civilizations

Bronze head from a ritual pit at Sanxingdui, China, c. 1200–1000 B.C.

*The bronze caster wiped the sweat from his brow with his apron, then took up the long tongs and drew the heavy crucible, full of molten bronze, from the furnace. With careful concentration he swung the crucible to one side until it was directly above the strange object of fired clay, with its funnel-like opening in the top. This was a piece mold, an intricate assemblage of pieces of fired clay, bearing the shapes and decoration of a ritual vessel on their inner face. Gently tipping the crucible, the worker poured the molten bronze slowly and steadily into the opening. There was a hiss as hot air issued from tiny holes in the sides of the clay mold, but silence returned as the bronze settled and began to cool. It would take several hours before the mold could be taken apart and removed. Then a little more work would be needed to finish the vessel, cleaning up the elaborate animal-mask decoration with a chisel, polishing the surface, and cutting away any excess metal that had formed between the joins of the mold. But he felt well pleased with the work. It would no doubt earn a handsome reward from the Shang nobleman who had ordered it. He would use it in banquets, invoking the ancestors, and pass it on to his heirs, until at last, one day, it would be placed with one of them in the grave, to serve them in the afterlife as it had in this.*

Bronze ritual vessels are one of the most famous products of the first Chinese civilization. It takes its name from the Shang dynasty, which ruled the valley of the Huanghe in the second millennium B.C. The ritual vessels were the mark and preserve of an elite group, those who governed the Shang and neighboring states. They relied on the ancestors to guide and protect them, seeking advice through divination and placating them by ritual banquets served in these sumptuous bronze vessels.

Our understanding of early civilization in China has been greatly modified in recent years by the realization that the Shang culture of the Huanghe valley was not the only center of bronze working and state formation at this period. Important discoveries in Mongolia, the Yangzi valley, and southwestern China (Sichuan province) have shown the existence of other traditions, contemporary with the Shang and combining Shang features alongside local material to create their own distinctive, elite cultures. Thus early civilization in China was not a single-center phenomenon but a pattern of multiple, interconnected core areas of varying size and importance. Shang elite culture was simply the most prevalent of these and the Shang state the best documented from historical records.

In this chapter we consider what may be learned of Bronze Age civilizations in China from the evidence of archaeology and written records, not least among the latter being the oracle bone inscriptions left by the Shang rulers at Anyang. First, however, we discuss the origin and development of the first Chinese civilization, beginning with the farming communities of the Neolithic period. Chinese society in historical times was characterized by the search for order and harmony and a strong respect for tradition. What is striking is that Chinese civilization accumulated its traditional features gradually over many centuries: from the basic cultigens, rice and millet, to drinking vessels, lacquer and jade, palaces and writing, and a rigidly hierarchical society (Table 6.1).

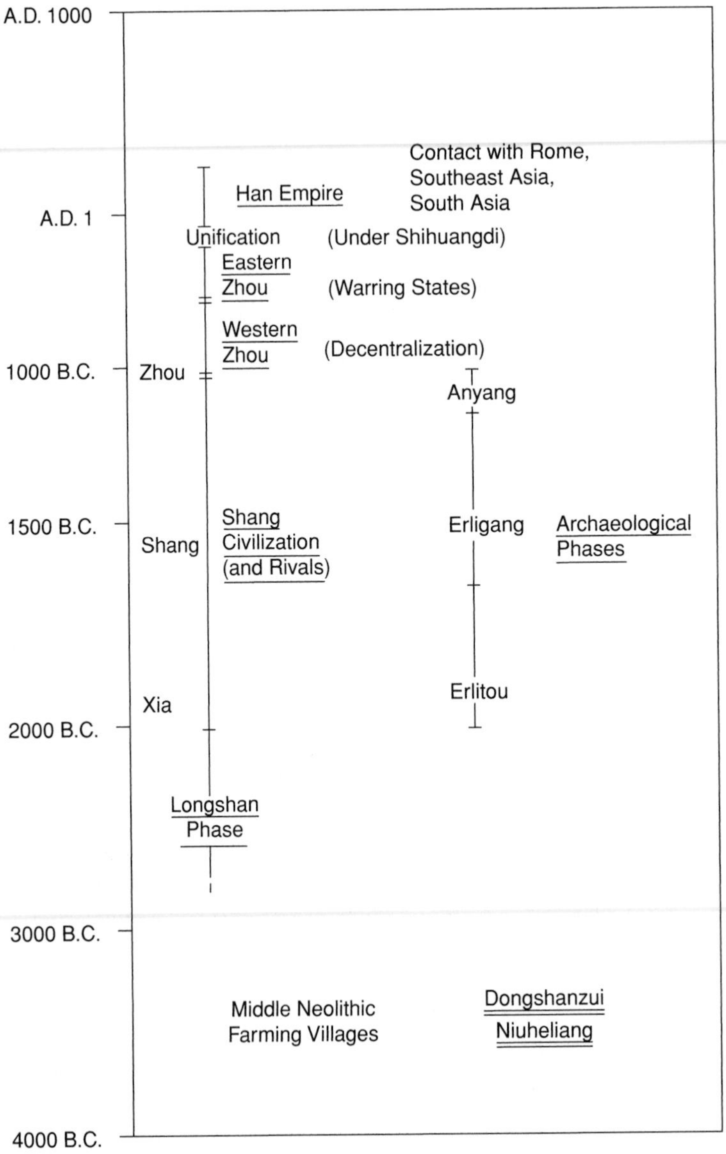


**Table 6.1** Chronological chart of Chinese civilization, Neolithic to Han.

## Setting

China encompasses an enormous area of Asia, from the very high mountains and plateaux of the Hindu Kush, Tibet, and the Himalayas in the far west; to the Pacific coast and low-lying, hot subtropical regions of the south; and to the great prairie-steppes that separate the boreal forests of Siberia from China's cultivated lands.

The great central plain of China in the north covers more than 300,000 square kilometers (115,000 square miles), bounded by the Huanghe (Yellow River) in the north and the Yangzi to the south. The Huanghe flows through rolling loess country, formed by vast accumulations of glacial windblown dust laid down during the Ice Age. In its upper reaches it turns sharply northward to encompass the arid Ordos Desert, upstream of the so-called Huanghe corridor where the Shang state was formed. In these northern lands, the dry and permeable loess soils and the cold winters necessitate the growing of drought-resistant cereal crops such as millet.

The boundary between northern and southern China follows the Qinling Mountains in the west and the Huai River to the Pacific coast. Southern China is much warmer and better watered, with more equable winters and hot summers, which are ideal for rice cultivation in waterlogged fields. Thus, for many centuries, two distinct agricultural traditions developed. Northern China had dry, rainfall-supported farming of hardy cereal crops, while southern farmers subsisted on many forms of rice. The boundaries between the two provinces were never rigid, however, with many variations in local farming practices that resulted from both cultural preferences and favorable and unfavorable climatic conditions.

## Millet and Rice (c. 7000–4500 B.C.)

The first Chinese farming cultures appeared suddenly in the archaeological record as early as 7000 B.C. But, right from the beginning, northern and southern Chinese farmers pursued quite different agricultural regimes.

### *The North: Yangshao and Cishan*

It was a Swedish geologist, J. G. Andersson, who must be credited with the discovery of the Chinese Neolithic. In 1921 he was given polished stone axes, similar to those of Neolithic Europe, and red pottery bowls, painted with elaborate designs in brown or black, from Yangshao-cun in the great loess plain of the Huanghe basin. These first discoveries of the Chinese Neolithic became known as the Yangshao culture. With the advent of radiocarbon dates, however, it has become clear that the Yangshao is far from the earliest Neolithic culture of northern China. Much earlier is the site of Cishan, at the foot of the mountains overlooking the lower plain of the Huanghe. The structural remains at Cishan are merely storage pits and sunken house foundations, but found among them were pottery vessels and evidence of agricultural activity: grindstones; hoes and reaping knives; bones of domestic dogs, pigs, and chickens; and abundant carbonized remains of foxtail millet. These leave no doubt that Cishan was a village of early Chinese farmers, growing millet and raising pigs and chickens on the edge of the northern plain. Radiocarbon dates from sites like Cishan fall in the late seventh or early sixth millennium B.C. and suggest that millet farming may have begun in this region as early as 7000 B.C. It was a pattern that was to continue for thousands of years.

Cishan pottery bears less sophisticated decoration than the later Yangshao painted wares, but the striking feature is the prominence of tripod vessels—bowls with three tapering feet, enabling them to stand upright on an uneven surface. They are not the first pottery in China; coarse-ware sherds from Nanzhuangtou in the northeast have been dated to around 10,000 B.C., and cord-marked sherds from cave sites such as Xianrendong in the south may be equally early. But the Xianrendong ceramics have pointed bases, and though domesticated rice has been found there it was in no sense a farming village. The Cishan tripod vessels, however, stand at the beginning of a long sequence. Tripod vessels—by then in bronze—were still being manufactured in the Shang period, over 4,000 years later.

## *The South: Hemudu and Pengdoushan*

Millet was, and remains, a primarily north Chinese crop, although it is also grown on Taiwan. Further south, the staple cultigen was rice. Here the key site is Hemudu, on the edge of a former lake south of modern Shanghai, beyond the Yangzi delta. This caused something of a sensation when it was investigated in the 1970s, for it demonstrated conclusively what had long been suspected, that the development of farming communities in southern China was both different from and independent of that of northern China. Radiocarbon dates showed that Hemudu was founded around 5000 B.C. and was hence somewhat later in date than the earliest farming villages of northern China. There was no question of influence from the north, however, since in almost every respect Hemudu was distinctive and original. The houses, for instance, were not pit-based dwellings but were made of wood, raised on posts a meter above the marshy ground; waterlogging was the reason for the well-preserved state in which they were found. There was also pottery—with cord decoration and occasional incised or painted designs of plants and animals—round or flat-based, without the tripod feet of the north but also without the pointed bases of the nearby, but earlier, Xianrendong cave. As we have seen, Xianrendong also has early remains of domesticated rice.

Recent discoveries at Pengdoushan have suggested that rice farming in the middle Yangze valley, upstream from Hemudu, might be even earlier. Rice husks of a large-grained domestic variety have been found at this site in levels dated between 7000 and 5500 B.C. and associated with remains of rectangular, timber-framed houses. If the Pengdoushan dates are confirmed, it will mean that rice farming in the Yangzi valley began at least as long ago as millet farming in the Huanghe basin. For the moment, however, Hemudu remains the best known of the early rice-farming settlements.

The finds from Hemudu testify to both large-scale farming and animal husbandry. There were hoes, made from animal shoulder blades; wooden sticks and mallets; bones of domestic dogs, pigs, and water buffalo; and enormous quantities of cultivated rice, both *Oryza sativa indica* and *Oryza sativa sinica*, the two major subspecies. These were found in rubbish layers up to 0.5 meters (2 feet) thick, which had accumulated on the waterlogged ground beneath the houses.

The marshy land around Hemudu made it an ideal location for the cultivation of wet rice. Much of the area is covered by peat today, and in prehistoric times it was a patchwork of ponds and rivers, with forests on the drier land between. Whether wild rice grew locally is still a matter of dispute. The wild progenitors grow today in a belt of territory stretching from southernmost China to northeast India. If that had been the same in the Neolithic, the inhabitants of Hemudu and similar sites must have taken the crop from further south. Rice farming at Hemudu, on the one hand, may have been the result of a steady attempt to expand rice's natural range, the grains being planted further and further north. On the other hand, around 5000 B.C. wild rice may have grown in natural conditions as far north as the Yangzi delta. Its domestication by the people of Hemudu might then have been purely a local undertaking. Cishan and Hemudu represent the twin pillars of early Chinese village life: millet and pigs and chickens in the north; rice and water buffalo in the south. Cishan, with its tripod vessels, also shows the first stage in the development of distinctive and traditional pottery types, the precursors of the ritual bronzes that were such an important feature of early historic society in China. Hemudu, too, has its cultural "first": a red, lacquered wooden bowl. Lacquerware was to become another typical feature of Chinese civilization.

## Symbolism in the Middle Neolithic (4500–2700 B.C.)

By 4500 B.C. farming villages had spread to many regions of China, and a wide diversity of cultural traditions had emerged. During the Middle Neolithic (4500–3000 B.C.), Chinese societies became increasingly complex, and evidence of social hierarchy began to appear. A number of separate centers developed: in Manchuria in the northeast; on the edge of the steppe zone in the northwest; in the lower Yangzi valley; in the Shandong peninsula; and in the Huanghe basin, traditional birthplace of the first Chinese civilization.

### *Liangzhu Jades*

The earliest and most significant of these regional developments is the appearance of a suite of special symbolic artifacts in the Yangzi delta area, associated with powerful individuals. At Sidun, one individual had achieved sufficient prominence to command burial under a mound 20 meters (65 feet) high, accompanied by over 100 objects of jade. These included rings, tubes, and other ornaments, all expertly worked. Sidun belonged to the Liangzhu culture (c. 3300–2200 B.C.), which is particularly renowned for its early tradition of jade working. Jade is a general term for a family of fine translucent stones, including nephrite, tremolite, and chrysolite. It was clearly a valued material in the Middle Neolithic and remained so in China until recent times, being considered even more precious than gold. The richness of the Liangzhu jade-working tradition may have owed much to the proximity of local sources near Lake Tai in the lower Yangzi plain. Its significance goes further than the mere use of jade, however, for the designs of many of the pieces continued into later periods. This is most notable in the case of the flat, polished rings *(bi)* and the rectangular tubes with square facets along their corners and a longitudinal central perforation *(cong)*. We do not know their meaning in Middle Neolithic times, but in historic China the *bi* was the symbol of heaven and the *cong* of earth. The discovery of the two together in the grave at Sidun suggests that even at this early date, these were symbols of particular potency.

Less spectacular than Sidun, but also very revealing for the nature of Liangzhu society, are two small cemeteries of elite graves excavated at Yao Shan and Fan Shan. There, too, carved jades were abundant, and some of the most elaborate have been reconstructed as ornaments attached to ritual headdresses. The individuals buried in these graves held high status and probably wielded political power. From the nature of the jades and by analogy with later periods, we can also suggest that they acted as shamans, intermediaries between the world of the living and the world of nature and the ancestors.

The geographical location of the Liangzhu culture gives these early jades further significance. The Liangzhu area lies outside the Huanghe basin, where the Shang civilization later emerged; yet many of the jades carry theriomorphic motifs very similar to the *taotie* designs of later Shang bronzes. Furthermore, Liangzhu *bi* and *cong* are not restricted to the Liangzhu area but are found in other regions of China, where they represent the spread of Liangzhu influence. All in all, it is clear that Liangzhu in the late fourth and early third millennia B.C. was a center of great cultural influence and innovation, perhaps a powerful chiefdom or protostate. The fact that it lost its preeminent position to the Shang in the second millennium B.C. should not obscure its important contribution to early Chinese civilization. The Liangzhu culture has one further claim to fame, which we consider again later: It has what is probably the earliest evidence of writing in China.

## *Neolithic Manchuria: The Niuheliang Temple*

A rather different tradition is represented in northeastern China, beyond the Great Wall. The key sites here are Dongshanzui and Niuheliang, which belong to the Hongshan culture (c. 4000–3000 B.C.). This culture is characterized by a settlement pattern of small scattered villages with ceremonial sites and elaborate burials. At Dongshanzui, Chinese archaeologists have recently discovered two related structures: a small, circular paved area, 2.5 meters (8 feet) across, and a rectangular area, 11.8 meters (38 feet 8 inches) long by 9.5 meters (31 feet) wide, defined by curbstones. These are interpreted as ritual monuments, a verdict reinforced by the discovery of fragments of clay statues. Similar statues, many of them life-sized but including parts of noses and ears three times as large, were excavated at Niuheliang. There was also a complete life-sized clay head, with blue-green jade inset for the eyes. This was found in a cruciform structure 25 meters (82 feet) long, with multiple subterranean chambers. The identification of the clay face as female has led archaeologists to label this structure the Goddess Temple. The Dongshanzui and Niuheliang sites are dated to around 3500 B.C.

The discoveries at these Manchurian sites indicate the presence of a flourishing regional tradition in northeast China in the fourth and third millennia B.C., running parallel with the Liangzhu culture in the southeast. It, too, may have been a major chiefdom or even a protostate. In most respects, the Manchurian and Liangzhu traditions are very different, but they do share one feature: the use of ritual jades. (Those of Liangzhu were discussed in the previous section.) In Manchuria, jade working is even older, beginning in the sixth millennium B.C. This is demonstrated by the discovery of eight carved jades at the important early farming site of Chahai near Fuxin. Four of the Chahai jades are of *jue* slit-disk form, a distinctive type that became traditional in the Shang and Zhou periods. Thus it seems that in Manchuria, too, as in the Liangzhu area, societies developed the use of ritual jades at an early date, and these ritual forms were later adopted in the Shang area. The conclusion must be that the elite Shang culture of the Huanghe basin was formed through a process of cultural eclecticism. It clearly owed much not only to its immediate local Huanghe antecedents but also to developments in surrounding regions of China.

## Elite Traditions in the Longshan Phase (2700–2000 B.C.)

So far we have been reviewing general developments in different parts of China during the early and middle phases of the Neolithic. If, however, we are searching for the immediate origins of the most famous of Chinese Bronze Age civilizations, that of the Shang, the obvious place to look is at the cultures that immediately precede it in the Shang core area: the middle valley of the Huanghe.

The Late Neolithic cultures of this area are known as Longshan. This phase is divided into some half a dozen regional types, which fall within the same time bracket (2700–2000 B.C.) and are sometimes described as forming an *interaction sphere*. This term indicates that these regional groups were in contact with one another and were actively borrowing cultural features from one another. The result was a process of cultural convergence that culminated in the Shang Bronze Age, which followed the end of Longshan. The fuel for this process was provided by the emergence of elite groups who struggled to emulate and surpass one another by acquiring the newly established trappings of power and status. This resulted in the rise of a cultural sphere of increasing homogeneity. It must be borne in mind, however, that most of China did not participate in this process and that rival traditions developed in other regions. These will be discussed later, but first we must turn to the Shang.

### *Pottery and Ritual*

Longshan potters made a highly distinctive form of glossy, black pottery, which showed a new competence in both form and firing. Shaped on the wheel, classic Longshan ware was plain or simply decorated and was fired at high temperatures to give a crisp, thin-walled product. The high temperatures needed for this pottery led to innovations in kiln design, resulting in kilns that could achieve temperatures of around 1,200 degrees centigrade (2,192 degrees Fahrenheit), sufficient for the smelting and casting of copper. It is no coincidence that some of the earliest copper objects from China are a pair of awls from the Longshan site of Sanlihe. Some of the pottery vessels seem to imitate metal types, and Wangchenggang has yielded a fragment of a copper alloy vessel. In Shang times, the possession of a set of bronze ritual vessels was the prerequisite for elite status. Wangchenggang may have been an elite center, just the kind of place one would expect such vessels to be found. The finest Longshan pottery—the black, lustrous box, jar, and cup—may have been the ceramic antecedents, and the Wangchenggang fragments might well mark the transition from pottery to metal for such elite ritual vessels.

Another innovation of the Longshan groups was the adoption of scapulomancy—the practice of divination by applying heated implements to animal shoulder blades and turtle shells. In Shang times, professional diviners interpreted the resulting cracks in terms of answers from the gods to specific questions from the ancestors, which had been put to them beforehand. We know this was the custom in Shang times because many of the so-called oracle bones were inscribed with details of both the question and the resulting answer. The Longshan oracle bones bear no inscriptions but are presumably evidence of the same practice in earlier centuries.

## *The First Chinese Writing*

Despite the absence of oracle bone inscriptions, there is evidence of the early use of writing in the Longshan culture. This takes the form of two potsherds, discovered in 1992 and 1993, having short incised "texts." Neither bears any evident resemblance to later Chinese writing, and they may well belong to a regional tradition that subsequently died out.

Of roughly the same age as the Longshan examples (c. 2500–2000 B.C.) are two incised pottery vessels from the later stages of the Liangzhu culture of southeast China. Here again, there are whole groups of signs that seem to indicate a running text. It is this that distinguishes the Liangzhu and Longshan inscriptions from the potters' marks used in parts of Neolithic China since at least the fifth millennium B.C. The potters' marks usually occur in isolation, not in groups.

The Liangzhu and Longshan inscriptions belong to two separate traditions, and their existence emphasizes once again how a number of cultural traditions were developing in parallel in different regions of China during the third millennium B.C. The Shang was only one of these, though on current showing it was by far the most spectacular.

## *Walls and Warfare*

Perhaps the most significant of all Longshan innovations was the appearance of rectangular defensive enclosures. These varied in size from 17 hectares (42 acres) at Chengziyai to 0.75 hectares (1.8 acres) at Wangchenggang. The walls were of a special Chinese construction known as *hang tu*, or "rammed earth," and were the earliest examples of this technique. It consisted of pouring regular layers of loose earth, some 10 to 15 centimeters (4 to 6 inches) thick, between parallel lines of timber shuttering—rather in the way that concrete is poured today. Then the workers compacted the layers by pounding them with long wooden poles, some 3 to 4 centimeters (1 to 1.5 inches) in diameter. Once one layer was finished another would be poured on top, and the process was repeated until the desired height was reached. Longshan walls made in this way were up to 10 meters (35 feet) thick and sometimes survive to a height of several meters; the horizontal marks left by the timber shuttering are clearly visible on their sides.

The gate structure at Pingliangtai confirms that these were defensive works since it boasts rectangular guardhouses of large sun-dried bricks on either side of the entranceway. There is other evidence, too, that these were violent times: At the Longshan settlement of Jiangou a number of people had been thrown into two dry wells, some decapitated and others showing signs of struggle. If the people of Jiangou suffered a violent fate, there is evidence that they themselves inflicted similar suffering on others. Six skulls had been placed as a foundation deposit beneath one of the houses, all with signs of wounds or scalping.

What is not clear is whether the rammed-earth enclosures were ordinary settlements or special elite residences. The construction of the walls indicates centralization of authority, and within them are houses and craft areas. Toward the end of the Longshan period, however, raised platforms of rammed earth began to appear within the enclosures. These rectangular structures are interpreted (by analogy with later periods) as the foundations of small palaces or elite residences, especially since they incorporate human sacrifices in their foundations.

The archaeology of the Longshan culture suggests a pattern of warring elites, struggling to maintain their position or gain greater ascendancy over their neighbors. It also indicates that ritual vessels (first high-quality pottery, later copper or bronze) were the all-important mark of elite status. In this as in so many respects, Longshan directly prefigures the full civilization of the Shang Bronze Age.

## Three Dynasties: Xia, Shang, and Zhou (before 2000 B.C.–1027 B.C.)

Contemporary written records of early Chinese history do not really begin until the Han period, in the last two centuries B.C. One reason for this is that many of them were written on perishable materials such as silk, bamboo, or wood. Another is that the first emperor of China, Qin Shihuangdi, acting on the advice of his prime minister, Li Si, ordered the destruction of all historical documents except those relating to his own home state, Qin. Nonetheless, enough survived for Chinese historians of the Han period (206 B.C.–A.D. 220) to trace the main events of Chinese history well back into the Bronze Age. The scheme they came up with was based on a sequence of three major dynasties: Xia, Shang, and Zhou, leading up to the accession of Qin Shihuangdi in 256 B.C.

"When Yi (founder of the Xia dynasty) assembled the lords at Tushan there were ten thousand states that came carrying jades and silks. At the time when Cheng Tang (of the Shang dynasty) received the mandate, more than three thousand states remained. When Wu Wang (of the Zhou dynasty) viewed the troops, there were eighteen hundred states" (Chang, 1986, p. 307). Thus did the historian Gu Zuyu, writing in the seventeenth century A.D., summarize the course of early Chinese history, outlining the increasing centralization of royal power as one dynasty replaced another. His concept was of a China gradually unified under a single ruling house. In this chapter and Chapter 14 we see just how well Gu Zuyu's outline history agrees with the evidence of archaeology for the pattern of development of the first Chinese kingdoms.

## *Xia and Shang*

The traditional Chinese historical narrative begins with three shadowy mythological rulers—Fu Xi, the common ancestor; Shen Nong, first planter of crops; and Zhu Rong, inventor of fire. Five equally mythological emperors follow before we arrive at the beginning of Chinese history proper, with the Xia, first of the Three Dynasties. We know from the sequence of the Three Dynasties that the Xia was supposed to precede the Shang, but both when and where the Xia dynasty reigned remains in doubt. Astronomical observations preserved in later records give a possible fix through an eclipse that took place in the reign of Zhong Kang, fourth king of the Xia dynasty. American historian Hung-hsiang Chou and astronomer Kevin Pang have calculated that if this observation is accurate, then the eclipse in question took place in 1876 B.C. As for location, the study of place-names associated with the Xia in historical records points to the modern province of Henan, in the middle valley of the Huanghe.

Henan is in the heart of the Longshan culture area and hence a perfectly logical place for the first Chinese states to appear. Its importance in developments of the period was borne out by the discovery in 1957 of the site of Erlitou, a major center that belonged to the very earliest period of the Chinese Bronze Age.

Here, a note on chronology and terminology may be helpful. Radiocarbon dates for sites of the Erlitou phase run from a little before 2000 B.C. to around 1750 B.C. This marks the first phase of the Chinese Bronze Age, a period that continues past the end of the Shang dynasty into the first millennium B.C. In archaeological terms, the Erlitou phase is followed by the Erligang and Anyang phases. Some authors incorporate all three phases under the heading Shang, so that Erlitou equals Early Shang, Erligang equals Middle Shang, and Anyang equals Late Shang. That may be a convenient archaeological classification, but in historical terms Erlitou is more probably equated with the period of the shadowy Xia dynasty and may indeed have been one of their capitals. The following dynasty, the more famous Shang, overthrew the Xia, probably in the eighteenth century B.C. But in terms of cultural style—in the decoration of bronze ritual vessels, for example—no distinction can be made between Xia and Shang. Thus the name *Shang* can be used for both the historical dynasty and the archaeological culture. The bronzes of the Erlitou phase are already described as Shang in style. The Xia and Shang dynasties are merely two parts of a single Shang culture, beginning in 2000 B.C. and ending when the last Shang king was overthrown by the Zhou dynasty in 1027 B.C. Therefore, we will set aside the historical distinction between Xia and Shang dynasties and deal with the centuries 2000–1027 B.C. as a single archaeological period, which we refer to as Shang (see Figure 6.1).

The origins of the first Chinese state lie, as we have seen, in the preceding Longshan culture of the central northern plains. In a recent study, archaeologist Li Liu has attempted to follow in detail the development of the Shang state from clusters of Longshan sites, which he interprets as chiefdoms. It might be expected that the state would emerge earliest from among the most complex of these chiefdoms, but this is not what his study has shown. The complex Longshan chiefdoms were probably located in the Taosi region within the sharp bend of the Huanghe, centered on the largest site of the period, Taosi, covering some 300

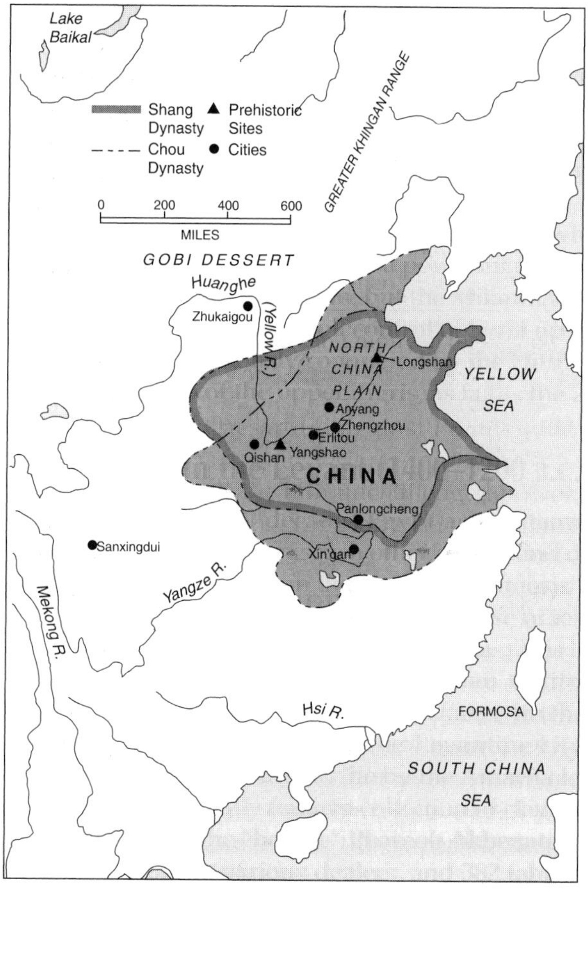


**Figure 6.1** Map of major Shang period sites: Anyang, Panlongcheng, Erlitou, Zhengzhou, Qishan, Sanxingdui, Zhukaigou, Xin'gan.

hectares. This is larger than many of the early cities of southern Mesopotamia or the Indus valley, but in terms of functions and complexity it is classified as the center of a large and complex chiefdom rather than a state. Further to the west, a much more fragmented pattern of smaller walled Longshan centers is found, including the sites of Chengziyai, Wangchenggang, and Pingliangtai, already described. It is from these smaller competing walled centers, however, that the early Shang state developed. Endemic warfare may have been the driving force, coupled with demographic growth and, perhaps, the destabilizing effects of the frequent flooding of the Huanghe river.

## *Shang Cities*

The key sites for the study of Shang civilization are the ancient cities of Erlitou (for the earliest, or Erlitou, phase, 2000–1750 B.C.), Panlongcheng and Zhengzhou (for the middle, or Erligang, phase, 1750–1300 B.C.), and Anyang (for the last, or Anyang, phase, 1300–1027 B.C.). A recently discovered city at Huanbei may fill a chronological gap between Zhengzhou and Anyang. These cities differ from the walled enclosures of the Longshan period in a number of important respects:

- They are much larger. A large Longshan enclosure such as Chengziyai covers 17 hectares (42 acres); the Shang city of Zhengzhou at 325 hectares (800 acres) is almost 20 times as big.
- The Shang walled enclosures seem to have served primarily as elite centers. They are surrounded by clusters of lower-status villages and workshop areas; Longshan villages seem to have been more self-contained and certainly included craft areas within the walls.
- The elite materials from Shang centers are more abundant and varied than those from Longshan sites, as befits the rise of a state-level society.
- Finally, the Shang walled enclosures are found over a much wider area of China, including the middle valley of the Yangzi; this represents the spread of Shang elite traditions into neighboring regions and the formation of more extensive political alliances.

A brief description of the key Shang centers will help to illustrate these points.

**Erlitou.** This site, discovered by Chinese archaeologists in 1957, belongs to the Early Shang period. As we have seen, it may have been one of the capitals of the Xia dynasty. Remains are scattered over a large area 1.5 by 2.5 kilometers (almost 1 by 1.5 miles), but the most conspicuous features are a pair of two-stage stepped platforms—large platforms that cover up to a hectare (2.5 acres) with smaller platforms built on top of them, usually toward one edge. These were of *hang tu* (rammed-earth) construction and seem to have been the bases of elite residences or palaces. In both cases the lower platform is fringed by a rammed-earth wall, no doubt to separate the elite zone from the areas occupied by the ordinary populace. The elite buildings themselves had been made of wattle and daub on a timber framework, with a gabled and probably thatched roof. Even elite residences did not use costly or durable building materials at this period.

One feature of Erlitou that deserves special mention is the general layout of the elite platforms: rectangular (or roughly so), facing south, with a main gate in the middle of the south side; the secondary platform with the principal elite building in the northern part of the enclosure. This is a common (though not universal) pattern in Chinese architecture from this period onward.

The smaller but better preserved platform at Erlitou had a large pit-grave, over 5 by 4 meters (16 by 13 feet), behind the main building. It had been plundered in antiquity, but traces of lacquer and cinnabar show that it was richly furnished. Other graves were found elsewhere on the site. Some had no grave goods of any kind, but a few were clearly elite graves, with lacquer coffins and bronze weapons and ritual vessels. The finds from Erlitou indicate a degree of social stratification a whole order of magnitude greater than that from Longshan sites. This is exactly what we would expect if (as seems clear) this was a state-level society.

**Zhengzhou.** Zhengzhou lies a short distance downstream along the Huanghe, where the river debouches from the mountains and flows toward the sea through a broad floodplain. This is rich farming country, with fertile loess soil brought down by the river from the higher lands to the west. Zhengzhou stands just south of the river at this strategic location. The Shang remains consist of two separate but interrelated elements. The first is an immense enclosure surrounded by a rammed-earth wall 7 kilometers (4.5 miles) long, still standing in places over 9 meters (30 feet) high. The second element is a halo of sites around the main enclosure, including bronze workshops, pottery kilns, cemeteries, and ordinary dwellings. These extend over an area of 40 square kilometers (15 square miles).

The Zhengzhou arrangement has been called an *urban cluster,* to distinguish it from the compact Chinese cities of the first millennium B.C. and later. The same pattern is found at Anyang, and the urban cluster seems to be typical of Shang centers. They are in a sense a spatial illustration of the hierarchical nature of Shang society and the interdependence of its parts. Within the Zhengzhou enclosure lived the elite and the ritual specialists. Here are found rammed-earth palace platforms, ritual pits with sacrificed dogs and humans, and inscribed oracle bones (Figure 6.2). One of these buildings was probably the ancestor temple of the ruling lineage. Outside the walls, in a series of small dispersed communities, lived and worked those on whom the elite depended: the bronze workers, who produced the all-important ritual vessels; craftspeople in bone and ceramics, who supplied more mundane items; and the farmers, who provided the privileged classes with food.

Zhengzhou suggests that by the Middle Shang period the social distance already seen in the palace platforms at Erlitou had developed into a rigid demarcation between elite and nonelite sectors of the population. Zhengzhou also shows how much the Shang centers differed from the cities of early Mesopotamia or Egypt; they may have had substantial populations, but these were essentially ritual or ceremonial centers surrounded by various support services and many subordinate farming villages. The same seems to be true of the most famous of all the Shang centers: Anyang.

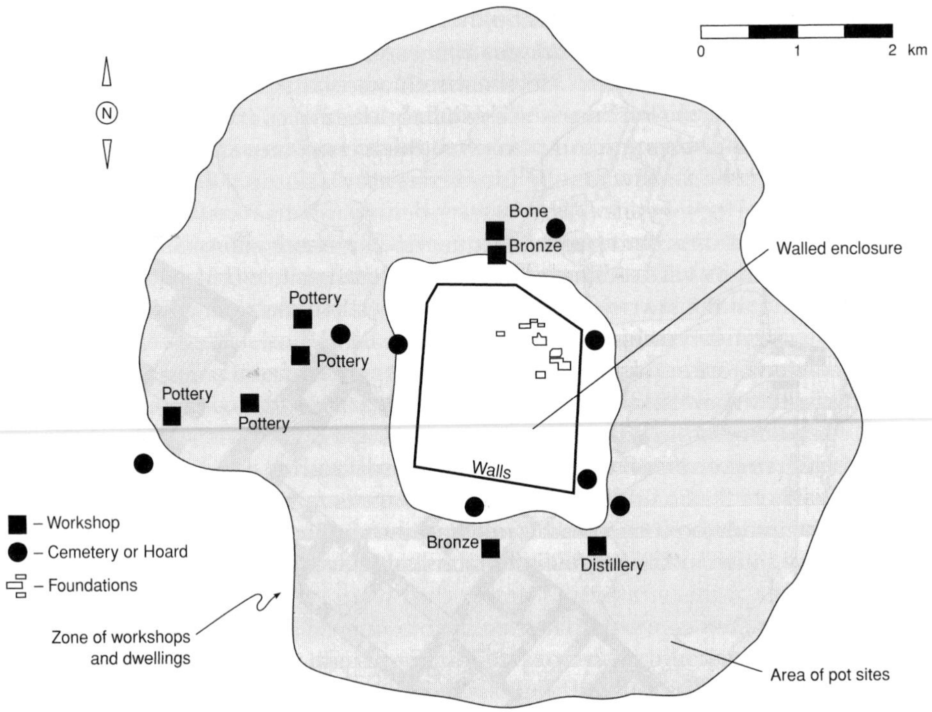


**Figure 6.2** Plan of the urban cluster at Zhengzhou.

**Anyang.** Chinese archaeologists have confidently interpreted the remains at Anyang as those of the last capital of the Shang dynasty, the city called Yin in historical sources. It is an enormous site, stretching for 5.8 kilometers (3.6 miles) along the banks of the Huan River. Inscribed oracle bones sold in a drugstore were traced in 1899 to Xiaotun, one of the villages in the Anyang area. These turned out to be records of the last Shang kings. In 1928 the Academia Sinica began excavations that have continued in different parts of this vast site up to the present day. Such is the scale of the work that archaeologist Kwang-chih Chang estimates that 90 percent of all the basic material for the study of Shang civilization comes from this one center.

In urban structure, Late Shang Anyang resembled Middle Shang Zhengzhou, though it lacked a prominent enclosure wall. There was a ceremonial or ritual center supported by a dispersed pattern of artisans' villages, industrial workshops, and both rich and poor cemeteries (Figure 6.3). The ritual center was at Xiaotun and consisted of a series of buildings raised on rammed-earth platforms. The whole complex covered roughly a hectare (2.5 acres) and served as part palace and part temple. In fact, Shang rulers were themselves ritual specialists, sole intermediaries with the ancestors (and beyond them, the gods) on behalf of their subjects. It is this religious role that legitimized the rule of the Shang kings. Thus it is not surprising that rituals were practiced within the palace precincts. Most oracle bones come

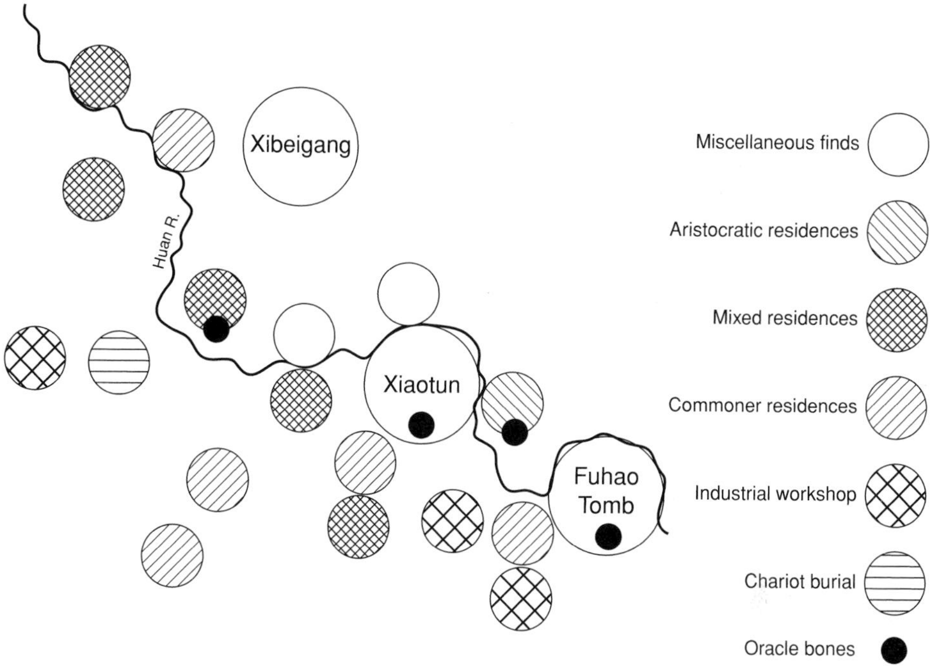


(a)

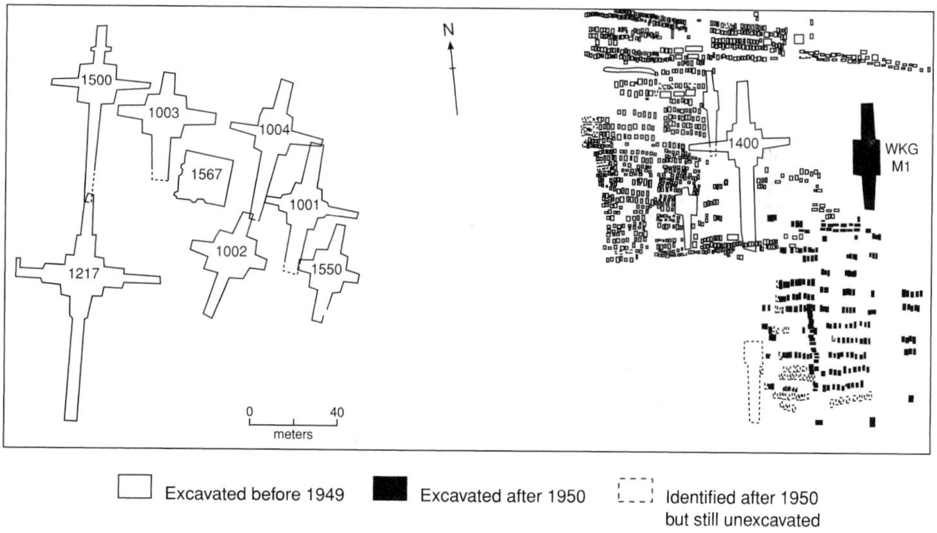


(b)

**Figure 6.3** Anyang: (a) Diagram of urban cluster; (b) plan of Xibeigang cemetery; (c) reconstruction of Xiaotun house; (d) diagram of shaft grave with single ramp.

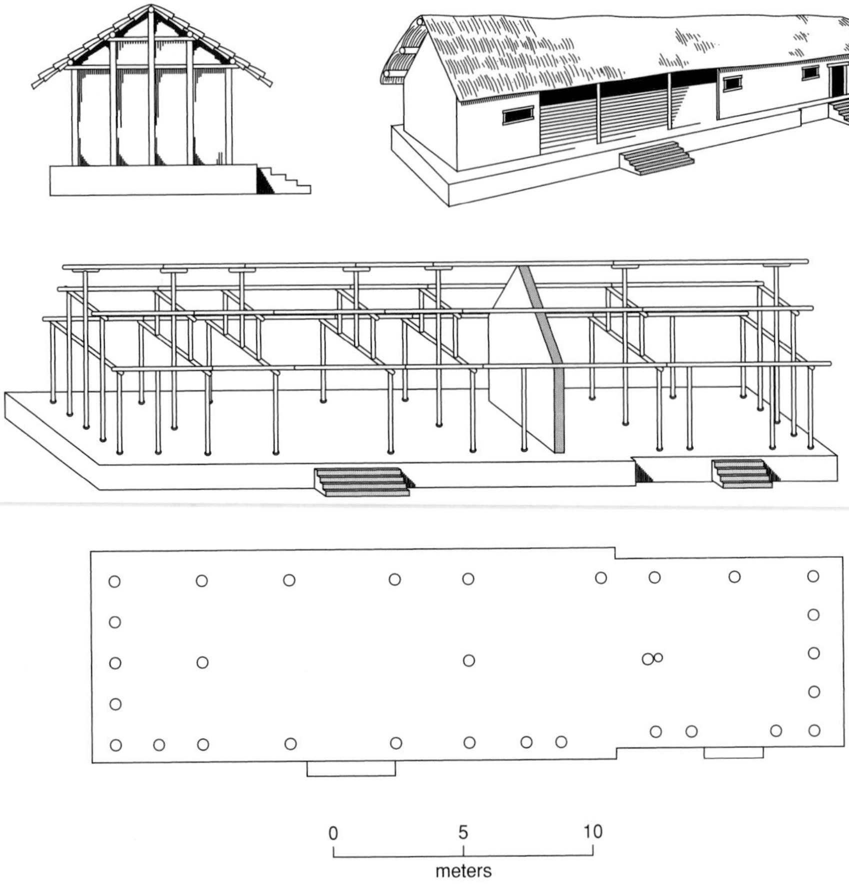


(c)

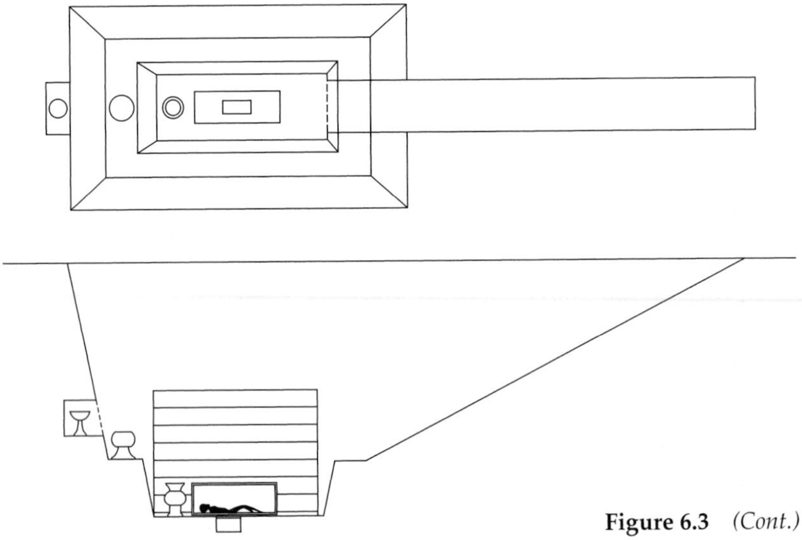

(d)

**Figure 6.3** *(Cont.)*

from Xiaotun, indicating that divination was a regular part of palace-temple rituals. Another aspect of Shang ritual was related to the building of the structures themselves: Large numbers of human sacrifices were found in the rammed-earth foundations. The buildings, like those of Erlitou some centuries before, were of timber-frame construction, with walls of wattle and daub and roofs of thatch; the only concession to grandeur was the bronze disks or stone bases used to support some of the timber uprights.

**Royal Tombs at Anyang.** Anyang is famous for its royal tombs, found in the Xibeigang cemetery some 2 kilometers (1.25 miles) northeast of Xiaotun, on the opposite side of the Huan River. The cemetery holds a total of 1,200 graves, but most of them are fairly small. Among them, however, 13 graves stand out because of their size, their shape (notably the sloping ramps), and their contents, although all of them had been looted in antiquity. Eight of the tombs are of a cruciform plan, with a ramp sloping down into the burial pit on each of the four sides. The others have one or two ramps only. The largest tombs are 10 to 11 meters (35 to 40 feet) deep, with ramps as much as 40 meters (130 feet) and more in length. The burial chamber was a wooden structure built in the center of the burial pit; it could be either rectangular or could itself be cruciform in plan, mirroring the shape of the tomb. The woodwork is not preserved, but impressions of intricate wood carving were found on a clay surface in one of the tombs, and another had fragments of red and black lacquer. These small clues suggest that the tombs' chambers were richly decorated and brightly colored.

Of the tombs' contents, only the vestiges left by the robbers survive. These include stone sculptures, carved jades, and bronze weapons and vessels. One tomb had a stash of over 500 bronze helmets, halberds, and spearheads at the foot of one of the ramps. Another tomb had 11 rows of headless corpses, 59 in all, laid out on the ramp. Human sacrifices were also found below the base of the tomb pit and in the step cut into the sides of the pit, level with the top of the wooden chamber. In death, as in life, the Shang elite were surrounded by the bodies of humans sacrificed to the ancestors—as many as 600 beneath one Xiaotun house alone; 164 in a single Xibeigang tomb.

Who was buried in the large graves at Xibeigang? For many years only 11 tombs were known, and this number tied in neatly with the 11 Shang kings recorded as having ruled from Anyang. (The twelfth and last king, Di Xin, was excluded from the reckoning since his body had been burned by the Zhou conquerors in 1027 B.C.) The discovery of further large tombs at Xibeigang complicates the issue, though it is still possible that the 11 kings are buried there, the others being graves of queens. The only definite queen's grave (indeed the only incontrovertibly royal grave) is located not at Xibeigang but at Xiaotun to the east. Though much smaller than the Xibeigang tombs, it had never been plundered. When excavated by Chinese archaeologists in 1976 it proved to contain 7,000 cowrie shells, 590 jades, and 440 bronzes, as well as items of bone and stone. This serves to remind us how much has been lost from the Xibeigang tombs. Sixty items from the grave bear the name of Fuhao, one of the 64 recorded wives of King Wu Ding, who reigned during the thirteenth century B.C.

## *Writing and Society*

Though most of our information about the Shang period comes from archaeology, in Late Shang times (when Anyang was the capital, c. 1300–1027 B.C.) written sources become available in the form of oracle bones. These enable us to investigate (among other things) the nature and extent of the Shang state.

**Oracle Bones.** Divination was an integral feature of Shang ritual from the outset and was used by rulers to put questions to the ancestors, who in turn were thought to intercede with the gods. It was by no means a new feature; oracle bones had been used in Mongolia as early as 3700 B.C. and are a common find at Longshan sites. But unlike their predecessors, the Shang oracle bones carry inscriptions.

Chinese scholars estimate that there are around 100,000 pieces of inscribed oracle bones in existence, either in China itself or in Japanese or Western collections. (There are also large numbers of fakes.) Most, if not all, come from Anyang. In addition to oracle bones made from cattle shoulder blades, the Shang also used the lower shells of freshwater turtles for divination. The technique in both cases was to cut rows of oval cavities around a centimeter (0.5 inches) across in the back face and apply heat to the cavities by means of a heated metal rod. The resulting pattern of cracks on the front face of bone or turtle shell was then interpreted by a diviner.

The process becomes clear to us through the inscriptions. These always give the date and the question that was being asked of the ancestors. Sometimes they also record the interpretation of the cracks and finally (more rarely) the actual outcome, that is, whether the divination was borne out by events. The following is an example from the reign of King Wu Ding:

> *Day Gui Si, divined.*
>
> *Ke inquired: No ill fortune during the xun? [the Shang ten-day week]*
>
> *The king prognosticated and said: There will be bad fortune. There will be trouble that will be inflicted, arriving three times.*
>
> *Five days later on day Ding Yu, trouble was indeed inflicted, from the west. Zhi Mu stated that Tu Fang reached the eastern border region and inflicted casualties on two towns. Gong Fang also came to graze in our fields in the western border region.* (Chang, 1980, p. 256)

The oracle bones were, of course, far from being the only writing produced by the Shang. Inscriptions cast on bronze vessels also survive, though they are rarely more than 50 words long. Most Shang writings must have been on perishable materials such as strips of bamboo or rolls of silk. Confirmation of this comes from the script itself: the Shang character *ce*, meaning a book, is a pictograph of wooden or bamboo strips tied together with strings. We do not know quite when the Shang script first came into use. We have already seen how writing of some kind was developed in the east and southeast of China by the Liangzhu and Longshan cultures during the late third millennium B.C. Neither of these bears close resemblance to the later Shang script, however, and whether they are connected in any way remains to be established.

The purpose for which the earliest Chinese script was developed remains subject to debate. Some scholars argue that the medium is misleading, and that had writings on perishable materials survived, as well as those on oracle bones and tortoise shells, then the apparently ritualistic focus of the script would be greatly broadened to include more mundane subjects. Others, however, argue that the intrinsic character of the Chinese script indicates that it was invented to serve a particular ritual use—for communication with the ancestors. The oracle script characters are logographs, recording spoken sounds, not ideographs conveying ideas or concepts. Thus they were probably written as they were spoken aloud, to commemorate and record particular ritual events. As Shang specialist David Keightley (1996, p. 75) suggests, "Just as the living heard the sounds of their ancestors in the divination cracks, so did Chinese characters provide the means to hear the sounds of the original words, bringing those words, as it were, back to life." Keightley links the development of the elite code of writing to the complex coded symbols carved on jades or cast on bronze vessels, and he sees it as part of a long-standing Chinese tradition of art and representation. The controversy about the origins of Chinese writing provides an excellent example of the tension between generalizing arguments that seek for underlying similarities between early state societies in different parts of the world, and more particularist views that consider each society the unique product of its own social and ideological circumstances.

Whatever the case, a writing system ancestral to the Shang was probably established in the Huanghe basin from the early second millennium B.C., perhaps under the Xia dynasty and certainly by Late Shang times. The new script was no doubt used to record events, to keep accounts, and to issue instructions, and it became an essential instrument of government. The writing system invented by Xia or Shang was so effective, indeed, that it endured in much modified form to become the foundation of modern Chinese scripts.

## *State and Society*

Though much of their information is by its very nature indirect, the oracle bones can throw light on military campaigns, political alliances, and the structure of the Shang state. One of the biggest questions is the extent of territory the Shang controlled. This is hard to answer, but the oracle bones do help since they refer to named places that can still be identified. They divide the Shang into two zones: an inner "capital" and an outer "domain." The capital is thought to be the area around Anyang itself, extending perhaps 160 kilometers (100 miles) to the south. The domain lay beyond that and may have included not only the Shang homeland but also allied states.

The Shang realm was clearly much smaller than the Shang cultural sphere. The latter is defined by characteristic Shang-style bronze ritual vessels, which were used both by the Shang themselves and several of their rivals. The question is given added importance by the discovery of a Shang-style walled center at Panlongcheng in the Yangzi valley. It is possible that at some periods Shang control did extend as far south as this. At other times, however, erstwhile allies became deadly enemies in a pattern of shifting alliances.

The Shang state itself, centered on the king and the royal lineage, was essentially feudal in nature. Local lords swore fealty to the Shang king but sometimes were still at war with one another. Much of the outer domain referred to in the oracle bones was probably under the control of semiautonomous lords.

The oracle bones also tell us something about warfare in the Late Shang period. They refer to squadrons of chariots, each vehicle carrying a driver, a halberdier, and an archer. The chariot itself was not an independent Shang invention (unlike writing or bronze metallurgy) but had reached China from the Near East by transmission across the steppes of Central Asia. It first appeared around 1300 B.C., and examples turn up in graves at Anyang. Chariots were for the elite and must have been little more useful in real warfare than they were in Mycenaean Greece or the Bronze Age Levant (see Chapter 10). The ordinary soldiers, grouped into units of 100 men, fought on foot with bows and arrows or halberds mounted on the ends of long poles.

## *Ritual Bronzes: Technology and Meaning in Shang Society*

One of the most distinctive features of Shang civilization was the production of elaborately decorated ritual vessels, manufactured from cast bronze (Figure 6.4). They followed and expanded on the shape of ceramic forms of the Longshan period and made use of the high-temperature kilns developed for high-quality Longshan pottery. Metalworking, too, had its origin in the Longshan period. The techniques used by Shang bronze workers far surpassed anything seen earlier, however, and laid the foundation for a continuing Chinese tradition of sophisticated bronze metallurgy (Figure 6.5).

Shang craftspeople made their bronze ritual vessels by using large ceramic piece molds composed of separate pieces of pottery carefully designed to fit tightly together. One of the striking features of the ritual vessels is the richness of surface decoration, formed by intricate shallow channels or low relief. In the Shang piece-mold technique, most of the decoration was carved on the ceramic molds, and thus cast in place when the molten bronze was poured in. Only minor finishing was needed at a later stage, when the vessel had cooled. This whole process was in strong contrast to the methods used for making metal vessels in Bronze Age western Asia and Europe. There, casting was used for small items such as daggers and axes, but large forms like open vessels were made by hammering and riveting sheets of bronze.

Apart from their technology, two other aspects of Shang bronze ritual vessels are worthy of particular note. The first is their decoration. The most regular element was the so-called *taotie* motif. This is a fantastic animal mask or face, split symmetrically on either side of a vertical line or casting seam and laid out flat along the sides of the vessel. Eyes, eyebrows, and sometimes fangs can clearly be seen. The face motif was not a Shang innovation: It first appears on jade objects of the Neolithic Liangzhu culture. Nor did it end with the overthrow of Shang rule. The *taotie* continued to be a standard feature of Chinese bronzes in the subsequent Western Zhou period (1027–771 B.C.).

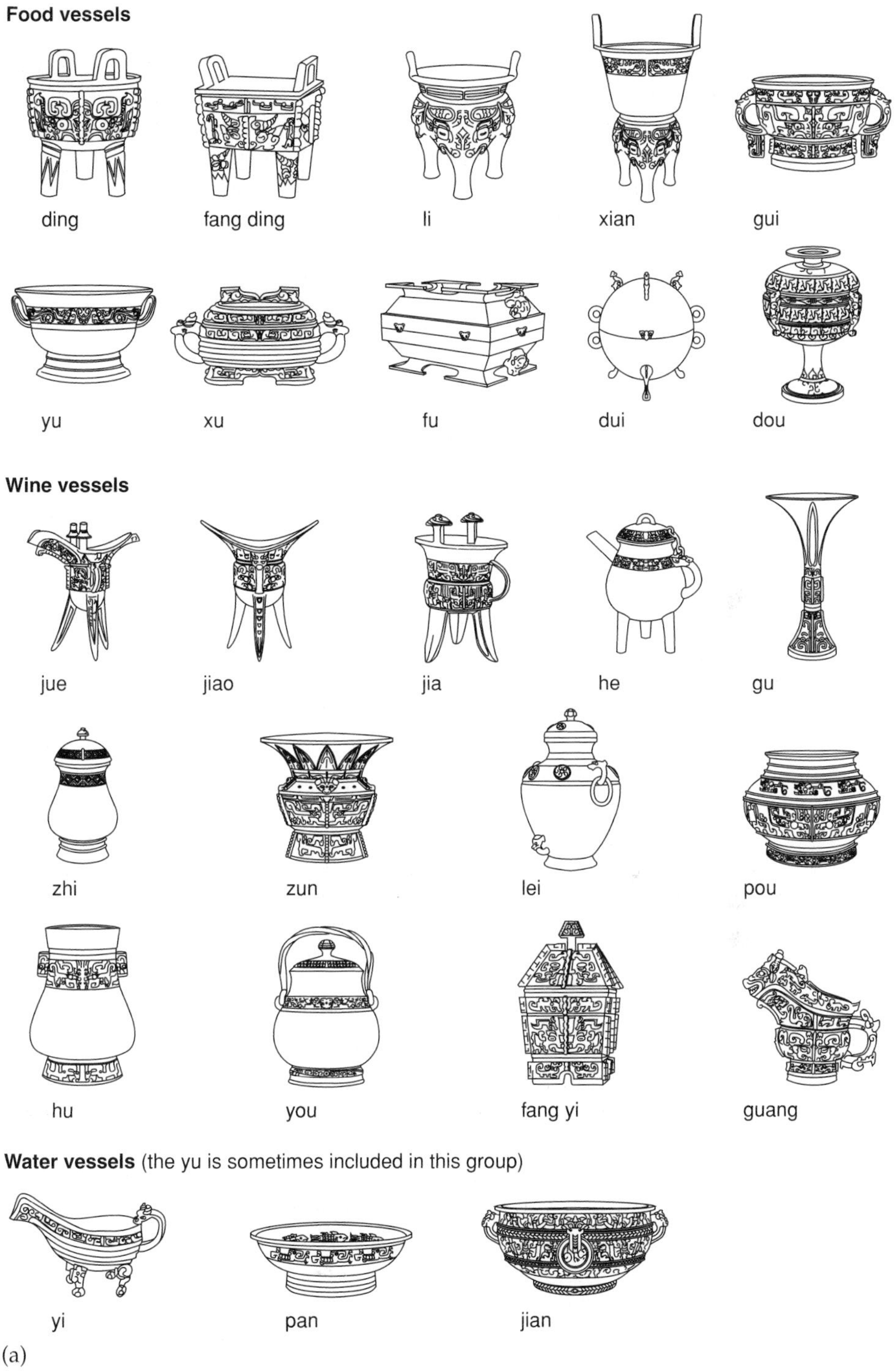


**Figure 6.4** Shang ritual vessels: (a) Diagram of food vessels, wine vessels, and water vessels with names; (b) close-up of *taotie* motif.

(b)

**Figure 6.4** *(cont.)*

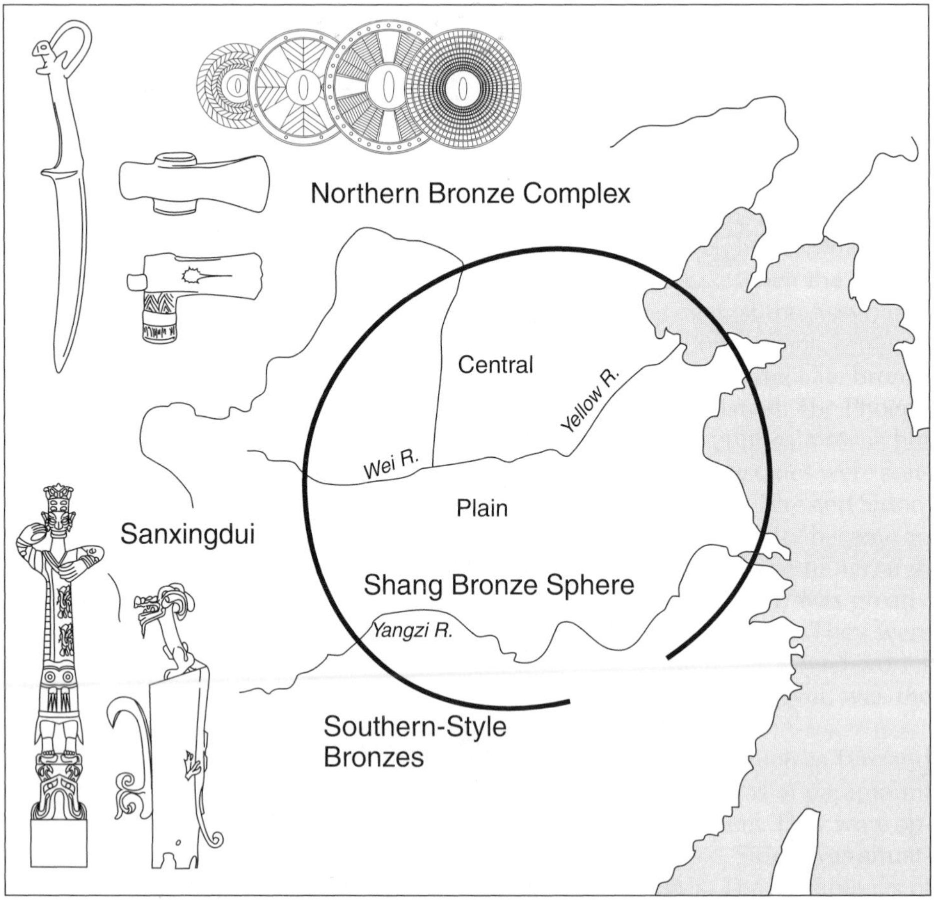


**Figure 6.5** Map of Shang period bronze traditions.

The second notable feature of Shang ritual bronzes is the restricted range of shapes. Shang craftspeople did not make their vessels to just any shape that came to mind. Instead, they followed a precise typology of shapes, each of which had its own name and was intended for a particular function. Thus vessels for food included the *ding, fang ding, yu,* and *gui.* For wine drinking there were the *jue, jiao, gu,* and *fang yi,* among others, while water vessels included the *yi, pan,* and *jian.* This highly regimented scheme gives us a clue to the meaning and importance of the bronze vessels. Shapes, decoration, and uses were ritually prescribed, and possession of these vessels was one of the key criteria for claiming and maintaining an elite rank. Inscriptions cast onto similar vessels of the Zhou period show that they were usually dedicated to the ancestors, and they were probably used in banquets held to show respect for the ancestors. It was through these very same ancestors that high-ranking families asserted their right to elite status.

## *Shang Civilization in Its Broader Context*

Archaeological and historical evidence show that the Shang was the most important early civilization in China. In geographical terms, however, it is essential to remember that the Shang state covered only a small area of northeastern China. Shang culture—especially the use of the characteristic bronze vessels—extended far beyond the confines of the Shang state. It was adopted by many states and peoples that were actively their enemies, notably the kingdom of Zhou to the west, which invaded and overthrew the Shang dynasty in 1027 B.C.

Beyond the zone of Shang bronzes were the independent bronze-working traditions of western, northern, and southern China. These underline the point that the Shang was only one of a number of regional bronze-working cultures in Bronze Age China. Recent discoveries have shown that some of these were not merely regional metalworking traditions but also the centers of independent states. This conclusion has revolutionized our understanding of Bronze Age China, which is now seen, not as a Shang zone surrounded by a halo of derived and dependent cultures, but as a multicenter pattern comprising several cultures of equal or near-equal status.

Excavations at Zhukaigou in Inner Mongolia, just within the bend of the Huanghe, have revealed a sequence of layers that spans the period from the late third millennium B.C. to the mid-second, parallel to the period from late Longshan to Middle Shang further south. The sequence is especially interesting for the light it throws on relations between peripheral areas and the Shang elite culture. In the third millennium (phase I), the Zhukaigou site belonged to just one of several northern Chinese Longshan-related groups. Metalworking started around the beginning of the second millennium B.C. (phases II and III), but it was in the middle centuries of the second millennium that specific features of Shang culture appeared. This began in Zhukaigou phase IV, with the adoption of dog sacrifice (an elite Shang custom) and drilled and polished oracle bones (though undrilled oracle bones had already been in use for some time). The big change came in phase V (c. 1500 B.C.), when bronze ritual vessels and weapons of classic Shang style appeared in the graves at Zhukaigou. Alongside these were other bronzes, of a kind already familiar in the steppe lands to the north. What seems to have occurred was the emergence of a local elite, who were drawing on products (notably metalwork) of established elites in adjacent areas to prop up their new-found status. When Chinese archaeologists analyzed the bronzes more closely, they found they had been made locally, with different proportions of tin, copper, and lead than contemporary bronzes of the Shang heartland. Zhukaigou does not therefore indicate an extension of Shang power but rather the adoption of Shang status items by an emerging elite in a peripheral region.

North of Zhukaigou is the area of the Northern Bronze Complex, on the edge of the steppe zone, with such typical products as circular mirrors, curved knives, and socketed battle-axes. This was an independent bronze-working tradition, unrelated to Shang but owing much to the cultures and technologies of the Eurasian steppes. Products of the Northern Bronze Complex appear, as we have seen, alongside Shang bronzes at Zhukaigou, illustrating the position of the latter at the intersection of Shang and steppe traditions.

More interesting still are recent excavations by Chinese archaeologists at Sanxingdui in southwestern China. Here they have found an early city site with a substantial defensive wall of rammed-earth construction, enclosing an area of 1 square kilometer (0.4 square mile), and the remains of buildings within. This is far from the Shang heartland, in an area that historical sources refer to as the kingdom of Shu. Within the city wall, the archaeologists discovered two rectangular sacrificial pits, 30 meters (98 feet) apart, filled with bronzes, ivories, and jade. The deposit in pit 2 was covered by a layer of no fewer than 60 charred elephant tusks. These finds have been divided into two categories: group A, consisting of bronze ritual vessels and other objects in Shang style, and group B, objects in a hitherto unknown style with a particular emphasis on the human form. Specialists propose that the group A objects were imports from the Shang cultural area, but the group B objects were clearly locally made and testify to another non-Shang cultural tradition. As American archaeologist Katheryn Linduff has argued, "Even the briefest look at Sanxingdui confirms that this was a culture with technological sophistication, social and religious complexity of the sort thought previously to have existed only in the Central Plain" [the Shang heartland] (Linduff and Yan Ge, 1990, p. 513). It was very likely the predecessor of a regional state, culturally and politically independent from the Shang.

The importance of these discoveries is that they allow us to put the Shang civilization in its broader Chinese context. Shang culture—especially the ritual vessels—clearly enjoyed great prestige among neighboring non-Shang elites. These were not simply poor relations of the Shang, however, but powerful regional groupings with their own cultural traditions. Some of them were state-level societies in direct competition with the Shang. Many of their traditions continued into the first millennium B.C. and contributed to the rich and varied cultural life of the historic kingdoms of the Zhou period.

The discoveries at Sanxingdui are leading to a radical reassessment of the Chinese Bronze Age, with the recognition that Shang was not the only powerful cultural tradition. We are now beginning to envisage a multicenter model of Chinese state formation, in which the Shang is only one of several major players.

This point has been driven home still more firmly by the recent discovery of a richly furnished tomb at Xin'gan in Jiangxi province, south of the Yangzi River. The Xin'gan tomb has been dated to the thirteenth century B.C., and it is the second richest Bronze Age tomb ever to have been found in China, surpassed only by the Fu Hao tomb at Anyang. Among the contents are 356 pottery vessels, 50 bronze vessels, 4 bronze bells, over 400 bronze weapons and tools, and 150 carved jades. Some of the bronzes are similar to Shang types, with *taotie* masks as decoration. Other bronzes and some of the carved jades are in a local style, without parallel in the Shang heartland. We should remember, too, that in this same region craftspeople of the Liangzhu culture had been carving *taotie* motifs on ritual jades over a thousand years before. Here again, the traditional primacy of the Shang civilization has to be called into question. Shang may have been the most important elite culture of early China, but it certainly was not the only one.

Twenty kilometers (12.4 miles) from Xin'gan is the settlement site of Wucheng, with evidence of bronze working and writing. It now seems that Wucheng was the center of a regional state contemporary with the Shang to the north. Its rulers were buried in richly furnished graves in the surrounding area.

## The Western Zhou Period (1027–771 B.C.)

In 1027 B.C. the last Shang king was overthrown by one of the rival states to the west, the Zhou. Though in historical terms this was a sharp dynastic break, archaeology shows considerable continuity in many aspects of Shang and Zhou culture. The Zhou had already fallen within the zone of influence of Shang material culture before the conquest. Zhou ritual bronzes followed Shang styles and were probably associated with similar beliefs and practices. Many of these bronzes started to carry inscriptions, recording special events or ceremonies. Some commemorated gifts of land from the king or the investiture of a particular official. A famous example is the Xing Hou *gui*, a four-handled bronze basin that the marquis of Xing had cast to commemorate the king's gift to him of control over three peoples. The inscription offers his thanks to the king and reaffirms his loyalty.

Both the Xing Hou *gui* and historical records show that the structure of the early Zhou state was similar to that of the Shang, with the king granting lands and office to lords and retainers in return for their loyalty and service. There does seem to have been some measure of greater centralization, however, since the Zhou realm was both larger in size than that of the Shang and comprised many fewer separate states (only 50 or so, compared with the hundreds reputedly controlled by the Shang dynasty).

Early Zhou urbanism and architecture also reflected Shang traditions. "Urban" centers, such as the Zhou capital at Qishan, remained a cluster of sites around a central palatial complex. Like the Shang, the Western Zhou rulers used oracle bones and lived in palaces of timber-frame construction raised on rammed-earth platforms. Monumentalism was beginning to creep into Western Zhou architecture, however: Timber posts were spaced in rows as much as 5.5 meters (18 feet) apart, indicating enormous roof spans, and ceramic tiles were used in place of thatch for roof coverings.

The Zhou capital remained at Qishan until 771 B.C., when raids by nomads from the north forced the rulers to move east, to the more sheltered location of Luoyang. This move is the basis of the traditional division of the Zhou period into Western Zhou (1027–771 B.C.), when the capital was at Qishan, and Eastern Zhou (771–256 B.C.), when the Zhou kings ruled from Luoyang. In archaeological terms, as we have seen, the Western Zhou period is very much a continuation of the Shang. During the Eastern Zhou, however, significant new developments began to take place: ironworking, compact cities, coinage, and markets. These mark the opening of a new phase in Chinese developments, leading toward the establishment of the first Chinese empire, as we see in Chapter 14.

## Summary

Bronze Age China was home to a number of civilizations. The most famous was that of the Shang, which takes its name from the dynasty who ruled in the middle valley of the Huanghe (Yellow River) in northern China during the second millennium B.C. The formative stages of this state-level society lay in the elite traditions of the Late Neolithic Longshan phase (2700–2000 B.C.), though some elements can be traced to the earliest farming villages of the seventh and sixth millennia B.C. Shang civilization (from 2000 B.C.) was characterized by dispersed urban sites known as urban clusters and by a heavy investment in the manufacture of ritual bronzes. The earliest decipherable Chinese writing comes from the Late Shang period and takes the form of inscriptions cast on bronze vessels and inscribed on oracle bones, used for royal divination.

In other regions of China, contemporary with the Shang, separate bronze-working traditions developed, some of them associated with state-level societies. These have hitherto received little attention but are coming increasingly to prominence as a result of recent discoveries. They suggest that a multicentered model of Chinese state formation may be more accurate than the traditional Shang-dominated view.

The Shang dynasty itself was overthrown by a rival power, the Zhou, in 1027 B.C.; but culturally, politically, and economically there was little change until the end of the Western Zhou period in 771 B.C.

## Guide to Further Reading

Much of the enormous literature of Chinese archaeology is unfortunately inaccessible to non-Chinese speakers. However, three books in English provide useful coverage of early Chinese civilizations and their archaeology: G. L. Barnes, *China, Korea and Japan: The Rise of Civilization in East Asia* (London: Thames and Hudson, 1992) is an up-to-date account that supplements Kwang-Chi Chang's two classic works, *Shang Civilization* (New Haven, CT: Yale University Press, 1980) and *The Archaeology of Ancient China*, 4th ed. (New Haven, CT: Yale University Press, 1986). For the post-Shang period see C. Y. Hsu and K. M. Linduff, *Western Chou Civilization* (New Haven: Yale University Press, 1988). Jessica Rawson, *Ancient China: Art and Archaeology* (London: British Museum, 1980) and Wen Fong, *The Great Bronze Age of China* (New York: Metropolitan Museum of Art, 1980) are also valuable. These can now be supplemented by Jessica Rawson, *Mysteries of Ancient China* (London: British Museum Publications, 1996), which contains details and illustrations of recent archaeological discoveries, including the striking bronze figures from Sanxingdui. An up-to-date review of the Chinese Neolithic, with lengthy bibliography, is provided by Anne P. Underhill, "Current Issues in Chinese Neolithic Archaeology," *Journal of World Prehistory* 11 (1997): 103–160.

The study of Shang oracle bones as historical records is the subject of David N. Keightley, *Sources of Shang History: The Oracle Bone Inscriptions of Bronze Age China* (Berkeley: University of California Press, 1978). For a general history of China, focusing mainly on later periods, see Jacques Gernet, *A History of Chinese Civilization* (Cambridge: Cambridge University Press, 1982).

Sarah M. Nelson, ed., *The Archaeology of Northeast China: Beyond the Great Wall* (London: Routledge, 1995) provides details of new results from the Dongbei region of China, better known to Western readers as Manchuria. For Huiheliang, see "The Ritual Landscape of 'Boar Mountain' Basin: The Niuhelinag Site Complex of North-Eastern China," by Gina L. Barnes with Guo Dashun, *World Archaeology* 28 (1996): 209–219. For the Hongshan culture and subsequent developments in northeast China, see also Gideon Shelach, *Leadership Strategies, Economic Activity, and Interregional Interaction: Social Complexity in Northeast China* (New York: Kluwer Academic, 1999).

Two periodicals, *Antiquity* and *Orientations*, have occasional articles on the Chinese Neolithic and the Bronze Age. They provide valuable English-language accounts of recent discoveries. On the Liangzhu jades, see Tsui-mei Huang, "Liangzhu—A Late Neolithic Jade-Yielding Culture in Southeastern Coastal China," *Antiquity* 66 (1992): 75–83 and Jean M. James, "Images of Power: Masks of the Liangzhu Culture," *Orientations* 22, no. 6 (1991): 46–55. The site of Zhukaigou in Inner Mongolia is described by Katheryn M. Linduff, "Zhukaigou, Steppe Culture, and the Rise of Chinese Civilization," *Antiquity* 69 (1995): 133–145. The important discoveries at Sanxingdui are described in the book by Jessica Rawson, referred to previously, and by Katheryn M. Linduff and Yan Ge, "Sanxingdui: A New Bronze Age Site in Southwest China," *Antiquity* 64 (1990): 505–513 and Robert W. Bagley, "A Shang City in Sichuan Province," *Orientations* 21, no. 1 (1990): 52–67. The newly discovered Shang city of Hunabei is briefly described by Jigen Tang, Zhichun Jing, and George Rapp, "The Largest Walled Shang City Located in Anyang, China," *Antiquity* 74 (2000): 479–480. The Xin'gan tomb is described by Robert W. Bagley, "An Early Bronze Age Tomb in Jiangxi Province," *Orientations* 24, no. 7 (1993): 20–36.

Up-to-date information on the origins of Chinese writing is given by Tao Wang in Nicholas Postgate, Tao Wang, and Toby Wilkinson, "The Evidence for Early Writing: Utilitarian or Ceremonial?" *Antiquity* 69 (1995): 459–480. The alternative view, that Chinese writing arose not from the need for accounting or economic recording as found in other early state societies but stemmed directly from Chinese ritual practice and artistic conventions, may be found in David N. Keightley, "Art, Ancestors, and the Origins of Writing in China," *Representations* 56 (1996): 68–95. The process of state formation in northern China, from Longshan to Shang, has recently been studied in detail by Li Liu, "Settlement Patterns, Chiefdom Variability, and the Development of Early States in North China," *Journal of Anthropological Archaeology* 15 (1996): 237–288.

# PART III

# Great Powers in the Near East

These broken hills were palaces; those long-undulating mounds, streets; this vast solitude, filled with the busy subjects of the proud daughter of the East. Now, wasted with solitude, her habitations are not to be found.

Sir Robert Ker Porter on the ruins of Nebuchadnezzar's Babylon, 1818.*

***Travels in Georgia, Persia, Armenia, Ancient Babylonia, etc.* 2 vols. (London: John Murray, 1822). *N.B.:* 1818 is the date of Porter's visit to Babylon.

*Chapter 7*

# Near Eastern Kingdoms

## (2000–1200 B.C.)

Boghazköy relief from the King's Gate. Warrior figure (Hittite).

*As the sun rose the donkeys were laden once again and the caravan made ready for the next stage of the westward journey. Packs of colored textiles were strapped into place, and the panniers of the valuable* **annakum** *(tin) that had been brought from Iranian sources to Assur, the home city. The* **annakum** *had been costly, but the merchants were content as they padded softly along beside their donkeys, thinking of the profits to be made when they arrived at their destination. They had many days' travel ahead of them, first across the level, dusty plains of northern Mesopotamia, then over the Taurus Mountains to the Anatolian plateau. But they had made the journey many times before and knew well the way-stations and inns where they would stop each night. They were also looking forward to a warm welcome when they reached their goal, the great Anatolian city of Kanesh. For they were carrying not only much-prized commodities for the market but also news and letters from Assur for the thriving Assyrian merchant colony that the king of Kanesh had allowed to be built just below the walls of his city.*

In the third millennium B.C., the story of the Near East had been dominated by southern Mesopotamia—the land of Ur and Uruk and the birthplace of writing and empire (see Chapter 3). For the second millennium, described in this chapter, we must broaden the geographical canvas as new regions such as Anatolia take an ever more prominent place in the mosaic of states and peoples (Table 7.1).

## Bronze Age Cities in Anatolia (2000–1700 B.C.)

This is not to suggest, of course, that Anatolia had been unpopulated or undeveloped before 2000 B.C. We have already seen how, thousands of years earlier, the inhabitants of southern Anatolia had established in Çatalhöyük one of the first towns. Sophisticated pottery and metalworking soon followed, but it was only in the third millennium that true cities made their appearance.

### *Alaça Höyük*

Two sites of the third and early second millennia B.C. deserve particular mention. The first is Alaça Höyük, a conspicuous city mound in northern Anatolia. (The Turkish word *höyük* is equivalent to Arabic *tell* or Persian *tepe,* all of which mean "a city mound." Later in the second millennium B.C., this became an important Hittite city. Today the site is dominated by the massive fortifications and monumental gates of that period. What concerns us here, however, is not the later city but the tombs that were found beneath it: 13 richly furnished "Royal Graves." These

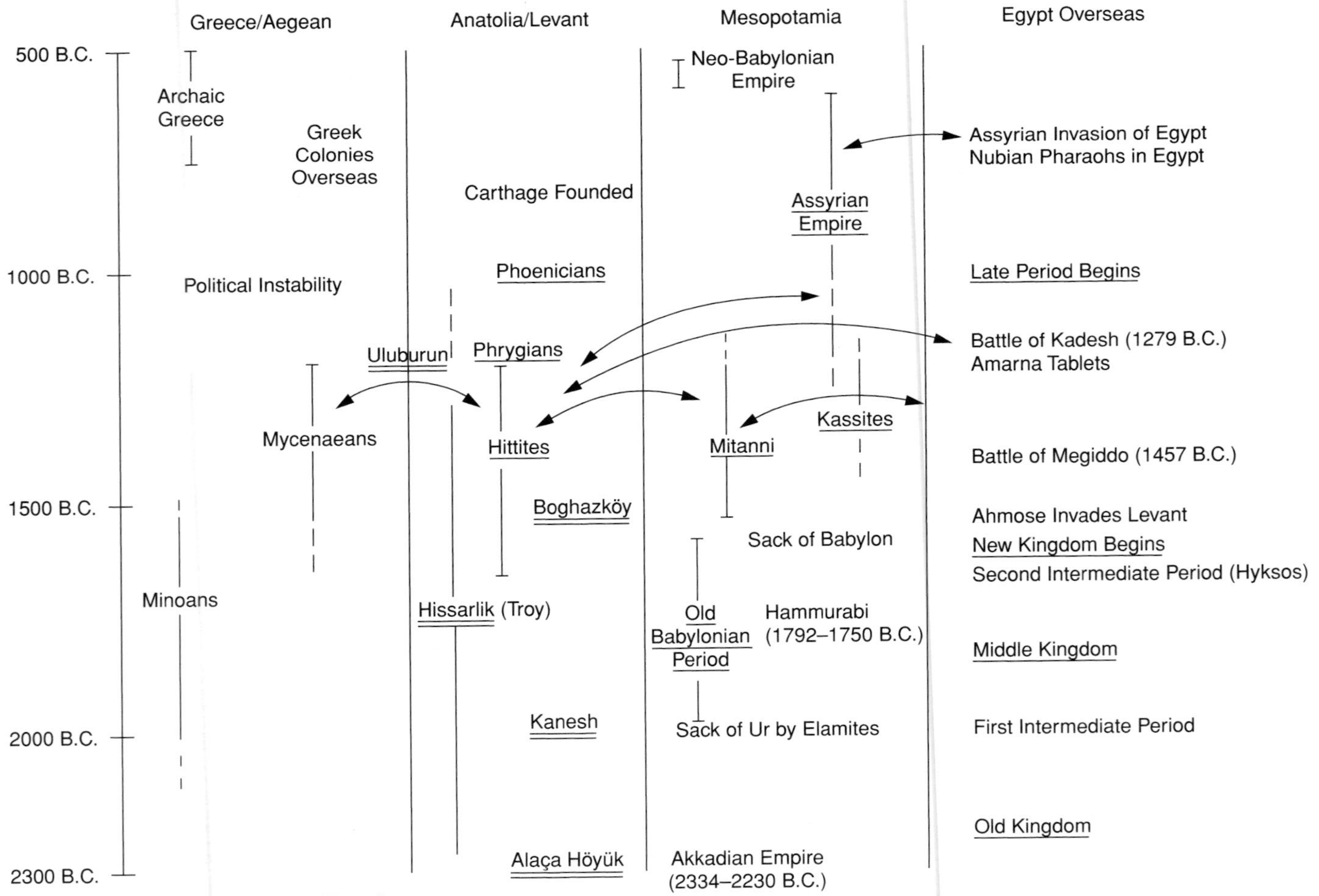


**Table 7.1** Later Near Eastern Kingdoms.

took the form of large rectangular pits with burial chambers up to 6 meters (20 feet) long and 3 meters (10 feet) wide at their base. The chambers were lined with stone and roofed in timber and contained the remains of people identified as the early rulers of Alaça Höyük—usually both a male and female body, though it could be seen that these had not in all cases been buried at the same moment. The "royal" character of the graves is shown most clearly by their rich furnishings: objects of copper, gold, silver, and even iron, which at that time was a rare and valuable metal.

The royal graves of Alaça Höyük show that already by around 2500 B.C., kingdoms and city-states had begun to appear on the Anatolian plateau. In the absence of written records, however, we are unable to chart the historical development of these kingdoms in any detail. We do know that they were in contact, or were soon brought into contact, with the cities of the Mesopotamian plain. Later legends record that King Sargon of Agade led an expedition into Anatolia against the city of Purushkanda. The exact location of this city is uncertain, but the southern fringes of Anatolia may well have formed part of the Akkadian sphere of influence for a period during the twenty-fourth century B.C. These contacts hastened the formation of larger political units in Anatolia. By 1900 B.C. we have clear evidence of several regional states, one of them centered on the city of Kanesh (see Table 7.1).

## *Kanesh*

Clay tablets from this general area, inscribed with Akkadian script, had begun to turn up on the antiquities market in the 1880s. It was not until 1925, however, that Czechoslovakian philologist Bedrich Hrozný succeeded in tracing their origin not to the city mound of Kanesh itself (where Germans and French had already dug in vain) but to a meadow just over 100 meters (300 feet) beyond the walls. Here he came across the remains of a trading colony inhabited by merchants from the Mesopotamian city of Assur on the Tigris. In all, well over 10,000 clay tablets have now been discovered at the site. These record a flourishing trade between the Assyrian merchants of Kanesh and their home base at Assur during the period 1900 to 1750 B.C. The commerce was in the hands of Assyrian merchant families, who shipped tin and textiles by donkey caravan to Kanesh in return for silver from Anatolia. This, in fact, was one arm of an international trading system, which linked the city of Assur not only with Anatolia but also with Iran (source of the tin), with southern Mesopotamia (source of the so-called Akkadian textiles), and possibly at a further remove with Dilmun (Bahrain) and Oman, a source of copper.

We learn from these records that Kanesh was only one of ten Assyrian merchant colonies at Anatolian cities. The cities themselves seem to have been independent, each controlling their surrounding area, and not always on friendly terms. One significant though shadowy historical event was the conquest of Kanesh and its Assyrian colony by Anitta, son of Pitkhana, a neighboring ruler, around 1820 B.C. After his victory and a successful campaign of military expansion in central Anatolia, Anitta transferred his main residence to "Nesa" (Kanesh), where a dagger inscribed with his name has been found. Anitta may have been an ancestor of the later Hittite rulers, for the Hittites referred to their own language as Nesili, the language of Nesa.

## The Struggle for Mesopotamia (2000–1800 B.C.)

In Chapter 3 we left the story of Mesopotamia with the capture of Ur by the Elamites in 2004 B.C. By that time, the Ur III empire had already collapsed through the secession first of Eshnunna and the far north, then of Susa and the east, and finally of Nippur at the heart of ancient Mesopotamia. Power passed to a new dynasty based at the city of Isin. The rulers of Isin managed to extend their control over much of southern and central Mesopotamia. Isin's supremacy was short-lived, however, for the south soon fell under the sway of the rival city of Larsa. Other powers then appeared on the scene: Kish in the north; Kazallu in the west; and the city of Babylon, which by 1800 B.C. had conquered its nearest rivals and was poised to advance on both Isin and Larsa.

The rivalry of Isin and Larsa has been given an archaeological dimension by American-led investigations in the late 1980s at Tell Abu Duwari, site of the ancient city of Mashkan-Shapir, due east of Babylon and not far from the modern course of the Tigris River. We know that Mashkan-Shapir was an outpost of Larsa, and its location suggests that it was founded for a special strategic purpose. Isin had one big advantage in its struggle with Larsa: Both cities lay on the Euphrates, but Isin was further upstream and could prevent supplies of traded materials from reaching Larsa by the river route. Mashkan-Shapir was Larsa's response, a new city north of Isin but linked to the Tigris rather than the Euphrates. By founding Mashkan-Shapir, Larsa aimed to sidestep its rival and secure an alternative supply route for essential raw materials from the north.

For archaeologists Elizabeth Stone and Paul Zimansky, Mashkan-Shapir had one outstanding recommendation: It was so short-lived (occupied for only 200 years) that it hardly had time to form a tell. Many features of the city were therefore visible on the surface. They set out to map these surface features, using a combination of field walking and aerial photography (a collection of 1,600 photos taken by a kite-mounted camera). From their results, Stone and Zimansky have estimated that no fewer than 30 million potsherds litter the surface of the site. They were able to map a network of canals that cut across the city area, separating it into five districts, and broadening out into two wider areas of water identified as internal harbors. Many of the major buildings faced onto canals rather than streets, emphasizing the importance of water transport. There were also copper-working areas, pottery kilns, and a religious quarter in the southeast sector, the whole enclosed within a mud-brick city wall. These results give us a unique insight into the layout of a south Mesopotamian city at the beginning of the second millennium B.C.

This period of political and military uncertainty was a time of flourishing trade in the Persian Gulf. Already in the third millennium merchants from southern Mesopotamia had been bringing copper from Oman. Sargon of Agade in the twenty-fourth century boasted how ships from Oman, Bahrain, and the Indus

## *Box 7.1 The City of Saar and the Dilmun Trade*

The island of Bahrain, ancient Dilmun, was a crucial trading center in the commercial networks that linked southern Mesopotamia with the Indus Valley. It seems to have reached its greatest importance during the so-called Early Dilmun period (2300–1700 B.C.). The prosperity of the Dilmun merchants was founded largely on their monopoly of the copper trade from Oman and the Indus Valley. This prosperity led to the establishment of several new towns in the northern part of the island, including Saar, where archaeologists began excavating in the 1980s. Around 2000 B.C., Saar was a town of stone houses fronting onto regular streets. The walls are still preserved in places to a height of 3 meters (10 feet). In the northern sector stood a temple with a central row of columns to support the roof and two altars—one against a column, the other against a side wall. The side altar had been replastered several times, and where the plaster had fallen away there were burned fishscales, indicating that fish must have been among the offerings made here. At the time Saar was on the edge of a coastal inlet. Judging from circular sealstones used for stamping impressions, many of its inhabitants were involved in the trade, which was the island's lifeblood. Similar sealstones have been found as far afield as Kanesh in Anatolia and the Indus Valley. Indeed, some Early Dilmun seals are actually inscribed with characters of the mysterious Harappan script, and the Harappan weight system appears to have been in use on the island. There could be no better illustration of the cosmopolitan nature of Bahraini society in the early second millennium B.C.

Valley tied up at his quaysides (Box 7.1). The Gulf trade seems to have reached its peak, however, in the early second millennium, when the kings of Larsa controlled the southern outlets of Mesopotamia. It was the southern counterpart to the flourishing Assyrian trade with Anatolia, and like that trade was in the hands not of state or temple but of wealthy merchant families. The object, as always, was to supply the populous cities of Mesopotamia with the valuable raw materials that they lacked, notably metals, hard stone, and timber.

A main beneficiary of the Gulf trade was the island of Bahrain (ancient Dilmun), which had few raw materials of its own but acted as intermediary and entrepôt (market) for traders from Mesopotamia and further afield. The international trade links of Bahrain at this period are shown by the discovery there of weights of the Indus Valley type, and one Gulf-style stamp seal has turned up at the Indus port of Lothal. Further light has been thrown by excavations at the site of ancient Saar on Bahrain.

## The World of the Mari Letters (1810–1750 B.C.)

While the city-states of southern Mesopotamia were fighting among themselves, important new developments were taking shape in the north. One was the rise of Assur, a city whose merchants, as we have already seen, were active in Anatolia.

Assur itself became a powerful political force, notably under the great ruler Shamshi-Adad (1813–1781 B.C.). His realm extended from the Zagros Mountains in the east to the Euphrates River in the west, but it collapsed at his death, leaving the field open to rival contenders.

One of the rivals was Zimri-Lim, ruler of Mari on the Euphrates. His father had been ousted by Shamshi-Adad, but after the latter's death Zimri-Lim returned to reclaim his throne. He ruled Mari for over 20 years, until in 1759 B.C. the city was captured and destroyed by King Hammurabi of Babylon. The destruction that accompanied this event proved to be an enormous benefit to twentieth-century archaeologists; it preserved Zimri-Lim's great palace under a pile of collapsed mud-brick, including a collection of over 20,000 clay writing tablets, which detail all aspects of court life at Mari from 1810 to 1759 B.C. (Figure 7.1). The tablets began in the reign of Shamshi-Adad (whose indolent son Yasmah-Addu had been installed as local ruler) and provide an outline of political events in the years that followed. One particularly graphic text—a letter to local tribal leaders—sums up the political conditions in Mesopotamia during Zimri-Lim's reign: "There is no king who by himself is strongest. Ten or fifteen kings follow Hammurabi of Babylon, as many follow Rim-sin of Larsa, Ibal-pi-el of Eshnunna, and Amut-pi-el of Qatna, while twenty kings follow Yarim-Lim of Aleppo."

This was a game of shifting allegiances and alliances, which ultimately Zimri-Lim lost. There are frequent references to warfare, involving sieges and large armies; on one occasion Shamshi-Adad planned to raise a force of 60,000 men. Other tablets concern food and drink. In one place we are told that a plague of locusts descended on a certain town; the local governor trapped some of them and sent them to Mari as a delicacy. Still more surprising was the building of icehouses in various places. The Mesopotamian plain is swelteringly hot and dry during the summer months, yet the rulers of Mari managed to collect ice in the winter and store it in these special icehouses for use during the rest of the year. For its time and place, this represented the height of luxury.

The Mari tablets also provide much information on social conditions in and around the royal palace. There were workshops for textiles and metalwork, where male and female prisoners of war were among those employed. The various departments were administered by officials who reported directly to the king; similar officials were placed in charge of dependent territories and were responsible for collecting taxes. The tablets tell us that women did not enjoy the opportunities open to men, but they were not kept in seclusion. Zimri-Lim seems to have had only a single wife, Shibtu, whom he left in charge of affairs at Mari when he was visiting other towns in his dominions or on military campaigns.

The accident that preserved the clay tablets of Mari brought disaster to Zimri-Lim and an end to the city's greatness. For in Hammurabi of Babylon, Zimri-Lim had come up against another formidable Mesopotamian empire-builder.

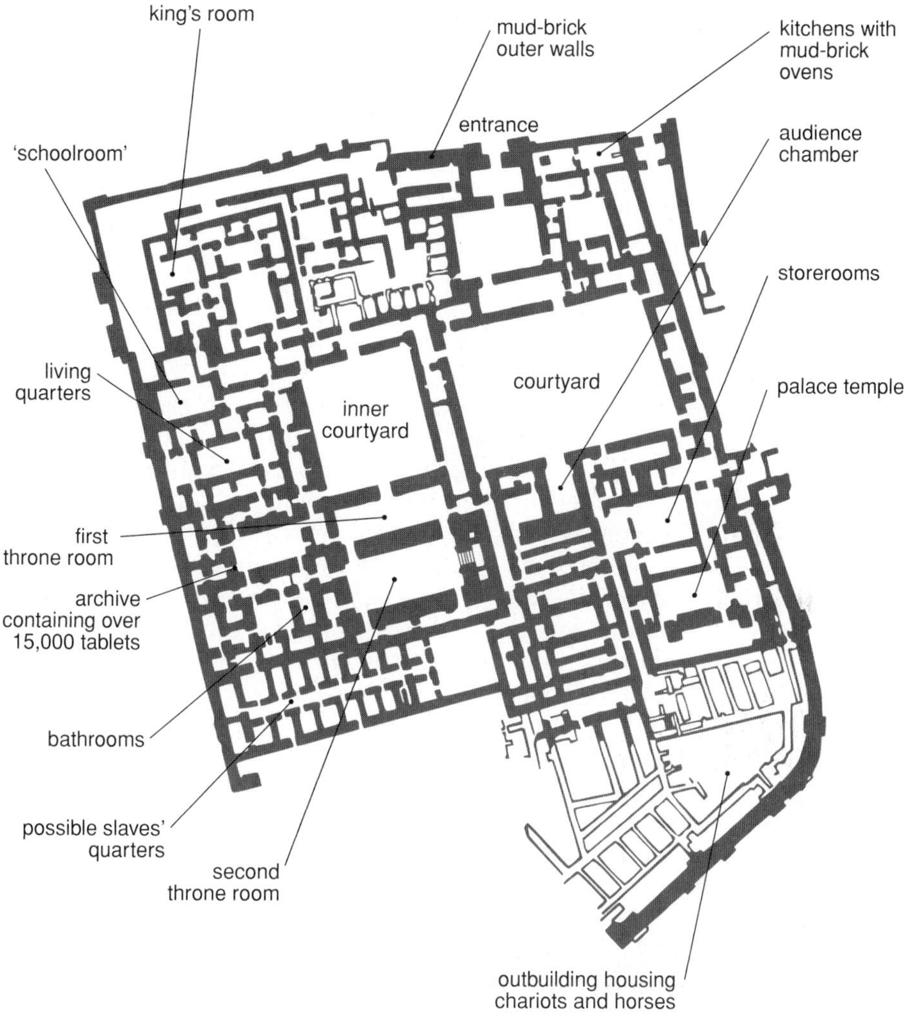


**Figure 7.1** The palace of Zimri-Lim at Mari. Mesopotamian cities of the third millennium B.C. were dominated by major temples. The king drew much of his power from also being high priest. In the Old Babylonian period, this pattern changed: Royal power became more secular and not so dependent on religious sanction. This trend is reflected in the increased size and importance of royal palaces in cities of the second millennium. Best known is that at Mari, an enormous mud-brick complex covering 2.5 hectares (6 acres) and dating in its present form from the reign of Zimri-Lim (1780–1759 B.C.). Painted frescoes adorned courtyards and principal rooms. There were also storerooms, workshops, and private apartments. One room was an archive, containing over 15,000 clay tablets, which have revealed many details of palace life. They also show Mari as the center of an important kingdom, engaged in war and diplomacy with its powerful neighbors.

## The Emergence of Babylon and the Old Babylonian Period (2004–1595 B.C.)

The city of Babylon, beside an old branch of the Euphrates in western Mesopotamia, had been a small and unimportant town in the third millennium. Yet during the early part of the second it achieved a position of preeminence in Mesopotamian affairs. As a result, the period from the fall of Ur (2004 B.C.) to the Hittite invasion (1595 B.C.) is conventionally known as the Old Babylonian period. Babylon became important once again in the Kassite period and in the first millennium B.C., notably under the Neo-Babylonian dynasty (625–539 B.C.) (Chapter 8). Here, however, it is the Old Babylonian period that concerns us.

The rise of Babylon was largely the work of one man: Hammurabi. In a reign of over 40 years (1792–1750 B.C.) he conquered Isin and Larsa in the south, then Mari and Eshnunna in the north, until he ruled the whole of southern and central Mesopotamia as a single, unified state. This was achieved not by some whirlwind campaign but through a consistent and determined combination of diplomacy and warfare. For example, Larsa did not fall to his armies until 1763 B.C.; Eshnunna, not until 1755 B.C. One of the casualties of these campaigns was the city of Mashkan-Shapir, which lost its strategic importance and was abandoned.

Hammurabi reorganized and centralized the territories under his control, tying large areas of conquered land directly to the crown by overriding the rights of previous owners. This ruthless policy was counterbalanced by the promulgation of Hammurabi's famous law code, proclaiming that the king was a just ruler despite his widespread confiscations (Box 7.2). Whether any of the code's provisions was actually used is open to doubt; it was largely an exercise in imperial propaganda.

Hammurabi's kingdom soon ran into difficulties after his death. The habit of political autonomy was still well entrenched in Mesopotamia. Though city-states might be forced to acknowledge an overlord, they did not give up their aspirations to independence and chose the earliest opportunity to rebel. Hammurabi's successor, Samsu-iluna (1749–1712 B.C.), fought a five-year war against Larsa and Uruk. At first he was victorious, but his hold over southern Mesopotamia was weak. By the end of his reign a local dynasty had seized control. Continuous fighting devastated many cities that had been flourishing centers in earlier centuries. The destruction of Ur, like that of Mari, buried numbers of cuneiform tablets and the mud-brick houses in which they were found by archaeologists. The tablets enable us to identify the occupants, including in one case a merchant active in the Dilmun trade and in another a schoolteacher. The exercise tablets of his pupils were scattered among the ruins.

American archaeologist Norman Yoffee has studied the fall of the Old Babylonian dynasty in an effort to understand its causes. Yoffee maintains that these were embedded in the structure of government that Hammurabi created. His policy of centralization brought wealth to the king, at least in the early days, when the empire was largely intact. But it placed heavy demands on the central administration and generated enormous resentment in the conquered territories. As more and

## *Box 7.2 Law Code of Hammurabi*

The most famous monument of the Babylonian ruler Hammurabi is the diorite pillar carved all round with a law code of 282 clauses (Figure 7.2). It was discovered in 1901 at Susa in southwestern Iran, where it had been carried by the Elamites as a trophy. At the top of the stone, Hammurabi himself is shown receiving the laws from Shamash, sun god and god of justice. The laws themselves are not a comprehensive code, but they cover a wide variety of subjects, from ransom of prisoners of war to pledges of land in payment for debts and punishment for adultery. The provisions make clear that Babylonian society was divided into aristocrats, commoners, and slaves; women held a subordinate position, although they were allowed to hold property and could divorce their husbands for maltreatment, provided they themselves were of good character. The examples below illustrate something of the range of subjects covered:

> *If fire broke out in a man's house and a man who went to extinguish it cast his eye on the goods of the owner of the house and has appropriated the goods of the owner of the house, that man shall be thrown into the fire.* (§25)
>
> *If outlaws have congregated in the establishment of a woman wine-seller and she has not arrested those outlaws and did not take them to the palace, that wine-seller shall be put to death.* (§109)
>
> *If a physician performed a major operation on a man with a bronze lancet and has caused the man's death, or he opened up the eye-socket of a man and has destroyed the man's eye, they shall cut off his hand.* (§219) (Pritchard, 1958, pp.142, 149–150, 162 [slightly adapted]).

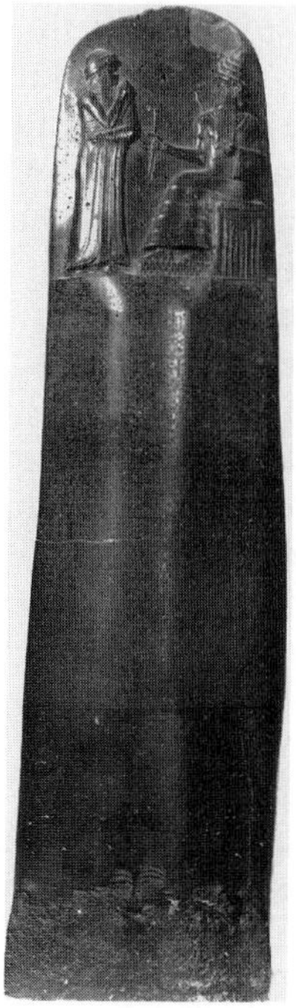

**Figure 7.2** The Law Code of Hammurabi. (Stele of Hammurabi. Hammurabi standing before the sun-god Shamash and 262 laws. Engraved black basalt stele. 1792–1750 BCE, 1st Babylonian Dynasty. Louvre, Paris, France. © Giraudon/Art Resource, NY.)

more cities seceded, the government fell into financial difficulties and attempted to offset its losses by exploiting the remaining lands even more thoroughly. Hammurabi's successors appointed many more royal officials, but this simply increased the size of the central administration. Eventually the officials became hereditary local aristocrats, depriving the kings of a further large slice of their dwindling power. The collapse of the Old Babylonian empire, when it came, was thus not so much the result of foreign attack as of decay from within; the central government simply lost the allegiance of its officials and local leaders.

Of Babylon, the capital, little is known at this period since the early levels are deeply buried beneath later deposits and below the water table. It must have possessed a luxurious royal palace, however, and a major temple to the chief god of Babylon, Marduk, perhaps on the site of the later ziggurat. The tablet evidence shows that the Old Babylonian period was a time of literary and scientific activity. The power of the state steadily dwindled, however, as parcels of territory were clipped away by neighboring peoples. The final blow was delivered not by one of these but by a more distant enemy: the Hittites from Anatolia. In 1595 B.C. Hittite King Mursilis I descended on Mesopotamia. Meeting little resistance, he sacked Babylon. With this event the center of power in the Near East moved decisively away from southern Mesopotamia to the north and west.

## The Rise of the Hittites (1650–1400 B.C.)

The Hittites remained one of the most mysterious peoples of the ancient Near East until the present century, when excavations by German archaeologist Hugo Winckler at Boghazköy recovered 10,000 clay tablets from the Hittite royal archives. Boghazköy, which had indeed been the Hittite capital from around 1650 B.C., was known by the name Hattusas. It lay in the northern part of the Anatolian plateau not far from Alaça Höyük, site of the third-millennium royal graves described earlier. Over the four centuries from 1650 B.C. the Hittite rulers turned Boghazköy into a vast fortress-city, sprawling over the rocky terrain, with craggy citadels and elaborate temples (Figure 7.3). It became the center of a powerful empire that covered not only most of Anatolia but also at times extended far to the south, into Syria and the Levant.

The Hittites were one of several peoples inhabiting the Anatolian plateau at this time. The tablets found at Boghazköy record no fewer than eight different languages. It is clear that not all of these languages were current in the Hittite heartland in equal measure. They do, however, reflect the polyglot world with which the Hittites came into contact during their imperial expansion. The Hittites first entered history in the seventeenth century B.C. Later tradition told of a King Labarnas, who extended his power from central Anatolia to the Mediterranean coast. It was his son, Hattusilis, who moved the capital to Boghazköy. Hittite armies campaigned vigorously during these years, meeting particularly strong resistance in western Anatolia; although the far west and the mountainous north may have remained unsubdued, the Hittites were widely successful and were soon ready for

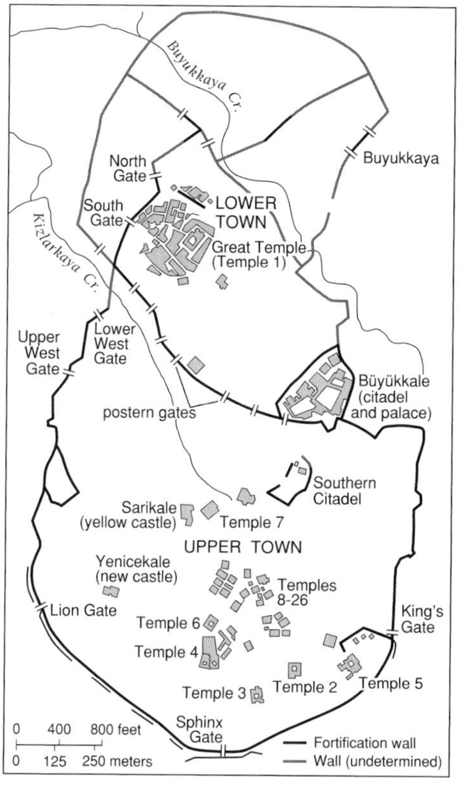


**Figure 7.3** Plan of Boghazköy, ancient Hattusas, capital of the Hittite empire from c. 1650 to 1200 B.C. The Hittites were skilled in fortification and made excellent use of the rocky terrain to strengthen their defenses. On the eastern side is the Büyükkale or Great Citadel, where remains of an imperial Hittite archive have come to light. A major feature of Boghazköy was its many temples within the defensive circuit.

exploits further afield. Hattusilis himself crossed the Taurus Mountains and reduced the major kingdom of Yamhad (Aleppo) to vassalage. For most Near Eastern states, however, the bolt from the blue came in 1595 B.C. when Hattusilis's adopted son and successor, Mursilis I, marched far to the south in a lightning raid and sacked Babylon. As we have seen, this brought an end to the Babylonian dynasty founded by Hammurabi.

The Hittites did not follow up the Babylon raid since Mursilis was murdered shortly afterward and royal authority collapsed. For almost a century and a half, the princes of the Hittite royal house struggled among themselves for power while the conquests of their predecessors slipped away. Hittite fortunes revived only toward the end of the fifteenth century B.C. when once again a Hittite king was campaigning in northern Syria. The great expansion of Hittite power south of the Taurus Mountains, however, occurred under their most famous king, Suppiluliumas I, who reigned from around 1350 to 1315 B.C. Suppiluliumas's reign ushered in the period known as the Hittite empire, but in order to follow these events it is necessary first to introduce the other leading players on the Levantine stage: Egypt and Mitanni (Figure 7.4).

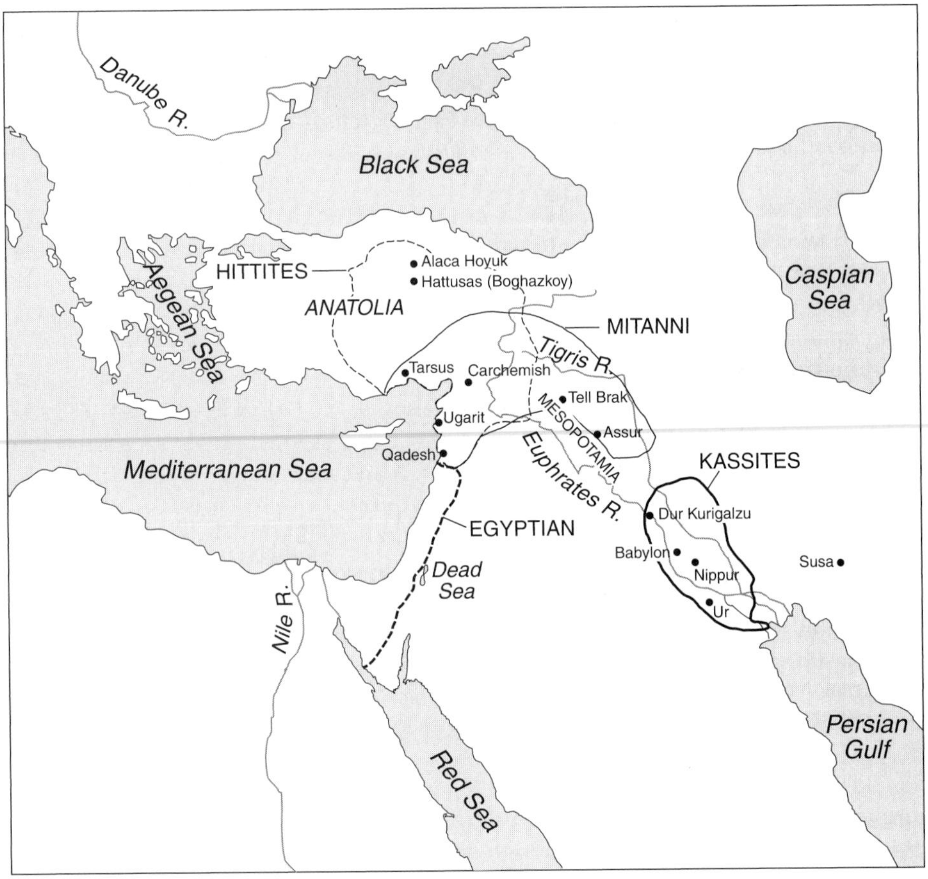


**Figure 7.4** Map of the Near East in the mid–second millennium.

# Egypt and Mitanni: War in the Levant (1550–1400 B.C.)

The Levant had been a land of cities long before the second millennium. Many of the early cities in the southern Levant had declined or been abandoned in the later third millennium B.C., however, and it was not until the Middle Bronze II period (c. 2000 B.C.) that there was an urban renewal. By the early second millennium, the Levant as a whole was divided up among a number of kingdoms ruled from major cities like Hazor and Qatna. Hazor is a good example of such a city, with a large lower town and a more strongly defended citadel, which probably contained the royal palace. Israeli archaeologist Yigael Yadin found that the lower town was laid out in the early second millennium and surrounded by a massive earthen rampart built around a mud-brick core. The front of the rampart was steeply sloping and faced with small stones—too steep to scale and too sloping to attack with a battering ram. On top of the rampart was a wall or breastwork of mud-bricks. The city gateways were flanked by square towers of mud-bricks on stone foundations. Similar defenses encircled the citadel or upper city.

The size of these fortifications hints that large-scale warfare was a fact of life in the Levant during the early second millennium. If so, it was largely internecine, for it was only in the sixteenth century B.C. that neighboring states began to interfere in the affairs of the region. It was at this time that a trio of "superpowers" emerged around the fringes of the Levant, each seeking to establish its dominance over the local kings.

First of the trio to campaign in the region was Egypt. The invasion of the southern Levant under Pharaoh Ahmose (1550–1525 B.C.) began as retaliation for the Hyksos domination of Egypt—the Hyksos being peoples of the Levant who had conquered the Egyptian delta (see Chapter 4). What began as retaliation soon turned into imperialism, as subsequent Egyptian rulers campaigned far to the north. Tuthmosis I (1504–1492 B.C.) even reached the Euphrates, and local rulers hurried to swear allegiance to such a powerful monarch, who had the immense resources of Egypt behind him. The problem for the Egyptians was that once their campaigns were over and they went home, the Levantine rulers grew less fervent in their support. Tuthmosis III (1479–1425 B.C.) sought to consolidate Egyptian power in the region by a 20-year series of military campaigns. In 1457 B.C. he won a great victory at Megiddo. Much of the southern Levant then became an Egyptian dependency. In the north, however, Egyptian ambitions were checked by the development of a rival superpower of northern Mesopotamia—the kingdom of Mitanni.

Mitanni arose around 1550 B.C. when a local ruler succeeded in defeating his rivals and established a powerful unified state. Its center lay east of the Euphrates, in the Khabur plain, but the Mitannian kings soon cast their eyes west and east. In the west, they took control of Syria up to the Taurus Mountains, including territories previously conquered by the Hittites. In the east, they captured Assur and the valley of the upper Tigris, as far as the Zagros foothills.

## The Hittites in the Levant (1400–1200 B.C.)

For several decades Egypt and Mitanni pursued a form of proxy warfare in the Levant, fighting each other's allies and dependents rather than attacking each other directly. Then in the reign of Tuthmosis IV (1401–1391 B.C.) they suddenly changed tack and made an alliance because of renewed activity by the Hittites, culminating in the conquests of Suppiluliumas. This Hittite monarch defeated and destroyed Mitanni and took over Mitannian territories in the northern Levant. His victory brought the Hittites face to face with the Egyptians.

The history of the Levantine city-states during the fourteenth century is brought vividly to life by the Amarna letters. In 1887 an Egyptian peasant woman accidentally found a collection of clay tablets at the site of Amarna, capital of Egypt under the "heretic" Pharaoh Akhenaten (see Chapter 4). The local people soon sold them to various dealers, and 382 tablets eventually found their way into Western museums. They proved to be diplomatic correspondence from the reigns of Akhenaten (1353–1335 B.C.) and his father, Amenhotep III (1391–1353 B.C.). Many of them concern affairs in the Levant.

Most of the Amarna tablets are written in Akkadian, the diplomatic language of the period. Most are from foreign princes to the pharaoh, but a few are copies of letters sent by the pharaoh. The general tone is of Levantine rulers protesting their loyalty to Egypt, accusing their neighbors of treachery, and asking for assistance against them. Many of these rulers may indeed have felt threatened by the rising power of the Hittites, for it was at this time that Suppiluliumas defeated Mitanni and became heir to its Levantine dependencies. It is clear, however, that the local princes themselves were engaged in shady diplomacy, defecting to the Hittites whenever that served their purpose.

Hostility between Egypt and the Hittites continued into the thirteenth century B.C., culminating in a great battle at Kadesh in 1279 B.C. The protagonists on this occasion were the vainglorious pharaoh Ramesses II and the Hittite ruler Muwatallis. We are fortunate in possessing a full account of the battle from the inscriptions and depictions of it that Ramesses had carved on temples in Egypt, including Abydos and Abu Simbel. These are, naturally, slanted to the Egyptian point of view but nonetheless make it possible to reconstruct the course of events.

A key feature of the battle was the war chariot. This was a light, two-wheeled fighting platform pulled by a pair of well-trained horses. The Sumerians in the third millennium had used heavy four-wheeled carts in battle; they are riding down on the enemy on one side of the famous *Standard* of Ur. The war chariot was a very different contrivance, however—lightweight in construction and capable of traveling at a high speed. Controlled by a driver, it carried an archer rapidly across the field of battle. This mobile firing platform was especially good for harrying slow-moving infantry formations. The war chariot became an essential element of Near Eastern armies during the second millennium B.C., though its effectiveness must always have been limited by the need for level terrain. That said, the Hittites used war chariots with great success in their encounter with Ramesses II at Kadesh.

Both sides claimed victory at Kadesh, but 16 years later Egyptians and Hittites officially recognized the futility of further conflict and negotiated a peace treaty that left the Levant divided into Egyptian and Hittite zones.

## The Hittites in Anatolia (1400–1200 B.C.)

Despite Hittite interest in the northern Levant, the heart of their empire remained central Anatolia, and it is here that one would expect their greatest monuments to be found. In fact, much less is known about Hittite archaeology than we might like or would expect, given this people's historic importance. The principal site remains Boghazköy, the capital, where the fortifications were rebuilt and strengthened during the reigns of Suppiluliumas and his successors. There were over two dozen temples within the walls, some (like the city walls themselves) built on foundations of massive stone masonry. For the clearest evidence of Hittite religion we must look 2 kilometers (1.2 miles) beyond Boghazköy to Yazilikaya (Figure 7.5 a and b).

It was here in the thirteenth century that one of the last Hittite kings, Tudhaliyas IV, had the gods and goddesses of the Hittite pantheon carved on the walls of a rock-cut defile.

The chief difficulty faced by the Hittite rulers was their insecurity within Anatolia itself. Expeditions to the Levant brought rich pickings and gave them direct control of wealthy and powerful Syrian cities such as Carchemish and Aleppo. All too often, however, these expeditions gave the local Anatolian peoples an opportunity to reassert their independence, sometimes even to attack the Hittites themselves. The Hittites controlled only central Anatolia directly (Box 7.3). To the north lay the troublesome Kaska, a highland people in the mountains fronting the Black Sea whom the Hittites were constantly defeating but never able to subdue. To the southeast and southwest lay, respectively, the kingdoms of Kizzuwatna and Arzawa, sometimes allies and sometimes enemies. Further west still, on the Aegean coast, was a land known as Ahhiyawa. Scholars have debated whether this could be a reference to the Achaeans of Homeric legend, the Mycenaean Greeks. During the thirteenth century the "Great King" of Ahhiyawa seems to have controlled the territory around Miletus. Further north along this same Aegean coast lay the site of Troy at the entrance to the Dardanelles. If the legend of the Trojan War has any historical foundation it would have taken place around the middle of the thirteenth century B.C. and would represent a further episode of Mycenaean Greek expansion along this seaboard.

The Aegean coast of Turkey lay at the extreme limit of Hittite influence; it was only very rarely that Hittite kings campaigned as far as the western sea.

The end of the Hittite empire is shrouded in mystery. Archaeology shows that all the major Hittite sites in Anatolia were destroyed and abandoned around 1200 B.C. The most likely perpetrators were the Phrygians, a new enemy settled in

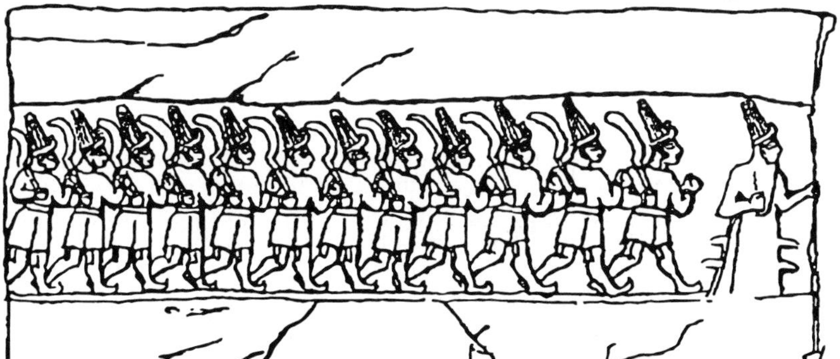

(a)

**Figure 7.5** Yazilikaya. (a) Drawing of reliefs.

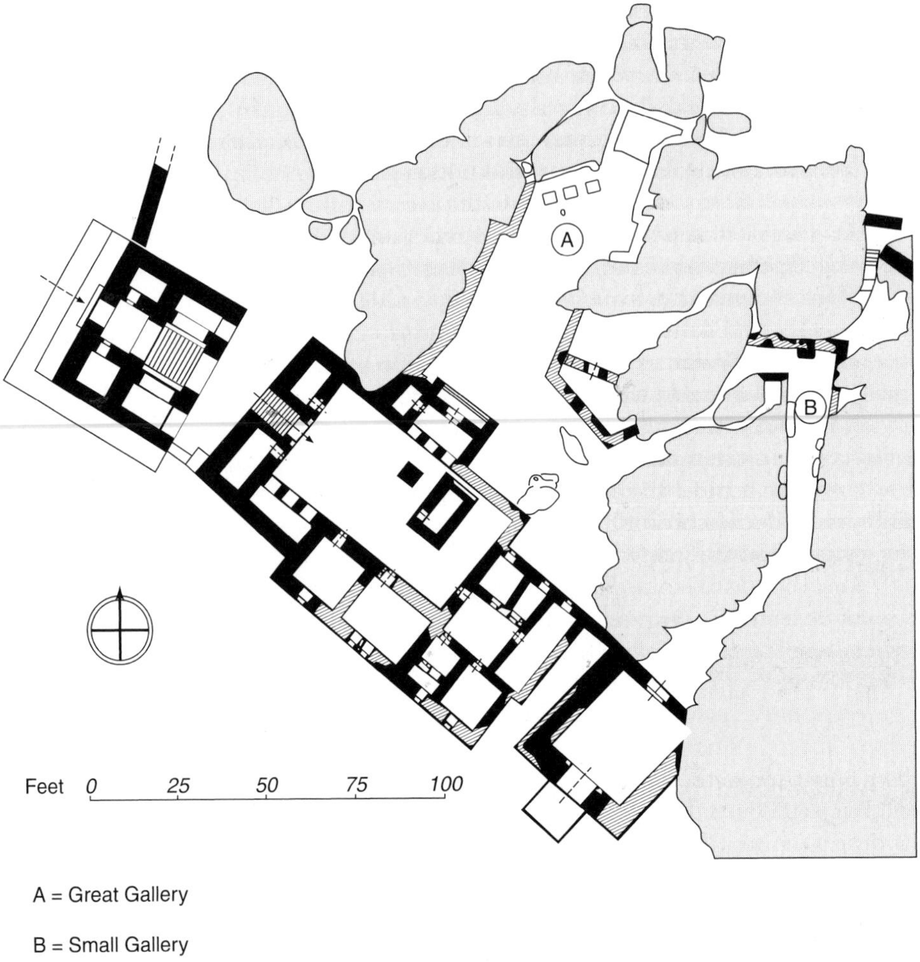


(b)

**Figure 7.5** *(cont.)* (b) Plan of sanctuary. The open-air sanctuary of Yazilikaya lies a little northeast of the Hittite capital, Boghazköy. It consists of rocky clefts carved with relief portraits of the Hittite pantheon. The figures are over 2 meters (6 feet, 6 inches) tall and are carved in continuous panels, as if in procession. The larger of the two decorated rock clefts, the so-called Great Gallery, has figures of 63 deities, with gods on the left and goddesses on the right. The two processions meet at the end of the gallery, where the chief god Teshub, "Weather God of Heaven," meets his consort, Hepat. The name of each deity is given in hieroglyphs. The only human figure to appear in these scenes is King Tudhaliyas IV (c. 1250–1220 B.C.), who was responsible for the carving both of the great gallery and the smaller side gallery. In the great gallery Tudhaliyas is shown as a god himself, whereas in the small gallery he is embraced by the god Sharruma. The small gallery also has three rectangular niches in the walls, and it is conjectured that these were used for burial urns of Hittite rulers, possibly Tudhaliyas himself and his parents, Hattusilis III and Puduhepa.

## Box 7.3 Kilise Tepe

During the second millennium B.C. Hittite power expanded from the Anatolian plateau to include the coastlands facing the Aegean to the west and the Mediterranean to the south. The narrow valley of the Göksü River is one of the principal routes linking the central plateau with the southern coast, and here, at a strategic fording point, stands the small tell site of Kilise Tepe. Occupation began in the third millennium B.C., but during the second millennium what may previously have been a small independent statelet was absorbed into the Hittite empire. The change is illustrated in Layer III by discoveries of standard unpainted Hittite pottery, which can be closely paralleled at the Hittite capital Boghazköy far away to the north. Kilise Tepe, however, also had links southward with the Mediterranean world, and these were confirmed by sherds of Mycenaean painted pottery found in the overlying Layer II. Layer III belongs to the period when the Hittite empire was at its strongest, but the Mycenaean pottery from Layer II dates probably to the twelfth century B.C., by which time Hittite centralized power was in eclipse. In this part of southern Anatolia, however, Hittite rule seems to have survived several decades longer than in the Hittite heartland, and though the site was destroyed by fire, Layer II also contained stone stamp seals with the names of officials in Hittite hieroglyphic (see Figure 7.6). But Kilise Tepe did not escape unharmed from the disturbed conditions of the late second millennium B.C., and the site suffered a second successive destruction by fire at about this time, perhaps from attack by the Sea Peoples. Such a strategically located site was not long abandoned, and Kilise Tepe became part of a small south Anatolian kingdom with strong connections to the Mediterranean in the early first millennium B.C. and eventually, as its name "Church mound" indicates, the site of a Byzantine ecclesiastical complex of the fifth to seventh centuries A.D.

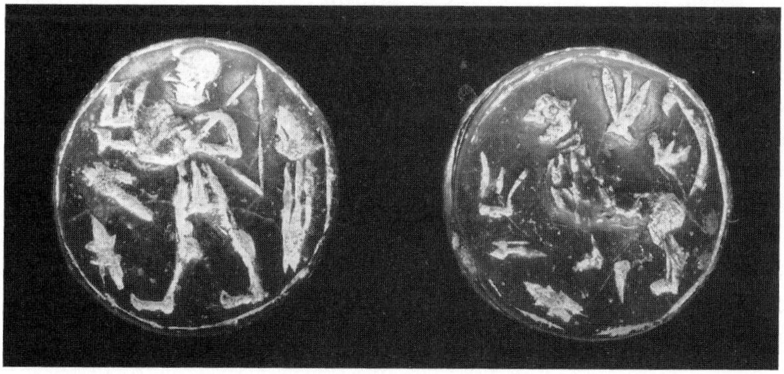

**Figure 7.6** Stamp seal of the Hittite official Tarhunta-piya, found in recent excavations at Kilise Tepe. He is carrying a bow, and his shoes (note the upward-pointing toes) are typically Anatolian in fashion. They illustrate the strong cultural links between the southern coastlands of Turkey and the Anatolian plateau, heartland of the Hittite empire.

the northern hills. Certainly it was the Phrygians who were in possession of the Anatolian plateau when written records resumed in the first millennium B.C. Hittite survivors, meanwhile, fled south to the cities of Syria and the Levant, which were now the sole remnants of the once-great Hittite empire. These cities, known in this final period as Neo-Hittite, remained a powerful political force until they were absorbed into the Assyrian empire in the ninth century B.C.

## Mesopotamia and Iran (1400–1200 B.C.)

This account of Hittites, Egyptians, and the struggle for the Levant has left to one side events in the rest of the Near East during the later second millennium. In Mesopotamia, political history in this period was dominated by two powers: Assyria in the north and the Kassites in the south. We have already encountered Assur as the homeland of the merchants stationed at Kanesh in Anatolia. In the fifteenth century B.C. Assur came under the control of the kings of Mitanni, but when the Hittites defeated Mitanni 150 years later, the Assyrians regained their autonomy and soon began to expand their territory. The result was the Middle Assyrian empire, which during the thirteenth century extended as far west as the border of Hittite territory along the Euphrates.

At around the same time as the kings of Mitanni were establishing themselves in the north, a new dynasty known as the Kassites took control of Babylonia. These outsiders ruled from Babylon and soon adopted the trappings of Babylonian culture and religion, though they also retained their own gods. Kassite kings are featured in the Amarna letters as the equals of Hittite and Egyptian rulers. In archaeological terms, the most striking Kassite remains are those of Dur-Kurigalzu (modern Aqar Quf), a city founded as a new capital by the Kassite king Kurigalzu II (1332–1308 B.C.). The royal palace covered an area of 9 hectares (22 acres), and the mud-brick core of the great ziggurat still stands to a height of 57 meters (187 feet).

Kurigalzu II was famous as a builder and as a warrior, leading his armies eastward against the kingdom of Elam. As in earlier periods (see Chapter 3), this realm lay along the edge of the Iranian plateau, partly on the plateau itself and partly on the lowland plain of Susiana at its foot. Like their Kassite neighbors—and probably following their example—one of the Elamite kings founded a new capital city, Choga Zanbil, centered on a religious enclosure that contained a massive ziggurat, originally over 60 meters (296 feet) high. Hittites, Egyptians, Assyrians, Kassites, and Elamites make up the complicated political map of the Near East in the thirteenth century B.C. The further development of the region into the first millennium B.C. and the growth of the great "international" empires of Assyria, Babylon, and Persia are described in Chapter 8.

## Summary

Kingdoms and states appeared on the Anatolian plateau in the later third millennium B.C., known to archaeologists from the royal burials at Alaça Höyük (c. 2500 B.C.) and excavations at Kanesh, where from 1900 B.C. the Assyrians maintained a trading colony. A period of political uncertainty in Mesopotamia after the collapse of the Ur III empire brought Babylon into prominence as trade with the Persian Gulf, and notably the island of Dilmun (Bahrain), flourished. In the north, Assur on the Tigris and Mari on the Euphrates became powerful, the latter being well known from the tablet archives at the palace of Zimri-Lim. Mari was overthrown by King Hammurabi of Babylon, who forged a major empire that covered both northern and southern Mesopotamia in the eighteenth century B.C. To the northwest, the Hittites came into prominence on the Anatolian plateau, raiding Babylon in 1595 B.C. The apogee of Hittite power came under King Suppiluliumas I (1350–1315 B.C.) when his armies competed with Egypt and Mitanni for control of the Levant. This power play culminated in 1279 B.C. in the battle of Kadesh between the Hittites and Egyptians, the latter led by the redoubtable Ramesses II. The Hittite empire collapsed around 1200 B.C., dissolving south of the Taurus Mountains into powerful neo-Hittite city-states, which were absorbed into the Assyrian empire in the ninth century B.C.

## Guide to Further Reading

Two general works guide us through this complex period of Near Eastern archaeology: Seton Lloyd, *The Archaeology of Mesopotamia* (London: Thames and Hudson, 1978) and Michael Roaf, *Cultural Atlas of Mesopotamia and the Ancient Near East* (Oxford: Facts on File, 1990). Joan Oates, *Babylon* (London: Thames and Hudson, 1986) covers the archaeology of this major site and the kingdoms of which it was the capital.

Trade between Ashur and Anatolia is the subject of Mogens Larsen, *The Old Assyrian City-State and Its Colonies* (Copenhagen: Akademisk Forlag, 1976); see also Larsen's analysis of the broader network, "Commercial Networks in the Ancient Near East," in Michael Rowlands, Mogens Larsen, and Kristian Kristiansen, eds., *Centre and Periphery in the Ancient World* (Cambridge: Cambridge University Press, 1987), pp. 47–56. Recent excavations at Saar on Bahrain are described by Harriet Crawford, "The Site of Saar: Dilmun Reconsidered," *Antiquity* 71 (1997): 701–708.

Excavations at Mashkan-Shapir in Iraq are described by Elizabeth C. Stone and Paul Zimansky, "The Tell Abu Duwari Project, 1988–1990," *Journal of Field Archaeology* 21 (1994): 437–455 and "The Tapestry of Power in a Mesopotamian City," *Scientific American* 272, no. 4 (April 1995): 92–97.

There are no good accounts in English of the palace of Mari, but Stephanie Dalley, *Mari and Karana: Two Old Babylonian Cities* (London: Longman, 1984) provides details of daily life drawn from the palace archives. For Norman Yoffee's analysis of the fall of the Old Babylonian empire, see *The Economic Role of the Crown in the Old Babylonian Period* (Malibu, CA: Undena, 1977); he summarizes the argument in "The Decline and Rise of Mesopotamian Civilization: An Ethnoarchaeological Perspective on the Evolution of Social Complexity," *American Antiquity* 44 (1979): 5–35. A recent account of the Elamites is provided by D. T. Potts, *The Archaeology of Elam: Formation and Transformation of an Ancient Iranian State* (Cambridge: Cambridge University Press, 1999).

For the Hittites, see Trevor Bryce, *The Kingdom of the Hittites* (Oxford: Oxford University Press, 1999) and J. G. Macqueen, *The Hittites and Their Contemporaries in Asia Minor* (London: Thames and Hudson, 1996). The Amarna letters are well covered by W. L. Moran, *The Amarna Letters* (Baltimore: Johns Hopkins University Press, 1992). On the destruction of the late Bronze Age's great centers and the identity of their attackers, see Trude Dothan, *People of the Sea: The Search for the Philistines* (New York: Macmillan, 1992). Excavations at Kilise Tepe and other sites are described in Roger Matthews, ed., *Ancient Anatolia* (London: British Institute of Archaeology at Ankara, 1998).

*Chapter 8*

# The Near East in the First Millennium B.C.

A Persian king in audience. A relief from the palace of Persepolis, Iran. Fifth century B.C. (Copyright SEF/Art Resource, NY)

*The doors of the great audience chamber swung open, and the attendants escorted them forward. On either side the walls of the room were decorated with bands of brightly painted reliefs that depicted cities falling to Assyrian attack and the king presiding over the torture and execution of rebels. There was no mistaking the message here as the foreign delegation was ushered forward into the presence of the king himself. There, at the end of the room, sat Assurnasirpal, on a throne emblazoned with gilded ivories. Around him stood his courtiers and attendants, richly attired in brightly colored clothes and jewels, hair and beards elegantly dressed and perfumed. Silence descended as the usher tapped the floor with his stick, and the king spoke: "Know ye not what I do to my enemies; how I flay some, burn others alive, immure them in the walls of their palaces, leave them to die as if they had never been? How I deal with captives, cutting off noses, ears, and fingers, putting out their eyes? Submit then, before it is too late!" [fictional quote]*

Such menacing scenes may have been a regular occurrence in the audience chamber of Assurnasirpal, ruler of the Assyrian empire in the ninth century B.C. We may still see today the king on his throne, surrounded by courtiers, depicted in the relief carvings taken from his palace. The palace itself survives only as a mud-brick ruin, a maze of courts and passages, revealing little of its former glory. Archaeology and imagination together are needed to restore its original appearance in the mind's eye. For the words of the king himself, however, we rely not on imagination alone but on Assurnasirpal's own royal inscriptions, which detail the refinements of cruelty he used to instill fear into his enemies. The weapon of terror was highly effective as the Assyrians built and consolidated their great empire.

This chapter describes developments in the Near East during the first half of the first millennium B.C. One feature of the period was the emergence of new kingdoms—notably that of the Israelites—in the Levant. To their north were the Phoenicians, enterprising merchants with an alphabetic script, precursor to our own. But, above all, a succession of empires dominate these centuries: first, the Assyrian empire; then the Neo-Babylonian; and finally the Persian, or Achaemenid, which brought Near Eastern rule to the shores of the Aegean Sea (see Table 7.1).

## A Reordered World (1200–1000 B.C.)

New peoples entered the archaeological record in the Near East after the dissolution or decline of the "great powers" around 1200 B.C. The two following centuries are sometimes called the "dark age," largely because of a dearth of historical records. It does not mean that there were no thriving Near Eastern communities during this period. Yet there was a measure of disruption as the old order collapsed. The Hittite empire disappeared around the end of the thirteenth century; Assyria slipped into decline after the murder of King Tukulti-Ninurta I in 1207 B.C.; and Egypt withdrew within its own borders under the combined effect of economic difficulty, internal unrest, and the onslaught of the so-called Sea Peoples. It was during these troubled times that the Philistines, one of the Sea Peoples, took control of the coastal plain.

We first meet the Sea Peoples in Egyptian historical texts of the thirteenth century B.C. They were an assortment of different peoples who operated around the shores of the eastern Mediterranean and were bent on raiding and plunder. They included a strong Mycenaean element, and Mycenaean pottery appears in many of the sites destroyed (presumably by the Sea Peoples) during this period in layers above the destruction horizon. One of the Sea Peoples is described in Egyptian accounts as *Peleset*. These are the Philistines, famous in the Bible as opponents of the Israelites. Goliath, slain by David, was a Philistine, and it was the Philistines who captured and blinded the Israelite hero Samson. During biblical times the Philistines lived in the coastal cities of the southern Levant, where they had settled after taking part in the attacks on Egypt. Archaeology shows that their pottery, painted with red or black geometric designs, was derived from Mycenaean prototypes. Their temples, too, owed little to local Canaanite forms of the late Bronze Age but had more in common with Mycenaean or Cycladic examples.

One significant innovation was the use of iron. Bronze, an alloy of copper and tin, is a useful metal but expensive because of the scarcity of tin, which had to be shipped over long distances from sources on the Iranian plateau. Equipping whole armies with bronze helmets and weaponry was beyond the means of all but the wealthiest states. Iron, in contrast, is a much more common metal, though it does require higher temperatures to extract from the ore. It is also worked differently; whereas bronze is poured into molds to give it a predetermined shape (casting), iron is usually hammered into shape while red-hot (forging). However, Chinese metalworkers did cast iron from an early period (see Chapter 14). These technological differences delayed the spread of iron. It had been known as early as the third millennium B.C. and appears in the royal graves at Alaça Höyük. The Egyptian pharaoh Tutankhamun was buried with an iron knife in the fourteenth century B.C., but the metal was still a rarity at that time and was considered more valuable than gold. It was only in the eleventh century that iron came into more widespread use in the Aegean and at various points throughout the Near East, probably because the collapse of the great powers disrupted the traditional trade routes. For a while, copper and tin became even more difficult to obtain. Many communities switched their efforts away from the old metal to the development of the nascent iron technology. Once the new technology was mastered, iron proved to have significant advantages over bronze. It was plentiful enough to be used for everyday items such as farming implements and military gear, and it could be worked to a harder edge than bronze.

Iron was among the innovations introduced to the Levant by the Philistines. From there it spread to other local communities, including the Israelites. Elsewhere in the Near East, iron technology was also developed by the city-states of Syria and Anatolia and by the Assyrians east of the Euphrates. This event forms the distinction, in conventional archaeological terms, between the Late Bronze Age of the later second millennium and the Iron Age of the first millennium B.C. The transition from bronze to iron was only gradual, however, and older theories of the impact of the metal on social structures and military advantage are now generally discounted. The important change at the end of the Late Bronze Age was not the appearance of a new metal but the collapse of the Bronze Age empires and trading networks.

## The Mediterranean Coastlands (1000–700 B.C.)

In archaeology and history it was not the Philistines but their neighbors to the east and north, the Israelites and Phoenicians, who were the leading Levantine powers of the early first millennium B.C.

The Israelites first come to historical prominence around 1000 B.C. when, according to the biblical account, Saul and then David founded and consolidated the kingdom of Israel, defeating their neighbors to the east and west, including the Philistines, to establish a measure of regional dominance. Tracing the earlier history of the Israelites is a more contentious business. The Old Testament recounts how the Israelites left Egypt after being oppressed by the pharaohs, an event (the Exodus) that some scholars have placed in the thirteenth century B.C. Led by Moses, they crossed the Red Sea before wandering 40 years in the Sinai Desert and then entering the land of Canaan from the east across the River Jordan. How does this account tie in with the archaeology?

The question has naturally been taken up with great interest by Israeli archaeologists, and some, such as Adam Zertal and Israel Finkelstein, have assembled evidence that supports an alternative version of events. Zertal identifies the Israelites with a swathe of rustic farming settlements of Early Iron Age date, the earliest of which lay on the desert margins of eastern Israel. As the Early Iron Age progressed, these settlements gradually spread westward into the hill country and the valleys. Finkelstein argues that the reason for this spread is not the military conquest of Canaan by the Israelites envisaged in the Bible but the economic collapse of the Canaanite cities in the late thirteenth century. This took place at the same time that the Hittites were defeated and the Sea Peoples attacked Egypt and then, as Philistines, settled the Levantine coast. According to the new theory of Israelite origins, then, the Israelites had long been present in Canaan as herders and farmers on the edge of the densely settled zone. Their takeover of the land was achieved by largely peaceful means. As the cities declined, the nonurban Israelites became the dominant power, eventually controlling the cities as well. Naturally, not all historians accept this version of events, but it is an interesting example of the discord that often arises between archaeological evidence and literary or historical records of the very distant past.

The archaeology of the early kingdom of Israel is no less contentious. The traditional view holds that David's son and successor, Solomon (c. 965–931 B.C.) was a great builder. Several key cities (Gezer, Hazor, and Megiddo) are held to show evidence of powerful new fortifications from this period, but according to the Old Testament sources, Solomon's greatest efforts were devoted to Jerusalem. He turned Jerusalem into a splendid royal capital by extending David's city and taking in the Temple Mount. This became the site of an impressive upper city, containing the royal palace and the famous Temple itself, which Solomon built with help from Phoenician craftspeople and architects.

This reconstruction of events is increasingly difficult to reconcile with archaeological evidence, which suggests instead that the great buildings of Megiddo and other "Solomonic" cities belong not to the tenth century but to the ninth century B.C., the period in which the northern kingdom of Israel arose as a significant regional power. There is still less archaeological evidence for major Solomonic buildings at Jerusalem in the tenth century B.C. Thus revisionist archaeologists argue that the true story of the region in the tenth and ninth centuries is the development of a northern kingdom of Israel, descended directly from Late Bronze Age Canaanite roots, during the ninth century; followed by a southern kingdom, that of Judah, which achieved statehood only in the eighth century B.C. Tenth-century Jerusalem, according to this view, was a small hill-country stronghold for a ruling family—that of David and Solomon—who achieved mainly posthumous fame as the founders of the royal house of Judah. This reading is, of course, in conflict with the biblical account, which holds that the United Monarchy of David and Solomon was a major power already in the tenth century B.C., before it split (after Solomon's death) into the successor kingdoms of Israel and Judah. Archaeology suggests a rather different reading of the evidence, with centralized kingdoms arising as modest players in the regional power game during the ninth and eighth centuries B.C. The first historical fixed point is the battle of Qarqar in 853 B.C., when the king of Israel appears among a confederacy of local rulers fighting against the Assyrians.

The greatest Levantine traders of this period were the Phoenicians, centered on the coast of present-day Lebanon (Figure 8.1). Here the cities of the Late Bronze Age had escaped the decline suffered by the Canaanite cities of Israel. The Phoenicians were not newcomers to the region, therefore, nor even to political power, but the direct descendants of the Bronze Age inhabitants. Their leading cities were scattered along the Mediterranean coast and were major ports, notably Tyre and Sidon. Freed from Egyptian overlordship in the twelfth century B.C., each city became an independent city-state, supported by the produce of an agricultural hinterland. Any fame that the Phoenicians may have had as farmers, however, was greatly overshadowed by their accomplishments as craftspeople and traders. They were particularly famed for the production of multicolored glassware and carved ivories designed as inlays for furniture. Their most important legacy, however, was the alphabet (Box 8.1).

Remains of several Phoenician cities survive, though many (such as Tyre and Sidon) are buried beneath later constructions. Access to the sea was of paramount importance since the Phoenicians were enterprising maritime traders. They were operating throughout the Mediterranean by the eighth century B.C. Sidon was situated on a rocky headland, Tyre and Aradus on offshore islands. The advantages of these locations, which provided natural defenses and sheltered anchorages, were

**Figure 8.1** The harbor of Byblos, on the coast of modern Lebanon, looking across toward the site of the ancient city. Already an important center for trade and commerce in the third and second millenniums B.C., the Phoenician city of Byblos was eclipsed by its rivals, Tyre and Sidon in the first millennium B.C. but has given us one of the earliest surviving alphabetic inscriptions, carved on the sarcophagus of its eleventh-century king Ahiram (see Box 8.1).

improved by the building of seawalls and harbor works, linking together offshore reefs and islets with substantial masonry walls. Some of these harbor works may date back to the Bronze Age, but we can be sure that they were added to or improved during the great centuries of Phoenician trade in the first millennium B.C. (Figure 8.3).

## Box 8.1 *Invention of the Alphabet*

The alphabet, one of the most significant inventions of the ancient Near East, replaced the cumbersome syllabic scripts that had hitherto been in use. Syllabic scripts rendered each syllable by a separate sign. The large number of syllables in any language meant that the number of signs usually ran into hundreds (almost 600 in the case of Akkadian). Alphabetic scripts break down the syllables into their constituent vowels and consonants and need only 20 to 30 signs to represent all the sounds used in a language. The Phoenician alphabet had 22 signs; classical Greek had 24; Etruscan and modern English have 26 (Figure 8.2).

The idea of alphabetic components first appeared in inscriptions found in Sinai, known as Protosinaitic and dated to c. 1700 B.C. These took Egyptian hieroglyphics as a basis but used a small selection of the full range of hieroglyphic signs to form the letters of an alphabet. The language of the inscriptions was not Egyptian but Canaanite, and it was in the Levant that the subsequent development of the alphabet took place. By the eleventh century B.C. a fully developed version of this early alphabet was being used by the Phoenicians. The Israelites and Aramaeans adopted and adapted the Phoenician alphabet in the ninth century B.C., and the Greeks adopted it from Phoenician merchants in the eighth century. From there it spread to Etruscans and Romans in the west. Being so much simpler to learn and use, alphabetic scripts gradually supplanted cuneiform during the final centuries of the first millennium B.C. The last known cuneiform tablet was written in Mesopotamia in A.D. 75, but syllabic scripts remain in use today in China and the Far East.

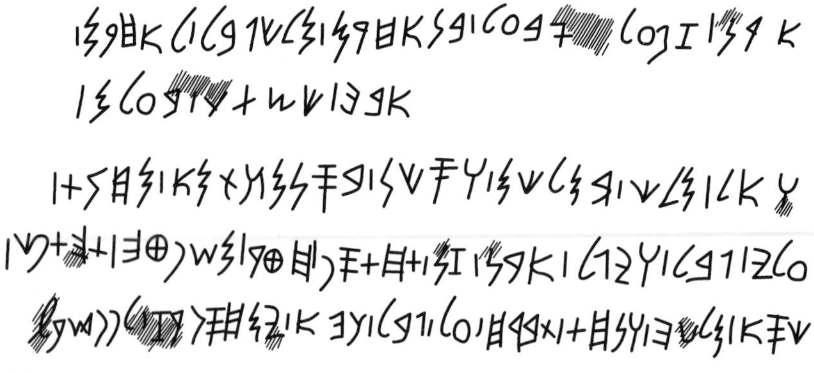

(a)

**Figure 8.2** (a) Phoenician inscription from the Ahiram sarcophagus at Byblos, eleventh century B.C.

| Phoenician | Hebrew | Classical Greek | Modern Alphabetic |
|---|---|---|---|
| 𐤀 | א | Α | a |
| 𐤁 | ב | Β | b |
| 𐤂 | ג | Γ | g |
| 𐤃 | ד | Δ | d |
| 𐤄 | ה | Ε | h |
| 𐤅 | ו | Υ | w |
| 𐤆 | ז | Ζ | z |
| 𐤇 | ח | Η | h |
| 𐤈 | ט | Θ | t |
| 𐤉 | י | Ι | y |
| 𐤊 | כ | Κ | k |
| 𐤋 | ל | Λ | l |
| 𐤌 | מ | Μ | m |
| 𐤍 | נ | Ν | n |
| 𐤎 | ס | Ξ | s |
| 𐤏 | ע | Ο | o |
| 𐤐 | פ | Π | p |
| 𐤑 | צ | | s |
| 𐤒 | ק | | q |
| 𐤓 | ר | Ρ | r |
| 𐤔 | ש | Σ | s |
| 𐤕 | ת | Τ | t |

(b)

**Figure 8.2** *(cont.)* (b) Table of Phoenician alphabet with Hebrew, Greek, and modern English equivalents.

The most graphic evidence of Phoenician maritime power is their foundation of colonies overseas. There is some uncertainty about when this process first began, but it is clear that by the eighth century B.C. new Phoenician cities had been founded in Spain, North Africa, and Sicily, always in coastal locations and with a view to trade. Southern Spain was particularly important as a source of metals, but the

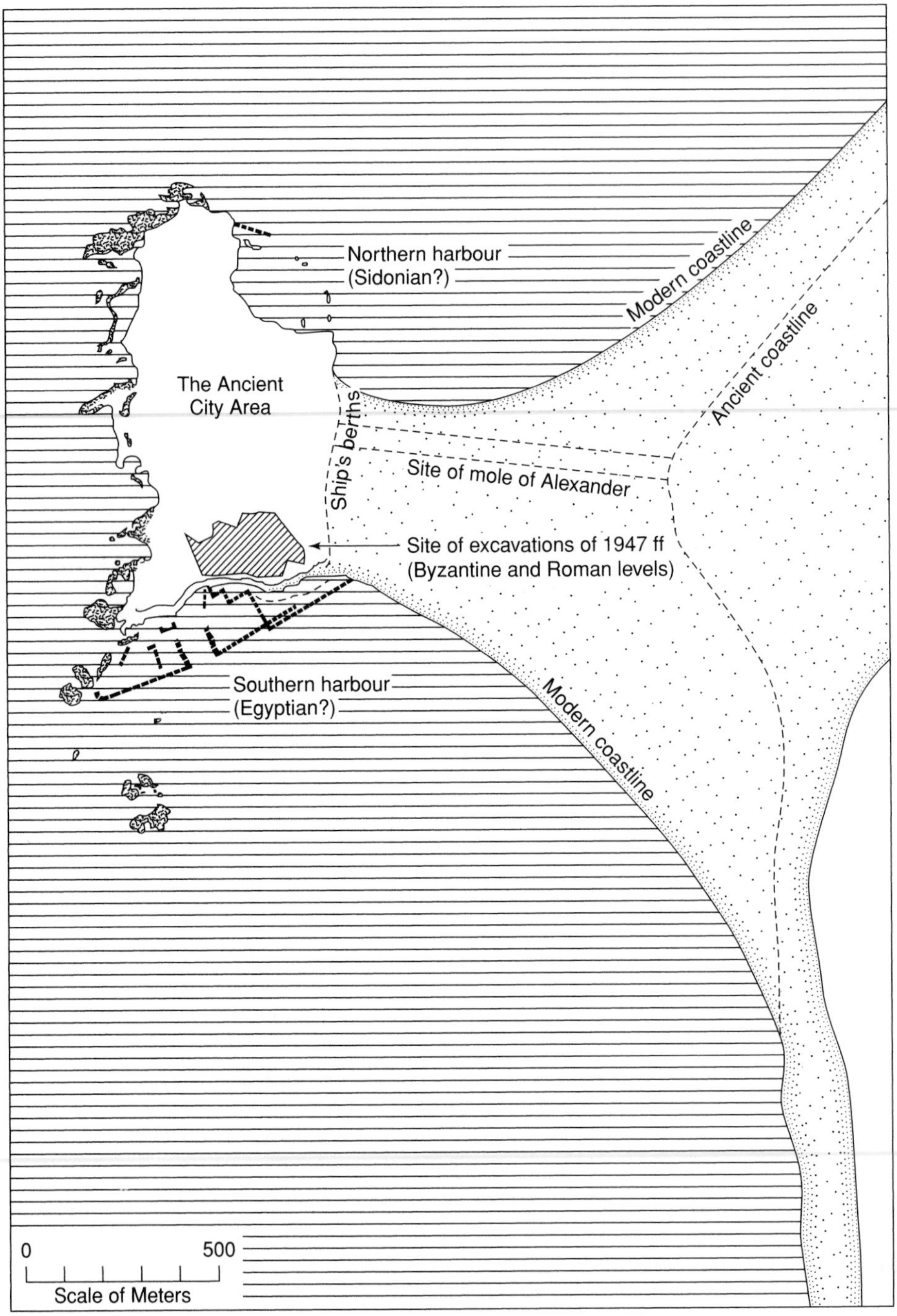


**Figure 8.3** Plan of Phoenician city of Tyre with harbor works. Tyre was a major Phoenician port, an offshore island with sheltered anchorages to north and south. It was joined to the mainland only in the fourth century B.C., when Alexander the Great built a causeway in order to capture the city.

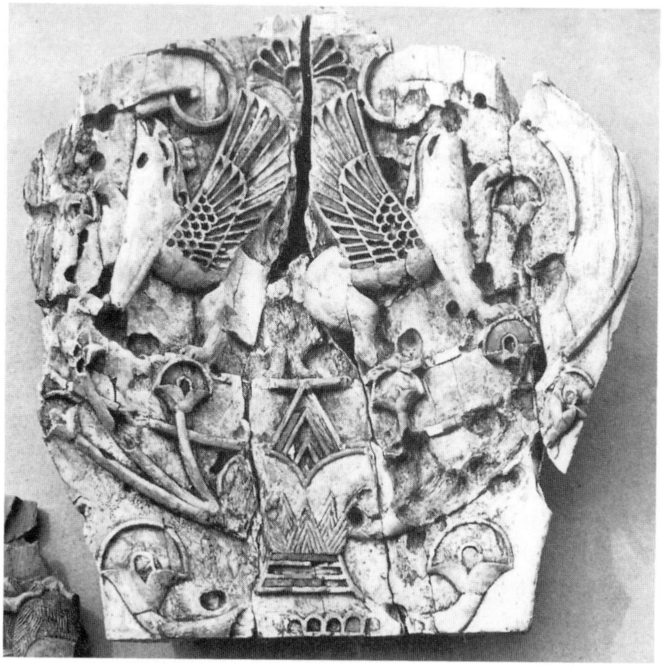

**Figure 8.4** Nimrud ivory found in the remains of Fort Shalmaneser, an Assyrian storehouse and military arsenal on the edge of ancient Nimrud. These ivories are of Phoenician origin and were probably taken by the Assyrians as booty or tribute. Pieces such as this, showing winged griffins (mythical beasts) and plants, were made as inlay for expensive pieces of furniture.

greatest Phoenician overseas foundation was undoubtedly the city of Carthage in modern Tunisia (see Chapter 10). At home, the Phoenician cities continued to flourish, first as independent states and then, from the late eighth century, as subjects of the Assyrian and Persian empires. This explains why many of the finest examples of Phoenician craftsmanship were found not in the Levant but in the Assyrian heartland of northern Mesopotamia. When British archaeologist Sir Max Mallowan was excavating the Assyrian capital of Nimrud in the 1950s, he discovered whole caches of carved Phoenician ivory panels in royal storerooms—the so-called Nimrud ivories. These had been taken by the Assyrians as plunder or tribute but were abandoned when Nimrud was destroyed by the Medes in 612 B.C. (Figure 8.4).

## The Archaeology of Empire

Reference to the Assyrians brings us to what may be considered the "grand narrative" of the Near East in the first millennium B.C.: the formation of the great empires. There had been earlier attempts to bind Near Eastern states into a larger political unit: Sargon and Ur-Nammu in the third millennium and Hammurabi in the second achieved some measure of success. Neither in size nor longevity, however, did their empires equal the great international states of the Assyrians, Neo-Babylonians, and Persians.

The archaeology of empire focuses on the mechanisms that integrated the imperial heartland with the dependent provinces and on the effects of imperial rule on both these elements. The distinction between a state and an empire is that an empire is an amalgam of several states that are allowed to retain a measure of cultural identity, and even political autonomy, provided they deliver tribute to the imperial heartland and do not deviate from their allegiance. In most empires, the dependent territories are acquired by military conquest, and there tends to be resistance to the central authority. Conquered territories become provinces, to be exploited for what they can yield in revenue. Imperial governments usually send direct representatives as governors of the provinces, supported by military garrisons to hold the subject peoples in check.

Empires, then, are larger than individual states and more internally diverse. They combine a number of areas with different languages, religions, economies, and cultural traditions. They are thus polyglot and heterogeneous and require powerful and sophisticated government mechanisms to bind them together. In archaeological terms, it is expected that the heartland of an empire will provide evidence of a flourishing population and economy. Revenues from the provinces are used to enrich the elite and build grandiose monuments in the major cities, which become impressive statements of imperial power. In the provinces, there may be a mixture of outcomes. Palaces of provincial governors and military fortresses of imperial garrisons may be found. These may follow a standardized imperial plan or contain features that link them artistically or architecturally with the traditions of the imperial heartland. Other provincial centers, as well as the rural areas, may suffer decline as the imperial power seeks to wrest from them what revenue it can. Provincial systems, however, are not the only way of governing dependent territories. Direct rule over conquered lands is a costly business and breeds resentment at the local level. Another strategy is to recruit local rulers to the cause of an imperial power, cowing them into submission by a show of force or allowing them—or perhaps a close relative—to continue in power after they have been defeated, though on carefully specified terms. This can be a better solution for the imperial government since it provides a steady flow of tribute for minimum effort once the initial show of force has been made.

Most historical empires consist of a patchwork of directly controlled provinces and subject kings. There is often a core-and-periphery pattern, in which territories near the center are organized into provinces while outlying regions are left in the control of local dynasties. Empires are wont to flaunt their power and success in grand imperialistic monuments and gestures. Paradoxically, however, their real success depends on the support of their subject territories. No imperial power can fight on all fronts at once. The long-lived empires are those that have developed a stable pattern of control or have been able to adapt flexibly as circumstances change.

We meet a number of empires in this and later chapters: notably the Roman Empire (Chapter 11), Han China (Chapter 14), the Aztec (Chapter 16), and the Inka (Chapter 18). Each developed a different solution to the problem of effective imperial control.

## Assyria Resurgent (911–700 B.C.)

The Assyrians were old players on the Near Eastern scene. Their history is conventionally divided into three stages, Old, Middle, and Late. We have already seen how in the Old Assyrian period (nineteenth and eighteenth centuries B.C.) merchants from Assur in the Assyrian heartland were trading with cities on the Anatolian plateau. The Assyrians entered a second period of power and prosperity when they threw off the Mitannian yoke in the fourteenth century and established the Middle Assyrian kingdom. This extended as far west as the Euphrates at times and lasted until the death of the powerful King Tiglath-pileser I in 1076 B.C. There followed a century and a half of Assyrian weakness, ending in 911 B.C. with the accession of a strong new ruler, Adad-Nirari II (911–891 B.C.), who established firm control over the Assyrian heartland and began the conquest of adjacent territories. His reign marks the beginning of the Late Assyrian period, which lasted until the destruction of the Assyrian capital, Nineveh, in 612 B.C.

The first of the great Late Assyrian rulers was Assurnasirpal II (883–859 B.C.). He repeated the exploits of his Middle Assyrian forebears, leading Assyrian armies to the shores of the Mediterranean and extorting tribute from the lesser kingdoms he encountered. Some of the wealth was plowed back into projects at home, notably the construction of a new Assyrian capital at Nimrud. The earlier capital, Assur, was not abandoned but became more a ritual and religious center than an administrative capital. The Assyrian kings were buried at Assur but governed from Nimrud.

The building of Nimrud was an enormous undertaking, demanding some 15 years of concerted effort by a veritable army of craftspeople and laborers. The city covered an area of around 350 hectares (864 acres) and was surrounded by a city wall incorporating an estimated 70 million sun-dried bricks. Pride of place went to the royal palace (the so-called North-West Palace) built on the raised citadel at one edge of the city. This was the first of many elaborate royal palaces built by Assyrian kings at their capitals. It was first in another sense, too, for it was Assurnasirpal who introduced the practice of decorating the walls of the principal rooms with friezes carved in low relief. These are often considered to be among the finest works of ancient Near Eastern art. This modern aesthetic judgment might be reconsidered, however, if we were to see the reliefs as they originally appeared, brightly painted in vivid colors, with further painted scenes on the plaster of the high walls above. Traces of paint still survive on some of the relief panels. It serves to remind us that the origin of Assurnasirpal's reliefs lay in an earlier Assyrian tradition of brightly colored wall decoration and in the carved bas-reliefs of the north Syrian Neo-Hittite cities he would have seen on his campaigns (see

Chapter 7). A few fragments of glazed brick wall decorations survive from Middle Assyrian Assur, as well as traces of wall paintings from other sites. Assurnasirpal's main innovation was to translate this tradition into stone.

This is not to deny the skill of the Assyrian stonecutters or the interest of the reliefs themselves, both as art history and as political propaganda. The slabs themselves are generally around 2 meters (6.5 feet) high and about twice that in width. They depict scenes of warfare (proclaiming the might of Assyrian arms), of gods and demons, and of the king hunting and at rest (Figure 8.5). They were dispersed about the walls of the palace in a conscious pattern, relating to the use of particular rooms. At the entrances to courtyards and reception halls there were enormous sculptures in the round—colossal bull figures with sweeping wings and human heads. These were *lamassu* figures, intended to provide ritual protection against the forces of evil. They also reminded the visitor of the awesome power of the Assyrian king. The completion of Assurnasirpal's palace was marked by an enormous ten-day party to which almost 70,000 guests were invited. Few could fail to have been impressed by this demonstration of royal magnificence, and in a real sense Assurnasirpal's reign marks the beginning of the Assyrian empire. His power rested on annual military campaigns, conducted with great ferocity, which ensured the submission of neighboring rulers.

The pattern continued under Shalmaneser III (858–824 B.C.), who consolidated Assyrian dominance over Syria and the Mediterranean coastlands; he had a rock relief carved at Nahr el-Kelb near Beirut and commemorated his victory over the Phoenicians and others on the bronze gates found at Balawat, not far from Nimrud, which show the rulers of Tyre and Sidon bringing tribute. Shalmaneser also campaigned in the north, against the nascent kingdom of Urartu. Most of these areas west of the Euphrates remained outside direct Assyrian control, however, and soon

**Figure 8.5** King Assurnasirpal (under umbrella) receives the surrender of prisoners of war.

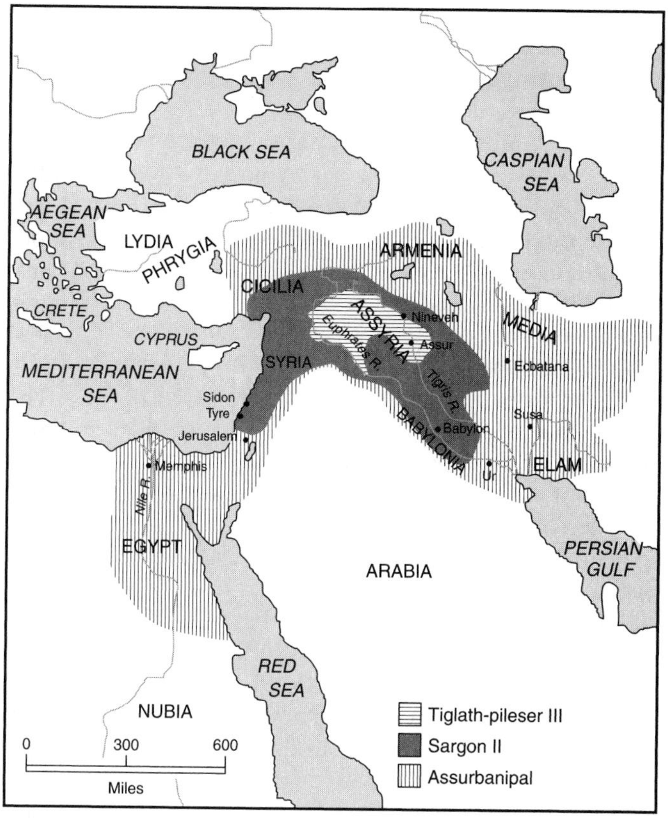


**Figure 8.6** Map showing the expansion of the Assyrian empire: the frontier of the empire under Tiglath-pileser III, Sargon II, and Assurbanipal.

broke free when Assyria itself was assailed by civil war in the declining years of Shalmaneser. Imperial fortunes were restored by Tiglath-pileser III (744–727 B.C.), who reduced the western kingdoms to the status of conquered provinces (Figure 8.6). Imperial expansion continued apace under Sargon II (721–705 B.C.) and Sennacherib (704–680 B.C.). Among Sargon's conquests was the kingdom of Israel. For his part, Sennacherib conquered and destroyed the city of Babylon, which had become a troublesome dependency of the Assyrian empire after its earlier centuries of independent greatness.

## The Mountain Kingdom of Urartu (c. 830–600 B.C.)

Assyrian records make clear that one of their doughtiest opponents lay in the north, in the mountainous terrain of Armenia. This was the kingdom of Urartu (biblical Ararat), with its capital, Tushpa, on the eastern shores of Lake Van. Armenia had long been divided among a number of minor rulers, but it was the growing threat from Assyria that caused these people to band together and form a single realm. Indeed, if any one event may be said to have forged the Urartian kingdom it was the five campaigns led against the Urartians by the Assyrian ruler Shalmaneser III (858–824 B.C.). Urartu successfully withstood further Assyrian attacks for almost 200 years.

The secret of Urartu's success was its geographical remoteness, coupled with the Urartians' skill at fortification. When the Urartian army was defeated and failed to hold the frontier, the people would retreat into their strongholds and simply wait for the enemy to depart. The mountainous nature of Urartian territory made it ideal for this strategy, with many a craggy rock easily turned into a near impregnable fortress. The capital itself, Van kale, is an excellent example. Almost a mile long but only 182 meters (600 feet) wide, the rock of Van was crowned with a line of mighty fortifications and cut through by a huge rock-cut ditch, dividing the core from the rest of the citadel (Figure 8.7). Later peoples have built on top of the earlier structures, remodeling and restoring the great fortress, but the large squared-stone blocks so typical of Urartian architecture can still be seen at the base of many of the walls. It was a considerable achievement, one that the Urartian kings were proud to record in cuneiform inscriptions.

Van kale was built by the first great Urartian king, Sarduri I, in 830 B.C. His successors added to his work but also embarked on a major irrigation project for the fields around the capital. Some of the canals and dams that they built can still be seen. The Urartians were also skilled bronze workers. The history of this important state, however, is only sketchily known. Urartian royal inscriptions show that in the eighth and seventh centuries B.C. the kingdom covered not only the Van region but also extended to the upper reaches of the Euphrates in the west and beyond Lake Urmia and Lake Sevan in the east. One of their best-excavated sites, Karmir-Blur, lies in the territory of the former Soviet Union. The end of Urartu, when it came, was due not to their traditional enemies, the Assyrians, but to a new power on the Iranian plateau to the east: the Medes and Persians discussed later in this chapter.

**Figure 8.7** View of Van kale, ancient Tushpa, the capital of the Urartian kingdom. Most of the visible buildings at the site are of more recent date, but they stand on large block foundations of the original Urartian fortress.

## The Assyrian Apogee (680–612 B.C.)

The last decades of Assyrian rule were marked by further conquests under Esarhaddon (680–669 B.C.) and Assurbanipal (669–627 B.C.), who brought the empire to its greatest extent. In 671 B.C. Esarhaddon conquered Egypt, and in 647 B.C. Assurbanipal finally defeated Assyria's eastern neighbors, the Elamites, sacking their capital city, Susa. Yet control of Egypt soon slipped from his grasp, his reign was afflicted by civil war, and the destruction of Elam was achieved only at great cost. During this final phase the Assyrian empire was governed not from Nimrud but from Nineveh, an old established city some 25 kilometers (16 miles) to the north. Sargon II had in fact established a new capital at Khorsabad, complete with royal palace and decorative wall reliefs, but this had been abandoned on his sudden death in battle in 705 B.C. It was the new ruler, Sennacherib, who moved the capital to Nineveh, building on the citadel of the ancient city a magnificent royal residence, the "Palace without a Rival." Sennacherib also laid out a lower city even larger than Nimrud, and around Nineveh he planted gardens and orchards. Elaborate canals were built to water them, drawing from springs in the mountains to the northeast of Nineveh. One of them crossed part of the intervening plain on the stone Jerwan aqueduct.

Sennacherib's palace had all the usual accoutrements of a major Assyrian residence: colossal guardian figures and impressively carved stone reliefs (over 2,000 sculptured slabs in 71 rooms). Its gardens, too, were exceptional. Recent research by British Assyriologist Stephanie Dalley has suggested that these were the famous Hanging Gardens, one of the Seven Wonders of the Ancient World. Later writers placed the Hanging Gardens at Babylon, but extensive research has failed to find any trace of them. Sennacherib's proud account of the palace gardens he created at Nineveh fits that of the Hanging Gardens in several significant details, such as the use of screw pumps (the famous Archimedean screw, already invented in Mesopotamia long before the Greek scientist Archimedes was born). These pumps were used to lift water to the top of the gardens, whence it could run down in channels and ornamental cascades.

One further discovery from Nineveh deserves mention. Austen Henry Layard was excavating here in 1849 when he came across two small rooms that contained a mass of clay tablets. These were the remains of the palace library. Another cache of tablets was found shortly afterward in the nearby palace of Assurbanipal in the northern part of the citadel mound. (Not content with Sennacherib's splendid residence, Assurbanipal built his own entirely new palace some 50 years later.) These two discoveries, totaling more than 25,000 pieces, form one of the largest and most important collections of clay tablets. They include not only diplomatic correspondence but also copies of earlier documents, including such Mesopotamian classics as the *Epic of Gilgamesh*. There are also scientific, religious, medical, and mathematical texts. Furthermore, we learn from letters that Assurbanipal's agents were scouring the cities of southern Mesopotamia, actually seeking ancient clay tablets. The palace reliefs portray the Assyrian kings as conquerors and lion hunters; the clay tablets reveal that the palaces were also centers of scholarship and learning.

## The Neo-Babylonian Empire (612–539 B.C.)

Assyria under Assurbanipal may have seemed unassailable, but it dissolved into chaos after his death, and the major Assyrian cities were sacked and destroyed by an alliance of Medes and Babylonians. The Medes were a people of the Iranian plateau who had established hegemony over neighboring regions and had created a powerful kingdom. Once Assyria had fallen, however, they had withdrawn from Mesopotamia, leaving the Babylonians in control.

The Babylonians had been unwilling subjects of the Assyrians for many years. When Assurbanipal died in 627 B.C. they declared their independence and fought a long war, which ended with the capture of Nineveh, the Assyrian capital, in 612 B.C. During the long reign of Nebuchadnezzar (605–555 B.C.) the powerful Babylonians sought to reconstruct the Assyrian empire, with themselves, rather than the Assyrians, in control. In addition, Babylon had its own distinguished past to look back to—it was Hammurabi's capital and that of the Kassites during the previous millennium. The attempt to restore their imperial fortunes was very largely successful. One notable event occured in 586 B.C., when Nebuchadnezzar captured and sacked the rebellious city of Jerusalem. The treasures of the Temple were looted, and many prominent Jews were carried off into captivity in Babylonia.

In archaeological terms, it is once again the spectacular nature of the imperial capital that grabs our attention. The city of Babylon had been an important center for many centuries, since at least the time of Hammurabi in the Old Babylonian period. To distinguish it, the dynasty of Nebuchadnezzar is known as the Late Babylonian or (more commonly) Neo-Babylonian period, and it runs from the accession of his father, Nabopolassar, in 625 B.C. to the fall of Nabonidus in 539 B.C. Nebuchadnezzar reconstructed Babylon, turning it into a capital worthy of a great empire. He also restored the walls of Ur and constructed magnificent new temples at Kish, as well as other buildings in other famous cities of southern Mesopotamia. This enterprise continued under Nabonidus (555–539 B.C.), who succeeded Nebuchadnezzar after an interval marked by three short-lived rulers. Nabonidus was remarkable for his interest in antiquity and in the origin of the temples he restored. In several cases, before beginning to rebuild, he dug into the foundations to discover the foundation deposit and the inscription that recorded the builder of the temple. This work was inspired by piety more than scholarship, though Nabonidus also collected inscriptions and other remains and housed them in a kind of museum in the residence of his daughter, Bel-shalti-nannar, who was high priestess of the god Sin at Ur. The most famous museum was at Babylon itself, in the so-called Northern Citadel (Box 8.2).

Babylon was not merely a royal capital and ceremonial center but also a major settlement with a population running into hundreds of thousands. The people lived in houses of two or three stories, though only the foundations survive. These were courtyard houses, the traditional Near Eastern type, with rooms arranged around a central open court, looking inward and with few openings to the outside world. Some houses contained private chapels with family burials beneath the floor. The city also had over a thousand temples of various sizes, culminating in the Temple

## Box 8.2 Imperial Babylon

Babylon under Nebuchadnezzar (605–562 B.C.) became the greatest city of the Near East. We learn this from the account given by Nebuchadnezzar himself, and it is confirmed by the writings of the Greek historian Herodotus and by the findings of archaeology. From 1899 to 1913, Babylon was the subject of extensive excavations led by the German archaeologist Robert Koldewey. The closeness of the water table to the ground surface made it impossible for him to make deep soundings, as he had originally hoped, so he and his team contented themselves with a thorough investigation of the Neo-Babylonian levels.

The Germans discovered city walls, the royal palace, the great Temple of Marduk and other shrines, and areas of ordinary housing. The site itself was vast. The outer fortifications enclosed over 15 square kilometers (6 square miles) within a moated rampart. At the center lay the inner city, itself measuring 1.6 by 2.4 kilometers (1 by 1.5 miles). The walls of the inner city were considered one of the wonders of the ancient world, a double line of baked-brick fortifications with frequent towers and gates, with room enough on top for two four-horse chariots to pass. The most magnificent of the gates lay next to the royal palace on the northern side of the inner city, at the head of the processional way leading to the Temple of Marduk (the so-called Esagila) and the ziggurat (Etemenanki). This, the famous Ishtar Gate, was decorated with a facing of blue-glazed bricks in which figures of lions and bulls were picked out in molded relief (Figure 8.8).

(a)

**Figure 8.8** (a) Detail of glazed brick panel from the famous Ishtar Gate built by Nebuchadnezzar.

*(Cont.)*

(b)

**Figure 8.8** *(Cont.)* (b) Reconstruction of Babylon, looking across the Ishtar Gate toward the city center.

of Marduk himself, chief god of Babylon, whose shrine contained a gold statue of the god 6 meters (20 feet) tall. The citizens of this great metropolis no doubt included rich and poor, master and servant, slave and free, but it was an impressive showcase for Nebuchadnezzar's New Babylonian empire.

## Phrygians and Lydians (Eighth Century–500 B.C.)

This chapter ends with the fall of Babylon to the Persians in 539 B.C., but it is necessary first to outline developments in other regions of the Near East. In Anatolia, the collapse of the Hittite realm in the thirteenth century B.C. initiated a period for which we have little historical or archaeological information. By the eighth century B.C. the central part of the Anatolian plateau had fallen under the control of the Phrygians, who ruled it from their capital at Gordion. American archaeologists have studied both the site itself and the impressive burial mounds in the plain around it. The city was modest by Assyrian standards—covering only 100 hectares (250 acres)—but included a citadel encircled by a powerful stone wall strengthened by timber framework. The lower city, too, was surrounded by a massive ashlar (hewn masonry) wall. Within the citadel was a building with a decorative floor mosaic, one of the earliest known. The burial mounds yielded the greatest surprises, however, especially the 50-meter-high (160-foot-high) "Tomb of Midas."

Midas is a semilegendary king of Phrygia, famous for his ability to turn objects into gold at his touch. The historical Midas was an eighth-century ruler who was first an enemy, then an ally, of Sargon II of Assyria. The gold-turning legend was a reference to the fabulous mineral wealth of the Phrygian kingdom, but remarkably enough the elaborate timber chamber found in the Tomb of Midas contained no objects of precious metal. Despite the absence of rich grave goods, this can clearly be judged (from its size alone) to be the burial place of one of the Phrygian rulers. The desire to link historical figures with archaeological finds is seductive and has persuaded many scholars to believe that this burial chamber may be that of Midas himself, as the traditional name of the mound suggests. Dating of a timber from the chamber shows that the tree from which it was taken was cut down around 757 B.C. If Midas reigned from 738 to 696 B.C., the timber must have been old when it was used in the burial chamber, but that is exactly what recent studies have shown—that many of the timbers were reused from earlier buildings on the citadel. Even the poverty of grave goods may be explained historically since Midas perished when Gordion was destroyed by the Cimmerians (a people from the Black Sea region), and the raiders probably looted much of the capital's wealth. It is equally possible, however, that the "Tomb of Midas" is in reality the grave of his predecessor, Gordias, or of another member of the Phrygian ruling dynasty.

Scientific study of residues from vessels placed in the Tomb of Midas have revealed the nature of the funerary feast consumed by the mourners during the burial ritual. The banquet had included a spicy dish of sheep or goat meat with pulses, washed down by a mixed drink of grape wine, barley beer, and honey mead. The size of the ceremony can be judged from the presence of more than 100 bowls in which it had been served.

Recent fieldwork at Gordion has clarified the original landscape setting of the city, and its dramatic impact on the local environment. The city was founded on a gravel knoll within a bend of the river Sakarya, rising from a marshy plain some 3 to 5 meters (10 to 16 feet) below the present ground surface. The rise in ground level is a direct consequence of the activities of the Gordianites, who used large timber beams in their early constructions and may have intensified agricultural activity on the surrounding hillslopes. Deforestation and massive erosion were the inevitable result, and low-lying areas of the city became vulnerable to flooding. The Gordianites laid down thick layers of fill to raise their city above the flood danger and built masonry flood defenses, but river-borne alluvium gradually buried most of the low-lying areas. Only the Citadel Mound and the smaller Küçükhöyük rise above these alluvial deposits today. The fact that the alluviation of the plain coincided exactly with the development of the city c. 700 B.C. illustrates the human origin of this environmental change.

The decline of Phrygia was balanced by the rise of a new Anatolian kingdom to the west, that of the Lydians. This kingdom, too, became famous for its wealth, especially during the reign of Croesus (c. 560–546 B.C.). The Lydian capital, Sardis, lay in a fertile plain near the western edge of the Anatolian plateau, close to gold-bearing hills and gold washings in the gravel of the River Pactolus. Some of the gold was in the form of electrum, a natural alloy of gold and silver, and the

Lydian kings used this material to strike the world's earliest known coinage. They also discovered the process for separating electrum into gold and silver. An installation where this was done has been excavated at Sardis, and it dates to the time of Croesus. The Lydian invention of coinage was soon copied by the Greeks and the Persians. The latter, however, also destroyed the Lydian kingdom, defeating Croesus and absorbing Lydia as a province of their vast empire.

## The Rise of the Persians (614–490 B.C.)

We end this chapter with the creation of the Persian Empire. The Persians were a people of southwestern Iran, living on the plateau alongside the Persian Gulf. To their north, facing Mesopotamia, was the land of the Medes, another major people of the Iranian plateau. It was the Medes from their capital at Ecbatana (modern Hamadan) who first welded the peoples of western Iran into a major political and military power. The Median King Cyaxares invaded Mesopotamia in 614 B.C. and played a major part in the destruction of the Assyrian empire. Cyaxares also extended his rule into eastern Anatolia. A battle with the Lydians in 585 B.C. was allegedly forestalled by an eclipse of the sun. The two powers took this as a portent and agreed to make peace, fixing their common frontier along the River Halys.

This left four major players on the Near Eastern scene: Lydia, Media, Babylonia, and Egypt. During this period the Persians were subjects of the Median kings, but in 550 B.C. the Persian ruler Cyrus "the Great" threw off the Median yoke and made the Persians the dominant power. Thus the Median empire became a Persian one, and Cyrus embarked on a policy of aggressive expansionism. First to be conquered was Lydia in 546 B.C. Seven years later Cyrus led his armies against Babylonia, capturing Babylon itself in a whirlwind campaign. In 525 B.C. Cyrus's son and successor, Cambyses, conquered Egypt, but it was during the reign of Darius (522–486 B.C.) that the Persian Empire reached its greatest extent, from Thrace in the west to the Indus Valley in the east. It was under Darius, too, that the Persian Empire first came into conflict with the Greeks in the episode known as the Persian Wars (490–479 B.C.), described in Chapter 10.

One of the most famous memorials of Darius's reign is the relief at Behistun in western Iran, which played a key role in the decipherment of the cuneiform script (Box 8.3).

## Summary

In this chapter we have followed the development of Near Eastern society from the collapse of the empires of Egypt and the Hittites in the thirteenth century B.C. to the formation of the ever-larger empires of the Assyrians and Persians in the ninth to sixth centuries B.C. The collapse of the Bronze Age empires was followed by the resurgence of the pattern of smaller kingdoms and city-states, such as those of the Israelites and Phoenicians, with their own languages, religions, and cultural traditions. During the ninth century B.C. these smaller polities fell under the influence and then the direct control of the Assyrians, who expressed their supremacy

## Box 8.3 The Decipherment of Cuneiform

Eighteenth-century European explorers made careful copies of the inscriptions they saw on the ancient monuments of the Near East, but the meaning of the texts was beyond them. These writings were in cuneiform, the script of wedge-shaped characters devised in Mesopotamia in the early third millennium B.C. for incising on clay tablets with a reed stylus. The decipherment of cuneiform was a crucial step in the development of Near Eastern studies since until the texts could be read and understood, historical knowledge of the ancient Near East had to rely on external sources such as the Bible or the Greek historian Herodotus. The complicated decipherment process involved solving two separate puzzles: the enigma of the script itself and the puzzle of the language or languages that lay behind it. The clue to decipherment lay in the grandiose rock-cut inscriptions of the Persian kings. By the end of the eighteenth century it was already realized that these inscriptions contained parallel texts in three different languages—as befitted the major memorials of the rulers of such a multilingual, multiethnic empire. The next breakthrough came in 1802, when German college lecturer Georg Friedrich Grotefend, working from copies, discovered that one of the three languages in these inscriptions was alphabetic, an early version of Persian (Old Persian).

Grotefend's findings were largely ignored at the time. The decipherment of cuneiform had to wait until the 1840s and the work of Henry Rawlinson at Behistun. The Behistun inscription, carved by the Persian king Darius, stands on a rock face high above the Hamadan-Kermanshah road (Figure 8.9). It was only in 1847, with the help of an agile

**Figure 8.9** The Behistun relief.

*(Cont.)*

Kurdish boy, that Rawlinson was able to take paper "squeezes" of the whole inscription. Ten years earlier, however, in 1835–1837, he had made his own careful copy of two of the texts (subsequently found to be in Old Persian and Elamite languages), and in 1846 he published a translation of the alphabetic Old Persian inscription that recorded Darius's victories over rebellious subjects.

The Elamite inscription was altogether more difficult, written in a syllabic script in which each of 123 signs represents a different syllable. Furthermore, Elamite is a dead language, related to no known spoken tongue. Despite these difficulties, with the help of the parallel Old Persian text deciphered by Rawlinson, Edwin Norris succeeded in deciphering the Elamite version of the Behistun inscription in 1855. Meanwhile, Rawlinson himself, assisted by Edward Hincks, worked on the 600 signs of the Babylonian (Akkadian) script. They were soon able to read not only the Behistun inscription but also the flood of clay tablets coming from Austen Henry Layard's excavations at Nineveh. These opened the way to a whole new understanding of the history, economy, religion, science, and literature of the ancient Near East.

in the wealth and political iconography of their imperial capitals, Nimrud, Khorsabad, and Nineveh. Beyond the limits of Assyrian control, however, other states rose and flourished, notably those of Phrygia, Lydia, and Urartu in Anatolia and of the Medes in Iran. If Babylonia and Assyria (Mesopotamia) were still the core of the Near East in terms of population density, the peripheral regions became increasingly well organized in political and military terms. The conclusion arrived when the periphery—in the form of the Medes and Persians—took control of the core (Mesopotamia) and extended its power to the Aegean and Egypt. The Persian Empire was nonetheless a multiethnic entity, and within its frontiers the various tributary peoples such as Phoenicians and Babylonians retained much of their cultural identity.

## Guide to Further Reading

The complex literature of this period taxes even specialists, but here are some general references: Michael Roaf, *Cultural Atlas of Mesopotamia and the Ancient Near East* (Oxford: Facts on File, 1990); Seton Lloyd, *The Archaeology of Mesopotamia* (London: Thames and Hudson, 1984); and the relevant chapters in Amélie Kuhrt, ed., *The Ancient Near East: c. 3000–330* B.C. (London and New York: Routledge, 1995). Seton Lloyd's *Foundations in the Dust,* 2nd ed. (London: Thames and Hudson, 1980) provides an admirable summary of the stirring history of archaeology in Mesopotamia. J. T. Hooker, *Reading the Past: Ancient Writing from Cuneiform to the Alphabet* (London: British Museum Publications, 1990) describes cuneiform decipherment and the development of the alphabet.

For the origins of Israel and the Israelites, see Neil A. Silberman, "Who Were the Israelites?" *Archaeology* 45, no. 2 (1992): 22–30; see also K. W. Whitelaw and R. B. Coote, *The Emergence of Israel in Historical Perspective* (Sheffield, England: Almond Press, 1987). The reinterpretation of the United Monarchy of David and Solomon is contained in two articles by Israel Finkelstein: "The Archaeology of the United Monarchy: An Alternative View," *Levant* 28 (1996): 177–187, and "Bible Archaeology or Archaeology of Palestine in the Iron Age? A Rejoinder," *Levant* 30 (1998): 167–174. The Phoenicians are well covered by the lavish exhibition catalogue edited by Sabatino Moscati, *The Phoenicians* (Milan: Bompiani, 1988). The archaeology of empire is reviewed on a broad canvas by Carla M. Sinopoli, "The Archaeology of Empires," *Annual Review of Anthropology* 23 (1994): 159–180.

There are few good general accounts of Assyrian history and archaeology. Seton Lloyd's *The Archaeology of Mesopotamia*, previously cited, provides a short outline. A study of one of the major palaces is John Malcolm Russell, *Sennacherib's Palace without Rival at Nineveh* (Chicago: University of Chicago Press, 1991). The best accounts of Babylon are by Joan Oates, *Babylon* (London: Thames and Hudson, 1986) and (for the sixth century B.C.) David J. Wiseman, *Nebuchadnezzar and Babylon* (Oxford: Oxford University Press, 1985). See also A. R. George, "Babylon Revisited: Archaeology and Philology in Harness," *Antiquity* 67 (1993): 734–746. Urartu and the highland kingdoms are covered by Charles Burney and David M. Lang, *The Peoples of the Hills: Ancient Ararat and Caucasus* (London: Weidenfeld and Nicholson, 1971).

The environmental setting of Gordion is described by Ben Marsh, "Alluvial Burial of Gordion, an Iron-Age City in Anatolia," *Journal of Field Archaeology* 26 (1999): 163–175. The analysis of food residues from the Gordion tumulus is reported by Patrick E. McGovern and colleagues in "A Funerary Feast Fit for King Midas," *Nature* 402 (1999): 863–864.

# PART IV

# The Mediterranean World

but now Odysseus
came to the famous house of Alkinoös, but the heart pondered
much in him as he stood before coming to the bronze threshold.
For as from the sun the light goes or from the moon, such was
the glory on the high-roofed house of great-hearted Alkinoös.
Brazen were the walls run about it in either direction
from the inner room to the door, with a cobalt frieze encircling,
and golden were the doors that guarded the close of the palace,
and silver were the pillars set in the brazen threshold. . . .

And within, thrones were backed against the walls on both sides
all the way from the inner room to the door, with fine-spun delicate cloths,
the work of women, spread out upon them. [Lattimore, 1967, *Odyssey*, Book VI, 81]

# Chapter 9

# The First Aegean Civilizations

Faience figure of a "snake goddess" from the Minoan palace at Knossos, Crete.

*The crowd looked on expectantly as the bull pawed the ground, then lowered its head and charged the young man directly in its path. For him this was no suicide mission but the culmination of months of training. As the bull drew near, the athlete deftly seized it by the horns and vaulted onto its back. The bull, puzzled and frustrated, came to a sudden halt, and the athlete with one bound leaped clear, landed on his feet, and threw his arms out wide in a dramatic flourish. His hazardous feat was completed, and the crowd of onlookers—ruling elite, priests, palace officials, and ordinary townspeople—broke into applause. Behind them rose the multiple tiers of the palace of Knossos, an impressive backdrop to this scene of ritual and athletic action. The bull had once again been overcome and outwitted by human ingenuity and skill.*

Such, at least, is the scene depicted in the frescoes of the Minoan palace at Knossos, Crete. Young men and women alike took part in this perilous ritual or so it seems—for some have doubted whether it is really possible to grasp the horns of a charging bull and leap over its back, suggesting that in real life the athletes approached the bull from the side. One carved stone vessel shows a young man transfixed by the horns of a bull, suggesting that some such dangerous acrobatic act was indeed part of Minoan palace ritual. But was it a real-life event that was being depicted, or some legendary feat? Some archaeologists have even argued that the bull-leaping frescoes represent the movement of constellations in the night sky, though the constellations themselves—and the names by which we know them—can only be traced back with confidence to the last few centuries B.C., fully a thousand years after the Knossos frescoes were painted.

The meaning of the ritual—whether an initiation rite for young men and women or an annual reenactment of some mythological event—still escapes us, but the bull-leaping frescoes from Knossos have become a well-known feature of the Minoan civilization, which developed on Crete around 2100 B.C. It takes its name from Minos, the legendary king who ruled the seas with a powerful fleet and kept a bull-headed monster, the Minotaur, in his labyrinth at Knossos. This beast was annually fed seven youths and seven maidens, until it was slain by the Athenian hero Theseus. There may be memories in this legend of a real historical event—the takeover of Minoan Crete by the Mycenaeans from mainland Greece—for around 1450 B.C. the Minoan palaces were destroyed. Only Knossos was rebuilt, and the earlier situation of multiple centers was replaced by a period in which Knossos was the sole center of power on the island. Furthermore, the Linear B texts found at Knossos show that when the palace rose again from the ashes, Mycenaeans from the Greek mainland rather than indigenous Minoans were in control.

Chapter 9 describes both the Minoans and the Mycenaeans (Table 9.1). They were the twin foci of an Aegean Bronze Age world which also included the island societies of the Cyclades. In chronological terms, Minoan civilization came first, its influence spreading widely through the Cycladic islands during the second millennium B.C. On the mainland, the separate, palace-based civilization of the Greek-speaking Mycenaeans arose during the sixteenth century B.C. (the period of the famous Shaft Graves, mentioned in Chapter 1). Mycenaean civilization in its formative stages owed a great deal to Minoan Crete. Mycenaean painted pottery, for example, was dependent in its development on Minoan styles, and Mycenaean luxury arts relied heavily on Minoan models. This is not to say that Mycenaean civilization was a mere copy of Minoan culture—that would be very far from the truth—but Minoan influence was clearly powerful. The positions were partially reversed, however, in the fifteenth century B.C., when the Mycenaeans took control of Crete. Thereafter the Aegean fell increasingly under Mycenaean influence, a situation that continued until the downfall of the mainland palaces around 1200 B.C. Crete and other regions retained their distinctive local identities, however, and did not simply become submerged in a broader Mycenaean world.

This chapter begins with developments on Crete, the Cycladic islands, and the southern Greek mainland during the Early Bronze Age (3200–2100 B.C.) (Figure 9.1).

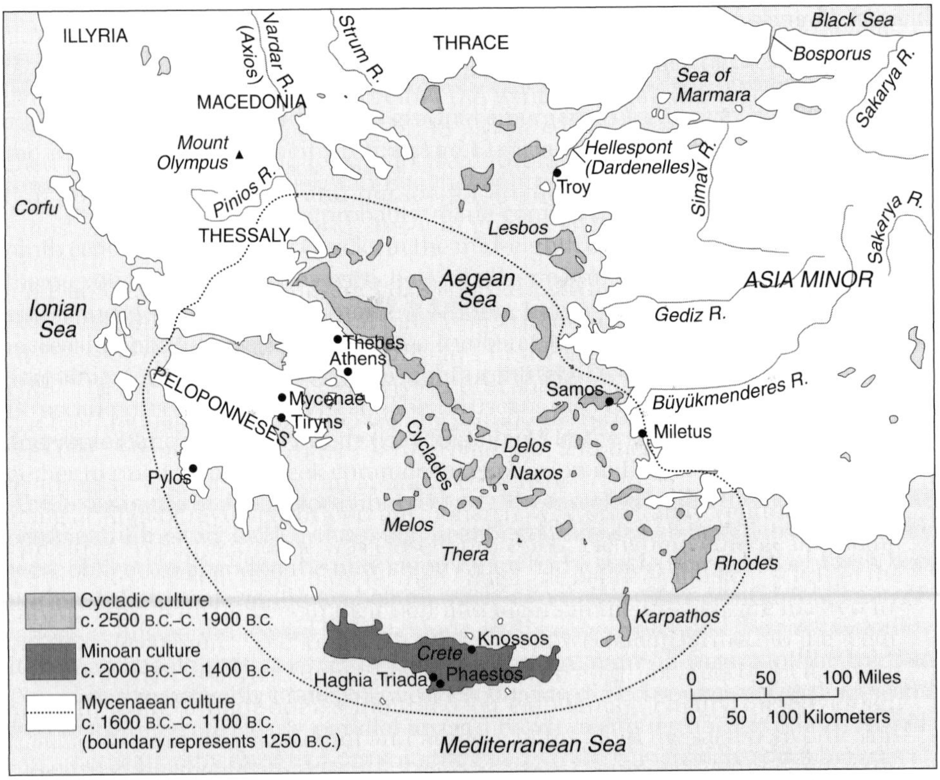


**Figure 9.1** Map of the Bronze Age Aegean, showing sites on Crete, the Cyclades, and the Aegean coast of Turkey.

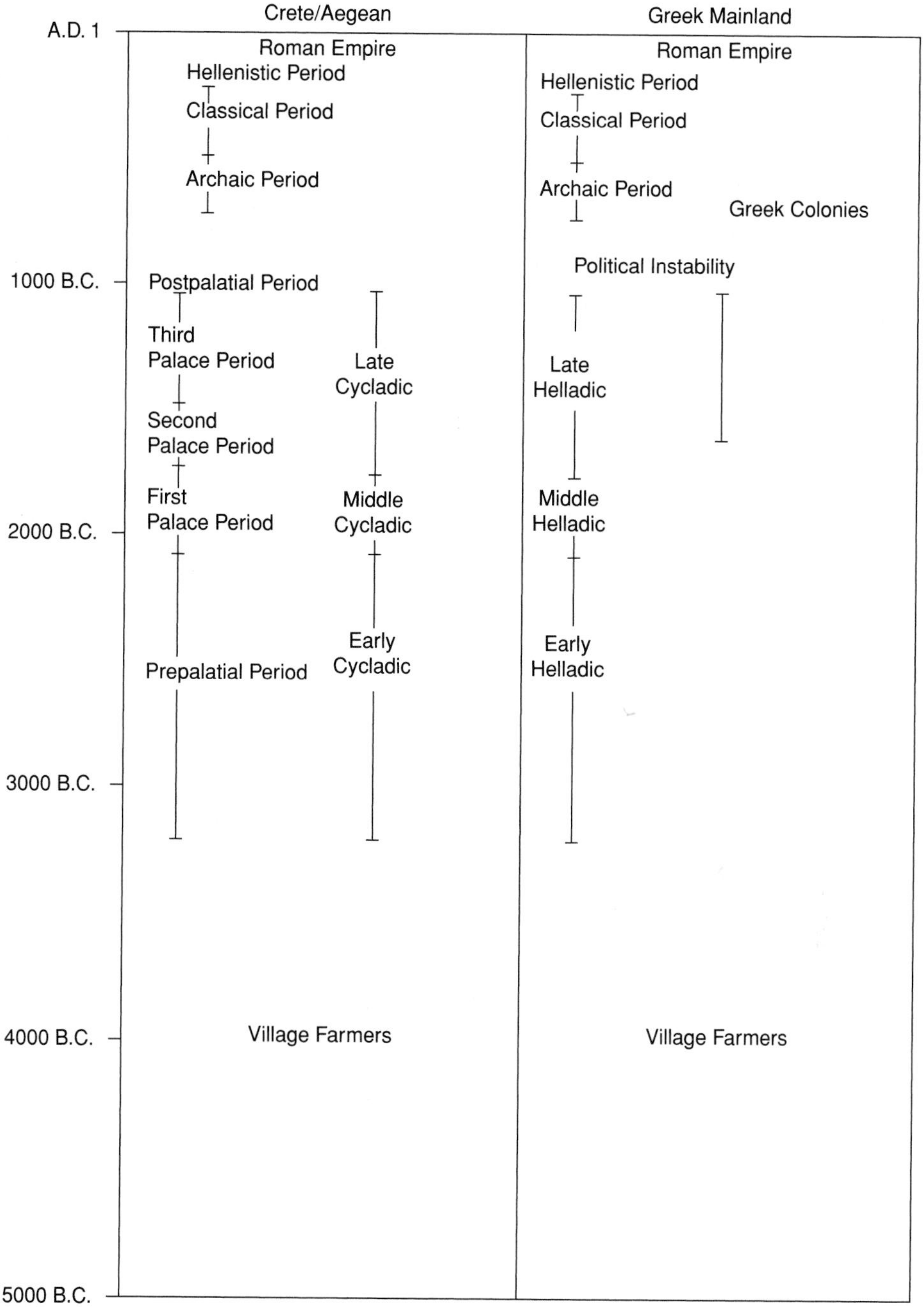


**Table 9.1** Chronological table of Aegean civilization

# The Aegean Early Bronze Age (3200–2100 B.C.)

## *Early Minoan Crete*

The island of Crete is long and mountainous, with peaks rising to 2,500 meters (8,000 feet). Within the rugged uplands lie sacred caves, one (Dikte) reputedly the birthplace of the classical god Zeus. To north and south of the mountain backbone, a handful of fertile plains stretch toward the coast and to the harbor towns on which, until air travel, the island depended for contact with the outside world. Crete indeed is relatively isolated within the southern Aegean. To the south, 320 kilometers (200 miles) of open water lie between it and the North African coast; to the north, the nearest of the Cycladic islands is some 80 kilometers (50 miles) distant. The Cretans were nonetheless great sailors, and from the third millennium B.C. onward there is evidence for sporadic, then regular, contact with Egypt and the Near East in the form of hippopotamus ivory and Egyptian stone vessels imported to Crete.

The third millennium on Crete is known as the Early Minoan or Prepalatial period.[1] This corresponds to the centuries before the construction of the first of the palaces for which Crete subsequently became so famous. One significant change from the previous Neolithic period was how metals were used, notably copper. A characteristic Early Minoan metal item was the dagger, with rivet holes at the heel of the blade for attachment to a haft or handle. Such daggers are significant in two respects: First, they were clearly too small to be effective as weapons of war and were probably as much for display as for use (though even today Cretans usually carry knives for cutting all manner of things); second, the material from which they were made—copper mixed with arsenic—not only required craftsmanship but also was not widely available on Crete and may have been imported (perhaps from Cycladic sources such as Kythnos) from an early date.

The use of copper thus implies access to imported materials and specialized skills. It reinforces other evidence that suggests the gradual development of a more hierarchical society on Crete in the Early Minoan period. The strongest evidence comes from the graves, where the offerings placed with the dead show increasing differences of wealth between family groups. We can also point to the growth of a

[1] A confusing feature of Aegean Bronze Age chronology is the use of two separate systems of terminology. The first is based mainly on pottery styles and is divided simply into Early (3200–2100 B.C.), Middle (2100–1700 B.C.), and Late (1700–1050 B.C.). The mainland sequences are labeled Helladic—thus Early Helladic (EH), Middle Helladic (MH), and Late Helladic (LH); those of the Cyclades are labeled Cycladic (EC, MC, LC); and those of Crete, Minoan (EM, MM, LM).

Alongside this system is an alternative periodization based on the Minoan palaces, beginning with the Prepalatial period (3200–2100 B.C.). This is followed by the First Palace, or Protopalatial, period (2100–1700 B.C.), corresponding to the first Cretan palaces to the period of their destruction by earthquake c. 1700 B.C. Then follows the Second Palace, or Neopalatial, period (1700–1450 B.C.), which ends with the destruction of the Cretan palaces and the beginnings of Mycenaean control at Knossos. The Third Palace period runs from 1450 B.C. to the fall of the mainland Mycenaean palaces in 1200 B.C. The final phase in this system is the Postpalatial period, from 1200–1050 B.C.

small number of larger settlements. Most important of these was Knossos, in the center of the fertile northern plain, which had already been a much larger than average settlement in the preceding Neolithic period. By the beginning of the Bronze Age it covered as much as 5 hectares (12 acres). Similar Early Minoan settlements may lie beneath the later palaces at Mallia and Phaistos. Whether these medium-sized settlements were really the centers of emerging small kingdoms is far from clear, given our only sketchy knowledge of the remains. Size alone cannot tell us about the function or internal divisions of these sites.

## Mainland Greece and the Cycladic Islands

Better evidence for emerging social complexity comes from mainland Greece and the Cycladic islands. At Lerna in the Peloponnese, a substantial Early Helladic mud-brick building known as the House of the Tiles stood within an enclosure wall with projecting, circular "towers." Doorways and stairs were made of timber, and the roof, as the name suggests, was of terracotta tiles and blue schist slates. Modest in scale (though much bigger than other buildings on the site), measuring 25 by 12 meters (82 by 39 feet), this building may have been the seat of a local ruler who controlled one corner of the fertile Argive plain during the second quarter of the third millennium B.C. Numerous sealings come from the House of the Tiles. These were produced by impressing a carved seal bearing a complex geometric design into the soft clay placed over the openings of boxes or jars to secure their contents. They denote some measure of ownership or administrative control, but their very diversity (70 different seal patterns) makes it difficult to see them as evidence of anything approaching a centralized bureaucracy. They are more likely to have been simply personal signatures.

On the Cycladic islands, the pattern is similar—with signs of modest social complexity in the form of longboats and fortifications. Here again, however, it would not do to overinterpret the evidence. The clearest fortifications are those of Kastri on Syros with its circular stone towers and a maze of small buildings within the walls. This nucleated settlement is associated with the cemetery of Chalandriani, which has more than 650 graves. Most Early Bronze Age cemeteries of the Cyclades have dozens rather than hundreds of graves, representing the burials of a nuclear family rather than a sizeable community, so Chalandriani is evidently exceptional. Its special status is underlined by the discovery of pottery objects known from their shape (but not their function) as "frying pans." These have richly incised decorations, including depictions of many-oared longboats, indicating perhaps the crucial role of sea traffic (possibly also piracy) in the prosperity of Syros. At least 7 of the 13 known frying pans come from Chalandriani, and the other 6 may also be from this cemetery.

Another striking feature of the Cycladic islands during the Early Bronze Age is the use of marble for vases and figurines. The figurines are especially distinctive in their repertoire of styles and have attracted the attention of art historians as well as archaeologists. Some, such as Patricia Getz-Preziosi, have gone so far as to suggest they can identify the work of particular sculptors. She has even assigned names to the supposed sculptors (based on museums where examples of their output are displayed), such as the "Berlin Master" or the "Goulandris Master." This places the figurines on the same footing as later artworks like classical vases or Renaissance paintings. It is much more likely that these relatively simple Cycladic figurines were the work of small-scale local craftspeople. Many people today have admired the purity of line of these white marble carvings, which has given them inflated values in the international art markets and encouraged the large-scale looting of the island graves in which they were deposited. The purity of appearance is in any case largely deceptive: Traces of paint show that the figurines were originally brightly colored, probably in a garish style that highlighted facial features and clothing.

### *Toward the First Palaces*

On Crete itself, most Early Bronze Age settlements were small villages of around half a dozen households. A famous example is Myrtos, on the south coast. Myrtos was initially interpreted as a special site, a "mansion," with coordinated functions that indicate a move toward a palace-type economy. Reanalysis, however, has suggested that it was not a protopalace but simply a cluster of ordinary houses built against each other.

There is evidence of social change in the tombs during the Early Minoan period, however, especially in eastern Crete. At Mochlos, for example, a small number of more elaborate tombs contained gold diadems and other valuables, whereas the majority of tombs were simpler and more poorly furnished. These were family burial places, so they must have been particular families who were gaining special status in society. The evidence suggests that a ruling elite had already emerged in some parts of Crete several centuries before the beginning of the Middle Minoan period—the age of the first palaces.

## Minoan Civilization: The Palace Period (2100–1450 B.C.)

Cretan palaces appear suddenly in the archaeological record, but as we have seen, the foundations for the new developments must have been laid over preceding centuries. It was only in the Middle Minoan period, however, from around 2100 B.C., that palace centers are evident at key points throughout the island, notably at Knossos and Mallia in the north and Phaistos in the south. These first palaces were joined in the Second Palace period by Zakro in the east, and other palace sites are suspected in the center and west of the island. Each was probably the administrative and political center of a small state or province, though the function of the palaces themselves—ritual complexes or royal residences—remains far from clear, and the term "palaces" should be used with caution.

In the 1970s, British archaeologist Colin Renfrew emphasized an interlinked series of factors to explain the rise of the Minoan palaces—intensification of agriculture, growth of foreign trade, and increased craft specialization (see Chapter 2). Renfrew's argument was that these factors interacted with one another in a positive manner, by the process of "positive feedback," to magnify and accelerate the scale of change (what he called the "multiplier effect"), resulting in the formation of palace-based states. Some parts of this model are now generally discounted. It implies, for instance, a steady evolution of complex society on Crete during the Early Minoan period—something that the available evidence does not support. Renfrew also ascribed an important role to vines and olives. These are not grown on the same land as cereals and therefore do not compete with them. Renfrew proposed that the introduction of domesticated vines and olives in the Early Bronze Age allowed a substantial expansion in the amount of land under cultivation and helped to power the emergence of complex society. Some archaeologists and palaeobotanists have recently questioned this view, pointing out that available evidence for cultivated vines and olives does not show their presence much before the Late Bronze Age. It is difficult to date their introduction with confidence from the scanty preserved remains, however, and some element of agricultural change would have been essential to support the larger population of palace-period Crete. Furthermore, elaborate drinking vessels appear in Crete during the Early Bronze Age and may indicate that the Cretans were already drinking wine at that period. But there is no firm evidence of extensive agricultural expansion on Crete during the Early Bronze Age. Agricultural change, rather than the driving force of Cretan state formation, was probably just one of several associated factors, along with social and ideological developments.

## *The Minoan Palaces*

The Cretan palaces—and Minoan civilization as a whole—have been known to archaeologists little more than a hundred years. The discovery is usually attributed to British archaeologist Sir Arthur Evans, who began digging at Knossos in 1900, although in fact a local Cretan enthusiast—appropriately named Minos Kalokairinos—had already uncovered parts of the palace some 20 years before. Evans dug systematically at Knossos from 1900 to 1905 and then intermittently for more than 25 years, revealing large areas of the palace complex. It was first thought that this was another Mycenaean palace, similar to those excavated by Schliemann at Mycenae and Tiryns on the mainland, discussed later in this chapter. Within a few years, however, Evans had come to quite a different conclusion—that what he was dealing with was not Mycenaean but a new civilization, which he termed Minoan after Minos, the legendary king of Crete.

The palace revealed by Evans was indeed an impressive structure. Spread over several hectares on the sloping edge of the earlier tell, it consisted of ranges of rooms around a rectangular central court, with a second court to the west. The key to the overall layout was the central open court, the heart of the palace. This gave access to all the other areas, which were basically arranged in a radiating fashion around it. The plan is an unusual one—very different, for example, from the megaron palaces of Mycenaean Greece (see p. 262).

The ground floors of Minoan palaces were constructed of rubble, faced with ashlar and reinforced with timber tie-beams as a precaution against earthquakes, which are a feature of the region. Indeed the first Knossos palace was destroyed by just such an earthquake around 1700 B.C. Upper floors, too, were timber-reinforced, with doorways and architectural details made of stone or wood. Mud-bricks were also used in the palace at Mallia. At Knossos, during the Second Palace period (and possibly earlier), the appearance of the rooms was transformed by the extensive use of painted plaster to produce the frescoes for which the site is justly famous. Surprisingly, there is little evidence of similar decorations at any of the other major palaces, but traces certainly remain at several of the "villas" (smaller palatial sites) such as Tylissos, Amnisos, and Ayia Triada. And there are elaborate wall paintings, surely Minoan-inspired, at such island sites as Phylakopi on Melos and Akrotiri on Thera.

The wall paintings at Knossos included both geometric and naturalistic designs. The walls of the ceremonial rooms were often divided horizontally into three painted bands, with plain colors or patterns above and below, framing a central band of figured scenes. Those with human figures were mainly religious or ceremonial in character. These included the famous "bull-leaping" frescoes or the long *Procession Fresco,* showing gifts being brought to a female figure. Other paintings were naturalistic in character—notably the well-known Dolphin scene (probably, in fact, a floor decoration) from the so-called "royal apartments" in the southeast corner of the palace (Figure 9.2).

The question of the royal apartments introduces one of the key problems in the analysis of the Minoan palaces: interpreting the function of the various rooms. Those of utilitarian character, such as the ground-floor rooms with rows of storage

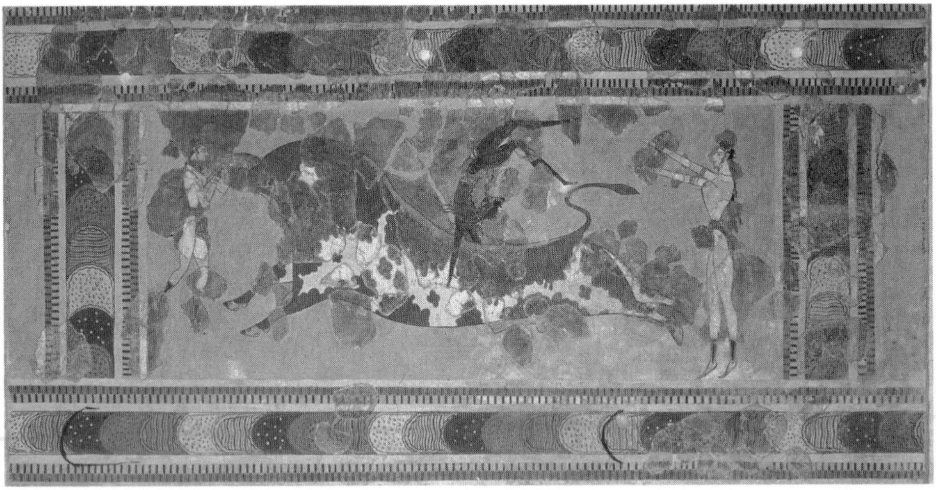

**Figure 9.2** Photograph of one of the so-called bull-leaping (Taureador frescoes) from the palace at Knossos, Crete, showing a man vaulting over the back of a charging bull and a woman standing behind with outstretched arms, waiting to catch him. The sex of the participants is confirmed by the Minoan convention (borrowed from the Egyptians) of painting men reddish-brown and women white. The figure on the left, grasping the horns of the bull, is wrongly reconstructed and probably comes from another fresco. (Minoan, ca. 1450–1400 BCE. Archaeological Museum, Heraklion, Crete, Greece. Scala/Art Resource, NY)

jars, are straightforward. They held materials like grain, beans, and olive oil, which probably came to the palace as tax or tribute or as the produce of palace-held farmlands. The extensive storage facilities show that the palace was designed to play a key role in the agricultural economy as consumer, producer of processed goods, storer of surpluses, and regulator of distribution.

On the west side of the main court was a series of rooms of ritual or ceremonial importance, including the famous Throne Room with its carved gypsum throne set against the center of one wall and flanked by frescoes of recumbent winged griffins. Here again Evans's interpretation may seem reasonable. We are on much less secure ground concerning his hypothesis about the function of the rooms in the southeast corner of the palace. Here, at the first-floor level, reached by what Evans called the Grand Staircase, were a series of rooms that he believed were used by the royal family who ruled at Knossos, notably the Queen's Megaron with adjoining bathroom; an adjacent corridor led to a lavatory with a wooden-seated toilet that discharged directly into a drain with provision for flushing. The hypothesis that the palace at Knossos was built by a ruling family may itself be farfetched, but the attribution of these particular rooms to a queen, well-appointed though they were, is more a flight of fancy than an archaeological fact.

## *The Political Geography of Minoan Crete*

The government of Knossos raises the issue of the political geography of Minoan Crete. The palace of Knossos that the visitor now sees is essentially a structure of the Second Palace (Late Minoan) period, though it follows earlier palaces of Middle Minoan date on the same site. Similar palaces of Middle or early Late Minoan date are known from other parts of the island, notably Mallia in the north, Zakro in the east, and Phaistos in the south. There may have been other such centers at Khania in the west and at Galatas inland. The existence of a number of contemporary palaces suggests that Crete was divided into a series of autonomous political units, each centered on a major palace.

The palaces of Minoan Crete provide an excellent case for the theory of "peer polity interaction." This approach argues that states (polities) that are in contact will influence one another's development as ruling elites seek to emulate and surpass their neighbors. The striking similarities among the different Cretan palaces and the artifacts found in them (even painted pottery styles) might well be explained by such a process of interaction.

In addition to the palaces, there were also substantial towns. At Knossos, the town covered an area of 75 hectares (185 acres) around the palace and must have been a populous settlement, although we do not know how densely built up it was. In eastern Crete, recent excavations have uncovered another substantial Minoan town with a large and as yet unexcavated "palace." Not all Minoan towns were centered on major palaces, however; the best-preserved example, at Gournia, has regular blocks of houses ranged along cobbled streets with a modest palace or governor's residence overlooking a public square. We may imagine that these towns, with their small palaces, were centers of local administration. Some idea of the houses' appearance can be gained not only from excavation of their ground plan but also from artistic depictions such as the "town mosaic" found at Knossos. This series of faience plaques shows two- or three-story structures strengthened by timber reinforcing beams with windows on the upper floors.

In addition to towns and palaces, the political geography of Minoan Crete incorporated a third category of site known as the "villa." Much smaller than the palaces but often incorporating palatial features (architectural refinements, luxury objects, and cult equipment), these, too, seem to have been centers of local administration. They appear only in the Second Palace period and were probably the residences of local lords or high-ranking officials, but they also had storerooms for agricultural produce. One of the best-preserved villas, at Vathypetro, south of Knossos, was equipped with presses for wine and olive oil, underlining its role in the local economy.

## *Minoan Writing and Crafts*

The Minoans used three major scripts, usually inscribed on clay tablets. Only the most developed of the three (Linear B) has been deciphered. The earliest script, commonly called hieroglyphic, came into use around 2000 B.C., near the beginning of the Palace period. It remained in use during the First Palace period. The script known as Linear A, developed during the eighteenth century B.C., became the standard Cretan script of the Second Palace period and is also found on a number of Cycladic islands, including Melos and Santorini, and at Miletos on the west coast of Turkey. Examples have also been found as far afield as Tell Hazor and Lachish in Israel. Linear A was inscribed on clay tablets, clay labels, stone offering tables, and jewelry. Although the script cannot yet be read and we do not even know what language it represents, the patterns of signs on the tablets suggest that they are generally lists of commodities—in some cases, taxes or inventories of stores; in others, records of offerings due to the gods. Linear A tablets are relatively rare finds but show that the palaces in Crete were run by a literate bureaucracy of scribes or clerks. The short texts on jewelry and offering tables suggest that Linear A was also used in ritual contexts.

The third Cretan script is known as Linear B. It originated from Linear A but was adapted to the needs of the early form of Greek spoken by the Mycenaeans, who took control of Crete at the end of the Second Palace period. It was used at Knossos (and on the Greek mainland) during the Third Palace period.

We have already seen in the construction of the Cretan palaces and the sophistication of the colorful frescoes the evidence of Minoan craft skill. Some of the finest examples are smaller objects such as pottery, gemstones, and figurines. The Minoans were consummate potters, producing high-quality thin-walled vessels and painting them with imaginative polychrome decorations. Stylized scenes of plants and marine life are among their most famous products. Some of the most elaborately decorated pottery was no doubt produced in the palace workshops and intended for the elite. Changing styles of painted pottery form the backbone of traditional Minoan chronology, though it is sometimes uncertain how far the styles are truly successive (rather than contemporary or overlapping), and it is very difficult to assign absolute dates or durations to the various phases on this basis alone. But the painted pottery serves above all to divide the Cretan Palace period into its traditional phases.[2]

Painted pottery, of course, represents only the finest wares, but even utilitarian vessels were skillfully made. At the other end of the scale, Minoan craftspeople also made vessels of gold and silver or carved from attractive stones like serpentine and banded marble. They produced finely carved gemstones and ivories, too, and knowledge of faience working is shown by the snake-goddess figurines from Knossos.

## *Minoan Religion*

Our knowledge of Minoan religion comes from ritual equipment (including figurines) and other artistic depictions on frescoes and sealstones and from the remains of Minoan shrines. Archaeologists have identified two contrasting types of Minoan shrine. The first are those in the palaces and villas, stone rooms or buildings with benches and basins for offerings. Figurines of deities such as those from Knossos may well have been displayed in these shrines.

The second type of Minoan shrine is in a natural setting, on a hilltop or (more rarely) in a cave. Some 25 hilltop, or "peak," sanctuaries are known, most of them dating to the First Palace period (c. 2100–1700 B.C.). Two of the most elaborate, Jouktas and Petsophas, were associated with the nearby centers of Knossos and Palaikastro, respectively, and may in a sense have been "state" shrines. More numerous were the simpler peak sanctuaries, such as that recently excavated by British archaeologists Alan Peatfield and Christine Morris at Atsipadhes in western Crete. Here there was no evidence for any building; the nearest thing to a structure was an area of pebbles, brought to the site from the valley floor below, in the middle of which an upright stone or similar sacred object had once stood. The most striking and abundant finds from Atsipadhes, however, are some 5,000 figurine fragments. These are mainly of cattle (especially horns and legs), but there are also human figurines, including both whole figures and votive limbs and phalli. The site itself, like other peak sanctuaries, is relatively difficult of access and distant from lowland settlements. It may have been visited only during special festivals, when local people walked to the shrine, made offerings there, and left votive figurines to remind the deity of their particular needs, whether these related to their animals or to their own bodily health.

Peak sanctuaries such as Atsipadhes are essentially shrines for local people and are scattered throughout the mountainous uplands of Crete. A significant change takes place during the Second Palace period (c. 1700–1450 B.C.), when most of the peak sanctuaries fell out of use. The six or eight that continued to flourish were all associated with palatial centers. Thus there appears to have been a suppression of local cults in favor of more centralized religious observance.

[2] The conventional classification scheme, based on vessel forms and decoration, is as follows: Middle Minoan IA, IB, IIA, IIB, IIIA, IIIB; Late Minoan IA, IB, II, IIIA1, IIIA2, IIIB, IIIC.

The objects of worship, gods or goddesses, are difficult to identify. One sealstone shows a goddess in flounced skirt standing on top of a mountain and flanked by dogs or felines. We have already mentioned the faience female figurines from Knossos, bare-breasted, with snakes on their arms or in their hands. A little later in date, the Linear B texts from Knossos mention offerings to the gods as well as "priestesses of the winds," and Minoan art shows scenes of animal (especially bull) sacrifices. The importance of religion in Minoan society is clear, as well as efforts by the state to harness it as a source of authority, but the details of cult and belief remain hazy.

## Crete and Its Neighbors

The Minoans were able sailors and kept in close contact with surrounding lands. Most of their metal (copper, lead, and silver) came from the deposits at Laurion in Attica, on the Greek mainland. Ivory, gold, and other luxury materials may have been imported from the Near East. Cretan merchants were known in Egypt, as tomb paintings of people from an island named Keftiu confirm. A remarkable and much closer link with Egypt is shown by recent excavations at Avaris, a city site on the eastern edge of the Nile Delta. Here a rubbish deposit yielded fragments of a Minoan-style fresco, depicting a typically Cretan bull-leaping scene. Avaris was the capital of the pharaoh Amenhotep I as Ahmose during the seventeenth century B.C. (see Chapter 4). They may have had particularly close links with Crete. In the converse direction, Cretan wall painting must itself have owed something to Egyptian models, for instance, the convention for painting men reddish-brown and women white.

Minoan culture had enormous influence in the Aegean islands, especially the Cyclades immediately to the north. There has been great debate about whether the Minoans actually controlled the Cyclades, or some of them, during Middle and Late Minoan times. Minoan-style frescoes occur in the islands, notably at Phylakopi on Melos, Ayia Irini on Kea, and Akrotiri on Thera (Santorini) (Box 9.1). Fragments of Linear A tablets also come from Phylakopi and other Cycladic sites, even though it is unlikely that Cretans and Cycladic islanders spoke the same language. Later Greek legends tell of a Minoan "thalassocracy," a maritime empire based on a powerful Cretan navy, but whether this is based on historical reality and, if it is, whether that reality relates to the Minoan period are questions difficult to answer from archaeological evidence alone.

Crete's relations with the outside world took on an entirely different aspect early in the Late Bronze Age. The major palaces had already been severely damaged by an earthquake c. 1700 B.C., which marks the division between the First and Second Palace periods. A second destruction occurred at the end of the Second Palace period, when all the major palaces except Knossos were abandoned. The villas, too, were destroyed. When the dust settled a new administration was in place at Knossos, and the palace officials were using a new script, Linear B. This is now known to record an early form of Greek, the language used by Mycenaean rulers on the Greek mainland. It seems, therefore, that early in the Late Bronze

## *Box 9.1 Dating a Bronze Age Catastrophe*

Akrotiri, on the Cycladic island of Santorini (Thera), has been labeled the "Pompeii of the Aegean." Early in the Late Bronze Age, this small town was buried in a volcanic eruption beneath several meters of ash and pumice. So quickly did the volcanic deposits accumulate that they have preserved the remains of houses still standing to a height of two or three stories, complete in many cases with colorful frescoes of scenes from ritual and daily life. Quite when this catastrophe occurred is the subject of heated and continuing debate. The pottery from the latest occupation at Akrotiri is of Late Minoan (LM) IA type. This has usually been dated to around 1500 B.C. on the basis of finds of LM IA material in dated Egyptian contexts. Scientific techniques, however, have been argued to give a much earlier date for the Santorini eruption. Large volcanic events emit enormous quantities of ash, which circulate in the upper atmosphere for many months, blocking the sun's rays and causing a nuclear winter effect over large areas of the northern or southern hemisphere. Hence the Santorini eruption should be visible in climatic records such as peat bogs and tree rings. There was thus great excitement when teams of scientists discovered a period of markedly narrower tree rings in material from both California and Northern Ireland, beginning in 1628 B.C. These suggested that periods of cool weather lasted over several years, consistent with the effects of atmospheric dust. Others have identified sulphur peaks in Greenland ice cores, dating to the mid–seventeenth century B.C. and thought to be the result of sulphur emissions from a huge volcanic eruption. Using this and related evidence, a number of archaeologists proposed 1628 B.C. as the date of the Santorini eruption; they believed that the conventional chronology of the Aegean Late Bronze Age, based on links with Egypt, was simply wrong. Recently, however, great doubt has been thrown on this claim by studies of volcanic glass trapped in the Greenland ice core, which show it to differ in composition from the Santorini material; hence the 1628 B.C. eruption might have been another volcano altogether. Furthermore, the dramatic scenarios proposed by earlier writers, who envisaged tidal waves sweeping down onto the Cretan coast and ash clouds covering the eastern end of the island in pumice, are now largely discounted. The Santorini caldera is thought to have collapsed gradually, in piecemeal fashion, after the eruption, and would not have created the huge waves once envisaged. What is very clear is that Crete suffered regularly, about every 80 years, from seismic events, which were hence almost a part of everyday life. Whether the effect of the Santorini eruption, whenever it occurred, was sufficient to disrupt the Minoan economy and render the island vulnerable to Mycenaean invasion is still unresolved.

Age, Mycenaeans took control (either peacefully or by force) of the island of Crete, ousting the earlier Minoan rulers with their non-Greek language. Henceforth, Crete was to be part of the Mycenaean world.

## Mycenaean Greece (1600–1050 B.C.)

The Mycenaeans take their name from Mycenae, the important citadel in the eastern Peloponnese, which was excavated by Schliemann in 1876–1877 (see Chapter 1). What he discovered in the Shaft Graves were the burials of the ruling elite who had governed Mycenae at the very beginning of the Late Bronze Age, in the early sixteenth century B.C. (Figure 9.3). The graves are among the earliest evidence of the change that the mainland experienced at this time, from the relatively unprepossessing Middle Helladic period to the Late Helladic, with fortresses, palaces, impressive tombs, and rich grave goods. These new features characterize the Mycenaean period (1600–1050 B.C.).

The landscape of mainland Greece makes it ideal for the development of autonomous, small-scale kingdoms. Mountains break the terrain into fertile coastal plains, each of which could naturally form the focus of a separate state. These kingdoms first became visible at the beginning of the Late Bronze Age, when the

**Figure 9.3** Gold mask of Agamemnon from the Shaft Graves at Mycenae. "I have gazed on the face of Agamemnon," telegraphed Heinrich Schliemann to the king of Greece in 1876 when he opened the fifth of the Shaft Graves at Mycenae. According to Homer, Mycenae was the seat of the Greek leader Agamemnon, who led the expedition against Troy. Just within the Cyclopean walls, Schliemann came upon five rectangular, rock-cut pits, which contained the remains of 19 individuals accompanied by lavish offerings of gold. A sixth was discovered by his assistant the following year. Some of the bodies had gold face-masks over the skulls. Schliemann, ever the romanticist, identified the finest of these as the "Mask of Agamemnon." We know now that this is a chronological impossibility. The Agamemnon who took part in the Trojan War must have reigned in the thirteenth century B.C. The leaders buried in the Shaft Graves lived some three centuries before, at the beginning of Mycenae's greatness. They provide graphic evidence for the rise of elite rulers in sixteenth-century Greece, an event that marks the opening of the Mycenaean period.

elites who governed them began to engage in long-distance trade with the hinterland of Europe and to proclaim their wealth and power through the richness of their grave goods. It was only in the later Mycenaean period, however, that writing was adopted for the administration of these kingdoms. Here, as in many other areas of life, the Mycenaeans owed a great debt to Minoan Crete. The Linear B script of Mycenaean Greece is indeed merely a version of Minoan Linear A adapted for the Mycenaean language.

The best-known sites of Mycenaean Greece are the major centers of Mycenae, Tiryns, and Pylos. Mycenae, as we have seen, was first excavated by Schliemann in 1876; significant work at Tiryns followed soon after in 1884. Both sites proved to be heavily fortified citadels built on rocky eminences. The enclosure or fortification of settlements on the Greek mainland goes back at least to the Early Bronze Age (third millennium B.C.), but the Mycenaean structures are on an altogether larger scale. Most impressive of all are the Cyclopean defensive walls of Mycenae, Tiryns, and Gla. The term *Cyclopean* refers to the use of large stone blocks carefully fitted together and takes its name from the legendary Cyclops, a race of giants. At Mycenae itself the Cyclopean enclosure is entered through a gateway of still more massive construction, with monolithic jambs and lintel and a "heraldic" sculptured relief panel above the gate that depicts lions supporting a column (Figure 9.4). Such walls reflect a serious concern with defense and security. The military character is enhanced by the careful disposition of bastions and postern gates. Defenses were not always built entirely of stone, however: The wall of Mycenaean Thebes was largely constructed of mud-bricks, although it rested on a stone foundation. Furthermore, it seems that some centers lacked defenses of any great substance; none

**Figure 9.4** The Lion Gate at Mycenae, principal entrance into the citadel. The gate takes its name from the sculptural group above the entrance, which shows a pair of lions on either side of a pillar. What originally stood on top of the pillar is unknown, but the lions are clearly merely heraldic supporters in the overall scheme. Note the massive "Cyclopean" blocks used in both the gate and the wall to its left.

were found at Pylos, for example. This raises the possibility that the western Peloponnese, where Pylos is located, was more peaceful than other parts of Mycenaean Greece: the Argolid, Attica, or Boeotia.

Natural citadels such as Mycenae were probably fortified from the outset of the Late Bronze Age, as early as the sixteenth century B.C., but the first major fortifications in Cyclopean style, here and at other sites, are only dated to the fourteenth century B.C. The first Mycenaean palaces date to the same period. Early in the thirteenth century, the needs of defense seem to have escalated. The walled area was enlarged at both Mycenae and Tiryns. At Mycenae, a new length of walling was built to enclose the southern slopes of the citadel. Grave Circle A, with the famous Shaft Graves, was thus brought within the fortified perimeter, though it was probably the need for a strategic defensive line rather than the desire to protect the graves themselves that was responsible; the more recent "tholos" tombs still lay outside the walls. At Tiryns, the fortifications were both extended and elaborated—extended to take in the lower citadel on the northern part of the ridge, and elaborated with the construction of massive new bastions provided with rows of arrow loops for a more active kind of defense (Figure 9.5a and b).

Mycenaean fortifications varied considerably in the extent of the area they enclosed. The largest, Gla, had walls almost 3.2 kilometers (2 miles) long, though this unusual site was perhaps a special military installation. At Thebes, too, it seems that the defensive wall encircled the whole of the site, but in other cases the fortified area appears to have been a citadel, with a lower town at its foot. Such was the case at Mycenae, where groups of houses were scattered among tombs on the slopes below the citadel. Some of the houses were richly appointed, with painted frescoes, but the settlements as a whole were not extensive and should be described as towns rather than cities.

## *Palace-Based Kingdoms*

The rulers themselves lived in palaces, the focus of which was an architectural complex known as a megaron. This consisted of a principal room with a central, raised hearth that was entered through an antechamber by a single door from a columned porch on the long axis: Porch, antechamber, and main room formed three elements of a single plan. Along the outside of the longer walls of this complex ran corridors giving access to adjacent suites. The main room with hearth was clearly a ceremonial chamber. The best-preserved example is at Pylos, where the hearth and the plastered floor still bear traces of their decoration; the floor was painted and polished to give the effect of variegated paving stones. The walls, too, were decorated with painted frescoes ultimately derived from Minoan models, though the Mycenaean fresco style is distinct from the Cretan in many respects. None of the palaces is standing above foundation level today, however, and their original appearance must be reconstructed from stone footings and fragments recovered through excavation. These suggest that, at Pylos at least, the upper story was made of mud-bricks.

As befitted their role as the administrative centers of small kingdoms, Mycenaean palaces contained storerooms for agricultural produce and luxury

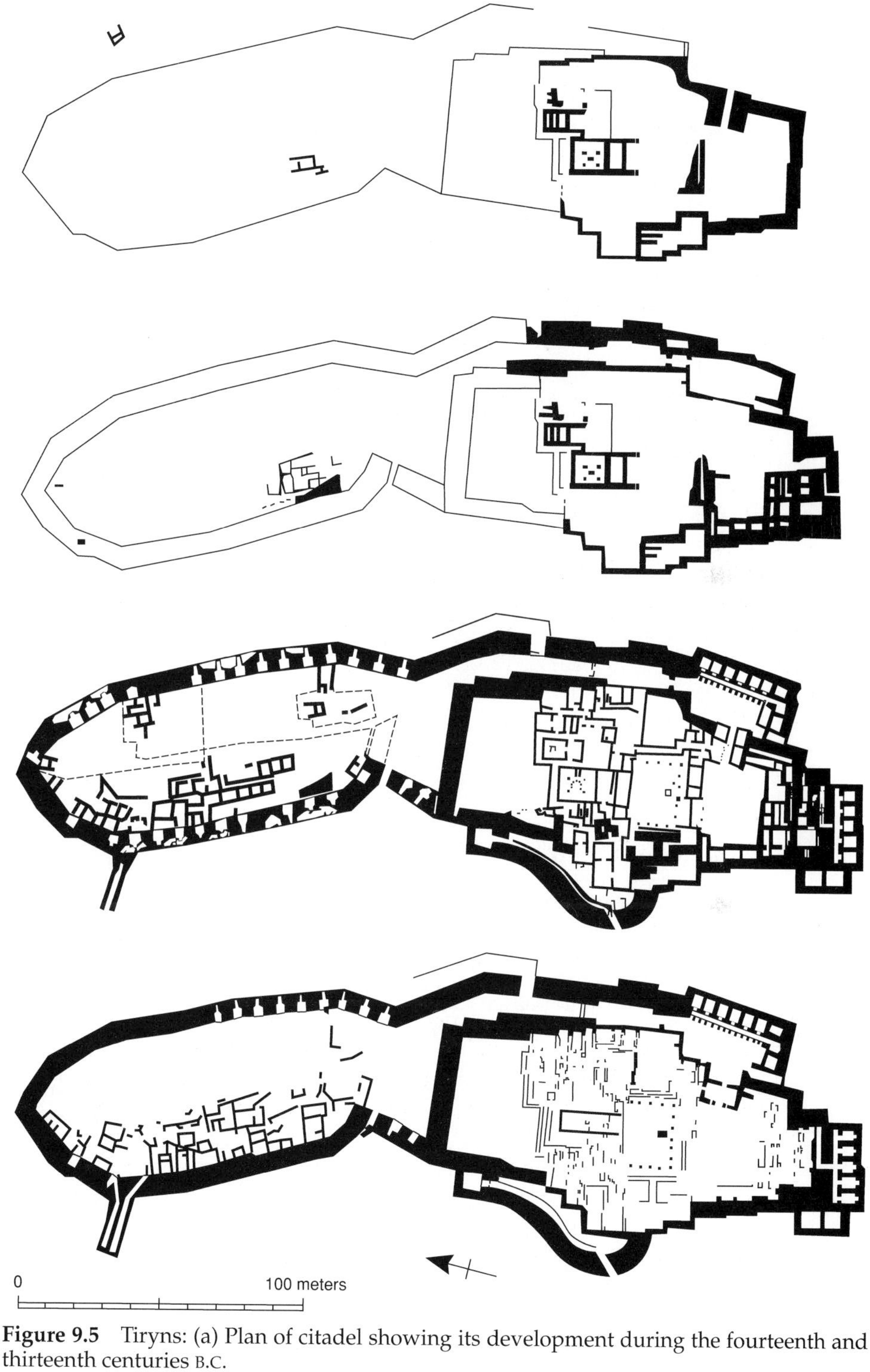


**Figure 9.5** Tiryns: (a) Plan of citadel showing its development during the fourteenth and thirteenth centuries B.C.

**Figure 9.5**(b) Photo of archery casemates.

manufactures. The rulers no doubt drew wealth from the surrounding countryside in the form of tribute and taxation. The Linear B tablets from Pylos contain references to bronze weapons and vessels, female textile workers, a perfume industry, and the allocation of bronze to metalworkers. These clues suggest that the palaces were centers of craft production under the direct control of the ruler, rather as the Mari tablets indicate in the Near East (see Chapter 7). There are also references in the Pylos tablets to palace furnishings: chairs of ebony and greenwood, for example, decorated with ivory or inlaid with gold and electrum figures of men, animals, and vegetation; or a footstool inlaid with blue glass and fitted with gold struts.

The Mycenaeans were not only builders but also engineers. This appears most clearly in the Argolid and Boeotia. Around Mycenae, a whole network of paved roads has been traced, complete with bridges and culverts where there were streams to cross. The roads may have been built to carry horse-drawn chariots, which would otherwise have found the broken terrain difficult to traverse. A more substantial undertaking was the dam built upstream of Tiryns in the thirteenth century B.C. This diverted the stream via an artificial canal, approximately 0.5 kilometers (a third of a mile) long, into a new course well south of the citadel and may have been a response to extensive flooding shortly before. The most extensive engineering works undertaken by the Mycenaeans were the dams and canals built to drain Lake

Copais, northwest of Thebes. These are evidence for powerful central direction by a ruler or dynasty based probably at Orchomenos, as suggested by the discovery of Linear B tablets and the impressive chambered "tholos" tombs (see next section).

## *The Political Geography of the Mycenaean Kingdoms*

The tombs, along with the palaces, are crucial evidence for the political geography of Mycenaean Greece. We have already described the famous Shaft Graves of Mycenae with their fabulous wealth of grave offerings. These date from the sixteenth century B.C. Most, though not all, later Mycenaean princely burials were laid in impressive stone burial chambers, circular in shape and covered by a corbeled vault, commonly known as tholos tombs. The most sophisticated is the so-called Treasury of Atreus at Mycenae, with smoothed stone facing and decorative slabs carved with spirals in relief. Clusters of such tombs at various locations in southern Greece probably represent local centers of power. Their presence close to a citadel, palace, or other major site may indicate the center of a small kingdom. If such evidence can be trusted, Mycenaean Greece was divided into a dozen or more separate states. These were not city-states on the Near Eastern model but princedoms ruled from palaces, without any large population centers. Many upland areas may have remained outside the system altogether. There is certainly nothing to suggest that the whole land formed a single unified kingdom, even if the Mycenaeans are to be equated with references in Hittite texts, which speak of a "King" or "Great King" of Ahhiyawa (see Chapter 7).

Linear B tablets provide important information on the political geography of Mycenaean Greece. Those that have survived, including substantial archives from Pylos and Knossos, relate almost exclusively to administrative matters. Writing was clearly an important tool for the government of Mycenaean kingdoms. The Pylos tablets provide valuable evidence for the internal organization of this Mycenaean state. They show that it was divided into two provinces: the Nearer province, consisting of the coastal area around Pylos itself, and a Further province, stretching inland into the mountains. Each province in turn was divided into 16 districts administered by a governor. At the apex of the administration was the king, or *wanax*, with his army chief and court companions.

## *Mycenaean Crafts*

As with the Minoans, pottery is one of the most widespread Mycenaean products and is the basis for the internal chronology.[3] Mycenaean pottery is a high-quality product, with thin-walled, wheel-made vessels and attractive, often elaborate

[3] Mycenaean pottery classifications are complex. In pottery terms the Mycenaean civilization comes under the Late Helladic Period (LH), to distinguish it from the Late Minoan (LM) of Crete and the Late Cycladic (LC) of the islands. Late Helladic is subdivided into three major units (LH I, II, and III), and these again into smaller divisions (LH IIA, IIB; LH IIIA1, IIIA2, IIIB1, IIIB2; IIIC; with regional and site-specific subdivisions) from the evidence of pottery shapes and decorations. There is a large literature on the subject, and these pottery styles are generally taken to represent successive time periods of around 50 years, though some (e.g., LH IIIB2) are not present in all areas.

shapes. Painted decoration, too, is of a high standard, ultimately derived from Minoan models but recognizably different. Floral and marine subjects are popular, slightly stiffer in composition than their Cretan counterparts. Special mention must be made of the "pictorial" vessels, which appeared in Late Helladic III times. These show painted scenes such as chariot processions, bulls, or in one case a line of marching foot soldiers. It must be remembered that painted pottery, though widespread, is always in the minority on Mycenaean sites. Most of the everyday pottery was undecorated, though still of high quality.

Mycenaean craftspeople displayed a wide range of skills, many of them for use by the palace elites. As we have seen, the palaces themselves were the setting for some of this craft activity. Here we may mention carved gemstones, gold jewelry, carved ivory, and metal vessels like the famous gold Vapheio cups. Some of the materials must have been imported: Tin for the bronze, for example, probably came from the Near East, and amber, used in jewelry, traveled to Mycenae and other sites across a network of trade routes from Baltic sources. Lapis lazuli was another exotic import, brought from sources as far away as Afghanistan.

The Linear B tablets refer to craftspeople in bronze and to storerooms with chariots. It is clear from this and the evidence for fortification that the Mycenaean world was a warlike environment, although not necessarily more so than neighboring regions. The supposed contrast between a warlike Mycenaean Greece and a peaceful Minoan Crete is in the process of reassessment, though it remains true that armor and weaponry are more prominent in the Mycenaean world, both in actual finds and in artistic depictions. A striking example is the bronze body armor from the rich tomb at Dendra, though this was probably exceptional and cumbersome to wear as well. A boar's tusk helmet was also found in this tomb; examples are known from other sites, and they are sometimes depicted in art. Shields, spears, and swords, however, were the commonest weapons. We suspect that the chariot, which appeared in art and on the tablets, can have been of little use as a war machine in the rugged Greek terrain, though the palaces evidently maintained large fleets of these vehicles. They were probably used as mobile archery platforms, as in the Near East. This is very different from the practice suggested by Homer's *Iliad*, where chariots ferry aristocratic warriors to and from the battlefield, but by Homer's day chariots had not been used in Greek warfare for several centuries. That the *Iliad* cannot be used as a reliable guide to Mycenaean military practices is underlined by other features (e.g., the use of iron swords and cremation) that clearly refer to a later age.

## *The Mycenaeans Abroad*

The Aegean world had had trade relations with the Near East from at least the third millennium B.C., but in the Late Bronze Age these take on a much greater (or more visible) importance. The evidence consists mainly of Mycenaean and, to a lesser extent, Minoan pottery, which is found in large quantities in Egypt, along the Levantine coast, and in Cyprus. A large proportion of the vessels are small containers, probably used for the transport of perfumed oils; in this case it was obviously the contents rather than the pottery itself that was important. Analysis of the pottery fabric by the technique known as optical emission spectroscopy has shown that most of it comes from the Argolid, which was evidently the key region of Greece that participated in these exchanges.

The large quantity of Mycenaean pottery at east Mediterranean sites could be taken to imply that Mycenaean traders were regular visitors at Syrian and Cypriot ports. While this may have been the case, it is clear that much Mycenaean pottery was carried in non-Mycenaean vessels. The evidence comes from excavations by George Bass and others at Bronze Age shipwrecks off the southern coast of Turkey (Box 9.2). These were not Mycenaean ships but Syrian or Canaanite vessels that carried Mycenaean pottery among a range of other wares. In both cases, the principal commodity appears to have been copper ingots, mainly of "ox-hide" shape (rectangular, with concave sides and projecting corners). The copper had been mined on Cyprus and was perhaps being shipped westward, along with some tin, for trade to the Mycenaean world. These sites divert emphasis from the Mycenaean decorated pottery, which is so prominent in the archaeological record, to the much more valuable trade in copper ingots, which would have been melted down and cast into finished goods upon arrival at their destination. The Uluburun wreck also contained finished metal goods: glass beads; unworked ivory, gold and silver ornaments; and ostrich eggshells from countries as far afield as Syria and Egypt.

The East Mediterranean was not the only area of Mycenaean overseas interest, however, and it is possible that in the central Mediterranean Mycenaean sailors and ships were the principal carriers. Mycenaean pottery has been found around the coasts of Sicily, southern Italy, and Sardinia. Some authorities have gone so far as to argue that the site of Scoglio del Tonno, overlooking the excellent natural harbor of Taranto Bay, may have been a Mycenaean trading station, an argument based on the quantities of Mycenaean and native Italian material it has yielded. Mycenaean pottery reached the island of Malta and even the coast of southern Spain. What the Mycenaeans were getting in return remains an enigma, but on Sardinia the main object was no doubt Sardinian copper. Copper ingots of the typical ox-hide form have also been found on Sardinia, and the Mycenaeans could actually have been involved in working the mines on the island. Surprisingly, analyses of the metal suggest that Sardinian ox-hide ingots are of Cypriot (rather than Sardinian) copper, though they may all be in reality of recycled metal.

Whatever the scale of Mycenaean involvement far afield, it was in the Aegean region that it had its greatest impact. As we have seen, at some point during the fifteenth century Minoan Crete was absorbed into the Mycenaean orbit and Greek-speaking leaders became the new rulers of Knossos. Mycenaean influence became particularly strong in the islands of the Dodecanese, including Rhodes. Whether this ascendancy was achieved by peaceful or violent means is uncertain, but the Linear B tablets from Pylos do mention substantial numbers of female captives and their children (but relatively few men) from places in the eastern Aegean like Chios, Lemnos, and Knidos. They were employed by the palace for spinning and food processing and received rations in return. Two interpretations are possible: Either they were purchased in slave markets of the eastern Aegean, or they were captives taken directly by the Mycenaeans themselves.

## Box 9.2 *The Uluburun Shipwreck*

Few archaeological finds rival the extraordinary cargo found aboard a Bronze Age ship wrecked off the rugged Uluburun cliffs in southern Turkey. Shipwrecks like this offer unique opportunities to study ancient trade, for each ship on the seabed is a sealed capsule, its holds a mirror of trading conditions at the time. George Bass and Cemal Pulak's excavation of the Uluburun ship has yielded a mine of information on the commercial world of the eastern Mediterranean in the fourteenth century B.C. The heavily laden ship was sailing westward from the eastern Mediterranean when it was shattered on the jagged rocks of Uluburun in about 1316 B.C. (a date from tree rings in firewood found in the wreck). It sank on a slope, between 17 and 48 meters (90 to 151 feet) below the surface. Bass and Pulak have plotted the exact position of every timber and every item of the ship's equipment and cargo as they lift artifacts from the seabed. They have recovered a unique portrait of eastern Mediterranean trade more than 3,000 years ago.

The Uluburun ship was laden with over 350 copper ingots, each weighing about 27 kilograms (60 pounds), a load of 10 tons, enough to equip a small army with armor and weapons (Figure 9.6). The tin may have come from southern Turkey. A ton of two-handled Canaanite jars from Palestine or Syria held olives, glass beads, and resin from the terebinth tree, incense used in religious rituals. The ship's hold contained Baltic amber that probably reached the Mediterranean overland, ebonylike wood from Africa, elephant and hippopotamus ivory, and ostrich eggshells from North Africa or Syria. Egyptian,

**Figure 9.6** Excavations on the Bronze Age shipwreck at Uluburun, near Kas, southern Turkey. Note copper ingots in the foreground.

Levantine, and Mycenaean daggers, swords, spearheads, and woodworking tools lay aboard, and also sets of weights, some fashioned in animal forms. There were costly glass ingots, Mesopotamian cylinder seals, a Mycenaean seal stone, even a gold cup and parts of a tortoiseshell lute. The ship carried Egyptian scarabs, dozens of fishing weights, fishhooks, and 23 stone anchors, vital when anchoring in windy coves. Even the thorny burnet shrub used to pack the cargo was preserved. One unique find: a diptych, a wooden cover for a wax tablet used to record commercial transactions.

By using artifact distributions from land sites and a variety of sourcing techniques, Bass and Pulak have reconstructed the anonymous skipper's last journey. They believe he started his voyage on the Levant coast, sailed north up the coast, crossed to Cyprus, then coasted along the southern Turkish shore. The ship called at ports large and small on its way west, along a well-traveled route that took advantage of changing seasonal winds, to Crete, some Aegean islands, and perhaps to the Greek mainland. The skipper had traversed this route many times, but on this occasion his luck ran out and he lost his ship, the cargo, and perhaps his life on Uluburun's pitiless rocks. From the archaeological perspective, the Uluburun shipwreck is a godsend, for it allows researchers to fill in many details of an elaborate trade network that linked the eastern Mediterranean with Egypt, the Aegean, and Greece more than 3,300 years ago. Bass and Pulak suspect that the Uluburun ship may have been carrying an unusually valuable cargo—perhaps for a monarch—but the owners remain a mystery.

The picture of Mycenaean seaborne warriors raiding settlements on the coasts and islands of the eastern Aegean may have provided the historical background for the Homeric story of the Trojan War. References in Hittite royal records to a king of Ahhiyawa who operated in a hostile manner in Aegean Turkey may also relate to "Achaean" (Mycenaean) military activity on the Turkish mainland. The coastal area around Miletus and Halicarnassus may even have become a Mycenaean enclave; it faces west toward the heavily Mycenaean-influenced Dodecanese. It is, of course, very difficult to be certain that we are dealing here with ethnic Mycenaeans rather than with the local adoption of Mycenaean fashions in pottery and burial.

## After the Palaces: Postpalatial Greece (1200–1050 B.C.)

The thirteenth century B.C. was a time of increased insecurity on the Greek mainland. New or enlarged fortifications were built at Mycenae, Tiryns, Athens, and several other sites. Work even began on a wall across the Isthmus of Corinth to protect the Peloponnese from landward attack, a project repeated in classical times when Greece was threatened by Persian invaders. Shortly afterward, around the end of the thirteenth century B.C., the palaces themselves were destroyed. Pylos went up in a huge conflagration, which proved to be of great good fortune to archaeologists since it baked hard and preserved the clay Linear B tablets in the palace archives.

The causes of this destruction, at Pylos and elsewhere, are unclear. There is no evidence to suggest that the countryside was overrun by foreign raiders or invaders.

Drought, crop failure, and internecine warfare among the various kingdoms may all have played their part. Whatever the causes, over a period of 50 years or so all the major palaces were abandoned, an event that ushers in the so-called Postpalatial period (c. 1200–1050 B.C.). This was generally a time of reduced prosperity, though the town of Tiryns, for example, grew to be even larger than before (maybe providing refuge for people from the surrounding countryside). Overseas contacts were maintained, but Crete and the Dodecanese, rather than the mainland, seem to have been the leading centers of trade in the Postpalatial period. By around 1000 B.C.,

**Figure 9.7** Fortifications of Troy VI. The *Iliad* tells of a war fought between the Achaeans (Greeks) against the city of Troy, near the Dardanelles at the northwest corner of Turkey, led by Agamemnon, high king of Mycenae. In the 1860s the site of Troy was identified with the mound of Hissarlik by British archaeologist and local resident Frank Calvert. Heinrich Schliemann's excavations in the 1870s uncovered a series of Bronze Age settlements, stretching back into the third millennium B.C. Among them was a fortified citadel of Late Bronze Age date (Troy VI), contemporary with the Mycenaean citadels of Greece. Schliemann himself erroneously equated Homer's Troy with Troy II, a much earlier third millennium fortress; his assistant Dörpfeld corrected the chronology some years later. Troy VI suffered severe destruction around 1250 B.C., for which both earthquake and human assault are possible explanations. It is tempting to link this destruction with the legend of the Trojan War. The Mycenaeans may well have been raiding this coast in the thirteenth century B.C., and local strongpoints such as Troy would have been natural targets in such a conflict. The Greek legends of the Trojan War contain many elements borrowed from later periods, however, including the use of iron and the emphasis on the burial rite of cremation, as in the description of Patroclus's funeral. Inhumation was the standard rite in the Mycenaean period. Recent excavations by German archaeologist Manfred Korfmann have shown that the Troy excavated by Schliemann was in fact only the citadel of a larger Late Bronze Age city.

however, even this economic activity had slowed. The demand for craftmanship declined still further, and settlements became small and dispersed. In areas of southern Greece such as Messenia and Laconia there is evidence of severe depopulation.

It was hardly an optimistic moment, but this was the economic and political matrix from which the world of classical Greece was to develop during succeeding centuries. By the eighth century B.C., city life and foreign trade had revived and the first Greek epics were being written in the newly adopted alphabetic script. These legends and epics contain echoes of the Mycenaean Palace age, most famously in the *Iliad* and the *Odyssey,* attributed to Homer. There is little doubt that such texts incorporate historical elements—the Trojan War may have been a real historical event—but their picture of swashbuckling heroes engaged in single combat is a far cry from the painstaking palace bureaucracies revealed by the Linear B tablets (Figure 9.7).

## Summary

The first Aegean civilizations, those of Minoans and Mycenaeans, flourished during the second millennium B.C. We have seen how they related to each other and to the rest of the Mediterranean world, with Mycenaeans replacing Minoans as the dominant regional power during the fifteenth century B.C. A major theme throughout this chapter is contrast and comparison among Crete, the Greek mainland, and the Aegean islands. Each had its own individual character yet drew on a common pool of cultural influences and borrowings. Another theme is the tantalizing glimpses provided by later Greek legends, which seem to tell of Bronze Age historical events. The discovery that Linear B script is a version of Greek shows that the Mycenaeans were the direct ancestors of the Greeks of the classical period, whose story we follow in Chapter 10.

## Guide to Further Reading

The archaeology of the Aegean Bronze Age is well summarized in a number of publications. Good starting points are Oliver Dickinson, *The Aegean Bronze Age* (Cambridge: Cambridge University Press, 1994) and Colin Renfrew, *The Emergence of Civilization: The Cyclades and the Aegean in the Third Millennium B.C.* (London: Methuen, 1972). Peter Warren, *The Aegean Civilizations,* 2nd ed. (Oxford: Phaidon, 1989) offers a more popular account. A comprehensive guide to the literature is provided by Tracey Cullen, ed., *Aegean Prehistory: A Review* (Boston: Archaeological Institute of America, 2001).

A recent study of the Cyclades, exploring their special character as island societies, is Cyprian Broodbank's *An Island Archaeology of the Early Cyclades* (Cambridge: Cambridge University Press, 2001). On Cycladic figurines see Colin Renfrew, *The Cycladic Spirit* (London: Thames and Hudson, 1991). Patricia Getz-Preziosi's analysis of individual masters is published in her *Sculptors of the Cyclades: Individual and Tradition in the Third Millennium B.C.* (Ann Arbor: University of Michigan Press, 1987). The tragedy of looting, which has left most of the Cycladic figurines without recorded provenance, is discussed in Chris Chippindale and David Gill, "Material and Intellectual Consequences of Esteem for Cycladic Figures," *American Journal of Archaeology* 97 (1993): 601–659.

A number of recent works deal specifically with Aegean Bronze Age chronology. Among the most useful are Peter Warren and Vronwy Hankey, eds., *Aegean Bronze Age Chronology* (Bristol: Bristol Classical Press, 1989) and Stuart Manning, *Absolute Chronology of the Aegean Early Bronze Age* (Sheffield: Sheffield Academic Press, 1995). For the tree-ring dating of the Santorini eruption, see M. G. L. Baillie, *A Slice Through Time* (London: Batsford, 1995).

Gerald Cadogan, *Palaces of Minoan Crete* (London: Barrie and Jenkins, 1976) and Nanno Marinatos, *Minoan Religion* (Columbia: University of South Carolina Press, 1993) deal with two key aspects of Minoan culture. For "peer polity interaction" and the Cretan palaces, see John F. Cherry, "Polities and Palaces: Some Problems in Minoan State Formation," in Colin Renfrew and John F. Cherry, eds., *Peer Polity Interaction and Socio-Political Change* (Cambridge: Cambridge University Press, 1986), pp. 19–45. Sir Arthur Evans, *The Palace of Minos at Knossos,* 4 vols. (Oxford: Clarendon Press, 1921–1935) is the classic but, of course, now dated account of the great palace. Robin Barber, *The Cyclades in the Bronze Age* (London: Duckworth, 1987) describes the archaeology of these Aegean islands. The spectacular site of Thera is described by Christos Doumas, *Thera: Pompeii of the Ancient Aegean* (London: Thames and Hudson, 1983); its wall paintings receive splendid coverage in Doumas's *The Wall-Paintings of Thera* (Athens and London: Thera Foundation, 1992).

For excavations during the twentieth century at two of the key mainland Mycenaean sites, see Alan Wace, *Mycenae: An Archaeological History and Guide* (Princeton, NJ: Princeton University Press, 1949); George Mylonas, *Mycenae and the Mycenaean Age* (Princeton, NJ: Princeton University Press); and Carl W. Blegen and Marion Rawson, *The Palace of Nestor at Pylos* (Princeton, NJ: Princeton University Press, 1966). John Chadwick, *The Mycenaean World* (Cambridge: Cambridge University Press, 1976) is a good general account of Mycenaean civilization from the evidence of the Linear B script. Chadwick's *The Decipherment of Linear B* (Cambridge: Cambridge University Press, 1958) tells the story of Michael Ventris and decipherment. Chadwick's account of Linear B in J. T. Hooker, ed., *Reading the Past* (London: British Museum Publications, 1990), pp. 136–195, brings the situation up to date. The craftsmanship of Mycenaeans and Minoans is well covered by Sinclair Hood, *The Arts of Prehistoric Greece* (Harmondsworth, England: Penguin, 1978). Michael Woods, *In Search of the Trojan War* (London: BBC Books, 1985), is a detailed discussion about the historicity of the Trojan War.

*Chapter 10*

# The Mediterranean World in the First Millennium (1000–30 B.C.)

Sarcophagus of a married couple on a funereal bed. (Etruscan, from Cerveteri, 6th B.C.E. Terracotta. Reunion des Musees Nationaux/Art Resource, NY. Photo: Lewandowski/Ojeda. Louvre, Paris, France)

*The twenty-eighth day of the month Hekatombaion, the first month in the Athenian calendar, dawned bright and clear. Already the city was astir with activity, for this was the festival of Athena's birthday, the day of the Panathenaia, the great procession. Early in the day the procession assembled on the edge of the city, marshals organizing the various groups into their proper order: young men on horseback, chariots, people on foot, youths bearing water jars, men playing pipes, and others with the stringed instruments known as* **citharas.** *Near the front of the procession were the key players in the ceremony. A group of men led cattle and sheep for sacrifice. More important still was the contingent of young girls, past puberty but not yet married, escorting the wheeled cart that carried the embroidered peplos itself, raised high above the crowd on a wooden mast. Slowly, the procession passed through the city gate and made its way along the stone-paved Sacred Way through the agora. Ahead of them stood the gleaming marble buildings of the Acropolis; there in the shrine of Athena Polias, the ceremony itself would take place. The ancient statue of the goddess would receive the* **peplos,** *her new robe, and the city would rejoice in another year of Athena's patronage.*

The Panathenaic Festival was one of the annual events of ancient Athens, the leading city-state of Classical Greece. In this chapter we discuss the rise of the Greek city-states from their beginnings in the eighth century B.C. We also consider the parallel development of city-states in Etruscan Italy and the implantation of Greek and Phoenician colonies around the shores of the Mediterranean. The chapter ends with an account of Classical Greece and the Hellenistic world (see Tables 9.1 and 11.1).

## The Recovery of Greece (1000–750 B.C.)

In historical terms, the centuries following the collapse of the Mycenaean palaces in Greece are shrouded in darkness. Later Greek historians such as Herodotus believed that Greece had been invaded by peoples from the north, the so-called Dorians. These newcomers, it was thought, had introduced iron tools and weapons and had replaced the heroic society of the Mycenaean age (as depicted by Homer) with a new social order. Yet several of the principal Mycenaean centers—Athens, Thebes, Sparta—remained important or regained their importance during these "dark" centuries. Furthermore, the language spoken by the Mycenaeans and recorded on the Linear B tablets is now known to have been an early form of Greek (see Chapter 9). Current theories of the "dark age" do not look to a wholesale replacement of the Greek population but to a decapitation of Mycenaean society—the fall of the aristocrats, with their palaces and clay tablets, leaving the uneducated villagers and farmers, with only their oral traditions and village-farming economy.

For several centuries Greece remained a basically peasant society, without cities, without writing, and without architecture of any significance. Yet as early as the tenth century B.C. there were signs of economic revival. This cultural and economic recovery, continuing during the ninth and eighth centuries B.C., had both domestic and international components. At home, population levels that had fallen dramatically at the end of the Mycenaean age began to rise once again, and prosperity grew (Figure 10.1). Overseas, there were renewed contacts with the ports around the eastern Mediterranean, and luxury items from Egypt and Cyprus were placed in graves at Lefkandi on the Greek island of Euboea.

The eighth century B.C. marks a watershed in Greek cultural and economic development. This is the century in which the Homeric epics attained their present form and were set down in writing, using the alphabet that in this same century the Greeks adopted from the Phoenicians. Another landmark of early Greek literature was the poetry of Hesiod, a younger contemporary of Homer, who lived in the small town of Askra in Boeotia around 700 B.C. In his *Theogony*, a long verse account of the gods and their origins, we find Zeus and Hera, Apollo and Athena, Ares, Artemis, and Aphrodite: the gods and goddesses of the classical Greek pantheon. They are also featured in Homer's writings. At about the same time, buildings recognizable as temples appeared in such places as Samos and Olympia, simple structures at first but the beginnings of a great tradition of classical architecture. The Greeks later maintained that the first Olympic Games had been held in 776 B.C.; this date was taken as the starting point of Greek historical chronology.

One of the most crucial developments was that of the city-state, or *polis*. As we have seen, Mycenaean centers had been relatively small settlements, clusters of houses around a fortress or palace. It is doubtful if any of them would have qualified for designation as cities. Classical Greece, by contrast, was a land of cities, and citizenship became a key feature of Greek politics and way of life. The concept of the city-state was the major organizing principle in the Greek world. Typically it comprised the city itself (usually fortified since they were often at war with each other) and the surrounding rural hinterland, dotted with farmsteads and villages. On the one hand, many such city-states were small both in extent and in population; some could field only a few hundred men of military age. On the other hand, some could afford to build grandiose temples and public buildings: not palaces for the wealthy but monuments to the prestige of their own city. This is a trend seen most obviously in fifth-century Athens, when the resources of the Athenian empire were poured into the reconstruction of the Acropolis and above all the Parthenon, with its gold and ivory statue of the patron goddess, Athena.

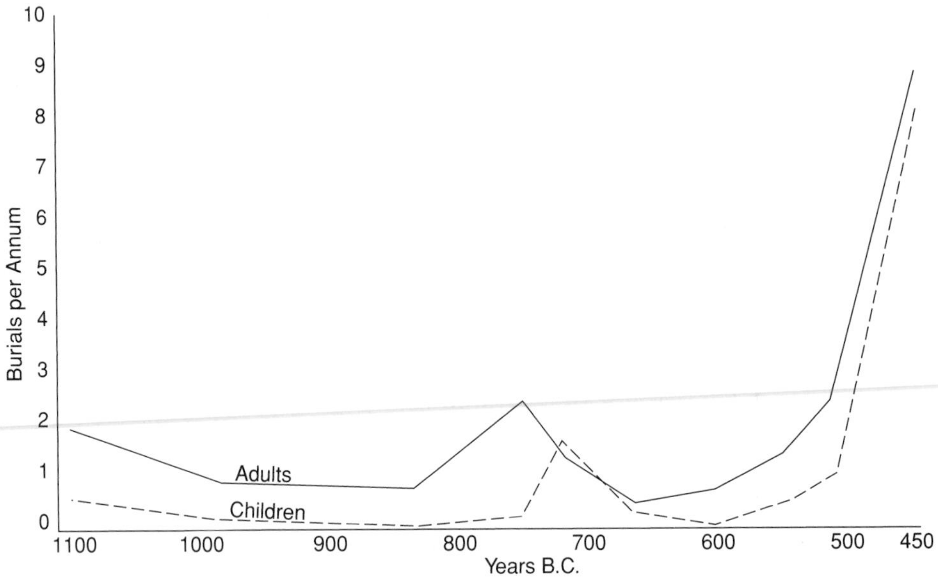


**Figure 10.1** Graph of burials at Athens, 1100–450 B.C. A key feature of the rise of the Greek polis, or city-state, was the development of a new social ideology that emphasized the concept of citizenship, that is, that citizens enjoyed equal rights, regardless of wealth and rank. This was a marked change from the situation during previous centuries, when Greek society had been dominated by wealthy families and most of the people were dependent peasant laborers. British archaeologist Ian Morris has argued that in the case of Athens, the transition from the master-peasant stage to the citizen-polis was far from smooth and suffered at least one temporary reversal. He bases this conclusion on burial evidence from Athens and its surrounding area, where he notes the exclusion of certain groups, including children and the poor, from formal burial in cemeteries during the prepolis period (eleventh to eighth centuries B.C.). Comparing the representation of children with that of adults, we see that the proportion of children rose during the eighth century B.C., along with an increase in the numbers of adults who had formal burials. This, Morris argues, indicates a trend toward citizens' burial, in which all citizens, whether rich or poor, have the right to cemetery interment. Several Greek cities (though not all) underwent a parallel process around the same time, resulting in the emergence of city-states at Corinth and other centers. At Athens, however, Morris shows that this pattern of change is reversed around 700 B.C., when burial reverts to the rich alone. The incipient rise of the Athenian polis seems thus to have been nipped in the bud. The resumption of the trend occurs only in the sixth century B.C., when there is a rapid increase in the numbers of both adult and child burials in Athenian cemeteries. This marks the final transition to the polis ideal, wherein the city-state was governed by and on behalf of the citizenship as a whole rather than by the wealthy families alone. The culmination of this process was the development of Athenian democracy shortly before 500 B.C.

## Phoenicians and Carthaginians (1000–750 B.C.)

The recovery of the Greek economy and the expansion of Greek overseas contacts were part of a much wider phenomenon that also involved the Phoenicians. These active Levantine traders began to engage in long-distance commerce and exploration perhaps as early as the tenth century B.C., reaching northwest Africa and southern Spain during the ninth century (see Chapter 8). One of the principal objects of this trade was the metal resources of southern Spain and Portugal (Iberia), the kingdom known as Tartessos. These included silver above all, but Iberia also yielded abundant resources of tin and copper and much gold. Spain was, of course, a long journey from Phoenicia itself, but the metals could be sold at great profit in the ports and markets of the eastern Mediterranean, and Phoenician merchants became rich through this trade. One result of their commercial success was the foundation of trading colonies on the shores of the Mediterranean. These served both as stopping-off points for long-distance merchant ships and as places for trade with the local populations. The main prerequisite in choosing a site for such a colony was a good natural harbor—offshore islands; deep, sheltered bays; or sandy promontories where ships could be hauled up and beached. Gades (Cadiz) in southern Spain is a typical example: a long island not far from the shore, with sheltered bay and river estuary behind. Such locations paralleled those of the main cities of Phoenicia itself, such as Tyre and Sidon.

Phoenician colonization got properly underway during the ninth century. It was then that the greatest of all their new settlements, the city of Carthage on the North African coast, was founded. The traditional date of the foundation is 814 B.C., and German excavators have located levels as early as the eighth century. The name itself means "new city" (Qart Hadasht), and it quickly grew to be the leading Phoenician center of the western Mediterranean and the head of a Carthaginian empire. It was a Levantine city transplanted in Africa, with the Phoenician gods Baal Hammon and Melkart and the goddesses Astarte and Tanit. One famous rite the Phoenicians brought with them was that of child sacrifice in times of crisis (for instance in 310 B.C., when the city was besieged by the Greeks). Confirmation of this gruesome rite came in 1921 when a local resident stumbled on the child cemetery, or *tophet*, near the southern limit of the ancient city. Estimates suggest that well over 20,000 urns may have been buried in this cemetery, most containing the cremated remains of one or more children, though roughly one in ten held the remains of young animals instead. The latter were probably substitutes for child sacrifices. In chronological terms they spanned virtually the whole of the city's early history, from 750 B.C. to its destruction by the Romans in 146 B.C. It is clear the Carthaginians practiced child sacrifice on a large scale throughout this period. Recent excavations by American archaeologist Lawrence Stager and subsequent analysis of the cremations by Jeffrey Schwartz have revealed important changes between the earliest burials, in the seventh century B.C., when newborn babies predominated, and the later burials in the fourth century B.C., when the bones were mainly those of infants between 1 and 3 years old. Greek and Roman sources suggest they probably had their throats cut before they were burned. Carthage is in fact only one of ten Phoenician cities in the western Mediterranean where cemeteries containing cremated remains of sacrificed children have been found. The children may have been sacrificed in fulfillment of a vow, making the gruesome ritual in reality an act of piety and religious faith.

We would know much more about Carthage and the Carthaginians had their own writings survived, but they perished in the Roman destruction of the city in 146 B.C. Thus we are dependent on sketchy details provided by Greek and Roman writers, who had no reason to admire a Carthaginian people with whom they were so often at war.

## The Greek Colonies (800–600 B.C.)

The Phoenicians planted colonies around much of the western Mediterranean basin, including southern Spain, North Africa, Sardinia, and western Sicily (Figure 10.2). But they were not the only colonizers of the first millennium B.C. The Greeks, too, built new cities around the shores of the Aegean, the central Mediterranean, and the Black Sea. The process began as early as the tenth century with the foundation of cities such as Miletus and Ephesus on the western coast of Turkey; these became so well established that in later years they were regarded as part of the Greek homeland. Some of the sites may indeed have been continuously occupied by Greeks from Mycenaean times.

The great phase of Greek colonization began in the eighth century B.C., when several cities on mainland Greece sent out colonies both eastward and westward. This was linked with a resurgence of interest in the sea, something that the Greeks had probably never lost but which was increasingly marked by ship designs painted on Athenian pots. The most active of the colonizing cities of the eighth century were Eretria and Chalcis on the island of Euboea. No fewer than

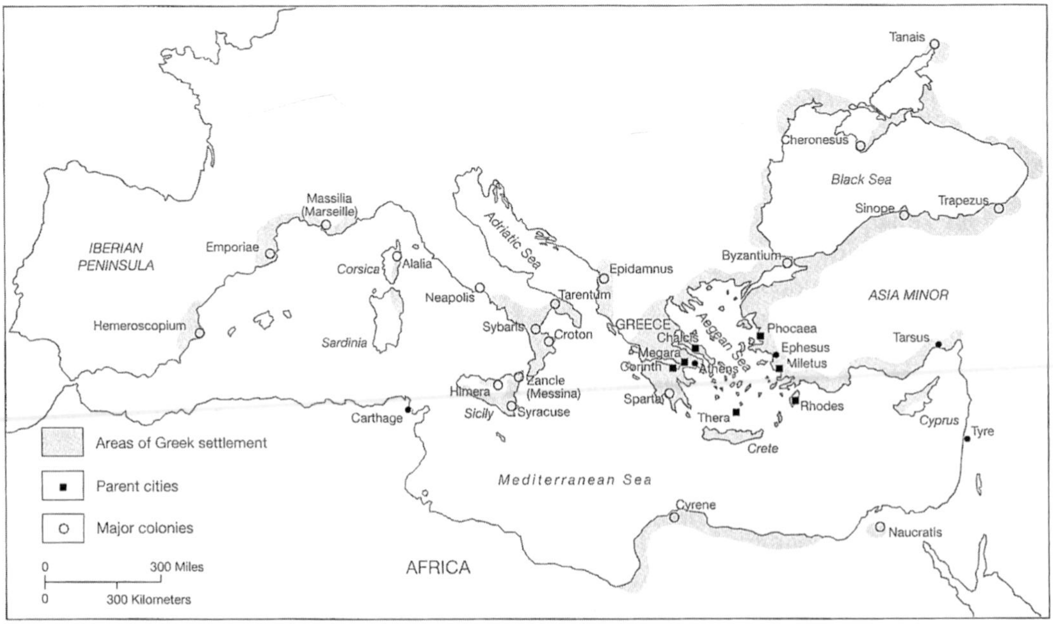


**Figure 10.2** Map of Greek and Phoenician colonies around the Mediterranean and Black Sea coasts.

19 Euboean colonies were founded, beginning around 750 B.C. with Pithekoussai in southern Italy. These were no mere footholds on a foreign coast but substantial settlements. The remains at Pithekoussai cover 75 hectares (185 acres), and already by 700 B.C. it must have had a population numbering several thousand. Within little more than a century the whole of southern Italy and much of Sicily was dominated by Greek colonies such as Neapolis (Naples), Cumae, Poseidonia (Paestum), Taras (Taranto), and Syracuse, so much so that it came to be known as Magna Graecia. Around 600 B.C. Greek colonists founded the cities of Massilia (Marseilles) in southern France and Emporion (Ampurias) in northern Spain, though their expansion further west was blocked by the Carthaginians.

The Greeks may have had to contest control of the western Mediterranean with the Carthaginians, but in the Black Sea they had no serious commercial rivals. The cities of Megara near Corinth and Miletus in Aegean Turkey began by founding colonies around the straits of the Dardanelles and gradually expanded their activities eastward. Byzantium (modern Istanbul) was founded by the Megarians in the middle of the seventh century B.C., and by the fifth century colonies had been established across the Black Sea as far as Phasis in the east. The northern shallows around the mouths of the great Russian rivers were a particular attraction for Greek colonists. The Black Sea here is only 100 meters (330 feet) deep but is rich in fish like sturgeon, salmon, and turbot. The rivers themselves also gave access to the interior and provided the opening for lucrative trade in grain and other commodities with the nomadic Scythians of the Eurasian steppes. Complex reasons lay behind Greek colonization. One common earlier theory pointed to land hunger at home, arguing that rising population levels in Greece itself during the eighth and seventh centuries B.C. stimulated the search for a new life overseas. It is doubtful, however, whether populations had grown so far by the eighth century that land at home was in short supply.

Another explanation emphasizes political tensions in the early cities and the increasing divisions between rich and poor. More than one historical account tells of defeated political factions who left their home city to begin again overseas. But other factors must also have played a vital role. One was commercial. The Greeks could not have established their overseas colonies in the teeth of determined local opposition, though there is some evidence to suggest that local residents were driven out. Nonetheless, the Greeks must have had something to offer these people to persuade them to accept or at least to tolerate their presence. An obvious advantage was that they provided a ready outlet for goods and manufactures such as foodstuffs, slaves, and raw materials; the local residents could make a tidy profit through traffic with Greek traders. The Greeks themselves were careful to back this up by diplomatic gifts to local rulers, such as the famous Vix krater found in a Celtic grave in eastern France—the largest ancient Greek bronze vessel to have survived anywhere.

Greek colonies grew rich on the proceeds of trade and agriculture, shipping surplus produce such as grain and salt meat to the growing cities of mainland Greece and Ionia. In return they provided Greek goods and manufactures, some imported from overseas and others made in the colonies themselves. And wherever they went, the colonists carried Greek language and culture, bringing large parts of the Mediterranean and Black Sea coasts within the Greek orbit and spreading Greek influence far into the interior through trade and interaction with native non-Greek peoples.

## Etruscan Italy (750–400 B.C.)

The Etruscans, long-time trading partners of the Greeks, occupied the area of northern Italy known as Etruria, facing the Tyrrhenian Sea (the western basin of the Mediterranean), a fertile hill country with access to important iron deposits on the island of Elba. The Etruscans spoke a language unrelated to any modern European language. In the eighth century B.C., through contact with the Greeks, they borrowed the Greek alphabet, dropping three of the Greek letters and adding others of their own invention. Yet although some 10,000 Etruscan texts are now known, only 6 are more than 50 words long and most are very short indeed. The script itself is easy to read, but the brevity of the texts makes it difficult to decipher their meaning, and the Etruscan language remains only partly understood. As a result, our knowledge of the Etruscans is dependent on the testimony of archaeology and the writings of their neighbors (often their enemies), the Greeks and Romans.

For many years it was believed, following the testimony of several classical writers such as Herodotus, that the Etruscans were newcomers from the east, who had invaded Italy at the end of the Bronze Age. This theory is now generally discounted, and archaeology shows a gradual emergence of Etruscan civilization from the indigenous societies of Bronze Age Etruria, the pace of change quickening through contacts with Greek and Phoenician traders.

Phoenician merchants probably made contact with the Etruscans during the ninth century, followed by Greeks in the mid-eighth century B.C. They brought with them exotic luxuries such as ostrich eggshells, raw and carved ivories, faience and glass, and gold and silver ornaments. Soon, Greek painted pottery appeared in increasing abundance in aristocratic tombs at leading Etruscan centers such as Tarquinia, Caere, and Vulci. By the eighth century, Greek merchants were active at Etruscan ports such as Graviscae. The Etruscans also entertained close commercial and diplomatic contacts with the Carthaginians. In the sixth century they acted together to put a stop to Greek commercial expansion in the western Mediterranean. At the sea battle of Alalia, fought in 540 B.C., the Greeks carried the day against the combined Etruscan and Carthaginian fleet but suffered such heavy losses that they were obliged to abandon the new colony they had founded on Corsica, which was the immediate cause of the war. Vivid evidence of close Etruscan-Carthaginian relations at this period is provided by three sixth-century B.C. gold plaques found by Italian archaeologists at Pyrgi in 1964. Two of them are in Etruscan, the third in Phoenician (or possibly Punic, the west Phoenician dialect spoken at Carthage), and two of the three are clearly parallel texts (direct translations of each other), recording a dedication by the Etruscan ruler of Caere to the Phoenician goddess Astarte. Pyrgi was the port of Caere (Cerveteri), one of the leading Etruscan cities, and the plaques indicate that Phoenician deities were worshipped in one of these temples.

The Etruscan period in Italy is divided into a series of phases.[1] The formative phase, which led to the appearance of the first cities, is known as Villanovan (900–700 B.C.). It is at this time, too, that the transition from simple cremation burials to inhumation burials in chamber tombs occurred, though the latter were no doubt reserved for the elite. The Villanovan phase is followed by the Orientalizing period (700–600 B.C.), marked by imports of Greek luxuries including painted pottery, and the Archaic (600–500 B.C.) and Classical (from 500 B.C.) periods, when the Etruscan cities reached their greatest power and influence. Greek imports, notably of Attic painted pottery, continued during these periods.

Etruria, like Greece, was a land of city-states. The 12 leading cities formed the Etruscan League, but each city was essentially autonomous. The cities first emerged during the eighth century B.C.—a time of growing contacts with Phoenicians and Greeks—but the increased trade was probably a symptom rather than a cause of Etruscan urbanization. The roots of Etruscan urbanization lay deep in the past, in the Iron Age Villanovan communities, which were home to the native inhabitants of northern Italy. As we have already seen, earlier theories, which held that the Etruscans were newcomers to the region in the eighth century B.C. and brought the concept of the city-state with them, can now be discounted. The development of the Etruscan cities may more plausibly be attributed to local causes, including population increase, social emulation, and economic growth.

Etruscan cities are not well known in archaeological terms; none has yielded remains to rival the contemporary cities of Classical Greece. It is clear that hilltop sites were favored, however, and in many cases these were protected by substantial walls constructed either of stones alone or of mud bricks on a stone foundation. The greatest Etruscan cities were equal in extent to any of those in the Aegean or eastern Mediterranean; the walls of Veii were 11 kilometers (7 miles) in length. Excavations have shown that the earliest houses in these cities were oval in plan, though from the seventh century B.C. the rectangular house became the dominant form.

## *Cerveteri and Etruscan Cemeteries*

Our best evidence for Etruscan houses comes paradoxically from tombs, notably those of the great Banditaccia cemetery at Cerveteri (Figure 10.3). Tomb chambers were carved in the form of houses, with doors, benches, ceiling joists, and columns to support them, all cut into the solid rock. In a few cases decoration extended to high-backed chairs, circular shields hung on the walls, or even (in the famous Tomb of the Reliefs) weapons of war, domestic utensils, and mythological scenes. These tombs were covered by burial mounds, the most famous being the large circular tumuli of the seventh and sixth centuries. Later tombs were built in rectangular blocks, paralleling the change in city planning from oval to rectangular houses. Usually several tombs were cut below a single tumulus, and each consisted of a sloping or

[1]There are a number of conflicting schemes for Etruscan chronology. The one used here broadly shadows the customary scheme for Classical Greece, a situation that reflects the fact that the dates of the Etruscan phases are based largely on imports of Greek painted pottery and Near Eastern artifacts.

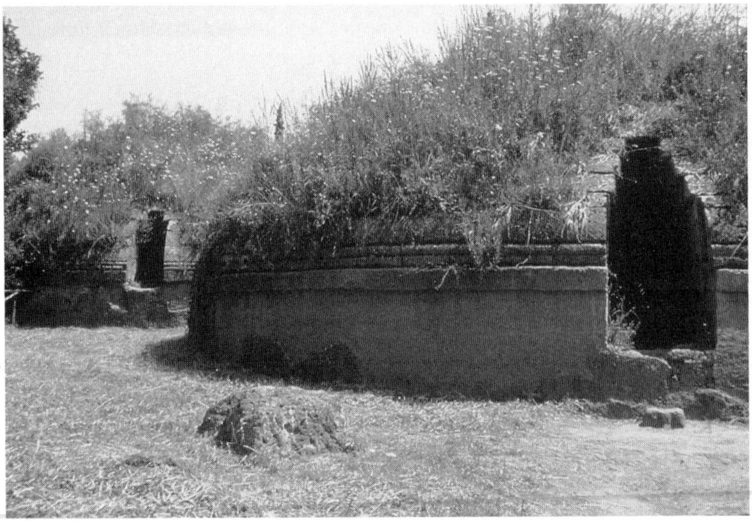

(a)

**Figure 10.3** The Etruscan cemetery of Banditaccia, near Cerveteri. (a) Photo of the burial mounds; (b) plan of the cemetery as a whole; (c) plan and elevation of the Tomba della Cornice (sixth century B.C.). Banditaccia was the principal cemetery of Cerveteri, one of the leading Etruscan cities of north-central Italy. The tombs show the combination of the techniques of above-ground construction and below-ground quarrying: The chambers and lower parts are cut into the rock, the upper parts built of carefully tooled blocks. The largest tombs, belonging to the seventh and sixth centuries B.C., are enormous circular monuments over 40 meters (131 feet) in diameter and capped by dome-shaped grassy mounds. They are the burial places of leading families in the early heyday of the city. These large tombs may contain up to four separate groups of chambers, not all of the same date; the four tombs of the Tumulo monumentale II, for example, range in date from the early seventh century to the second half of the sixth century B.C. Each complex is entered by steps or a sloping ramp cut into the side of the tumulus. At the bottom a doorway leads to a short passage from which open the burial chambers themselves.

A typical example is the sixth-century Tomba della Cornice. Here doorways on either side of the passage lead to square side chambers, each with a bench on either side of the door on which a body would have been laid. The benches, like the chambers, are carved from the rock and have semicircular shelves at the head end. Beyond these side chambers, the main passage leads into the principal chamber, which also has built-in benches against the walls. A feature of this particular tomb (and certain others in the cemetery) is a pair of rock-cut, straight-backed chairs that face into the chamber on either side of the doorway. From the opposite side of this main chamber, three identical doorways with carved cornices and surrounds lead into separate chambers, each with a pair of benches, as in the side chambers.

One revealing feature of the burial chambers is the way they represent, cut into the rock, features of Etruscan domestic architecture. Chairs and doorways have already been mentioned. In a number of cases the ceiling is carved to represent wooden beams, and sometimes these are further supported by rock-cut pillars. Such tombs were the burial places of the powerful Etruscan families who dominated Cerveteri from the seventh century B.C.

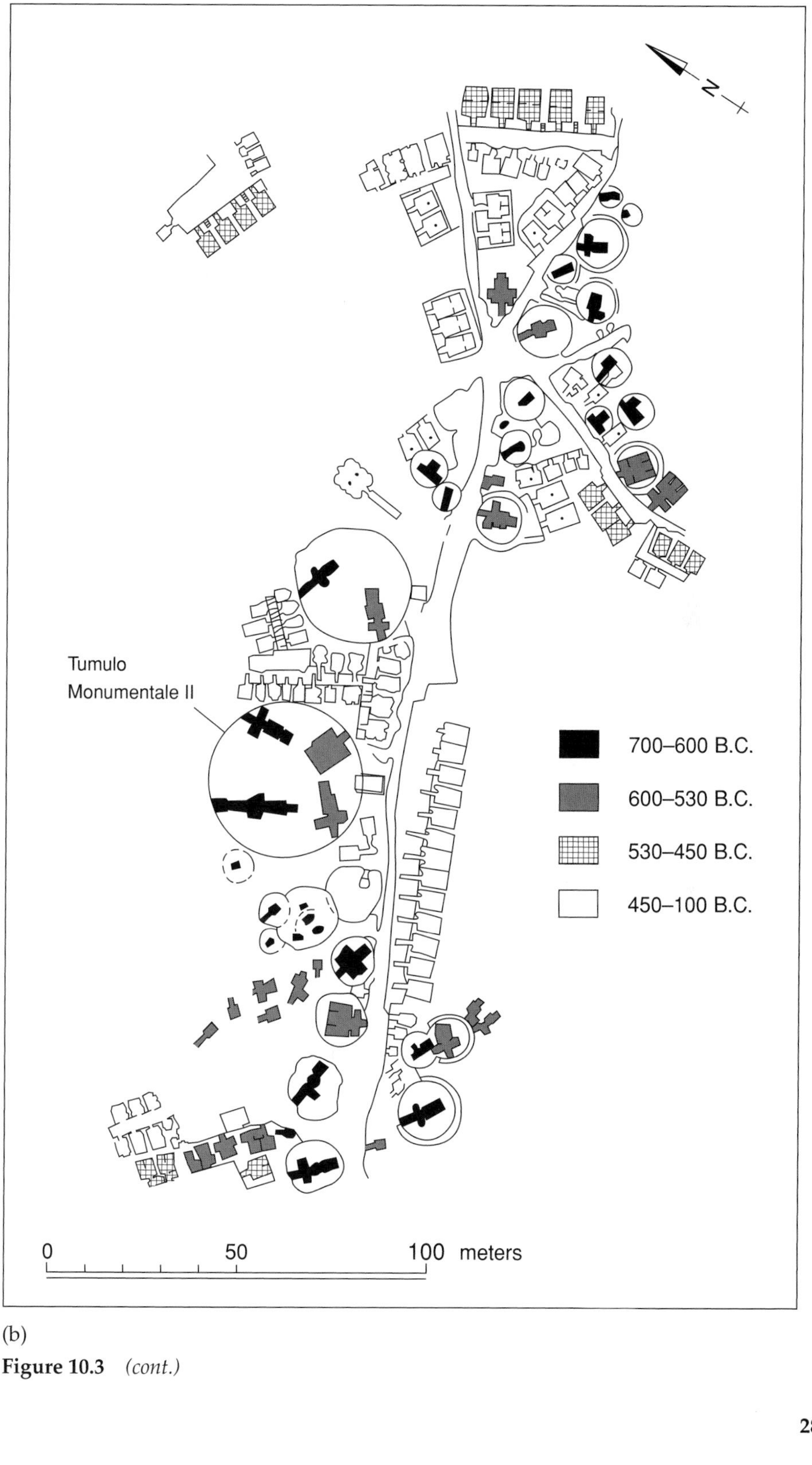


(b)

**Figure 10.3** *(cont.)*

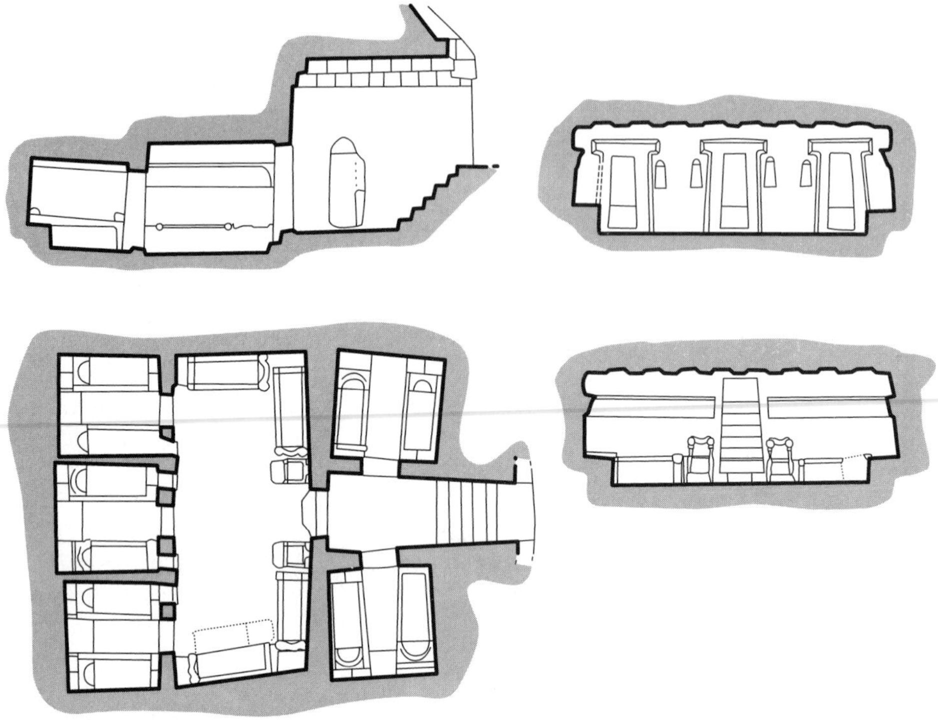

(c)
**Figure 10.3** *(cont.)*

stepped entrance leading to a main chamber, which was surrounded by a number of side chambers. The bodies themselves were laid out on benches carved to resemble beds or couches, with pillows at the head end. Other burials were placed in sarcophagi of stone or terracotta with figures of the deceased on top, as if reclining on a bed or couch; the most famous examples are the two sixth-century terracotta sarcophagi showing a husband and wife from Cerveteri (see chapter opener, page 273).

Etruscan civilization is famous for its painted tombs. Around 100 of these are now known, from a number of major Etruscan cemeteries, but the most famous are those at Tarquinia, which date mainly to the sixth century B.C. Several of them have been known only since the 1950s, when Italian engineer Carlo Lerici drilled into them from above and inserted a periscope and camera. He was able by this means to investigate tombs without the effort and disturbance required for a full excavation. Only a tiny fraction of the tombs he explored were decorated, and it is estimated that altogether only 2 percent of the tombs at Tarquinia were painted. Those that were, however, are justly famous both for the quality of their decoration and for the information they provide about Etruscan beliefs. A painted doorway, giving access to the world of the dead, is a common feature. Many of the tombs also have scenes of feasting, which seem to represent a funerary banquet held in honor of the deceased. Here we see husbands and wives reclining on couches together, something that would never have been allowed in contemporary Athens or early Rome, where women were kept firmly in the background on social occasions. Women in Etruria may indeed have enjoyed relatively high status in comparison with other regions of the Mediterranean at this period.

Etruscan temples are much less well known, and certainly none survives in anything like the state of preservation of the Parthenon at Athens, mostly because the superstructures of Etruscan temples were built mainly of timber, a much less durable material. Foundations and tomb models show squat, rectangular buildings with heavy, oversailing pitched roofs. The temples stood generally on a raised podium reached by a flight of steps and were fronted by rows of columns. Among the most striking features were the brightly painted terracotta ornaments that decorated the edges and ridge of the roof, including large-scale statues of gods and goddesses. Attempts have recently been made at the site of the Portonaccio temple at Veii to convey something of the appearance of such an edifice in a partial reconstruction. It is also of note that the first temple of Jupiter on the Capitol Hill at Rome was probably of just this kind since Rome at the time (late sixth century B.C.) was under Etruscan control. Better preserved, though of a slightly later period (fourth century B.C.), are the remains of the temple known as the Ara della Regina from the site of Tarquinia. This, too, was decorated with terracottas, including a splendid pair of winged horses that may once have pulled a chariot containing the figure of a god. The subtle modeling and striking realism of this piece is evidence of the impact of Greek sculpture on Etruscan art from the fifth century B.C. onward.

The people buried under the great burial mounds at Cerveteri or in the lavishly painted chambers at Tarquinia were the leaders of Etruscan society. The elaborate and monumental chamber tombs were built and used by aristocratic Etruscan families. During the sixth and fifth centuries B.C. these families suppressed the earlier institution of kings and replaced it by an oligarchic system of government under which they themselves held the reins of power in the great cities.

Though the Etruscan city-states were never a single, unified territorial power, they engaged in a conscious policy of expansion in two separate directions. First, during the seventh century B.C. they took control of several cities around the Bay of Naples, forming an Etruscan enclave centered on Nola, Capua, and Pompeii. This brought them into direct contact with the Greek colonies founded on the coast of southern Italy during the previous century and led to hostilities between the two. The Etruscans also took control of Rome, a small Latin settlement that commanded an important crossing over the Tiber River. An Etruscan dynasty, the Tarquins, transformed Rome from a village to a city, though it slipped from Etruscan grasp again when the last of the Tarquins was expelled in 510 B.C.

The second area of expansion was in the north, where the Etruscans occupied the Po plain and planted a series of planned towns such as Marzabotto, where the grid-plan layout of the streets has been revealed with striking clarity by aerial photographs. The Etruscans even had some kind of presence in the coastal city of Spina, the ancient predecessor of Venice and, like it, situated just to the south of the Po delta. The Etruscans consolidated their hold on this region in the fifth century B.C., but during the fourth century the Etruscan cities of the Po plain came under pressure from Celtic peoples from north of the Alps and eventually fell under their control. (For later Etruscan history, see Chapter 11.)

## Archaic Greece (750–480 B.C.)

In Greece, the period from 750 to 480 B.C. is known as Archaic since it is seen as the formative phase of the Classical period that follows (480–323 B.C.).[2] It was during the Archaic period that Greek history properly began, with sufficient sources and inscriptions to chart the development of the major city-states. It was also the time during which Greek sculpture and architecture came to maturity.

In sculpture, at least, the Greeks owed much to their contacts with Egypt. During the seventh century B.C., the Egyptian demand for mercenaries led many young Greeks to seek their fortunes there. Their bronze helmets and body armor made them a particularly formidable fighting force. Greek armored infantrymen were known as hoplites and fought in disciplined massed formations. They were first employed in Egypt by Pharaoh Psammetichus I in 664 B.C., and the policy was followed by Psammetichus II (595–589 B.C.). During the latter's reign Greek soldiers returning from a campaign in Nubia carved graffiti on the leg of one of the colossal statues of Ramesses II at Abu Simbel. These are among the very earliest Greek inscriptions.

Egyptian influence on Greek sculpture is particularly evident in the pieces known as *kouroi* (singular *kouros*), standing statues of naked youths. Though they are essentially Greek in origin, the idea of large-scale stone sculptures was almost certainly taken from Egypt. There was definitely no Mycenaean tradition of large-scale sculptures to look back to, and certain details of the pose, such as the clenched fist and slightly advanced right leg, seem to have been borrowed directly from Egypt. Together with their female equivalents, the *korai* (singular *kore*), the *kouroi* provide one of the clearest indicators of the distribution of Greek culture during this period (Figure 10.4).

Greek architecture, too, came of age in these formative centuries. Both of the major Greek orders—Doric, with its simple cushion capitals, and Ionic, with its more decorative volutes and leaf ornaments—originated in the late seventh and early sixth centuries B.C. The simpler Doric was the principal style in Greece itself and in the western colonies; it was used, for example, in the Temple of Apollo at Corinth and in three temples at Paestum. The most famous of all Greek temples, the fifth-century Parthenon at Athens, has an exterior colonnade in the Doric style. The more elaborate Ionic style originated in the wealthy Greek cities of western Turkey, where it was used in ambitious structures of breathtaking scale: the great Temple of Artemis at Ephesus and the unfinished Heraeum on Samos. These were statements in stone, proclaiming the power and confidence of the eastern Greek cities. They are also the largest Classical temples ever begun.

[2]We have chosen to use the term *Archaic* to cover the whole of this period, though some authorities divide it into two: Orientalizing (750–600 B.C.), and Archaic (600–480 B.C.).

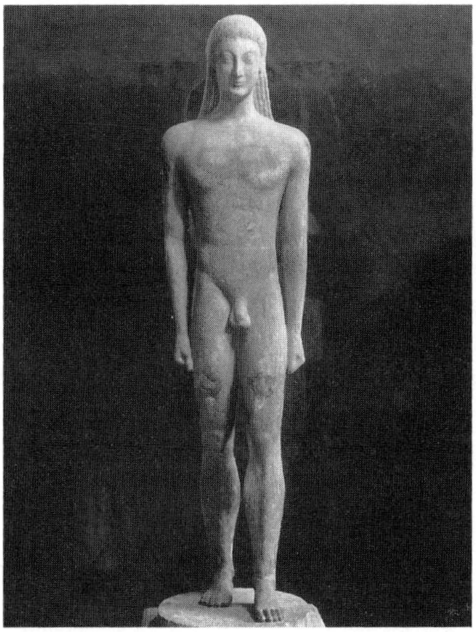

(a)

**Figure 10.4** (a) Greek *kouros* (National Archaeological Museum, Athens, Greece. ©Alinari/Art Resource, NY); (b) distribution map of *kouroi.*

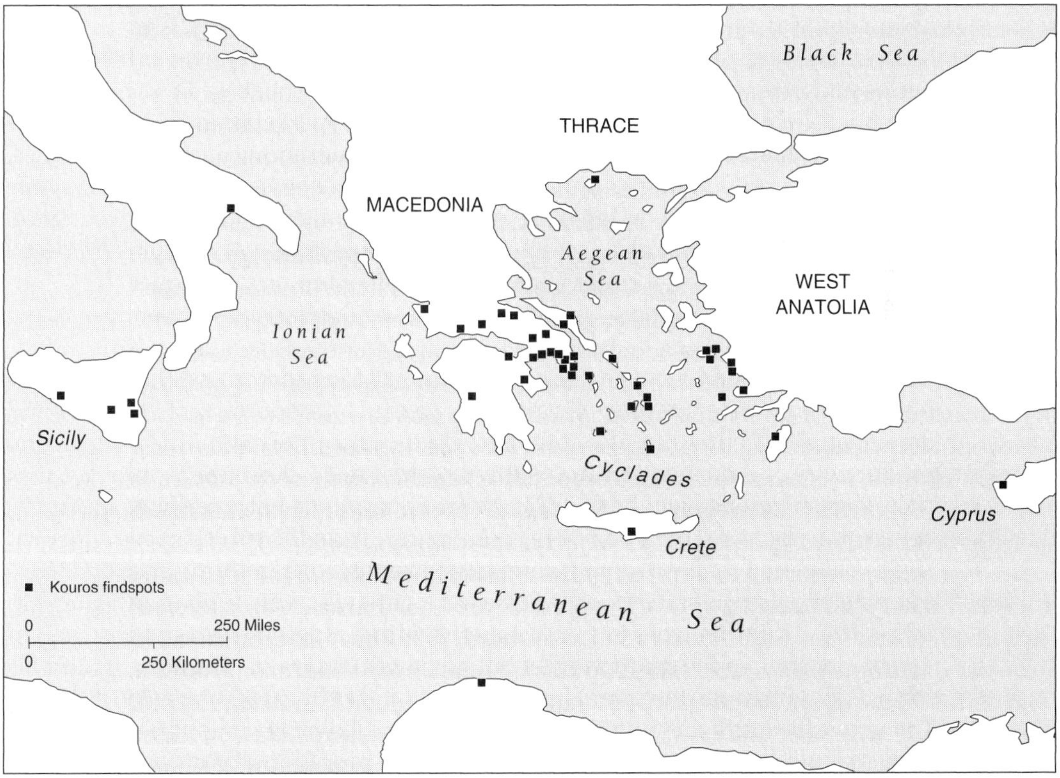


(b)

## Three Greek Cities: Athens, Corinth, Sparta

Corinth was probably the wealthiest city of mainland Greece in the sixth century B.C. It was a great manufacturing center with extensive trading activities, building on its strategic location at the base of the narrow isthmus that divides the rest of Greece from the Peloponnese. It was governed by a series of "tyrants," not the oppressive kind of rule we associate with the word today, but a government headed by one man, often backed by a citizen army to thwart the domination of powerful aristocratic families. The economic power of Corinth in the age of the tyrants is vividly reflected in the spread of Corinthian pottery. The most famous products are the miniature *aryballoi,* or perfume jars. The painted decoration of these vessels borrowed eastern motifs such as winged griffins to create an attractive polychrome style (known as Orientalizing), which circulated widely in both the east and west Mediterranean until supplanted by the popular Attic black-figure ware in the late sixth century B.C.

In contrast, Sparta, the other great Peloponnesian state, remained predominantly agricultural in its economy and concentrated its efforts not on overseas commerce (though it did found the important Italian colony of Taras—modern Taranto) but on territorial expansion at home. This began with the conquest of the neighboring region of Messenia in the late eighth century B.C., consolidated in the face of a major Messenian revolt in the middle of the seventh century. The conquered Messenians were reduced to servitude and added to the class known as helots, who performed most of the agricultural labor, handing over half of their produce to their Spartan masters. It was during this period that Sparta became a rigidly disciplined state dominated by military ideals. Almost alone among ancient Greek cities, Sparta dispensed with the idea of a city wall and relied instead on its redoubtable army for protection. The Messenian wars had one other important consequence: They established the dominance of the armored infantryman, the hoplite, in Greek warfare for over three centuries (Box 10.1). Sparta went on to conquer the southeastern Peloponnese in the sixth century B.C., establishing its ascendancy over the whole peninsula.

Athens underwent a slower development during this period. Economically, it stood somewhere between Corinth and Sparta, an important commercial and manufacturing center but also a territorial power supported by the agricultural productivity of Attica. Sparta and Athens were indeed exceptional among Greek city-states in having such large agricultural hinterlands. Early tensions at Athens between the rich and the poor were eased in the 590s B.C. by the famous Athenian lawgiver Solon, who instituted a number of constitutional reforms intended to reduce the oppression of the poorer classes and outlaw slavery among Athenian citizens. These reforms were important in providing a basis for the introduction of democracy later in the century. After Solon, however, tyrants (Peisistratus and his sons) took control of Athens and held it on and off for almost 50 years (556–510 B.C.). The tyrants beautified the city, building new temples, patronizing the leading poets of the day, and elaborating the Panathenaia—the procession held every year (and with special ceremony every fourth year) in honor of Athena, the city's patron

## Box 10.1 The Rise of the Hoplite

The hoplites were the armored infantrymen who provided the backbone of Classical Greek armies. They were essentially ordinary citizens—neither aristocrats nor the very poor—who could afford to equip themselves with the heavy infantry armor that was adopted by Greek armies from the end of the eighth century. This consisted of a bronze breastplate, fashioned to reflect the shape of the male torso; a bronze helmet with nose and cheek pieces; bronze greaves to protect the lower legs; and a circular or elliptical bronze shield. The outfit was known as a panoply. Offensive weapons were an iron-tipped thrusting spear and a straight iron sword. Fighting in close formation on suitable terrain, the hoplite army was a slow-moving but highly effective military formation, which could even withstand cavalry charges. The bronze body armor made the soldiers largely immune to arrows and other missiles. The new weaponry placed military power in the hands of ordinary citizens; Greek armies were no longer dominated by a handful of mounted aristocrats, supported by a body of ill-armed, peasant foot soldiers. Instead it was the toughness of the male citizenry as a whole that was responsible for a city's safety. The introduction of the hoplite was one of the changes that helped undermine the power of the aristocracy and promote the rise of citizen assemblies as the ruling force in the Greek city-states.

deity. It is this procession that many people think is depicted on the later Parthenon frieze (the so-called Elgin marbles). Athens during the sixth century also became a center of innovation, producing the new Attic black-figure pottery in enormous quantities and shipping it to overseas markets as far afield as Scythia and Celtic Gaul. Athenian-decorated pottery retained its popularity into the fifth century B.C., though black-figure was replaced by the new red-figure technique around 530 B.C. (Box 10.2).

## Classical Greece (480–323 B.C.)

The transition between the Archaic and Classical periods of ancient Greece is marked by the successful resistance of the southern Greek city-states to the Persian invasion of 480 B.C.

One of the key features of ancient Greek society was the emphasis on Greek ethnicity. The fifth-century historian Herodotus puts a speech into the mouths of the Athenians that expresses this view very clearly, referring to "the kinship of all Greeks in blood and speech, and the shrines of the gods and the sacrifices that we have in common, and the likeness of our way of life." The Greeks recognized themselves as different and separate from the "barbarians" around them. The very word *barbarian* was a Greek invention, intended to convey the sound of a foreign (non-Greek) language (*barbarbar . . .*). In a negative sense, the Greeks came

## *Box 10.2 Black- and Red-Figure Pottery*

Painted pottery is one of the most distinctive products of Classical Greece. The most famous vessels are those produced in Attica (the area around Athens) during the late seventh, sixth, and fifth centuries B.C. These fall into two broadly successive styles, known from their decoration as black-figure and red-figure (Figure 10.5). The basis of both techniques is the liquid clay slip applied to the surface of the vessel. In a special sequence of oxidation and reduction firings, the slip turns black and the rest of the vessel orange. In the black-figure technique, the figures or designs were black, whereas in the red-figure case the surrounding surface was black, leaving the figures or motifs standing out in red silhouette. In black-figure pottery, internal details of the figures could be marked by carefully scratching away the black layer to reveal the red beneath; other details were sometimes added in white or purple paint. This was the technique taken over by the Athenians from Corinthian potters in the seventh century B.C. and enhanced by them until Athenian black-figure ware led the field. Red-figure ware was an invention of Athenian potters themselves, probably around 530 B.C., though it was some years before it supplanted the popular black-figure ware. Red-figure decorations were simple, bold shapes, with internal details of the figures painted in black; to many eyes it represents the height of Athenian vase painting. It remained in vogue well into the fourth century B.C.

(a) (b)

**Figure 10.5** (a) Athenian black-figure vessel; (b) Athenian red-figure skyphos, depicting Amazons (legendary female warriors from the Black Sea region). Note the typical decorative "Greek key" frieze around the base (fifth century B.C.). (Two Amazons. Museo Etrusco Gregoriano. © Alinari/Art Resource, NY)

Some Attic vessels carry the name of an individual potter. Well-known examples include Amasis, Ergotimos, and Kleophrades. Potter and painter were not usually the same person, though both operations were probably carried out in the same workshop. These were generally small, family-run establishments. Vase painters sometimes moved among them. Identification of the individual vase painters is a straightforward matter when they signed their products, but otherwise it must depend on the less secure process of stylistic analysis. This kind of analysis is associated especially with the name of British art historian Sir John Beazley, who carried out a comprehensive study of Athenian black- and red-figure wares and grouped them, where possible, according to their painters. He worked on the basis (already accepted in the field of Renaissance art) that it is in the minor details, such as ears, ankles, and drapery, that a painter is most likely to reveal himself. Hundreds of painters have been identified in this way, though only a few (e.g., Exekias, Brygos, and Euphronios) are known by their real names on the basis of their "signatures." Others are named after some famous subject (e.g., the Nausikaa painter), by the potter with whom they were associated (e.g., the Amasis painter), by where their products were found (e.g., the Agrigento painter), or even by some peculiarity of their style (e.g., the Elbows-Out painter).

In recent years there has been a revised view on the value of this pottery in ancient Greece and the status of Athenian potters. It is now accepted that the craft was a lowly one and that the vessels themselves were not especially valuable, despite the skill that went into their manufacture. Some features of black- and red-figure pottery, however, were expressly designed to imitate the much more valuable gold and silver vessels used by the wealthiest citizens.

to distinguish themselves as civilized and the barbarians as vicious and cruel. This assessment was narrow-minded and arrogant, not least since it included as barbarian all the urban societies of the Near East. Nor could the modern student consider ancient Greece an entirely civilized society, given its heavy reliance on slaves, whatever the glories of Greek art and literature. But the Greeks' recognition of their ethnic identity did have more positive results. It led to a concept of Hellenism—of essential "Greekness"—that was widely shared, whether in the colonies of the Black Sea or western Mediterranean or in Greece itself. It also found expression through pan-Hellenic festivals, which all Greeks were permitted to attend, accompanied by athletic and other contests in which they could all compete. These festivals were held at four major shrines: Olympia (site of the Olympic Games), Delphi, Nemea, and Isthmia.

Although sharing a common language and culture, ancient Greek society had a highly competitive ethos (seen in the games); the Greek city-states were never politically united, nor did they share a unified political purpose. This became especially clear during the Classical period (480–323 B.C.). The period opened with a determined attempt to conquer Greece by the Persian rulers Darius and Xerxes. The failure of the invasions, secured by Greek victories at

Marathon (490 B.C.), Salamis (480 B.C.), and Plataea (479 B.C.), was embroidered by Greek writers who emphasized Greek heroism and cooperation in the face of overwhelming odds. In fact, there were serious divisions among the Greeks throughout the campaigns, and in the final battle almost as many Greeks fought alongside the Persians as against them.

Victory in the Persian Wars was exploited by the Athenians for their own advantage. The Athenian fleet had ensured success in the battle of Salamis, and their ships had led the follow-up operations in the Aegean as the Persians withdrew. The Athenians used the Persian threat as a means of persuading many Greek cities, especially those in the vulnerable island or coastal areas, to form a defensive league (the so-called Delian League). Athens was so much the dominant partner in this arrangement that what began as a defensive league was soon transformed into an Athenian empire. The fleet gave the Athenians the means to extort tribute from their fellow members; actual records of the tribute assessments and the amounts paid survive in fragments of the marble slabs set up at Athens.

The ascendancy of Athens led to challenges from other cities, which banded together under the leadership of Sparta and fought against Athens in the Peloponnesian War (431–404 B.C.). Athens was defeated, its fleet destroyed, and for a while Sparta and then Thebes was dominant in Greek affairs. But still the city-states retained their autonomy, and it was only with the victory of Philip of Macedon at Chaeronea in 356 B.C. that they lost their independence. Henceforth they were units within a broader Macedonian empire. The Classical period ends with the conquests of Alexander of Macedon (Alexander the Great) and his death in 323 B.C.

This sketch of political developments provides the backdrop for an account of society and culture in the most famous of the Greek city-states, Athens, in the period between the Persian and Peloponnesian wars.

## Democracy and Slavery

Fifth-century Athens is famous both for its writers, sculptors, and architects and for its political institutions. The key political innovation was democracy—the rule of the people (from Greek *demos*, "the people," and *kratos*, "power"). The origins of this idea lay in an earlier tradition that placed the government of the city-state in the hands of an assembly of citizen-soldiers. Women, children, slaves, and noncitizens were therefore excluded. For most of ancient Greece, including sixth-century Athens, real power lay in the hands of wealthy aristocrats. The change at Athens occurred in 508 B.C., when a disenchanted aristocrat reformed the citizens' assembly, giving it new powers, and introduced the institution of ostracism—which allowed the assembly to exile any one citizen for a period of ten years without giving a reason. The word *ostracism* derives from *ostrakon*, a "potsherd," since those voting for ostracism scratched the name of that person on such a sherd. A number of sherds have survived, some marked with the names of known Athenian politicians such as Themistocles. The aim of ostracism was to avoid the rise of overmighty citizens who could dominate the state. No evidence of malpractice was required to justify the ostracism, merely a secret ballot.

The Athenian democracy reached its greatest development in the later fifth century, after important reforms in 462 B.C. From this time on all Athenian officials were chosen by lot. Since not all citizens were wealthy, the state compensated for their loss of earnings while they were engaged on state duties. Remains of a remarkable machine for selecting jurors and magistrates have been found in the Agora at Athens. Eleven columns of slots held the name-tickets of potential jurors, but which column was chosen depended on whether a white or black ball appeared from the bronze tube mounted on the side of the machine when the crank handle was turned.

Impressed though we may be by the lengths to which the Athenians went to ensure fairness in their political system, we cannot ignore the fact that Athens was far from being a free society. Indeed, it has been estimated that there were as many slaves working in the Athenian silver mines at Laurion as there were male citizens of Athens itself. Furthermore, as already noted, women had a subservient position and could play no role in politics.

## *The Great Age of Athens*

In a famous speech recorded (or invented) by Thucydides, the Athenian leader Pericles called Athens the "school of Hellas." It is certainly true that the cultural life of fifth-century Greece was nowhere livelier than at Athens. Here lived and worked the great dramatists Aeschylus, Sophocles, Euripides, and Aristophanes; the historian Thucydides; and the philosopher Socrates. Unusual in any ancient society, a high proportion of Athenians could read and write, more so than in the rest of Greece. In archaeological terms, the most vivid testimony to Athens's status and power is provided by the remains of buildings, monuments, and sculptures.

The most famous of all Athenian monuments are the temples and the sculptures that adorned them: the Parthenon, sacred to the city's patron deity, Athena Parthenos (Box 10.3); the smaller jewel-like temple of Athena Nike, reconstructed in modern times from the blocks built into a bastion during the Turkish occupation of Greece; the Erechtheion, the holiest shrine of Athens, with the columns of its porch carved in the shape of standing maidens; and the most perfectly preserved of Athenian temples, that of Hephaistos on the edge of the Agora (known as the Theseion from its sculptures, which depict the legendary Athenian ruler Theseus). Fifth-century Athens could boast of many other outstanding buildings: the Theater of Dionysus on the southern slopes of the Acropolis; the famous Long Walls, which connected the city with its harbor at Peiraeus some 8 kilometers (5 miles) to the west; and the civic buildings and offices clustered around the Agora, including the bouleuterion (or city council chamber), the smaller prytaneion for the executives, the law courts, and a number of stoae (covered colonnades). One of the stoae (the Stoa Poikile) was a gallery of paintings; another (the Stoa of Zeus), a favorite meeting place of philosophers, including Socrates and the so-called Stoics (who took their name from this very building). The Agora was indeed the commercial and administrative heart of the city, just as the Acropolis was the religious center (and could in times of war revert to its original role as the citadel of Athens) (Box 10.3).

## *Box 10.3 The Building of the Parthenon (447–432 B.C.)*

The Parthenon, built between 447 and 432 B.C., is often considered the climax and culmination of Greek architecture (Figure 10.6). As the principal temple of Athens, which was at the time the leading city of Greece, such an achievement is perhaps only to be expected. The podium of the present structure measures 31 by 70 meters (102 by 230 feet), making it far from the largest temple of ancient Greece, though what it yields in size it gains in detail and refinement. These refinements include minute adjustments to the vertical and horizontal lines of the columns and podium to counter optical illusions, which make long straight lines seem curved from a distance. Thus the surface of the podium slopes gently upward toward the center by a factor of only 11 centimeters (4.3 inches), while the external columns are placed to lean slightly inward, by 6.5 centimeters (2.6 inches) in a height of 10.4 meters (34 feet); their surfaces are not rigidly straight but have been given a slightly convex profile (a feature known to Greek architects as *entasis*). The marble for the Parthenon came from Pentelikon, in the mountains east of the city. There it was quarried, roughed out, and placed on carts to be brought to the Acropolis for final finishing. Only after many years was the work sufficiently advanced for the famous Parthenon sculptures to be put in place. These were designed by Pheidias, the greatest Greek sculptor of the day, who had also created the enormous gold and ivory statue of Athena Parthenos, over 11 meters (36 feet) tall, to stand inside the sanctuary. Paradoxically, though it is far and away the most famous temple of ancient Greece, the Parthenon may never have been intended as a functioning temple at all since there was no provision for an altar, and no official cult of Athena Parthenos existed when it was built. It was nonetheless a powerful symbol of Athenian greatness.

(a)

**Figure 10.6** (a) Photograph of the Parthenon; (b) cut-away of east side of Parthenon, showing the position of architectural sculptures; (c) detail of the Parthenon frieze, showing young aristocrats riding in procession.

(b)

(c)

**Figure 10.6** *(cont.)*

Among all these buildings, one feature stood out: the wealth of images. Ancient Greek cities were full of them: bronze statues, now largely melted down and lost; marble statues, originally painted in vivid colors and making a far different impression from that of the chaste white marble in which they have come down to us; reliefs and wall paintings on temples and public buildings. Many showed gods and goddesses and scenes from Greek mythological tales or legends such as the Trojan War. Others represented civic heroes and leading statesmen and generals: citizens who had deserved a place on the roll of fame in the service of their city. Even victors in the Olympic Games might be commemorated in this way. Such images were the visual counterpart of the democratic constitution, promoting civic values and imbuing Athenians with a sense of pride in their city.

## The Ancient Greek Countryside

Around the well-known cities of ancient Greece lay the rural landscapes, which provided them with the food they needed for their rising populations. Transport was expensive, and most cities relied on the produce of their local area. One exception may be Athens, which by the end of the fifth century B.C. had grown so much that it outstripped its local agricultural capacity. The response was to import cereals by ship from the Hellespont and Black Sea region. In general, however, Classical Greek city-states depended on food grown within their own territories.

Recent years have seen a number of regional surveys that have attempted to trace the pattern of activity across the whole of the Greek landscape (Box 10.4). These surveys have identified the locations of individual farmsteads and small villages. Without resorting to expensive and time-consuming excavation, the researchers have used surface finds such as pottery to provide dating evidence for the sites and have thus been able to show changing patterns of settlement from prehistory to the present day. At the same time, they have found evidence for ancient Greek farming practices, one being the "halo" of artifactual material that surrounds many sites. Some ancient cities have halos that extend over several square miles. In the Boeotia region these were interpreted as the result of the intensive use of manure: Animal dung, night soil, and other organic wastes (including the accidental admixture of discarded pottery and other cultural material) were carted to the edge of town and spread over the fields to increase fertility. Not everyone is convinced by this "manuring hypothesis," but such an intensive agricultural practice would be an indication of the high population density of many regions of Classical Greece. It was probably during this period, too, that extensive stone-walled terraces were built on the hillsides, again reflecting population growth and the need to increase agricultural productivity, in this case by creating new fields.

Excavations show that fifth- and fourth-century farmsteads comprised the farmhouse itself, with a central court and outbuildings, and an attached walled enclosure, sometimes subdivided, in which livestock could be kept (Box 10.5). Other parts of these enclosures may have been gardens or orchards of cultivated fruit trees. In one case a complete farm boundary wall has been found, enclosing an area of 9 hectares (22 acres). Farmsteads rather than villages seem to have been

## Box 10.4 The Classical Argolid

What did the landscape of Classical Greece look like? Between 1979 and 1983 a team from Stanford University, led by Michael Jameson, Curtis Runnels, and Tjeerd Van Andel, made an intensive field survey of the southern Argolid at the eastern end of the Peloponnese. In the course of this work they discovered several hundred archaeological sites of all periods and collected 45,000 ceramic pieces, mainly potsherds. Analysis of this huge body of material, coupled with the study of the soils and landscape, enabled them to chart changes in the settlement of the region from prehistory to the present day. The number of sites reached a peak during the fourth century B.C., when the area around the Classical town of Halieis (Figure 10.7) became an important center of olive production. This is shown by a combination of different kinds of evidence. On the one hand, rural

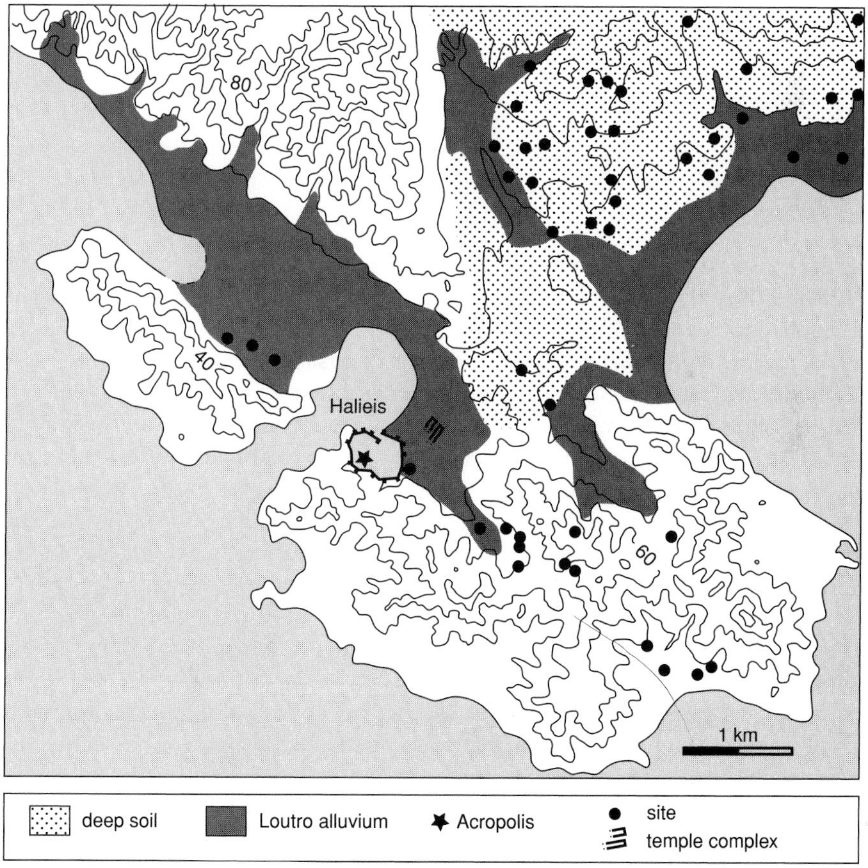


**Figure 10.7** Map of Halieis and its surroundings (c. 300 B.C.–30 B.C.).

*(Cont.)*

settlements appeared at this time on stony alluvium and lower slopes, areas that give poor cereal yields but are ideal for olives. Olives were probably grown on terraces built on the hillsides, indicating a more labor-intensive use of the landscape. Further evidence for the production of olive oil comes from oil presses found both at rural farmsteads and at Halieis itself. At the same time, cereal growing continued on the fertile and water-retentive deeper soils. Runnels and Van Andel suggest that the importance of olive production in the fourth-century Argolid may well be linked to political events in neighboring regions of Greece, notably the destruction of Athenian olive groves by Spartan forces during the Peloponnesian War (431–404 B.C.). Olive trees take many years to mature, and Athens would have been dependent on imported supplies for several decades. The Argolid is geographically close to Attica and would have been well placed to supply that need. It would also have supplied newly expanding cities such as Thebes and Megalopolis that were situated in regions poor in olive groves. Thus the southern Argolid survey is an illustration of the intimate way in which rural fortunes may be linked to the politics of the wider world.

## *Box 10.5 The Greeks at Home*

In Classical Greece, sometimes credited with the invention of politics, the importance of public life and the citizen is well known from literary and historical texts. But what of the domestic settings in which much of everyday life was lived? In an archaeological study of Greek houses of the fifth and fourth century B.C., Lisa C. Nevett was able to show how domestic space was organized to accommodate and define the respective spheres of men and women, guests and household members. The best evidence came from the city site of Olynthos in Chalkidiki (northern Greece), where many of the houses were identical in size and shape and aligned in blocks along street frontages (Figure 10.8). The central element was the open court (pastas), reached from the street door along a passageway. The rooms of the house were arranged around this court, which was often decorated with painted plaster and frequently had a portico along one side. Passing through the portico and an anteroom led one to the *andron*, also decorated with painted plaster, where male guests were entertained. Study of literary sources had led to the theory that, in the Greek house, male and female space was carefully segregated. The archaeological evidence from Olynthos and other sites shows, instead, that no such segregation was possible, as all the rooms were reached from the open central court. The seclusion of the andron behind a portico and antechamber does show, however, how guests, while being welcomed into the heart of the house, were kept somewhat apart from other household members. Thus, as Nevett concludes, the archaeological analysis of domestic space enables us to look beyond the stereotype of the ancient Greek house divided physically into separate male and female quarters and to explore the way in which the Greek household is likely to have operated in practice.

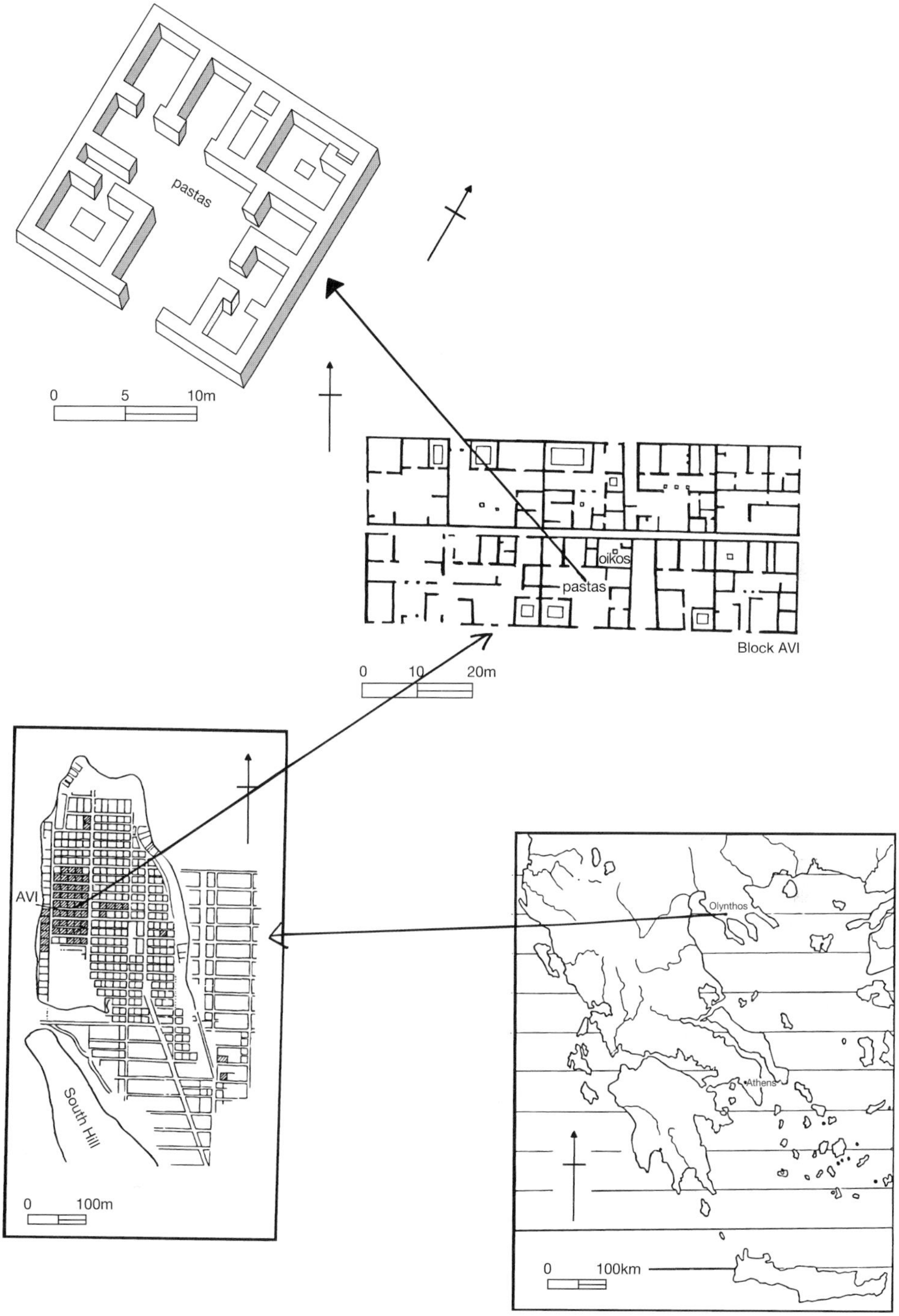


**Figure 10.8** Greek houses at Olynthos. A city block and its residences.

the principal rural settlement in many regions of Classical Greece. In some cases (for example, the southern Argolid in Box 10.4), it has also been possible to relate survey results for the rural economy to broader political and military events. One common feature documented by many regional archaeological surveys is a sharp decline in rural activity in the post-Classical, or Hellenistic, period (323–30 B.C.). Greek fortunes, as far as the countryside was concerned, did not reach fifth- and fourth-century levels again until the later Roman period.

## Sequel: The Hellenistic World

The reign of Alexander the Great (336–323 B.C.) marks a turning point in the history of Greece and the Near East. When he came to power as ruler of Macedonia (a kingdom immediately to the north of Greece), his rule extended from the Adriatic to the Hellespont and as far south as the Peloponnese, but no further. Profiting from the decline of the Persian Empire, however, Alexander embarked on a campaign of conquest that took Greek and Macedonian armies to the Indus Valley in the east and brought Persia, Asia Minor, Mesopotamia, and Egypt under his sway. For a brief period the whole of this vast empire was united, but at Alexander's premature death in 323 B.C. the bonds of power quickly began to dissolve and his generals divided the empire among them—one taking Egypt and another Macedonia, while others squabbled over Asia Minor and the Near East.

The death of Alexander marks the end of the Classical age and the beginning of a new period known as Hellenistic. It was marked by the expansion of Greek artistic traditions throughout the lands conquered by Alexander. Though not a Greek himself, Alexander was a keen promoter of Greek art and culture and sought to consolidate his conquests by founding colonies of Greek and Macedonian citizens. One of the most exciting discoveries of recent decades has been at Ai Khanum, on the banks of the Oxus River in northern Afghanistan, where remains of a Hellenistic city, probably one of those established by Alexander, has been excavated. The finds include typical Greek architectural elements such as column capitals, indicating the existence of elaborate public buildings. There was a typically Greek gymnasium and a theater. Still more vivid are fragments of Greek philosophical writings and copies of maxims from the oracle of Delphi. Despite its remoteness from the rest of the Hellenistic world, this region (known as Bactria) survived as an independent Greek kingdom until 140 B.C., a period of almost 200 years. During these centuries, Greek Bactria had a major impact on sculptural traditions further east. The so-called Gandharan art of Pakistan and eastern Afghanistan embodies Classical principles in a composite style best represented by a series of splendid seated Buddhas.

The heart of the Hellenistic world lay in the lands around the eastern Mediterranean. Here again, many new cities were founded by Alexander and his successors. Most famous of all was Alexandria, on the western edge of the Nile Delta. This grew to be the largest city of the Western world in the first century B.C., a great center of craftsmanship, commerce, and learning. The Ptolemaic rulers of Egypt embellished the city with a lighthouse (the famous Pharos) and a House of the Muses, or Museion (Museum), which included the famous Library of Alexandria.

The city itself was a polyglot place, with Greeks, Egyptians, Jews, and others rubbing shoulders on its crowded quays and colonnaded streets. Like flourishing cities of more recent times, it also gained an unsavory reputation for street violence.

In the Greek-speaking cities of the Aegean and east Mediterranean, the Classical art style was replaced at the end of the fourth century B.C. by a new style, known (like the period itself) as Hellenistic. In portrait sculpture, one of the major new trends was the emphasis on the realistic portrayal of individuals. Classical sculptors had presented a naturalistic but idealized image of the human body. Their Hellenistic successors showed their subjects as recognizable individuals, leaving us an impressive portrait gallery of famous figures that includes rulers, athletes, and philosophers.

Changes in sculpture and portraiture are only one element in a whole suite of Hellenistic artistic innovations. The technique of decorative mosaic, using colored cubes of cut stone or glass (*tesserae*), was a Hellenistic invention of the third century B.C. Houses were decorated with vivid wall paintings, some portraying historical events or mythological scenes, and others depicting landscapes or architectural fantasies. But many of the greatest examples of Hellenistic art were intended for public display, such as the Great Altar of Pergamum, with its 2-meter-high (6-foot-high) frieze of warring gods and giants. The cities were the showcases of the Hellenistic dynasties, and Hellenistic rulers expended considerable wealth on statues, theaters, temples, and colonnaded streets.

One of the greatest differences between the Hellenistic world and Classical Greece was that of scale. The cities of Classical Greece, for all their achievement, had generally been only modest in size and territory; Athens stands out partly because it was so exceptional. The conquests of Alexander the Great gave Hellenistic rulers vast realms to govern and placed enormous resources of wealth and manpower at their disposal. For ordinary people, the Hellenistic rulers were just the latest in a whole series of masters who sought to derive maximum profit from their toil. In many of the conquered areas, there is archaeological evidence of increased commercial and agricultural activity, the latter probably linked to an imperialist-style exploitation of the new territories.

Another major difference lay in the multicultural character of the Hellenistic kingdoms. Greek language and Greek culture may have been powerful, but they by no means extinguished local traditions that stretched back many thousands of years. In Egypt, for example, royal inscriptions were written in hieroglyphic even though the ruling family, the Ptolemies, were Macedonians, did not intermarry with the local population, and habitually spoke Greek. In other regions of the Hellenistic world, a curious hybrid culture developed, combining Greek elements with local styles.

The political history of the Hellenistic kingdoms is one of almost continual warfare and intrigue. By the end of the third century B.C., the Hellenistic world was divided into three major kingdoms: Ptolemaic Egypt, Seleucid Syria and Mesopotamia, and Macedonia. In western Asia Minor, the smaller kingdom of Pergamum had managed to establish itself among these major powers. Despite their size and resources, none of these kingdoms was able to resist the advance of

Rome from the west. Macedonia, Greece, and Pergamum became Roman provinces in the mid–second century B.C.; Syria and most of the rest of Asia Minor followed by the middle of the first century. The last of the great Hellenistic kingdoms, Egypt, fell to the Romans with the death of the last Ptolemaic ruler, Cleopatra, in 30 B.C. Hellenistic art and culture, however, continued to thrive under the Roman Empire.

The rise of Rome and the archaeology of the Roman Empire are the subjects of Chapter 11.

## Summary

We have reviewed the development of Mediterranean civilization from the beginning of the first millennium B.C. to the end of the Hellenistic age in the first century B.C. The treatment has focused on three separate peoples: Greeks, Phoenicians (or Carthaginians), and Etruscans. Two further themes run through the chapter: the foundation of new cities by the process of colonization and the government of the cities themselves, which formed autonomous political units (city-states). The wealth of textual evidence gives a much richer account of the Classical world in the fifth century B.C. than any earlier period. Our ability to comprehend the texts, however, should not blind us to the reality that the world of fifth-century Athens, for example, was very different from our own, with attitudes toward women and institutionalized slavery that would be unacceptable today. The demise of the city-states of Greece and Etruria coincided with the rise of territorial polities much larger and more powerful than an individual city—the empires of Macedon and Rome. The conquests of Alexander the Great initiated a new phase in the development of the Classical world, one in which Greek culture spread widely throughout the Near East, providing a superficial level of unity and a heightening of civic and commercial activity. This continued as the Hellenistic kingdoms were steadily absorbed into the Roman Empire.

## Guide to Further Reading

An excellent overview of Mediterranean history over the past 3,000 years is provided by P. Horden and N. Purcell, *The Corrupting Sea* (Oxford: Blackwell, 1999). Phoenician and Greek activity in the western Mediterranean and the Atlantic is described by Barry Cunliffe, *Facing the Ocean: The Atlantic and Its Peoples 8000 B.C.–A.D. 1500* (Oxford: Oxford University Press, 2001).

For ancient Greece, good starting points are William R. Biers, *The Archaeology of Greece: An Introduction*, 2nd ed. (Ithaca, NY: Cornell University Press, 1996) and James Whittey, *The Archaeology of Ancient Greece* (Cambridge: Cambridge University Press, 2001). They can be supplemented by Ian Morris, ed., *Classical Greece: Ancient Histories and Modern Archaeologies* (Cambridge: Cambridge University Press, 1994), which illustrates the contribution being made by modern archaeological approaches. For a more traditional historical account, J. B. Bury and Russell Meiggs, *A History of Greece*, 4th ed. (London: Macmillan, 1975) provides an overview of Greek history to the end of the Classical period.

The rise of the Athenian city-state is set against the background of burial evidence from Attica by Ian Morris in his influential case study, *Burial and Ancient Society: The Rise of the Greek City-State* (Cambridge: Cambridge University Press, 1987). It may be contrasted with the very different approach, focusing on Corinth, taken by Michael Shanks, *Art and the Early Greek State: An Interpretive Archaeology* (Cambridge: Cambridge University Press, 1999). See also Ian Morris, *Archaeology as Cultural History* (Oxford: Blackwell, 2002), which combines written and archaeological evidence for developments in

Greece during the period 1000–600 B.C. The contribution of evidence from archaeological surveys to the rise of Greek city-states and their fortunes during the Classical, Hellenistic, and Roman periods is provided by John Bintcliff, "Regional Survey, Demography, and the Rise of Complex Societies in the Ancient Aegean: Core-Periphery, Neo-Malthusian, and Other Interpretive Models," *Journal of Field Archaeology* 24 (1997): 1–38.

Greek colonization is well covered by John Boardman, *The Greeks Overseas: Their Early Colonies and Trade,* 2nd ed. (London: Thames and Hudson, 1980). The evidence from Pithekoussai, the earliest western colony, is placed in its broader background in David Ridgway, *The First Western Greeks* (Cambridge: Cambridge University Press, 1992). See also the splendidly illustrated *The Western Greeks*, edited by G. Pugliesi Carratelli (London: Thames and Hudson, 1996).

For Phoenician activity in the Mediterranean, see Sabatino Moscati, ed., *The Phoenicians* (Milan: Bompiani, 1988) and Maria Eugenia Aubet, *The Phoenicians and the West: Politics, Colonies and Trade* (Cambridge: Cambridge University Press, 1993). Among the best recent accounts of ancient Carthage is David Soren, Aicha Ben Abed Khader, and Hedi Slim, *Carthage: Uncovering the Mysteries and Splendors of Ancient Tunisia* (New York: Simon & Schuster, 1990). Serge Lancel's *Carthage: A History* (Oxford: Blackwell, 1995) is also useful. On the Carthaginian practice of child sacrifice, see John Day, *Molech: A God of Human Sacrifice in the Old Testament* (Cambridge: Cambridge University Press, 1989) and Shelby Brown, *Late Carthaginian Child Sacrifice and Sacrificial Monuments in Their Mediterranean Context* (Sheffield: JSOT Press, 1991).

For the archaeology and history of the Etruscans, the classic work is Massimo Pallottino, *The Etruscans* (Harmondsworth, England: Penguin, 1978). This can be supplemented by Larissa Bonfante, ed., *Etruscan Life and Afterlife* (Detroit: Wayne State University Press, 1986); Mario Torelli, ed., *The Etruscans* (London: Thames and Hudson, 2000); and Nigel Spivey and Simon Stoddart, *Etruscan Italy: An Archaeological History* (London: Batsford, 1990). A recent review of evidence for the rise of the Etruscan city-states is provided by Alessandro Guidi, "The Emergence of the State in Central and Northern Italy," *Acta Archaeologica* 69 (1998): 139–161. The symbolism of Etruscan temples is discussed by Vedia Izzett, "Form and Meaning in Etruscan Ritual Architecture," *Cambridge Archaeological Journal* 11 (2001): 185–280.

The literature on Greek architecture is immense, but see especially W. B. Dinsmoor, *The Architecture of Ancient Greece,* 3rd ed. (New York: Norton, 1975); A. W. Lawrence, *Greek Architecture,* rev. T. A. Tomlinson (Harmondsworth, England: Penguin, 1983); and J. J. Coulton, *Greek Architects at Work* (Ithaca, NY: Cornell University Press, 1977). Athenian buildings are covered by R. E. Wycherley's excellent *The Stones of Athens* (Princeton, NJ: Princeton University Press, 1978). For the most famous of all Greek temples, the Parthenon, see John Boardman and David Finn, *The Parthenon and Its Sculptures* (London: Thames and Hudson, 1985) and Ian Jenkins, *The Parthenon Frieze* (London: British Museum Publications, 1994). The recent program of reconstruction work on the Acropolis is described and lavishly illustrated in Richard Economakis, ed., *Acropolis Restorations* (London: Academy Editions, 1994). The architectural development of the Acropolis is discussed by Robin F. Rhodes, *Architecture and Meaning on the Athenian Acropolis* (Cambridge: Cambridge University Press, 1995). Finally, Richard A. MacNeal, "Archaeology and the Destruction of the Later Athenian Acropolis," *Antiquity* 65 (1991): 49–63, describes the political background to the clearance of medieval and Turkish buildings from the Acropolis during the nineteenth century.

An up-to-date general survey of Classical art and architecture to the Roman period is John Boardman, ed., *The Oxford History of Classical Art* (Oxford/New York: Oxford University Press, 1993). For early Greek sculpture, see Boardman's excellent series of volumes, *Greek Sculpture: The Archaic Period; Greek Sculpture: The Classical Period,* rev. ed.; and *Greek Sculpture: The Late Classical Period* (London: Thames and Hudson, 1978, 1991, 1995). J. J. Pollitt's *Art and Experience in Classical Greece* (Cambridge: Cambridge University Press, 1972) is also invaluable. Black- and red-figure pottery are covered by R. M. Cook, *Greek Painted Pottery*, 2nd ed. (London: Methuen, 1972); Martin Robertson, *The Art of Vase-Painting in Classical Athens* (Cambridge: Cambridge University Press, 1992); and Tom Rasmussen and Nigel Spivey, eds., *Looking at Greek Vases* (Cambridge: Cambridge University Press, 1991).

For regional surveys of Classical Greece and the debate over the "manuring hypothesis," see Susan E. Alcock, John F. Cherry, and Jack L. Davis in Morris, *Classical Greece:* "Intensive Survey, Agricultural Practice and the Classical Landscape of Greece," pp. 137–170. The domestic context, and relations between women and men, family and outsiders in the domestic context is analyzed by Lisa C. Nevett, *House and Society in the Ancient Greek World* (Cambridge: Cambridge University Press, 1999).

A general account of farming practices in the Classical period is given by Signe Isager and Jens Erik Skydsgaard, *Ancient Greek Agriculture: An Introduction* (London: Routledge, 1992). The southern Argolid survey used here as a case study is described by Tjeerd van Andel and Curtis Runnels, *Beyond the Acropolis: A Rural Greek Past* (Stanford, CA: Stanford University Press, 1987). The fuller definitive account of this project has since been published: Michael Jameson, Curtis Runnels, and Tjeerd van Andel, *A Greek Countryside: The Southern Argolid from Prehistory to the Present Day* (Stanford, CA: Stanford University Press, 1994).

The standard history of the Hellenistic period is Peter Green, *Alexander to Actium: The Hellenistic Age* (London: Thames and Hudson, 1990). For Hellenistic art see J. J. Pollitt, *Art in the Hellenistic Age* (Cambridge: Cambridge University Press, 1986). The impact of Greek art on other areas of the Hellenistic world and on India and beyond is covered by John Boardman, *The Diffusion of Classical Art in Antiquity* (London: Thames and Hudson, 1994).

# *Chapter 11*

# Imperial Rome

Cameo portrait of the Emperor Augustus (31 B.C. to A.D. 14) cut in sardonyx.

*The rain blew gustily across their faces as they made their way along the parapet walk, cloaks wrapped tightly around them to keep out the worst of the weather. You could well imagine that you were near the edge of the known world, with the vast expanses of the ocean only a few days' travel to the west. Their harness clinked in time to their measured footsteps as the soldiers returned from their tour of duty at the watchtowers along Hadrian's Wall. It was a far cry indeed from the sunny Mediterranean. These men were not Italian legionaries, however, but auxiliary troops, Tungrians from the low-lying lands near the mouth of the Rhine. Their job was to watch for any sign of trouble from the Celtic Votadini to the north. It was dull work, especially unpleasant when the winter rain drove horizontally. Soon, now, they would be in their messroom at the fort of Vercovicium (Housesteads), warming themselves by the fire and enjoying a good meal. While the tribes beyond the wall remained quiet, frontier duty seemed a pointless task. But the very presence of the soldiers, part of an army of 300,000 men, deterred the barbarians from even contemplating hostile action. And the wall itself, a massive masonry barrier 120 kilometers (80 miles) long, was a constant reminder of the might and majesty of Rome.*[1]

Chapter 11 describes the last of the great civilizations of the Western Old World: ancient Rome. This was not only a cultural entity but also a political one: a vast empire, binding together peoples of different languages and skin color and different religious beliefs and cultural values. How it succeeded in doing so and in surviving as an empire for over 500 years is one of the main themes of the chapter (Table 11.1). Rome began life as an unexceptional settlement on the banks of the Tiber River. Tradition, supported by Livy and other historians, held that it was founded in 753 B.C., perhaps through the coalescence of several earlier villages. The legendary founder, Romulus, is now thought to be pure fiction, but remains of early Iron Age huts have been found on the Palatine Hill, which may represent one of the early villages, and there are cemeteries of cremation and inhumation graves nearby. The great change occurred in the seventh century B.C., when Rome fell under the control of its Etruscan neighbors to the north. These new rulers drained the low-lying marshland at the foot of the Palatine and Capitoline hills and laid it out as a public, open space: the Forum, or marketplace of Rome, which also became the seat of civic administration. The Etruscans also built the first large-scale buildings at Rome, including a temple to Jupiter Optimus Maximus (Jupiter Best and Greatest), the principal god of the Roman pantheon, on the Capitoline Hill.

[1]Eighty Roman miles equals 117 kilometers (73 twentieth-century [statute] miles).

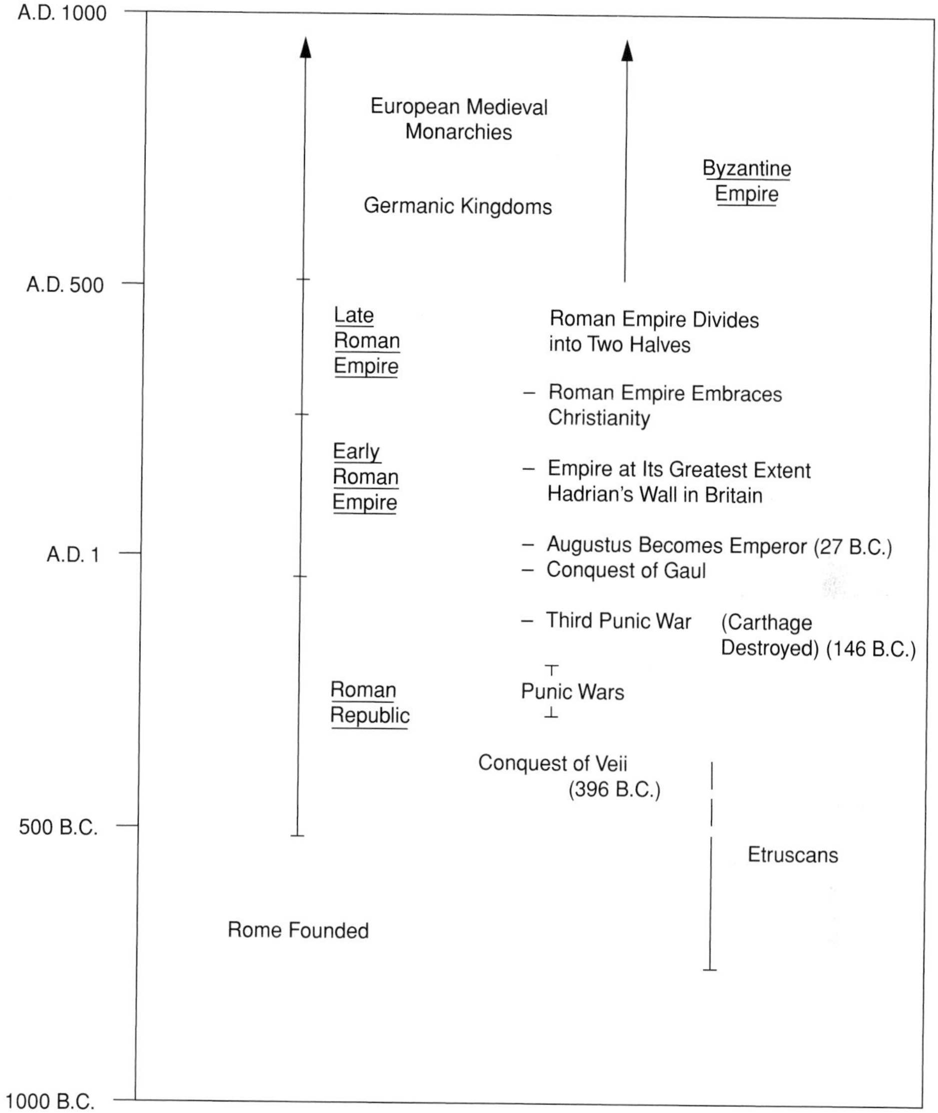


**Table 11.1** Chronological table of ancient Rome.

# The Roman Republic (510–31 B.C.)

Early Rome was governed by kings (Roman and Etruscan), but in 510 B.C. the leading families overthrew the last of them and established a republican constitution. This mirrors the pattern in many Etruscan cities, where kings were replaced by oligarchies (groups of aristocrats) in the sixth century B.C. (see Chapter 10). Rome at this stage was still a city-state, a small town surrounded by the rural territory under its control. It was also thoroughly Italian, in the sense of being Latin (in the region of Latium), with Etruscan influences from the north (including the *fasces*, or bundles of rods, symbols of power that are the origin of the modern word *fascism*); it was certainly not Greek. The Greek-style temples and statues came much later, in the second century B.C., as the original city-state of Rome grew to become the capital of a regional empire.

This process began with the conquest of Italy. As early as 396 B.C. the Romans had captured and annexed the important Etruscan city of Veii, their nearest rival and a city as large as Rome itself at the time. Over the next century and a half they extended their sway throughout the whole of Italy, not by force of arms alone, but by an astute mixture of war and diplomacy. Once they controlled Italy, they became a rival to the other major power of the western Mediterranean: the Carthaginians. The Romans defeated them in two major wars, the First Punic War (264–241 B.C.) and the Second Punic War (218–201 B.C.). It was in the Second Punic War that Italy was invaded by the brilliant Carthaginian general, Hannibal. Despite crushing victories at Lake Trasimene (217 B.C.) and Cannae (216 B.C.), Hannibal was unable to capture Rome itself, and the Romans eventually invaded North Africa and defeated Hannibal at Zama (202 B.C.). Carthage was never again a major power. Victory in these wars gave the Romans control over their first territories beyond the Italian peninsula: the island of Sicily and former Carthaginian possessions in Sardinia and southern Spain.

The pace of overseas conquest quickened during the second century B.C., when the Romans cast their eyes eastward and absorbed Greece and parts of Asia Minor, as well as the region known to them as Africa (modern Tunisia), after the final defeat and destruction of Carthage in the Third Punic War (149–146 B.C.). The conquered territories became provinces of the Roman Empire, ruled by a governor appointed by the Senate at Rome. Governors had wide powers and often abused their position, lining their pockets at the expense of provincial populations. The provinces were also exploited by ruthless Italian entrepreneurs, who gained mining concessions and trading monopolies, not always by the fairest of methods. Roman Italy grew increasingly wealthy and increasingly cosmopolitan in culture. The greatest cultural impact came from the Greek territories of the Aegean and (since Alexander the Great's conquests) the Near East. A famous Roman writer quipped that conquered Greece had taken her fierce victor captive (*Graecia capta ferum victorem cepit*), and indeed the face of Rome itself became increasingly hellenized as Greek architectural features and Greek sculpture—some looted from Greece, the rest Roman copies—became the fashion of the day. Greek even began to replace Latin as the language of educated discourse.

The Roman Empire continued to expand during the first century B.C. and for the first time spread beyond the Mediterranean basin with Julius Caesar's conquest of Celtic Gaul (58–51 B.C.) (Figure 11.1). By this time the power of the Senate, the traditional governing body, was increasingly overshadowed by the leading generals of the day, who could call on the support of large bodies of highly trained soldiers. The result was civil war, as over-mighty subjects used their military followings to fight against each other and overthrow the traditional constitution—as

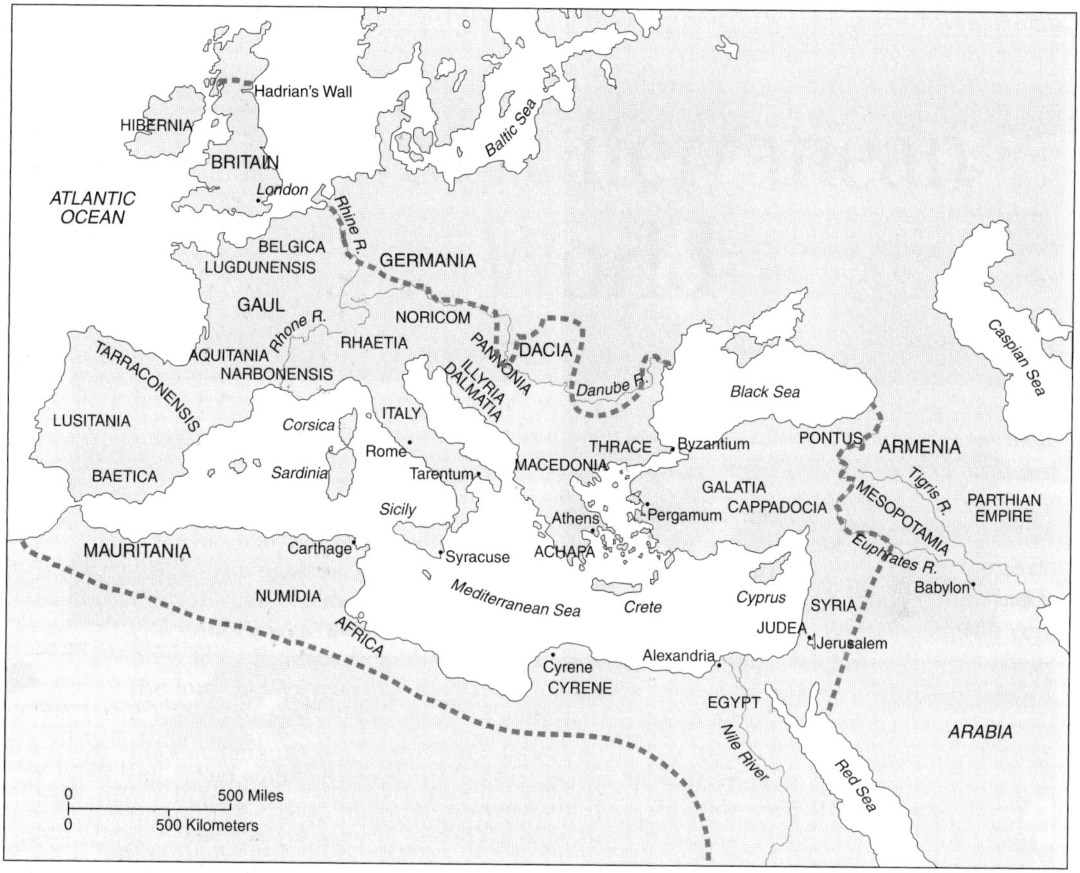


**Figure 11.1** Map of the Roman Empire in the second century A.D.

Julius Caesar did against Pompey the Great in 48 B.C. (battle of Pharsalus) and Octavian against Mark Antony in 31 B.C. (battle of Actium). Octavian's victory at Actium gave him unchallenged power and enabled him to transform the Roman constitution. He became the first Roman emperor, taking the title Augustus.

## The Early Roman Empire (31 B.C.–A.D. 235)

Augustus (31 B.C.–A.D. 14) consolidated and expanded the Roman Empire, conquering the northern Balkans in order to take the frontier to the Danube, though in the west, campaigns beyond the Rhine overstretched his resources and led to a serious military retreat (Figure 11.2). Several further provinces were added to the empire during the first and second centuries A.D.: Mauretania, Britain, Dacia, and Arabia. One reason may have been strategic—the desire to stabilize and reinforce the frontiers—but the emperors' desire for military glory was an equally powerful motive.

**Figure 11.2** Statue of Emperor Augustus in military regalia from Prima Porta, c. 20 B.C. Military success was an essential ingredient in the propaganda of imperial office. However, many Roman emperors claimed to be constitutional rulers, supported by the Senate and people, but it was control of the army that formed the bedrock of their power. (Vatican Museums, Vatican State. © Alinari/Art Resource, NY)

The empire reached its greatest extent early in the second century A.D. By this date, Rome's domains stretched from Mesopotamia in the east to the Atlantic in the west and from Hadrian's Wall in the north to the Sahara in the south. It was a polyglot, multiethnic, multicultural realm, incorporating territories as diverse as the urbanized lands of the Greek east and the tribal territories of the Celtic west. Latin, the official language, provided a veneer of uniformity, but in the eastern provinces Greek remained the dominant language and was used even for official documents. Cities were founded in the less developed provinces, and local elites were encouraged to adopt the trappings of Roman culture. In some areas, such as Gaul, Spain, and Africa (modern Tunisia), families of native origin came to play a major part in running the empire. This was part of the crucial change that took place during the first two centuries A.D., which saw the empire transformed from a series of tributary provinces, governed and exploited by Italians, to something that more resembled a commonwealth of provinces. The change is reflected in the origin of the emperors themselves: The first were wealthy Romans of aristocratic background (the Julio-Claudians, 31 B.C.–A.D. 68); then came middle-class Romans from central Italy (the Flavians, A.D. 69–96) and Roman families who had settled in Spain (Trajan and Hadrian, A.D. 98–138); finally Africans and Syrians who had only recently become Roman citizens (the Severans, A.D. 193–235). The process went still further in the third century, when the empire was under intense military pressure, and career officers of humble Illyrian background assumed the imperial purple.

Romanization is one of the key issues in the expansion of the empire. Most authorities now believe this was not a conscious Roman policy, but largely an indirect result of Roman rule and the economic, social, and political possibilities that it opened up to provincials. It is also debatable how far the empire in its different provinces marks a break with the past. In the east, as we have seen, there was continuity in commerce and city life. The Romans, indeed, learned many new skills from their eastern subjects and were heavily influenced by Greek architectural and artistic traditions. Greek literature was taken as a model by many Roman writers, some of whom even preferred to write in Greek. In the west, however, the picture was very different. Some have argued that the Celtic peoples of Gaul were already organized into states, with towns and coinage, before the Roman conquest. This argument proposes that these territories were in some sense preadapted to Roman rule, with aristocracies already won over by Roman luxuries and with systems of government ripe for annexation by a foreign power. Yet despite the existence of coinage and of large defended sites known as *oppida*, it is far from clear how centrally organized these societies really were; many of them, if not all, are better described as peoples than as states. On the one hand, the imposition of Roman rule marks a rupture in their development, not merely the acceleration of an existing trend toward statehood and cities. On the other hand, this is not to say that native culture disappeared or was suppressed by the Romans; far from it. Native languages continued (for a while at least) to be spoken alongside Latin, and native deities retained their local followings, even though Roman deities (including the cult of the emperor) were established in major temples.

## The Culture of Empire

At the center of the Roman Empire lay Rome, the greatest city of its day. By the reign of Augustus, it had a population of probably half a million people. He and his successors poured money into new building projects, some of them utilitarian, designed to improve the basic facilities of the city (such as aqueducts and amphitheaters); others were monuments to the imperial rulers and their dynasties. The most overtly propagandist were the triumphal arches and victory columns erected in the principal public places: Trajan's Column, recording his conquest of Dacia in a frieze of spiraling reliefs; the arches of Titus and Septimius Severus, commemorating victories over Jews and Parthians; and many more. The first emperors also built a series of imperial *fora*, to supplement the facilities of the original Roman Forum, now too cramped to accommodate the needs of an imperial capital. Julius Caesar began the tradition, buying up land next to the old Forum, though he was murdered before the work could be completed. It was taken up by his adoptive son, Augustus, who also built his own Forum—complete with temple and colonnades, adorned with marble and colored stone, and statues proclaiming the emperor's supposed descent from the legendary hero Aeneas. Further imperial fora were built by the emperors Vespasian (A.D. 69–79), the "Forum of Peace"; Nerva (A.D. 96–98), the "Forum of Nerva," in reality largely the work of his predecessor, Domitian (A.D. 81–96); and Trajan (A.D. 98–117). Together with new buildings in the Forum Romanum they turned the area into a splendid imperial showcase.

The emperors themselves lived on the Palatine Hill, in a residence that has given us the word *palace*. Augustus was careful to avoid any outward show of monarchy, mindful perhaps of the murder of his less cautious predecessor, Julius Caesar. He lived in a rich but not palatial house on the Palatine. Later emperors built more lavishly. Nero (A.D. 54–68) famously bought up a large area of central Rome for his Golden House, a series of buildings set within parkland. It incorporated such ingenious features as ceilings that could shower perfumes and petals on assembled dinner guests. After Nero's death, however, the Golden House was abandoned, and it was left to Domitian to build most of the huge, 4-hectare (10-acre) palace that is on the Palatine Hill today.

Domitian's palace was a far cry from the conditions in which the majority of Rome's inhabitants lived. Wealthy citizens could afford luxurious mansions with courts and gardens, but many people lived in crowded tenement blocks, several stories high. We get a better impression of these from the actual remains of Roman tenements at Ostia, the harbor town downstream from Rome. Roman writers made clear that tenement blocks were not always soundly built and that collapses were relatively common. Laws were passed to limit the height of buildings along street fronts, first to 18 and later to 21 meters (60 to 70 feet). There could have been no more vivid illustration of the enormous wealth differences in ancient Rome than the crowded tenements of the poor compared with the spacious garden suburbs of the rich.

## *Artists and Architects*

The Romans were consummate architects and engineers. They developed new methods and materials for building and also drew on the rich heritage of Greek and Hellenistic architecture. In the eastern provinces, indeed, the earlier traditions continued to flourish under Roman rule. Many of the greatest surviving Roman buildings are found in Asia Minor and the Levant: the temples of Baalbek in modern Lebanon, for example, which illustrate the development of a baroque style of architecture and architectural decoration also present at Petra and Palmyra. The cities of Asia Minor, too, saw major rebuilding during the Roman period, and theaters, baths, and libraries were founded by wealthy citizens. By the second century A.D. even relatively minor cities possessed colonnaded streets and ornamental fountains.

The North African provinces also prospered under Roman rule, and here again there is a rich legacy in art and architecture. The amphitheater at El Djem (ancient Thysdrus), for example, is one of the largest and best preserved in the Roman world, built from the profits of the local olive oil industry. In North Africa, as elsewhere, some of the greatest buildings were imperial projects, funded by the emperor himself, for example, the baths at Carthage built by Antoninus Pius (emperor A.D. 138–161) and the basilica at Lepcis Magna begun by Septimius Severus (emperor 193–211), dedicated by his son and successor, Caracalla, in 216.

During the first and second centuries A.D., Roman architects devised new ways of using their materials to make innovative and daring structures. Most major buildings were constructed of brick and concrete, with marble or other expensive stone used only for columns or facings. The culmination of these developments was the Pantheon at Rome, built by Emperor Hadrian between 116 and 126. Its massive concrete dome, 43 meters (142 feet) across, is larger even than the dome of St. Peter's in the Vatican. The interior is decorated with stucco and marble veneer, completely masking the structural materials behind. Similarly daring in engineering terms, and equally opulent in their fittings, were the great bath complexes built at Rome by Caracalla (emperor 211–217) and Diocletian (284–305).

The prosperity of the Roman Empire created a great demand for artworks from wealthy individuals and municipal patrons. There were statues—often copies of Greek originals—to fill niches and adorn pedestals. Roman artists were also experts in relief sculpture, especially on public monuments and on sarcophagi. The finest reliefs date to the period between the reign of Augustus and the death of Marcus Aurelius (A.D. 180). They were boldly executed, making full use of naturalism, skilled composition of the various elements, and depth of carving.

Perhaps even more famous than Roman sculpture are Roman mosaics. Many of the finest surviving examples came from North Africa. Mosaic was used to portray mythological scenes, landscapes, buildings, and people. In addition to mosaics for the floors, wealthy Romans also had the walls of their houses decorated with paintings, again with a wide choice of subjects. Special mention must also be made of glassware, in which Roman products surpassed anything made in Europe until the Renaissance.

We call all this Roman art, but it is important to recognize that not all the artists, architects, and craftspeople responsible for these works were Romans. This is especially true in the provinces, where local workshops would have absorbed new fashions and innovations alongside existing practices and techniques. Yet there is a certain homogeneity of style throughout the empire, as well as regional diversity. Poor people—most of the population—may have known little and cared even less about what was happening in distant provinces, but the elite were living in an imperial milieu, aware of new models and ideas, and it was the elite who commissioned the artworks and set the trends.

## The Military Establishment

The Romans sought to rule their empire with the support of the local aristocracies. These wealthy men were encouraged to think of themselves as part of the Roman system; they responded by taking on magistracies and endowing their cities with public utilities such as libraries and water supplies and monuments to civic pride. The backbone of Roman rule, however, was the Roman army. This was at one and the same time an instrument of conquest, a machine for guarding the frontiers, and a force for stamping out rebellion or internal unrest. The key element was the 30 or so legions, units of 5,000 highly trained, well-equipped infantrymen. They were supported by an equivalent number of smaller units, the so-called auxiliaries. While the legions were drawn from Roman citizens, the auxiliaries were recruited from among the subject peoples of the empire and sometimes formed specialized units (for example, Batavian cavalry, Syrian archers, and Tigris River boatmen).

In archaeological terms, the impact of the Roman army is most vividly seen in forts and frontiers. Roman forts originated from the marching camps, which were part of standard Roman field procedure. When operating in enemy territory, Roman forces would build a temporary camp each night for protection against a surprise attack. This usually consisted of a bank and ditch, strengthened by wooden stakes, that enclosed a rectangular area with rounded corners (the so-called "playing-card" shape) in which the soldiers erected their tents. Traces of these temporary camps survive in several regions, notably northern Britain, where archaeologists have sought to date and use them as a basis for reconstructing particular military offensives.

When Augustus stabilized the frontiers he also reduced the size of the army to 28 legions, plus an equivalent number of auxiliaries, resulting in a total fighting force of 300,000 men. Most of these were posted on or close to the frontiers, in permanent camps. The defenses were made of earth and timber in the early days, but by the second century A.D. stone forts were the norm. They followed the plan of the temporary camps, although within the playing-card enclosure the buildings that housed the soldiers and their stores were made of timber or stone. Rectangular barrack blocks were divided into ten rooms *(contubernia)*, each holding eight men, with larger quarters for an officer and his household at one end. Thus each barrack block held around 80 men, the normal size of a Roman "century," and the officer was known as a centurion. Cohorts of auxiliary troops were made up of 5 or 10 centuries; legions, of 60 centuries. Even when a fort has not been excavated, the regularity of Roman military planning usually makes it possible to deduce the size of the unit stationed there simply by measuring the ground plan.

Alongside barrack blocks there were all the other buildings we would expect to find in a military compound, plus one or two that were perhaps less usual. At the center of the fort was the headquarters building *(praetorium)*, with a room for the standards ("eagles" in the case of a legion) and the strongroom (sometimes below ground) that held the soldiers' pay. Next to the *praetorium* was the *principia*, the residence of the commanding officer, who unlike the ordinary soldiers was allowed to marry and live there with his family. Workshops, granaries (with raised floors to avoid the damp), a hospital block, and stables (larger in the case of a cavalry unit) were also regular elements, the whole being laid out on a rigid orthogonal street plan. A less obvious inclusion was that of a bath block, containing hot and cold rooms and a plunge pool; this was often to be found outside the fortified perimeter but was no doubt a welcome feature to soldiers returning from drill or duty.

## *Imperial Frontiers*

Aside from occasional foreign campaigns, the army spent much of its time guarding and patrolling the frontiers. These, like the forts, underwent a transformation during the first and second centuries A.D., becoming less fluid. The frontiers of the Roman Empire can be divided into three categories. River frontiers, notably the Rhine, Danube, and Euphrates, provided a continuous natural marker or barrier. It was sufficient to place forts at fords or bridging points and watchtowers along the banks to warn of any unauthorized incursion. Deserts provided relatively secure frontiers, notably those of Syria, Arabia, and North Africa. There the Romans built networks of forts and roads and occasionally went so far as to construct a physical barrier, such as the 60-kilometer (37-mile) length of stone wall and ditch across the Oued Djedi in eastern Algeria, though seasonal movements by nomads were still permitted.

Frontiers unprotected by either desert or river gave Roman military planners the greatest cause for concern, and it was in these regions that the concept of a continuous frontier defense reached its fullest expression. The two key sectors were northern Britain and the awkward terrain between the upper reaches of the Rhine and Danube in modern Germany. The Emperor Hadrian (A.D. 117–138) built a continuous timber palisade in Germany, which was later in part rebuilt in stone. But the real strength of the frontier lay in the closely spaced network of watchtowers and forts behind it. In northern Britain the frontier work (known as Hadrian's Wall) was built largely of stone from the outset, and those stretches that were not at first constructed of stone became so a few decades later. This was an enormous undertaking: a solid wall up to 3 meters (10 feet) wide at the base and originally some 3.7 meters (12 feet) high, stretching for 117 kilometers (73 statute miles) from coast to coast (Figure 11.3). Again, forts, fortlets, and watchtowers were an

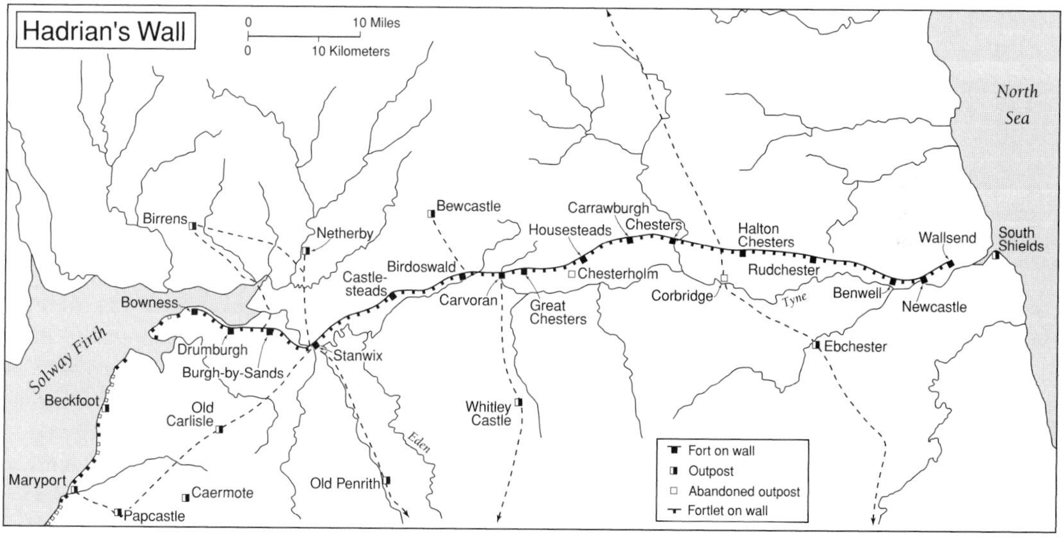


(a)

**Figure 11.3** (a) Map of Hadrian's Wall, on the northern frontier of Roman Britain; (b) photograph of the wall. The wall itself was a continuous stone structure, running 117 kilometers (73 miles) from the mouth of the River Tyne in the east to the Cumbrian coast in the west. Along its length were milecastles (fortlets) at every mile with turrets (watchtowers) between. Larger forts, which held units of 500 (or, in one case, 1,000) men, were located either on the wall itself or a few kilometers to its rear. This elaborate frontier defense was built on the orders of Emperor Hadrian in the 120s A.D.

(b)
**Figure 11.3** *(cont.)*

integral part of the scheme, for it was in the forts that the soldiers who patrolled the wall actually lived. Hadrian's Wall also shows something of the rigidity of Roman military planning, which we have already encountered in the standardized layouts of the forts themselves. Fortlets (known as milecastles) were placed at every mile along Hadrian's Wall, with a pair of watchtowers (known as turrets) evenly spaced between.

Archaeologists and historians have long debated whether Hadrian's Wall was an effective military barrier. Evidence of rebuilding, which some have interpreted as repairs after hostile attacks, has been regarded by others as merely routine refurbishment. Whatever its military effectiveness, however, it was clearly a powerful symbol of Roman military might. The biographer of Hadrian remarks that the emperor built the wall to separate the Romans from the barbarians. In the same way the Chinese emperors built the Great Wall to separate China from the barbarous steppe peoples to the north. In both cases, in addition to any military function, the physical barriers served in the eyes of their builders to reinforce the conceptual divide between civilized and noncivilized. They were part of the ideology of empire.

# Arteries of Empire: Roads and Sea-Lanes

## *Roman Highways*

Along each of the Roman frontiers ran a strategic military road, enabling troops to be rushed to any threatened sector in the shortest possible time. Roads also linked the frontiers and provinces to the heart of the imperial administration in Italy and formed an essential part of the communications network through which the empire was governed.

Roman roads have remained one of the Romans' most famous achievements. They lie beneath many modern roads and can often be detected where a highway runs for miles in a straight line. As conquerors, the Romans did not need to pay great heed to existing property boundaries, and in any event the roads were initially a strategic military device, overriding local interests. It was only later, as more and more local tracks were paved to link together the main arterial routes, that the Roman road system became an intricate, all-embracing network. The first Roman roads were built in Italy and carried the names of the leading politicians responsible for their construction, for example, Via Appia after Appius Claudius (312 B.C.) and Via Flaminia after Gaius Flaminius (220 B.C.). Their primary aim was to facilitate rapid troop movements from Rome to the boundaries of Roman territory. They also served the official postal service, with relay stations holding fresh horses in readiness at regular intervals. This system was first established by Emperor Augustus as part of his imperial reform, and it allowed messengers to travel up to 241 kilometers (150 miles) a day.

All Roman roads had dry, all-weather surfaces. The actual techniques of construction varied somewhat from region to region. In the eastern provinces, gravel surfaces were the norm, held in place by curbstones and drained by gullies. Italy and the western provinces boasted of more elaborate roads, surfaced with carefully fitted paving stones. Along with the roads themselves came the need for bridges. Small spans would be bridged by stone arches; long widths, by timber superstructures supported on stone pillars. The engineers applied the same technical skill to the construction of aqueducts and large vaulted halls. In the latter case, as in much of their architecture, the invention of a kind of concrete had a revolutionary impact, enabling grander and more daring structures to be built than the Greeks or Etruscans would ever have attempted.

## *Roman Seaways*

Roman concrete had one further advantage: It would set under water, making it suitable for artificial harbor works. As a Mediterranean empire, sea traffic was particularly important to the Roman world. Much of the trade was shipborne, and most of the major cities were near the sea or on the banks of navigable rivers, where they could be supplied by water transport. An official price list of A.D. 301 makes clear that it was as cheap to ship grain from Spain to Syria as to cart it 120 kilometers

(75 miles) inland. The population of Rome, the capital, was heavily dependent on seaborne supplies of grain, brought mainly from Egypt and distributed free in a monthly dole to Roman citizens. Yet Rome itself was too far upriver to be reached

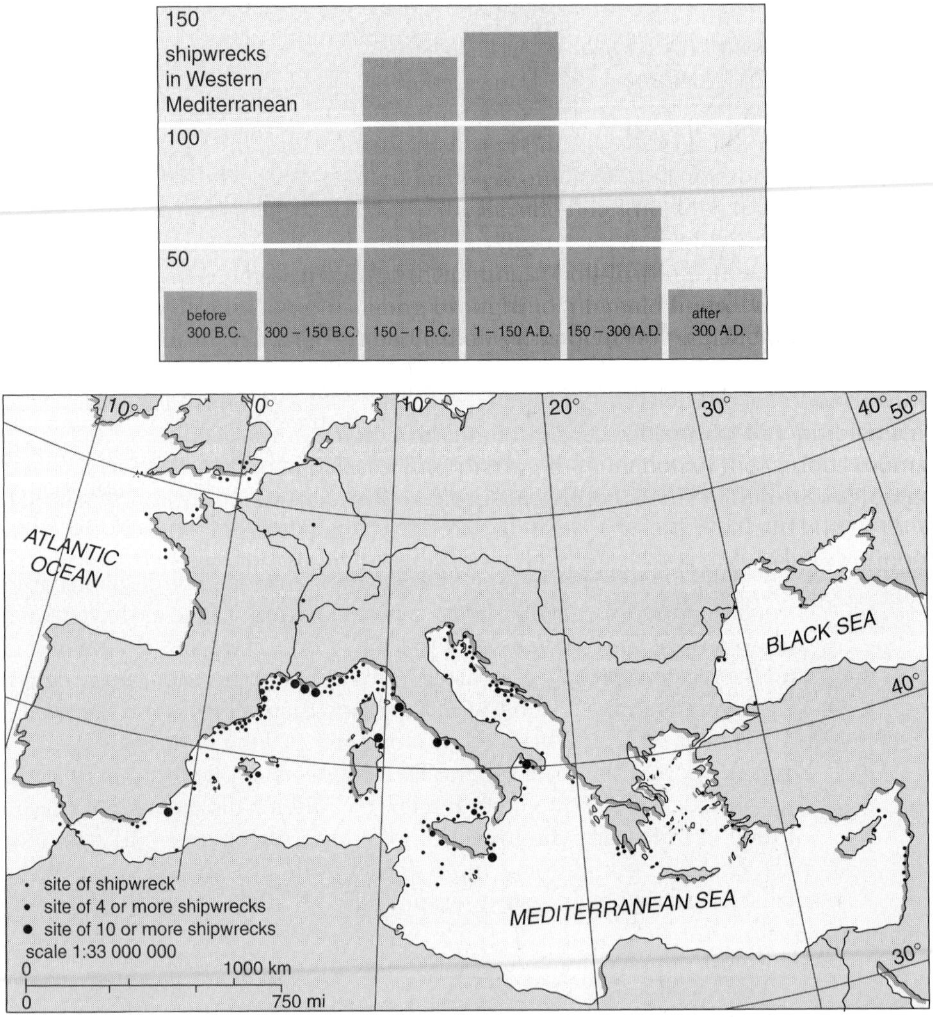


(a)

**Figure 11.4** (a) Graph and maps of the numbers and locations of Roman shipwrecks in the Mediterranean, first century B.C. to third century A.D.; (b) Ostia mosaic of a ship and lighthouse. Seaborne transport was a key element in the Roman economy, allowing bulky goods such as grain to be shipped over long distances to feed city populations and army units. The rise and fall in the number of Mediterranean shipwrecks is thus a good indication of the health of the Roman economy. Major harbors such as Ostia, the seaport of Rome at the mouth of the Tiber River, were provided with lighthouses to aid navigation.

(b)
**Figure 11.4** *(cont.)*

by large ocean-going vessels; thus great efforts were made to improve the harbor facilities of Ostia, at the Tiber mouth, by building massive artificial breakwaters and then by constructing a huge inland basin, linked to the sea by a canal. Artificial harbors were also built at several other cities around the shores of the Mediterranean, notably Caesarea in modern Israel and Lepcis Magna in North Africa. All too often, however, the engineers found themselves fighting a fruitless battle against the forces of nature, and many Roman harbors, including those of Ostia and Lepcis, gradually became blocked by silt.

Many Roman harbors were equipped with lighthouses to guide vessels into port. The idea of a tower with a beacon on top may well be old—examples from the sixth century B.C. are known on the Greek island of Thasos—but the immediate inspiration for the Romans was the massive Pharos lighthouse at Alexandria, which was considered one of the Seven Wonders of the Ancient World. Useful though they were, lighthouses had negligible success in reducing the risks of sea travel and could not guard against storms or piracy. Shipwrecks were the inevitable outcome, but however tragic these were to merchants and voyagers, they have provided vital information for archaeologists. By studying the vessels themselves, so far as they are preserved, we can learn how Roman ships were built. By studying the cargoes, we can discover what they were carrying and even reconstruct the course of the voyage. And by studying the incidence of shipwrecks in space and time, we can chart the relative importance of sea traffic in the Mediterranean, noting a peak around the first centuries B.C. and A.D. and a steady decline thereafter. This provides a direct measure of the changing fortunes of the Roman mercantile economy (Figure 11.4).

(a)

**Figure 11.5** (a) the Arch of Septimius Severus (dedicated A.D. 203) in the Forum in Rome in honor of his victories over the Parthians; (b) plan of imperial Rome. During its heyday in the first and second centuries A.D. Rome was a thriving metropolis of perhaps half a million people. Unlike many Roman cities it was not planned around a regular grid of streets but had grown up haphazardly over the centuries. Though most of the ancient city has been built over, many of the major monuments survive to this day as ruins. Archaeological excavations, contemporary documents, and fragments of a marble plan of c. A.D. 200 enable us to fill in further details. From these we learn that most of Rome's inhabitants lived in cramped tenement blocks several stories high. They were not always soundly built and occasionally collapsed; they also became death traps in a fire. Yet in the fourth century A.D. records show that Rome had 46,000 tenement blocks and fewer than 2,000 private houses. The latter were the preserve of the wealthy and might, in extreme cases, include leafy gardens and parks. The wealthiest citizen of all was, of course, the emperor, who lived in a splendid residence on the Palatine Hill. He could look down on the south to the Circus Maximus, the main racetrack and athletics ground, and on the north to the Forum. The Forum was the heart of Roman civic life. First laid out as a public square in the seventh century B.C., it was a showpiece for Roman power and magnificence, with colonnaded temples and halls and massive triumphal arches erected to commemorate imperial victories. Only a handful of these arches have survived, but they include some of the most familiar monuments of ancient Rome.

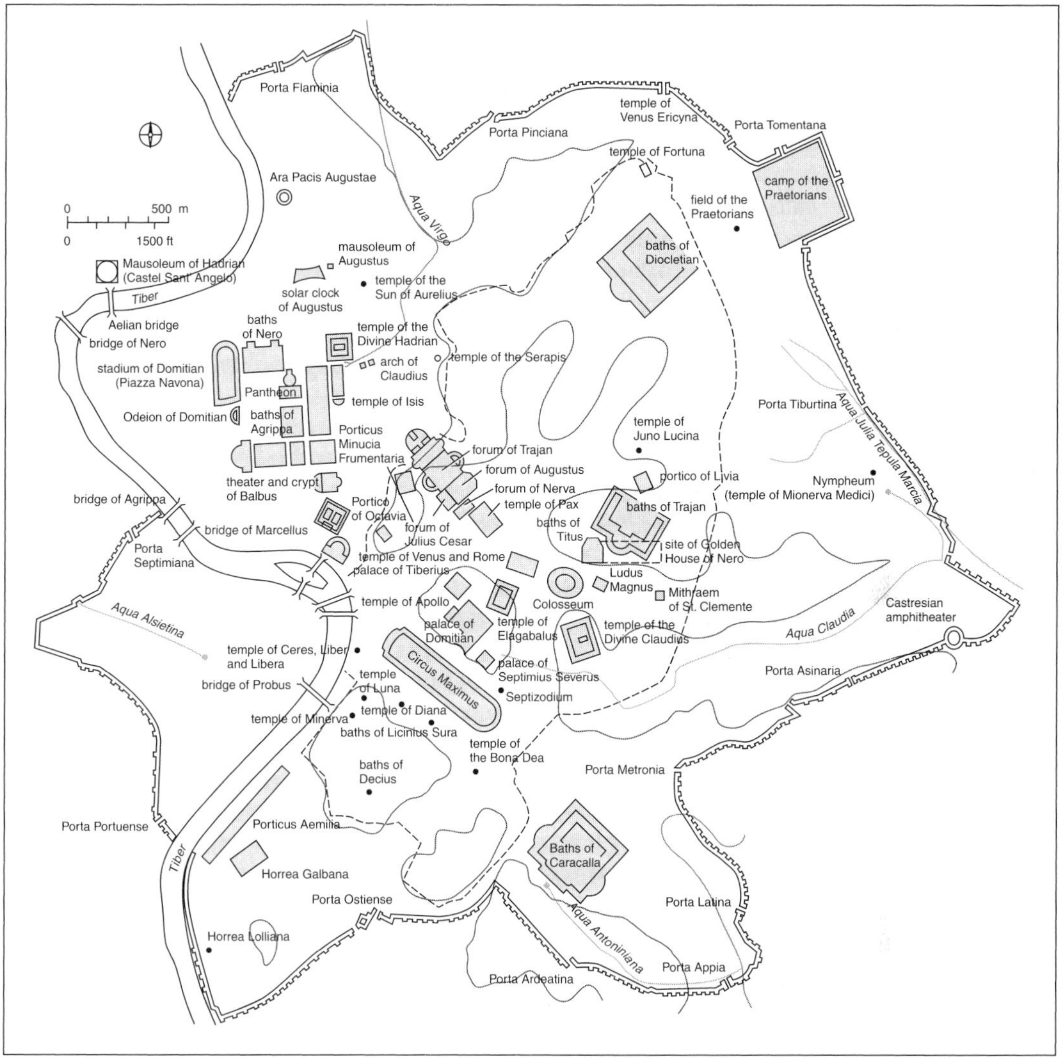


(b)

**Figure 11.5** *(cont.)*

# Cities

Roads, ships, and aqueducts all converged on the cities, which were the focal points of the Roman Empire. The cities, of course, were dependent on their rural hinterland—the Roman economy remained very much agrarian in nature. But the cities assumed the greatest prominence in the affairs of the empire, and it is they that have yielded the most vivid archaeological evidence in the form of monuments, artifacts, and housing (Figure 11.5).

Roman cities varied greatly in size. At one end were the leading cities of the empire, with populations running into the hundreds of thousands—Alexandria, Antioch, Carthage (refounded by Augustus as a Roman city), and above all Rome itself, probably the first city in the Western world to have half a million inhabitants. At the other end were the small cities, some little more than villages by modern standards, with a few thousand residents. Each city had its public buildings, but their scale and magnificence very much depended on the generosity of local patrons. A rich citizen might give money to repair a temple, pave a marketplace, improve a water supply, or even build a theater—not necessarily because of altruism but as a way of promoting his own political ambitions. The result in either case was a rash of building in cities throughout the empire during the first two centuries A.D., though lessening in the third century as the empire experienced political and military problems.

Pompeii, in the shadow of Vesuvius, not far from modern Naples, is one of the best-preserved and best-known Roman cities. Vesuvius erupted in A.D. 79, engulfing Pompeii in dense ash and lava, and the abandoned city remained deeply buried until archaeologists began working there in the eighteenth century. Now much of the city has been unearthed once again. No single city can be taken as representative of Roman city life as a whole, but Pompeii comes nearest to that role (Figure 11.6).

Like many Roman cities, Pompeii was laid out on an orthogonal plan, with streets crossing each other roughly at right angles. The plan was not perfectly square, and the southwest corner was on a different axis (part of an earlier settlement), but this does not detract from the general intention. The streets were paved with stone slabs, flanked on either side by raised sidewalks. The crisscross pattern of the streets divided the buildings of the city into rectangular or trapezoidal blocks—known to the Romans as *insulae*—which were often modified substantially in the course of their occupation. An example is the Insula of the Menander, so-called after a painting of Menander, a third-century Athenian dramatist, in the garden colonnade of the principal house. The *insula* was planned in the third century B.C. when the city was extended to take in that area. It was divided into a number of separate properties, all perhaps belonging to a single owner, who may have lived in the House of the Menander on the north side of the *insula*. In its early days the Insula of the Menander was an aristocratic neighborhood. By the end of the third century B.C., however, if not before, it was completely built up; the density of occupation increased during the late first century B.C., when an upper story was added to many of the buildings.

The last years of the *insula* are a commentary on the changing values of Roman imperial society. At the one end of the scale, the wealthy owners of the House of the Menander decided to extend their holdings, buying an adjacent property on the east side of the block and building a magnificent banquet hall on the site. At the other end, shops and taverns were opened on the street frontages; the principal houses stood behind them, arranged around open courts, with only modest doorways opening onto the outside world. The wealthy wanted security and seclusion. Yet it is strange to note how the entrance to the House of the Menander was thus next door to a

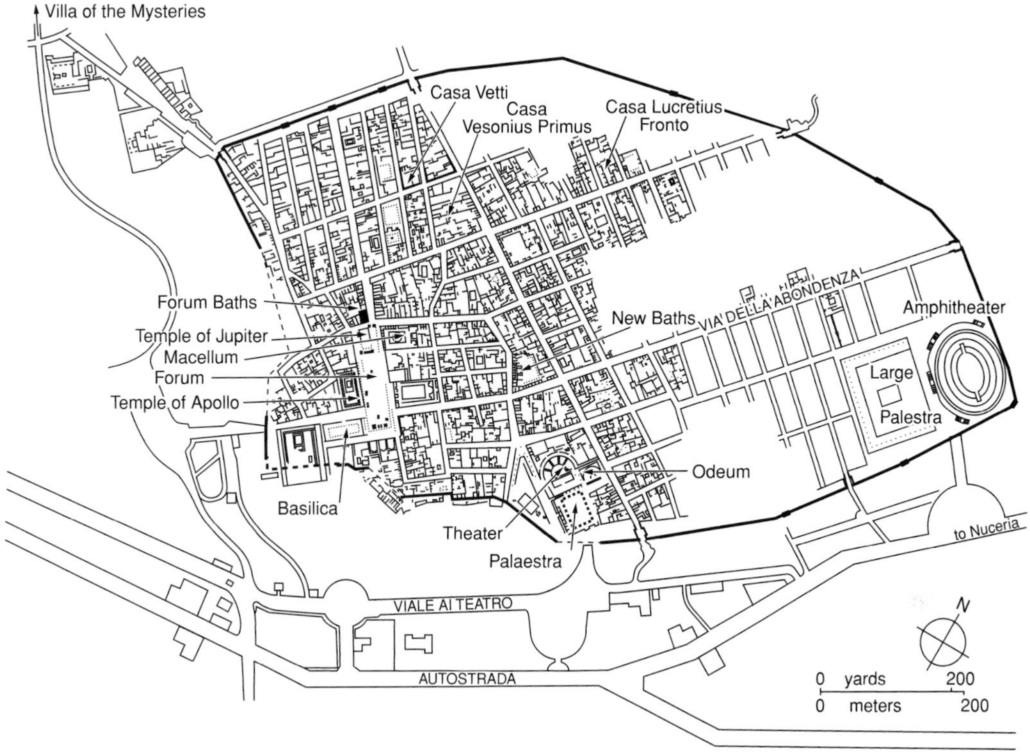


**Figure 11.6** Plan of Pompeii.

stairway that gave access to a first-floor brothel. From its origins as an aristocratic neighborhood, the Insula of the Menander had become a thriving if less salubrious mix of private and commercial activities (Figure 11.7).

In addition to shops and houses, Pompeii possessed the amenities of a prosperous Roman city, including a forum area, originally the city's market but later converted into a setting for public buildings. A temple of Jupiter stood at one end, a temple of Apollo to the west, and a temple and colonnade dedicated to Augustus to the east, along with a covered market that provided space for the stall-holders. At the southwest end of the forum was a basilica, a covered hall where lawsuits were heard and public business transacted. One of the buildings to the south may have been the city prison; another, the city treasury. Other buildings provided for the entertainment of the citizens. A theater had been built in the second century B.C. It was rebuilt and remodeled by two wealthy patrons in the reign of Augustus. Other patrons had built a second, smaller theater and the large amphitheater for gladiatorial games in the first century B.C. The latter, a smaller but older version of the famous Colosseum in Rome, was used to stage the kind of bloodthirsty games for which the Romans were notorious: gladiatorial contests (nearby Capua was the leading school for gladiators); artificial fights or hunts in which wild beasts were

**Figure 11.7** Wall painting from the Villa of the Mysteries at Pompeii. The wealthier houses of Roman Pompeii are famous for their elegance and luxury. They had colonnaded courts and gardens and were decorated with eye-catching wall paintings, which reveal some of the imaginary world of the Romans. They include idealized landscapes, scenes from mythology, and simple decorative patterns. Specialists have divided the paintings into four successive styles, showing how Roman tastes had changed during the three centuries before the eruption of Vesuvius, which destroyed Pompeii in A.D. 79. The First Style (200–80 B.C.) is severely rectilinear and simply mimics such architectural features as fluted columns and facings of colored stone. The Second and Third Styles (80 B.C.–A.D. 50) develop this tradition by creating a fantastic illusionary architecture, framing panels some of which are like windows open to country scenes. The paintings of the Fourth and final style (A.D. 50–79) are the most elaborate and baroque, combining ornament and illusionism in subtle and often whimsical fashion. In some cases the paintings indicate the particular interests of the owner. One house, for instance, has a whole series of scenes from Greek plays. Another, the so-called Villa of the Mysteries, just outside the city, has a room decorated with paintings of the initiation of a Roman woman into the cult of the god Dionysus. This cult promised immortality after death and was one of several religions (including Christianity) that became popular in the Roman Empire by offering a more "personal" belief than the traditional state religion.

slaughtered; even executions of condemned criminals, who were sometimes forced to fight to the death to entertain the populace. At one event blood flowed in the aisles as well as in the arena. Among the spectators at a gladiatorial show in A.D. 59 were people from the neighboring town of Nuceria. Nucerians and Pompeians soon progressed from shouting abuse at each other to throwing stones and drawing swords. Many died in the ensuing riot, and Emperor Nero banned gladiatorial games in Pompeii for ten years (Box 11.1).

## Box 11.1 The Colosseum

Most Roman cities in Italy and the western provinces had an amphitheater, where games were held at various times throughout the year. The largest was the Colosseum, begun by Emperor Vespasian (A.D. 69–79) and completed by his son and successor, Titus, in A.D. 80. It stood at the very heart of Rome and was capable of seating 50,000 spectators

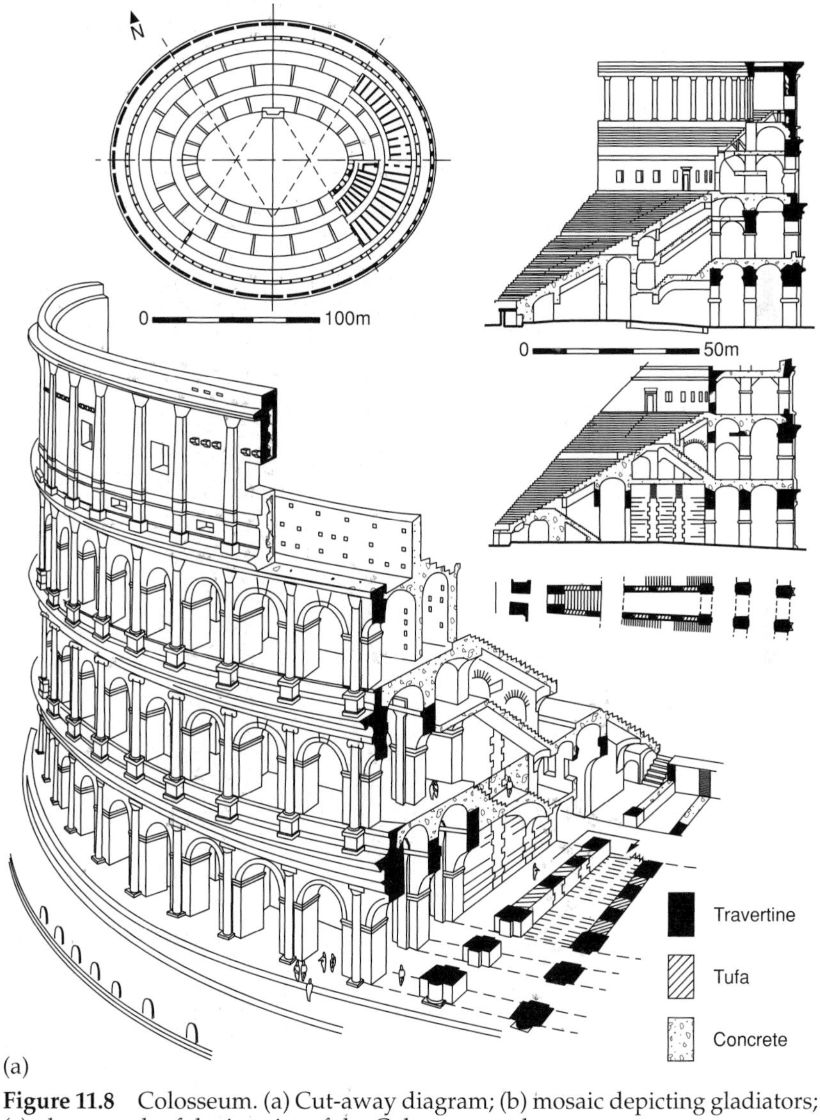


**Figure 11.8** Colosseum. (a) Cut-away diagram; (b) mosaic depicting gladiators; (c) photograph of the interior of the Colosseum today.

*(Cont.)*

(b) The Hunt. (4th century mosaic. Galleria Borghese, Rome, Italy. © Alinari/Art Resource, NY)

(c)

**Figure 11.8** *(cont.)*

(Figure 11.8). The oval structure was constructed of concrete and faced and reinforced with blocks of travertine, a local stone. The seats rose in four sloping tiers around the central arena. The front rows were reserved for senators and magistrates; women and slaves were restricted to the highest tier at the back. The emperor had his own special, marble box. Below the wooden floor of the arena was a maze of passages and chambers, some of them for holding the wild animals that took part in the games. There were rope-operated lifts to raise the animals to the level of the arena. The Colosseum is a masterpiece of Roman engineering. It is also a monument to the violent tastes of Roman society. When Emperor Titus inaugurated the Colosseum in A.D. 80, the games lasted 100 days, and no fewer than 9,000 animals were slaughtered. Gladiators armed with nets and tridents or shields and helmets also took part and sometimes became great popular heroes. Roman writers describe mock sea battles in specially flooded arenas and mock hunts with forests of trees in tubs of earth. These were elaborate shows, very popular with the common people. Educated men like the philosopher Seneca were not so amused:

> In the morning men are thrown to the lions and the bears, at noon they are thrown to the spectators. The spectators call for the slayer to be thrown to those who in turn will slay him, and they detain the victor for another butchering. The outcome for the combatants is death. . . . "But one of them was a highway robber, he killed a man! . . . Kill him! Lash him! Burn him!" And when the show stops for intermission, "Let's have men killed meanwhile! Let's not have nothing going on!"

After a day at the games, male Pompeians could have sought relaxation in baths, taverns, or less reputable places of entertainment. They would have had a choice of three public baths and a number of wine bars or taverns, many of which doubled as brothels. Roman law held that a woman who worked in a tavern or wine bar was little better than a prostitute. The main inn at Pompeii was directly opposite the city's principal brothel. The same bill might itemize wine, food, fodder for the mule, and a girl. Respectable women stayed indoors and were accompanied by male relatives or attendants (if they could afford them) when they went out. Roman cities were not always peaceful places. Even a small town like Pompeii had its riots, and larger cities—Alexandria in particular—were notorious for their street violence.

## *Commerce and Coinage*

Like most Roman cities, Pompeii was a center of production and manufacture. There were at least 13 workshops for metalworking, identified not only by casts, molds, and specialized metalworking tools but also by signs and inscriptions. Pompeii was a highly literate place. Textile production was also practiced: There were workshops for dyeing, fulling, and weaving, though not on a large scale. Most of the end products were probably intended purely for local consumption rather than export. The same is true of the bakeries, with tall millstones of coarse volcanic stone turned by donkey power to produce flour. However, Pompeii did export a much sought-after, fine-quality fish sauce known as *garum*.

Pompeii was typical of many Roman towns in producing goods mainly for local consumption. Yet commerce did flourish in the Roman world, especially by sea. Some of the clearest evidence is provided by finds of the pottery containers or amphorae used to carry wine and olive oil and even *garum*. Enormous rubbish heaps of discarded amphorae accumulated behind the riverfront at Rome, where boats tied up and unloaded. Many of them had once contained Spanish or North African olive oil, and some had been stamped with the name of the potter and marked in ink with the name of the shipper, the year, the export authorities, and the weight of the amphora and its contents. In some cases, archaeologists can use the distribution of stamped amphorae to reconstruct the pattern of trade from a particular center. A good example of this are the so-called Sestius amphorae from France and the western Mediterranean. Gaius Sestius was a prosperous wine producer who owned vineyards near Cosa in northern Italy. He made his own amphorae, stamped with his name, on his estates. The pattern of finds shows that Sestius was exporting wine to barbarian Gaul (northern France) long before it was conquered by the Romans (Figure 11.9).

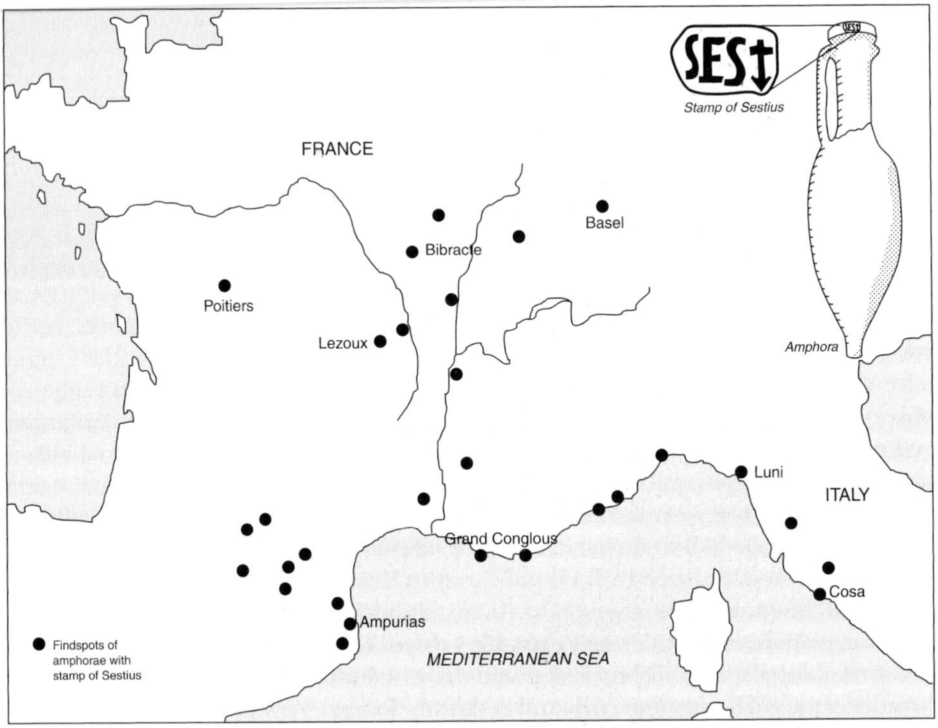


(a)

**Figure 11.9** (a) Map and stamp of Sestius amphorae; (b) amphora label from Spain. Amphorae, large pottery vessels, were the standard containers for transport of a whole range of produce in the Roman world, including wine, olive oil, and a fermented fish sauce known as *garum*. Many amphorae were locally manufactured and stamped with the name of the estate owner. Hence, the mapping of archaeological finds of amphorae bearing that particular stamp can reveal the extent of distribution of one estate's produce. Such is the case with the Sestius amphorae produced near Cosa in Italy for wine export in the first century B.C. Some Spanish amphorae were even labeled in ink with the weight of the amphora and its contents, the name of the shipper, and an official export mark.

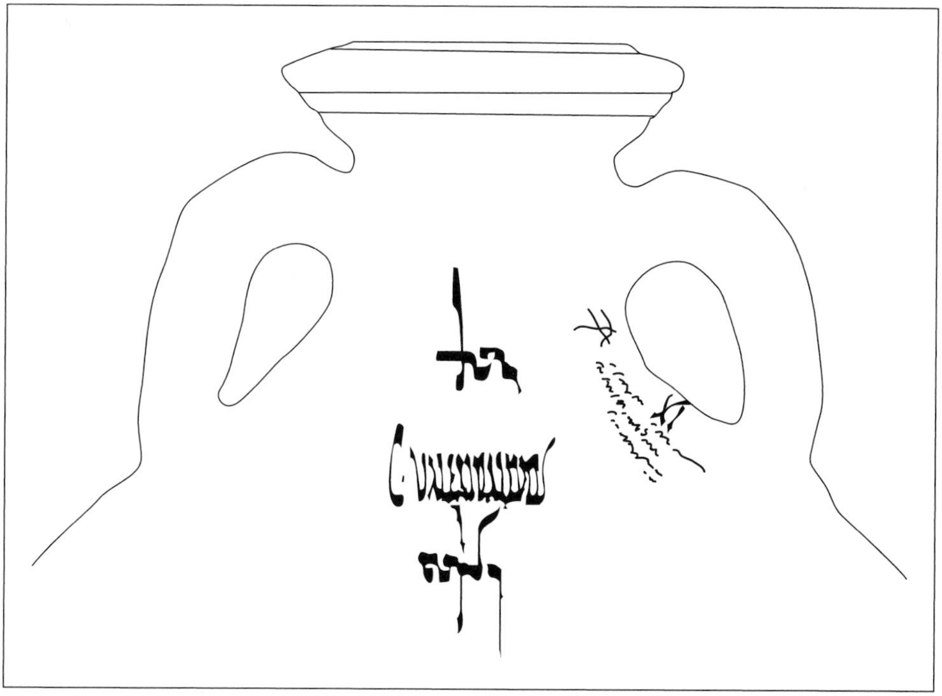

(b)

**Figure 11.9** *(cont.)*

In two particular respects, Roman society seems more similar to our own than all earlier ancient civilizations: One was the pursuit of literature and the widespread use of writing; the other was the use of coinage. As we move toward the electronic age of plastic credit cards and direct transfers, it is becoming easier to imagine a world without coinage. For the Romans, however, with their far-flung empire, coinage was a great facilitator of commerce and finance. Previously, barter had been the main method of buying and selling. Values might be thought of in terms of weights of precious metals like gold and silver. The invention of coinage in Lydia during the seventh century B.C. did not at first change anything very much. The first coins were gold or silver, precious items in themselves, and were not very useful for everyday marketplace transactions. It was rather like carrying a sheaf of $1,000 bills. The big change came when bronze coins began to be used alongside gold and silver, giving rise to a trimetallic (three metal) currency system. This began in the third century B.C., both in Rome and in the as-yet-unconquered cities of the eastern Mediterranean. The principal Roman coin was the *denarius* (plural *denarii*), a silver coin originally weighing 4.5 grams (0.16 ounces). The main bronze coin was the *as* (plural *asses*), a heavier piece that weighed around 55 grams (2 ounces) but was worth only one-sixteenth of a *denarius*. At the other end of the scale was the gold *aureus*, worth 25 *denarii*.

This system of coinage meant that it was possible to go to the marketplace, buy some bread and fish with a silver *denarius,* and receive change in the form of bronze *asses*. Higher-value commodities such as property or land could be purchased with *aurei*. The state or local municipality issued the coins and guaranteed their quality. In the imperial period, one face (the obverse) depicted the head of the reigning emperor, with his name and titles in abbreviated form. On the opposite face (the reverse), there might be a special motto, such as *Libertas restituta* (Liberty restored), a propaganda statement commemorating Emperor Vespasian's victory in the civil war of A.D. 69. This, together with the imperial titles, allows the coin to be dated to a specific year. Coins are an invaluable tool for dating Roman sites.

Roman coins also tell us about the state of the Roman economy. In times of crisis or economic difficulty, the emperors devalued the coinage, either by reducing the weight of the coin or by mixing the silver or gold with the less valuable bronze. During the first and second centuries A.D., when the empire was at the height of its power and prosperity, the coins declined very gradually in weight and quality. In the troubled times of the third century, the coins deteriorated rapidly, although quality improved again when the empire was put on a sounder footing by Diocletian (A.D. 284–305) and Constantine (A.D. 306–337).

## *Literacy and Writing*

Writing was vital to Roman society: the inscriptions on temples and public buildings; the rich literary output of letter writers, poets, and historians, which give us such a vivid glimpse into the thoughts and feelings of Romans themselves; and the fragments of bureaucratic records, which the Romans used to organize their lives and their empire. Although we cannot be sure how many Romans could read and write, the shop signs and electoral graffiti on the walls of Pompeii show that writing was not the mysterious preserve of an educated few, as it had been in early Egypt and Mesopotamia, but was a more widely accepted part of everyday life.

The key works of Roman literature survive almost exclusively in the form of copies made by medieval monks. For Roman writing in everyday use we must look to the snippets on amphorae or walls or to the rather rare remains of actual letters and administrative documents. In the eastern provinces, the main writing material was papyrus (the Egyptian marsh plant from which we get the word *paper*). In the west, parchment and vellum (the hides of cattle, sheep, and goats) or wafer-thin slivers of wood were used instead. These last were so thin they could be folded, and an address might be written on the outer face. A large collection of wooden tablets was found at the Vindolanda Fort near Hadrian's Wall in northern Britain. Papyrus documents (including an early fragment of St. John's Gospel, which may date to the second century A.D.) have survived in the desert sands of Egypt and Syria. These exceptional discoveries make very apparent to us the enormous quantity of Roman writings that have not survived the ravages of time (Box 11.2).

## *Box 11.2 The Vindolanda Tablets*

In 1973, in a modern drainage ditch just outside the fort of Vindolanda on Hadrian's Wall, two thin slivers of wood were found with traces of writing in ink still dimly visible. Chance circumstances of preservation had allowed the survival of Roman writing tablets almost 2,000 years old. In the more than 20 years that have followed that initial discovery, British archaeologist Robin Birley has recovered literally hundreds of wooden writing tablets from this same waterlogged deposit. They date from around A.D. 100 and cover a whole range of subjects, including military reports and personal letters. The ink writing can be read only with the aid of infra-red photography, and it needs a specialist to decipher the spidery handwriting, but as Birley himself has written, "The tablets can provide answers to questions that before we never dared to ask." One of the most evocative is a letter to Sulpicia Lepidina, wife of Flavius Cerialis, the camp commandant at Vindolanda, from her friend Claudia Severa, wife of Aelius Brocchus, the commander of a neighboring fort: "Claudia Severa to her Lepidina, greetings. I send you a warm invitation to come to us on September 11th, for my birthday celebrations, to make my day more enjoyable by your presence. Give my greetings to your Cerialis. My Aelius greets you and your sons. I will expect you sister. Farewell, sister, my dearest soul, as I hope to prosper, and greetings." (Birley, 1994, p. 28) (Figure 11.10).

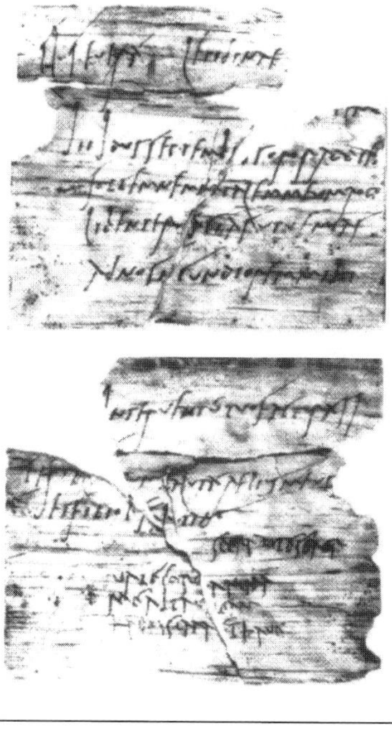

**Figure 11.10** The Lepidina letter (Vindolanda tablet LVII).

## The End of the Ancient World

This chapter has covered several aspects of ancient Rome: the growth of the empire; roads, forts, and frontiers; commerce, coinage, and city life; engineering and literacy. In recent years, archaeologists have also studied the rural landscape, using field survey techniques to plot the location of individual farmsteads and villas. The latter were a regular feature of the Roman landscape, the center of a rural estate that might be worked by dependent laborers or slaves. Some Roman villas were simple farmhouses. Others were palatial country residences, decorated with frescoes and mosaics and equipped with luxurious gardens and steam baths. Drainage, a water supply, and underfloor heating were standard items in these grandiose dwellings and were often found even in relatively modest houses (though not those of rural laborers or of the urban proletariat). All this prosperity depended on secure frontiers—the famous *Pax Romana* (Roman peace)—and on economic prosperity. For the first two centuries A.D. this security and wealth endured, but during the third century the empire became embroiled in internal and external crises. There was civil war as rival emperors were proclaimed by the powerful frontier armies. Successful emperors were often killed by their own disgruntled troops. Groups of provinces tried to break away and become independent empires. At the same time, the frontiers themselves were breached by a whole range of foreign enemies, from Persians in the east to Goths and Germans in the north and west. Vital reforms were instituted at the end of the third and beginning of the fourth centuries by the emperors Diocletian and Constantine. They improved the coinage, strengthened the armies, and restored a measure of peace and stability. But the nature of the empire was changing, and Constantine accelerated the process by making Christianity the state religion.

The Roman Empire never really collapsed; it merely transformed itself into something else. Around A.D. 400 it was divided officially into two halves, each ruled by a separate emperor. The eastern empire, with its capital at Constantinople (modern Istanbul in Turkey), survived for another thousand years as the Byzantine Empire (Byzantium being the original name of Constantinople). The western empire, by contrast, collapsed in the course of the fifth century and became a mosaic of independent kingdoms, controlled by Germanic leaders who became the first kings of medieval Europe.

Thus did the ancient world come to an end in the West. The last Roman emperor was pensioned off in A.D. 476, to spend the rest of his life in comfortable retirement on the Bay of Naples. But while Roman rule fragmented and vanished, many of the key features of Roman life persisted in Western civilization, even to the present day. The Roman language, Latin, is the origin not only of modern Italian but also of French, Spanish, and Romanian. Roman law is the basis of most Western legal systems. The stately colonnades of Roman architecture, reinterpreted through the Renaissance, decorate many public buildings in Europe and the Americas, including the White House and the Capitol at Washington, DC.

## Summary

The Roman Empire was one of the greatest empires of the ancient world, uniting Greece, Egypt, North Africa, and the Near East with the Celtic lands of Europe under a single system of government. The population of the empire as a whole was probably around 50 million, small by modern standards but enormous compared to the average Greek or Mesopotamian city-state. This polyglot, multiethnic empire was controlled and protected by the highly trained Roman army and the well-defined and carefully patrolled imperial frontiers. Within the frontiers, a network of roads and sea-lanes held the empire together, joining the cities to one another and to the centers of government. Trade—especially maritime trade—grew and prospered, but most inhabitants of the empire were engaged in agricultural activities rather than manufacture or commerce. Cities, a key feature of Roman life, provide many of the best remains and monuments of the Roman period. The legacy also lives on more directly in language, in legal codes, and in the religion that the Romans first opposed, then later espoused as the official religion of the empire: Christianity.

## Guide to Further Reading

One of the best general accounts of Roman history is M. Cary and H. H. Scullard, *A History of Rome to the Reign of Constantine,* 3rd ed. (London: Macmillan, 1975). T. J. Cornell and J. Matthews, *Atlas of the Roman World* (Oxford: Phaidon, 1982) is also useful. Chris Scarre, *The Penguin Historical Atlas of Ancient Rome* (Harmondsworth, England: Penguin, 1995) is a shorter account, based also on maps and concentrating on the imperial period.

The origins and early development of Rome from a historical and archaeological viewpoint are discussed by T. J. Cornell, *The Beginnings of Rome* (London: Routledge, 1995) and R. Ross Holloway, *The Archaeology of Early Rome and Latium* (London: Routledge, 1994).

The literature on the Roman Empire is immense, and only a small selection of general references can be given here. The transitional period from the late republic to the early empire is covered by two excellent accounts: Sir Ronald Syme's classic, *The Roman Revolution* (Oxford: Oxford University Press, 1939) and H. H. Scullard, *From the Gracchi to Nero* (London and New York: Routledge, 1982). A good general history is Colin Wells, *The Roman Empire,* 2nd ed. (London: Fontana, 1992). Many aspects of Roman archaeology, including frontier studies, are covered in John Wacher, ed., *The Roman World,* 2 vols. (London: Routledge, 1987). For more specialized topics this can be supplemented by Kevin Greene, *Archaeology of the Roman Economy* (London: Batsford, 1986); Yann Le Bohec, *The Imperial Roman Army* (London: Batsford, 1994); and D. P. S. Peacock and D. F. Williams, *Amphorae and the Roman Economy* (London: Longman, 1986). Population estimates for Rome itself are discussed by Glenn R. Storey, "The Population of Ancient Rome," *Antiquity* 71 (1997): 966–978. Recent work in the heart of ancient Rome is reviewed by James Packer in "Report from Rome: The Imperial Fora, A Retrospective," *American Journal of Archaeology* 101 (1997): 330–337.

Excellent studies of Roman impact in individual provinces are Greg Woolf, *Becoming Roman: The Origins of Provincial Civilization in Gaul* (Cambridge: Cambridge University Press, 1998); Martin Millett, *The Romanization of Britain: An Essay in Archaeological Interpretation* (Cambridge: Cambridge University Press, 1990); Susan E. Alcock, *Graecia Capta: The Landscapes of Roman Greece* (Cambridge and New York: Cambridge University Press, 1993); and Warwick Ball, *Rome in the East* (London: Routledge, 2000). Diversity and identity are the subject of the essays in Ray Laurence and Joanne Berry, eds., *Cultural Identity in the Roman Empire* (London: Routledge, 2001).

For Roman architecture, two standard authorities are J. B. Ward-Perkins, *Roman Imperial Architecture* (Harmondsworth, England: Penguin, 1991) and William L. MacDonald, *The Architecture of the*

*Roman Empire*, 2 vols. (New Haven, CT: Yale University Press, 1982 and 1986). For sculpture, painting, and mosaic, see Donald Strong, *Roman Art*, rev. Roger Ling (Harmondsworth, England: Penguin, 1988) and Roger Ling's own *Roman Painting* (Cambridge: Cambridge University Press, 1991).

For the later Roman Empire, see A. H. M. Jones, *The Later Roman Empire: A Social, Economic and Administrative Survey* (Oxford: Blackwell, 1964) and Averil Cameron, *The Later Roman Empire* (London: Fontana, 1993). Klaus Randsborg, *The First Millennium* A.D. *in Europe and the Mediterranean* (Cambridge: Cambridge University Press, 1991) sets these developments within the broader European context. The transformation of Roman art from Classical to early Christian is discussed by Jas Elsner in *Imperial Rome and Christian Triumph: The Art of the Roman Empire A.D. 100–450* (Oxford: Oxford University Press, 1998). Finally, for the early history of Christianity to the reign of Constantine, a readable account is Robin Lane Fox, *Pagans and Christians* (New York: Knopf, 1986).

# PART V

# Northeast Africa and Asia

Immediately after this harbor begins the country of Arabia, extending lengthwise far down the Erythraean Sea. It is inhabited by a variety of tribes speaking languages that differ, some to a certain extent, some totally. . . . They plunder any who stray from a course down the middle and fall among them, and they enslave any who are rescued by them from shipwreck.

The ship captain Hippalus, by plotting the location of the ports of trade and the configuration of the sea, was the first to discover the route over open water. . . .

Beyond this region, by now at the northernmost point, where the sea ends somewhere on the outer fringe, there is a very great inland city called Thina from which silk floss, yarn, and cloth are shipped. . . . It is not easy to get to Thina; for rarely do people come from it, and only a few. . . .*

## Introduction: The Erythraean Sea

The Roman Empire was an omnivorous consumer of exotic luxuries, many of them—like drugs, gems, silks, and spices—from India and lands beyond. By the time of Christ, East and West were joined by increasingly complex webs of economic interconnectedness, through caravan routes that linked China with Iran over the Silk Road of central Asia and India with the Red Sea and Egypt by routes across the Indian Ocean. These land and sea routes had developed over many centuries.

The gems and spices of the East commanded enormous prices in the markets of the eastern Mediterranean. Roman merchants had nothing to trade that could equal the value of these products, so they paid for them in gold and

*Lionel Casson, trans., *The Periplus of the Erythraean Sea* (Princeton, NJ: Princeton University Press, 1989), pp. 63, 87, 91.

silver. The result was a net flow of precious metal from the Mediterranean to India, which caused concern to the Roman government as early as the reign of Tiberius (A.D. 14–37). The Roman historian Tacitus states that in A.D. 22, Tiberius contemplated measures to control luxurious living among the rich; he wrote to the Senate, complaining of "the specially female extravagance by which, for the sake of jewels, our wealth is transported to alien or hostile countries." In the reign of Nero, the Elder Pliny, a Roman statesman and writer, estimated that the annual trade deficit between Rome and India totaled the enormous sum of 60 million denarii (the denarius was the Roman silver coin).

The growth of the Indian Ocean trade linked together a number of separate trade networks. One of these was the famous incense trade. Frankincense and myrrh are the aromatic resins of trees that grow only in restricted areas of southern Arabia and Somalia. Frankincense was extensively used in temples, especially in Egypt, during the last few centuries B.C. Myrrh was an important component in the embalming of Egyptian corpses. The growing demand for frankincense and myrrh led to the development of lucrative trade between the eastern Mediterranean and the so-called incense states of southern Arabia, such as Saba (Sheba) and Hadramaut. At the other end of the network were trade routes bringing materials like tortoiseshell from Malaysia to southern India and Sri Lanka.

Even in Sumerian times, merchant ships coasted along age-old inshore routes, sailing from port to port in the Persian Gulf, along the southern shores of Arabia, into the Persian Gulf, and down to the west coast of India. The coasting routes of the Indian Ocean were like desert caravan tracks to those who plied them, as predictable and unchanging as the seasons of the year, whatever the political conditions ashore. With their lateen sails, short masts, and huge yards that could lie close to the wind, an Arabian dhow (sailing ship) leaving the Red Sea would sail on the same tack against the northeast monsoon for days along the desolate shores of southern Arabia. Once well to windward, the skipper would head offshore and ride the northeast monsoon to Indian shores, the Indus, the Malabar coast, and even Sri Lanka at the southern tip of India. Then, some time late in the first millennium B.C., Indian skippers mastered the secrets of the monsoon winds. Throughout the summer months, from June to September, these winds blow steadily across the Indian Ocean from the southwest. In November they reverse their direction and until March blow from the northeast.

Knowledge of the monsoon winds passed from father to son, from ship owner to apprentice. Both Arabians and Indians kept their knowledge to themselves, as mariners usually do. Thus, the monsoon cycle remained a closely held secret until an Indian ship was wrecked and its skipper brought to Alexandria. With his help, a Greek adventurer, Eudoxus of Cyzicus, made two journeys from the Red Sea to India around 115 B.C. It was either on this expedition or soon afterward that a Greek named Hippalus worked out a strategy for much faster, direct voyaging. Instead of following the coast of Arabia, he rode in August the rough and boisterous southwest monsoon directly to India's Malabar coast. The much gentler northeast monsoon of winter carried him home a few months later. Hippalus's strategy made it possible for large sailing vessels to make a circular voyage from the Red Sea to India and back within a year.

In about A.D. 70, an anonymous Egyptian-Greek captain compiled *The Periplus of the Erythraean Sea*, a set of sailing directions to the Indian Ocean (Erythraean means "red"). The *Periplus* is a much compressed work that has been described as a trade directory combined with a volume of the British *Admiralty Pilot*. Its unknown but well-traveled author describes ports and headlands, the inhabitants of coastal towns and villages, and the trade to be conducted at each landfall. The manual begins from the Egyptian ports of Myos Hormos and Berenice and first guides the traveler down the African coast as far as Zanzibar. We learn that Arabian traders sailed far south down the East African coast as far as Zanzibar to trade for "a great amount of ivory . . . ; rhinoceros horn; best quality tortoise shell; a little nautilus shell." More important by far, however, was the Indian Ocean trade. The *Periplus* describes the ports of southern Arabia—Muza, Eudaemon Arabia (Aden), and Qana—and then follows the route to the west coast of India. The main ports there are Barbarikon, near the mouth of the Indus River; Barygaza, near the mouth of the Narmada River; and Muziris and Nelykanda, in the south of the peninsula. These southern ports could be reached by sailing directly across the Indian Ocean, using the monsoon winds. It was there that the most exotic goods were to be found: locally produced pepper and cinnamon, diamonds and sapphires, as well as luxuries brought there for resale from lands to the east—Chinese silks and Malaysian tortoiseshell.

At the time of the *Periplus*, the Erythraean Sea still lay at the very boundaries of the classical world, but the peoples living on its shores were now connected by an intricate web of land and ocean routes. Downwind sailing ships carried the ivory, rhinoceros horn (prized as an aphrodisiac), and tortoiseshell of Africa to distant lands. They transported incense and spices to the heart of the Mediterranean world and cotton cloth and fine silks to city bazaars. The domestication of the camel (see Chapter 12) and the Indian Ocean's monsoon winds linked the Mediterranean world, Asia, and tropical Africa in new and lasting economic relationships. They were among the catalysts that fashioned a new world economic system from the smaller, more regional trading networks of earlier times. Fleets of ships that carried Greek, Syrian, or Italian merchants set off each summer from the Red Sea ports, making the crossing to India and then waiting in Indian ports for the winter monsoon to begin before making the return voyage. The profits were enormous.

In archaeological terms the extent of the trade is manifest in the quantities of Roman gold and silver coins that have been found in southern India. Still more graphic was the excavation by British archaeologist Sir Mortimer Wheeler of an actual Roman trading colony on the Indian coast at Arikamedu near Pondicherry, on the southeastern side of the peninsula. Imported items show that it was already in contact with the West in the second century B.C., but around the time of Emperor Augustus (27 B.C.–A.D. 14) the local port was transformed by the establishment of the Roman merchant colony. The foreigners imported amphorae of wine, olive oil, and spicy fish sauce from the Mediterranean. They also used fashionable Italian tableware.

Roman maritime trade with India and the East flourished throughout the first and second centuries A.D. Soon Greek and Roman traders were not only exploring the coastal areas but penetrating inland as well. They visited the courts of Indian rulers, and these rulers in return sent official embassies, which were received by Roman emperors such as Hadrian and Antoninus Pius. Merchants born in the Roman Empire came in touch with people from distant lands far to the east, with Buddhists and Hindus, who told stories of fabulous countries beyond the eastern ocean, such as the island of Chryse (Malaysia)—the golden, most eastern extremity of the inhabited world, lying under the rising sun itself—or of the very great inland city called Thina (China).

The establishment of the Indian Ocean trade routes brought South and Southeast Asia, as well as southern China, into regular contact with the Western world. And this ever more elaborate web of interconnectedness affected the lives of individuals and states living thousands of miles apart. The unchanging cycles of the monsoon winds were the Silk Road of southern latitudes, one of the catalysts that, centuries later, ushered in the development of the world economic systems of today. The civilizations described in Chapters 12 to 14 were part of the new world of the monsoon winds.

## Guide to Further Reading

Lionel Casson, trans., *The Periplus of the Erythraean Sea* (Princeton, NJ: Princeton University Press, 1989) is a superb analysis of the Periplus.

*Chapter 12*

# Northeast Africa: Kush, Meroe, and Aksum

Nubian soldiers march in the tomb of a Middle Kingdom Egyptian official, Meshti.

*The aromatic smell of wood charcoal hangs heavily over the arid landscape, light clouds of wood smoke mantling the tall clay furnaces where the bellows snore. The only sound is the monotonous "chuff," "chuff," of the smiths' goatskin bellows, which continues day and night throughout the smelt. Steep piles of iron slag surround the furnaces, which are open to the prevailing winds so that the natural draft helps to keep the temperature high. Each furnace has its own team of workers, led by an experienced smith who watches the fire closely, adding charcoal from the heaps of charred acacia wood nearby. A smelt takes over seven hours of intense firing, with teams of bellowsmen rotating at 20-minute intervals so that the fire is always red-hot. At last, the smith is satisfied. The bellows cease as he breaks open the mouth of the furnace and rakes out a glowing lump of slag about the size of a soccer ball. The sweating workers rest as he examines the cooling lump. They know that in a few hours their labors will start all over again as a new smelt begins.*

The iron smelters of Meroe lived deep in Nubia, a land far up the Nile River, at the very fringes of the Classical world. "When you have passed this portion of the river in the space of 40 days, you go aboard another boat and proceed by water for 12 days more, at the end of which time you reach a great city called Meroe, which is said to be the capital of the other Ethiopians." The Greek traveler Herodotus visited Egypt during the fifth century B.C. He never traveled above the First Cataract but was profoundly curious about Nubia, the arid country upstream of Egypt's southern frontier. He questioned the Egyptians about the mysterious land from which they obtained gold, ivory, and semiprecious stones.

To the Egyptians, Nubia (perhaps from the Egyptian word for gold, *nebew*), "the Land of Kush" in southern Egypt and the Sudan, was the home of the Ethiopians, the "burnt faces." The Arabic word *Sudan* (from Beled es Sudan, "the country of the blacks") means much the same thing. The Egyptians had little respect for their Nubian neighbors. Government scribes labeled Nubia "miserable" or "abominable." As archaeologist William Adams remarks, "For millennia Egypt treated [Nubia] as a kind of private hunting preserve for human and animal game." But archaeology and historical records show that Egypt and Nubia, while linguistically and racially distinct, were linked to each other by commercial, and sometimes political, ties for more than 3,000 years. For a short period, between 730 and 663 B.C., Nubian kings actually ruled over the land of the pharaohs.

Few scholars except the most ardent Afrocentrists (see Chapter 4) now believe that Egyptian civilization developed from Nubian or Ethiopian roots; a large-scale state-organized society appeared in Egypt much earlier than in the south.

This chapter describes the distinctive Nubian and Ethiopian kingdoms, which developed upstream quite independently and in partial response to developments downstream.

## Nubia and the Middle Nile

Above the First Cataract at Aswan, the floodplain landscape of green fields and shimmering irrigation canals gives way to a harsh, rocky terrain, where the desert presses down to the river. Nubia was desolate and inhospitable to strangers, a land of arid ravines and rocky cliffs, where travel, even along the river, was never easy. The desert formed a natural barrier between Egypt and Nubia, but people on either side of the frontier were in regular contact from the earliest times. Ancient trade routes followed the river and led to mineral-rich outcrops deep in the desert. Most farming communities lay at the mouths of large wadis, where alluvial soils were thickest. The local people adopted many Egyptian customs, although there was not enough farmland to attract dense agricultural settlement or to support large cities.

Nubia straddled a long and narrow strip of sometimes fertile land that begins at the First Cataract and ends at the confluence of the Blue and White Nile near Khartoum, far to the south in the Sudan (Figure 12.1). The most fertile lands

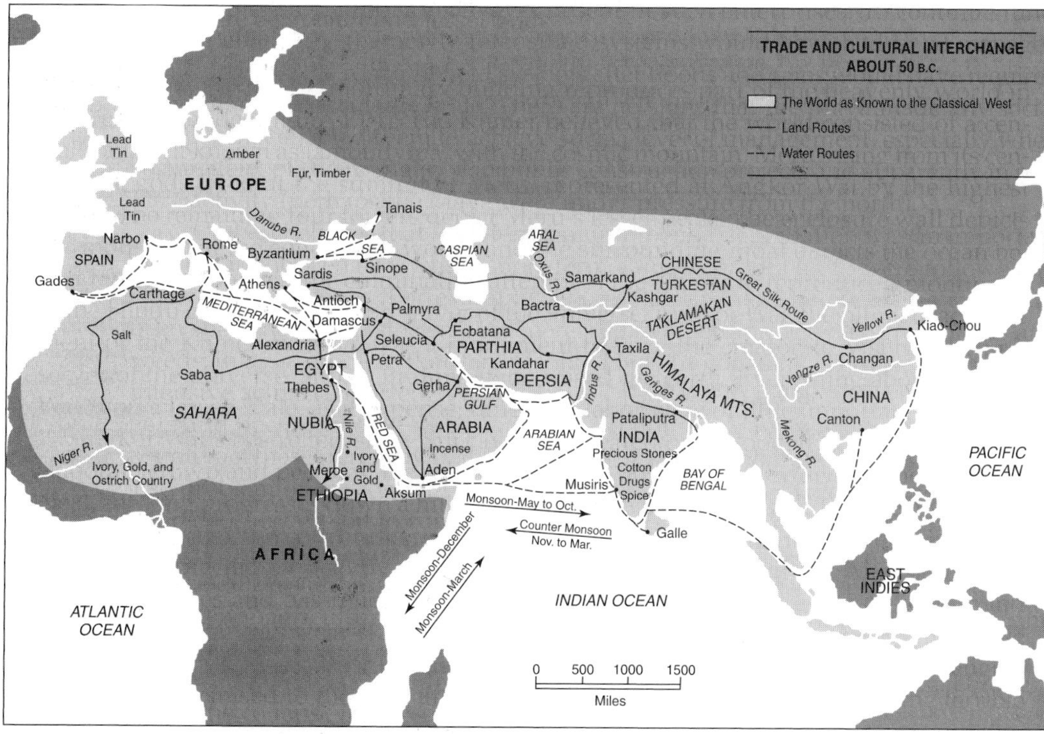


**Figure 12.1** Map of archaeological sites and states mentioned in Chapter 12 and major trade routes across the Indian Ocean.

lie between the Third and Fourth Cataracts, the famous Dongola Reach, where the Nile passes through featureless, sandstone landscape, flooding the surrounding lowlands each summer, just as it did in Egypt far downstream. Dongola was home to some of the earliest Nubian kingdoms. Far upstream, desolate country gives way to the Shendi Reach. There the river flows though semiarid grasslands, where people grazed their herds of cattle for thousands of years. Shendi ends at the junction of the Blue and White Nile. The city of Meroe flourished in this reach at the time of Christ.

## *"The Shadow of Egypt" (3500–2100 B.C.)*

In 3500 B.C., sedentary farming cultures flourished along the Middle Nile, where people lived in reed and grass hamlets, anchored to their gardens on the nearby floodplain. They were humble folk, buried in desert cemeteries, where they crouched in small, shallow graves and were often wrapped in linen shrouds. These were not self-sufficient communities. The river, in its more tranquil reaches, was a natural highway between neighbors and between communities near and far. By the time Egypt became a state, the Nubians were exchanging foodstuffs, ivory, and other exotic commodities along the river, among themselves, and with the Egyptians living below the First Cataract. Even before 3000 B.C., what William Adams calls "the shadow of Egypt" was falling across Nubia. Its raw materials were irresistible to a civilization where wealth went hand-in-hand with divine kingship.

The Old Kingdom pharaohs sent their armies to subdue Nubia and secure their southern frontier. They called Nubia Ta-Sethy, "the land of the bow," a reference to the expert archers pitted against them. As the pharaohs' armies raided, so parties of Egyptian prospectors traveled far and wide through Nubia in search of minerals and semiprecious stones. Each party probably consisted of a few soldiers and one officer, a scribe and overseer, and a small number of expert miners, who knew the telltale signs of precious metals. Some Nubian diorite (a black rock) was used for the flagstones of Khufu's mortuary temple at the Pyramids of Giza (Box 4.1). By the end of the Old Kingdom in 2134 B.C., Nubia had become part of the vast trade network that linked the pharaohs with the Near East and with Arabia and the coasts of the Red Sea (Box 12.1).

Thanks to excavations by Harvard archaeologist George Reisner in the early years of this century, we know that the Nubians made characteristic black and white incised bowls and red-surfaced pots. Such unimaginatively named "C-Group" vessels occur all the way from Lower Nubia, many miles into the desert on either bank of the Nile, and as far south as the Ethiopian highlands. The densest populations flourished along the Dongola Reach, ruled by village headmen who owned large herds. Nubian society was not hierarchical, like that of the pharaohs, but it had great disparities in wealth and power.

The Middle Kingdom pharaohs established a permanent Egyptian presence in Nubia by the simple expedient of fortifying the strategic Nile reaches below the Second Cataract. They built a series of forts along the Dongola Reach, principal among them Buhen, designed to guard the junctions of key trade routes and to

## Box 12.1 Voices: Egyptians in Nubia

The Egyptian pharaohs depended heavily on Nubia for raw materials, especially gold and tropical products. In later centuries, they manned their armies with Nubian mercenaries, who were famous as bowmen. The Old Kingdom pharaohs raided Nubia and campaigned against rebellious tribes. Their generals returned with plentiful prisoners and many head of cattle. The process was called "setting the fear of Horus [the pharaoh] among the southern foreign lands, to pacify [them]." Many campaigns were little more than slave raids, which brought back as many as several thousand captives and depopulated Lower Nubia. One fourth-dynasty graffito refers to as many as 17,000 Nubian prisoners of war. Once in Egypt, they were set to work on the land or on construction projects and enrolled in the military. Carefully organized prospecting expeditions brought back ebony and ivory, incense, myrrh, wild animal skins, and semiprecious stones.

Harkhuf, a sixth-dynasty Governor of Upper Egypt, led no less than four trading expeditions into Nubia. His four trips southward took him not up the Nile, but along the so-called Oasis Road. The overland route led from Middle Egypt through a chain of four desert oases before regaining the Nile valley at Toshke in Nubia. Harkhuf and his parties traveled on hundreds of donkeys, which enabled him to complete one successful journey in seven months and to travel on other occasions deep into Nubia to the kingdom of Yam, which was centered on the town of Kerma south of the Third Cataract. He exchanged gifts with the ruler of Yam and returned with "three hundred donkeys laden with incense, ebony . . . elephant tusks, throw sticks, and all sorts of good products." His entourage also included a dancing dwarf. Harkhuf had sent a courier ahead to the court reporting on his doings. The youthful pharaoh Pepi II wrote back in his own hand in great excitement: "Come north to the residence at once! Hurry and bring with you this pygmy whom you brought from the land of the horizon-dwellers live, hale, and hearty, for the dances of the god, to gladden the heart. . . ." When traveling on the Nile, men were to guard him lest he fell into the water. Twenty were to watch over him as he slept in camp lest he come to harm. "My majesty wishes to see this pygmy more than the gifts of the mine-land [Sinai] and of Punt [the Red Sea lands]."

The Old Kingdom pharaohs treated Nubia and its people with disdain and their lands as something to be exploited, but they never attempted conquest or colonization above the First Cataract. The Middle Kingdom pharaohs pressed southward in their ambition to control the increasingly lucrative ivory and gold trade. The Nubians were formidable enemies. Many of their commanders and soldiers had long served bravely in the Egyptian army and had taken the measure of their enemy. The pharaoh Senusret III (1878–1841 B.C.) fortified Lower Nubia heavily with a row of fortresses that stretched from the First Cataract to Semna at the southern end of the strategic Second Cataract region. He described the Nubians as cowards, " not people he [Senusret] respects, they are wretches, craven-hearted." The inscriptions tell of the women and children he enslaved, the cattle he slaughtered, the crops he burned. To encourage his successors, he set up a statue of himself "at this border which my majesty has made so that you

*(Cont.)*

maintain it and so that you fight for it." The royal statue glowered at a row of imposing fortresses that stretched downstream as far as Elephantine at the very gates of Egypt itself. The most impressive of all was Buhen, at a critical strategic point at the foot of the Second Cataract, a vast mud-brick construction that had much of the sophistication and impregnability of a European medieval castle.

During the New Kingdom, Nubia became an Egyptian colony, but not without some bloody engagements. A veteran soldier named Ahmose, son of Abana, accompanied the pharaoh Ahmose (no relation) on a Nubian campaign. He recalled: "Now when his majesty had slain the nomads of Asia, he sailed south . . . to destroy the Nubian Bowmen. His majesty made great slaughter among them, and I brought spoil from there: two living men and three hands. Then I was rewarded with gold once again, and two female slaves were given to me. His majesty journeyed north, his heart rejoicing in valor and victory. He had conquered southerners and northerners." In 1522 B.C., the pharaoh Thutmose I, an experienced soldier, campaigned vigorously in rebellious Nubia. He fought his enemies at Buhen, by then occupied by Nubians. "His majesty became enraged like a leopard. His majesty shot, and his first arrow pierced the chest of that foe." One can imagine the heat and choking dust, the swarms of deadly arrows shot at close range with deadly effect. Men clasp arrow shafts in their chests and choke to death. Others turn and run, only to be felled by showers of missiles in the back. Then the fierce war cries of the charioteers and the drumming of hooves as the pharaoh orders a charge into the churning Nubian regiments. As the Egyptians count their casualties and round up hundreds of prisoners, crows and vultures circle overhead. Thutmose sailed north laden with booty, with the rebel leader's body pinned head downward to his bow. (Quotes in this box from Lichtheim, 1973, pp. 151ff; Lichtheim, 1976, pp. 212–213, 216)

ensure the safe passage of goods up and down the river. Further south, the commerce was in the hands of powerful Nubian rulers, whose territory extended far upstream to Kerma and beyond. This was the fabled Land of Kush, so rich in gold and ivory that its fame spread throughout the Mediterranean world.

## *Kerma: The Lords of Kush (c. 1570–1528 B.C.)*

The Nubian chieftains of Kush owed their power and wealth to their strategic position astride a long stretch of navigable and fertile river valley. When the pharaohs were strong and political conditions in Egypt were stable, the rulers of Kush kept within their boundaries. But when pharaonic control weakened and soldiers were withdrawn from the Second Cataract forts, the Nubians extended their influence upstream, even occupying some of the abandoned fortresses. This is exactly what happened in the sixteenth century B.C., when the Asian Hyksos ruled Egypt from the far north.

Kush's rulers lived at Kerma in the heart of the Dongola Reach, where a natural basin with fertile soils floods every year. By 1570 B.C., between 2,000 and 3,000 people lived in what had become a small town. The closely packed settlement had no formal layout. Narrow alleys twisted and turned between small dwellings. Most were one- or two-room mud-brick houses. One common design had two rooms on either side of an interior courtyard, with a small courtyard outside, where food was stored and cooked, cattle penned, and pottery fired in special pits.

Charles Bonnet of the University of Geneva has excavated at Kerma for more than ten years, uncovering not only much of the town but also a 61-meter-long (200-foot-long) palace with a throne room and other chambers. Another complex of buildings serviced the riverside harbor with warehouses. The entire town was fortified with elaborate defenses—wide, massive walls, protected with rectangular, projecting watchtowers, all surrounded with dry ditches to prevent undermining. The four gates, placed at the cardinal points, were flanked by defense walls. Although Kerma's defenses were inadequate against professional New Kingdom armies, they were highly sophisticated for the time (Box 12.2).

In their heyday, the Kerma rulers enjoyed great wealth. They were interred under large burial mounds near the town, most of them about 91 meters (300 feet) across, each with an internal chamber. The three largest mounds had a remarkable internal structure of long, parallel mud-brick walls that ran across the tumulus. It is as if they were a framework for the mound itself. The important personage buried in the tomb was placed on a bed with his weapons and personal possessions. Dozens of sacrificial victims lay both in the chamber and in a corridor that ran across the mound (see Figure 12.3). George Reisner estimated that as many as 400 people perished with one ruler, one of the largest number of sacrificial victims on record anywhere.

All this wealth came from trade connections with desert peoples and communities living much further upstream. The lords of Kush maintained regular trading connections with the Hyksos court in the faraway Delta, employing a small cadre of Egyptian officials to oversee the trade on their behalf. But Kush was an entirely African kingdom, created by local chiefs who seized the economic and political initiative when their more powerful neighbors faltered. They acquired many Egyptian artifacts and perhaps some of their religious beliefs and customs, but they presided over the earliest black African state.

## *King's Son of Kush (1528–1100 B.C.)*

Around 1535 B.C., New Kingdom King Ahmose pounced on Nubia and refortified the river, apparently in the face of little resistance. This time, Egypt needed Nubia's wealth to support its nobility and to finance ambitious public works at home, as well as military campaigns in distant lands. As the era of Egyptian imperialism dawned, Ahmose's successors crushed the rulers of Kerma, occupied Kush, and extended Egyptian rule to the Fourth Cataract. Nubia became, to all intents and purposes, an Egyptian dependency. From trade monopolies organized from afar, the New Kingdom pharaohs turned to direct exploitation of their new possession. The Egyptian-appointed Viceroy of Kush, known as "The King's Son of Kush," was a powerful official, responsible for delivering a vast annual tribute to Thebes.

## Box 12.2 Kerma

In its heyday around 1550 B.C., Kerma was a colorful and powerful kingdom, with a strong economy based on agriculture, cattle, and a growing gold trade with the north. The town covered about 26 hectares (65 acres), a striking indigenous metropolis. Its ruler controlled all of Lower and Upper Nubia. He lived in the fortified city core, protected by massive 30-foot mud-brick walls with four gateways and projecting, rectangular towers. A huge white temple (*deffufa*) rose high above the walls, its white pylons visible from miles away (Figure 12.2). Kerma's temple covered an area of 325 square meters (3,500 square feet), a large building even by Egyptian standards.

Superficially, the *deffufa* resembled an Egyptian temple, but the interior reflects very different religious beliefs. It also housed workshops for the production of prestige goods. Instead of entering at the front, a side entrance and a stairway lead to a small sacrificial chamber, where goats and sheep were offered on a circular marble altar. Another stairway climbs to the roof, where outdoor rituals, perhaps for the sun-god, were once performed. A 5-meter (16-foot) mud-brick wall surrounded the religious precincts, enclosing not only the *deffufa* but small shrines and living quarters for the priests. Perhaps 2,000 people lived within the larger fortifications, in the royal palace and the dwellings of the nobility.

Kerma's ruler originally held audience in a large circular hut with mud-brick walls that stood to a height of at least 10 meters (30 feet). A conical thatched roof covered the structure, later abandoned in favor of a rectangular mud-brick palace with an imposing audience hall where the ruler sat on a dias to conduct official business. A great deal of trading activity centered on this large complex, aligned with the main temple entrance,

**Figure 12.2** The *deffufa* at Kerma, Sudan.

as if the ruler's public appearances were carefully orchestrated. The palace had large storage chambers and an archive room, where archaeologists unearthed thousands of clay seal blanks, used to mark goods or to close messages.

Kerma was a sprawling city, a walled community surrounded by clusters of much smaller settlements. The central precincts housed a diverse population, not only the ruler and his family and court, but also officials, soldiers, and a hierarchy of priests, as well as a large population of commoners, most of whom lived outside the city walls. Its artisans were expert in gold and ivory and created some of the finest clay vessels ever made in Africa: red and black colored, and of eggshell thinness. The city's houses reflect a complex, wealthy society, with many two-room dwellings fronted by a courtyard and others with more complicated ground plans. Vast enclosures between the city and the river housed enormous numbers of animals stored for food. Excavators have even found the imprints of cattle hooves in the soil! Lines of small villages once flourished along now dry Nile channels in the hinterland around the capital. They grew grain for Kerma and stored it in special structures with raised wooden floors.

The vast Kerma cemetery about 3 kilometers (2 miles) east of the city provides a fascinating window into Nubian society of the day. More than 30,000 people lie there. Commoners were buried with few possessions. Wealthier members of society lay on well-made wooden beds, provided with a box of personal possessions such as bronze razors and stone vessels for eye pigment or ointment. They wore linen and leather garments, occasionally caps decorated with mica ornaments. Four exceptionally large royal burial mounds lie along the southern edge of the cemetery associated with mud-brick mortuary shrines. Averaging about 88 meters (290 feet) across, they once housed the royal corpse, laid out in all its finery on a magnificent bed. Lavish supplies of locally made inlaid furniture, weapons, and pottery accompanied each ruler. The mourners lined the area outside the burial chamber with statues and statuettes of Egyptian pharaohs and officials, plundered from abandoned fortress towns and cemeteries now under Nubian control.

On the day of the funeral, large crowds gathered at the great burial mound, where narrow corridors led to the burial chamber. A long procession of mourners walked to the tomb carrying offerings amidst great wailing and chanting. Trusted priests and officials closed the doors of the burial chamber. The ruler's attendants, his entire harem in their best finery, their children, and dozens of slaves filed into the earthen passageway and crowded tightly together close to the burial chamber. Excavator George Reisner tells the tale: "The cries and all movements cease. The signal is given. The crowd of people assembled for the feast, now waiting ready, cast the earth from their baskets upon the still, but living victims on the floor and rush away for more. The frantic confusion and haste of the multitude is easy to imagine" (Figure 12.3). Death came quickly to many of the victims, who pressed their hands over their faces or their heads between their elbows. "At that last moment we know from their attitudes in death that a rustle of fear passed between them and that in some cases there was a spasm of physical agony." The passageway filled, the assembled crowd enjoyed a great feast of beef from the oxen slaughtered to accompany the dead lord.

*(Cont.)*

**Figure 12.3** Kerma royal burial mound. The people are hastening to complete the mound after the interment.

Considerable debate surrounds the nature of Egyptian imperialism in Nubia. As archaeologist Bruce Trigger, Egyptologist Paul Frandsen, and others have pointed out, the people of Nubia, including Kerma, were considered barbarians by their northern neighbors. The Middle Kingdom pharaohs had garrisoned Nubia, but Egyptian culture made few inroads into local communities, perhaps a reaction to military occupation. After the withdrawal of the garrisons, however, there was more peaceful interaction and Egyptian technology came into widespread use. At the same time, many Nubians served as mercenaries in Egyptian armies, fighting against the alien Hyksos rulers of lower Egypt. By the time the New Kingdom pharaohs descended on Nubia, much of the population was more amenable to integration into Egyptian social and economic systems. But the pharaohs were concerned with the security of their frontiers, with the need to eliminate the threat of a powerful Kerma state, so they colonized Nubia and made it part of Egypt.

Everyone agrees that Nubia effectively became a province of Egypt. The destruction of Kerma made strategic sense to the pharaohs, but why did they incorporate Nubia into Egypt, something their predecessors never did? Archaeologist Stuart Smith hypothesizes that the colonization and acculturation of Nubia made good sense to the New Kingdom Egyptians. Nubia's conquerors intensified agriculture and herding and increased food surpluses dramatically. These they reinvested in a local temple and estate system modeled on that in Egypt itself. Both Egyptian officials and settlers and coopted local leaders ran this system, while the latter's sons were held as hostages in Egypt and educated as Egyptian nobles. As the generations passed, the population became increasingly acculturated. The farmers and commoners became impoverished, just as they were downstream, while the Egyptian-born and Nubian elite enjoyed increasing wealth. The reinvestment of resources into the maintenance of the local economic system was very cost-effective, for it paid for most if not all of the infrastructure required to extract minerals and run the trade routes that carried Nubia's exotic goods to Egypt and the wider world. These were the goods that were vital to Egypt's foreign policy in the Near East and for the maintenance of its rulers and nobility. In other words, says Smith, New Kingdom Nubia became a self-supporting enterprise that was run to finance key state enterprises such as mineral exploitation and the trade in Africa's luxury goods. Under these circumstances, the pharaohs' imperial policy made very good sense.

Nubia changed from a country of village farmers and herders into something more closely resembling a vast plantation state, whose inhabitants worked for the benefit of absentee landlords and sometimes for Nubian officials who were indistinguishable from high Egyptian nobles. Kush was carefully organized to provide commodities at the cheapest possible price. *The Annals of Tuthmosis III* (c. 1480 B.C.) quotes figures for Nubian tribute that include 830 kilograms (1,830 pounds) of gold received over three years of his reign alone, gold with a value of well over three million dollars today.

## *"The Shadow of Nubia" (1100–730 B.C.)*

The economic and political shock waves that rolled across the eastern Mediterranean in the thirteenth century B.C. overthrew the Hittites (Chapter 7) and also rippled up the Nile as far as distant Nubia. The Egyptians abandoned Kush to its own devices. Many Nubians still clung to Egyptian ways, forming a new elite that was to create its own distinctive civilization in the centuries ahead. Much of the wealth and military power that had been Egypt's now remained in Nubia. As William Adams says, "For two thousand years the shadow of Egypt had lain on Nubia; at the end of the New Kingdom the shadow of Nubia was beginning to be visible in Egypt." The end of direct Egyptian rule left a political vacuum, but the tradition of divine monarchy and the cult of Amun survived. The flat-topped sacred mountain named Jebel Barkal stands close to the north bank of the Nile at the Fourth Cataract, near the town of Napata. Tuthmosis III and Ramesses II both chose this magnificent setting for a Temple of Amun. The great shrine built by Ramesses—brilliantly reconstructed with three-dimensional computer graphics by Timothy Kendall of the Boston Museum of Fine Arts—ranks among the

**Figure 12.4** The Jebel Barkal temple, Nubia.

finest examples of its kind (Figure 12.4). It was here that the traditions of kingship and ancient religious beliefs were kept alive. And, in due time, the cult of Amun became the ideological thread that sustained Nubian civilization for more than a thousand years.

No one knows exactly how Nubian civilization arose with such dramatic suddenness. A common hypothesis is that the priests of Amun at Jebel Barkal kept alive the ancient traditions, dwelling among people who had reverted to traditional ways. In time, alliances formed between the priests and the local chiefs, the ancestors of men who were to rule a new kingdom of Kush and Egypt itself. It was a close connection between secular and spiritual power that sustained Nubian kings and validated their authority for many centuries. The wealth of this new state was based entirely on exports to Egypt. Those who controlled this trade along the Dongola Reach achieved great secular and economic power.

The first signs of new rulers come not from historical texts but from 36 royal tombs in a cemetery at El Kurru, downstream of Jebel Barkal. These are the sepulchers of the first kings and of the Nubian pharaohs who were to seize power in Egypt a century later. Every Nubian ruler was buried under a pyramid of unashamedly Egyptian design, much smaller than those of Giza but proportionally much taller, with a 60- to 70-degree slope. The continuity of Nubian royal burial is remarkable; George Reisner and others have located five cemeteries, three of them near the Fourth Cataract and two others upstream at Meroe. A provisional but controversial list of rulers and reigns begins around 806 B.C. and ends in A.D. 320, 1,100 years later.

## *Nubian Pharaohs (730–663 B.C.)*

The first Napatan king we know by name is Kashta, at least the sixth generation of the dynasty to which he belonged. We know little of him, only that he journeyed north to Thebes, where he was confirmed as ruler by the priests of Amun. He was received with relief by the Theban priests, for Nubian mercenaries kept them in power and threats from the north in check. Kashta's son Piye (Piankhi) spent the first 20 years of his reign in Nubia. Then came word from Thebes of a threat from a Delta king named Tefnakht, "the great chief of the Ma" (Libyans), who sought to control all Egypt. Piye dispatched an army to repel the intruders, then arrived himself to finish off the task. With brilliant diplomacy, he celebrated the festival of Opet, which honored Amun at the Temple of Luxor, establishing himself as the protector of the god and a man with a sacred mission. Then he marched north, took Hermopolis and Memphis, and overthrew the warring princes of the Delta. Having assumed the full titles of a pharaoh of Egypt he quietly returned to Napata, where he ruled for another decade without returning to Thebes.

A commemorative stela set up in the Jebel Barkal temple records how Piye marched down the river, "raging like a panther" and seizing towns "like a cloudburst." The forceful and thoroughly competent Piye was not only a skilled general but also an expert politician. We read how he sent his wives and female relatives to cozy up to the consorts of defeated lords and of his dismay at the condition of the horses in the royal stables at Hermopolis after the siege. "It is more grievous in my heart that my horses have suffered hunger than any evil deed that thou hast done in the prosecution of thy desire," he complains to their vanquished owner. By all accounts, Piye was a merciful conqueror, who allowed his rivals to keep their thrones once they had pledged allegiance to him.

Piye's successors, Shabaqo and Shebitqo, established the royal seat at Thebes, effectively founding the Twenty-Fifth Dynasty of Egyptian pharaohs. Now the tide had turned completely, for the servant had become the master, the conquered the conquerors. But there was a major difference: The Nubians, unlike earlier pharaohs, were not exploiters. All the Nubian pharaohs embarked on ambitious temple-building programs in honor of Amun. They patronized artists and artisans, had ancient papyri copied, and ordered long-forgotten rituals to be performed. Such was their piety that they restored temples all along the Nile and sponsored a revival of ancient styles, but with one difference: Their artists always recorded the kings' distinctive racial differences and the Nubian costumes they wore.

The Nubian dynasty ruled until 663 B.C., when King Taharqa fled ignominiously to Napata before the invading Assyrians. For three-quarters of a century, his successors tried to recover their throne. But in 591 B.C. an obscure pharaoh named Psamtik II (Psammetichus) routed the Kushite ruler Anlamani at Pnubs near the Third Cataract. Psamtik's soldiers "waded in Kushite blood as if it were water." The Egyptian army marched to Napata unopposed and sacked its towns and temples. Aspelta fled to the safety of Meroe on the Shendi Reach, some 480 kilometers (300 miles) upstream. There Nubian civilization took on a new lease of life for a time. But Meroe's royalty always revered Napata and its shrines. For centuries the kings were crowned at the shrine of Amun and were buried within sight of Jebel Barkal.

## Camels and Monsoons

Egyptian knowledge of the desert and the Indian Ocean region expanded dramatically with the domestication of the camel, and, later, with the discovery of the monsoon wind cycle of the Indian Ocean.

Egyptian rulers had long prized tropical products from Red Sea ports. Queen Hatshepsut ruled Egypt from 1498 to 1483 B.C., a strong-willed woman who effectively usurped the authority of the child-king Tuthmosis III. Hatshepsut was not known for her military prowess, but she was an ambitious trader. A famous relief on the wall of her mortuary temple commemorates a memorable expedition to the "Land of Punt," probably in northern Somalia or Djibouti. The queen's envoys crossed overland to the Red Sea, then sailed southward to exchange young incense trees, ivory, and semiprecious stones for Egyptian manufactures (see Figure 12.1).

No Egyptian ships ventured further than Socotra until several centuries after the Nubian kings had retreated upstream to Meroe. But in 25 B.C. the Greek geographer Strabo accompanied the Roman prefect of Egypt far up the Nile to the borders of Kush. Far from the Mediterranean, Strabo learned that "as many as one hundred and twenty vessels were sailing from [the Red Sea] to India, whereas formerly, under the Ptolemies, only a very few ventured to undertake the voyage and to carry on traffic in Indian merchandise."

The downwind sailing ship and the monsoon winds linked Africa with India and Southeast Asia. The camel, the "ship of the desert," was the equivalent of the ocean-going sailing ship in arid lands. After 500 B.C., this beast revolutionized desert travel and the land-borne spice trade between southern Arabia and the eastern Mediterranean world. Camels are seemingly ungainly beasts, but they are ideal for crossing deserts. Their padded feet enable them to travel on soft sand, their bodies absorb heat efficiently, and they store fat in their humps. They conserve water through an efficient kidney system and can distribute immense amounts of liquid through the body tissues within 48 hours. Inevitably, camels became beasts of burden because they were perfectly adapted to travel in arid lands, provided they were properly ridden. The saddle turns the camel—in its various configurations—into a fighting vehicle, a racing steed, or a superb load carrier.

Camel breeding on a large scale began after the twelfth century B.C., when Semites from the north took control of the Arabian frankincense trade. The real revolution occurred between 500 and 100 B.C. with the appearance of the so-called North Arabian saddle—a rigid, arched seat, mounted over the camel's hump, that distributes the rider's weight evenly on the beast's back. A pack load can be slung on either side of the saddle. Even more important, a warrior could fight from camelback with sword or spear. The North Arabian saddle gave the hitherto despised camel-breeding nomads of the desert unprecedented military, political, and economic power. The camel-borne warrior mounted on a sturdy saddle made those who supplied desert transportation a political force to be reckoned with. The camel breeders thus controlled the desert caravans of the Near East, so much so that wheeled carts vanished from the Near Eastern world for many centuries. The camel was simply more efficient.

By the third century B.C., desert nomads like the Beja of the northeastern Sudan, with their military saddles acquired from across the Red Sea, could threaten law and order in Egypt. They and their camels dominated the lucrative trade routes that linked the Red Sea with the Nile. Two centuries later, camels were commonplace far to the south, in Kush. By the time of Christ, the southern Red Sea became the crossroads between Asia and Africa and between India and the Mediterranean world.

The Nubian kings of Meroe were quick to adapt to changing economic times. Because of the camel, they ruled over a kingdom at a strategic economic crossroads. To the east, large camel caravans linked the Nile with Red Sea ports. More camel tracks stretched westward, deep into the Sahara, and southward, into tropical grasslands where ivory could be obtained. Then the camel was a load carrier rather than a weapon of war. The Saharan saddle was mounted on the beast's shoulders forward of the hump. The new design provided better control for long-distance riders, who could steer their steed with a stick or their toes. This was highly adaptive when transporting heavy loads of gold, ivory, and salt over hundreds of miles of extremely harsh landscape.

## Meroe (c. 350 B.C.–A.D. 300)

Meroe lay on the outer fringes of the Mediterranean world, a remote and exotic land that was reputed to be awash in gold and ivory. The Nile was the life blood of Meroitic civilization, which at its height influenced a long strip of land about 1,125 kilometers (700 miles) along the river from near Dakka in Lower Nubia as far upstream as Sennar on the Blue Nile. Stories of Meroe's fabled wealth attracted King Cambyses of Persia, but his army perished of starvation in the desert before reaching the city. Alexander the Great sent a small expedition there in 331 B.C. In later centuries, Meroe's rulers maintained friendly relations with the Ptolemies of Egypt, who obtained from them not only gold but also war elephants. A fine bust of Emperor Augustus has come from Meroe, a war trophy from more unsettled times. The Roman writer Pliny tells us that a small party of Roman soldiers visited the city around A.D. 60 at the command of Emperor Nero, who was contemplating a campaign against Meroe. They reported that "the grass in the vicinity of Meroe becomes of a greener and fresher color, and that there is some slight appearance of forests, as also traces of rhinoceros and elephant." The Romans were used to great, teeming cities like Rome and Alexandria and were unimpressed with the diminutive city of Meroe, though their hosts boasted unconvincingly that they maintained "250,000 armed men and 3,000 artisans."

For all the Romans' scorn, the kings and queens of Meroe administered a complex, exploitative economic enterprise for their own benefit, controlling by force trade routes to the outside world through a network of carefully policed routes. They portrayed themselves as the descendants of the great pharaoh Piye and his successors, preserving many of the institutions of Egyptian society but with a distinctive African slant. They perpetuated the worship of Egyptian gods and built temples and sepulchers that were derived from ancient architectural convention. Even Meroitic hieroglyphs were based on pharaonic models, although the scribes developed a cursive script to write their own tongue, a script as yet undeciphered.

Meroe lies on the east bank of the Nile, 200 kilometers (124 miles) downstream of Khartoum. Today, the ruins of the once-famous town lie in a barren, arid landscape of low hills and dry scrubland, where the sun beats mercilessly on those who dig within its precincts (Figure 12.5). It is hard to imagine that this same desert was well wooded during the first millennium B.C., enabling the inhabitants not only to raise cereal crops like millet and sorghum but also to maintain large herds on nearby semiarid grasslands. They would also fell large numbers of trees to make charcoal, an essential fuel for smelting the rich iron ores that lay in abundance nearby. "[Meroe] contains great forests," wrote the Greek geographer Strabo in 25 B.C. He said that the Meroites subsisted "on millet and barley, from which a drink is also prepared. . . . They live also upon the flesh and blood of animals, milk, and cheese. They reverence their kings as gods, who are for the most part shut up in their palaces." Today's arid wilderness results partly from chronic drought conditions but also from the handiwork of Meroe's inhabitants, who overgrazed the nearby grasslands and stripped the forests for firewood and charcoal burning.

The Meroitic state was headed by a divine ruler, and the society was apparently matrilineal, for queens played an important role in Meroe's history. The prominence given to queens in Meroitic temple reliefs strongly suggests that royal property and the succession itself were transmitted through the female line. They appear in temple reliefs as massive, corpulent women, with elaborate jewelry and costumes, looming over their dying enemies in symbolic depictions of royal power.

**Figure 12.5** General view of Meroe's royal cemeteries. A natural iron ore outcrop is in the foreground.

We know little of Meroitic society or its people. Apparently, many Meroites had distinctive tribal scarifications on their faces, a mark of beauty characteristic of Africa rather than the Nile, while wealthier women made extensive use of imported cosmetics. Most people lived at the subsistence level, for the trade in gold, ivory, elephants, and other commodities was to the benefit of only a tiny minority of the population. As time went on, an increasing number of commoners were engaged in a new, labor-intensive industry: iron smelting.

Iron is a prosaic, everyday metal that was known to ancient metalsmiths long before it was turned into tools and weapons. It was known to the Egyptian pharaohs as early as the New Kingdom; indeed, a fine iron-bladed dagger was found in Tutankhamun's tomb. But the conservative Egyptians were slow to adopt the new metal, which was one reason why their armies were overwhelmed by invading Assyrian forces in the seventh century B.C. By that time ironworking had become a significant industry at Meroe, perhaps for military reasons. Iron-tipped tools and weapons gave Meroe's armies strategic advantages over their desert neighbors, who were often armed with only stone- or copper-tipped missiles and close combat arms. Meroitic smiths fashioned swords that were worn in scabbards over the shoulder, just as they are today by central Saharan nomads.

Iron ore was plentiful, for a low-grade ironstone formation caps the nearby sandstone hills. Every day, small parties of charcoal burners would set out from the city armed with iron axes. By evening, they would return with large bundles of acacia branches, which would be burned slowly in special fires to convert them into charcoal. It has been estimated that half a million tons of hardwood were cleared from the surrounding landscape over the centuries, for at least 0.9 kilograms (2 pounds) of charcoal are needed for every 0.45 kilograms (1.0 pound) of iron ore. So much iron was smelted at Meroe that large slag heaps lie close to the city, but we have no idea how long they took to accumulate or how much iron was smelted.

Meroe's greatest prosperity was in the first century A.D. A century later, Kush was in a slow decline, perhaps because of a shift in trading activity further southward in the Red Sea and because of the overgrazing of local soils. Between A.D. 325 and 350, King Ezana II of Aksum in the Ethiopian highlands went to war against the nomadic groups on the Atbara River. But his main objective was Meroe, where inscriptions tell of his victory: "I burnt their towns, those of masonry and those of straw, and my people seized their corn and their bronze and the dried meat and the images in their temples." His armies returned home with rich booty—more than 600 prisoners, 10,500 cattle, and 51,050 sheep, if Ezana's boastful inscriptions are to be believed. From this time, Aksum overshadowed its neighbor, which fragmented into small kingdoms.

## Aksum (A.D. 100–1100)

We know of Aksum from both archaeological and literary sources. The anonymous author of *The Periplus of the Erythraean Sea* wrote in around A.D. 70 of a prosperous Red Sea port named Adulis and of the "city of the people called Aksumites," high in the nearby Ethiopian highlands. By his time, Aksum had long been a major player in the Indian Ocean trade.

Aksum came into prominence as a result of its strategic position at the mouth of the Red Sea. Here, less than 32 kilometers (20 miles) of water separate southern Arabia from Ethiopia and its nearby highlands, making it easy for people and ideas to flow freely back and forth from Arabia to Africa. The highlands form a great triangle of mountainous terrain that drains westward into the Nile. The terrain is varied and the soils relatively fertile, allowing the cultivation of cereal crops including a native grass called *teff*, which became an Ethiopian staple. In some places, one can grow two or three crops a year or even plant and harvest within any month. The highlands are seemingly an environment of plenty. By Roman times, the highland Ethiopians were even using oxen to drag plows, the only people in tropical Africa to do so. The highlands sound like another Egyptian Nile, until one looks closer at the environmental constraints. Much of the plateau is rocky, very rugged, or too exposed to constant winds to have much value. The rainfall is irregular, and sudden frosts can decimate growing crops. Swarms of locusts sometimes wipe out ripe gardens in a few days. But the highland Ethiopian farmers flourished and soon came into contact with other lands.

By the late second and early first millennium B.C., the people of the highlands were in regular communication with southern Arabia, across the Red Sea. By 500 B.C., an indigenous monarchy appeared at the northern end of the highlands. These African kings adopted many Arabian institutions and assumed Arabian titles and religious beliefs. Yeha, in the fertile heartland of what was to become the Aksumite state, boasted of a large palace. Its masonry temple, built during the fourth or fifth century B.C., is similar in many ways to contemporary shrines in southern Arabia. Some inscriptions from the town are written in south Arabian script.

These south Arabian influences resulted from the Red Sea trade, for the highland peoples had access to gold, ivory, and other products. Like Meroe, Ethiopia became a gateway to Africa's riches for traders operating in distant markets in the Mediterranean world and along the northern and eastern shores of the Indian Ocean. The early centuries of the trade brought technological innovations like plows and ironworking and exotic imports from many lands. They also carried new religious ideas from the wider Arabian and Mediterranean world, which permeated an African society under the control of relatively few families, those engaged in trade. Archaeologist Graham Connah hypothesizes that it was the unpredictable, often harsh environment of the northern highlands that lay behind the major changes in Ethiopian society. Perhaps, he argues, those families that held monopolies over foreign trade also controlled the irrigation systems that provided surplus grain in drought years. Within a few generations, the northern highlands were ruled by a hereditary elite, headed by an absolute monarch.

As time went on, Arabian influences, especially in written script, gave way to a more indigenous syllabary written in Ge'ez, the ancestor of modern Ethiopian languages like Amharic. Ethiopian culture assumed a strong identity of its own, as the Aksum civilization blossomed into full flower from indigenous roots during the first century A.D. This flowering occurred when Meroe was at the height of its powers and resulted, in part, from friendly relations and close trading partnerships with Rome.

Adulis, on the Red Sea coast, was the gateway to the capital at Aksum and to the African interior, a bustling hub of international trade. From Adulis, one traveled inland to Aksum in eight days, precisely the same time required in the nineteenth century A.D. The same route took one onward to the Nile Valley near Meroe. Another long caravan route passed northwestward from Aksum for 30 days across the Nubian desert to Aswan. Adulis became so important that Aksum eventually overshadowed Meroe as the age-old Nile Valley trade declined.

The powerful monarchs (*negusa nagast*) who presided over this remarkable state lived at Aksum itself, dwelling in imposing palaces built in a highly distinctive architectural style. The palace of Enda Mika'el stood on a massive stone platform with stepped sides that served to increase its height and enhance its appearance. Both the platform and the exterior walls were indented to give an impression of great strength. According to its German excavators in 1906, Enda Mika'el was a four-story structure, the upper floors built of timber-reinforced masonry. The ends of timber beams projected from the walls. Four towers added to the general impression of stability and power. Another palace, at Ta'akha Mariam, was a huge complex of courtyards, towers, and multistory buildings, covering an area 120 by 80 meters (394 by 263 feet). The architectural styles of both palaces are distinctively Ethiopian yet owe something to Arabian, and perhaps Roman, inspiration.

The kings of Aksum are known to us from the portraits embossed on gold coins. They wear crowns and sometimes sit on thrones. Their main preoccupation was with wealth; with the colossal and gigantic; with the construction of fine palaces, mansions, and sepulchers. From the first to fourth centuries A.D., their authority was based on southern Arabian deities like the moon god, Almouqah, and Mahrem, the deity of war and kingship. The crescent and disk appear on coins, symbols of the moon and the sun. Successive kings expended vast sums on the construction of shrines and temples that helped validate their secular and spiritual authority.

Nowhere is the power of these monarchs better documented than at Aksum itself, where tall, thin stelae stand high above the ruined city. No fewer than 199 such columns once stood in two groups at Aksum, marking subterranean, rock-cut tombs. The largest towered over 33 meters (108 feet) high, carved to represent a building with 13 stories, one of the largest carved blocks of stone from the ancient world. The tallest stela still in place is 21 meters (69 feet) high, a symbolic depiction of a ten-story building, complete with false door (Figure 12.6). All this stonework required extraordinary engineering skills, not only to quarry massive stone slabs used to form the stelae and some royal tombs, but also to carve them and set them in place. Relatively few people were expert carvers or scribes. Most of the work was in the hands of unskilled laborers, who used levers and rollers to transport enormous granite blocks in the name of the king.

Like all preindustrial civilizations, Aksum was ruled by people who were masters at commanding and organizing village labor. Everything gives the impression of enormous wealth, which was concentrated in relatively few families, a hereditary nobility capable of monopolizing the export trade. They used their wealth to deploy large numbers of people as laborers in agricultural works, temples, and palaces and in other, menial tasks. The nobility and the artisans and merchants, who might be called a "middle class," lived in cities like Adulis and Aksum or Matara, about halfway between the two. Most of the people were commoners or slaves. Human beings were one of Aksum's major exports.

**Figure 12.6** A royal stela at Aksum, Ethiopia.

For seven centuries after the death of Christ, Aksum, through its port at Adulis, became a gateway to tropical Africa for a rapidly changing Mediterranean and eastern world. Aksum's connections extended to Rome and Byzantium, far into Syria and Armenia, to the shores of the Persian Gulf, and to India. Byzantine bronze weights have been found at Aksum itself. Roman coins of the second and third centuries A.D. have been found in Matara, midway between Aksum and the coast. Another site has yielded 104 third-century Indian coins. With Mediterranean wine amphorae, Egyptian and Roman glass flasks, and Mesopotamian and Egyptian fabrics, Aksum became a marketplace of the Classical world, the first African state to mint its own gold coins (in the third century). Its monetary system was the same as that of distant Byzantium, a measure of Aksum's integration into a much wider commercial world. Aksum was a symbol of a new, much more international world, which sprang from the ruins of the Roman Empire, a world that, in later Islamic hands, was to transform the face of Africa and Indian Ocean lands. For centuries, Aksum lay at the center of a giant web of trade routes that linked tropical Africa with the Red Sea trade and with the wider world of the Indian Ocean. At the height of its powers, Aksum's kings presided over a well-organized state of great wealth, so much so that a Byzantine ambassador was received by an Aksumite monarch who was standing in a chariot drawn by four elephants.

Aksum's connections with the wider world brought new spiritual beliefs to its court. In the fourth century, King Ezana, conqueror of Meroe, adopted Christianity as the official religion of the state. Christianity replaced earlier faiths so effectively that it survived as the Coptic church of Ethiopia long after Aksum itself had fallen. Aksum remained part of the Indian Ocean world until the mid–seventh century A.D., when the growing influence of Islam disrupted long-established trade routes through the Red Sea and cut off the flourishing state from its Mediterranean markets. In A.D. 702, only nine years before the Arabs crossed into Spain, the Aksumites are said to have attacked Islamic ships in Jedda harbor. It was a foolish move, for the Arabs inflicted savage revenge on a much weakened Aksum.

Aksum subsequently declined and withdrew from the world at a time when the quantity of rainfall was apparently somewhat higher than it is today. Its population rose rapidly, resulting in intense land use, widespread deforestation, and soil erosion, all of which may have sown the seeds for economic and social collapse. By the tenth century, more erratic rainfall may have caused much of the population to move further south into better watered grassland areas, where Christianity continued to flourish and Aksum's cultural legacy survived in magnificent rock-cut churches.

## Summary

Nubian civilization developed out of indigenous roots but under strong Egyptian influence. Egyptian pharaohs exploited Nubia for its wealth in ivory and semiprecious stones, garrisoning the Dongola Reach to protect their trade routes. The cattle-owning chieftains of Nubia developed powerful kingdoms when the Egyptian kings were politically weak, as they were during the First and Second Intermediate Periods. New Kingdom Egypt turned Nubia into a colony, which reverted to local control after 1100 B.C. During the seventh century, Nubian rulers from Kush became the kings of Egypt, only retreating upstream when confronted by Assyrian armies in the sixth century. After a crushing defeat in 663 B.C., the Nubian rulers retreated from Napata upstream to Meroe, at a time when the camel was assuming increasing importance in long-distance trade. The Meroitic kingdom flourished as the focus of trade moved southward and Egyptian captains discovered the monsoon wind cycles of the Indian Ocean. Meroe became a major center for ivory and other African commodities around the time of Christ, when it was also a major iron-working city. After the first century, the Aksumites of the Ethiopian highlands became major powers in the Red Sea and Indian Ocean trade.

## Guide to Further Reading

For Nubia generally, W. Y. Adams, *Nubia: Corridor to Africa* (London: Allen Lane, 1977) is the definitive source, although outdated in parts. Derek Welsby, *The Kingdom of Kush* (London: British Museum Publications, 1996) and Timothy Kendall, *Kush, Lost Kingdom of the Nile* (Brockton, MA: Brockton Art Museum, 1982) give up-to-date accounts of recent research, as does John Taylor, *Egypt and Nubia* (London: British Museum, 1991). Graham Connah, *African Civilizations*, 2nd ed. (Cambridge: Cambridge University Press, 2001) has strong chapters on Nubia. Torgny Save Soderbergh, *Temples and Tombs of Ancient Nubia* (London: Thames and Hudson, 1987) is very useful. For Kerma, see George Reisner, *Excavations at Kerma* (Cambridge, MA: Peabody Museum, Harvard University, 1923). Reisner's many other monographs on Nubian excavations can be found in W. Y. Adams's bibliography. For the latest excavations, Charles Bonnet has published progress reports on his long-term excavations in the journal *Geneva* (1978 onward). For the Jebel Barkal reconstruction, see Timothy Kendall, *The Gebel Barkal Temples 1989–90: A Progress Report on the Work of the Museum of Fine Arts, Boston, Sudan Mission* (Geneva: Seventh Conference for Nubian Studies, 1990). See also D. M. Dixon, "The Origin of the Kingdom of Kush," *Journal of Egyptian*

*Archaeology* 50 (1964): 121–132. Egyptian imperialism in Nubia has generated an extensive literature, for example, Paul John Frandsen, "Egyptian Imperialism," in Mogens Trolle Larsen, ed., *Power and Propaganda: A Symposium on Ancient Empires* (Copenhagen: Akademisk Forlag, 1979), pp. 167–191. See also Stuart T. Smith, "A Model for Egyptian Imperialism in Nubia," *Gottinger Miszellen* 122 (1991): 77–102.

For Meroe, Peter Shinnie, *Meroe* (London: Thames and Hudson, 1967) is still the authoritative source on the ancient city; John Robertson, "History and Archaeology at Meroe," in Judy Sterner and Nicholas David, eds., *An African Commitment* (Calgary: University of Calgary Press, 1993) provides useful background. Peter Shinnie and Rebecca Bradley, *The Capital of Kush I* (Berlin: Akademie-Verlag, 1980) is a key monograph. See also Peter Shinnie and François Kense, "Meroitic Iron Working," *Meroitica* 6 (1982): 17–28 and R. F. Tylecote, "Metal Working at Meroe, Sudan," *Meroitica* 6 (1982): 29–42. Laszlo Torok, "Kush and the External World," *Meroitica* 10 (1989): 49–215 discusses foreign trade.

Richard W. Bulliet, *The Camel and the Wheel* (Cambridge, MA: Harvard University Press, 1975) is a brilliant study of this remarkable animal. See also Hilde Gauthier-Pilters and Anne Innis Dagg, *The Camel: Its Evolution, Ecology, Behavior, and Relationship to Man* (Chicago: University of Chicago Press, 1981).

Stuart Munro-Hay, *Aksum: An African Civilization of Late Antiquity* (Edinburgh: Edinburgh University Press, 1991) is a comprehensive account of this remarkable society, which makes use of both historical and literary sources. See also Graham Connah, *African Civilizations*, 2nd ed. (Cambridge: Cambridge University Press, 2001). David W. Phillipson, *Ancient Ethiopia: Aksum: Its Antecedents and Successors* (London: British Museum Press, 1998) offers a comprehensive assessment.

# *Chapter 13*

# Divine Kings in Southeast Asia

Head of Vishnu. (Late 9th or early 10th CE. Cambodia, Prassat Phom Bok, distric of Banteay Srei, province of Sièmreap. Sandstone, H: 48cm. Inv.: MG 18102. Photo: Thierry Ollivier. Musee des Arts Asiatiques–Guimet, Paris, France. © Reunion des Musees Nationaux/Art Resource, NY)

*The rain never stops, pouring inexorably from the low, grey clouds onto a watery landscape. The water buffalo strains at the iron-tipped plow, his master beating him with a stick. The plow cuts deep into the waterlogged soil, turning over thick clusters of rotting weeds and churning them into the mud. Blue-green algae cascade around the buffalo's hooves, as rainwater held back by low banks at the edge of the field flows through a narrow defile and across the plowed soil toward a nearby stream. At the edge of the rice paddy, the women, oblivious to the wet, transplant new plants from a large seed bed, setting the seedlings in long rows. A well-dressed official watches the planting under the shelter of a red ceremonial umbrella, mentally assessing the potential yield from the crop.*

Rice agriculture was the foundation of civilization in south India and of village life in Southeast Asia long before complex societies appeared east of the Bay of Bengal. But the productivity of "wet" rice agriculture lies at the very center of the debates over early civilization in Southeast Asia. Were the early states of this region indigenous developments, or did they arise as a result of pervasive contacts between Indian civilizations and regions to the east? As voyaging increased, especially from southern India to Southeast Asia, a strong cultural influence began to be felt. The tribal societies of Southeast Asia were introduced to many alien products and some of the foreigners' philosophical, social, and religious beliefs. According to traditional South Asian histories, the Mauryan Emperor Asoka himself sent three missionaries to spread Buddhism in Southeast Asia. In a few centuries, kingdoms appeared that were run according to Hindu or Buddhist ideas of social order. These uniquely Southeast Asian states are the subject of this chapter.

## The Rise of States in Southeast Asia (c. 2000 B.C.–A.D. 150)

Ten thousand years ago, the Southeast Asian mainland extended far offshore, most of it low-lying marshland intersected by several major river systems. As Ice Age sea levels rose, so the continental shelf shrank. The three major river systems of Southeast Asia are much reduced versions of earlier rivers, each with its own fertile delta (Figure 13.1). The middle Thailand and Chao Phraya delta forms one such system; the lower Mekong and Tonle Sap plains (the major concern of this chapter), a second; and the Red River and Ma and Ca rivers of Vietnam, a third. All these rivers flood seasonally, inundating large areas of farmland with shallow water, where long-stalked, fast-maturing rice can be grown. These three river valleys, the homelands of complex societies for many centuries, are fertile enclaves surrounded by higher ground, where deciduous, drought-resistant forest and moist tropical forest

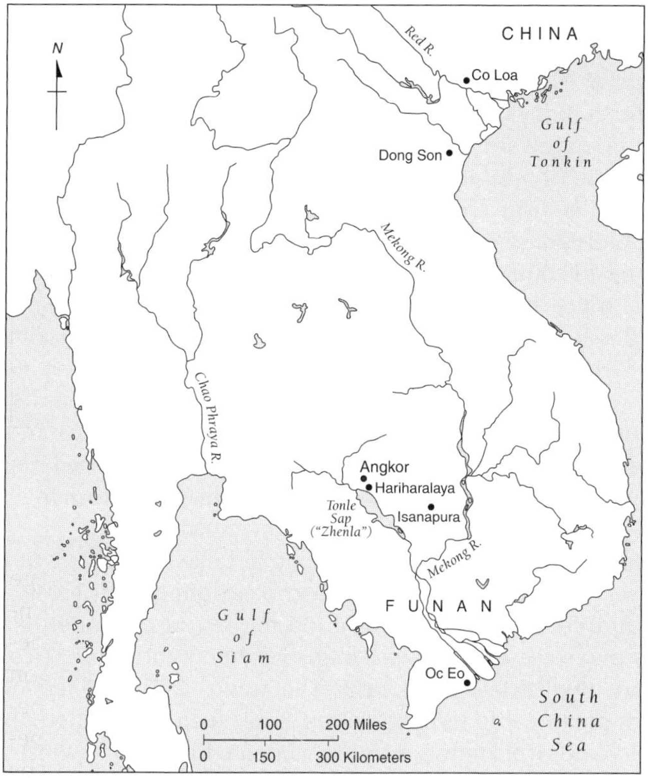


**Figure 13.1** Map of archaeological sites described in Chapter 13.

flourish. The same rivers have formed important communication arteries for many thousands of years. Watered by monsoon cycles and marked by considerable local variations in climate and topography, parts of Southeast Asia have supported high population densities only within the past 2,000 years.

The staple crop in ancient Southeast Asia was rice, domesticated in China's Yangzi River Valley before 6500 B.C. Rice farming was well established in Southeast Asia by 2000 B.C., but agricultural populations were never large. Between 1500 and 500 B.C., Southeast Asia's egalitarian farming communities adopted bronze metallurgy and traded widely with one another. Both mining and smelting were important activities, probably during the agriculturally quiet dry season. The Ban Na Di site in northern Thailand contains an important cemetery, where the dead lay in orderly clusters, with clear evidence of social ranking within the village and trade with other communities.

By 500 B.C., iron technology was in use as local populations rose and settlements grew much larger, some of them with as many as 25,000 inhabitants. The new metallurgy was grafted onto existing bronze technology, but it is uncertain whether ironworking was introduced from India, where forging (smelting in a small furnace) was used, or from China, which developed sophisticated casting methods that involved molten iron at very high temperatures. During the same centuries glass beads and other ornaments of Indian origin appeared for the first time, passed from one community to the next by already-existing exchange networks. For the first time, larger communities appeared, usually important centers for craft production.

In earlier times, rice cultivation was concentrated in small stream valleys and along the margins of major river floodplains. The appearance of larger settlements may have coincided with both intensive wet farming and the advent of plowing and double cropping, which greatly magnified food production and produced much larger surpluses. Those who had control of salt, copper, or tin deposits or who lived in a strategic location where trade routes passed or who had a monopoly over specific trade goods like glass beads or iron implements could achieve unusual wealth and political power. These were the centuries when Southeast Asians began to participate in maritime trade routes that linked the mainland and offshore islands, New Guinea and the Philippines, as well as India and China. Carnelian beads and a carving of a lion found at Ban Don Ta Phet in central Thailand reveal trade links with India as early as the fourth century B.C., while bronze bowls traced from their alloys back to Southeast Asia have been found in the Indian subcontinent.

A portrait of society at the time comes from the Noen U-Loke site in the Mun Valley of northeastern Thailand, where a sample of 126 graves dating from 400 B.C. to about A.D. 300 show a dramatic increase in the amount of effort expended on burying the dead. Some of the deceased were laid in graves filled with burnt rice. Others were lined and capped with clay, like coffins. The graves lay in clusters of men, women, and children, presumably family groups. One cluster contained almost all the carnelian jewelry and rice, another was associated with spindle whorls, a third with most of the clay-lined caskets. Three of them featured exceptionally wealthy males, adorned with bronze belts, bangles, ear disks, and other elaborate ornaments. These were not peaceful times, perhaps the product of an increasingly crowded landscape. One man lay prone with an iron arrowhead buried in his spine.

Throughout Southeast Asia, population densities and social complexity increased, as rich and warlike chiefdoms appeared at the end of the first millennium B.C. Expert seafarers and traders, they were active participants in a much larger world that linked the Han Empire of China with India and the mainland to islands far offshore. This trend toward complexity and competition was an indigenous development, even if innovations from outside fueled political and social change. Larger communities developed, usually centers for craft production. In earlier times, rice cultivation had been concentrated in small stream valleys and along the margins of major river floodplains. Such dry rice farming was much less productive than wet cultivation in waterlogged fields (paddies), which produced much higher and more predictable crop yields. The appearance of larger settlements may have coincided with both intensive wet farming and the advent of plowing and double-cropping, which greatly increased food production and produced much larger crop surpluses.

More centralized governance also developed, focused on large centers ruled by highly ranked lineages. Their power was underwritten by their control of food surpluses and rice lands, by their support of expert artisans, and by carefully managed exchange monopolies over high-status imports and exotic materials. The leaders of these societies wore fine ceremonial weapons and badges of rank, and they lived in finely decorated houses. Over a period of several centuries, far more complex societies developed, especially in fertile riverine areas—societies whose leaders controlled maritime and inland trade over large areas. The exposure to artifacts, technologies, and ideas from China and India grew alongside these major changes as powerful leaders surrounded themselves with all the panoply of public ceremony, ritual feasting, and ostentation.

## *The Dong Son Culture (c. 1000 B.C.–A.D. 43)*

Complex societies developed in Vietnam's Red River Delta and lowland coasts, the Khorat plateau, and Laotian uplands. The best known is the Dong Son culture of the Red River Valley, where a moist climate allows two rice crops a year.

The indigenous origins of the Dong Son culture go back to at least 1000 B.C., when bronze smiths were already at work in the valley. After 500 B.C., bronze artifacts proliferated in Dong Son graves, not only utilitarian artifacts but also numerous ceremonial objects, including weapons, buckets, and drums. The intensification of bronze working required enormous quantities of metal and much larger food surpluses, obtained by extensive wet rice agriculture in the Red River Delta. Dong Son metalworkers were masters of their craft, casting elaborate, richly decorated artifacts, and they eventually adopted the iron technology of their Chinese neighbors to the north. Drums, in particular, became symbols of high social status in Dong Son society. One from the Co Loa site weighed no less than 72 kilograms (159 pounds). Many Dong Son drums bear incised and modeled scenes of important lords in large boats with cabins and fighting platforms, crowded with paddlers and warriors. They even show drummers beating their drums, scenes that testify to the importance of music in Dong Son ritual.

The Lac lords, paramount chiefs, warriors, and keepers of the drums, ruled over this prosperous society. One of them ruled from Co Loa near Hanoi, founded by the third century B.C. Co Loa boasted of three sets of ramparts and moats supplied with water from a tributary of the Red River. The fortifications enclosed 600 hectares (1,500 acres). Unfortunately, most of our knowledge of the Dong Son culture comes from cemeteries, so we do not know how large various chiefdoms were or anything about lesser settlements.

The Chinese were well aware of the Dong Son chieftains. The Han knew of them as the most distant of "southern barbarians" and traded and fought with them for centuries. Finally, in A.D. 43, the warrior-nobles of Dong Son succumbed to their powerful neighbors. Their domains became a Chinese protectorate, but Han records tell us that they retained their traditional rights over land.

## *Trade and Kingdoms*

By about A.D. 1, the sea-trading networks of Southeast Asia were part of a much larger commercial universe. Finds of sewn-plank boats dating to the third to fifth centuries A.D. testify to a long tradition of seafaring. Chinese records tell us that some oceangoing vessels were up to 50 meters (164 feet) long and weighed as much as 500 tons. Striking evidence of the monsoon trade comes from the Sembiran site in Bali, where archaeologist A. W. Ardika has found Indian trade pottery from the southern Indian coast 4,350 kilometers (2,700 miles) westward as the crow flies. The traders themselves were an entirely maritime people of no particular nationality, called *Mwani*, or "barbarians," by the Chinese of the time. They spoke polyglot tongues and were of many lands, some Malays, some Indians, true wanderers who ventured as far east as the South China Sea. The Gulf of Tonkin and south China were served by *Jiwet*, Chinese mariners who brought luxuries to the coast, whence the goods were transported overland to the imperial capital.

That India had a profound influence on the development of Southeast Asian civilization is unquestionable. Between 300 B.C. and A.D. 300, Southeast Asian chiefdoms came in increasing contact with Indian merchants and Chinese officials and armies. The Mauryan empire was based, as we have seen, on Buddhist beliefs and on political principles said to have been set by Katilya, chief minister of Chandragupta Maurya, founder of the empire. His tract, the *Arthasastra*, argued that the king had a divine nature. He was like a father, supervising his ministers and protecting the people. He controlled crime through the legal system and encouraged agriculture, manufacturing, and trade. In this formulation, the state was a centralized system sustained by taxation and backed by force or the threat of force. Katilya's ideas coincide quite closely with archaeologists' definitions of early states and were to influence ideas of statehood in Southeast Asia for many centuries. Indian merchants used the monsoon cycles to travel back and forth across the Bay of Bengal, remaining for some months in Southeast Asia waiting for the change of seasons. They carried cargo and passengers, among them Hindu Brahmans and Buddhist monks, educated men with sophisticated and mature views of statehood.

Southeast Asia was a vital link in the chain of trading ports that connected China to India, and Asia to the Roman Empire. The maritime trade brought a vigorous exchange of ideas and new cultural influences. Inevitably, argues Sinologist Paul Wheatley, Southeast Asian chieftains learned a new way of seeing society and the world, perhaps by assembling the collection of commodities for trade and acquiring organizational skills. The authority and powers needed to expand and maintain the commerce were not part of the kin-linked society in which the chieftains had lived all their lives. In time they became familiar with the Brahman and Buddhist conceptions of divine kingship. There was even a brahmanic rite by which chieftains could be inducted into the ruling class, a group whose authority was vested in an assumption of divine kingship.

Toward the end of the first millennium B.C., some Southeast Asian societies had become highly ranked, centralized kingdoms, presided over by an aristocratic class to whom formal display, feasting, and ritual were of paramount importance. They ruled by virtue of their close relationships with their ancestors. As in Maya society in Mesoamerica (see Chapter 15), rank and ancestry were closely connected. The growing complexity of such societies came in part from the ability of their overlords to attract loyal followers and to organize people. In time, many such rulers aspired to even greater status, to presiding over far larger kingdoms carved out by force, charisma, or the creation of magnificent palaces and temples that served as the focus for elaborate public ceremonials and prestigious displays.

These Southeast Asian kingdoms were in a constant state of political flux and without fixed boundaries. The currency of political life was external, but always fluid. Alliances developed between neighboring rulers. Everything revolved around the principal overlord, whose ability to cement alliances and deal with potential enemies dictated his relationships with his rivals. Some experts use a Sanskrit word, *mandala*, an Indian political doctrine, to describe the relationships between these rulers, whose territories are thought of as circles. It is as if they were concertinas, which expanded and contracted as different polities interacted with one another. Each society focused on its own center and on its own religious ruler and his retinue. The personal and spiritual qualities of each leader were important variables in a complex, ever-changing political equation.

Divine kingship revolutionized social and political organization in Southeast Asia. Kingdoms flourished in riverine and lowland areas, along the lower Mekong and in the middle Mekong Valley, including the celebrated Tonle Sap plains, the homeland of Khmer-speaking peoples. (Khmer is an Austroasiatic language of considerable antiquity.) There were also kingdoms on the Khorat plateau, along the central Vietnamese coastal plain, and in the Red River area, the latter under Chinese control.

The Chinese also had well-defined views of statehood, forged from a turbulent historical tradition, which culminated in the unification of China under Emperor Shihuangdi in 221 B.C. By this time, iron was all-important in Chinese agriculture and warfare as the Han emperors waged wars of conquest on the northern and southern frontiers. Thus it was that the Dong Son kingdoms of the Red River came under Chinese protectorship in A.D. 43. Almost two centuries later, the Han dynasty ended and the Southeast Chinese state of Wu came into being. Wu was cut off by its rivals from the lucrative northern trans-Asian trade routes with the West, so its rulers and their successors investigated the possibilities of southern and western maritime routes. Generations of Chinese officials visited Southeast Asian kingdoms, investigating southern sea routes to India, while *mandala* rulers in turn visited Wu. For centuries, the peoples of Southeast Asia came under the direct influence of Chinese and Indian ideas.

The Chinese called the lower Mekong region Funan, which meant "the port of a thousand rivers," but the term has little real historical meaning. According to Chinese records, the ports of the delta handled bronze, silver, gold, spices, and even horses brought by sea from central Asia. One such port was Oc Eo, linked to the coast by a canal, a large town excavated by French archaeologists. Another was Angkor Borei. The two communities were linked by canals that drained water and also carried trade goods. Populations were densely concentrated, land was acquired through territorial conquest, and marshes were drained for more farmland. Whether there was a single kingdom or a series of competing chiefdoms is a matter for debate. Chinese accounts of Funan extol its rich trade. They tell of a drainage and transport system that rapidly transformed much of the delta from barren swamps into rich agricultural land. The development of these fields took the communal efforts of hundreds of people living off the fish that teemed in the bayous of the delta. Most Funanese lived in large lake cities fortified with great earthworks and moats swarming with crocodiles. Each major settlement was a port connected to the ocean and its neighbors by a canal network.

The coastal region prospered greatly from the third to the sixth centuries A.D., thanks to its long traditions of indigenous metallurgy and other crafts and trading expertise. In the sixth century, many more Indian Brahmans arrived in the region. They brought the cult of the god Siva. He appeared in the temples in the form of a linga, a phallic emblem of masculine creative power. Where rulers were worshippers of Siva, the royal linga stood in a temple that symbolized the center of the capital.

The political situation along the lower Mekong was always volatile, especially since the kingdoms upstream had only indirect contact with foreign traders. Leaders inland responded by carving out new routes to the coast, bypassing the delta. In this, they were successful. By the sixth century A.D., the center of economic and political gravity had shifted to the middle Mekong and the Tonle Sap, an area the Chinese called Zhenla.

The Tonle Sap, the central basin of Cambodia, was fed by numerous rivers, its fluctuating water levels supporting many acres of fertile soil. Most of the year, the basin is a shallow series of muddy pools some 66 kilometers (40 miles) long, drained by the Tonle Sap River, which runs into the Mekong. However, so much water floods into the Mekong Delta between August and October that the Tonle Sap's course is reversed and the pools become a vast lake, 133 to 167 kilometers (80 to 100 miles) long, 25 to 50 kilometers (15 to 30 miles) wide, and up to 16 meters (50 feet) deep. Late in October, the water starts receding, trapping millions of fish in the muddy bayous. In the twelfth century A.D., the environment was so bountiful that it supported dense urban populations and generated large food surpluses, sufficient to support a glittering, wealthy civilization. This favored region could provide ample food supplies if reservoirs and water control systems stored and distributed the annual flood over thousands of hectares of agricultural land. Local leaders competed with one another, forged alliances, sometimes waged war. Stronger chiefdoms conquered their neighbors or remained independent. The weaker ones succumbed to neighbors. Constant warfare and political maneuvering led eventually to the emergence of hereditary rulers and small states.

## *The Rise of the God-Kings*

Competing Zhenla rulers acquired sufficient food surpluses to embark on ambitious conquests and, eventually, to develop a new political concept of divine kingship that united their far-flung domains in a common purpose: the glorification of the god-king on earth. Devotion to the Hindu creator, Siva, became a mechanism which provided divine justification for kingship, as well as a focus for the loyalty and devotion of a ruler's retinue, who would endow temples in return for royal favors.

Between the time of Christ and the end of the eighth century, centralization and high status were so unstable that they could fluctuate considerably within an individual's lifetime. Ambitious men would try and try again to raise themselves above others and their kingdoms to supreme rule. Throughout the centuries, these were never states in the Western sense of the word. Rather, the "concertina" effect of kingdom politics was constantly at work, with competing polities asserting independence at times, becoming tribute givers and vassals at other times.

The Mekong River linked the Khorat plateau and the enormous drainage basin of the Tonle Sap with the sea. The Tonle Sap itself was fed by numerous rivers, its fluctuating water levels supporting many acres of fertile soil. At the time of Christ, the farmers of this favored region lived under local chiefs, who controlled local reservoirs, water control being critically important for successful agriculture. Small *mandala*s, which developed over the next few centuries, maintained their independence or coalesced, depending on the abilities of individual overlords to assert their authority. Some of the leaders of royal families were men of exceptional ability, remembered in Sanskrit inscriptions on their temples.

## *Supreme Kings*

Excavations at Sambor Prei Kuk (ancient Isanapura), the capital of the historically known ruler Isanavarman, revealed a large settlement surrounded by square or rectangular moats. There were three separate walled precincts, each dominated by a large central sanctuary set on a platform and reached by a flight of steps. Each was a gift from the ruler. Isanavarman is described in temple inscriptions as energetic and wise, a ruler like the sun in the sky, and the issue of revered kings of the earth. Foremost among the virtuous, Isanavarman "exceeded the limits of his parents' domain."

Hinduism in India embraced the notion of supreme devotion to the god Siva through control of mental and physical forces. An aspiring ruler would obtain proximity to Siva, the divine creator, by extreme asceticism, humility, and personal devotion. He absorbed Siva's physical and spiritual power and acquired an aura of divinity. Devotion to Siva became a mechanism that provided divine justification for kingship and a focus for the loyalty and devotion of a ruler's retinue, who would endow temples in return for royal favors. Such was the case along the Mekong Valley, where rulers like Isanavarman became divine kings, governing with the aid of a deeply embedded and inherited Indian political philosophy. Some rulers were aided by Indian brahmans, who consecrated overlords and served as important legal and political advisers. Great and wealthy families became ministers and physicians, governors, poets, and learned scholars, deeply involved in public affairs and in the accumulation of wealth through trade and taxation to sustain the kingdom.

The Mekong *mandala*s were organized on the principle that successful overlords accumulated wealth and power for themselves in a highly competitive environment. The acceptance of Buddhism and Hinduism by the local elite enhanced their sanctity, with the emerging cities of Southeast Asia serving above all else as symbolic and ritual centers where divine kingship reigned supreme. Scholarly opinion differs concerning the relative importance of Indian notions of kingship, but it certainly played a major role in binding the elite to the center through a blind devotion to the god Siva and the divine king associated with him.

## The Angkor State (A.D. 802–1430)

The overlords of the Tonle Sap all shared one ambition: to establish hegemony over as large an area as possible. The earlier kings were unable to hold the kingdom together until a dynamic Khmer monarch named Jayavarman II came to power in A.D. 802. He conquered his competitors and set up his new territories as tribute kingdoms, giving his loyal generals land grants. Jayavarman II is said to have merged the cult of the ancestors with that of Siva in the form of a linga to consolidate his new kingdom. A much later inscription tells us he called himself Supreme King. His subjects were taught to worship him as a god. All resources of an increasingly centralized government were devoted to the preservation of the cult of the god-king. Everyone, whether noble, high priest, or commoner, was expected to subordinate his or her ambitions to the need to perpetuate the existence of the king on earth and his identity with the god in this life and the next. This remarkable leader reigned for 45 years, the first of at least three dynasties of Khmer rulers, who often came to power after vicious fighting and presided over an ever-changing state that reached the height of its prosperity between A.D. 900 and 1200.

Previous monarchs had encouraged the worship of Siva in the form of the phallic image, but now Jayavarman II presented himself as the reincarnation of Siva on earth. He was the *varman*, the protector, and his priests were the instruments of practical political power. The high priests were invariably energetic, imposing nobles who presided over a highly disciplined hierarchy of religious functionaries. The ruler himself headed a bureaucracy of high-status families, which included generals and administrators who settled land disputes. The bureaucracy supervised every aspect of Khmer life, from agriculture to warfare, tax collection, and the rituals of the state religion. As always with pre-industrial civilizations, there was a close link between food surpluses and the control of the enormous labor forces needed to construct temples, reservoirs, and other public works. Most building activity probably took place during the dry months. The custom of building a new majestic and holy temple to house the royal linga of each king was the most important of all the religious rituals.

Jayavarman II's new strategy was brilliantly successful. He reigned for 45 years, founded a civilization that prospered for 600 years, and united the Khmer *mandala*s into a colorful state that reached the height of its prosperity between A.D. 900 and 1200. Successive Khmer kings presided over a civilization whose religious institutions functioned on the basis of consensus. Their society flourished on notions of conformity—on the belief that by giving to the temple, and therefore to the royal elite, people earned merit for themselves. For the next three centuries, each Khmer king ruled as "great master, king of kings." When the people were admitted to a king's presence, they prostrated themselves not before the gods but before the god-king. The Khmers' unique form of kingship produced a society that carried the cult of wealth, luxury, and divine monarchy to amazing extremes.

## *Holy Cities*

Five kings succeeded Jayavarman over the century after his death in A.D. 850. They unified his domains and consolidated his conquests. One of his nephews, Indravarman I (A.D. 877–889), started an architectural tradition followed by Khmer kings for almost four centuries. He built a large reservoir 3.2 kilometers (2 miles) long and 0.8 kilometers (0.5 miles) wide at Hariharalaya; then be built a raised temple platform, which housed images of the deified royal ancestors; and finally a temple mausoleum for himself, which was usually associated with the linga that bore the name of his preferred god. The water in the reservoir served practical irrigation and residential requirements but was also a symbolic lake at the foot of the royal mausoleum, itself a representation of Mount Meru, the mythical home of the Hindu gods north of the Himalayas. Indravarman's temple pyramid, the Bakong, was built of stone and surrounded by a moat 800 by 650 meters (500 by 404 feet). The scale of these buildings and waterworks was stupendous compared to anything built by the king's predecessors. The reservoir alone was 150 times larger than any earlier humanly made lake in the region. Hariharalaya became the first Angkor, a Sanskrit word meaning "holy city."

Indravarman's successor, Yasovarman, moved the royal capital slightly to the west, where a small hill rises 65 meters (213 feet) above the plain. This became his symbolic Mount Meru. Atop it rose the Bakheng, located within an enormous rectangular enclosure surrounded by a moat and earthen walls. The enclosure encompasses an area of nearly 1,600 hectares (4,000 acres). The Bakheng has a perfectly symmetrical plan, so from any angle the viewer sees only 33 of the 108 smaller towers erected around the central temple tower. These 33 towers correspond to the number of gods in Indra's heaven. The temple has 7 levels, representing the 7 heavens. Moreover, the 108 towers have important cosmic imagery, being divided into 4 sets of 27, each representing the phases of the lunar cycle. Each terrace contains 12 towers, representing the 12-year cycle of the planet Jupiter. Thus, the Bakheng is a symbolic representation of Mount Meru, the center of the *mandala*, the capital, and the universe. Its plan is an astronomical calendar in stone, which shows the positions and paths of the planets as conceived within the Indian notion of cyclical time.

Many of the 30 monarchs who followed Jayavarman II left massive religious edifices to commemorate their reigns. These they built on artificial mounds in the center of their capitals, the hub of the Khmer universe, an area known today as Angkor. The Khmer's unique form of kingship produced, instead of an austere civilization like that of the Indus, a society which carried the cult of wealth, luxury, and divine monarchy to amazing lengths. This cult reached its apogee in the reign of Suryavarman II, who built the temple of Angkor Wat in the twelfth century (see Box 13.1).

Angkor Wat was a temple and mausoleum, as well as a giant astronomical observatory. At the western entrance, the sun rises over the central lotus tower on the day of the spring equinox. As the sun moves during the seasons, its rays illuminate the bas-reliefs on the walls of the third gallery. It shines first on the creation

## Box 13.1 Angkor Wat, Cambodia

Four years after his succession in A.D. 1113, King Suryavarman II commenced building his masterpiece, an extraordinary shrine which is a spectacle of beauty, wonder, and magnificence, the largest religious building in the world. Angkor Wat (Figure 13.2) is 1,500 meters (5,000 feet) by 1,200 meters (4,000 feet) across. The central block measures 215 by 186 meters (717 by 620 feet) and rises more than 60 meters (200 feet) above the forest. It dwarfs even the largest Sumerian ziggurat and makes Mohenjodaro's citadel look like a village shrine.

One approaches Angkor Wat through an entrance gallery with a tower by a paved causeway 150 meters (500 feet) long that is flanked with balustrades adorned with mythical, multiheaded snakes (Figure 13.3). It opens into a cruciform terrace in front of a rectangular tower that rises in three imposing tiers to a central cluster of five towers. Each bears a lofty pinnacle, which from afar looks like a giant lotus bud. The causeway leads across a huge moat 180 meters (600 feet) wide and enclosed by masonry walls 6.4 kilometers (4 miles) in circumference. The engineers built the walls with a total error of less than two centimeters (an inch). The moat is still a beautiful sight, with floating water lilies, wild orchids, and other shimmering blooms. Angkor Wat was built in three great rising squares. A central group of chambers and then long open galleries extend all around each square, with a double square of columns on their outer face. A gallery interspersed with corner towers, pavilions, stairways, and other structures surrounds each terrace. On the highest level, the central tower is tied to axial pavilions by galleries that are supported by pillars, dividing this level into four paved courts. The towers themselves are without interior windows or staircases and are finished with superb lotus-bud cones.

**Figure 13.2** Aerial view of Angkor Wat, a representation of the Hindu universe.

**Figure 13.3** Paved causeway at Angkor Wat.

Every detail of this extraordinary building reproduces part of the heavenly world in a terrestrial mode (Figure 13.4). The Khmer believed that the world consisted of a central continent known as Jambudvipa, with the cosmic mountain, Meru, rising from its center. The gods lived at the summit of Meru, represented at Angkor Wat by the highest tower. The remaining four towers depict Meru's lesser peaks; the enclosure wall depicts the mountain at the edge of the world, and the surrounding moat depicts the ocean beyond. Angkor Wat was the culminating attempt of the Khmer to reproduce a monument to the Hindu god Vishnu, the preserver of the universe. Angkor Wat, the ultimate achievement of the Khmer *mandala*, was a monument to Siva, the creator, to Vishnu, the preserver of the universe, and to Brahma, who raised the earth. Everything about Angkor Wat is on a lavish scale, as if expense, time, and labor were of little importance.

Angkor Wat's bas-reliefs show Suryavarman seated on a wooden throne wearing an elaborate crown and pectoral. He receives his high officials as they declare their loyalty. Next, the king progresses down a hillside on an elephant accompanied by the high priest and his generals. The court rides with him through a forest, with noble ladies in litters, everyone protected by heavily armed soldiers. Scattered throughout Angkor Wat are scenes of battles and bas-reliefs of celestial maidens. Naked to the waist, slender and sensuous, the dancers wear skirts of rich fabric. Their flowered background, the subtle rhythm of their gestures, their jeweled necklaces and diadems bring to light the delights of paradise promised to the king after his death. Inscriptions also spell out the terrible punishments that awaited ill-doers.

(Cont.)

**Figure 13.4** Bas-relief of dancing girls at Angkor Wat. (Detail of the frieze of the Apsaras. From Angkor Wat. Musee des Arts Asiatiques-Guimet, Paris, France. © Guiradon/Art Resource, NY)

Angkor Wat was constructed using a measurement of 0.435 meters (1.43 feet), a Khmer unit of measurement known as a *hat*. The length and breadth of the central structure of the temple corresponded to 365.37 *hat*, while the axial distances of the great causeway corresponded with the four great eras of Hindu time. Someone standing in front of the western entrance on the spring equinox was able to see the sun rising directly over the central lotus tower. During his lifetime, Suryavarman used Angkor Wat as the place where he, as a divine monarch, communicated with the gods. When he died, his remains were placed in the central tower, so that his soul entered his divine image and made contact with the royal ancestors. Here the immortal ruler became as one with Vishnu, master of the universe.

in summer, on a bloody battle in autumn, and then leaves the north wall of the gallery in darkness during the dry season; then it illuminates the kingdom of death. Everything about Angkor Wat had profound cosmic and religious symbolism.

Jayavarman VII succeeded to the Khmer throne in A.D. 1181 after a period of warfare and political chaos, which resulted in the sack of Angkor. Soldier and devout Buddhist, Jayavarman VII was a prolific monument builder. He built a new capital, Angkor Thom, with a 12.8-kilometer (8-mile) outer wall and a crocodile-filled moat 162 meters (540 feet) across, which symbolized, as always, the mountain range and ocean boundaries of the sacred world. Angkor Thom was an entire city, not just a mausoleum, but it was still laid out according to a sacred design. Inside the enclosure rose a sacred world in stone, its gates guarded by stone representa-

**Figure 13.5** The Bayon at Angkor Thom, the temple-mortuary of Jayavarman VII.

tions of epic battles between heavenly and underworld gods over a serpent. The serpent's extended back reaches the central temple mountain, the Bayon (Figure 13.5). The battle represents an ancient myth, in which the gods and demons churned the ocean to extract the liquor of immortality. The cosmic serpent Vasuki was a rope, Mount Meru serving as the churning stick. Great triple-headed elephants protect the flanks of the gates, and four huge Buddha faces adorn the towers above the massive doorways.

A Chinese official named Zhou Daguan visited Angkor as part of a delegation between August 1296 and August 1297. The visitors traveled up the Mekong River and across the Tonle Sap by large, oar-driven boats to Angkor, where they admired the Bayon, "the tower of gold," and the royal palace. Angkor was a cosmopolitan capital with a large market, where precious metals, silks, ceramics, and imports of all kinds could be purchased. Thousands of people lived in or near the royal capital, most of them lowly servants and slaves, who endured harsh lives of unrelenting drudgery. This was a society that was deeply concerned, even obsessed, with grandiose displays and public spectacles (see Box 13.2).

The Grand Plaza of Angkor Thom was the scene of ceremonies and contests and of vast military reviews. Long bas-reliefs of animals and kings walking in procession above seas of snakes and fish lead to the plaza and look down on its wide spaces. One frieze of elephants extends over 360 meters (1,200 feet) of sculpted wall. The Bayon's towers bear representations of the Buddha, perhaps multiplying himself miraculously to confuse his enemies. Fish carved around the exterior

## Box 13.2 Zhou Daguan Visits Angkor

China traded extensively with the Khmer, trading gold, silver, silk, porcelain, and many other commodities for a variety of tropical products. The Chinese considered the Cambodians "barbarians," but many sailors deserted and settled there, noting with pleasure "that it is not necessary to wear clothes . . . rice is easily had, women easily persuaded, houses easily run, and trade easily carried on."

Zhou Daguan was a Chinese diplomat who spent nearly a year with an embassy to the Khmer court at Angkor in 1296–1297. His famous *Notes on the Customs of Cambodia*, written soon after his return to China, provide vivid insights into Khmer civilization at its height. He described Angkor Thom as a city with walls 8 kilometers (5 miles) in circumference, forming a perfect square. The "Golden Tower" of the Bayon rose in the center of the vast enclosure, "flanked by more than twenty lesser towers and several hundred stone chambers." He added: "These are the monuments which have caused merchants from overseas to speak so often of 'Cambodia the rich and noble.'"

The embassy visited the royal palace with its long colonnades and open chambers "interlaced in harmonious relation." "Every time I was admitted to the palace for an audience with the king, he came forward with his chief wife and took his seat in the embrasure of the golden window in the main audience hall. The ladies of the court were drawn up on both sides of the veranda below the window, changing places now and then to get a better look at us." The elaborate, tile-roofed palace contrasted with the humble, thatched dwellings of commoners, who were forbidden tiles. When high officials appeared in public, their insignia and number of attendants was carefully regulated. Only the most eminent rode in palanquins with golden shafts and four parasols with golden handles.

Khmer life unfolded in a constant series of elaborate festivals. At the New Year, a huge platform was erected in front of the royal palace and decorated with lanterns and flowers. For two weeks, spectacular firework displays lit the night sky, each financed by a high official. "The fire crackers, large as swivel-guns, shake the whole city with their explosions." Zhou Daguan comments on how the Cambodians could rely on three or four rice crops a year, irrigated by the waters of the Tonle Sap, and there were also water buffalo, many forms of vegetables, and an abundance of fish.

Everything at Angkor revolved around the monarch, who only rarely ventured outside the royal precincts. When he did, he was closely protected. He would emerge in solemn procession, preceded by marching soldiers, then "flags, the banners, music." "Girls of the palace, gaily dressed, with flowers in their hair and tapers in their hands, are massed together in a separate column." The king's bodyguard followed them, armed to the teeth, then "chariots drawn by goats and horses, all adorned with gold." Bearers of sacred parasols marched in front of high nobles mounted on elephants. "Finally the Sovereign appeared, standing erect on an elephant and holding in his hand the sacred sword. This elephant, his tusks sheathed in gold, was accompanied by bearers of twenty white parasols with golden shafts. All around was a bodyguard of elephants, drawn close together, and still more soldiers for complete protection, marching in close order." As the King passed, everyone knelt and touched the earth with their foreheads under the close eye of the parade marshals.

The Khmer state maintained a glittering facade and kept order with draconian severity and religious zeal. But the supreme ruler could not appear in public without a major display of force. Writes Zhou Daguan, himself from a despotic state: "These people, though barbarians, know what is due to a prince."

point to the underworld under the oceans, making the Bayon the home of the gods. Each of the 50 towers of the Bayon may represent a province of Jayavarman's domains. Each bears an image of Jayavarman, the living god on earth, gazing in all four directions.

Jayavarman's building frenzy extended far beyond his capital. He built large reservoirs in and near Angkor, allowing more land to be irrigated. His close relatives received mortuary temples. The king ordered the construction of guest houses and hospitals, the former spaced about 15 kilometers (9 miles) apart on the roads that radiated out from Angkor. One linked Angkor with another large center, Banteay Chmar—225 kilometers (140 miles) northwest—complete with bridges over major waterways.

It is said that a million people once lived in or near Angkor Thom. One temple dedicated to the king's father contained no fewer than 430 images, with more than 20,000 in gold, silver, bronze, and stone in the wider precincts. An inscription in the Ta Prohm temple nearby, dedicated to the king's mother in the image of the Buddha's mother, records that 306,372 people from 13,500 villages worked for the shrine, consuming 38,000 tons of rice a year. An inscription in the nearby temple of Ta Prohm inventories a staff of 18 senior priests, 2,740 minor functionaries, 615 female dancers, and a total of 66,625 "men and women who perform the service of the gods." The same temple owned gold and silver dishes, thousands of pearls, 876 Chinese veils, and 2,387 sets of clothing for its statues. The temple of the king's father contained no fewer than 430 images. A further 20,000 images in gold, silver, bronze, and stone stood in the wider precincts.

## *A Religious Utopia*

All this royal construction was designed to make merit for the king and his followers. He also built fully staffed hospitals and pilgrims' shelters to gain further credit. The result of Jayavarman's building projects was a totally centripetal religious utopia in which every product, every person's labor, and every thought was directed to embellishing the hub of the universe and the kings who enjoyed it. All these resources came from a flow of wealth toward the center, amassed by taxes on produce and manufactured goods. Moreover, the people raised defensive walls, built temples, and dug reservoirs as tax obligations to the state; the central court, not outlying centers, supervised all taxation. Everything was done in the service of the gods and the king, who was at the apex of Khmer society. He was served by his own relatives and other aristocratic families, who lived under an elaborate system of royal patronage and badges of rank—defined by the styles of litters and the staffs of umbrellas. Succession to important offices such as the chief priesthood was often hereditary. This small circle of high nobles controlled land ownership and tribute assignments from the provinces, sometimes making dozens of villages vassals to major temples to obtain food and labor. Standing armies and navies maintained security and subdued regional unrest. Elephants were a major strategic force in Khmer wars with their neighbors.

All labor, all material goods, flowed toward the center, to benefit those at the hub of civilization. Angkor itself was the center of a court society that strove to achieve material and spiritual perfection. Successive kings built great buildings; controlled water supplies through their vast reservoirs, which overcame the uncertainties of rainfall; and organized thousands of people to ensure the continuation of the perfection of the *mandala*, the sacred territorial circle.

The impression of prosperity and stability was illusory in a society where the ruler's power depended on the granting of favors, on his successful patronizing of the major aristocratic families. There was no stable bureaucracy with appointed officials to run the state. The king mediated with the gods for rain, settled disputes, and used the rich resources of the land to redistribute wealth among his subjects. He sat at the center of the circle represented by the *mandala*, its boundaries defined only by the loyalties of the aristocrats who ruled the outlying provinces. A Khmer king's hold on the reins of power depended on the control of the center, the Angkor. Thus, when the central administration was weak, the kingdom tended to break up into regional components.

## Collapse

By Jayavarman VII's death, Buddhism had gained a strong foothold, but religious dissension became common until Theravada, a form of low Buddhism preaching equality, became popular. Theravada did not mess with traditional ideas of kingship, so building activity slowed. Warfare was endemic. In 1430–1431, Angkor was sacked by the Thai after a long siege and the great state finally dissolved.

Late in the thirteenth century, the strategic trade routes through the Malay Straits came under Islamic control in a new chapter of international trade. Melaka became an important port and stronghold on the northern shore of the straits. The rest of the kingdoms and ports of the islands soon adopted the new religion, which preached a message of religious egalitarianism in the face of centuries of Indian statecraft based on notions of divine kingship. Within three centuries, the rulers of inland Java had adopted Islam, perhaps to maintain control over their subjects, who were welcoming the new beliefs with open arms. Islam and trade went hand in hand in island Southeast Asia, until the arrival of Portuguese gun-bearing sailing ships at Melaka in 1519.

The Khmer state is a classic example of how a combination of cultural processes and able individuals can lead to the appearance of powerful, yet volatile states. Yet these same states face constantly the problem of controlling not only the center but the periphery, especially in times of weak rule and menacing competition from outside.

## Summary

The origins of civilization in Southeast Asia had both indigenous and foreign roots. During the first millennium B.C., powerful chiefdoms arose among rice-farming groups in areas like Vietnam's Red River Valley, where the Dong Son culture flourished. About the time of Christ, Indian merchants brought Hindu and Buddhist beliefs to Southeast Asia, while Chinese armies conquered the Red River region. The Southeast Asian state was based on Indian notions of statecraft and was cast in the model of the *mandala*, a sacred circle. During the first millennium A.D. *mandala*s ebbed and flowed in the Mekong Delta and then inland in the Tonle Sap region of Cambodia. None of these states achieved any long-term stability, but they culminated in the great *mandala* founded by King Jayavarman II in the late eighth and ninth centuries A.D. Jayavarman carved out a large kingdom by conquering his neighbors, and he established new philosophies of divine kingship, which endured for five centuries. Political power in the Khmer state was vested in the person of the divine king, who governed by force; by judicious use of patronage; and by using his status as a god to acquire tribute, control ownership of the land, and collect taxes in goods and labor. The symbol of royal power was the mortuary temple—sites like Angkor Wat, which were built as symbolic replicas of the Hindu world. *Mandala*s were flexible forms of state without fixed boundaries, which were centripetal and rarely able to achieve long-term political stability. Islam spread widely in the Southeast Asian islands in the centuries before Portuguese contact in 1519.

## Guide to Further Reading

Charles Higham, *The Archaeology of Mainland Southeast Asia* (Cambridge: Cambridge University Press, 1989) is the definitive archaeological analysis of the Southeast Asian region and contains a comprehensive bibliography. Charles Higham and Rachanie Thosarat, *Prehistoric Thailand* (Bangkok: River Books, 1998) is a useful popular account. David Chandler, *A History of Cambodia* (Boulder, CO: Westview Press, 1983) provides a broader historical perspective. See also Paul Wheatley, *The Golden Khersonee: Studies in the Historical Geography of the Malay Peninsula to A.D. 1500* (Kuala Lumpur: University of Malaya, 1961). Wheatley's *Nagara and Commandery* (Chicago: University of Chicago Department of Geography Research Papers, 1983) is a fundamental source. O. W. Wolters, *History, Culture, and Region in Southeast Asian Perspective* (Singapore: Institute of Southeast Asian Studies, 1982) is invaluable on *mandala*s. For Khmer kingship, see I. W. Mabbett, "Kingship at Angkor," *Journal of the Siam Society* 66, no. 2 (1965): 1–58. For Angkor Wat, see E. Mannika, *Angkor Wat: Time, Space, Kingship* (Honolulu, HI: University of Hawaii Press, 1996). A series of valuable essays on such topics as the life of commoners will be found in R. B. Smith and W. Watson, eds., *Early South East Asia* (Oxford: Oxford University Press, 1979).

*Chapter 14*

# Kingdoms and Empires in East Asia

## (770 B.C.–A.D. 700)

An officer figure from the pottery army of the first Chinese emperor Shihuangdi at Mount Lishan, China.

*"A fast horse and a slow horse set out together on the 3,000-li (900-kilometer or 563-mile) journey from Changan to Qi. The first day the fast horse travels 193 li, thereafter increasing its speed by 13 li each day. The slow horse covers 97 li on the first day, thereafter reducing its speed by 0.5 li each day. After reaching Qi the fast horse starts its return journey and meets the slow horse. When does the meeting take place and how fast has each horse traveled?" The teacher sat cross-legged on the dais, looking down as his pupils struggled with the problem. Their heads were bent in concentration as they plied their ink-charged brushes and made rapid calculations on thin wooden boards. It was hard work but essential, for these young men would soon be candidates in the great state-run examinations. If they failed, they would return to their homes to make their own way in a family business or as a local town scribe. If they succeeded, the door would be open to high office in the Han empire and a chance to play their part in governing its 58 million inhabitants.*

The Han empire, which created this elaborate bureaucratic system, was the culmination of developments that extended over several centuries. The demise of the Shang state in 1027 B.C. (see Chapter 6) was followed by a period of increasing decentralization, the so-called Western Zhou period (1027–771 B.C.), when subject kingdoms freed themselves from central authority. The ensuing Eastern Zhou period (770–221 B.C.) saw revolutionary developments in Chinese civilization, including a new urbanism, the development of ironworking technology, and an upsurge of commerce coupled with the invention of coinage. There was also warfare on an unprecedented scale, so endemic that the second part of the Eastern Zhou period is known as the Warring States period (458–221 B.C.). It ended with the unification of China under the ruler of the state of Qin, who became known as Shihuangdi, "First Emperor." The Han empire was founded some 15 years later. We begin this chapter by discussing the radical changes in Chinese society and economy during the Eastern Zhou period before describing the monuments of Shihuangdi, notably his famous terracotta regiment. The Han empire that followed was itself divided into two phases: Western Han (206 B.C.–A.D. 8) and Eastern Han (A.D. 25–220). We end with an analysis of the formation of early states in Korea and Japan during the fifth to seventh centuries A.D.

## Society Transformed: The Eastern Zhou Period (770–221 B.C.)

### *Urbanism*

We saw in Chapter 6 how urban centers first developed in China during the Shang period (c. 2000–1027 B.C.). We have also noted that these were not urban in the same way as early Mesopotamian cities, for example. Shang cities consisted of elite enclosures surrounded by a scatter of workshops and artisans' villages, a pattern that we have termed an "urban cluster." It could be argued that these were not true cities since they did not comprise large-scale residential areas with commercial, as well as administrative, functions. If that is our preferred definition of urbanism, the first urban centers in China were those of the Eastern Zhou period.

Hundreds of Eastern Zhou cities are known from historical texts, but fewer than 40 have been studied archaeologically. In the eighth century B.C., cities covered large areas—confined within *hang tu* defensive walls—but had relatively few inhabitants. Residential occupation was usually limited to particular sectors, with cemeteries in others, and there was little pressure on space. Three centuries later, as both texts and archaeology show, cities had become densely built-up, with tens or even hundreds of thousands of inhabitants. The largest, Yanxiadu, may have housed as many as 316,000 people. Furthermore, the cities themselves were larger than those of the Western Zhou period. State capitals such as Yanxiadu and Handan covered around 20 square kilometers (7.5 square miles), twice the size of the largest Western Zhou cities, and were much more densely built within their walls (Figure 14.1). State capitals were the seats of the dynasties who ruled the Eastern Zhou kingdoms. These ruling elites lived in palace areas either within or alongside the cities. The palaces themselves are marked archaeologically by rammed-earth platforms on which the buildings were constructed. On the one hand, the idea of a separate royal city, surrounded by its own wall, was no doubt a device to keep the ruling elite apart from the urban populace as a whole. It enhanced the impression of social distance and mystique. On the other hand, clusters of rammed-earth platforms do appear in other city areas in the later part of the Eastern Zhou period. This suggests that palacelike complexes were being built by other than the ruling family, and it perhaps reflects a weakening of royal power in some of the states as time went on.

Eastern Zhou cities were also important centers of both commerce and manufacturing. From the fifth century B.C., iron foundries were both large and numerous. The cities, with their major markets, may well have supplied the surrounding populations with iron tools for farming. There were also mints for coinage in some cities and workshops for jade and bone. These, then, were true cities: substantial concentrations of population and commercial, manufacturing, and political centers, linked with the surrounding countryside in a relationship of mutual interdependence.

### *Ironworking*

Just when the Chinese first began to smelt iron is open to some doubt. Dates as early as the seventh century have been proposed, but the latest consensus is that

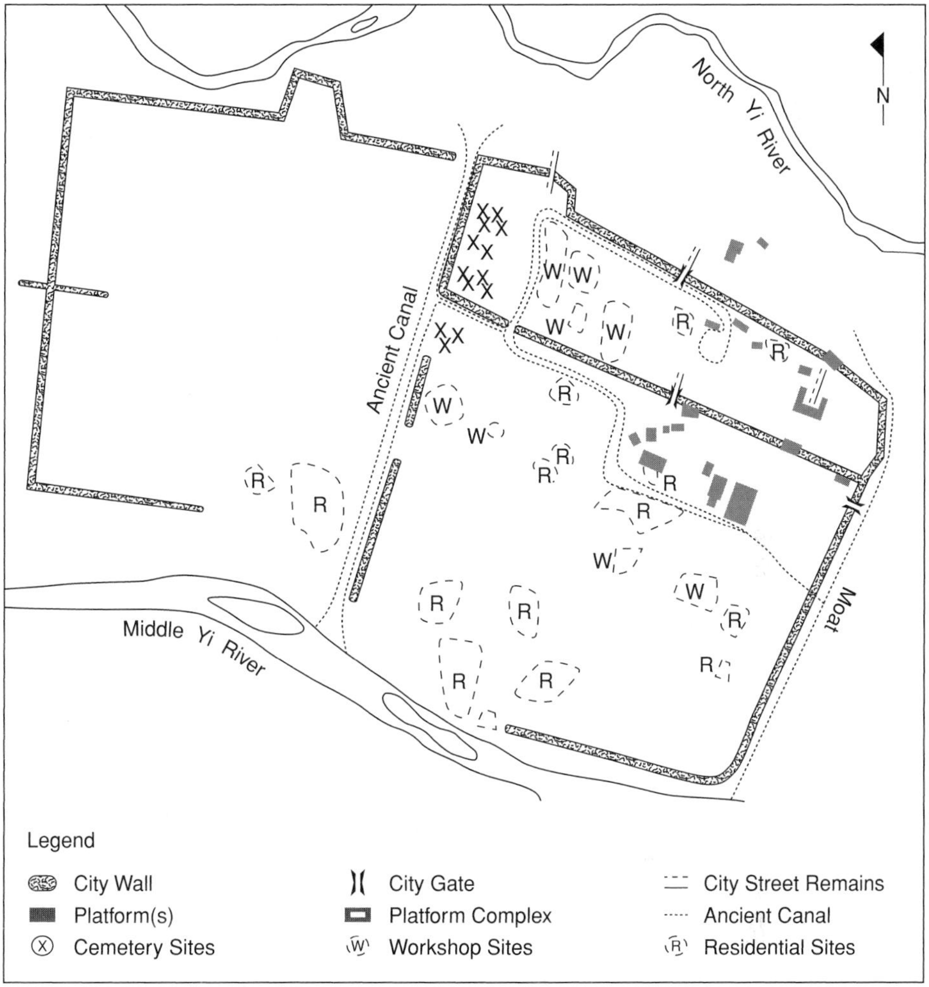


**Figure 14.1** Plan of Eastern Zhou city of Yanxiadu.

by at least 500 B.C. ironworking was well established in some regions of China, notably in the southern kingdom of Wu. Ironworking developed several centuries later in China than in western Asia or the Mediterranean, but there is no reason to suggest that knowledge of the metal spread from one region to the other. Chinese metallurgists had already for some time been producing bronze objects with a high iron content. Furthermore, Chinese ironworkers used very different techniques for working the metal than their Western counterparts. In the West, iron was smelted without added carbon, giving a spongy "bloom," which was then shaped by repeated hammering and heating (the process known as forging). In contrast, the Chinese added extra carbon, in the form of charcoal, to the iron during smelting. This lowered the melting point of the iron and yielded not spongy bloom but molten ore, suitable for casting in the same way as bronze. Within a couple of centuries, Chinese metalworkers had discovered ways of regulating the amount of carbon taken up by the iron and were able to produce a form of mild steel, far superior to anything available in the West until the late Middle Ages.

Iron is a cheaper and more abundant metal than bronze, and the ability to cast it made it possible for Chinese metalworkers to mass-produce iron farming tools. This in turn allowed competing Eastern Zhou states to invest in agricultural expansion as they sought to increase both farming yields and population size. Massive iron-producing establishments were set up on the edges of the forested zones, where abundant supplies of wood were available for charcoal. The northern kingdom of Yang was an especially prolific producer of iron tools and weapons. Bronze continued to be used for ritual and decorative items, however, including impressive sets of bells. A major copper mine of the period has been discovered at Tonglushan in east-central China, complete with wooden shuttering and pit props for shafts and galleries. These mines are further evidence of the increasing importance of the metal industry in China during the late first millennium B.C.

## *Coinage and Commerce*

Coins may first have been made in China in the seventh and sixth centuries B.C. By 400 B.C. most Eastern Zhou kingdoms were minting their own. The shapes of the earliest coins provide a hint of their ancestry: Those of central China were shaped like knives, while the coins of the Shandong peninsula in the east took the form of miniature spades. Both were made of bronze and were intended for relatively utilitarian transactions (unlike the earliest coinages of western Asia and the Mediterranean, of about the same period, which were made of gold and silver and could not have been intended for everyday use). Spade and knife coins were cast rather than struck, and each carried an inscription that recorded the name of the state and the city that produced it (Figure 14.2).

**Figure 14.2** Chinese spade and knife bronze coins from the Warring States period (458–221 B.C.).

The circular coin with a square, central hole for stringing on a cord appeared at the very end of the Eastern Zhou period. This was the form chosen by the state of Qin, whose ruler unified China and became the first emperor in 221 B.C. The Qin emperor made the circular coin the standard type throughout the whole of China, and so it remained up to recent times.

## *Warring States*

The invention of coinage in China must have stimulated trade and commerce, removing the need for barter. Just as important, it made it easier for the rulers to gather revenues from their kingdoms.

By the end of the Western Zhou period in 771 B.C., when the Zhou rulers moved their capital from Qishan to Luoyang, their authority as overlords of their domains was little more than nominal. Instead, real power was in the hands of more than 130 separate states, small and large, many of them grouped into alliances. Hardly surprisingly, the history of the following five centuries was one of warfare and annexation. At first, in the so-called Chunqiu (Spring and Autumn) period (770–458 B.C.), the wars were relatively small-scale. Particular prestige attached to the number of chariots each side could field.

The nature of warfare changed significantly in the Zhan'guo (Warring States) period (458–221 B.C.). The wars of the spring and autumn period had already reduced the number of independent kingdoms to 22. By the fifth century B.C. the effects of population growth and mass-produced iron weaponry had given wars a very different character. Armies now numbered tens of thousands. Chariots were largely abandoned as weapons of war in favor of cavalry and massed squadrons of infantry. Iron swords came into use, sometimes with fine jade fittings for the pommel. One of the most interesting military innovations was the crossbow, a Chinese invention, capable of propelling an arrow with much greater speed and force than an ordinary bow.

The crossbow was particularly suitable for defending the walled cities of the period. Walls were also built between the separate kingdoms to protect them from one another or from the horse-riding nomads on their northern frontier. These long interstate walls represented an enormous investment of resources and are eloquent testimony to the centralized organization of Eastern Zhou states. The Wei kingdom built its wall of sun-dried brick; the Qi built partly in stone; most others were of rammed earth. Whatever the material, they provide stunning confirmation of the effective bureaucracies of the various kingdoms.

Even these elaborate precautions failed to protect the states that built them. By 300 B.C., only five major kingdoms survived: Qin, Zhao, Wei, Han, and Chu, plus the tiny state of Zhou, which still held nominal suzerainty over the rest. In 260 B.C. the ruler of Qin defeated his greatest rival, Zhao, slaughtering 400,000 prisoners in the process. The next ruler of Qin then went on to complete the conquest not only of Zhao but also of Zhou, Wei, Han, and Chu. Having brought all these lands under his sole rule, in 221 B.C. he officially proclaimed himself Qin Shihuangdi, "First Emperor" of a united China.

## The First Chinese Empire (221–206 B.C.)

### *Qin Shihuangdi (221–210 B.C.)*

An enormous burial mound, 50 meters (164 feet) high, rises amid fields of irrigated cereals and vegetables some 40 kilometers (25 miles) east of Xian, the modern capital of Shaanxi province. Around its base run two huge rectangular enclosures, one inside the other, enclosing an area of 2 square kilometers (0.75 square miles). Between outer and inner walls once lay the "Sleeping Palace," occupied by guards, attendants, and concubines, whose duty was to tend the grave of the dead ruler. Legend has it that 700,000 convicts were conscripted to complete the burial complex and that the artisans who designed and built the chamber within the mound were killed to conceal its secrets. Despite this precaution, news leaked out of a fabulous tomb chamber, equipped with rivers of flowing mercury and booby-trapped crossbows to deter any would-be pillager. It was probably the greatest tomb ever built in China, and it has never been fully excavated (Figure 14.3).

This tomb is the resting place of Shihuangdi, First Emperor of China. It was begun in 221 B.C., shortly after his victory over the last of the rival Warring States, and was completed by his son and successor after Shihuangdi's death in 210 B.C. It was this successor who decided to kill the artisans who might divulge details of the tomb's security features. We know of these features through the writings of later Chinese historians. Long regarded as fanciful, they gained credibility in 1974 when direct evidence of Shihuangdi's burial arrangements came to light in the form of vast pottery regiments. Four huge pits had been dug to the east of the tomb enclosure, facing any danger that might approach from that side. The largest (Pit 1) contained 3,210 life-size terracotta statues of Qin soldiers, discovered when the local people were digging wells in the vicinity. The pit itself measures 210 by 60 meters (689 by 197 feet). The soldiers are arranged in 11 marching columns, standing 4 abreast. Some are depicted wearing armor of bronze or iron plates, and all originally carried long spears with bronze spearheads, though these have now gone, looted by rebels in 206 B.C.

This first pit was astonishing enough, but more was to follow. In 1976 Chinese archaeologists discovered a second, smaller pit, containing 1,400 terracotta figures of men and horses. If Pit 1 represented an infantry unit, then here were the cavalry and chariots that accompanied them, including a division of kneeling crossbowmen. A third pit, found in 1977, contained a command and control unit: the commander-in-chief in his war chariot, surrounded by 64 officers and bodyguards, the latter clearly selected for their height (1.9 meters, or 6 feet, 2 inches).

The pottery regiment was evidently intended to provide ritual protection for the dead emperor. It has echoes of earlier times, when soldiers themselves were sacrificed and placed in the graves—in the Xibeigang tombs at Anyang, for example (see Chapter 6)—although not in these numbers. For archaeologists today, it provides striking evidence of the power of Qin Shihuangdi and also illustrates in vivid detail the nature, equipment, and organization of the army that gave the Qin dynasty its victory over rival states.

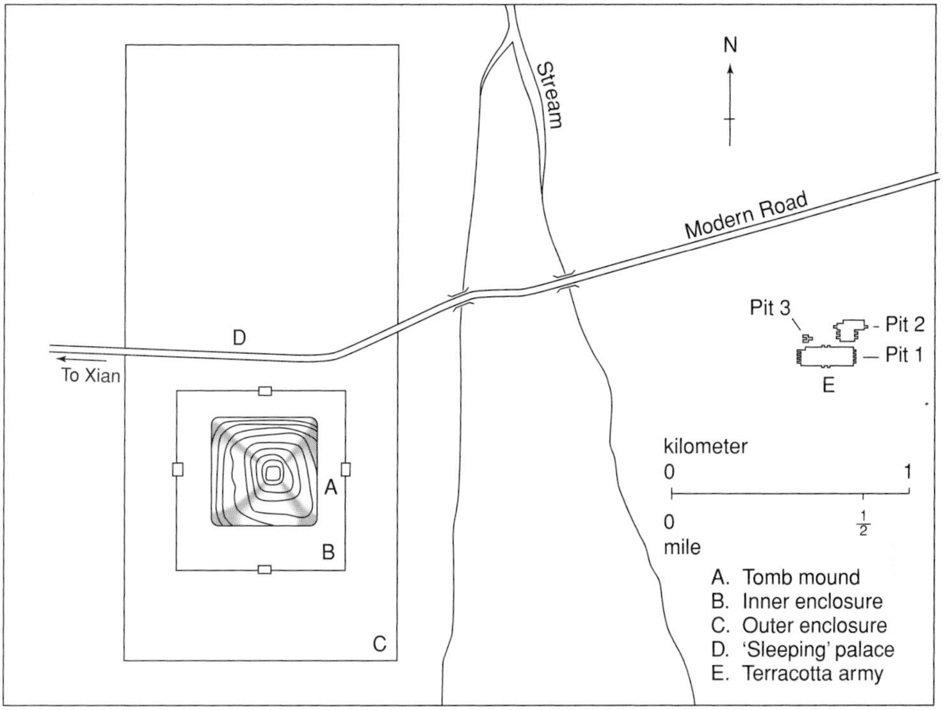


(a)

(b)

**Figure 14.3** The tomb of Qin Shihuangdi. (a) Plan of the tomb complex; (b) view of excavations in Pit 1 and ranks of terracotta soldiers.

## *The Qin Empire*

The success of Shihuangdi was based on his formidable and battle-hardened army and also on his bureaucratic and administrative reforms. Earlier rulers had allowed conquered territories to survive under subject lords, in a feudal arrangement. Shihuangdi broke with this tradition by dividing the kingdoms into provinces of roughly equal size and appointing governors answerable to himself to rule over them. This created a centralized imperial administration. In newly conquered territories the administrative centers of the new provinces were known as *commanderies*.

Shihuangdi reinforced the power of central government by ordering the destruction of books of a political nature and all histories except those relating to his own forebears, the rulers of Qin. His intention was to suppress rival histories and establish a new, unified state ideology. He not only dismembered the former kingdoms and divided them into provinces, he also suppressed the very memory of their separate pasts. The Mexican ruler Tlacaelel followed a similar policy 17 centuries later when establishing the Aztec empire, suppressing rival histories to create a new myth of Aztec dominance (see Chapter 16).

The emperor consolidated his domains by an ambitious road-building program. Five trunk roads led from the imperial capital at Xianyang, each provided with police forces and posting stations. Most of these roads were of rammed-earth construction and were 15 meters (50 feet) wide. The longest ran southwest over 7,500 kilometers (4,500 miles) to the frontier region of Yunnan. So precipitous was the countryside that sections of the road had to be built out from vertical cliff faces on projecting timber galleries. Despite these efforts, parts of southern China remained beyond imperial control until the Eastern Han period (first century A.D.).

In the north, the threat of nomad incursions from the steppes was met by the building of the Great Wall. This was the not the stone structure known from tourist photographs today; those well-known stretches of the Great Wall date only from the sixteenth century A.D. and were built to defend Beijing from the Manchurians. Shihuangdi's Great Wall was at one and the same time both more and less impressive—less impressive in its construction, which was mainly of traditional rammed earth or sun-dried brick, but much more impressive in its enormous length. It stretched for over 5,000 kilometers (3,000 miles) across hill and plain, from the boundaries of Korea in the east to the troublesome Ordos Desert in the west. It was an enormous logistical undertaking, though for much of its course it incorporated lengths of earlier walls built by the separate Chinese kingdoms to defend their northern frontiers in the fourth and third centuries B.C.

We have dwelt at some length on the achievements of the First Emperor of China since they demonstrate graphically the centralization of power he achieved through ruthless and sometimes paranoid rule. History remembers Shihuangdi as a superstitious tyrant, and the dynasty did not long survive his death in 210 B.C. In 206 B.C. the imperial capital, Xianyang, was sacked by a rebel army, and a new dynasty, the Han, took control. They were to rule China for over four centuries.

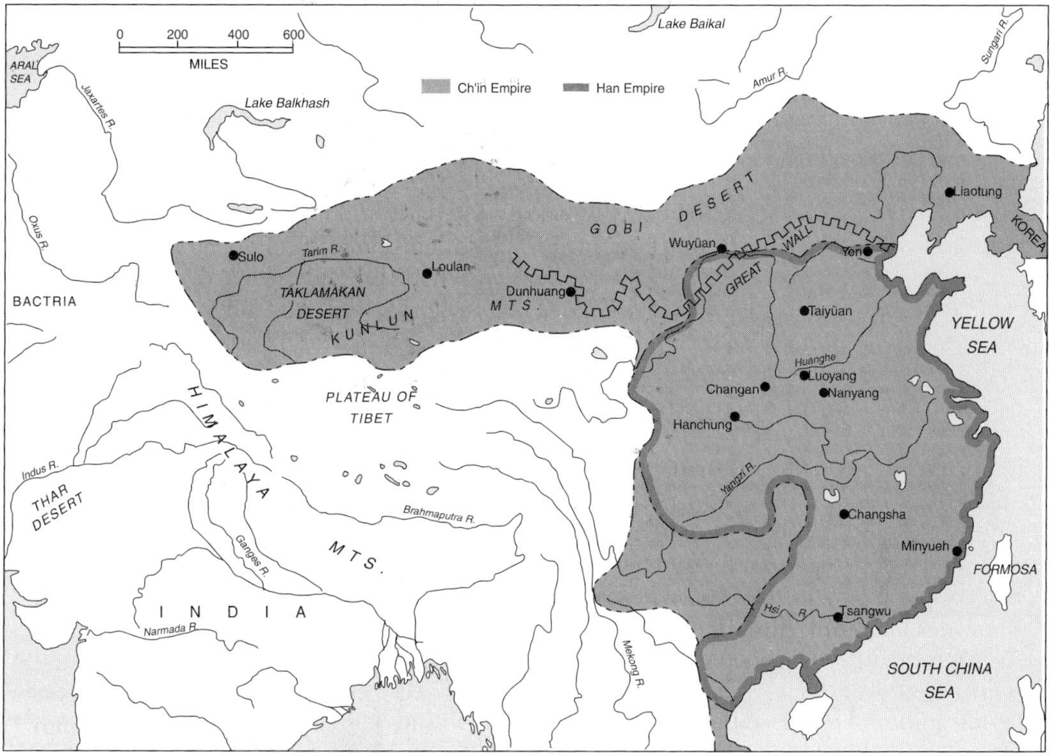


**Figure 14.4** Map of the Ch'in (Qin) and Han empires.

# The Han Empire (206 B.C.–A.D. 220)

The rulers of the Han dynasty took over the government machinery and infrastructure established by Shihuangdi (Figure 14.4). The empire was ruled primarily through commanderies, though there were also a number of small subject "kingdoms," entrusted to members of the Han royal family. In 1971 Chinese archaeologists discovered the tomb of one of these subject rulers, Marquis Dai of the Changsha kingdom, together with the even better preserved burial of his wife. These tombs, dating to c. 160 B.C., provide vivid evidence of the luxury of courtly life during the early Han period (Figure 14.5).

## *Aristocratic Burials*

Archaeological material from the Han dynasty is much more abundant than from earlier periods of Chinese civilization. Much of it comes from tombs, which contain both luxury and everyday objects. Many of them also contain terracotta

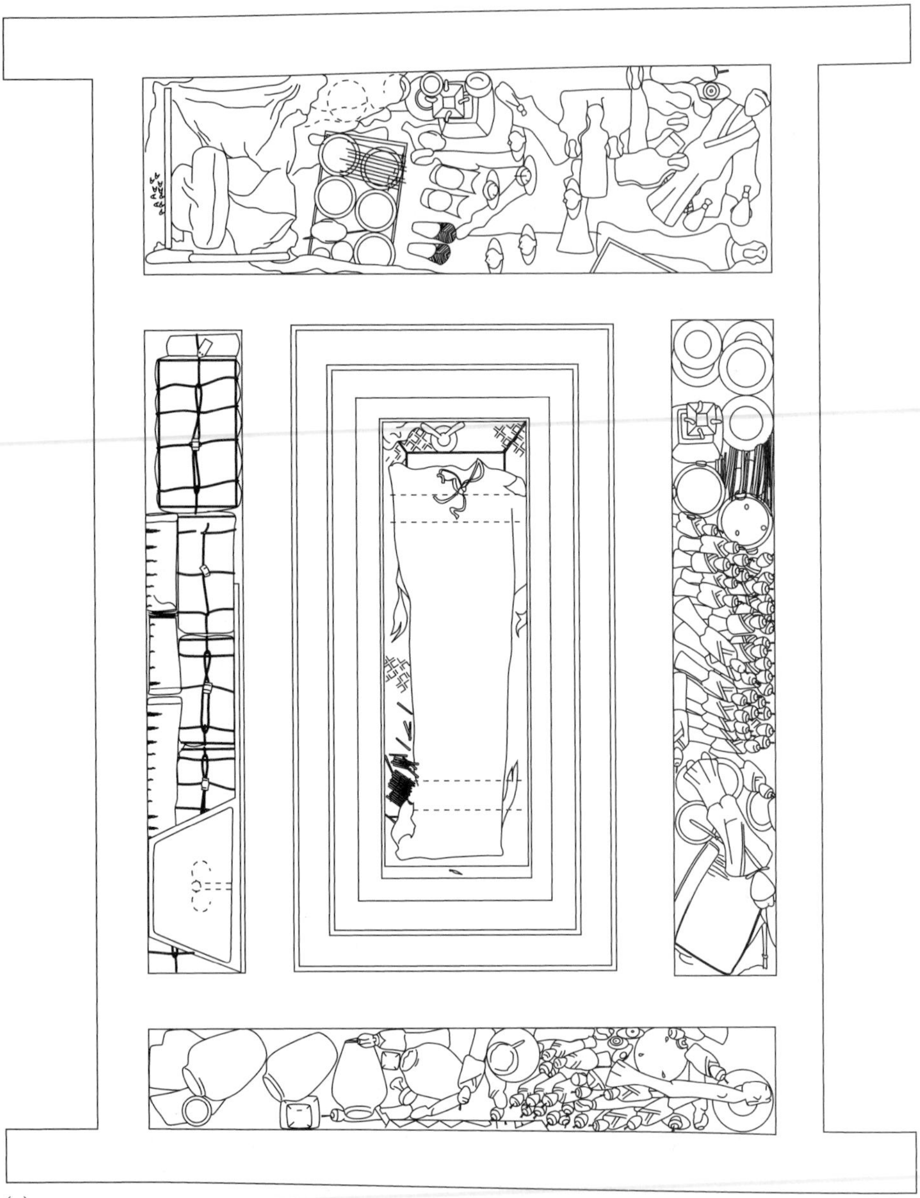

(a)

**Figure 14.5** (a) Plan of the Mawangdui tomb. When Chinese archaeologists opened Tomb 1 at Mawangdui in central southern China they came upon one of the best-preserved Han tombs ever discovered. Documents show that it was the resting place of the wife of Marquis Dai of Changsha, who died around 160 B.C. The wooden burial chamber had been sealed in by layers of charcoal and white clay and was almost perfectly preserved; the flesh of the woman's body was still soft to the touch. She had died around age 50 from a heart attack brought on by acute pain from gallstones. In small compartments around the main burial chamber, archaeologists found hundreds of priceless luxury artifacts, including decorated silks, lacquerware trays and food bowls, cosmetic equipment, and tiny wooden figures playing musical instruments. One of the finest items was a T-shaped silk banner, painted with sun and moon and mythological scenes.

(b)

**Figure 14.5** *(cont.)* (b) Lacquer bowl from the tomb of the wife of Marquis Dai at Mawangdui, second century B.C. Lacquerware, a Chinese invention, became increasingly sophisticated during the Zhou and Han periods and eventually replaced pottery tableware in aristocratic households. The item illustrated here shows that traditional Chinese eating habits—using bowls and chopsticks—have a very long history.

models of buildings, including simple farmsteads with courtyards and towers. These provide a much better image of the ordinary architecture of the Han countryside than do the excavated remains of such buildings. Other tomb models represent domestic livestock or agricultural equipment such as rice hullers and winnows. Scenes from court and country life are depicted in relief on molded bricks.

The greatest Han tombs were those of princes and aristocrats. The largest of all were naturally the tombs of the Han emperors themselves. In general form they copied the pattern set by Shihuangdi: a truncated, four-sided pyramid mound, surrounded by a wall and accompanied by a temple where the cult of the dead king was observed. The reigning emperor would visit the tombs of his dead ancestors on specified occasions. The burial mounds were sometimes of enormous size: 230 meters (750 feet) square and 46 meters (150 feet) high in the case of the tomb of Wu Di (141–87 B.C.), the greatest Han emperor. Tradition held that the emperors devoted one-third of their revenues to the construction of their tombs. The main imperial cemetery was located northwest of Changan, the capital. No fewer than nine of the early Han emperors were buried here, each in his own mounded tomb, with the smaller burial mounds of consorts, courtiers, and retainers scattered over the surrounding plain. Each imperial tomb was also attached to a settlement of the living, whose inhabitants (numbering several thousands) were charged with the upkeep of the royal necropolis and the continued observance of the necessary rites and rituals. The whole arrangement was remarkably reminiscent of the pyramid cemeteries of ancient Egypt (see Chapter 4).

One of the most extraordinary discoveries of Chinese archaeologists in recent years has been a series of pottery armies, resembling those of Qin Shihuangdi but associated with the Han imperial tombs. The main difference is that the Han figures, dating to the second century B.C., are only around 60 centimeters (2 feet) tall. The largest group, found in 1990, comes from a site 50 kilometers (31 miles) northeast of Xian and is part of the tomb complex of Emperor Jang Di (156–140 B.C.) and his wife, Empress Wang. Twenty-four separate pits have been discovered, containing thousands of pottery warriors; one estimate puts the total number at 40,000, far more than the 6,000 discovered near the tomb of Shihuangdi. One of the pits contained figures of oxen, dogs, sheep, and pigs. Another had a group of soldiers guarding a granary, complete with well-preserved contents of wheat and millet. The soldiers had wooden arms, which could be rotated at the shoulders, and held miniature weapons, including iron swords and wooden crossbows. The figures themselves were originally painted and clothed in silk.

None of the imperial Han tombs has been excavated, so for knowledge of the below-ground structures (and tomb contents) we must turn to the princely tombs in the provinces. One of the most famous is the tomb of Liu Sheng, Prince of Zhongshan (died 113 B.C.), at Mancheng in northeastern China. This consisted of an entrance ramp leading to chambers cut more than 50 meters (170 feet) deep into the solid rock of a hillside. The passage was closed by a door of cast iron, which had been poured in situ. Behind it, side galleries held suites of chariots and other equipment. Beyond them lay the main chamber, large enough to accommodate a timber-built palace hall with tiled roof. Deeper still within the mountain, behind a white marble door, was the burial chamber itself. When Chinese archaeologists at last penetrated this far in 1968, they were met by a fantastic sight: the burial suit of Prince Liu Sheng himself, made of 2,498 wafer-thin pieces of jade sewn together with gold thread. Liu Sheng's wife, Dou Wan, clothed in a similar jade burial suit, was found in a second rock-cut tomb nearby.

More recently, another elaborate tomb has been found at Beidongshan near Xuzhou in eastern China. This, too, was dug into a hillside, but in architectural terms it was considerably grander than the tomb at Mancheng, though its contents had been looted in antiquity. To one side of the long passage that led to the burial chamber was a reception complex, comprising a kitchen, storerooms, an ice cellar, a lavatory, a well, and a hall for music and dancing. These were finely built of cut stones and covered by a roof of stone slabs, which still preserve traces of the painted numerals that indicated how they were to be placed in position. At the far end of the passage was the burial place of the prince, a small group of chambers entirely painted with cinnabar, in accordance with ritual precepts of the period. Still more remarkable was the discovery in Xuzhou itself, 10 kilometers (6 miles) south of the tomb, of a pit containing over 500 miniature pottery warriors. This discovery shows that not only members of the imperial family were provided with pottery armies to protect them after death.

More recently still, another tomb at Xuzhou has been identified as that of Liu Wu, third king of Chu, who died in 170 B.C. Here again the tomb was tunnelled deep inside the mountain, but in this case the burial furnishings survived. They included a shroud of 4,000 wafer-thin jade plaques and a gold-decorated belt, the latter perhaps a gift from the nomadic peoples far away on China's northern frontier.

These, of course, are exceptional finds. Most people of the Han empire received relatively simple burial, with few or no grave goods. Only the rich could afford to be buried in such style.

## *Economy and Government*

The Han empire was one of the earliest states in the world to try to establish the size of its population. A census taken in A.D. 2 gave a total of 12,233,062 households, suggesting a total of around 58 million people, mostly located in the lower valley of the Huanghe (Yellow River). This population is probably of about the same order of magnitude as the Roman Empire at around the same period.

Most Han subjects were peasant farmers who lived on the land, but cities were also an integral part of the landscape. These were true cities, many of them major centers of settlement, manufacture, and commerce. The capital, Changan, lay just across the River Wei from the Qin imperial capital, Xianyang, which had been looted and destroyed in the civil war that ended the Qin dynasty. With a population of a quarter of a million people, Changan was the greatest Chinese city of its day. It followed a rectangular grid plan, 6 by 7.65 kilometers (3.7 by 4.7 miles) in size. The protective walls were of rammed earth—16 meters (52 feet) thick at the base and protected by a moat—and had 12 city gates, 3 on each side. Just outside the western wall was an imperial pleasure garden, expertly landscaped and stocked with botanical and zoological rarities. Within the walls were palaces and markets, temples and shrines, and residential and industrial quarters. Of the buildings themselves, constructed mainly of timber and tile (only occasionally of brick), little has survived. Contemporary accounts tell of dwellings crowded together "as closely as the teeth of a comb." Wealthy families lived in multistoried houses, dressed in silks and furs, and traveled the streets of the capital in fine horse-drawn carriages (Box 14.1).

A constant concern of the Han government was to supply Changan and the other main cities with food. In 55 B.C., 60,000 soldiers were employed to carry 4 million measures of grain by barge to feed the capital. In some places canals were dug to facilitate bulk transport. During the first century A.D., the state embarked on a major project of building dikes and digging channels to control the Huanghe, which regularly overflowed its banks and devastated large areas of fertile farmland. Not for nothing did this mighty river become known as "China's sorrow."

During the course of the Han period the southern region of China, with its abundant deposits of iron and its high agricultural productivity, became increasingly important at the expense of the north. The government made both iron and salt into state monopolies in 117 B.C. Salt was obtained either from coastal pans around the Shandong peninsula or from brine wells inland. Iron was important as the main material for weapons; its control gave the state not only an important source of revenue but also a means to forestall internal rebellion. Five years later, in 112 B.C., the minting of coins also became an imperial monopoly.

These and other state enterprises were placed in the hands of trained bureaucrats, appointed and promoted on the basis of merit. As early as 196 B.C., an imperial edict ordered the commanderies to send suitable candidates for official posts to the capital, Changan, where their abilities could be assessed. These candidates were soon expected to take formal written examinations before appointment to

## Box 14.1 Changan: The Han Capital

Relatively little survives of the Han capital at Changan, although the massive rammed-earth walls still stand in places to a height of several meters (Figure 14.6). Chinese archaeologists have been able to reconstruct much of the internal layout with the aid of ancient descriptions. Thus the south of the city was occupied by two enormous imperial palaces, the Changlegong and the Weiyanggong, covering, respectively, one-sixth and one-seventh of the entire city area. Each of them had its own rammed-earth enclosure wall, complete with towers. Chinese archaeologists have recently excavated quantities of arms and armor at the southwestern watchtower of the Weiyanggong, showing that it was heavily garrisoned. The most conspicuous surviving feature is the base of the Qian Dian, or Audience Hall, at the center of the Weiyanggong—an

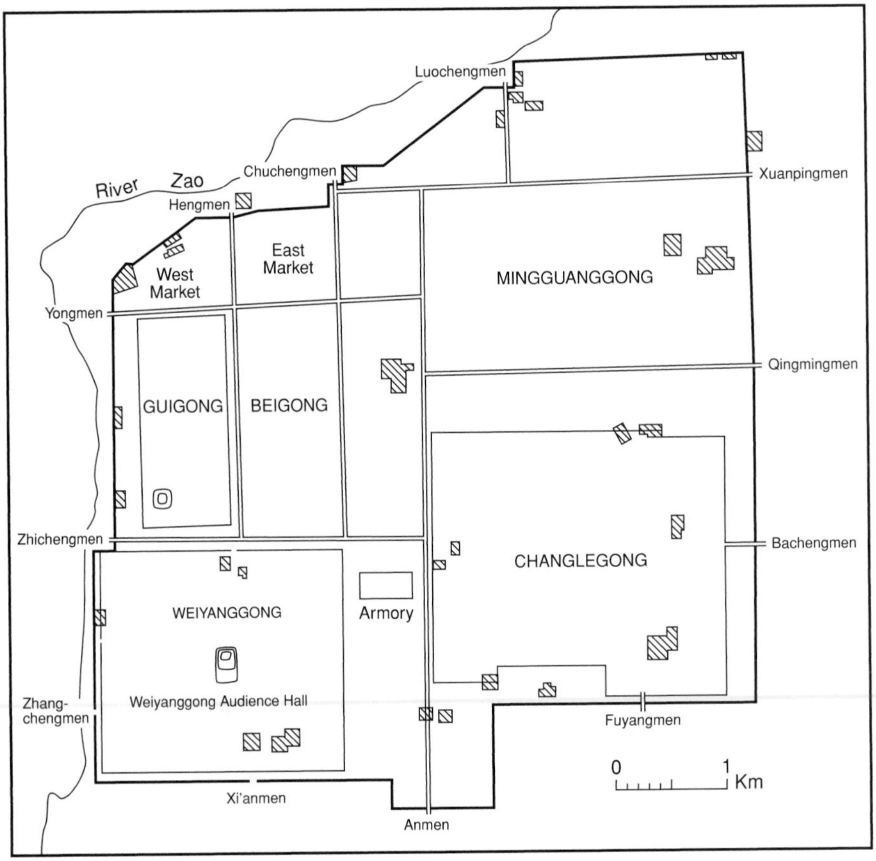


**Figure 14.6** Plan of Han Changan.

enormous stepped foundation platform, 350 by 200 meters (1,150 by 650 feet), in plan and rising to a height of 15 meters (50 feet) at its highest northern point. Here, the emperor dealt with state affairs. In another part of the Weiyanggong compound part of the imperial archives has been unearthed, consisting of slips of cattle bone inscribed with records of tribute received by the government over a period of 200 years. The Changlegong was originally the home of the Dowager Empress. Between the two palaces was a third large imperial structure: the arsenal, a cluster of warehouses up to 230 meters (759 feet) long and almost 50 meters (160 feet) wide. Chinese archaeologists excavating here in the 1970s found iron swords, spearheads, halberds, and armor. Three other imperial palaces, only a little smaller in size, were located in the northern part of the city. One, the Mingguanggong, housed Emperor Wu Di's 2,000 concubines. Here, too, were nine markets and evidence of coin casting and pottery making. Houses of the nobility were built near the gateways to the palace enclosures, but the dwellings of the ordinary populace seem to have been concentrated in the northeastern corner of the city. They were grouped into walled compounds, or "wards," to ensure strict central control.

official positions. They were mainly members of the flourishing middle class, literate and articulate, and more likely to be loyal to the central government than were the old noble families.

## *The Northern Frontier*

The Han army consisted largely of conscripts since all able-bodied males were required to serve two years between the ages of 23 and 56. Many of them were posted to the northern frontier, which faced the greatest security threat. The people of the steppes, beyond the Great Wall, regarded northern China as a land of rich pickings, and raids and invasions were an ever-present menace for the Han population of the northern provinces. The main enemy was the Xiongnu, warrior nomads from Central Asia who had established a powerful confederacy on the northern steppes by the second century B.C. Emperor Wu Di (141–87 B.C.) decided to take decisive action against them and mounted a series of major campaigns, fielding armies of between 50,000 and 100,000 men. Wu Di extended Shihuangdi's Great Wall far to the west, eventually to the Tarim basin, and established commanderies throughout the region. Towers along the line of the wall, built of sun-dried brick, served as signal stations, sending messages by flags or torches. They were manned by small detachments of conscripts, who found themselves far from their homelands in the Yangzi or Huanghe valleys, in desert terrain that was burningly hot in summer and bitterly cold in winter. It must have been a harsh tour of duty, though in military terms the conscripts were well provided with armor and crossbows to resist any nomad assault (Box 14.2).

## *Box 14.2 The Tarim Mummies*

The Taklamakan Desert on China's northwestern frontier is one of the harshest regions in the world, but it was skirted by important routes linking China to Central Asia and the West. In oasis settlements along the desert fringe lived communities whose dead have been extraordinarily well preserved by the dessicating desert sands (Figure 14.7). One of the best known graves is that at Zaghunluq where in a heavily looted cemetery a pit held the remains of a man and three women. The man and one of the women, dated to c. 600 B.C., had been naturally mummified. At another cemetery, Qizilchoqa, tartan fabrics were found closely similar in weaving technique to those found in Europe at the same period. Study of the bodies themselves suggests that most (though not all) have features described as Caucasoid (rather than the Mongoloid features of the majority of Chinese), and this finds some support in the DNA discovery of the typically European Haplotype H in a sample from one of the bodies. It is also known that an Indo-European language (or rather a related group of languages) known as Tocharian was spoken in the Tarim basin in the sixth to eighth century A.D. Taken together, these findings indicate

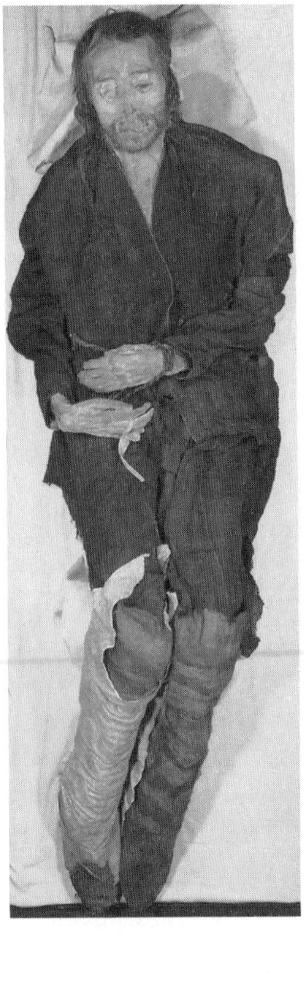

**Figure 14.7** Tarim mummy from Zaghunluq, Xinjiang, China.

that the Tarim basin may first have been settled by nomads from the Eurasian steppe, genetically and linguistically related to peoples further west. In the Han period, and later during the Tang dynasty, the Tarim basin came under Chinese political control, but from the ninth century A.D. it was dominated by Turkic-speaking Uyghur peoples, and the latest western-looking figures in the local Buddhist art date to the thirteenth century A.D.

Early in the twentieth century, a series of Western explorers mounted expeditions to the remote lands of northwest China. They were rewarded by the discovery of documents written on bamboo strips, which had been preserved by the arid sands of the desert. These documents, when deciphered, proved to be records of the Chinese military garrisons stationed in these remote border outposts. They included letters, inventories, duty rotas, and ration lists. Other documents reported the results of the annual archery tests that the troops had to undertake or occasional lapses in military discipline. They throw vivid light on a soldier's life on the Great Wall during the Han period (Box 14.3).

One reason for extending the Great Wall to the west was to provide a protected corridor from China into Central Asia. This was the first leg of the famous Silk Road, a series of routes running from Han China to the Near East. Overland transport was expensive, and only luxury products made commercial sense in such long-distance trade. Silk was one of the most valued materials to travel in this way, reaching India, Persia, and the Roman Mediterranean. Few traders, if any, traveled the whole distance; the idea was to carry the goods so far, then sell them at a profit to local merchants. Those local merchants, in turn, would carry them to the next trading station and sell them there. Eventually they might reach Alexandria, Antioch, or even Rome. The Silk Road trade was not a unidirectional enterprise. Goods and ideas also flowed into China along this route. The most important of these was Buddhism, which arrived from India in the first century A.D.

It was not only commerce that carried Chinese cultural influence into Central Asia. Still more important was the Han government practice of giving gifts and subsidies to the nomadic peoples, sometimes to buy peace and sometimes to cement alliances. Once again, silks were a major commodity, though only rarely have they survived to be found by archaeologists. More tangible evidence of contact is provided by the distinctive circular bronze mirrors with decorated backs. These mirrors were often placed in Han tombs and were thought to assist the spirits of the dead. Beyond the frontiers, they have turned up in the territories of the various nomadic groups with which the Han government was in contact.

## *Korea and the South*

Emperor Wu Di's expansionist policies were not only directed at northwestern China. He also launched campaigns in the south, against the Dian people on the Vietnamese frontier. By 110 B.C. most of this region had been absorbed. The Yue

## Box 14.3 Writing and Literacy

Writing began in China during the Shang period, but the Han government standardized the script and used it to administer the vast empire. In so doing it established a single script throughout the whole of China, one that remained in use without significant change into the twenty-first century. The Han period also saw a great expansion in literacy and the use of writing in many areas of life. Writing was generally done with a brush and ink. For important documents or wealthy households, rolls of silk might be used (as also for maps or diagrams such as those found in several Han tombs). Ordinary documents were written on long wooden strips, so narrow that they could hold only a single column of characters. The strips were then tied together by hempen strings so that they could be rolled up for storage. Wood was cumbersome and bulky, silk expensive and rare. Toward the end of the Han period (traditionally in A.D. 105) an imperial official invented a new writing material: paper. This could be made from discarded rags and woodchips and hence was much cheaper to buy, although it did not become widely used in China until the fourth century, well after the fall of the Han dynasty.

people of the southeast coast held out somewhat longer and were only fully assimilated in the late Han period. These campaigns were important in setting the southern boundaries of Chinese control for centuries to come. The Han emperors and their successors maintained commercial and diplomatic ties with the states of Southeast Asia. Their ships traveled as far as India, bringing Chinese markets within the orbit of the maritime trade networks of the Indian Ocean (see Chapter 13). Though central power might weaken and be divided, Han Chinese culture was as strongly established in the south as in the traditional heartlands of the north.

In the northeast, Wu Di's forces came up against the Choson kingdom of Korea, which they defeated in a short series of campaigns. In 108 B.C. most of the Korean peninsula became the Han commandery of Lelang. In the 1930s, Japanese archaeologists excavated an enormous walled enclosure covering 42 hectares (104 acres) at the Tosongni site on the west coast of Korea. They identified this as the Chinese capital of the Lelang commandery, a well-planned town with brick-paved lanes and a ceremonial palace. On the hills nearby were almost 1,500 burial mounds. Some of them belonged to Chinese officials, immigrants from the west. Others were probably the graves of local people, culturally assimilated by the Han Chinese. When the first native Korean states arose in the fourth century A.D., they owed much to Chinese influence.

### *The Fall of Han China*

In A.D. 25, after the brief interregnum of the Xin dynasty (A.D. 8–23), the Han emperors abandoned Changan and moved their capital east to Luoyang. This marked the beginning of the second period of Han China (known as the Eastern Han). Within little more than a century, however, signs of decline were evident. A census taken in A.D. 140 recorded only 48 million people, 10 million fewer than in A.D. 2. At the same time, the central government was losing power to local lords, many of whom were building up massive estates that were exempt from taxes. The lot of the ordinary farmer did not improve, however, and there were serious peasant rebellions. From A.D. 187 the Han dynasty was steadily shorn of real power, and in A.D. 220 it was officially abolished.

The unified Chinese empire was now fragmented. The following centuries saw the rise and fall of many states and dynasties, coupled with serious incursions by the northern nomads. Central control was not restored until the Sui (581–618) and Tang (618–907) dynasties, which lie beyond the scope of this book.

## Secondary States: Korea and Japan

No account of early civilization in eastern Asia would be complete without a review of state formation in Korea and Japan during these post-Han centuries. Korea and Japan are examples of secondary state formation (see Chapter 1): regions that came under the influence of a powerful adjacent state (in this case Han China) and underwent social and political changes, which led them in turn to develop their own state-level societies.

### *Korea (A.D. 220–700)*

The process is clearest in Korea. The foundation of the Lelang commandery by Han China in 108 B.C. is an example of centralized political organization, even though this commandery was merely one of the provinces of a larger empire. Local elites were conscripted into running the province, and they acquired new ideas and aspirations. After the collapse of the Han empire the Lelang commandery was revived by the Wei dynasty of northern China and did not finally disappear until A.D. 313. It is during the following decades that we find the first evidence of native kingdoms in Korea.

The kingdoms in question are Koguryo in the north and Silla and Paekche in the south, as well as the more amorphous polity known as Kaya. Each had at its heart a cemetery of mounded tombs, the burial places of the ruling dynasty. These had tomb chambers for the body of the deceased, accompanied by wealthy offerings: lacquerware, gold and silver ornaments, wine cups, and chopsticks. The richest tombs had chambers of squared stone or brick, plastered over and decorated with mural paintings of episodes from daily life—the dead person hunting and feasting—and mythological scenes with dragons and spirits.

The best known of the Korean tombs are those of the Kyongju cemetery, in the kingdom of Silla. One of the largest mounds was Tomb 98, the so-called Great Tomb at Hwangnamdong. This fifth-century tomb was in fact a double burial of king and queen, with their individual tomb chambers in separate mounds, built against each other. The king's grave was notable for a pit adjacent to the tomb chamber that contained over 2,500 iron weapons and pottery vessels. The queen was buried with a gold crown and gold belt with pendants. The king, too, had a crown, though his was only of gilt bronze. Both tombs also contained imported materials from far afield, including a striped glass goblet, probably manufactured in Alexandria, Egypt.

Throughout what is known as the Three Kingdoms period (A.D. 300–668) Silla, Paekche, and Koguryo vied and fought for political supremacy. In the north, Koguryo captured the seat of the Chinese Lelang commandery in A.D. 313 and moved its own capital there a century later. It then began to expand southward, absorbing parts of Paekche. All three kingdoms maintained contacts with China, adopting the Chinese script and the Buddhist religion from their western neighbors. With Buddhism came cremation, and from the seventh century onward Korean rulers were no longer buried in large mounded tombs. State resources were directed instead to the construction of Buddhist temples with tall pagodas, sometimes of wood and sometimes of brick or stone. Paekche craftspeople were particularly noted for their building skills, just as Silla was a center for gold working and Kaya a region of iron production.

During the seventh century the southern kingdom of Silla emerged as the major Korean power, conquering Kaya and Paekche and then going on to defeat Koguryo. This victory marks the beginning of the Unified Silla period (A.D. 668–918). The Silla kings built themselves a new city immediately to the north of their existing capital. This new city, Kumsong, followed a gridded plan in emulation of the great Tang dynasty capital of Changan (a new city built alongside Han Changan). Silla also adopted features of the Tang administrative system, including a provincial structure of government. There can be no doubt about the powerful impact of Chinese civilization on the early states to its east.

## *Japan (A.D. 100–700)*

Japanese developments closely paralleled those of Korea during these centuries. There were diplomatic contacts between China and Japan during the Han period. Japanese envoys visited Luoyang in A.D. 57 and 107. The greatest formative influence on the early Japanese state, however, appears to have come not from China itself but from southern Korea.

The first known Japanese state (aside from these hazy mentions in Chinese records) is the kingdom of Yamato, centered on the Nara basin of southern Honshu. During the Kofun (mounded tomb) period (A.D. 300–710), burial mounds were built throughout much of southern Japan. The largest were those of the early Yamato leaders, such as the enormous Nintoku burial mound. (Nintoku was a late-fifth-century ruler—reputedly the fifteenth emperor—of the Yamato state.) This mound is almost 485 meters (1,600 feet) long, contains an estimated 1,405,875 cubic meters (49,647,736 cubic feet) of material, and is shaped in the distinctive "keyhole" plan characteristic of many of the Nara tombs (Figure 14.8). The surface of this mound (and indeed of all Japanese mounded tombs of the period) was once covered in fields of *haniwa*, intended to indicate the status of the deceased and to provide magical protection against evil. Most *haniwa* take the form of simple pottery cylinders, though some are shaped as horses or armored warriors, where the intention was to show the tomb was that of a ruler or warrior.

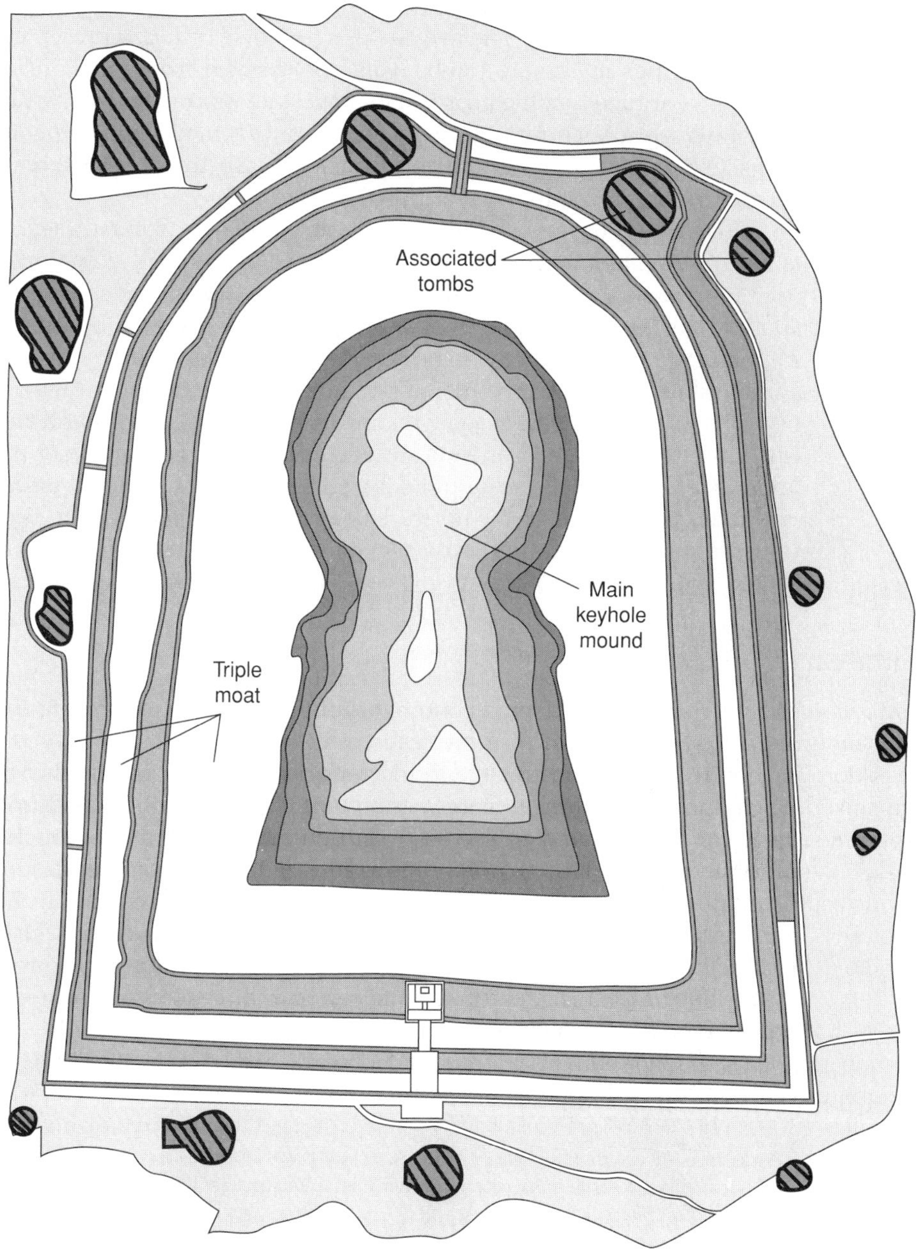


**Figure 14.8** Plan of the Nintoku keyhole tomb.

How directly the Yamato state was influenced by Korea remains a point of contention. Close links with the Kaya region of southern Korea are not disputed. It was from this region that Yamato rulers obtained much of their iron and adopted iron armor and weapons. The new fashion for horse riding, represented by finds of horse trappings in Yamato tombs, was also derived from the Korean peninsula. Many have argued that the incipient Yamato state was taken over by Koreans in the early fifth century, and it owed much of its subsequent development to their impetus. Others maintain that the opposite is the case, that the Kaya region of Korea became a Yamato colony.

Like Korea, the early Japanese state came under growing influence from mainland China in the sixth and seventh centuries. Yamato rulers reorganized their kingdom into a series of provinces linked together by trunk roads. Chinese script was adapted for the Japanese language. Buddhism was adopted by the ruling elite in A.D. 552 and led, as in Korea, to the demise of the burial mound. The maturity of the Yamato state was confirmed by the founding of the grid-plan capital of Fujiwara in 694. This was modeled once again on the Tang capital, Changan, and along with residential zones contained an enormous palace, covering an area of over a square kilometer (a third of a square mile). Sixteen years later a second grid-plan capital was founded at Heijo, to the north. This remained the center of the Japanese state until the end of the eighth century, when the capital was transferred to Heian (modern Kyoto), superseded only in 1869 by Tokyo, the present capital.

## Summary

Major social, political, and economic changes transformed the nature of Chinese society in the sixth and fifth centuries B.C. True cities made their first appearance, along with ironworking and coinage. China was divided among a number of rival kingdoms during the Warring States period (458–221 B.C.), but in the third century B.C. these were unified into an empire by Shihuangdi, First Emperor of China. The empire founded by Shihuangdi was continued under the Han dynasty (206 B.C.–A.D. 220). Wealthy burials provide particularly rich evidence of the lives led by the Han rulers and aristocracy. Roads, canals, and frontier works indicate the development of centralized bureaucratic control. After the fall of the Han empire, "secondary" states were formed under Chinese influence in the neighboring regions of Korea and Japan during the fourth to seventh centuries A.D.

## Guide to Further Reading

Gina Barnes, *China, Korea and Japan: The Rise of Civilization in East Asia* (London: Thames and Hudson, 1993) provides a reliable guide through later East Asian archaeology. Qian Hao, Chen Heyi, and Ru Suichu, *Out of China's Earth: Archaeological Discoveries in the People's Republic of China* (Beijing: China Pictorial, 1981) covers spectacular finds. Jessica Rawson, *Ancient China: Art and Archaeology* (London: British Museum Press, 1980) is a good summary.

For the archaeology of Eastern Zhou cities, see Shen Chen, "Early Urbanization in the Eastern Zhou in China (770–221 B.C.): An Archaeological View," *Antiquity* 68 (1994): 724–744.

The terracotta army of Shihuangdi and the reign of Shihuangdi himself are described by Arthur Cotterell, *The First Emperor of China* (Harmondsworth, England: Penguin, 1981). For the Han empire, see Wang Zhongshu, *Han Civilization* (New Haven, CT: Yale University Press, 1982); for tomb remains, see S. L. Caroselli, ed., *The Quest for Eternity* (London: Thames and Hudson; Los Angeles: Los Angeles County Museum of Art, 1987). The recent discoveries at Beidongshan and Xuzhou are illustrated in *Orientations* 21, no. 10 (1990). For a general account of Han China see Michael Loewe, *Everyday Life in Early Imperial China* (London: Batsford, 1968).

For Indo-Europeans in the Tarim basin see J. P. Mallory and Victor H. Mair, *The Tarim Mummies* (London: Thames and Hudson, 2000). The best account in English of Korean archaeology is S. M. Nelson, *The Archaeology of Korea* (Cambridge: Cambridge University Press, 1993).

# PART VI

# Early States in the Americas

Oh dew of the world
Viracocha
inner dew
Viracocha
you who dispose by saying
"Let there be greater and lesser gods"
great Lord
dispose that here
people do multiply
fortunately.*

*From John H. Rowe, "Eleven Inca Prayers from the Zithuwa Ritual," *Kroeber Anthropological Society Papers* 8–9 (1953): 92.

*Chapter 15*

# Lowland Mesoamerica

A seated Maya woman depicted on a pot, wearing rich textiles and a bloodletting headdress.

*The vast, colorful crowd falls silent, all eyes turned toward the dark entrance of the temple high on the pyramid's summit, above the great plaza. Mist swirls around the brightly painted temple and its grotesque carvings, casting layers of shadows across the artificial hilltop. It is as if the mountains are wreathed in clouds. A man clad in white emerges from the temple, supported by high nobles. Strong-smelling incense rises high above the temple as the priests bring forward the white bark paper and the sacred fish spine. The lord gashes himself deliberately, blood cascading from his genitals onto the waiting paper. The incense thickens, and the lord falls into a shamanistic trance in full view of the crowd. As he communicates with the ancestors and chants loudly, the people wait in awe, for their ruler has departed from his body for the sacred world of the ancestors.*

Intricate calendars, great ceremonial centers and superb architecture, mysterious glyphs, and spectacular shamanistic rituals—the colorful Maya civilization fascinates archaeologist and layperson alike. Exotic, and until recently little understood, the Maya epitomize the ancient traditions of civilization in Central America. But how did Maya civilization begin? What were the origins of the spectacular pre-Columbian states of lowland and highland Mesoamerica? The nineteenth-century traveler John Lloyd Stephens wrote brilliantly of Maya cities in the 1840s; he set the stage for all subsequent fieldwork with his statement that this great civilization had "a distinct, separate, indigenous existence; like the plants and fruits of the soil, indigenous." No serious research since then has cast doubt on Stephens's contention of 150 years ago. Thus, to discover the origins of the Maya and other Mesoamerican civilizations, we must travel back nearly four millennia to the village farming communities that flourished in this region when Egyptian civilization was at its height and the Shang state was dominating northern China. This chapter describes the origins and growth of Maya and other lowland civilizations in Central America. Chapter 16 surveys the peoples of the nearby highlands, who interacted constantly with their lowland neighbors.

## Mesoamerica

We must begin by defining the term *Mesoamerica.* Archaeologists conventionally use it to describe the large area of Central America where indigenous American states flourished. Anthropologist Paul Kirchoff used ethnographic and linguistic data to define the distinctive Mesoamerican culture area in 1942. He pointed out that the peoples of Mesoamerica were remarkable for their elaborate religious beliefs and ceremonial rites, including human sacrifice; for their spectacular public architecture of temples, plazas, and pyramids; and for their codices and calendar

(18 months of 20 days, plus 5 extra days). Such cultural and social attributes occurred wherever Mesoamerican civilization flourished, on lowlands and highlands, in tropical rainforest and in semiarid terrain. Volatile, sophisticated, and sometimes ardently militaristic, the unique Mesoamerican civilizations encountered by the Spanish conquistadors had developed over more than 3,000 years (Table 15.1).

The boundaries of Mesoamerica lie in northwest Mexico, dipping south onto the central plateau before extending north and east to the gulf near Tampico. A line from Punta Arenas on the Costa Rican coast northwest to the Gulf of Honduras forms the southern frontier (Figure 15.1). But these boundaries shifted constantly over the years as the focus of political and economic power shifted from one area to another. Two great mountain chains form the backbones of highland Mesoamer-

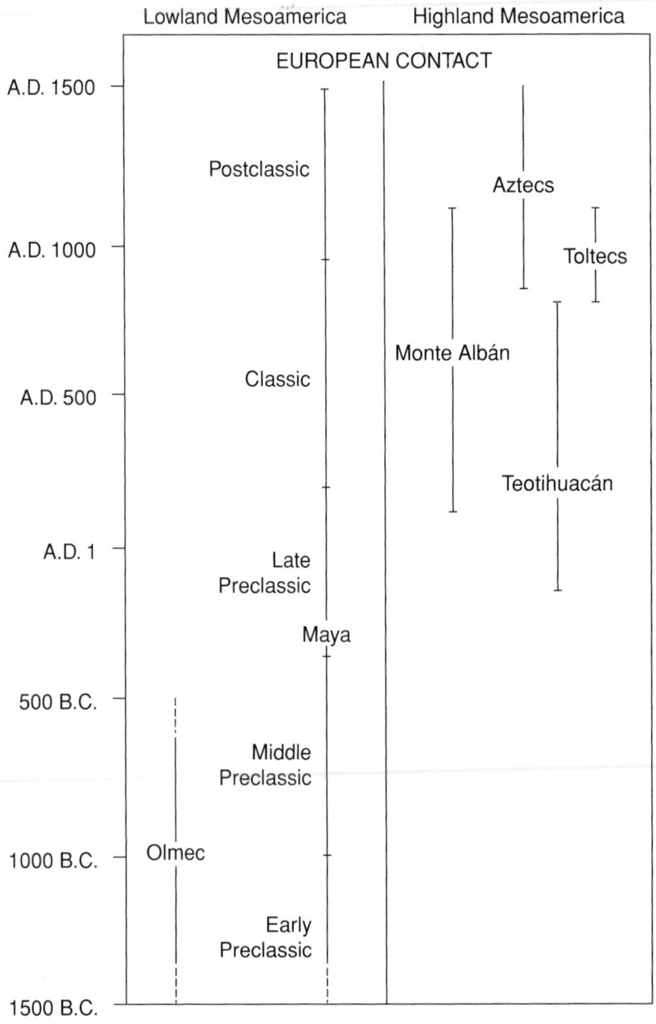


**Table 15.1** Chronological table of Mesoamerican civilizations.

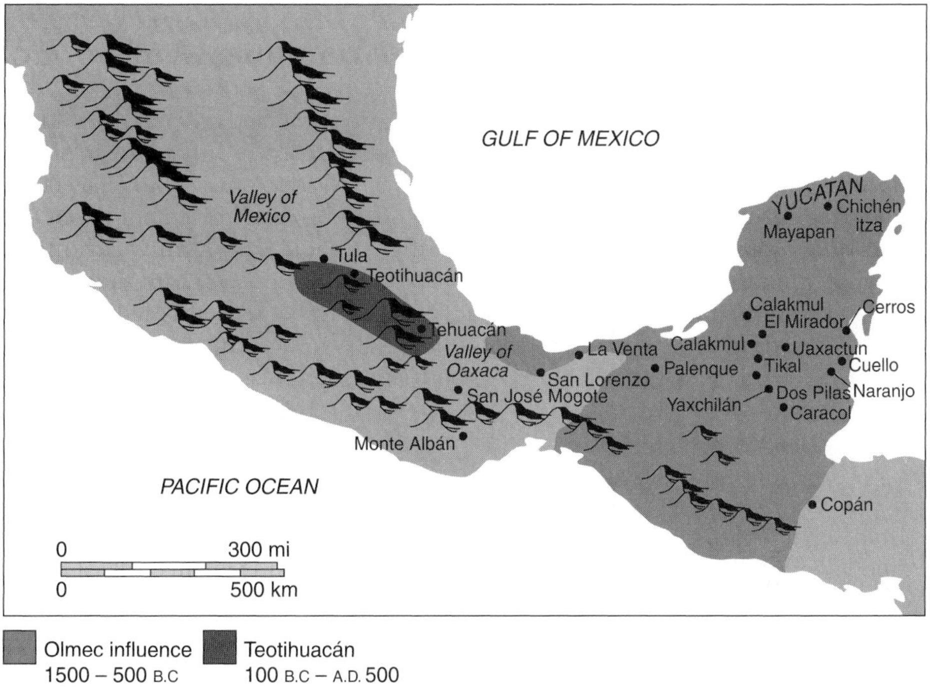


**Figure 15.1** Map of archaeological sites and states mentioned in Chapter 15.

ica, running down the coastlines until they reach the east-west volcanic chain that forms the Mesa Central, the central plateau. The inland basin of the Valley of Mexico, with its five lakes, forms the heart of the plateau, for thousands of years the center of political and economic life in highland Mesoamerica.

The highland regions of southern Mesoamerica are mountainous, with the highland plateau of Oaxaca offering some of the rare flat terrain in the region. Even further south, great mountain ranges enclose the highland plateau, where modern Guatemala City is situated. The peoples of the basin of Mexico and the southern highlands enjoy a cool climate; most rainfall occurs between June and November, sufficient to allow a single crop a year. The more southerly plateaus are still fertile but warmer.

To the northeast, the serried mountains of the highlands give way to the low-lying limestone peninsula of the Yucatán, the so-called Maya lowlands. Highland climatic conditions contrast dramatically with those in the lowlands, which are hot and humid throughout the year. The southern two-thirds of the Yucatán make up the Petén, hilly limestone formations covered with dense tropical forest intersected with lakes and swamps. The limestone plains of the northern Yucatán are much drier, with a drainage pattern based on underground water channels. The shores of the Gulf of Mexico are low-lying and hot—the low coastal plains of Veracruz and Tabasco, the Yucatán Peninsula, and the heavily forested coastal strip along the Gulf of Honduras.

The great civilizations of the Mesoamerican lowlands have always been dependent on commodities obtained from neighbors near and far, in every kind of highland and lowland environment imaginable. Therein lies a crux of Mesoamerican civilization: the constant interactions and exchanges of both commodities and ideas among people living in dramatically contrasting environments, often within only a few hundred miles of one another.

## Village Farmers (c. 7000–2000 B.C.)

The roots of Mesoamerican civilization lie deep in the remote past, among hunting-gathering and farming cultures on both highlands and lowlands. Palaeo-Indian groups settled in Mesoamerica at least 12,000 years ago, soon after the end of the Ice Age. We know little of these peoples except for their stone projectile points and occasional scatters of animal bone fragments. As big-game animals became extinct in the Americas after 9000 B.C., small foraging groups throughout the continent adapted to local environments, developing strategies for the intensive exploitation of small game, aquatic resources, and plant foods. By 7000 B.C., some groups were experimenting with the deliberate cultivation of wild plant foods, experiments that eventually led to agriculture.

The American Indians domesticated an impressive range of native plants, some of which, like maize, potatoes, and tobacco, were rapidly adopted by European farmers after the fifteenth century A.D. The most important staple crops in Mesoamerica were maize, beans, squash, amaranth, and sweet potatoes, all developed from hardy native plants. In contrast to Old World farmers, the Mesoamericans never had the benefit of plow- and load-carrying animals like the camel, horse, or ox. All highland and lowland civilizations based their economies on intensive maize and bean agriculture.

Most experts now agree that the more than 150 strains of maize (*Zea mays*), developed in the Americas over more than 4,000 years, share a common ancestor in a wild Central American grass known as teosinte (*Zea mexicana*). But when did teosinte become maize, and why did Mesoamericans take up farming?

At the Guilá Naquitz Cave in the valley of Oaxaca, Kent Flannery excavated seven cultural layers, of which six represented transitory, sporadic, seasonal visits by a small group of foragers in late summer to late fall between about 8800 and 6700 B.C. A meticulous study of the environmental data and seed remains from the cave revealed people who were experts at exploiting the plant foods in an area where rainfall was always unpredictable. Computer simulations show how the people scheduled their foraging of these plants through the various seasons of the years. Under these circumstances, the collective memories of successive generations are of vital importance, for past experience forms the basis for survival decisions in famine years. On the basis of the Guilá Naquitz excavations, Flannery believes that the first experiments with agriculture in Mesoamerica were attempts to alter the densities of specific plants. The deliberate planting of maize, beans, and squash began as a logical extension of people's need to increase predictable food supplies in environments with irregular rainfall. In such climates, food supplies vary in abundance dramatically from one year to the next. A logical strategy is to experiment with the planting of such commonly eaten plants as wild beans and cereal grasses such as teosinte, the wild ancestor of domesticated maize. Successful cultivation of small amounts of edible plants provided more predictable food supplies. Successful experiments of this kind in many areas soon transformed the economies of Mesoamerica.

The earliest maize cultivation in the Americas currently dates to the sixth and fifth millennia B.C. Cobs at Guilá Naquitz have been AMS (accelerator mass spectrometry) radiocarbon dated to about 4300 B.C.; even earlier maize cultivation is claimed on the basis of pollen grains at the San Andrés site in lowland Veracruz, Mexico, dating to about 5000 B.C.

Between 1960 and 1964, Richard MacNeish studied dry caves in the Tehuacán Valley of the Puebla Basin in the semiarid highlands. He discovered 24,000 maize fragments, as well as the remains of squash and beans in a series of sites spanning more than 6,000 years. A series of small cobs from his San Marcos cave excavations have been radiocarbon dated by AMS to about 2750–2650 B.C. The modern teosinte populations biochemically most similar to maize flourish in the central Balsas River drainage, more than 250 kilometers (155 miles) west of the Tehuacán Valley. Perhaps it was here that the first farming communities appeared: in riverside locations scattered throughout western and southwestern Mexico. Wild beans were probably domesticated at about the same time in the same general region, but archaeological evidence is still lacking. Later, maize, beans, and squash combined to form a distinctive and remarkably successful agricultural partnership that sustained all Mesoamerican civilizations.

Once established, maize farming spread rapidly throughout Mesoamerica and further afield. Maize appeared in the North American Southwest between 2000 and 1500 B.C. and in northern South America by about 1000 to 800 B.C. (see Chapter 17). By 2000 B.C., sedentary villages were common throughout Mesoamerica, dispersed in small communities across highly diverse agricultural environments in both lowlands and highlands. Many farmers in more arid regions combined maize and bean slash-and-burn cultivation with foraging—clearing small areas in forests and woodlands and fertilizing the soil with the ash from the burned trees. In the basin of Mexico, some communities used floodwaters and canals to bring lake water to their gardens. They piled up natural vegetation and lake mud to form grids of naturally irrigated fields near the lake shores. These plots were the ancestors of the extensive *chinampa* garden systems developed by later highland civilizations (Chapter 16). The people of the tropical lowlands used slash-and-burn agriculture like their highland neighbors. But some communities also developed small areas of raised fields in swampy locations, the predecessors of more extensive field systems in Maya times. In some areas, the sedentary villages became small towns, part of increasingly elaborate hierarchies of human settlement that were to develop in later centuries. (The San José Mogote village in the valley of Oaxaca is described in Chapter 16.)

The very diversity of the Mesoamerican environment, with its widely distributed food resources and raw materials, made everyone dependent on neighbors, communities living in very different surroundings. From the earliest times, barter networks linked village to village and lowland groups to those living on the semiarid highlands or in the basin of Mexico. The same exchange networks spread compelling ideologies, which were to form the symbolic foundation of ancient Mesoamerican civilization.

## Preclassic: The Olmec (1500–500 B.C.)

The first signs of political and social complexity appear in many parts of highland and lowland Mesoamerica between about 2000 and 1000 B.C., during the so-called Preclassic, or Formative, era. In many regions there appeared small but often powerful chiefdoms, headed by a chief and a small nobility. A similar pattern of greater social and political complexity arose in Mesopotamia, Egypt, China, and other areas where early state-organized societies evolved. In Mesoamerica, as elsewhere, the new social complexity can be identified by differences in house designs, by the appearance of small shrines, and through prestigious trade goods such as fish spines and seashells from the gulf coast that were used in bloodletting and other religious ceremonies. Here, as in other areas, control of trade in exotic, prestigious objects and knowledge of distant lands were vital to the ideology of chiefdoms. Such objects, and the ideology associated with them, symbolized and legitimized the authority of leaders to control both human and natural resources.

There was no one region where this emerging sociopolitical complexity occurred first. Rather, it was a development that took hold more or less simultaneously in many regions of Mesoamerica, not in isolation but with each region interacting with others. This process of interaction between neighbors—between communities and chiefdoms living in different environments—was a critical element in the development of the distinctive religious beliefs, art traditions, and economic and political institutions of Mesoamerican civilization. The most famous of these early societies was the Olmec.

The Olmec occupied a revered place in the legend and lore of later Mesoamerican civilizations. Maya priests recognized the great cultural legacy they owed to these little-known ancestral Mesoamericans. The Aztec rain god, Tlaloc, may have originated among the primordial deities of the Olmec. Earlier scholars thought in terms of a "mother civilization," of an Olmec state that was the ancestor of all later Mesoamerican civilizations. Today, we know that Olmec was a series of chiefdoms along the gulf coast of Veracruz and Tabasco, which may have exercised some influence over adjacent areas of Chiapas and central Mexico in early Preclassic times. During the middle Preclassic, Olmec society flourished in a period when art motifs, religious symbols, and ritual beliefs were shared among developing chiefdoms in many regions as a result of regular contacts among the leaders of widely separated communities and through day-to-day trade. Olmec art and artifacts have been found over an area 20 times that of the gulf coast heartland, testimony to the wide contacts of La Venta and other centers. Olmec-like artifacts have come from Cuello in the Maya lowlands and were found in pre-Maya burials under the city of Copán (both sites discussed later in this chapter). Arthur Demarest has called this phenomenon a "lattice of interaction" over many centuries, which produced the complex and sophisticated traditions of Mesoamerican civilization that developed later.

Olmec peoples lived along the Mexican south gulf coast from about 1500 to 500 B.C. Their homeland is low-lying, tropical, and humid, with fertile soils. The swamps, lakes, and rivers are rich in fish, birds, and other animals, creatures that formed an important part of a new and remarkably sophisticated art style, which was to leave a permanent imprint on Mesoamerican life. The origins of the Olmec are a complete mystery, but their culture undoubtedly had strong local roots.

Some of the earliest artifacts from an Olmec settlement come from a platform at San Lorenzo, in the midst of frequently inundated woodland plains. The first village had few distinctive Olmec traits; but by 1250 B.C. the people of San Lorenzo were farming both dry gardens and fields on river levees, which produced exceptional crop yields. This mosaic of gardens played a critical role in the appearance of a more hierarchical society in the region. Soon, San Lorenzo's leaders were erecting ridges and earthen mounds around their platform, on which they built pyramids and possibly ball courts. A century later, magnificent monumental carvings adorned San Lorenzo—apparently portraits of rulers—which were often mutilated by the Olmec themselves, perhaps when the rulers died (Figure 15.2). The people of San Lorenzo traded obsidian and semiprecious stones with many parts of Mesoamerica until their center fell into decline after 900 B.C. It was superseded by La Venta, the most famous Olmec site, nearer the Gulf of Mexico.

San Lorenzo was far from unique, for large Olmec sites abound elsewhere in the lowlands. There were no Olmec cities as defined in Chapter 1; most people lived in settlement hierarchies of occasional large ceremonial centers or even towns that presided over many smaller villages dispersed throughout the countryside. Was Olmec society a large, homogeneous state or a series of smaller kingdoms linked by kin, religion, and trade? Current opinion favors the second alternative, arguing that originally village land was owned communally by large kin groups. Over many generations, certain families probably acquired control of the most fertile lands and the prime fishing and waterfowl-hunting preserves. They became the dominant elite in Olmec society.

**Figure 15.2** Giant Olmec stone head from San Lorenzo, made from basalt, approximately 2.4 meters (8 feet) high. The heads may be portraits of rulers, and glyphs on the "helmets" may represent their names.

To give symbolic and ritual expression to their newfound power, the elite built awe-inspiring artificial mountains and strategically placed open spaces, designed to give an impression of overwhelming supremacy. It was there that the rulers performed carefully staged public rituals and displays designed to confirm supreme authority. Those who ruled over these settings adorned their precincts with colossal statues of themselves.

Nowhere are these buildings and sculptures more spectacular than at La Venta, built on a small island in the middle of a swamp. A rectangular earthen mound, 120 by 70 by 32 meters (393 feet long by 229 feet wide and 105 feet high), dominates the island. Long, low mounds surround a rectangular plaza in front of the large mound, faced by walls and terraced mounds at the other end of the plaza. Vast monumental stone sculptures litter the site, including some Olmec heads with expressions of contempt and savagery, perhaps portraits of actual rulers. Thronelike blocks depict a seated figure, perhaps a ruler, emerging from a deep niche carved into the stone. He leans slightly forward with arms extended to grasp thick, coiled ropes that run along the base to seated figures on the sides, perhaps relatives linked to him by a symbolic kin cord (Figure 15.3). The sides also bear stylized depictions of jaguars, perhaps symbolizing the mythic origins of the rulers from such animals. Every stone for these sculptures and temples had to be brought in from at least 96 kilometers (60 miles) away, a vast undertaking; some sculpted blocks weigh more than 40 tons. For about 400 years, the La Venta people traded ceremonial jade and serpentine from as far away as Costa Rica, during a time when Olmec

**Figure 15.3** An Olmec altar or throne sculpture from La Venta. A ruler is connected to his parents on the side by an umbilical cord. The sculpture is about 2 meters (6 feet) high.

ideas of kingship and religious ideology spread far across the lowlands and highlands. Then, sometime around 400 B.C., La Venta was destroyed, its finest monuments intentionally defaced.

One of the most important institutions to come into being in Olmec society was kingship, known to us only from distinctive art styles centered on a mysterious half-jaguar, half-human figure. Olmec lords were the first Mesoamericans to portray their power in enduring form—in carvings, paintings, and sculptures. Their artists used a complex symbolism, including jungle animals of all kinds. But the most powerful was the jaguar. Jaguars are strong beasts, endowed with great cunning and endurance. They flourish on land and in water and in the "upperworld" of trees. They are aggressive and fearsome, like brave warriors; they hunt at night and cross different environmental boundaries at will. For many thousands of years, American Indians have associated this formidable animal with rain and fertility and the power of shamans, who were capable of passing effortlessly from the living world into the spiritual realm and back again. Olmec lords may have grafted the ancient ideology of the jaguar onto an emerging institution of kingship, where the ruler was a shaman-king with awesome supernatural powers. The Olmec rain god may have been a half-human, half-animal figure with snarling jaguar teeth, but this was only one of many combinations of mythical beasts that came from the hallucinogenic mind, as opposed to the forest itself. Olmec artists grafted eagles' feathers and claws onto serpents and other beasts to form mythical creatures; the "Feathered Serpent," Quetzalcoatl, was perhaps the most enduring of all Mesoamerican deities and central to highland civilization for many centuries (see Chapter 16). Powerful shamanistic rituals and public ceremonies of bloodletting and human sacrifice were dominant issues in Mesoamerican civilization.

The Olmec left a powerful legacy of art, architecture, and ideology. They were not the mother culture of Mesoamerican civilization but an important catalyst for the elaborate cultural developments that followed. Their ideas of kingship and governance, as well as religious beliefs, spread rapidly in an area of great environmental diversity, where everyone depended on their neighbors for important commodities and exotic artifacts.

By 300 B.C., late Preclassic societies were changing rapidly as common ideologies united much of Mesoamerica for the first time. The leaders of the new religious orders validated their rule with elaborate public ceremonies in spectacular architectural settings, commemorating potent and widely recognized deities. Distinctive art and architecture accompanied the new religion, the practice of which required precise measurements of calendar years and of longer cycles of time. Writing and mathematics were developed to affirm religious practices, a unifying political force in the sense that they welded scattered village communities into larger political units.

By the time the classic Mesoamerican civilizations of highlands and lowlands arose, dynasties of lords had been ruling Mesoamerica along well-established lines for nearly 1,000 years. A dramatic find of a 4-ton basalt stela at La Mojarra on the Acula River bears the figure of a great ruler of the second century A.D., known from accompanying glyphs to be the "Harvest Moon Lord." The inscription is written in an ancient form of the Zoquean language, perhaps the ancestral Olmec tongue, using signs that show some resemblance to later Maya script. The earliest such kingly inscription known, it commemorates his accession to the throne and his triumphant suppression of a rebellion by his brother-in-law.

A broadly similar pattern of emerging social and political complexity appeared in Mesopotamia, Egypt, China, and other areas where early state-organized societies evolved. This pattern is well illustrated by Maya civilization.

## Preclassic Maya Civilization (before 1000 B.C.–A.D. 200)

### *Origins: Cuello (c. 1200–400 B.C.)*

The roots of ancient Maya civilization lie in much earlier cultural traditions in the Mesoamerican lowlands. Unfortunately, the Maya homeland, with its dense forest cover, is unsympathetic to the archaeological record. The perpetual humidity and high rainfall militate against the preservation of organic remains, while the dense vegetation makes it hard to find even enormous pyramids and plazas. But when Boston University archaeologist Norman Hammond found the Cuello site in northern Belize in the early 1970s, he was able to trace the roots of Maya culture back to the second millennium B.C. Village life in the region goes back to at least 2500 B.C.

Cuello is a small Maya ceremonial center, today comprising a platform—0.4 hectare (1 acre) square and 3.6 meters (12 feet) high—and a low pyramid. Hammond knew that the Maya habitually rebuilt shrines and major centers on the same sacred sites, in the belief that supernatural power accumulated over the generations. He excavated layer after layer of occupation under the main plaza, until he found a pole-framed, palm-thatched house set on a lime-plaster platform, dating to about 1200 B.C. The Cuello people maintained the same basic plaza layout for many centuries, making it larger and larger until about 400 B.C. At this point, the villagers converted their ceremonial precinct, with its wood and thatch temples, into a large public arena. They burned their existing shrines, tore down their facades, and desanctified them; then they filled the square with rubble to create a raised platform covering more than an acre. Hammond unearthed the fragmentary skeletons of more than 30 sacrificial victims in the rubble, some with hacked-off skulls and limbs, others sitting in a circle around two young men. Six carved bone tubes buried with the victims bore the interlacing, woven-mat motif symbolic of later Maya kingship. Such mats were royal thrones. This motif may document the appearance of a Maya elite by 400 B.C.

Cuello provides striking evidence of cultural continuity in part of the Maya lowlands at a time when village farmers were improving maize strains and increasing agricultural productivity. This one site contains all the fundamental elements of later Maya civilization: more intensive agriculture and widespread trade connections, emerging social stratification (revealed by the fine-quality jade beads from the Motagua River in southern Guatemala, found with a few burials), and the first appearance of specialized crafts.

## *Nakbé and El Mirador (c. 1000–300 B.C.)*

The Nakbé ruins are 346 kilometers (215 miles) from Guatemala City and 13.6 kilometers (8.5 miles) from the early Maya city at El Mirador, which covers 15.5 square kilometers (6 square miles). The two settlements were once linked by a causeway, but smaller Nakbé was occupied much earlier, by about 1000 B.C. Even in its early stages, it was ruled by a powerful elite identified from their teeth, which were inlaid with jadelike stone, a common artifice among later Maya nobles. Between 650 and 450 B.C., Nakbé's leaders embarked on an ambitious building program. They constructed huge platforms over their earlier ceremonial structures, raising pyramids with blank facades on top of them. By 300 B.C., the builders were carving monsters with grotesque features into the limestone, then covering them with stucco. The pyramids themselves were crowned with three small temples clustered at the top of a steep stairway bounded with panels and masks. The same general design continued to be used in later centuries, as successive rulers used intricate hieroglyphs and stelae to commemorate their deeds and reigns.

Like their Olmec contemporaries, Nakbé's artists focused on gods and mythical beings. One architectural sculpture found at the base of a 46-meter-tall (150-foot-tall) pyramid consisted of a stylized head of the Maya god Celestial Bird, a symbol of the natural world. Celestial Bird later became associated with Maya kingship. Archaeologist Richard Hanson wonders if the complex religious ideology represented at Nakbé was the compelling force behind the development of Maya civilization. He believes the great buildings at Nakbé were built with the labor of people whose leaders played on the reverent relationship between humans and gods, precisely the kind of relationship found in Mesopotamian and early Chinese civilization in earlier times. Hanson's theory is highly controversial, but Nakbé's temple facades certainly reflect the emerging notion of Ch'ul Ahau, divine kingship, in Maya society. In lavish public ceremonies, important lords donned the masks of gods, symbolizing their role as living gods. Nakbé reached the height of its power around 300 B.C. but subsided into complete political and economic obscurity within a few generations, at a time when its neighbor, El Mirador, rose to prominence.

El Mirador enjoyed more reliable water supplies than its neighbor, as well as a better defensive position. Between 150 B.C. and A.D. 50, the city grew to about 16 square kilometers (6 square miles). Brigham Young University archaeologists have uncovered at least 200 buildings, including a great complex of pyramids, temples, and plazas. The Danta pyramid at the eastern end of the site rises from a natural hill more than 70 meters (210 feet) high. A little over 2 kilometers (a mile) west is the Tigre complex, a pyramid 55 meters (182 feet) high, surrounded by a plaza and smaller buildings (Figure 15.4). El Mirador is yielding some of the earliest examples of Maya writing, inscribed on potsherds and occasionally on stucco sculpture. A raised road (*sacbeob*) connected El Mirador with another important Preclassic center, Calakmul, 38 kilometers (24 miles) to the northeast.

**Figure 15.4** Reconstruction of the central precincts of El Mirador.

This stupendous and still little-known city collapsed suddenly in the early centuries A.D. The dynamics of this collapse are little understood but are mirrored at other Preclassic Maya communities, where the institution of kingship rose and was then abandoned. The volatility of many Maya centers may be connected to endemic warfare, but despite this constant change many centers, among them Calakmul, Tikal, and Uaxactún, developed continuously from Preclassic into Classic times.

## *Early Maya Kingship: Cerros (50 B.C.–A.D. 150)*

The same dynamics of rise and collapse can be seen elsewhere. In 50 B.C., the small late Preclassic town of Cerros near the eastern coast of the Yucatán was a modest fishing and trading community. But within two generations, the tiny community transformed itself into a large center. The village disappeared under plazas and temples. The central precincts became a ceremonial center, transformed into a symbolic landscape that depicted the sacred world—that is, the sacred mountains, a gateway to the Otherworld that was so important in Maya religion. Everyone in the community helped to build the ceremonial structures, which signaled the arrival of kingship in the community. The first temples were followed by later shrines, all of them settings for the ritual bloodlettings and sacrifices that served to legitimize the roles of the nobility, who led the community. Then, suddenly, Cerros's temples fell into disuse, and the once-important center again became a small fishing village. The anonymous leaders of Cerros, like those of

El Mirador and Nakbé, left no records of their names or their personal histories. Their only legacy to their successors was a distinctive architectural heritage that stressed social ranking and the use of large-scale structures to perpetuate royal dynasties. The rituals performed by these shaman-lords took place on the pyramids and in the plazas of the great Maya centers, which were symbolic replicas of the sacred landscape created by the gods at the beginning of the world. The architecture of the great ritual structures replicated forests, mountains, and caves as stelae, pyramids, and temple openings. The rituals were powerful, so powerful that the places where they were conducted became more and more sacred as successive rulers built new temples on the same spots. Generations of rulers replicated the iconography and sculpture of earlier buildings, elaborating on them to produce the sacred settings within which the strategies of political competition between neighbors were carried out.

## *The Maya Calendar and Script*

Maya civilization was also embedded in a matrix of unfolding cyclic time. Maya priests used the movements of planets and stars to mark the passage of time. They tried to understand the cycles of the cosmos, deciding which days were propitious for ritual, trade, royal marriages, war, and so on. The entire routine of Maya civilization operated according to a complex pair of interlocking calendars (see Box 15.1).

The calendar was vital to Maya life, for the complex geography of sacred time helped determine political strategies and social moves. The records kept by Maya scribes in hieroglyphic codices (books) were incredibly intricate records of divine actions on each day of the cyclic calendar. Each day had a character, a distinctive identity in the *tzolkin* and *haab*, and a position in all the permutations of cyclic time (Figure 15.5). Each Maya king developed a relationship to this constantly moving time scale. Some events, like planting and harvest, were regular events on the calendar. Others, like dates of accession, important victories, and royal deaths and births, left their marks on the calendar, sometimes as days that assumed great significance in the history of an individual dynasty. Maya rulers linked their actions to those of the gods and the ancestors, sometimes legitimizing their descent by claiming that it reenacted mythical events. Maya history was connected to the present and the Otherworld, to the legendary Olmec civilization of the past. Society was embedded in a matrix of sacred place and time.

The Maya developed a hieroglyphic script for calculating calendars and regulating religious observances. The script was also much used to record genealogies, king-lists, conquests, and dynastic histories. Owing to poor preservation conditions and the destruction wrought by Spanish friars, we do not know to what extent Maya writing was an administrative device. Certainly, its use was confined to rulers and the elite, and it figured large in display and ceremonial life. Politically, scribes were considered of great importance, so much so that captured scribes were mutilated to prevent them writing. The symbols are fantastically grotesque, consisting mostly of

## *Box 15.1 The Maya Calendar*

Maya civilization was embedded in a matrix of unfolding, cyclical time. The best way to think of its calendar is to imagine an interlocking set of gears (Figure 15.5). One cycle, the *tzolkin*, a 260-day count unrelated to any astronomical phenomenon, consisted of 13 numbers and 20 names. As the days advanced, the numbers and then the names were recycled; when the entire cycle was complete, the calendar returned to the original number and name combination with which it began. Each of the 260 days of the *tzolkin* had its own deity. The length of the cycle was arbitrary and probably established by long tradition. The *tzolkin* was used to regulate religious events and was intermeshed with the *haab*, a secular year of 365 days related to the solar cycle. This astronomical calendar was used to regulate state affairs, but the connections between the two calendars were of great im-

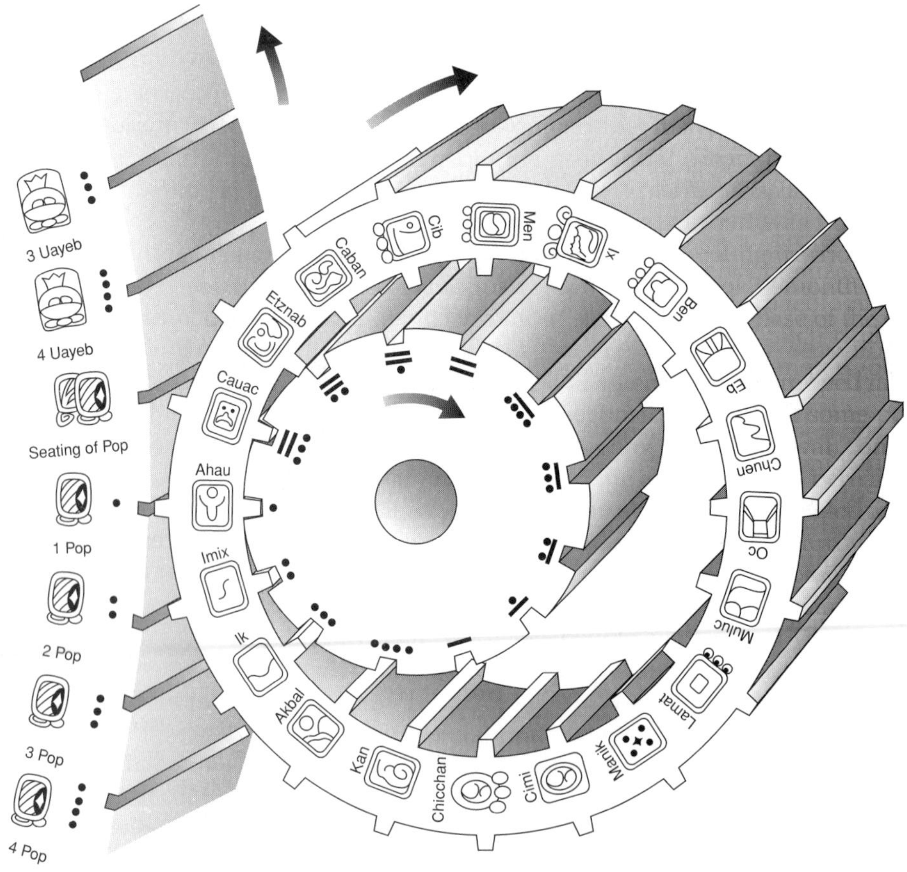


**Figure 15.5** The Maya calendar.

portance in Maya life. Each day had a character, a distinctive identity in the two calendars, and a position in all the permutations of cyclical time. Every 52 years a complete cycle of all the variations of the day and month names of the two calendars occurred, an occasion for intense religious activity. Each Maya king developed a personal relationship to the cycles of the calendar. Certain days of accession and royal deaths and births left their mark on the calendar and assumed great importance to the history of a royal dynasty. Thus, Maya history was linked to the present and to the Otherworld, and thus to the past and to the future.

The Maya also had a third, linear calendar of unique days, which did not repeat themselves. The starting point of this calendar, the famous "Long Count," was a mythical date, August 11, 3114 B.C., perhaps representing the day when the universe began. The Long Count was broken up into a notational system of units of days, the largest of which was the *baktun*, 400 360-day years, made up of 20 *katuns*, each 20 years.

humans, monsters, or god's heads. After more than a decade of intensive research, over half the extant Classic inscriptions have been deciphered. In its emphasis on religious and cosmological matters, Maya writing is closest to ancient Egyptian script in terms of its role in society (Box 15.2).

Hieroglyphic records were of cardinal importance in Maya life, for the institution of kingship was based on the principle that the royal crown passed from father to son, or brother to brother to son, in a line that led back to a founding ancestor. From there, families and clans were carefully ranked by their distance from the central royal descent line. This system of family ranking and allegiance was the basis of political power, a system that worked well but that depended on a careful documentation of genealogies.

Social status was highly prized in Maya society, as we can see at the great center of Copán, a major frontier capital of the Maya world at the edge of the Central American chiefdoms. Its pyramids, temples, and stelae are a remarkable record of Maya kings exercising political and social power. Although cosmology was a feature of Copán's building designs, the main function of the civic structures there, as elsewhere, was to commemorate major events in the lives of kings and the political histories of kingdoms. Each building was dedicated by the king who built it in the context of a specific event, everything from a royal accession to an important victory or a new alliance.

Among its many buildings, Copán features a ball court, two parallel platforms with sloping sides on either side of a narrow playing alley, a stadium used for an elaborate ceremonial contest in which sacrificial victims and kings descended through a symbolic "abyss" into the Otherworld (Figure 15.11). The players wore protective padding and used a rubber ball, which perhaps they aimed at markers—sometimes stone rings or macaw heads high on the side walls. Vase paintings show that the opposing teams bounced the ball off the sloping sides of the court, keeping it from touching the floor of the alley. Where rings were used, the game was won when one team bounced a ball through the ring. The ancient game originated in Olmec times. When

## Box 15.2 Voices: The Decipherment of Maya Script

The decipherment of Maya script ranks among the greatest scientific achievements of the twentieth century. The first person to record the elaborate, sometimes grotesque glyphs was Spanish Bishop Diego de Landa in the sixteenth century. Landa was a controversial figure, who studied traditional Maya life, on the one hand, and persecuted the Indians ruthlessly in the name of the One True Faith, on the other. He destroyed hundreds of Maya documents, codices written on bark and deerskin, but took the trouble to record details of the vanishing script. It was not until Englishman Alfred Percival Maudslay recorded thousands of glyphs in the 1880s and 1890s that an adequate body of inscriptions was widely available for serious study. For generations, the experts argued over whether Maya glyphs were picture writing or phonetic script. Were they historical records or merely calendrical or astronomical observations (Box 15.1)? Most Mayanists assumed that they were used to record the calendar and that the ancient Maya lords were peaceful astronomer-priests. But in 1952 Russian epigrapher Yuri Knosorov demonstrated that Maya script was a phonetic and syllabic hieroglyphic script, just like Egyptian writing. A decade later architect Tatiana Proskouriakoff discovered that the glyphs on stelae at the Maya site at Piedras Negras formed distinct patterns. She realized that the inscriptions were a record of once-living men and women. At nearby Yaxchilán, she identified two rulers from their distinctive glyphs, Shield Jaguar and his son, Bird Jaguar. For the first time, Maya lords became individuals with historical identities.

Twenty years passed before a group of scholars succeeded in assembling the dynastic history of Palenque from the earth—from seventh century A.D. until its demise, including the reign of Lord Pacal, who built the magnificent Temple of the Inscriptions (see page 430). Thus Maya archaeologists could attribute individual buildings to specific royal builders. More than 15 years of rapid-fire, intensive team work have since resulted in the partial decipherment of Maya script, although many difficulties await resolution. Unlike Egyptian or Sumerian script, the Maya archive is limited in scope and confined to inscriptions on clay pots, monumental inscriptions on buildings and stelae, and only four codices that survived the Spanish conquest. These are public statements of royal accessions, triumphant military campaigns, and important ceremonies. They are the political propaganda of Maya lords, the literature of a nobility intent on justifying their deeds and their ancestry. Of the everyday literature of the Maya, we know nothing. But the surviving texts tell us that Maya rulers were not peaceful astronomers but bloodthirsty lords who presided over a patchwork of competing city-states. Decipherment has clothed the archaeologists' chronology of pyramids and ceremonial centers with political and religious garments and revealed Maya civilization as a constantly shifting quicksand of diplomatic marriages, political alliances, and brutal conquests. The account of Maya civilization here is based on both archaeology and deciphered glyphs.

Spanish visitors saw the game played in the Yucatán in the sixteenth century A.D., the rules of play were at least 2,000 years old. The ball game had profound religious and sacrificial undertones, serving as a form of ritual combat—dramas in which the players acted out the deeds of the Maya gods. One Maya legend has the Heavenly Twins battling the Lords of the Underworld in an epic ball game; thus a ruler who sponsored or took part in a game was performing an important ritual act, which helped ensure the continuity of the universe. The entire ball court was a contest of political and religious significance between deadly opponents. The losing team became sacrificial victims and were decapitated. We do not know the rules of this ball game, but the games were associated with human sacrifice and much pomp and circumstance.

By combining archaeological excavation at Copán with historical art interpretation and text translations, scholars have been able to trace a lineage of nobles who specialized in hieroglyphic writing, a skill that gave them special prestige. Members of another noble rank, the *sahalob* ("vassals"), served as expert administrators and received many privileges for their skill. Status was inherited and was one way in which the legitimacy of society as a whole was maintained.

## Classic Maya Civilization (A.D. 200–900)

Copán is just one of many sites where archaeologists have documented the complicated political and social history of Maya civilization. The public monuments erected by the Classic Maya emphasize not only the king's role as shaman, as the intermediary with the Otherworld, but also his position as family patriarch. Genealogical texts on stelae legitimized his descent, his close relationship to his often long-deceased parents. Maya kings used both the awesome regalia of their office and elaborate rituals to stress their close identity with mythical ancestral gods. This was a way in which the kings asserted their kin relationship to and political authority over subordinate leaders and every member of society.

The king believed himself to have a divine covenant with the gods and ancestors, a covenant that was reinforced again and again in elaborate private and public rituals. The ruler was often depicted as the World Tree, the conduit by which humans communicated with the Otherworld. Trees were the living environment of Maya life and a metaphor for human power. So the kings of the Maya were a forest of symbolic human World Trees within a natural forested landscape.

The Maya calendar ensured a constant round of ceremonies and rituals at the great ceremonial centers erected by the labor of hundreds of people, farmers who also fed the kings, priests, and artisans. Yet the Maya worldview created serious and binding obligations among the king and his nobility and all the people, reflected in the king's responsibilities in gathering and redistributing commodities of all kinds and in implementing agricultural schemes that turned swamps into organized, productive landscapes. The lives of Maya rulers and all their subjects were interconnected in vital, dynamic ways. The king was state shaman, the individual who enriched everyone's life in spiritual and ceremonial ways. His success in organizing trade and agriculture gave all levels of society access to goods and commodities. The great ceremonial centers built by Maya leaders created a setting in which elaborate rituals and ceremonies took on intense significance. The "histories written and pictured by the kings on the tree stones standing before human-made mountains gave form to time and space in both the material and spiritual worlds" (Schele and Freidel, 1990, p. 319).

## Political Organization and Political History

Maya civilization was far from uniform. It appears to have been a mosaic of political units, large and small, and it is difficult to be specific about the political relationships between Maya settlements, divided as the people were into many small and multicenter polities. One possible approach is through the identification of "emblem glyphs," titles that were carried by kings and their highest nobility in the major kingdoms. The emblem glyph of Palenque was Ch'ul Bac Ahaw (Holy Bone Lord), and that of Tikal was Mutul (tied bundle or tied flower), depicting a man's hair topknot seen from the rear. The emblem glyphs can be taken as statements of political affiliation with particular kingdoms, for subordinate centers would sometimes use their overlord's glyph. They would identify political control over a territory by stating that events occurred *u cab* (in the land of).

Many Mayanists have thought of Maya civilization in terms of small competing kingdoms. But Joyce Marcus has studied Maya political territoriality using a combination of epigraphy (the study of inscriptions), iconography, and settlement patterns, assuming that site emblem glyphs and their distributions would reflect the structure and ranking of ceremonial centers. She has observed a remarkable similarity in the ways in which Mesoamerican states rose, reached their peak, and then collapsed. She notes a remarkably consistent scenario in both the lowlands and the highlands, not only in Maya civilization but also in Toltec and Aztec civilizations (see Chapter 16).

This scenario unfolds as follows: First, a new city-state, say, Maya Tikal or Teotihuacán, expands its territory through diplomacy, political marriage, and military conquest. The new state reaches its maximum territorial limits early in its history. Then, once some provinces have attained a significant level of cultural complexity and development, they break away from their nominal master and become an independent polity. Far from being weakened, the core state still prospers, investing its energy and resources in its own local area rather than in expansion. But sometimes the old provinces, now independent states, ally themselves against their old overlord and conquer it, so they become a second center.

This cycle of rise, expansion on the margins, fission, and then decline at the expense of others repeated itself again and again, to the point that it can be considered a consistent pattern of Mesoamerican civilization. Thus Marcus's scenario is well documented in Maya political history. She has also developed a general scenario for Maya political history and organization that envisages four major city-states during the Classic period, rather than dozens of smaller polities, as shown in the following paragraph.

Between A.D. 292 and 434, there were no regional capitals, no well-defined hierarchy of settlement, and different monument styles in the various regions of the Maya homeland. Most centers were, on average, about 27 kilometers (18 miles) apart, apparently autonomous and competitive, and of roughly equal rank. Tikal and Uaxactún appear to have been the earliest dominant centers. By A.D. 514 to 534, a standardized symbolic system was being used at monuments at even the most dispersed Maya centers. There were now four regional capitals, each with its own emblem glyph and each ruling over a well-defined hierarchy of lesser settlements, an arrangement suggesting a form of pyramidical state dominated by a few ruling dynasties. A hieroglyphic text of A.D. 731 from Copán, perhaps a biased source, lists these four capitals: Tikal, Palenque, Calakmul, and Copán. This quadripartite political structure is consistent in a loose way with ancient Maya cosmological structure, in which each major capital was associated with a cardinal direction. The four capitals were separate quadrants of the lowland Maya region.

Marcus believes the Maya capitals enjoyed some form of military alliance between A.D. 672 and 751, the ruler of each communicating with his neighbors of equal rank, a situation reflected by the adoption of a uniform lunar calendar and a homogeneous style and iconography of monuments. Within each region, the ruler achieved integration by strategic marriage alliances with ruling families from lesser, dependent centers—between, for example, Palenque and nearby Yaxchilán. But these arrangements did not last long. After A.D. 830 to 909, over 60 percent of all monuments were erected at what had previously been lesser centers, as if the authority of the original capitals had been replaced by more appropriate mechanisms for governing smaller, more dispersed populations. This changeover coincides with the so-called Maya collapse (see page 435).

There were many elements common to all Maya polities, among them the calendar and the hieroglyphic script, essential to the regulation of religious life and the worship of the gods. Architectural and artistic styles in ceramics and small artifacts varied from center to center as each developed its own characteristics and cultural traditions. The Maya were unified more by religion than by political or economic interests, in much the same way, perhaps, as the spread of Islam unified diverse cultures.

The political mechanisms used by the Maya included warfare, which had strong ritual overtones and was probably very destructive. It may have been aimed more at economic hegemony than territorial expansion. Much art and many inscriptions concentrate on the ceremonial and ideological aspects of war—the capture and sacrifice of prisoners as a way of validating political authority. Whether this was the primary purpose of going to war is uncertain. However, judging from emblem glyphs, most wars were between immediate neighbors, the capture and sacrifice of a ruler sometimes leading to the dominance of one capital by another for generations, at other times apparently having little effect. The inscriptions tell us that visits by rulers or their representatives to other capitals were important occurrences, usually to commemorate significant political events such as an accession or occasions when a ruler designated his heir. At the core of all these diplomatic and military maneuvers were ongoing rivalries between powerful noble families, which endured over many centuries. For example, the Jaguar Paw clan seems to have risen to prominence at Preclassic El Mirador, then spread its influence to Tikal, Caracol, and ultimately to Dos Pilos. Much Maya warfare was more between factions of powerful clans than between different ones.

## *The Rise of Tikal (c. 200 B.C.–A.D. 900)*

With this general scenario in mind, one can lay out the beginnings of a narrative of Maya political history from as early as the third century A.D. With constant new discoveries and decipherments, the snapshots given here, based on individual site histories, are, necessarily, an incomplete picture.

Cerros and El Mirador were major centers during the late Preclassic, but even as they prospered, new centers were emerging a short distance away. Tikal and Uaxactún were growing during the late Preclassic and stepped into the economic and political vacuum left by the decline of El Mirador. Tikal rose in a strategic position atop some low hills where extensive chert deposits occur. Nearby seasonal swamps may have provided a basis for intensive agriculture and some protection against sudden attack. The growing settlement also sat astride a critical river portage between water systems that carried trade goods from east to west across the Maya lowlands. Important trade routes to highland cities like Teotihuacán also passed through Tikal. At the same time, Tikal had powerful supernatural associations as the current seat of one of the oldest royal dynasties in the region (Figure 15.6).

Even as El Mirador collapsed, perhaps because its trading connections had faltered, Tikal and Uaxactun came into prominence. The two centers were fewer than 20 kilometers (12 miles) apart, too close for bitter rivals to coexist.

Tikal was perhaps the greatest Maya city, but it remained buried under thick rainforest until 1848. For more than a century, the only access was along narrow tracks, preventing any extended archaeological investigations. In 1951, the

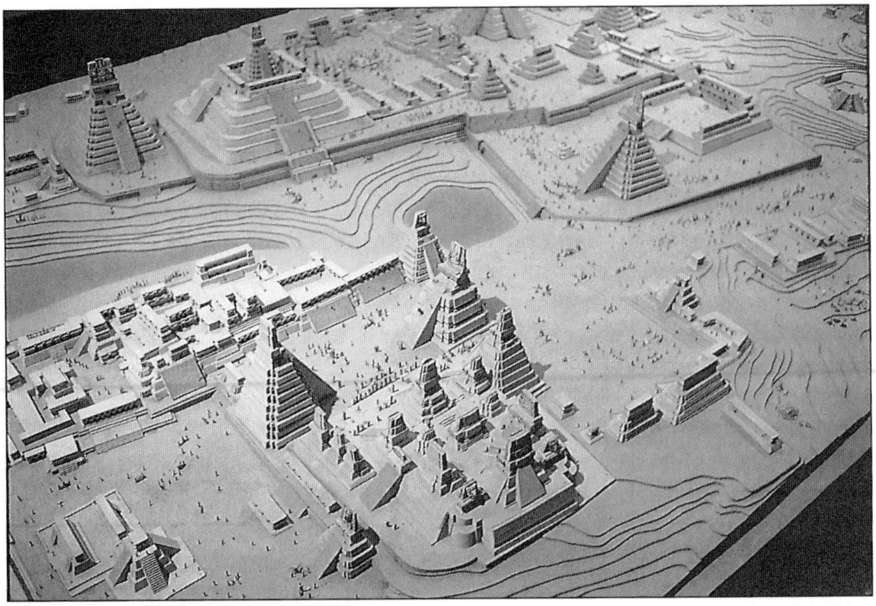

**Figure 15.6** The central precincts of Tikal.

Guatemalan air force built a small airstrip close to the site, which enabled the University of Pennsylvania to begin a 15-year research project at Tikal. More than 100 archaeologists participated in excavations and surveys, which uncovered more than 500 buildings and a detailed architectural history of the central precincts. Tikal began life as a small farming village in about 600 B.C. but soon developed into a much larger community. By the second century A.D., more than 40,000 people lived in and around an urban core. Tikal and its outliers covered more than 65 square kilometers (25 square miles).

As El Mirador collapsed, the rulers of Tikal built an elaborate complex of more than 100 buildings—monumental structures, pyramids, and royal burial vaults now known as the North Acropolis. This lay on the north side of the Great Plaza, which formed the heart of the city. Now grass covered, the plaza was originally plastered, an imposing setting for public ceremonies conducted on the surrounding pyramids—symbolic mountains topped by small temples, whose doorways served as gateways to the Otherworld. Over many centuries, successive lords erected new temples and pyramids in the central area. Their burials reveal taller, more robust individuals than the common people, perhaps a sign of a better diet. One noblewoman's tomb was adorned with portraits of fellow nobles, perhaps kin or ancestors. Another grave contained a headless and thighless corpse tied into a bundle, with a greenstone portrait head that was once the chest pectoral of the deceased. The human head on the pectoral bears the Jester God headdress, which centuries of Maya kings were to wear.

Constant remodeling of the central precincts buried much Preclassic art, such as a group of six temples whose facades were covered with stucco masks. One depicts the Maya cosmos—the great monster swimming in the primordial sea, on one level, and another monster above who represents the sacred mountain that rose from the waters to become land. The Vision Serpent penetrates the head of this monster, his sinuous body symbolizing the complex path to the Otherworld taken by the lords in shamanistic trances. For the first time, one temple bears the portraits of a ruler who is standing on a woven mat. At the same time, Tikal's public art reveals a major shift away from depictions of gods and the cosmos toward portraits of individual rulers.

The continuity of Maya kingship depended on smooth transitions from one generation to the next, on maintaining alliances between factions of the nobility, and on good relationships with neighbors. Deciphered glyphs record the founding of an enduring Tikal dynasty by a ruler named Yax-Ch'aktel-Xok (A.D. 219–238). Thirty-one lords inherited Tikal's throne from this founding ancestor and maintained dynastic continuity for more than 600 years.

At both Tikal and Uaxactún, Maya kings memorialized themselves on their temples, but the two centers were political and economic equals during the first century A.D.

Tikal's inscriptions are the chronicle of a remarkable dynasty that ruled one of the four Maya capitals from the early Classic until the ninth century A.D. The earliest recorded monarch is Yax-Ch'aktel-Xok (First Scaffold Shark), who is thought to have reigned around A.D. 200, although the city had a long and much earlier history. During his reign, strong influences from Teotihuacán on the highlands appear, shown by pottery styles and green obsidian from the city's closely controlled sources. This strong influence on political, military, and religious affairs at Tikal continued until A.D. 550.

Yax-Ch'aktel-Xok was not the earliest king but was the one who served as founding ancestor for the great royal clan of Tikal that ruled in coming centuries. Tikal's hieroglyphic texts identify 31 rulers (18 known by name) after the founder, the earliest dating to A.D. 292, the last known one to A.D. 869, making for 669 years of recorded history. Uaxactún also fostered a powerful royal dynasty, whose monuments, like those of the Tikal kings, soon depicted rulers with sacrificial victims cowering at their feet, noble victims taken in hand-to-hand combat for later sacrifice in public rituals. These portraits signal a crucial development in Maya history: the increasing role of warfare and campaigns of deliberate conquest.

Between A.D. 320 and 378, Great-Jaguar Paw, the ninth successor of Yax-Ch'aktel-Xok, sat on the throne of Tikal, at a time when rivalries with nearby Uaxactún came to a head. He died in 378, at a moment when a warrior named Fire-Born arrived, a warrior from the "west," presumably Teotihuacán. The connection between Great-Jaguar Paw's death and Fire-Born's arrival is unclear, but it was the former who defeated the armies of Uaxactún on January 16, A.D. 378. His army ignored long-established rules of combat and sacked Uaxactún, setting up Fire-Born as the founder of a new dynasty. The war was associated with new rituals first developed at Teotihuacán in the highlands, and it linked the god Tlaloc and the planet Venus. Tikal's military expansion took place with assistance from Teotihuacán during a period of regular trading contacts between the great highland city and many Maya centers, marked by many finds of the distinctive green obsidian mined by the great city. The same contacts may have brought new philosophies of war and conquest and the rituals associated with them. These rituals were to become part of the Mesoamerican religious tradition for many centuries.

Tikal's rulers continued to prosper in later centuries, eventually presiding over a multicenter kingdom acquired through conquest and diplomatic marriage. At the height of its powers in the early sixth century, Tikal's territory covered 2,500 square kilometers (965 square miles), with an estimated population of more than 360,000 people, a kingdom with an area somewhat larger than most Sumerian city-states in Mesopotamia 3,000 years earlier. Tikal's royal dynasty eventually headed a multicenter polity, extending its influence by conquest and long-distance trade and by judicious political marriages that gave neighboring rulers maternal kin ties to the center. At the height of its powers, Tikal's territory may have supported an estimated population of as many as 300,000 people, the city and its immediate hinterland perhaps 200,000: These are perhaps high estimates. But several outlying kingdoms, among them Calakmul and Dos Pilos, split off from Tikal and became independent domains.

In about A.D. 557, Tikal went into decline after its defeat by the lord of a new rising state, Caracol, then prospered anew during the Late Classic.

## *Calakmul and Caracol (Preclassic times–A.D. 800)*

Caracol, in south-central Belize, 70 kilometers (43 miles) southeast of Tikal, controlled important crystalline rock supplies and was an important rival to Tikal. Its imposing ceremonial core covered at least 2.25 square kilometers (0.9 square miles) during the seventh century, when between 30,000 and 50,000 people lived there, and as many as 100,000 in the surrounding countryside. Caracol commenced hostilities against Tikal in A.D. 557, soon after Tikal had captured and executed a prominent lord. The Caracol ruler Lord Water defeated Tikal, apparently capturing the city's then-ruler, Double Bird. Tikal became a tribute dependency of Caracol, which grew in size and prestige as its vassal declined. Lord Water's successors dominated Tikal for at least 150 years and embarked on ambitious conquests against neighboring Calakmul and Naranjo. But eventually Caracol paid the price for its military adventures. But both Calakmul and Tikal rose again during the Late Classic.

Calakmul, in the southern lowlands, was one of the largest Maya regional states of the late Classic period, but it remained virtually unknown until recently. Once split off from Tikal, Calakmul became a major force in the Maya world. In the eighth century, a supreme lord of Copán commissioned an inscription that referred to Calakmul as one of the "four on high," the leading Maya centers. A 12-year program of mapping and excavation has revealed a major city, one that ruled over at least six secondary centers, which were equidistant from the central capital.

Calakmul was linked to its subordinate centers by raised roads elevated above swamplands, which traversed the countryside in straight lines. Perhaps some of these roads once extended over much longer distances, linking the city to even more distant dependencies and, conceivably, to rivals far beyond the 34-kilometer (21-mile) radius of its secondary centers. The essence of efficient government is rapid communication, in this case achieved by earth- or stone-packed roads raised above swampy ground. Such roads have been known to connect different parts of large Maya cities, but it is only recently that they have been traced over longer distances. These road systems may account for Calakmul's importance as a regional capital in the Maya lowlands, one of three or four states that dominated Maya civilization during the late Classic. At its height, Calakmul had a ceremonial precinct covering about 2 square kilometers (0.7 square miles) and a surrounding residential area over 20 square kilometers (7.7 square miles) in extent. At least 50,000 people lived in the urban core of a great city and important rival of Tikal between at least A.D. 514 and 814.

Like Tikal, Calakmul sat astride an important overland trade route. The rivalry between the two cities may have been both a power play and a struggle for dominance of long-distance exchange. There may have been family ties between the two cities. The rivalry was intense, culminating in warfare and constant shifts in allegiance between Tikal, Calakmul, and Caracol, which are virtually impossible to decipher today.

Tikal had few allies in its immediate vicinity, but maintained friendlier relations with two more distant city-states—Palenque and Copán.

## *Palenque (A.D. 431–799)*

The great city of Teotihuacán on the highlands had a profound influence on Maya civilization until the end of the sixth century, when its powers waned. As Teotihuacán faded, so a number of important Maya centers achieved greater power and competed ferociously for people, resources, and territory. The overall political situation was in a state of constant flux, as lord vied with lord in a maze of ever-changing diplomatic alliances and short-lived military campaigns. Palenque's lords were among them.

The city of Palenque, another Maya capital, but in the western lowlands, is remarkable not only for its fine buildings but also for its rulers' obsession with their ancestry. Two Palenque rulers, Pacal the Great (Shield) and his oldest son, Chan-Bahlum (Snake-Jaguar), who ruled in the seventh century A.D., stand out for their vision and wisdom (Box 15.3). Palenque's dynastic history began on March 11, A.D. 431, when Bahlum- Kuk (Jaguar-Quetzal) became ruler, and lasted until sometime after A.D. 799. The experts have used the rich inscriptions left by Pacal and others to reconstruct a dynasty of no fewer than 12 kings, with, however, some minor sidesteps. These sidesteps accounted for the obsession with history that was so remarkable in Pacal and Chan-Bahlum's day.

Succession was through the male line, yet Pacal inherited the throne from his mother, Lady Zac-Kuk, who served for a time as ruler. She must have been a remarkable woman, although we know nothing of her. Pacal claimed the throne as her son and, in so doing, had to change the genealogical rules so that he could override the age-old rule of descent through the father and claim succession. In short, he, and later his son, orchestrated orthodox belief with clever fictions. First, they declared Lady Zac-Kuk to be equivalent to the first mother of gods and kings at the beginning of the present creation. This mother deity was the mother of the three major gods of Maya religion. Next, Pacal and Chan-Bahlum claimed that Pacal had been born on the very day of the calendar that coincided with that of the goddess's birth. Thus, both Pacal and the goddess were of the same divine substance. Pacal inherited the throne from his mother because this was what had happened at the beginning of creation: Authority had been transmitted through both males and females.

It may have helped that Pacal ascended to the throne at the age of 12, while his mother was still alive, and that she lived for another 25 years. The real power may have been in her hands for all those years, for it was only after her death in 640 that Pacal commissioned major inscriptions that justified his own rule.

Toward the end of his long reign, which lasted 67 years, Pacal built the Temple of the Inscriptions, a masterpiece of Maya architecture under which his tomb lies. His artists carved the images of his direct ancestors around his coffin deep under the temple; on this sarcophagus his strategy of dynastic legitimization was recorded (see Box 15.3).

Pacal's sons built additional temples at Palenque, maintaining the center as a major power for about a century after the great ruler's death. The great Palenque dynasty flourished during a period of Maya history that has been called the Warring

## *Box 15.3 The Lord Pacal*

Under the lord Pacal's stewardship, Palenque became a masterpiece of Maya architecture. Lying in the foothills of the Sierra of Chiapas, Palenque is a compact center by Maya standards, dominated by Pacal's Temple of the Inscriptions, built, so glyphs tell us, in A.D. 692. The temple rests on a stepped pyramid rising 23 meters (75 feet) above the plaza. A densely wooded hill supports the back of the pyramid. In 1952, Mexican archaeologist Alberto Ruz Lhuillier noticed some holes in a large slab that formed part of the temple floor. He lifted the slab and uncovered a rubble-filled stairway leading to the heart of the pyramid. After four months of arduous work, Ruz uncovered the steep stairs, which made a U-turn in the middle. The skeletons of six young male sacrificial victims lay at the foot by a triangular slab that sealed a vaulted doorway. Behind it lay a burial chamber measuring 9 by 4 meters (30 by 13 feet). A vaulted ceiling soared 64 meters (21 feet) overhead. The sepulcher lay 23.4 meters (80 feet) below the floor of the temple and 1.5 meters (5 feet) below the plaza ground surface. Otherworld figures adorned the chamber walls. Most of the floor was taken up by a massive, carved stone slab, 25 centimeters (10 inches) thick, weighing about 5 tons (Figure 15.7). Ruz lifted the sarcophagus lid with great difficulty and gazed on the skeleton of a tall man covered with jade ornaments. A magnificent jade mosaic mask covered the ruler's head.

When Ruz originally uncovered the tomb, he had no way to identify its occupant. But the decipherment of Maya script has enabled epigraphers to identify the owner as Pacal himself, who was born in 603, ascended to the throne in 615, and died in 683 at the age of 80. The sarcophagus, commissioned by Pacal years before his death, is a remarkable

**Figure 15.7** Tomb of Pacal, Palenque. The tomb lid commemorates his genealogy.

*(Cont.)*

commentary on Maya kingship. His genealogy appears in the metaphor of an orchard of fruit trees, that is, an orchard of the ancestral dead. Each ancestor rises with a fruit tree, the earliest in the southeast corner; Pacal's mother and father are in the north and south sides. On the lid, the king's artists have depicted the Sun Lord falling down the trunk of the World Tree into the waiting jaws of the Otherworld. They have included the resurrection as well, a half-skeletal monster who is carrying a sacrificial bowl bearing the glyph of the sun. Like the sun, Pacal would rise again in the east after his journey through the Otherworld.

States. Just as in China, small state vied with small state in a constant quest for economic and political power, which began when Lord Water of Caracol attacked his mighty neighbor—and then other states such as Dos Pilos and again Tikal—and achieved brief domination. But the Maya lords lacked the organization and military logistics to control wide areas and garrison conquered cities, so the diplomatic and military landscape changed constantly, even when large regional states were dominant. During the very late Classic period after A.D. 771, signs of political stress became more common, as minor nobles and others took advantage of the constant instability to carve out their own independent domains, often on the periphery of large states. This stress is well documented at the city of Copán.

### *Copán (before A.D. 435–800)*

Copán in Honduras is adorned with pyramids and plazas covering 12 hectares (30 acres), rising from the vast open spaces of the Great and Middle Plazas to an elaborate complex of raised enclosed courtyards, pyramids, and temples known to archaeologists as the Acropolis (Figure 15.8). Here successive rulers built their architectural statements atop those of their predecessors in an archaeological jigsaw puzzle of the first magnitude.

The earliest inscription at the site dates to December 11, A.D. 435 and was the work of ruler Yax-Ku'k-Mo' (Blue Quetzal Macaw), although there may have been earlier rulers. For four centuries, Blue Quetzal Macaw's successors formed a powerful dynasty at Copán and became a major force in the Maya world. At one point, Copán ruled over neighboring Quirigua. More than 10,000 people lived in the surrounding valley. But on May 3, 738, the subordinate ruler of Quirigua turned on his master and captured and sacrificed him. Yet Copán seems to have maintained a measure of independence and survived. In 749, a new ruler, Smoke Shell, ascended to the throne of the once-great city. He embarked on an ambitious campaign of rehabilitation, even marrying a princess from distant Palenque. He also embarked on a building frenzy which culminated in the Temple of the Hieroglyphic Stairway, built in 755, one of the oldest and most sacred of Copán's precincts. Smoke Shell's son from his Palenque marriage, Yax-Pac (First Dawn) ruled during troubled times, with internal factionalism on the rise. By this time, the city was top-heavy with privilege-hungry nobles and rife with political intrigue. Collapse was imminent.

**Figure 15.8** Tatiana Proskouriakoff's reconstruction of the central area of Copán.

The diplomatic and military landscape was constantly changing as alliances were formed and just as rapidly collapsed again. During the very late Classic, after A.D. 771, a new political pattern emerged, indicative of changed conditions and stressful times. Carved inscriptions began to appear in the houses of local nobles at Copán and other sites, as if the rulers were now granting the privilege of using inscriptions to important individuals, perhaps as a way of gaining their continued support in times of trouble. This proliferation of inscriptions in the Petén and elsewhere may also reflect minor nobles' taking advantage of confused times and a disintegrating political authority to claim their own brief independence. The confusion accelerated. By A.D. 800, Maya populations were declining sharply, and both monument carving and major construction soon came to an end.

The lowlands were never unified politically during the Classic period. What the Maya elite did share was a set of highly complex traditions and a network of contacts between rulers that transcended the local interests of individual kingdoms and considerable local diversity. Only when a few aggressive and exceptionally talented leaders appeared did several centers coalesce into multicenter states, such as archrivals Tikal and Calakmul.

There are intriguing parallels between Classic Maya and early Mesopotamian civilizations. The Sumerians were governed by independent rulers with strong ritual powers, presiding over independent city-states that were in a constant state of change and interaction. The city-state remained the practical political unit long after Sargon created a theoretically unified Mesopotamia around 2350 B.C. (Chapter 3).

## Box 15.4 Architecture as a Political Statement: The Hieroglyphic Stairway at Copán, Honduras

Today's Maya archaeologist works closely with epigraphers, using carefully deciphered glyphs and inscriptions to reconstruct complex architectural events, as well as the ritual or political motives behind them. William and Barbara Fash combined both lines of evidence to reconstruct the Hieroglyphic Stairway at Copán, erected by the ruler Smoke Shell in A.D. 755 on one of the city's most sacred precincts.

In the 1930s, archaeologists of the Carnegie Institution restored much of the ruined stairway, replacing the glyph blocks in approximate order. They were unable to read the inscriptions, which made the task difficult. In 1986, a team of archaeologists and epigraphers headed by the Fashes set out to restore and conserve the building, while establishing the true meaning of the stairway. Using meticulous excavation, the archaeologists recovered thousands of tenoned mosaic fragments from the structure, which were drawn and photographed, then pieced together in a precise reconstruction of the building. They recovered a powerful political statement (Figure 15.9).

More than 2,200 glyphs ascend the sides of the stairway and provide an elegant statement of the Maya kings' supernatural path. William Fash believes the building was an

**Figure 15.9** Reconstruction of the Hieroglyphic Stairway at Copán by Tatiana Proskouriakoff.

attempt by Smoke Shell to relegitimize the conquered dynasty of earlier times. Portraits on the stairs depict Copán's lords as warriors carrying shields, with inscriptions recounting their deeds. A figure, perhaps Smoke Shell himself, stands where an altar forms the base of the stairway, in the form of an inverted head of the rain god Tlaloc. Tlaloc seems to be belching forth the inscriptions, his lower jaw forming the top of the stairs. Inside his head lay an offering of decorated flints in the form of portraits and artifacts perhaps used by Smoke Shell himself in the sacrificial and bloodletting ceremonies that dedicated the stairway.

Unfortunately, the stairway was shoddily, and hastily, built. It soon collapsed, at a time when Copán was rapidly losing its political authority.

Just as in the Maya lowlands, larger political units forged by leaders of exceptional ability eventually fragmented back into their city-state parts. Maya civilization was a local phenomenon in the sense that its constituent regional states were relatively small and short-lived. Regional ties were crucial, far more so than in Mesopotamia. These ties were forged through common religious beliefs, alliances, and marriage ties. The central institution of Maya civilization was kingship, for it was the concept that unified society as a whole. Maya kings lived and carried out their deeds in the context of a history they recorded in building projects at Tikal, Palenque, and elsewhere. Maya elites lived out their lives in the context of the kings that ruled them, and in turn thousands of commoners lived out their lives with respect to the nobility.

We would know little about the lives of commoners except for a fortunate archaeological discovery. A humble Maya village at Cerén in San Salvador was buried under many feet of volcanic ash by an unexpected eruption in sixth century A.D. The people fled for their lives, leaving their possessions behind them. Payson Sheets and a team of Salvadoran archaeologists have located several houses by using ground-penetrating radar. Each Cerén household had a thatched dwelling for eating, sleeping, and other activities, as well as a storehouse, kitchen, and sometimes other structures. The villagers stored grain in clay vessels with tight lids, suspending corncobs and chilis from the roof. They kept many implements, including sharp-bladed stone knives, in the rafters, out of the way of children. The excavations have revealed three public buildings, and in the nearby fields, where the maize plants were doubled over, the ears still attached to the stalk—a "storage" technique still used in parts of Central America today. Judging from the mature maize, the eruption came at the end of the growing season, in August.

## The Ninth-Century Collapse

Maya civilization reached its peak after A.D. 600. Then, at the end of the eighth century, the great ceremonial centers of the Petén and the southern lowlands were abandoned, the long court calendar was discontinued, and the structure of religious life and the state decayed. Within a century, huge sections of the southern lowlands were abandoned, never to be reoccupied. At Tikal, perhaps the greatest

Maya center, the elite vanished and the population declined to a third of its earlier level. The non-elite survivors clustered in the remains of great masonry structures and tried to retain a semblance of their earlier life. Within a century, even they were gone. All this is not to say that Maya civilization vanished completely, for new centers may have emerged in neighboring areas, taking in some of the displaced population. Maya civilization continued to flourish in the northern Yucatán.

Everyone studying this ninth-century collapse agrees that a multiplicity of factors—some ecological, some political and social—led to catastrophe in the southern lowlands. The theories of the 1970s argued that the collapse of Teotihuacán gave the Maya a chance to enlarge their managerial functions in Mesoamerican trade. According to these theories, the elite became increasingly involved in warfare and competition between regions. The late Classic saw a frenzy of public building and increased pressure on the people, the source of both food and labor for prestige projects. Agricultural productivity fell, disease may have reached epidemic proportions, and population densities plummeted, so that recovery was impossible. There is some evidence of disease, stature decline, and malnutrition, but the evidence is incomplete.

More recently, endemic warfare has been invoked as a powerful factor in the collapse. At Dos Pilas in northern Guatemala, 105 kilometers (65 miles) from Tikal and founded by a renegade noble from Tikal in A.D. 645, Arthur Demarest uncovered evidence of civil war and prolonged conflict. Dos Pilas's later rulers embarked on campaigns of expansion, which had enlarged their territory to more than 3,884 square kilometers (1,500 square miles) by the mid-eighth century. Dos Pilas now controlled major jade and obsidian routes. Its lords lavished wealth on ornate palaces and a pyramid topped by three temples. Demarest and Juan Antonio Valdés dug deep under a small temple behind a stela that commemorated "Ruler 2," who reigned between A.D. 698 and 726, and uncovered the ruler's burial chamber. He wore a shell mosaic headdress adorned with monster faces, a heavy jade necklace, and jade bracelets. At his waist hung a stingray spine, once used for genital bloodletting. Hieroglyphs associated with the grave tell of the lord's carefully contrived diplomatic marriages with neighbors and of his delicate political alliances and his military campaigns.

Dos Pilas flourished until A.D. 761. By then, its rulers had overextended themselves, despite frantic efforts to maintain their domains. In that year, nearby Tamrindo attacked its former sovereign and killed "Ruler 4," despite desperate resistance by the Dos Pilas inhabitants. The invaders tore down the royal palace and robbed temple facades to build rough defensive walls with wooden palisades to surround the central precinct. Here, the people clustered in a small village of crude huts while the nobles fled and built a new center at Aguateca. The new center lay atop a steep cliff above a deep chasm, protected on three sides by natural features, as well as by massive defense walls. The Aguatecans held out for another half century, despite repeated attacks. In the early ninth century A.D., Demarest believes, intensive warfare drove these survivors of Dos Pilas into fortified towns and villages, where they erected defensive walls even around large tracts of agricultural land. Local conditions may have become so insecure that farmers were limited to defended acreage, so that crop yields may have been affected dramatically. In a last desperate stand, the remaining Aguatecans dug three moats, one 140 meters (460 feet) long, across a peninsula in Lake Petexbatun, creating an island fortress. The bedrock from the canals became defensive walls and a walled wharf for a canoe landing. The outpost did not last long, for the inhabitants abandoned it in the 800s.

The various collapse theories have been subjected to exhaustive analysis by researchers that involve both simulation studies and examinations of trading patterns and demographic and ecological stresses that could have affected population densities. Patrick Culbert has examined population densities and the potential for agricultural production in the southern lowlands. He has shown that population densities rose to as many as 200 persons per square kilometer (518 per square mile) during the late Classic over an area so large that it was impossible for people to adapt to bad times by moving to new land or emigrating. He believes that the magnitude of the population loss during the two centuries after A.D. 800 was such that social malfunction alone cannot account for it. Failure of the agricultural base must have been an important component in the collapse equation at the local level.

Maya agriculture became increasingly intense as populations rose, and both terrace and raised-field systems covered large areas in many parts of the lowlands. At some of the larger sites like Tikal, the people may have been transporting great quantities of foodstuffs from distances of between 50 and 100 kilometers (31 and 62 miles) away. In the short term, the intensification strategies worked, but they carried the seeds of collapse. The risks of climatic change, plant disease, erosion, and long-term declines in soil fertility are always present in such enterprises. To continue functioning efficiently, the newly intensified systems would have had to be managed constantly. Just the repair of field systems after floods and rains would have required watchful effort on a large scale. There are no signs that the Maya made any social changes that enabled them to achieve such a level of management, especially when so many people were engaged in public construction projects and apparently in military activity (perhaps the Maya were under pressure from the north).

Culbert believes that long-term environmental degradation was an important element in the scenario, where short-term gains in productivity were followed by catastrophic declines. For example, as populations rose, fallow cycles may have been shortened, so that there was increased competition between crop plants and weeds; this is a problem that can be solved only by constant weeding, a very labor-intensive activity. Shortened fallow cycles also lead to lower levels of plant nutrients and declining crop yields, and we do not know whether the Maya tried to counteract these trends by systematic mulching or by planting soil restoring crops. The problem of erosion may have been even more acute. There are signs that the people lost much soil to runoff in the lowlands, for they did not build the terraces needed in time to retain the soil. Some of this erosion may have resulted from extensive deforestation. At the same time, severe drought cycles played havoc with subsistence agriculture in an environment with only moderately fertile soils and already overly dense populations, phenomena now well documented in Mesoamerican lake sediments. Such droughts may, indeed, have been the trigger that brought about the collapse in the southern lowlands.

The sediments of Lake Chichancanab in the Yucatán show a recurring pattern of drought, occurring about every 208 years. These cycles coincide with the documented

206-year record in records of cosmogenic nuclide production (carbon-14 and beryllium-10) that are thought to reflect variations in solar activity. The period between 800 and 1000 was the driest of the middle to late Holocene, with two arid peaks, the first coinciding with the Classic Maya collapse. Such serious droughts were devastating to large-scale agricultural societies depending on surface water and dry agriculture.

Long-term field surveys of Copán and its hinterland have documented dramatic population changes during the collapse period. Between A.D. 550 and 700 the Copán city-state expanded rapidly, with most of the population concentrated in the core and the immediate periphery. There was only a small, scattered rural population. Between 700 and 850, the Copán Valley reached its greatest sociopolitical complexity, with a rapid population increase to between 18,000 and 20,000 people. These figures, calculated from site size, suggest that the local population was doubling every 80 to 100 years, with about 80 percent of the people living within the core and the immediate periphery. Rural settlement expanded outward along the valley floor, but it was still relatively scattered. But now people were farming foothill areas, as the population density of the urban core reached over 8,000 people per kilometer (0.3 square mile) and the periphery housing about 500 people per square kilometer (0.3 square mile). Eighty-two percent of the population lived in relatively humble dwellings, an indication of the extreme stratification of Copán society.

Copán's ruling dynasty ended in A.D. 810, just as serious urban depopulation began. The urban core and the periphery zones lost about half their population after 850, while the rural population increased by almost 20 percent. Small regional settlements replaced the scattered villages of earlier times, in response to cumulative deforestation, the overexploitation of even marginal agricultural soils, and uncontrolled soil erosion near the capital. By 1150, the Copán Valley population had fallen to between 5,000 and 8,000 people.

Culbert draws an interesting parallel with Mesopotamia, where at Ur an abundance of water from an expanded canal system led to overirrigation, shortened fallow cycles, and high levels of salt in the soil. There, long-term agricultural decline was in some ways a direct consequence of its earlier apparent success. The expanding Maya population was dependent on an agricultural system that made no allowance for long-term problems. Eventually, the system could produce no further riches, could not expand, and could only decline—with catastrophic results. But it would be a mistake to think of the Maya "collapse" as a universal phenomenon. Rather, the collapse of the ninth century was a marked episode in a long series of periodic flowerings and collapses characteristic of Maya civilization—indeed, of Mesoamerican civilization generally.

## Postclassic Maya Civilization (A.D. 900–1517)

Despite the collapse in the southern lowlands, Maya religious and social orders still endured in the more open country of the northern Yucatán. Just as Tikal and other famous cities collapsed, northern centers like Uxmal, Kabah, and Sayil in the Puuc region and Chichen Itzá in the northeast came into prominence during the Postclassic period.

The tenth and eleventh centuries saw unsettled political conditions throughout Mesoamerica caused by population movements and intergroup warfare. War and violence assumed great prominence in Mesoamerican ideology as militaristic rulers achieved power throughout the region. In the highlands, the Toltecs eventually stepped into the chaotic political vacuum left by the fall of Teotihuacán (see Chapter 16). In the lowlands, the Maya center at Chichen Itzá, in the northeastern Yucatán, may have come under some Toltec influence in the ninth century A.D. The extent of this influence is much debated, but a new elite encouraged artistic and political styles that separated functions of state from the personality of the individual ruler. The Chichen lords developed a flexibility and resilience that enabled them to be far more adaptive to changing political conditions than their southern predecessors. They fostered a truly regional state, peopled with talented artisans, and they traded salt from coastal pans over long distances.

Chichen Itzá itself has never been fully mapped, so its area and exact population remain a mystery (Figure 15.10). The city's central core is well known; its central plaza is dominated by the Castillo—the Temple of Kukulcán (Quetzalcoatl)—a square, stepped pyramid about 23 meters (75 feet) tall, crowned with a temple with stairways on all four sides. The Temple of the Warriors, west of the Castillo, is an

**Figure 15.10** The Castillo at Chichen Itzá.

inner temple with sculpted pillars masked by a later, more elaborate structure. The mosaics, carved facades, and sculpted serpents and warriors on the later temple show Toltec influence. A road extends 274 meters (300 yards) north from a dance platform to the celebrated Sacred Cenote, a natural sinkhole 55 meters (180 feet) deep with steep walls. Diving and scuba investigations have recovered human remains—probably those of victims sacrificed to the rain god—as well as gold, jade, and obsidian offerings. Chichen Itzá has the largest ball court in Mesoamerica, with walls 83 meters (272 feet) long (Box 15.5). During its heyday, this great city maintained contacts with the Putun Maya of the gulf coast lowlands; through them, with Oaxaca and the highlands; and through a port at Isla Cerritos, north of Chichen Itzá, with communities in what is now Honduras.

The Puuc Maya city of Uxmal, near modern Merida, east of Chichen Itzá, represents the peak of Maya city planning. Uxmal has imposing masonry buildings, finished with veneers of well-cut stone. The upper portions of buildings like the Nunnery Quadrangle and the Governor's Palace are decorated with snakes with barlike bodies, stone lattice work, and panels of mosaiclike masks and simple columns. At Uxmal, the Mayas succeeded in creating a truly monumental architecture, which conformed to humanly inspired, abstract rules of order and form.

But the Postclassic Maya civilization was marked by as much volatility as that of earlier years. First the Puuc centers declined, then Chichen Itzá in the thirteenth century. Political infighting and ecological problems may have been part of the cause. The city of Mayapan moved into the economic and political vacuum created by the demise of earlier kingdoms and became the dominant city in the northern Maya world. Mayapan was situated in the center of the northern Yucatán, a densely populated, walled city, with about 12,000 inhabitants, built near a series of natural wells. Its leaders headed a confederacy of smaller kingdoms, but the city's public buildings were much humbler than those of its illustrious predecessors. It was a trading center, dependent on an expanding waterborne trade in bulk goods like cacao, salt, and obsidian. Its confederacy fell apart in the mid-fifteenth century. Three-quarters of a century later, in 1517, some Spanish ships under the command of Francisco Hernandes de Cordoba arrived off the Mexican Yucatán. They coasted along the densely populated coast, landed several times, and collected some golden ornaments, taking with them some "idols of baked clay . . . some with demons' faces." Two years afterward, Hernán Cortés and his motley band of conquistadors landed on the gulf lowlands, changing the face of Mesoamerica forever. His objective was not the lowland Maya but the gold rich kingdom of the Mexica in the distant highlands, described in the next chapter.

## Summary

Mesoamerica, the area of central America where indigenous states developed, is marked by great environmental diversity between highlands and lowlands and within each of these zones. Village farming took hold throughout Mesoamerica in the third millennium B.C., with maize and bean agriculture becoming the foundation of later, complex states.

## Box 15.5 The Mesoamerican Ball Game

The ancient Mesoamerican ball game originated in Olmec times. When Spanish visitors saw the game played in the Yucatán in the sixteenth century A.D., the rules of play were at least 2,000 years old. Most major Maya centers had a ball court, built near the central precincts. One of the best preserved is the restored court at Copán (Figure 15.11), two parallel platforms with sloping sides on either side of a narrow playing alley. Two rectangular end zones turn the court into an I-shape. Some ball courts were equipped with stone rings on either side of the playing alley. Small stone buildings, perhaps ceremonial structures or dressing rooms, overlook the sides of the Copán arena. The ball game had profound religious and sacrificial overtones, serving as a form of ritual combat—dramas in which the players acted out the deeds of the Maya gods. One Maya legend has the Heavenly twins battling the Lords of the Underworld in an epic game; thus a ruler who sponsored or took part in a game was performing an important ritual act, which helped ensure the continuity of the universe.

The rules of the game are unknown, but Classic Maya contestants used a large, hard rubber ball, at least 0.3 meter (1 foot) in diameter, batting it about with their thighs, shoulders, or torso. Hands and feet could not be used. The players wore thick elbow and knee pads and a bulky waist protector of hide or wood. Vase paintings show that the opposing teams bounced the ball off the sloping sides of the court, keeping it from touching the floor of the alley. Where rings were used, the game was won when one team bounced a ball through the ring.

The Maya ball game was a contest of political and religious significance between deadly opponents. The losing team became sacrificial victims and were decapitated.

**Figure 15.11** The ball court at Copán.

The Preclassic period of Mesoamerican prehistory lasted from approximately 2000 B.C. to A.D. 250, a period of major cultural change in both lowlands and highlands. Sedentary villages traded with each other in raw materials and exotic objects. These exchange networks became increasingly complex and eventually came under the monopolistic control of larger villages. Increasing social complexity went hand in hand with the appearance of the first public buildings and the evidence of social stratification. These developments are well chronicled in the Olmec culture of the lowlands, which flourished from approximately 1500 to 500 B.C. Olmec art styles and religious beliefs were among those that spread widely over the Mesoamerican lowlands and highlands during the late Preclassic period.

Religious ideologies, ritual organization, and extensive trading networks were key factors in the development of Maya society in the lowlands after 1000 B.C. Classic Maya civilization flourished from A.D. 250 to 900 and consisted of an ever-changing patchwork of competing states. Maya glyphs show that Maya civilization was far from uniform. The Maya were unified more by religious beliefs than by political or economic interests. Until about A.D. 600, the largest states were in northeast Petén, with a multicenter polity headed by the "Sky" rulers of Tikal. Maya civilization reached its height in the southern lowlands after the seventh century, collapsing suddenly in the Yucatán after A.D. 900. The reasons for the collapse are still uncertain, but environmental degradation, pressure on the labor force, and food shortages were doubtless among them.

New Postclassic states developed in the northern Yucatán, based on Chichen Itzá and other centers. Postclassic Maya civilization flourished until the arrival of the Spanish in the early sixteenth century.

## Guide to Further Reading

Michael Coe, *Mexico*, 2nd ed. (London: Thames and Hudson, 1994) is a widely read, popular account of Mesoamerican civilization. For the beginnings of agriculture, see Bruce Smith, *The Emergence of Agriculture* ( New York: Scientific American Library, 1994). Kent Flannery, ed., *The Early Mesoamerican Village* (Orlando, FL: Academic Press, 1976) is a classic, remarkable for its irreverent essays on the archaeological scene of the day. See also Michael Coe and Richard Diehl, *In the Land of the Olmecs* (Austin: University of Texas Press, 1980) and Robert Sharer and David Grove, eds., *Regional Perspectives on the Olmec* (Cambridge: Cambridge University Press, 1989). Joyce Marcus, "Political Fluctuations in Mesoamerica," *National Geographic Research and Exploration* 8, no. 4 (1992): 392–411 offers a tentative scenario for the rise and fall of Maya city-states.

An enormous popular and specialist literature surrounds the ancient Maya. Michael Coe, *The Maya*, 6th ed. (New York: Thames and Hudson, 1999) gives a general account, and Coe's *Breaking the Maya Code* (New York: Thames and Hudson, 1992) and Robert J. Sharer, *The Ancient Maya*, 5th ed. (Stanford: Stanford University Press, 1994) give vivid descriptions of the triumph of decipherment. Jeremy A. Sabloff, *The Cities of Ancient Mexico* (New York: Thames and Hudson, 1989) and *The New Archaeology and the Ancient Maya* (New York: Scientific American Library, 1990) are strongly recommended general sources. Linda Schele and David Freidel, *Forest of Kings* (New York: William Morrow, 1990) and *Maya Cosmos* (New York: William Morrow, 1993) provide a complex, popular summary of the Maya world, controversial in parts but provocative. Peter Harrison, *The Lords of Tikal: Rulers of an Ancient Maya City* (New York: Thames and Hudson, 1999) summarizes what is known about this great city. William Fash, *Scribes, Warriors, and Kings* (New York: Thames and Hudson, 1991) describes excavations at Copán. For the Maya collapse, see T. Patrick Culbert, "The Collapse of Classic Maya Civilization," in Norman Yoffee and George Cowgill, eds., *The Collapse of Ancient States and Civilizations* (Tucson: University of Arizona Press, 1988), pp. 222–263. See also David Webster, *The Collapse of Maya Civilization* (New York: Thames and Hudson, 2001). For cycles of rise and collapse, see Joyce Marcus, "The Peaks and Valleys of Archaic States," in Joyce Marcus and Gary Feinman, eds., *Archaic States* (Santa Fe: School of American Research, 1998), pp. 59–94.

*Chapter 16*

# Highland Mesoamerica

A jade sculpture of the Aztec earth goddess Tlazolteotl giving birth.

*The mother and her 12-year-old daughter kneel side by side on small mats, their backstrap looms attached to wall posts. Comfortable straps also attach the looms to their waists. Cross beams of rolled-up, finished cloth lie across their bodies. Patiently, the mother shows her daughter how to keep the sheds apart, beating down the weft of the brightly colored cloth with a strong stick. Together, they pass fresh yarn over and under, creating an intricate pattern in the fine cotton fabric. The mother examines the girl's work with a critical eye, for she is in the final stages of an important apprenticeship. For generations, the family has woven fine garments for the nobility, passing on patterns, ties, and carefully nurtured technique from mother to daughter, each working alongside one another until the quality of the young woman's work matches, perhaps exceeds, that of her teacher. They know their work is important, for the decoration, even the fabric itself, denotes the exact rank and privilege of the noble wearer.*

Throughout the long history of Mesoamerican civilization, lowlands and highlands were linked inextricably to each other. (Frequent references to Chapter 15 will be made in this chapter.) Trade routes and common ideologies joined the societies of both environmental zones. The influence of great highland civilizations like that of Teotihuacán pervaded the lowlands for centuries, although only the vast but closely knit Aztec empire of the fifteenth century A.D. brought the two contrasting regions under common political leadership. Chapter 16 describes the highland Mesoamerican civilizations, which culminated in the complex, rapidly changing world of the Aztecs, disrupted catastrophically by the Spanish conquest of 1519 (see Table 15.1; Figure 16.1).

## The Rise of Highland Civilization (2000–500 B.C.)

Many of the foundations of highland Mesoamerican civilization were laid in two areas: the valleys of Mexico and Oaxaca. Thanks to the long-term study by a large University of Michigan research team, the complex processes that led to the growth of cities and complex societies are best known from Oaxaca.

The warm, semiarid Oaxaca Valley is the homeland of the modern-day Zapotec people. The valley has three arms and is shaped like an inverted Y. Because water could be found close to the surface, by 2000 B.C. maize and bean agriculture supported dozens of small villages and hamlets of 50 to 75 people. In time, some of these settlements grew to considerable size, with as many as 500 inhabitants, some of them nonfarming artisans and priests. The earliest farming villages were situated on the valley floors, where water supplies were more plentiful. Modern Oaxacan farmers use a simple form of "pot" irrigation in low-lying areas. That is,

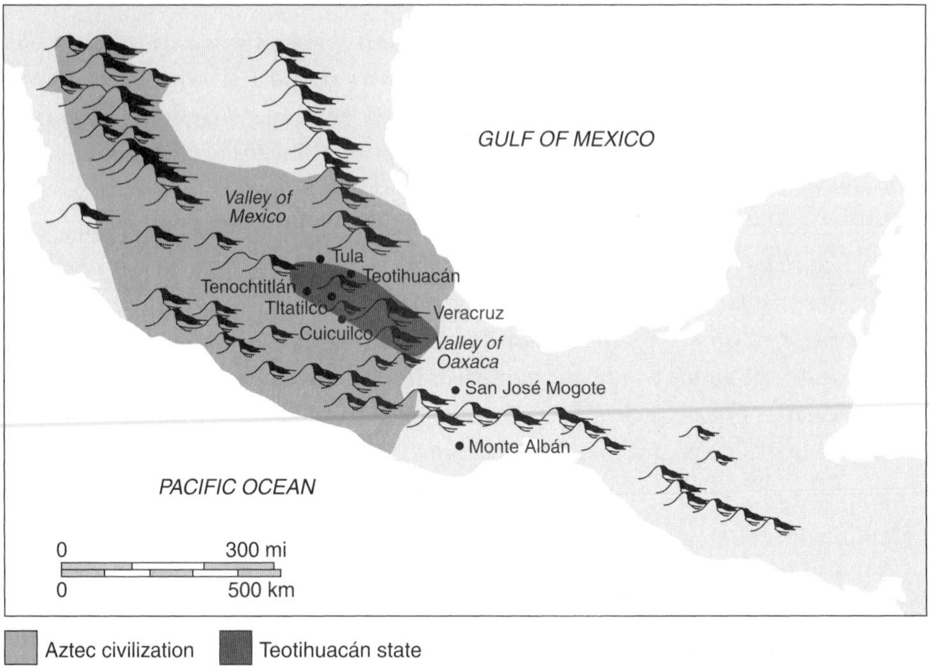


**Figure 16.1** Map showing archaeological sites and civilizations mentioned in Chapter 16.

they plant their crops close to shallow wells and water the growing plants by dipping pots into the exposed water table. Kent Flannery has argued persuasively that the early Oaxacans used the same technique, which does not require large numbers of people to irrigate the fields. As local population densities rose, the Oaxacans were able to build on their simple and effective farming techniques, expanding onto slopes and into more arid lands with great success. Eventually, argues Flannery, the economic power generated by these rising farming populations gave highland areas like this an edge over their neighbors.

The evolution of larger settlements in Oaxaca and elsewhere was closely connected with the development of long-distance trade. Simple barter networks of earlier times evolved into sophisticated regional trading organizations in which Oaxacan and other village leaders controlled monopolies of obsidian and its distribution. Soon magnetite mirrors (important in Olmec ritual), tropical feathers, and ceramics were traded widely between highlands and lowlands. The influence of the lowlands was felt most strongly in Oaxaca, where Olmec pottery and other ritual objects appeared between 1150 and 650 B.C. Many of them bear the distinctive were-jaguar motif of the lowlands, which had an important place in Olmec ideology (Chapter 15). By this time, many parts of highland and lowland Mesoamerica were joined by common religious beliefs, even if local deities and cults varied considerably. The exotic objects handled in long-distance trade were vital to the legitimacy and prestige of the new leaders.

By 1300 B.C., the largest settlement in the valley of Oaxaca, at the junction of three side valleys, was San José Mogote, a village of thatched houses with about 150 inhabitants sharing one lime-plastered public building. During the next century, San José Mogote grew rapidly into a community of 80 to 120 households (400 to 600 people) living in rectangular houses with clay floors, plastered and white-washed walls, and thatched roofs, over an area of about 20 hectares (50 acres). Public buildings, raised on adobe and earth platforms, began to appear in larger Oaxacan settlements. Fragments of conch shell trumpets and turtleshell drums were found in these structures. Clay figurines of masked, costumed dancers were found in San José Mogote's ceremonial buildings. There were marine fish spines, too, almost certainly used in personal bloodletting ceremonies performed before the gods (Chapter 15). The appearance of ritual artifacts of all kinds in communities like San José Mogote is no coincidence, for they arrived at a time when common art styles had come into use throughout Mesoamerica. Increasingly elaborate religious rituals brought the various elements of increasingly diverse societies together. At the same time, the new Oaxacan elites may have aspired to the status of their chiefly lowland neighbors and slavishly copied their rituals and beliefs. The iconography of the jaguar and of the feathered serpent linked people in highlands and lowlands alike.

The new style of leadership coincided with centuries of rapid population growth and increased economic activity. By 400 B.C., there were at least seven small chiefdoms in the valley of Oaxaca. One of these, Monte Albán, soon assumed dominance.

Parallel processes were taking place at this time in other parts of the highlands, including the Valley of Mexico. Tlatilco, in the valley of Mexico, was first settled by 1300 B.C.; it was a large village, covering over 65 hectares (165 acres) near a lake shore. The village has now been destroyed by industrial activity, but 340 burials have yielded lavish decoration, remarkable for the time. The dead were buried with clay figurines: figures of women who are carrying children or dogs; dancers with rattles around their legs; even males who are wearing hand and knee protection used in ball games, although no courts are known from this early date. Some Tlatilco art has strong Olmec overtones, again evidence for the pervasive influence of Olmec beliefs over much of Mesoamerica at the time.

The basic Mesoamerican pattern of civilization was developed over more than 1,000 years in the highlands. In the valley of Mexico, in Oaxaca, and elsewhere, a large center was ruled by an elite and served by a rural population living in lesser villages scattered throughout the surrounding countryside. By 50 B.C., at least some of the centers, like Monte Albán, had achieved considerable size and complexity. The new highland elites presided over hierarchies of priests and officials and commanded the labor of hundreds, if not thousands, of farmers to build and maintain temples, pyramids, and palaces. They controlled large food surpluses, which supported a growing population of nonfarmers, that is, merchants and artisans. Their political power rested on their ability to coerce others, on well-established notions of social inequality, and above all on a complex and often publicly reenacted social contract between rulers and their subjects. The people saw their leaders as intermediaries between the living and the ancestors, between their plane of existence and the spiritual world. An elaborate calendar and, later, writing regulated every aspect of ceremonial and daily life and helped generations of rulers in many kingdoms to legitimize their dynastic origins and their relationship to the gods. Highland civilization, with its carefully regulated agriculture, marketplaces, and lucrative trade monopolies, was to flourish for 2,000 years.

## Monte Albán (900 B.C.–A.D. 750)

Two major city-states dominated the Mesoamerican highlands in the early first millennium A.D., the time when Classic Maya civilization flourished in the lowlands: Monte Albán in the valley of Oaxaca and Teotihuacán in the valley of Mexico.

Monte Albán was founded around 900 B.C. on a hill overlooking three arms of the Oaxaca Valley 400 meters (1,300 feet) below (Figure 16.2). The new settlement grew rapidly, soon boasting more than 5,000 inhabitants. The chosen hill commands a spectacular view and a unique setting, but it did not make economic sense as a site for a major ceremonial center because it is far from the fertile agricultural lands in the valley below. Archaeologist Richard Blanton theorizes that Monte Albán may have been built on a neutral site between competing neighbors as a political capital for defense against common enemies. But there is no evidence that Oaxaca was ever attacked from the outside. More likely, San José Mogote's leaders simply chose an imposing site overlooking their domains as a symbol of their power and political domination. In any event, Monte Albán soon assumed great importance, becoming a major state by 150 B.C.

Between 350 and 200 B.C., more than 16,000 people lived in the city, the population rising to a peak of 30,000 during the late Classic period, between A.D. 500 and 700. Here, again, the Marcus model of rapid expansion, growth in the center,

**Figure 16.2** The central precincts of Monte Albán, valley of Oaxaca.

and decline (see Chapter 15) may hold true. The earliest period of occupation dates from about 900 to 300 B.C., when the elite developed a form of hieroglyphic writing, used a calendar, and were under some Olmec influence. By this time, they worshipped a pantheon of at least ten deities, including a rain god named Conijo. The celebrated Temple of the Danzantes (dancers), originally built during this period, contains stone slabs depicting more than 150 nude male figures in grotesque poses (sometimes with Olmec-like downturned mouths), probably the corpses of noble prisoners of war sacrificed to the gods. Sometimes scroll motifs flow from their groins, as if depicting bloodletting from their penises. The Danzante figures, with their implications of ritual bloodletting, link the rulers of Monte Albán with the underlying shamanistic beliefs that nurtured all Mesoamerican civilization (Chapter 15). Carved glyphs from several buildings seem to imply that this ancient capital was once called Hill of the Jaguar, another strong association with ancient concepts of leadership.

Between 300 and 100 B.C., Zapotec rulers constructed the main plaza on top of the now artificially flattened hilltop. Monte Albán became an elaborate complex of palaces, temples, and plazas, some of which served as ritual settings, others as markets. Its rulers built roads, defensive walls, and water control systems that stored rainfall for domestic use and channeled it to fields on the slopes below. The city straddled three hills, with at least 15 residential subdivisions, each with its own plazas. Most inhabitants lived in small houses erected on stone-faced terraces built against the steep terrain. Each dwelling had a central courtyard, where the family tomb was located. Years of archaeological excavation and survey have mapped more than 2,000 houses and an enormous ceremonial precinct centered around a paved main plaza. This ritual ward evolved over more than 1,000 years of continuous rebuilding and modification, which had the effect of progressively isolating the plaza and those who lived around it from the rest of the city.

The late Classic plaza of A.D. 500 to 720 was 300 meters long and 150 meters across (975 by 480 feet), bounded on its north and south sides by 12-meter-high (37-foot-high) platform mounds with staircases leading to buildings on top (see Figure 16.2). A ceremonial ball court and other platform mounds delineated the eastern and western boundaries, with a central line of buildings between the northern and southern mounds. One of these structures, stone-faced Building J shaped like a great arrowhead facing southwest, is honeycombed with dark chambers. More than 40 slabs in the lower walls of the building depict sacrificed corpses. The undeciphered glyphs with them may record battles, days, and places, perhaps a record of conquered kingdoms. Conceivably, too, Building J was used as an observatory. Astroarchaeologist Anthony Aveni believes he has identified a zenith sighting line for the bright star Capella, which appears during the solar zenith passage. The rulers and their families lived in a complex of buildings on the north platform, which also served as the formal setting for meetings with high officials and with emissaries from other states.

Monte Albán reached the height of its power after 200 B.C., when it rivaled another expanding state, Teotihuacán, to the north. The two great cities coexisted peacefully and traded with each other for centuries. Archaeologists have identified a Oaxacan merchants' quarter in the heart of its rival. Monte Albán's domains did not expand dramatically, but it held its own against its more powerful neighbor until about A.D. 750. Then the main plaza was abandoned, and its buildings fell into disrepair. For unknown reasons, the city's population declined rapidly, although parts of Monte Albán were still occupied until the Spanish conquest. The once great city never regained its importance and became just one of several competing Postclassic towns in the valley of Oaxaca.

## Teotihuacán (200 B.C.–A.D. 750)

As early as 600 B.C., a series of chiefdoms ruled over the valley of Mexico. Five centuries later, two of them, Cuicuilco in the west and Teotihuacán to the east, were vying for leadership. At that time, nature intervened with a major volcanic eruption, which buried and destroyed Cuicuilco completely, leaving Teotihuacán the master of the valley and adjacent parts of the central highlands.

Teotihuacán grew rapidly during the ensuing centuries as thousands of people moved from outlying communities into the metropolis. Whether they moved voluntarily or as a result of conquest and compulsory resettlement is unknown. At least 80,000 people lived in the city by A.D. 100. Like Monte Albán, Teotihuacán may have grown from constant military conquest, another example of the Marcus model of initial rapid expansion. Between A.D. 200 and 750, Teotihuacán's population grew to more than 150,000 people, making it similar in size to all but the very largest cities of the contemporary Near East and China.

### *The City*

We know more about Teotihuacán than almost any other ancient city because of systematic excavation, mapping, and restoration projects conducted by both American and Mexican archaeologists. Archaeologist René Millon's map of the city reveals an enormous community, which grew over many generations, not haphazardly, but according to a long-term master plan. The architects thought of Teotihuacán not as a city but as a vast symbolic landscape of artificial mountains, foothills, caves, and open spaces that replicated the spiritual world. Over more than eight centuries, the Teotihuacános built 600 pyramids, 500 workshop areas, a great marketplace, 2,000 apartment complexes, and precinct plazas. These were all constructed on a grid plan and anchored by the 5-kilometer (3-mile) Street of the Dead (a post-Conquest name), which bisects the city on a north-south axis (oriented exactly 15.5 degrees east of north, an orientation established by astronomical observation) (Figure 16.3). Even today, deserted, partially restored, and devoid of its inhabitants, Teotihuacán overwhelms one with its sheer size and with the monumental scale of its pyramids and plazas, which dwarf mere people into insignificant dots—as, indeed, their builders intended them to.

Between A.D. 1 and 100, the colossal Pyramid of the Sun rose on the east side of the Street of the Dead. Sixty-one meters (200 feet) high, with 215-meter-long (700-foot) sides, its five stages and immense staircase dwarf the nearby plaza and

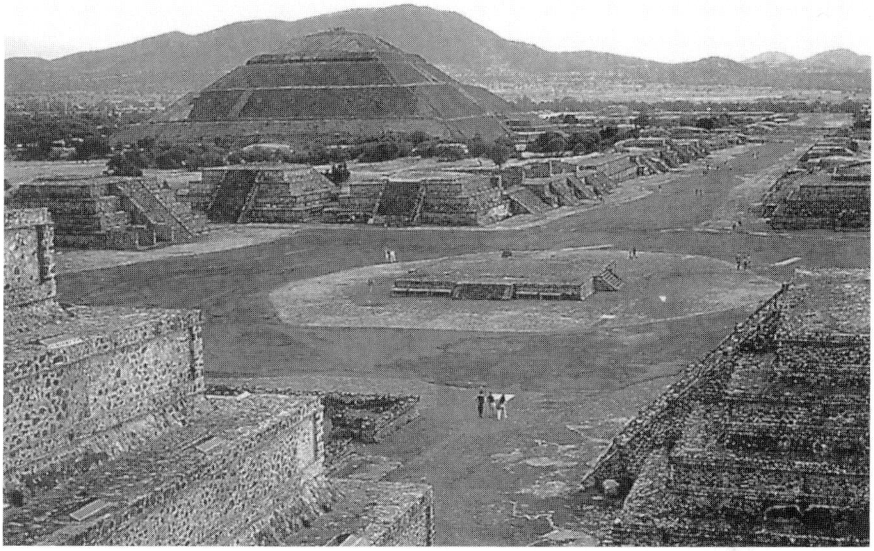

**Figure 16.3** Teotihuacán, showing the Pyramid of the Sun (*back left*) and the Street of the Dead, with the Pyramid of the Moon in the foreground.

buildings. More than 1,175,000 square meters (12,648,008 square feet) of rubble and sun-dried brick form the core of this stupendous construction, which was erected on the remains of an earlier pyramid. A wood and thatched temple stood on the summit. While digging trenches for the installation of a sound-and-light show in 1971, archaeologists chanced on a natural lava cave in the underlying bedrock. Enlarged in ancient times, it runs 100 meters (330 feet) eastward and 6 meters (20 feet) below the pyramid from the position of the main stairway, ending in a cloverlike set of four chambers. This cave was used for worship before the Pyramid of the Sun was built and remained a cult center for some time after construction. The excavation of the cavern has never been published, but elsewhere in Mesoamerica such dark chambers were thought of as symbolic wombs from which the sun and moon gods, as well as human ancestors, emerged in ancient times. The smaller Pyramid of the Moon, built perhaps half a century later, overlooks a building-surrounded plaza at the northern end of the Street of the Dead. In recent years, human sacrifices have been unearthed from the foundations of the pyramid.

The broad avenue extends southward for just over 3 kilometers (2 miles), where it intersects with an east-west avenue, thereby dividing the city into four quadrants. The huge square enclosure, known as the Ciudadela, with sides over 400 meters (1,300 feet) long, is situated at the intersection. Here lies the Temple of Quetzalcoatl (the Feathered Serpent), a six-level pyramid adorned with tiers of inset rectangular panels placed over a sloping wall. Figures of the Feathered Serpent alternate with what may be a Fire Serpent, the bearer of the sun on its daily journey across the heavens (Figure 16.4). The facade is thought to depict the moment of

**Figure 16.4** Temple of Quetzalcoatl, Teotihuacán.

creation, when opposed serpents—one representing lush greenness and peace; the other desert, fire, and war—cavort in the primordial ocean, painted blue in the background. Two apartment complexes, perhaps royal precincts, lie in the north and south halves of the Ciudadela. The Temple of Quetzalcoatl was built to the accompaniment of at least two hundred human sacrifices, young warriors with their hands tied behind their backs in groups of 18, the number of 20-month days in the year. The victims lay in burial pits on all four sides and at the base of the pyramid. Single victims lay at the four corners.

The Teotihuacán map suggests that the planned city was grouped into wards based on both kin ties and more commercial considerations. At some point, the city's rulers embarked on a systematic campaign of urban renewal, constructing standardized housing for what must have become a teeming and perhaps uncontrollable urban population. Most people lived in standardized, walled residential compounds up to 60 meters (200 feet) on each side, connected by narrow alleyways and compounds. Some of these barrios (neighborhoods) were home to craftspeople like obsidian workers and potters. There were also military quarters. Foreigners from Monte Albán and the Oaxaca Valley, as well as lowland Veracruz, lived in their own neighborhoods. More important priests and artisans lived in dwellings around small courtyards (Box 16.1).

Prominent nobles occupied elaborate palaces with central, sunken courts. Their palaces were flat-roofed, with numerous rooms and forecourts, the walls adorned with religious murals of standardized designs. The most famous murals come from the Tepantitla palace, where a deity—perhaps the Spider Woman, the goddess who created the Teotihuacáno universe—dominates a landscape that

## Box 16.1 Life In Teotihuacán's Barrios

Teeming neighborhoods of single-story, flat-roofed, rectangular apartment compounds complete with courtyards and passageways lay beyond Teotihuacán's ceremonial precincts. Narrow alleyways and streets about 3.6 meters (12 feet) wide separated each compound from its neighbors. Each housed between 20 and 100 people, perhaps members of the same kin group. Judging from artifact patternings, some sheltered skilled artisans, families of obsidian and shell ornament makers, weavers, and potters.

What was life like inside Teotihuacán's anonymous apartment compounds (barrios)? Mexican archaeologist Linda Manzanilla has investigated one such complex close to the northwest edge of Teotihuacán, searching for traces of different activities within the complex. The stucco floors in the apartments and courtyards had been swept clean, so Manzanilla and her colleagues used chemical analyses of the floor deposits to search for human activities. She developed a mosaic of different chemical readings, such as high phosphate readings where garbage had rotted, and dense concentrations of carbonate from lime (used in the preparation of both tortillas and stucco) that indicated cooking or building activity. Manzanilla's chemical plans of the compound are accurate enough to pinpoint the locations of cooking fires and eating places where the inhabitants consumed such animals as deer, rabbits, and turkeys. She was able to identify three nuclear families of about 30 people who lived in three separate apartments within this community inside a much larger community. Each apartment had specific areas for sleeping, eating, religious activities, and funeral rites.

Teotihuacán's barrios have revealed intense interactions between people who knew one another well and between these tight-knit communities and the wider universe of the city itself. Walking along one of the cleared streets, you can imagine passing down the same defile 1,500 years earlier, each side bounded by a bare, stuccoed compound wall. Occasionally, a door opens onto the street, offering a view of a shady courtyard, of pots and textiles drying in the sun. The street would have been a cacophony of smells and sounds—wood smoke, dogs barking, the monotonous scratch of maize grinders, the soft voices of women weaving, the passing scent of incense.

Teotihuacán was a vast urban community made up of hundreds of smaller communities, with a market that sold commodities and exotic luxuries from all over the Mesoamerican highlands and lowlands. The Teotihuacános valued their foreign trade so highly that they allowed foreigners to settle among them in special barrios occupied over many centuries. Immigrants from the Veracruz region of the lowlands lived in a neighborhood on the city's eastern side, identified from the remains of distinctive circular adobe houses with thatched roofs identical to those of the inhabitants' Gulf Coast homeland. These people, easily identified by their orange-, brown-, and cream-painted pots, probably traded in exotic tropical luxuries such as brightly colored bird feathers. Another neighborhood on the western side housed Zapotec traders from the valley of Oaxaca, 400 kilometers (250 miles) south of Teotihuacán. Potsherds from their segregated compounds allow us to identify their presence in the crowded city.

depicts a mountain with springs at the base. People dance and sing nearby, while butterflies play among flowering trees. But only a minority of Teotihuacános enjoyed any wealth. Life for the lower classes of society was one of brutal hard work and ruthless exploitation with a short life expectancy. The city needed a constant influx of newcomers to sustain the economy.

Teotihuacán was a unique city, covering at least 21 square kilometers (8 square miles). It teemed with traders and artisans from all corners of the Mesoamerican world and was a major place of pilgrimage, a sacred city of the greatest symbolic importance. Its prosperity came from trade, especially in the green obsidian found nearby; this was exchanged for all sorts of tropical products, including bird feathers, shells, and fish spines from the lowlands. Food supplies came from the intensive cultivation of valley soils and from acres of swamp gardens built up in the shallow waters of the nearby lakes. This was a brightly colored city, a landscape painted in every hue; the houses were adorned with polished whitewash, which still sticks to wall fragments. But above all, the great city spoke a powerful symbolic language, which has come down to us in architecture, art, and ceramics. Its leaders perpetuated an origin myth that established the city as the place where the cosmos and the present cycle of time began. Every ritual within Teotihuacán's precincts fostered the belief that its people were honored and were responsible for maintaining the cosmos. A cult of war and sacrifice, governed by an eight-year cycle, ensured the well-being of the cosmos, the city, and its inhabitants. Teotihuacán's armies were formidable in battle, their victories the source of the prisoners sacrificed to the gods.

At the very core of Teotihuacán's being was the Sacred Cave under the Pyramid of the Sun, an entryway to the underworld. The cave was the focus of the powerful creation myth perpetuated by the city's leaders. A sight line from the mouth of the cavern to the western horizon may have associated such astronomical phenomena as the setting sun to specific dates in the local calendar. Teotihuacán's first, and very able, leaders embarked on a massive program of public works, using a master plan that made the entire city a symbolic landscape that commemorated the creation and the principal gods. The Street of the Dead was perpendicular to the Sacred Cave. A small pyramid was dedicated to what scholars call "the Great Goddess," associated with the sun, on the site of the present Pyramid of the Moon, framed with a sacred mountain on the horizon. They then constructed a Pyramid of the Sun on the site of the Sacred Cave, dedicated to the Great Goddess and to a deity of fire, rain, and wind. The city's third main god was the Feathered Serpent, Quetzalcoatl.

## *The Center of the World*

Between A.D. 150 and 225, the city's leaders remodeled the Pyramid of the Sun in its present form; enlarged the Pyramid of the Moon; and extended the Street of the Dead more than 3.2 kilometers (2 miles) southward to two great enclosures, forming the city's new political and religious center—the Ciudadela. An even larger Great Compound became Teotihuacán's major marketplace and bureaucratic center. An east-west avenue intersected the Street of the Dead at this location, dividing Teotihuacán into four quadrants. No one knows why the center of religious and political power suddenly shifted southward. René Millon suspects that an ambitious ruler "with a passion for immortality" wished to commemorate his power with a new architectural complex for a new ritual setting.

Millon believes the changeover took place during a period of successful conquests and great prosperity. The architects took Teotihuacán's centuries-old symbolism of the Sacred Cave as a passageway and built it into the Temple of the Feathered Serpent at the Ciudadela. Here, Millon explains, the sculpted serpent heads of the god emerge from a "great facade of feathered mirrors," representing caves as passageways in Mesoamerican iconography. A powerful cult of sacred war and human sacrifice, sometimes called "Star Wars," became associated with the Feathered Serpent, the Storm God, and the cyclical movements of the planet Venus. The Feathered Serpent's great temple was the place where the cult was commemorated with human sacrifices, which served to maintain the cosmos and human well-being. The sacrificial victims dispatched at the dedication of the temple were a powerful reminder of the importance of war and human sacrifice in highland civilization. The beliefs associated with this Star Wars cult spread widely in Mesoamerica and had a profound effect on Maya civilization (see Chapter 15). The Ciudadela lay at the very center of Teotihuacán, at the crossroads of the city, and was the symbolic center of the cosmos, the axis around which the universe revolved.

The unknown ruler who dedicated the Temple of the Feathered Serpent may have been the last great leader of the city. He enjoyed staggering, absolute powers, so much so that the burden of supporting him may have been too onerous. Over the next 400 years, the leadership of Teotihuacán became collective and more bureaucratic, rationalized by ideological shifts that placed much greater emphasis on ritual. The successful performance of ritual kept the cosmos in motion, ensured fertility, and ensured the continuity of human life. Rituals were performed in the privacy of individual households within apartment compounds (whose walls reflected the sacred orientation of the city) and in public, where human sacrifices commemorated the war-and-sacrifice cult and where great lords (no longer absolute rulers) performed bloodletting ceremonies in their roles as shaman-rulers, intermediaries with the deities and the ancestors.

To be a Teotihuacáno was to be honored, for one dwelt at the very center of the world. But this honor carried important obligations to the city, to the lords, and to the gods. Every citizen served the state through artisanship, by laboring on public works, and by serving in Teotihuacán's armies. These obligations were fulfilled through the ties of kinship, which underlay every household, every apartment compound, and every royal palace, linking everyone in the city in the common enterprise of maintaining the cosmos. On occasion, the government attempted the planned resettlement of city dwellers on adjacent, underutilized lands (especially irrigable lands near the lakes), where agricultural production could be maximized. But most people lived in the city, the heart of a large, loosely knit state about the size of the island of Sicily in the Mediterranean, some 26,000 square kilometers (10,000 square miles). Teotihuacán's rulers controlled the destinies of about half a million people, but the city's main impact on lowland and highland Mesoamerica was economic, ideological, and cultural rather than political. Its power came from conquest and trade and, above all, from a carefully nurtured ideology that made the great city the place of creation, the very cradle of civilization. So successful was this religious propaganda that a ruined Teotihuacán was still deeply revered by the Aztecs and other highland peoples at the time of the Spanish conquest.

### *Collapse*

After about A.D. 650, Teotihuacán's ideology became increasingly militaristic, at a time when the state may have become more oppressive, perhaps with a return to more individual rule. The city's enormous population, combined with uneven exploitation of the valley of Mexico's resources, may have created serious economic problems that threatened to undermine the state. From all appearances, a rigid and inflexible hierarchy ruled the city, incapable of responding to serious dissent and pressures from its citizens. The end, when it came, was cataclysmic. The Ciudadela was attacked around A.D. 750, and its temples and palaces were burned and razed. The destruction was part of a systematic desanctification of Teotihuacán, both politically and ritually, to prevent new rulers from rising from the ashes. Every temple and every shrine was reduced to rubble. No one knows who the agents of total destruction were, but Teotihuacán and its state vanished from history, only to be remembered in legend as the place where the Toltec and Aztec world of later times began. Seven centuries later, the city was still a revered place of pilgrimage.

## The Toltecs (A.D. 650–1200)

Teotihuacán had acted as a magnet to the rural populations of the highlands for many centuries. When the great city collapsed, its inhabitants moved outward as other central Mexican cities expanded into the political vacuum left by its conquerors. None of them achieved the stature and ritual authority of Teotihuacán, and political authority passed rapidly from one growing city to the next. Eventually, one group achieved a semblance of dominance: the Toltecs.

"The Tolteca were wise. Their works were all good, all perfect, all marvelous . . . in truth they invented all the wonderful, precious, and marvelous things which they made," an Aztec informant once told the famous Spanish chronicler of ancient Mexican civilization, Fray Bernardino de Sahagun (Dibble and Anderson, 1969, pp. 165–166). The Aztecs considered the Toltecs great warrior heroes, magnificent conquerors who swept all before them. To be of Toltec ancestry was to have high social status in Aztec society. Righteous and wise, expert astronomers and artists, the Toltecs were painted as the very founders of militaristic civilization.

Early Toltec history is confusing at best, but like other highland peoples the Toltecs comprised various tribal groups, among them the Nahuatl-speaking Tolteca-Chichimeca, apparently semicivilized people from the fringes of Mesoamerica. (Nahuatl was the common language of the Aztec empire at the time of the Spanish conquest.) Their first leader was the legendary Mixcoatl (Cloud Serpent), who brought his people into the valley of Mexico to settle at Colhuacán. He was succeeded by his son Topiltzin Quetzalcoatl, born in the year 1 Reed (A.D. 935 or 947; Mesoamerican days had a number and name). It was he who moved the Toltec capital to Tollan, "the Place of Reeds," in its heyday a city of some 30,000 to 60,000 people, far smaller than Teotihuacán. (Tollan has been identified with the archaeological site of Tula.) Bitter strife broke out between the followers of the peace-loving Topiltzin Quetzalcoatl and those of his warlike rival, Tezcatlipoca (Smoking Mirror), the god of warriors and of life itself. The Tezcatlipoca faction prevailed by trickery and humiliation. Topiltzin and his followers fled from Tula and eventually arrived on the shores of the Gulf of Mexico. There, according to one account, the ruler set himself on fire while dressed in his ceremonial regalia. As his ashes rose to heaven, he turned into the Morning Star. The Spanish conquistadors learned another version of the legend in which Topiltzin Quetzalcoatl "fashioned a raft of serpents. . . . There he placed himself, as if it were his boat. Then he set off across the sea" (Dibble and Anderson, 1969, pp. 165–166). It was said he vowed to return in the year 1 Reed (see page 466).

Does this legend have a core of historical truth? Maya oral traditions from the northern Yucatán speak of the arrival of a highland conqueror named Kukulcán (Feathered Serpent) in the year A.D. 987, whose rule may be reflected in the signs of Toltec influence at Chichen Itzá, which are, however, much debated (see Chapter 15).

In the years following Topiltzin Quetzalcoatl's departure, the Toltec state reached its greatest extent, controlling much of central Mexico from coast to coast. If Aztec legends are to be believed, this was a period of great prosperity, when the Toltecs acquired great wealth and a reputation for brilliant craftmanship. But a serious drought cycle in the late twelfth century caused bitter factional disputes. The last Toltec ruler, Huemac, abandoned Tula and moved the capital to Chapultepec, now a park in Mexico City. There he committed suicide as his kingdom fell apart, his people migrating to all parts of Mesoamerica, even as far afield as the Maya highlands of Guatemala. All these groups and their leaders claimed descent from the ruling families of the once-great capital Tula, which lay in ruins.

## *Tula*

Tula itself is on a natural promontory, surrounded by steep slopes on three sides. Human settlement on the site dates back to the Preclassic period. A sizable village flourished here when Teotihuacán was all-powerful. By A.D. 900, Tula was a prosperous town of Tolteca-Chichimeca artisans, which soon grew into a city of 40,000 people covering 16 square kilometers (5.4 square miles). By A.D. 1000, the Toltec lords had laid out their capital on a grid pattern, with a wide central plaza and ceremonial center bordered by imposing pyramids and at least two ball courts. Only Pyramid B has been excavated, in its final form a pyramid with five tiers, each 10 meters (33 feet) high (Figure 16.5). A colonnaded hall, adorned with bas-reliefs of marching warriors, stands in front of the pyramid. A staircase leads to the temple entrance on the summit, flanked by stone columns modeled in the form of feathered serpents, with their heads on the ground. Four colossal warriors, carrying spearthrowers and incense bags, support the roof of the first room. Behind lies the sanctuary, its altar carried by small human figures. Four carved columns adorned with Toltec warriors hold up the roof. Pyramid B is remarkable for its reclining "chacmool" figures, perhaps incarnations of the rain god, ready to receive human hearts in the bowls carved into their stomachs.

**Figure 16.5** Colossal warriors atop Pyramid B at Tula, the Toltec capital.

The sides of the pyramid bear bas-reliefs that symbolize the powerful warrior orders of the state interspersed with composite beasts, perhaps a mythic Quetzalcoatl. A grim "Serpent Wall," 40 meters (131 feet) long, runs along the north side of the pyramid, with friezes of serpents consuming skeletal humans. Everything points to a militaristic society, obsessed with human sacrifice. One altar near a ball court was still covered with fragmentary human skulls when excavated in modern times.

We know little of the city itself, of its palaces and domestic architecture. Tula appears to have been organized into formal wards of households, each about 600 meters (1,970 feet) square. Inside lay flat-roofed, square or rectangular houses clustered in groups of as many as five dwellings, which shared a common shrine. Many of these households were engaged in obsidian mining and tool manufacture, much of it for export. But archaeology does not corroborate the persistent legends of Toltec artistry, despite abundant evidence for trade and tribute in fine ceramics and, presumably, perishable materials like tropical feathers and jaguar skins.

Tula's temples, pyramids, and ball courts were razed around 1200, when the Toltec empire fell apart. The capital may have been attacked by Chichimeca, people from outside the civilized valley of Mexico who were pressing southward onto prosperous, cultivated lands.

## The Rise of Aztec Civilization (A.D. 1200–1519)

During the next century, a political vacuum existed in the valley of Mexico, where a series of moderate-sized city-states prospered and competed. Powerful lords of Toltec ancestry became the leaders of these kingdoms, establishing the precedent that only those of Toltec descent could assume the throne. An emerging nobility shared this common ancestry. Upstart rulers of other states, with humbler beginnings among barbarian Chichimeca, strove to emulate their more established neighbors. Into this competitive world stepped a small and obscure group, the Azteca, or Mexica. Within a mere two centuries, these insignificant players on the highland stage presided over the mightiest pre-Columbian empire in the Americas.

The Aztecs' history, as they tell it, reads like a rags-to-riches novel. They claimed they came from Aztlan, an island on a lake west or northwest of Mexico, migrating into the valley under the guidance of their tribal god Huitzilopochtli (Hummingbird on the Left), who was soon reborn as the sun god himself. This was the official version perpetuated by official Aztec historians and recorded by the Spaniards. Such migration legends were common in ancient Mesoamerica and should not be taken at face value. The Aztecs had certainly settled in the valley by the thirteenth century, but they were unwelcome arrivals in the densely populated area. Eventually they settled on some swampy islands in the marshes of the largest lake in the valley, where they founded twin capitals, Tenochtitlán and Tlatelolco, sometime after 1325. Fierce and ruthless warriors, the Aztecs became mercenaries for Lord Tezozomoc of the expanding Tepanec kingdom in 1367. The Aztecs shared in the spoils of his expanding domains, soon adopting the institutions and empire-building strategies of their employer.

After Tezozomoc's death in 1426, the Aztec ruler Itzcoatl and his exceptionally able adviser, Tlacaelel, attacked the Tepanecs and crushed them in one of the great battles of Aztec history. The Aztecs became the masters of the valley of Mexico and set out to rewrite society and history itself. The great Tlacaelel ordered all the historical codices of the Aztecs' rivals to be burnt, creating a mythic, visionary history of the Mexica in their place. The Aztecs were thus the chosen of the sun god, Huitzilopochtli, and the true heirs of the Toltecs, great warriors destined to take prisoners in battle to nourish the sun in its daily journey across the heavens. A series of brilliant and ruthless leaders embarked on aggressive campaigns of conquest, determined to fulfil Aztec destiny. The greatest Aztec ruler was Ahuitzotl (1486–1502), the sixth *tlatoani*, or "speaker." His armies marched far beyond the valley, to the borders of Guatemala. Just as in Teotihuacán and Tikal, his initial conquests rapidly delineated the broad outlines of his domain. The Aztec empire covered both highlands and lowlands and affected the lives of over 5 million people. Brilliant strategist and able administrator, Ahuitzotl was a single-minded militarist, who believed fervently in his divine mission to nourish the sun god. Twenty thousand prisoners are said to have perished in 1487 when he inaugurated the rebuilt Great Temple of Huitzilopochtli and the rain god, Tlaloc, in the central precincts of Tenochtitlán.

## *Tenochtitlán* (A.D. *1487–1519*)

"And when we saw all those towns and villages built in the water, and other great towns on dry land, and that straight and level causeway leading to Mexico, we were astounded. These great towns . . . and buildings rising from the water, all made of stone, seemed like an enchanted vision. . . . Indeed some of our soldiers asked whether it was not all a dream" (Diaz, 1963, p. 214). Thus did conquistador Bernal Diaz, one of Hernán Cortés's followers, describe his first sight of the Aztec capital, Tenochtitlán, in 1519. Diaz wrote his vivid account of the Spanish conquest of Mexico 50 years later, when he was in his 70s. But his descriptions of Tenochtitlán read as if he had walked through the plaza the day before. It is this immediacy that makes Aztec civilization unique among early preindustrial states, for we have eyewitness accounts of it in its heyday.

Cortés and his companions marveled at a city larger than Seville and certainly better planned than many European capitals of the day. Tenochtitlán was a sophisticated and cosmopolitan city with a social, political, and economic organization flexible enough to integrate large numbers of outsiders—merchants, pilgrims, foreigners, and thousands of laborers—into its already large permanent population. The Aztec capital reflected a society that depended on military strength and on its ability to organize large numbers of people to achieve its ends. Thousands of acres of carefully planned swamp gardens (*chinampas*), intersected with canals, provided food for the large urban population.

The city originally consisted of two autonomous communities, Tenochtitlán and Tlatelolco, each with its own ceremonial precincts. By 1519, Tenochtitlán was the center of religious and secular power, while the main market was at Tlatelolco. The capital was divided into four quarters, which intersected at the foot of the stairway up the Great Temple of Huitzilopochtli and Tlaloc in the central, walled plaza. The rectangular plaza was about 460 meters (500 yards) square, large enough to accommodate nearly 10,000 people during major public ceremonies ( Figure 16.6).

Because of recent excavations by Eduardo Matos Moctezuma, we know that the temple (Templo Major) stood on the north side of the plaza, a stepped pyramid with two stairways and two shrines, dedicated to Huitzilopochtli and Tlaloc,

**Figure 16.6** Reconstruction of the central precincts of Tenochtitlán, with the Temple of Huitzilopochtli and Tlaloc at left.

respectively. Huitzilopochtli's red chapel was situated to the right; Tlaloc's blue shrine, to the left. Moctezuma unearthed no fewer than six earlier phases of the temple, the second dating to about 1390 and virtually complete (Figure 16.7). Successive generations of rulers had encased earlier structures with larger pyramids, each with its own shrines, sculptures, and offerings. Moctezuma excavated more than 6,000 artifacts from 86 separate offering caches, most of them tribute or booty from wars of conquest in distant parts of the empire. Magnificent jade, obsidian, and terracotta artifacts were offered to the gods, as were ancient stone masks from Teotihuacán, perhaps dug from the site by the Aztecs themselves. The excavators found one stone-lined pit containing the dismembered bodies of 38 children sacrificed to Tlaloc.

Moctezuma points out that the great pyramid depicts the four celestial levels of the Aztec cosmos, the original ground surface being the earthly plane of existence. It was from this point that the four cardinal directions of the Aztec world radiated, each associated with colors that were different personifications of gods and goddesses. From here a vertical channel led to the heavens above and the underworld below. Tenochtitlán was the symbolic center of the universe, a city set in a circle of water—Aztlan itself, the mythic island surrounded by water. The greatest festivals of the Aztec world unfolded at the great pyramid, ceremonies marked by rows of brightly dressed prisoners climbing the steep stairway to their death. The

**Figure 16.7** The Templo Major excavations, Mexico City.

victim was stretched out over the sacrificial stone. In seconds, a priest with an obsidian knife broke open his chest and ripped out his still beating heart, dashing it against the sacrificial stone. The corpse rolled down the steep pyramid into the hands of butchers at the foot, who dismembered the body and set the skull on the great skull rack nearby (Box 16.2).

The Spanish conquistadors were horrified by the shrines of Huitzilopochtli and Tlaloc, which reeked from the blood of fresh sacrifices. They claimed the Aztecs were cannibals, who killed their victims and then consumed their flesh. Nineteenth-century historians like William Prescott went further and regaled their readers with stories of "banquets teeming with delicious beverages and delicate viands" (Prescott, 1843, p. 345). Some modern scholars have claimed that human flesh was consumed regularly to make up for chronic protein deficiencies in the Aztec diet. However, most experts believe that the Mexica consumed only small amounts on ritual occasions, perhaps as an act of spiritual renewal.

## *The World of the Fifth Sun*

The Aztecs were militaristic, but every deed, every moment of living, was filled with symbolic meaning and governed by ritual. They inherited the cyclical view of time, established by the movements of the heavenly bodies, which had lain at the core of Mesoamerican civilization for millennia. Their 365-day secular calendar measured the passing of seasons and market days. A ritual calendar on a 260-day cycle consisted of 20 "weeks" of 13 days each. Each week and each day had a patron deity, all of them with specific good and evil qualities. Once every 52 years, the two calendars coincided, a moment at which time was thought to expire until rekindled by the priests who lit a sacred fire in a sacrificial victim's chest. Then a new cycle began amid general rejoicing.

Aztec creation legends spoke of four suns that preceded their own world, that of the Fifth Sun. A cataclysmic flood destroyed the world of the Fourth Sun. Primordial waters covered the earth. The gods gathered at the sacred city, Teotihuacán, where they took counsel. Two gods were chosen to represent the sun and moon. They did penance for four days, then immolated themselves in a great fire in the presence of the other gods. They emerged as the sun and moon, blown on their cyclical courses by the wind god, Ehecatl. Thus was born the world of the Fifth Sun, but a world doomed to inevitable, cyclical extinction. A strong sense of fatalism underlay Aztec existence, but the people believed they could ensure the continuity of life by nourishing the sun with the magic elixir of human hearts. This was why human sacrifice was so prevalent in Mesoamerican society—it was a means of returning food and energy from living people to the earth, the sky, and the waters. Feeding the sun was warriors' business, for they were the chosen people of the sun, destined to conquer or to suffer the "Flowery Death" (death on the sacrificial stone) when captured in battle. From birth, in formal orations; in schools; through art, architecture, and poetry; even in dress codes, the Aztecs were told that theirs was a divine quest—to carve out an empire in the name of Huitzilopochtli.

## Box 16.2 Aztec Human Sacrifice

The offering of human blood was the most profound Aztec religious act. Human sacrifice was the touchstone of all Aztec virtue, the key to their spiritual world. The gods themselves had originated the rite of sacrifice by immolating themselves on the summit of the Pyramid of the Sun at Teotihuacán to create the world of the Fifth Sun. The Aztecs believed they had acquired the custom from the gods themselves, a lineage sufficient to clothe it with a powerful divine sanction.

Sacrifice not only renewed the god to whom it was offered but also provided an ultimate test of manhood for the victims. Human beings counted in the cosmic order insofar as their offerings nourished the gods. The more valorous the offering, the more the gods were nourished—thus the celebrated "Flowery Death," in which a prisoner of war went to his death painted and dressed in the god's regalia so that he or she became a symbolic god. Elaborate rituals surrounded the more important sacrifices. The flawless young man chosen to impersonate the war god, Tezcatlipoca, assumed the role of the god for a full year. He wore divine regalia and played the flute. A month before his death, he was married to four young priestesses, who impersonated goddesses and sang and danced with him as he walked around the capital. On the day of sacrifice, the young man climbed willingly and alone to the sacrificial stone. On occasions like these, human sacrifice was not an earthly but a divine drama (Figure 16.8).

**Figure 16.8** Aztec human sacrifice.

(Cont.)

No one knows how many sacrificial victims perished each year, but estimates of 20,000 people a year throughout the entire empire are often quoted. As many as 800 victims may have died at major festivals in Tenochtitlán. In truth, the prestige of the victim was probably more important than sheer numbers.

## *The Aztec State*

The Aztec empire was far from a monolithic and highly centralized state. It was a mosaic of ever-changing alliances, cemented together by an elaborate tribute-gathering machine. The state itself was controlled by a tiny group of rulers, the lord of Tenochtitlán being principal among them. Everything was run for the benefit of a growing elite, who maintained their power by ruthless and efficient taxation campaigns, political marriages, and the constant threat of military force. Tribute was assessed on conquered cities and taken in many forms, for example, as raw materials like gold dust or tropical bird feathers for ceremonial mantles and headdresses. Fine ornaments, even capes, were assessed from communities that specialized in such products. Twenty-six cities did nothing but provide firewood for one royal palace alone. Metal artifacts were important tribute items, for they were of vital importance in Aztec and earlier Mesoamerican states. Expert smiths made musical instruments, such as bells, and alloyed copper to bring out shimmering gold and silver hues. Color and sound were central parts of Mesoamerican ideology, commemorating the sun and moon and the sounds of rain, thunder, and rattlesnakes, thus helping to bring symbolic order to the world.

Both settlement data and other archaeological data suggest that the Aztec empire was less centralized, both as a society and an economy, than its great predecessor, Teotihuacán. To what extent it was structured by decision making at the top, as opposed to market dynamics such as supply and demand, is still unknown. For example, pottery distributions show that political considerations such as alliances were more important than proximity to major markets in determining access to certain types of clay that were used in vessels. And both archaeology and ethnohistorical studies of market locations hint that imperial rulers located markets and decided the craft specializations within them to the advantage of their cities and at the expense of subordinate communities. Ornaments such as lip plugs served as material symbols of rights to land and created ideologies of dominance. There is clear evidence of major changes in standards of living under imperial Aztec rule. For example, in the western Morelos area of central Mexico, agricultural and textile production increased under Aztec rule, while living standards declined.

Under the highly visible and much-touted imperial veneer lay a complex foundation of small kingdoms, towns, and villages, all integrated into local economies. Many of them existed before the Aztec or even earlier civilizations arose, and they continued after the Spanish conquest. At the same time, the economic and political patterns of the empire were highly variable, both regionally and socially, in everything from land tenure to craft specialization, patterns of urbanization, and merchants and markets. This intricate social mosaic, only now being revealed by a new generation of archaeological research, lay behind a facade of political and economic uniformity and centralization.

Tribute and trade went together, for the Aztec empire depended heavily on professional merchants, *pochteca*. The Aztec merchants formed a closely knit class of their own, serving as the eyes and ears of the state and sometimes achieving great wealth. Tenochtitlán's great market at Tlatelolco was the hub of the Aztec world, attended, so the Spanish chroniclers record, by at least 20,000 people a day, and 50,000 on market days. Bernal Diaz walked through the market, amazed at the orderliness that prevailed. There were gold and silver merchants, dealers in slaves and tropical feathers, sellers of capes and chocolate, and every kind of merchandise imaginable. The market was supervised closely by officials appointed to ensure that fair practices prevailed.

The state itself was run for the benefit of the rulers and the nobility, a privileged class who controlled land and had the right to use communal labor. Through birthright, tribute levies, and appointed positions, nobles controlled nearly every strategic resource in the empire, as well as the trade routes that handled them. An elaborate dress code covered everything from ornaments to cape and sandal styles, regulations designed to restrict the size of the nobility (Figure 16.9). The tribute and labor of tens of thousands of commoners supported the state. The humble commoners with their coarse capes and work-worn hands supplied a small number of

**Figure 16.9** Aztec warriors in their elaborate uniforms with their captives. The Aztecs had strict sumptuary laws, which governed the uniform of every warrior and every citizen.

people with an endless supply of food, firewood, water, fine clothing, and a host of luxury goods that came from all over the lowlands and highlands. Only slaves and prisoners were lower in the social hierarchy.

Every Aztec was a member of a *calpulli*, or "big house," a kin-based group of families that claimed descent through the male line from a common ancestor. The four quarters of Tenochtitlán were organized into neighborhoods based on such groups. The *calpulli* served as the intermediary between the individual commoner and the state, paying taxes in labor and tribute and allocating people to carry out public works. Depending on its size, each *calpulli* was expected to raise a company of soldiers in times of war. Each had its own temple and ran its own school. Most important, the *calpulli* held land communally and allocated it to its members. An elected leader maintained special maps, showing how the land was being used, and interacted with government tribute collectors. The *calpulli* afforded a measure of security to every member of society, while also providing an efficient device for the state to govern a teeming and diverse urban and rural population and to organize large numbers of people for armies or work projects at short notice. The closely knit ties of family and *calpulli* provided the framework for an often harsh existence, carefully regulated by the state from birth to death. None of the Aztecs' social and political institutions were new. They had been used with ruthless success centuries earlier by the Toltecs and the rulers of Teotihuacán, but in the Aztec case they worked within a more flexible and diverse milieu.

## The Spanish Conquest (A.D. 1517–1521)

The Aztec empire was at its height when the aggressive and militaristic ruler Ahuitzotl died in 1501. The following year, Moctezuma Xocoyotzin (the Younger) was elected to the throne; he was a complex man, said to be a good soldier but given to introspection. When reports reached Tenochtitlán in 1517 of mountains moving on the Gulf of Mexico and of white, bearded visitors from over the eastern horizon to the Maya of the distant Yucatán, Moctezuma became obsessed with ancient Toltec legends concerning the departure of Topiltzin Quetzalcoatl, who had sailed over the eastern horizon, vowing to return in the year 1 Reed. The east was the direction of the rising sun, of renewal and fertility, of Quetzalcoatl himself. By grotesque historical coincidence, Hernán Cortés landed in Veracruz in the year 1 Reed (1519), convincing Moctezuma that "Topiltzin Quetzalcoatl . . . had come to land. For it was in their hearts that he would come to land, just to find his mat, his seat (Dibble and Anderson, 1975, p. 23).

The story of the Spanish conquest that followed unfolds like a Greek tragedy (Box 16.3). The seemingly mesmerized Moctezuma watches as Cortés advances from the coast at the head of an army swelled by dissatisfied allies. The two men meet on a causeway outside Tenochtitlán, by which time it is clear that the Spaniards are no gods. Two years later, the greatest city in the Americas lies in smoking ruins, its empire collapsed like a deck of cards. "Today all that I then saw is overthrown and destroyed: nothing is left standing," wrote Bernal Diaz (1963, p. 214). The conquest pitted an isolated, battle-hardened expeditionary force of about 600 men

## Box 16.3 The Spanish Conquest through Aztec Eyes

Fray Bernardino de Sahagun (c. 1499–1590) was a Franciscan friar who arrived in Mexico in 1529, less than a decade after the fall of Tenochtitlán. Sahagun soon learned the Aztec lingua franca, Nahuatl, then busied himself studying traditional Indian society as a means of combating what the friars called "idolatry." Fortunately, Sahagun realized that Aztec history was still walking around, although vanishing rapidly as many of the older generation died without passing on their cherished traditions. He began by enlisting the help of prominent Aztec elders, some of them merchants, and used young Spanish-speaking Indians as interpreters. For days on end, Sahagun conversed with his informants, recording formal orations and other discourses from earlier times.

To speak well in public was considered the mark of an Aztec gentleman, just as weaving was that of a woman, hardly surprising in a society where most education and knowledge was transmitted orally. Sahagun's informants produced hidden codices, taking the friar back to the vanishing world of their ancestors, and recited half-forgotten orations that spoke of early Aztec history; of the pantheon of gods and goddesses; of philosophy, poetry, and the universe. Aztec script was used mainly for record keeping, especially of the vast quantities of tribute that flowed into the capital from all corners of the Mesoamerican world. But it also served as a prompt for formal orations. Not content with codices and orations alone, Sahagun prepared questionnaires about the characteristics of gods and other matters, using techniques remarkably like those of modern anthropologists and ethnohistorians.

Between 1547 and 1569, Sahagun compiled his master work, *General History of the Things of New Spain*, a 12-volume compendium of Aztec civilization. This remarkable work encompasses the "gods worshiped by the natives" and rituals, sacrifices, and cosmology. Sahagun discusses astronomy and theology, natural history, and Aztec history and philosophy. The final volume describes the Spanish conquest through Aztec eyes. Sahagun's informants tell of strange portents, of the arrival of white strangers in mountains moving on the sea, and of Moctezuma's wavering in the face of the inexorable advance of Cortés and his men. They reveal how Moctezuma made a fatal error in assuming that Cortés was the returning Feathered Serpent, Quetzalcoatl. His ambassadors "put him [Cortés] into the turquoise serpent mask with which went the quetzal feather head fan. . . . And they put the necklace on him" (Dibble and Anderson, 1975, p. 168). Cortés responded by offering them European swords and challenging them to a fight. The puzzled ambassadors fled back to Moctezuma, who caused two prisoners to be sacrificed in their presence for "they had gone to see, to look into the faces, the heads of the gods—had verily spoken to them" (Dibble and Anderson, 1975, p. 165).

Bernardino de Sahagun's masterpiece was considered potential heresy by the Catholic authorities, who forbade its publication and buried the manuscript in church archives, where it remained until scholars discovered the *General History* in the nineteenth century. Today, Sahagun's work is of such seminal importance that an entire academic literature surrounds his writings.

against a brave, driven people, who were convinced, like their illustrious predecessors, that every act of war was imbued with deep symbolism. The Aztecs had long used war to feed the relentless appetite of the gods and to keep a loose patchwork of vassal states in order. With a skilled enemy exploiting their uneasy allies, they found themselves on their own. All they could do was defend themselves desperately against a puzzling foe, one quite unlike any adversary they had ever encountered. This small and determined band of gold-hungry adventurers was accustomed to long and arduous military campaigns, and it was inevitable that they would prevail.

Ten years passed before the whole of Mexico (New Spain) was under secure Spanish control. Tens of thousands of people died in bloody encounters, hundreds of thousands more from exotic diseases like influenza and smallpox, which were introduced by the newcomers. A rapid breakup of Mesoamerican society was inevitable in the face of a civilization armed with overwhelming technological superiority. Inevitably, those at a technological disadvantage lost, simply because their leaders could not call on the huge reservoirs of labor that had fought their wars, built their temples, and fed their city populations in the past. And instead of the divine benevolence of Quetzalcoatl, the conquerors brought suffering, death, exotic diseases, and slavery. More than 3,000 years of Mesoamerican civilization passed rapidly into centuries of historical obscurity.

## Summary

Like lowland Mesoamerican civilization, highland states developed from increasingly complex village societies in areas like the valleys of Mexico and Oaxaca during the first millennium B.C. The city of Monte Albán in Oaxaca Valley was in its heyday in the early first millennium A.D., when it was a major religious center and a rival to the dominant highland state of Teotihuacán. The latter grew rapidly from a small village in 200 B.C. into a vast metropolis with over 150,000 inhabitants. Teotihuacán's rulers designed their city as a symbolic landscape that reflected the place of creation, erecting imposing temples and public buildings. Teotihuacán became increasingly militaristic and the most powerful state in the highlands until its downfall around A.D. 750. Subsequently, the Toltecs achieved dominance until A.D. 1200, when their collapse left a political vacuum in the valley of Mexico. Between 1325 and 1500, the Aztecs forged a vast empire based on their capital at Tenochtitlán, which collapsed in the face of Hernán Cortés and his conquistadors in 1519–1521.

## Guide to Further Reading

Again, the literature is enormous. Michael Coe, *Mexico*, 2nd ed. (London: Thames and Hudson, 1994) covers much of the ground in this chapter. For the Valley of Oaxaca, see Kent Flannery and Joyce Marcus, *Zapotec Civilizations: How Urban Society Evolved in Mexico's Oaxaca Valley* (London and New York: Thames and Hudson, 1996) and Richard Blanton et al., *Ancient Oaxaca: The Monte Albán State* (Cambridge: Cambridge University Press, 1999). For Teotihuacán, Kathleen Berrin and Esther Pasztory, eds., *Teotihuacán: Art from the City of the Gods* (New York: Thames and Hudson, 1993) gives an up-to-date and lavishly illustrated summary. See also René Millon, *Urbanization at Teotihuacán,*

*Mexico,* Vol. 1: *The Teotihuacán Map* (Austin: University of Texas Press, 1973) and Janet Berlo, ed., *Art, Ideology, and the City of Teotihuacán* (Washington, DC: Dumbarton Oaks, 1992). For the Toltecs, see Richard Diehl, *Tula* (London: Thames and Hudson, 1984) and David Hanson, ed., *Tula of the Toltecs* (Iowa City: University of Iowa Press, 1989).

The Aztecs are well covered in Richard F. Townsend, *The Aztecs* (New York: Thames and Hudson, 1992); also by Inga Clendinnen, *Aztecs: An Interpretation* (Cambridge: Cambridge University Press, 1991). See also Michael Smith, *The Aztecs* (Oxford: Blackwell, 1996). Geoffrey W. Conrad and Arthur Demarest, *Religion and Empire: The Dynamics of Aztec and Inca Expansionism* (Cambridge: Cambridge University Press, 1984) gives a provocative comparative perspective. Eduardo Matos Moctezuma, *The Great Temple of the Aztecs* (London: Thames and Hudson, 1988) describes excavations in the heart of Tenochtitlán. Recent economic research on the Aztecs is revolutionizing our perceptions of their civilization. For a selection of essays, see Mary G. Hodge and Michael E. Smith, eds., *Economies and Polities in the Aztec Realm* (Albany, NY: Institute for Mesoamerican Studies, 1994). Bernal Diaz, *The True Story of the Conquest of New Spain,* trans. J. M. Cohen (Baltimore: Pelican Books, 1963) is a vivid account of the Spanish conquest. Charles E. Dibble and Arthur J. O. Anderson, *Florentine Codex; General History of the Things of New Spain,* 12 vols. (Salt Lake City: University of Utah Press, 1950–1975) is a definitive analysis and translation of Fray Bernardino de Sahagun's studies of Aztec civilization.

*Chapter 17*

# The Foundations of Andean Civilization

Andean textiles: A Paracas shaman in animal costume. ("Ceremonial Cloth" [detail]. Tabby weave, painted cotton, W. 254. 2cm. Peru, South Coast, early Nazca Phase 'A', ca. 1st–2nd c. AD. © The Cleveland Museum of Art, 2001, The Norweb Collection, 1940.530)

The Andean World: Poles of Civilization

The Preceramic Period (3000–1800 B.C.)

- *The Coast*
- *The Highlands*
- *Domestication of Animals and Plants*
- *El Paraíso (1800 B.C.)*
- *The "Maritime Foundations" Hypothesis*

The Initial Period (1800–800 B.C.)

The Early Horizon (900–200 B.C.)

- *Highlands: Chavín de Huantar (800–200 B.C.)*
- *Lake Titicaca Basin: Chiripa and Pukara (1400–100 B.C.)*
- *The Coast: The Paracas Culture (c. 500 B.C.)*

*The families gather on that cold winter's day 4,000 years ago. They huddle in their thick capes, greeting fellow kin quietly, as they enter the small, one-roomed shrine. Snow is deep on the nearby hills at Huaricoto, but the tightly fitting door keeps out the worst of the cold. The audience looks down on a smoking hearth, located on the higher level of the split-level floor. The shrine is dark, except for the flames, redolent with the scent of wood smoke and roasted chili peppers. The shaman chants, ingesting the powerful elixir of the hallucinogenic cactus. Mucus flows from his nostrils as he goes into a trance, chanting as his spirit enters the realm of the ancestors. As he chants and cavorts, an assistant interprets the messages from the ancestors, the guardians of life.*

The Inka called their domains Tawantinsuyu, the "land of the four quarters." In the fifteenth century A.D., their empire extended along the Andes Mountains and across the altiplano (high plains) of the Titicaca basin. Inka roads descended in tortuous zigzags down precipitous foothills into some of the driest landscape on the earth, along the Peruvian coast. Tawantinsuyu straddled the Andean world, bounded on its eastern side by the dense forests of Amazonia and on the west by the bountiful waters of the Pacific (Table 17.1; Figure 17.1). Both contributed to the fabric of the great civilizations that had developed centuries before the Inka mastered one of the most diverse landscapes on earth. Chapters 17 and 18 describe the origins and development of Andean civilization from its beginnings over 3,000 years ago until its overthrow by Spaniard Francisco Pizarro and a small band of conquistadors in A.D. 1531.

## The Andean World: Poles of Civilization

The Andes Mountains form the spine of South America, thrusting up like a wedge between the low, narrow coastal plain of the west and the sprawling tropical lowlands of the Amazon basin to the east. The mountains are wider and higher in the south and narrower and lower in the far north; the western and eastern lowlands resemble each other more closely, both environmentally and culturally. Two great mountain chains, the Eastern and Western Cordillera, form the boundaries of the altiplano in the south, the gap between them narrowing to the north. Climatic conditions vary greatly from north to south and with altitude. The low-lying coastal plains of the west are warm and very dry, the more mountainous regions, cooler and wetter, but there is enormous local variation. Over many centuries, two "poles" of Andean civilization developed—one in the south-central Andes, the other along the north coast of what is now Peru. Only the Inka

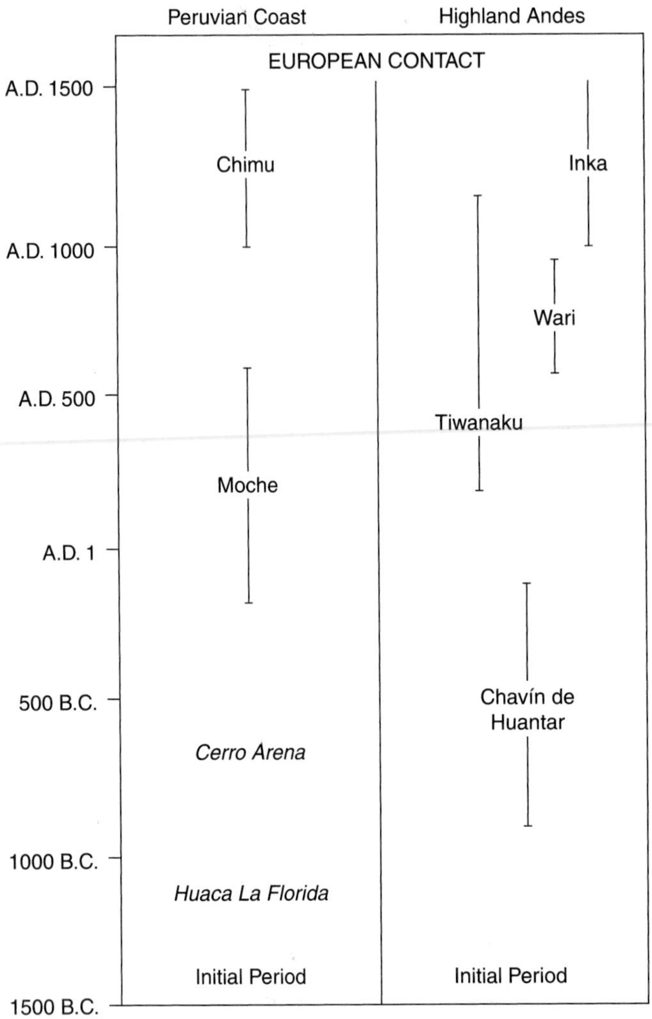


**Table 17.1** Chronological table of sites and cultures in Chapters 17 and 18.

succeeded in joining the two into one vast empire. (For the purposes of this book, the terms Andean and Andean region refer to the area covered by the Inka empire, Tawantinsuyu.)

The southern pole embraces the altiplano and the Lake Titicaca basin, highland Bolivia, and parts of Argentina and northern Chile in the south-central Andes. Much of the altiplano is too dry and cold to sustain dense human populations. The northern end of the Lake Titicaca basin is somewhat warmer and better watered, making both alpaca and llama herding and potato and quinoa agriculture possible. This was where the powerful Tiwanaku state flourished in the first millennium A.D. The puna grasslands of the higher altiplano were used to graze alpaca and llama, the economic exploitation of the plains varying with altitude. The civilizations of

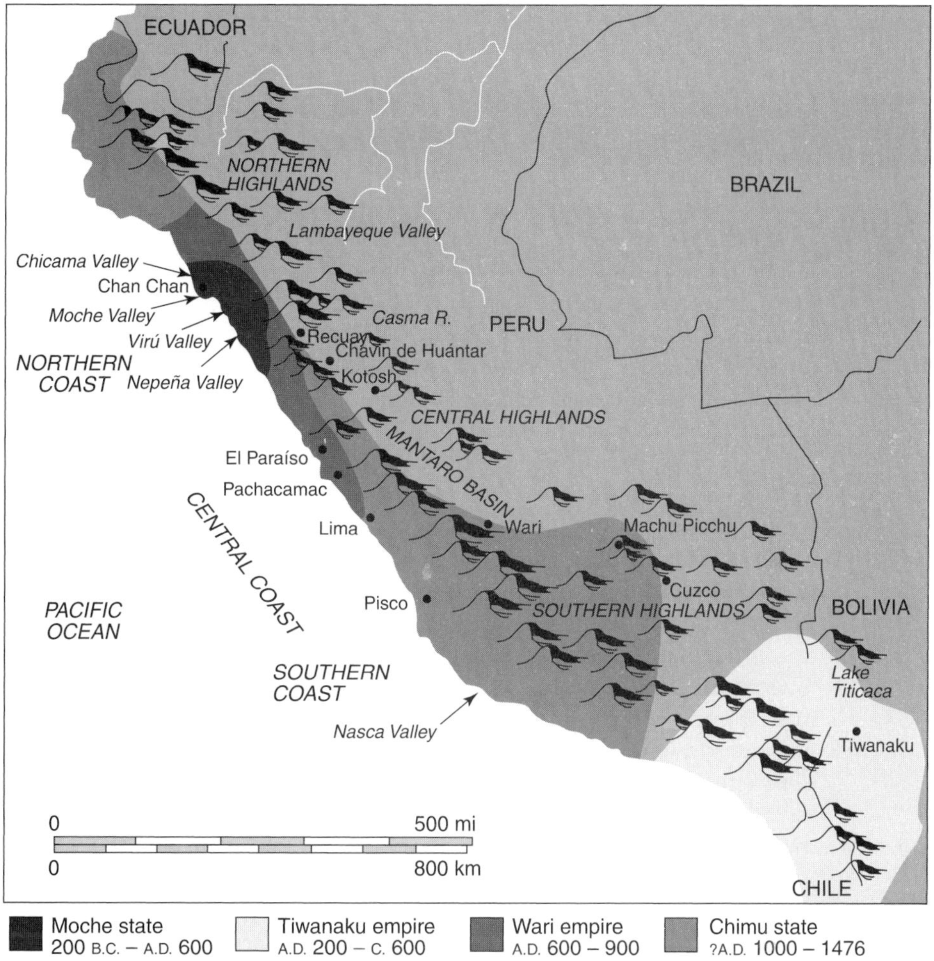


**Figure 17.1** Map of the Andean region and archaeological sites mentioned in Chapter 17.

the southern highlands traded regularly with the southern coast, bounded in the north by the Ica River and in the south by the Moquegua Valley. The arid plain is narrow, with deeply incised river gorges in the south, widening near the Ica Valley, where small rivers were canalized for irrigation.

In effect, highland Andes valleys were "stacks" of environmental zones, stratified one above the other. The highest elevations were given over to alpaca and llama herding, while potatoes and quinoa were grown at slightly lower altitudes. Below them came fields where a much greater variety of crops, including maize and beans, could be cultivated. Farming in the high Andes has always been a struggle against hostile environmental conditions. Ever-growing human populations moved upward and outward into harsher environments. As they did so, they tried to encourage animals and plants living in one zone to adapt to another, to extend their range onto unoccupied land. By seeding beans and cereals and transplanting roots and fruit trees, they struggled constantly to maintain a foothold outside natural floral and faunal ranges. This same struggle began more than 3,000 years ago, resulting in the breeding of dozens of strains of native plants such as potatoes.

The northern pole is centered on the bleak and effectively rainless Peruvian desert plain, which extends south nearly 550 kilometers (350 miles) along the coast as far as Collasuyu, reaching a width of up to 100 kilometers (62 miles) in the area of the Lambayeque River. Some 40 rivers and streams fueled by mountain runoff flow across the plain, but they can only be used for irrigation in areas where the surrounding desert is low enough. Four such locations were the most densely settled in ancient times. The two largest were located on the north coast, in the Chicama Moche area and in the Motupe-Lambayeque-Jequetepeque region. Local topography allowed farmers to link their field systems to canals that brought water from several rivers, permitting far higher population densities.

The Peruvian coast forms a series of related microenvironments: rocky outcrops, where shellfish are abundant; areas where wild plant foods nourished by damp fogs are common; and the floors or sides of river valleys. Close offshore, natural upwelling brings phytoplankton from deep water, providing nourishment for great schools of fish. For thousands of years, a combination of these microenvironments provided a rich constellation of food resources. In favored locations, even quite dense hunter-gatherer populations could live in relatively sedentary base camps occupied over many centuries. The predictable coastal fishery was disrupted by periodic El Niños, profound changes in Pacific currents that reduce the fisheries to a shadow of their normal selves for several years at a time. El Niño brings unfamiliar fish species and violent rainfall to the coast, the latter with the potential to cause catastrophic damage to irrigation systems. No one could store food against the eventuality of an El Niño, so the only strategy was to limit population densities to the lowest levels of available resources until such time as the people developed alternative food supplies by growing cereal crops, such as maize, through intensive irrigation agriculture. As in the south, there was constant interaction between coast and neighboring highlands, for each provided products needed by the other. And the fabric of Andean civilization developed out of this interaction.

## The Preceramic Period (3000–1800 B.C.)

### *The Coast*

Fishing and shellfish collecting were important from the moment of first human settlement, as early as 10,000 years ago. After 5000 B.C., however, fishing became more important, while coastal groups intensified their hunting and foraging. The Preceramic period dawned as this process took hold. Some people moved into larger, relatively sedentary communities near the coast. Best known is Paloma on the central coast's Chilca River, where the inhabitants relied heavily on fishing, using sophisticated spears and other artifacts to catch deep-water fish from canoes. They also netted millions of anchovies from rafts close to the shore. Their crowded settlement of simple, semisubterranean houses and grass-lined storage pits has yielded middens of fishbones and numerous plant species such as tuberous begonias, gourds, squash, and peppers. Paloma, occupied until about 2500 B.C., was less than 4.5 kilometers (3 miles) from the ocean, surrounded by lush patches of edible plants.

Fishing was always a staple along the coast, but long-term population growth did not occur until new, relatively reliable sources of nutrition were developed from more efficient plant gathering and from beans and other species planted deliberately as supplemental foods. Such deliberate manipulation began some time after 5000 B.C., but early coastal horticulture was never on a large scale until the arrival of maize and more intensive irrigation agriculture around 800 B.C.

## *The Highlands*

Somewhat similar cultural developments took hold in the Andean highlands between 2500 and 1500 B.C., when substantial Preceramic settlements flourished in the north-central highlands. Huaricoto, at 2,750 meters (9,000 feet) above sea level, was an important ritual center as early as 2260 B.C. and remained in use for 2,000 years. Detached, one-roomed structures with plastered floors and a central hearth served for private rituals that involved fire and offerings and were attended by only a few people, perhaps kin. Over the centuries, these sanctuaries became rectangular or square chambers with tightly fitting doors and split-level, plastered floors. The higher level served as a bench for the audience, with a recessed, rectangular floor for the central hearth. A clever ventilation system fed air to the fire, while permitting the chamber to be sealed as rituals unfolded.

The Preceramic occupants of Kotosh built two terraced platform mounds surrounded by numerous chambers, a form of architecture that defined the Kotosh Religious Tradition for many centuries. The Temple of the Crossed Hands, the most elaborate chamber, 9 meters (29.5 feet) square, was built of cobbles set in mud mortar. Thick plastered walls held rows of ornamental niches; the wall facing the entrance was adorned with a large central niche and two smaller ones set to each side, with sets of human hands crossed at the wrists below each of them. Both niches and friezes first appeared in Andean sacred buildings in Preceramic times and endured as symbols of high-status architecture in the Inka empire. The ceremonial chambers found at Kotosh and other sites formed the core element in an early set of religious beliefs, the Kotosh Religious Tradition, which endured for the next 1,500 years.

The same form of shrine design also appears at La Galgada, where mound construction began before 2200 B.C. The multilayered and oval north mound was faced with fine masonry and fronted by a circular, sunken court. The structures on the La Galgada platforms were made of rounded stones set in mud, plastered and painted white, and ornamented on the inside with wall niches. The log roof was plastered with clay, and a narrow entrance led to the easily sealed interior, with a ventilation system bringing air to the fire on the lower part of the split-level floor. Several such floors yielded white, orange, and green tropical bird feathers and deer antlers. At La Galgada, the shrines sometimes served the living and were then turned into burial vaults, where men, women, and children were deposited. Thus huacas, sacred places, used to invoke spiritual forces, became ancestral shrines, foreshadowing an important feature of later Andean civilization. After 1700 B.C., the many shrines on La Galgada's mounds became larger, more integrated structures that could hold as many as 50 people, perhaps marking a shift to more public rituals. Finally, around 1200 B.C., the summit of the largest mound assumed a U-shaped configuration—with three elevated platforms that surrounded a lower central court leading to the front of the tumulus—providing a setting for elaborate rituals that involved even larger audiences. La Galgada's long architectural history documents a long-term trend toward greater political and social complexity in the highlands, marked by great variation between different valleys and regions.

## *Domestication of Animals and Plants*

Intense speculation surrounds the origins of animal and plant domestication in South America, focusing in particular on the vast Amazon rainforest (where root crops may have been tamed) and on the central spine of the Andes mountains (where alpacas, llamas, and guinea pigs were domesticated, as well as a variety of important root and cereal crops). The vicuña and guanaco, native to the high-altitude puna grasslands of the Andes, are the camelid ancestors of the alpaca and llama. Both are gregarious, social animals, who live in close-knit herds. Specialized hunting of both the wild forebears is well documented at several caves high in the Andes. It would have been relatively easy for human herders to take advantage of the existing social structure of wild herds to manage and manipulate them. Once domesticated, llamas became invaluable pack animals, capable of carrying loads of up to 16 kilograms (35 pounds). Both llamas and alpacas are important sources of meat and wool. Studies of the age profiles of camelid bones from the Lake Junin basin of highland Peru show that domestication may have occurred as early as 2500 B.C. Camelid dung within the confines of a wood-posted corral dates to 2000 B.C. in the Asana site southwest of Lake Titicaca.

Nothing is yet known of early root crop cultivation in the Amazon basin, where preservation conditions are poor. But at least four species of tuber were vitally important to the Andeans. Three—oca, mashua, and ullucu—were grown in the highlands. The fourth, the potato, was cultivated throughout the Andes and has become a major world staple in recent centuries. Potatoes were probably first domesticated in the Lake Titicaca region, where the greatest genetic diversity of cultivated forms occurs. Wild potatoes were gathered at least as early as 10,000 B.C. in south central Chile; domesticated forms along with other major Andean root crops were probably developed between 3000 and 2000 B.C., the time when animals were first tamed. The changeover occurred in many valleys and sheltered highland basins, where hunter-gatherers were beginning to intervene in the life cycles of wild plants and increase their food supplies in harsh environments.

The staple cereal crops of the highlands were quinoa and maize. According to plant geneticists, quinoa (*Chenopodium quinoa*) was probably first domesticated in the south-central Andes of southern Peru and Bolivia and then diffused rapidly north along the mountains and to the coast. Excavations at Panaulauca Cave in the Junin Basin have yielded quinoa seeds, AMS-dated to between 3000 and 2000 B.C.

As we saw in Chapter 15, maize was first domesticated in Mesoamerica, perhaps as early as 5000 B.C. From there, it spread into the North American Southwest and into South America, but the date for the introduction into the Andes is controversial. Some experts believe maize reached the region as early as 5000 B.C., but their research predates the AMS dating of actual corncobs, which suggests maize was first grown in the highlands by 1250 B.C., arriving on the Peruvian coast perhaps as early as 800 B.C. This chronology is still highly tentative, for it is fully 1,500 years later than originally thought. Once on the coast, maize was combined with beans domesticated from Andean wild strains to form a major staple of later states.

But agriculture remained a secondary activity until comparatively recently in the lowlands. Despite this, sedentary settlements of several hundred, even thousands, of people flourished along the coast after 2600 B.C. Their inhabitants lived off sea foods, combined with beans and squash cultivated in irrigated valley fields.

Caral in the Supe valley, 193 kilometers (120 miles) south of Lima, and some 22.5 kilometers (14 miles) from the Pacific, was a large town as early as 2600 B.C. The 81-hectare (200-acre) settlement is dominated by a central zone comprising six platform mounds, built of quarried stone and river cobbles, arranged around a huge public plaza. The highest stands 18 meters (60 feet) high and measures 137 by 152 meters (450 by 500 feet) at its base. All six central mounds were constructed in only one or two phases, compelling evidence for a strong, centralized authority capable of marshaling large labor forces. Hundreds of villagers were needed to carry fiber nets full of boulders and rocks and heap them up to form the pyramids.

The Huaca Prieta site on the north coast was occupied soon afterward, an important community whose inhabitants were remarkably skilled cotton weavers. Even at this early date, Andean weavers devised elaborate designs, such as a double-headed snake with appended rock crabs, the double-headed motif persisting through more than 3,000 years of later Andean art (Box 17.1).

## *El Paraíso (1800 B.C.)*

The El Paraíso site, near the mouth of the Chillón Valley near Lima, dates to about 1800 B.C., to the very end of the Preceramic period. Six huge square buildings constructed of roughly shaped stone blocks, cemented with unfired clay, form a vast, U-shaped ceremonial complex. Tiers of platforms reached by staircases surround each platform, the clay-faced outer walls polished and painted in brilliant hues. As much as 100,000 tons of rock excavated from the nearby hills were used to build the El Paraíso buildings, the largest of which was more than 250 meters (830 feet) long and 50 meters (166 feet) wide, standing more than 10 meters (30 feet) above the plain (Figure 17.2). The rooms inside were covered with matting roofs supported by willow posts. A huge elongated patio covering more than 2.5 hectares (6.5 acres) lies inside the U, the precursor of a pervasive form of public architecture along the coast after 2000 B.C.

## Box 17.1 Andean Textiles

The first Andean textiles date to about 2500 B.C., soon after cotton was domesticated. The earliest textiles had rather coarse and uneven yarns, produced by twisting untreated yarn. After 2000 B.C., the weavers began to use delicate wood and thorn spindles mounted in a special clay, gourd, or wooden cup that minimized vibration. Thus they could produce much finer cloth. Most Peruvian textiles were made on the so-called backstrap loom, just like those used today in the Andes and Mesoamerica. The disadvantage of this type of loom is that the width of the cloth is limited by the span of the weaver's arms, so the Andeans sometimes combined several backstrap looms to create wider cloths for garments and wall hangings. The weavers were expert dyers and used about 200 hues from plant dyes, most commonly blue, red, and a multitude of other bright colors. Decorative motifs included simple checkerboards, filled squares, and stylized depictions of birds, felines, and other animals, as well as anthropomorphic figures. Some of the finest textiles were made in the Paracas area of the southern Peruvian coast, where the women sometimes used alpaca wool, which holds a wider range of dyes. They embroidered fine cloaks, mantles, and tunics with intricate designs, among them depictions of ornately dressed people wearing gold nose ornaments that resemble cats' whiskers. They carry staffs of office and hold trophy heads from sacrificial victims. The weaver has been likened to a spider that is creating a web, for the textile motifs of the Andeans again reveal the animistic roots of early civilization in this region: Both animals and humans had souls, and shamanistic rituals of transformation played a central role in defining the universal spirituality of the Andean world.

What is surprising is that the large El Paraíso structures were erected by people from dozens of scattered villages. For reasons as yet not understood, they united in a building project that channeled most of their surplus energies into a vast monumental center, a place where few people lived but where everyone congregated for major public ceremonies. The villagers themselves lived a life of seeming simplicity, remarkable only for their cotton textiles, adorned with basic geometric patterns and stylized animal-like motifs.

El Paraíso raises a fundamental question about early states. Did people need to control their food production to sustain a complex society, or were the surpluses from maritime resources sufficient for this purpose? While some archaeologists argue that this was the case, others point to the periodic El Niños, which disrupted normally predictable food supplies without warning. They believe El Paraíso was built when new agricultural economies were transforming coastal society, causing people to move inland and develop irrigation schemes. Significantly, El Paraíso's U-shaped layout coincided with the appearance of similarly shaped ceremonial centers further inland. Irrigation technology required a major reorganization of labor, which coincided with the appearance of new artistic traditions and architectural

**Figure 17.2** El Paraíso.

devices. We know El Paraíso was occupied for only a short time at the end of the Preceramic period, for residential debris is sparse. Perhaps its building coincided with rapid social changes, intense pressure on traditional food resources, and the adoption of new economies.

## *The "Maritime Foundations" Hypothesis*

El Paraíso epitomizes one of the fundamental issues of Andean archaeology. How did coastal states develop and from what economic and social base? In the 1970s, Michael Moseley developed his "maritime foundations" hypothesis for the development of early Andean civilization. He argued that the unique maritime resources of the Pacific coast provided sufficient calories to support rapidly growing, sedentary populations, which clustered in large communities. The same food sources also provided sufficient surplus to allow time for people to erect large public monuments and temples, work organized by the leaders of increasingly complex coastal societies. This scenario runs contrary to conventional archaeological thinking, which regards agriculture as the economic basis for state-organized societies (see Chapter 2). Along the Peruvian coast, the economic basis was fishing, argues Moseley. For thousands of years, coastal populations rose gradually, and their rise preadapted them to later circumstances, when they would adopt large-scale irrigation and maize agriculture. Large fish and mollusks were important, but the real staple was the anchovy and other small schooling fish, which could be netted easily from inshore canoes. The fish offered predictable food supplies, which could be dried or ground into storable fish meal. Such harvests provided an abundance of protein, capable of supporting large numbers of people.

Moseley's hypothesis has been much criticized, especially by those who argue that large coastal settlements could not have been supported by marine resources alone. Such arguments tend to ignore the overwhelming importance of anchovies, attested to both by their bones and by fine-mesh nets preserved in the dry middens of the coast. Other critics cite the catastrophic and irregular El Niños, which reduce the fisheries to below normal levels, with their potential for causing widespread famine. But overall, the maritime foundations hypothesis has stood the test of time well, provided it is seen as just one component in a much broader developmental process, which also occurred inland, in the highlands, and in areas where the width of the coastal shelf precluded extensive anchovy fishing.

Like Mesoamerica, the Andes region was one of dramatically contrasting environments, where highland and lowland communities depended on one another for essential commodities. The highland Andeans domesticated plants like quinoa, potatoes, and beans by at least 2500 B.C., transforming diet at higher elevations in dramatic ways. But the farmers needed lowland commodities like salt, protein-rich fish meal, and seaweed. Seaweed is rich in iodine, making it an important medicine for combating endemic goiter (a thyroid condition) and other medical problems. Carbohydrate foods like the tubers oca, ullucu, and white potatoes, which could not be grown at low elevations, have been found on archaeological sites in the Ancón-Chillón region of the north coast. The formation of states in both lowlands and highlands may have been fostered by continuous, often highly localized exchanges between groups on the coast and in the foothills and highlands inland.

The maritime foundations hypothesis argues that the rich maritime resources of the coast supported large, densely concentrated populations in favored areas near river valleys. Once irrigated, these valleys could grow large crops of such warmth-loving plants as beans, maize, and cotton, the last vital to the textiles that were such an important part of Andean society. The leaders of these societies were able to organize the large labor forces needed not only for building large ceremonial centers but also for transforming river valleys with sizable irrigation schemes into highly productive lands. In this scenario, irrigation farming was in the hands of a well-defined group of authority figures, who took advantage of existing simple technology and local populations to create new economies. This transformation, based as it was on trade, maize agriculture, and a maritime diet, acted as a catalyst for radical changes in Andean society.

Moseley argues that Andean civilization evolved in many ways, in a wide variety of ecological zones, ultimately from highland, tropical rainforest, and lowland subsistence strategies that were all of great antiquity, some dating to the earliest millennia of human settlement.

## The Initial Period (1800–800 B.C.)

The Initial period of Andean civilization lasted about 1,000 years, manifested by profound changes in settlement patterns and subsistence and by new concerns with the cosmos and powerful religious beliefs.

As maize and cotton cultivation assumed greater importance, coastal communities tended to move inland, closer to the growing irrigation systems in river valleys. Judging from excavated skeletons, the transition to agriculture was not an easy one. Much of the population had a short life expectancy and suffered from frequent malnutrition. Agriculture may have supported more people, but the dietary stress found at Paloma and other earlier foraging sites seems to have intensified in many places during the Initial period. By this time, coastal fishing villages were much larger communities, with highly organized social institutions, capable of building large ceremonial sites like El Paraíso and a large earthen mound 24 meters (80 feet) high at Salinas de Chao. The increasing complexity of coastal society was reflected in a wave of monumental construction in both the lowlands and highlands. By 2000 B.C., early ceremonial sites featured rectangular platform mounds fronting on a circular, sunken court that was usually housed in a rectangular forecourt. This ensured that people entered the forecourt of the sacred complex at ground level, descended into the sunken court, and then climbed the temple platform.

After 2000 B.C., coastal ceremonial buildings were greatly enhanced; the distinctive U-shaped platform employed at El Paraíso—with the open end facing eastward, or upstream—became commonplace. Pyramids formed the base of the U and surrounding mounds enclosed the courtyard, which usually featured several sunken courts. Such sunken plazas were being built at Caral as early as 2600 B.C. At least 45 U-shaped ceremonial centers are known to have existed on the north coast alone, all of them designed to communicate a powerful visual imagery and often adorned with intricate adobe friezes.

The most elaborate centers, each with its own complex architectural history, are in the Casma Valley. Sechin Alto, which covers 45 hectares (140 acres), is a huge ceremonial complex dominated by a stone-faced, 40-meter-high (130-foot-high) platform. This mound, nearly 300 meters (1,000 feet) long and over 250 meters (800 feet) wide, forms the base of a U-shaped ceremonial center with sunken courts, plazas, and flanking mounds. A vast sprawl of houses and platforms lies around this largest of all early ceremonial structures. One small building, erected around 1300 B.C., is surrounded by a mosaic of carved monoliths that depict a procession of armed men and dismembered human remains. The shrines at Sechin Alto employ one of the persistent themes of ceremonial architecture in the Andes region: artificially raising or lowering sacred spaces relative to one another in complementary opposition along a horizontal axis.

What does this ceremonial architecture mean in ritual terms? In many parts of the Americas the ritual manipulation of smoke and water served as a way of bridging stratified layers of air, earth, and bodies of water in the cosmos. Thus, it is argued, the early ceremonial centers of the coast, and also the highlands, reflect an ancient tradition of using these substances to maintain communication with the spiritual world. At the most famous highland center, Chavín de Huantar (described in the next section), galleries and ritual waterways flowed through the ceremonial platform and beneath a circular, sunken court, allowing the water to resonate underground so that the temple "roared." The vast, open courts of the coastal

U-shaped ceremonial complexes may have housed sacred orchards and gardens irrigated with manipulated water supplies. Such ritual waterways achieved great elaboration in the Chimú state of the north coast many centuries later.

Despite its enormous size, Sechin Alto, as well as other centers, probably supported a relatively small residential population, perhaps no more than a few thousand people. Most people probably lived in smaller villages or near the nearby irrigation systems in major river valleys. By this time, hierarchies of smaller settlements were ruled by a small elite, perhaps prominent kin leaders who owed their position to their religious abilities and political connections. Coastal society was undergoing major change at a rapid pace, change reflected in much larger monumental construction than that on the highlands at the time.

But in social and political terms, the Initial period remains somewhat of a mystery. There are few signs in burial rituals of any social ranking or personal wealth. Decision making and leadership were apparently not inherited and may have rotated from one person to the next on a regular schedule. The many ceremonial centers suggest that different kin groups commemorated their identities by erecting their own shrines, perhaps on a competitive basis. There were probably some larger kingdoms that extended over several river valleys, but who held sway over each of these political units is unknown. Were the leaders of centers like Sechin Alto presiding over a highly organized society, where the elite forced their subjects to create large irrigation schemes and to build enormous platforms as a form of taxation by labor, so common in later Andean societies? Or were the earliest irrigation canals built communally, while platform mounds were erected gradually in small layers by villagers as a conscious act of religious devotion conducted again and again over many generations? Many more excavations will be needed to resolve this controversy, but significant variations in settlement size, diet, and ceremonial centers show that major social and political change was underway.

## The Early Horizon (900–200 B.C.)

The Initial period saw a series of small kingdoms develop along the north and central coast. Major political units grew in the Moche, Casma, Chillón, and other river valleys, where large-scale irrigation was feasible. These polities traded constantly with one another and with highland communities, much of the exchange being in fish meal and in cotton, which was grown on the coast but in demand throughout the Andean region. Great sites like Huaca La Florida, about 13 kilometers (8 miles) inland of El Paraíso, were situated in the midst of an artificial environment created by irrigation. By the end of the Initial period in 800 B.C., coastal irrigation works were on a far larger scale. Conditions for the intensification of agriculture were favorable: gentle, cultivable slopes inland; a population expert in farming cotton and other crops; and an ample labor force that could subsist off grain and plentiful Pacific fish. The desert was reclaimed by building canals along the steeper areas of the coastal valleys, where the gradients made the diversion of river water an easy task. At first every family may have irrigated its own sloping gardens, but gradually each community grew so large that essential irrigation works could be handled only by cooperative effort. Eventually, simple cooperative works between families and neighboring communities evolved into elaborate public works that embraced entire inland valleys, controlled by a central authority who monopolized water supplies and the land they irrigated.

This process of organization, which may have taken centuries, was the result of many complex, interacting factors, among them population growth and an increase in the number of nonfarmers, such as priests and artisans, whose food needs had to be met by other people. At some time before 1000 B.C., the leaders of Huaca La Florida and other coastal centers may have devised a forerunner of the celebrated *mit'a* tax used 2,000 years later by the Inka, by which people worked a certain number of days per year for the state as either construction laborers or farmers. When one worked for the state, pay was given in food and shelter, sometimes in the form of a share of crops from state lands.

By 800 B.C., many exchange networks linked coastal river valleys with one another and with the highlands. New religious beliefs and ideologies spread along these networks from the highlands after 800 B.C., marking the beginning of the Early Horizon of Andean civilization.

## *Highlands: Chavín de Huantar (800–200 B.C.)*

In 1919, Peruvian archaeologist Julio Tello excavated the ruins of a unique stone temple-pyramid at the village of Chavín de Huantar in the Pukcha River basin in the Andean foothills. He recovered stone carvings and pottery adorned with a remarkable array of forest animals like jaguars, birds of prey, caymans, and mythical part-animal and part-human beasts. Soon afterward, Tello recognized the same animal motifs on pottery and goldwork from the north coast, far from Chavín de Huantar itself. He also found Chavín-like motifs on pottery and textiles buried with the dead on the arid Paracas peninsula in the southeast and on the shores of Lake Titicaca. He became convinced that Chavín was the "mother culture" of Andean civilization, the southern equivalent of the Olmec in Mesoamerica and a pan-Andean precursor to the later Tiwanaku and Inka civilizations of the highlands. Chavín was, he believed, originally a jungle culture from east of the mountains, which would account for the forest animals in its artistic tradition. Although Tello's notion of a mother culture remained controversial, most Andeanists agreed that Chavín influence was strong throughout much of the highlands and lowlands between 800 and 200 B.C., a period now known as the Early Horizon. By the 1970s, they thought of the Chavín culture as a religious cult, which spread from the north central highlands over a wide area. The distinctive Chavín iconography, reflected in art and ceremonial architecture, was thought to have brought "civilization" to much of the Andes, spreading along widespread trade routes that had existed for centuries.

This scenario suffers from the serious objection that neither Chavín culture nor its art style has been accurately defined or even dated. Recent fieldwork sees Chavín as a much more short-lived phenomenon. Furthermore, there is abundant evidence for complex, highly organized societies on the central and north coasts long before Chavín de Huantar became an important cult center. The great U-shaped ceremonial centers of the Moche and Casma valleys were at their height and then abandoned during the Initial period, before the appearance of Chavín. And the most intense occupation of Chavín de Huantar itself occurred between 400 and 200 B.C., long after elaborate kingdoms flourished along the coast. Most experts now believe that Chavín was indeed a religious cult, but one of limited distribution with little influence beyond the north-central highlands. The Chavín culture itself may have enjoyed considerable complexity, including some of the earliest social stratification in the central Andes, for there are clear signs of a privileged elite in burials and more elaborate dwellings. But its distinctive art and architecture were inspired, like those at other sites, by earlier cultures in the highlands and in the jungles to the east of the Andes.

Chavín de Huantar is in a small valley 3,100 meters (10,000 feet) above sea level, midway between the Pacific and the tropical rainforest. The inhabitants could cultivate maize in irrigated fields on the valley floor, grow potatoes on the surrounding slopes, and herd camelids on highland grasslands within easy range. Between 900 and 460 B.C., Chavín de Huantar was a small farming village with a local shrine, located at a strategic river crossing for trade routes between lowlands and highlands. Marine shells, imported potsherds, and the bones of forest animals like the jaguar testify to centuries of trading. Between 460 and 390 B.C., Chavín de Huantar suddenly became an important pilgrimage center. The village population settled along the river banks close to an imposing temple at the heart of the community. A century later, the settlement housed between 2,000 and 3,000 people and was four times its previous size, covering over 40 hectares (100 acres). The once humble shrine had become an Andean "cathedral," a place of pilgrimage known for miles around, as well as a highly organized trade and production center for the manufacture of ritual objects. Archaeologist Richard Burger has found fragments of pink Spondylus seashells of such ritual importance that they were traded from the Ecuadorian coast, 800 kilometers (500 miles) to the north.

Chavín de Huantar's Old Temple is a U-shaped structure, perhaps inspired by much earlier coastal centers. The terraced and truncated pyramid and temple structures enclose a rectangular court on three sides and stand up to 12 meters (40 feet) high (Figure 17.3a). The court is open to the east, the direction of sunrise and the rainforest. The Old Temple was rebuilt several times, resulting in a maze of passages, galleries, and small rooms, ventilated with special rectangular tubes. Conspicuous but inaccessible, the Chavín shrine was a mysterious structure. A white granite monolith built into the floor and ceiling, known as the Lanzón, "the lance," stands in a cross-shaped chamber near the central axis of the oldest part of the temple (Figure 17.3b). The Lanzón's connections to floor and ceiling suggest that it may have served as a conduit between the underworld, the earth, and the heavens. Julio Tello found a smaller gallery above the head, so close to the figure that one could reach the top of the Lanzón by removing a single stone block. Thus pronouncements could be arranged in such a way that they appeared to be responses from the Lanzón itself.

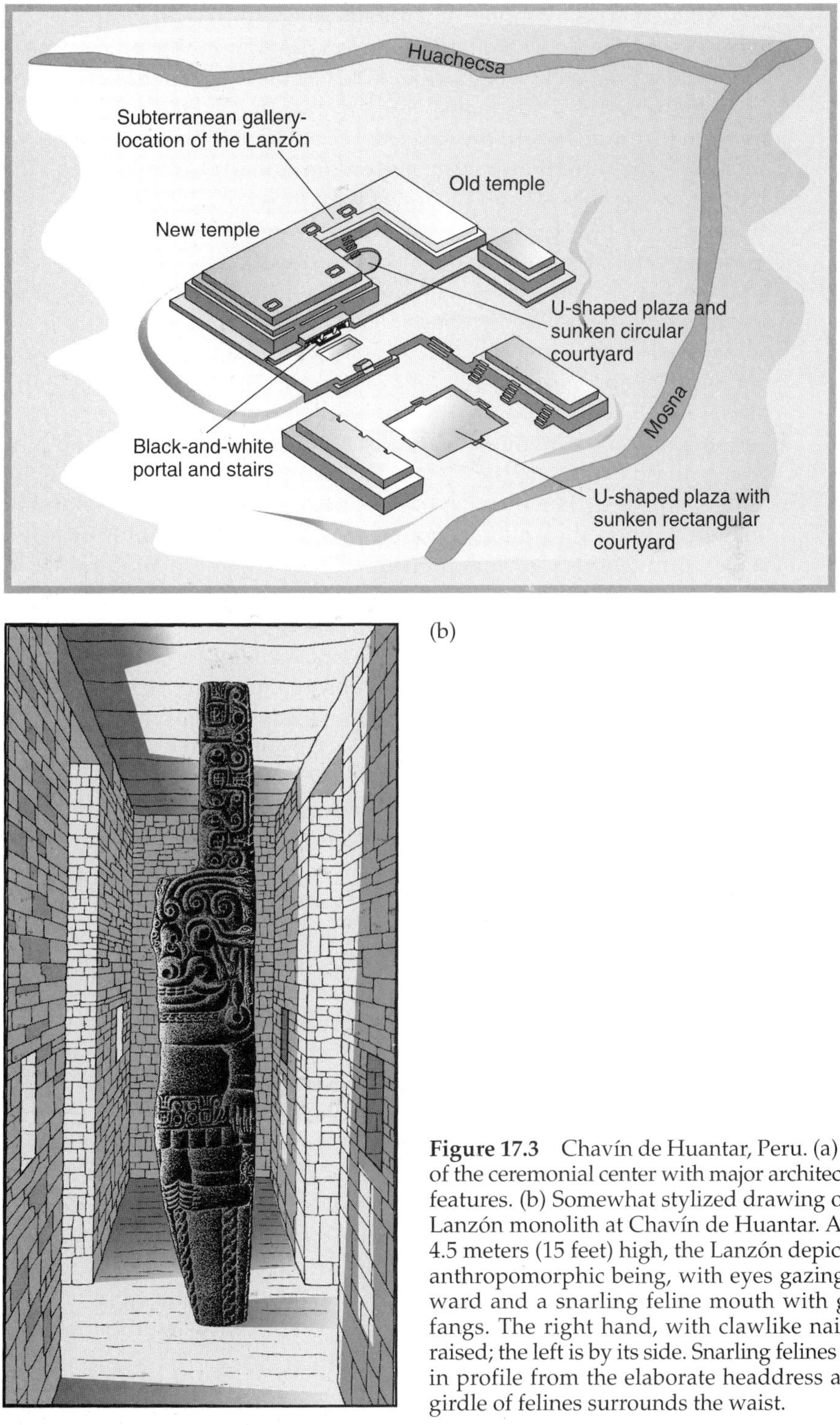


(a)

(b)

**Figure 17.3** Chavín de Huantar, Peru. (a) Plan of the ceremonial center with major architectural features. (b) Somewhat stylized drawing of the Lanzón monolith at Chavín de Huantar. About 4.5 meters (15 feet) high, the Lanzón depicts an anthropomorphic being, with eyes gazing upward and a snarling feline mouth with great fangs. The right hand, with clawlike nails, is raised; the left is by its side. Snarling felines stare in profile from the elaborate headdress and a girdle of felines surrounds the waist.

Chavín art is a dramatic combination of animals and humans. Mythical and living beasts mingle with snarling humans. Jaguar motifs predominate—humans, gods, and animals have jaguarlike fangs or limbs and snakes flow from the bodies of many figures. Caymans, jaguars, and snakes, the most common animals, are from the rainforest to the east, part of a compelling imagery that seems to reconcile the dichotomy between high mountain and humid jungle, bringing together ancient beliefs from the forest with those of farmers in deserts and remote mountain valleys. Experts believe there were two major deities at Chavín: the "Smiling God" depicted on the Lanzón, a personage with a human body and feline face, hands, and feet; and the "Staff God," a standing male with downturned, snarling mouth and serpent headdress. He grasps two staffs, each adorned with feline heads and jaguar mouths. Both of these supernatural beings were anthropomorphic gods, perhaps symbols of complex rituals of transformation that took place in the Old Temple.

These transformations may stem from the evergreen, humid jungle, with its broad, muddy rivers, to the east of the mountain. Rich but little known artistic traditions still flourish in the lowlands. The elaborate artifacts that form this tradition involve complex metaphors of animism (a belief in the total spirituality of the universe). Bird feathers, carnivore teeth, and seashells are all examples of animated transformations of natural forms into artifacts, made possible by the rich natural resources of the forest environment. Most of these artifacts are ephemeral, destined to rot back into the forest within a few years. As natural objects they are infused with the belief that the entire universe has spiritual meaning, that every living thing—anything that grows, moves, or develops—has a soul, just as humans do. This view is reinforced by the spiritual transformations of people into beasts or birds by ingesting hallucinogenic drugs and through complex shamanistic rituals. The anthropomorphic beings at Chavín may symbolize this transformation. A granite slab from Chavín de Huantar's plaza depicts the figure of a jaguar-human wearing jaguar and serpent regalia. He grasps a hallucinogenic San Pedro cactus, a plant species still used by shamans today. The mescaline in this cactus has mind-altering effects, producing multicolored visions, shapes, and patterns and giving the shaman great powers. The hallucinogen sends the shaman on flowing journeys through the subconscious, transforming him into a fierce, cunning jaguar. Animals, humans, and plants are always interconnected, depending on one another—all equals in an intensely spiritual world.

Chavín ideology was flamboyant and compelling, born of forest, mountain, and desert beliefs that wove a complex relationship among animals, humans, and shamans. The new religious beliefs were powerful, influencing both human societies and art styles over a large area of the Andes. Chavín was one of the many catalysts for later Andean civilization, some of them technological. For example, its ideological messages were painted on textile wall hangings, as well as on artifacts in clay, gold, stone, and wood. These powerful images, with their cosmic, shamanistic visions, brought together the institutions and achievements of increasingly sophisticated Andean societies and were Chavín's legacy to later Andean civilizations.

## *Lake Titicaca Basin: Chiripa and Pukara (1400–100 B.C.)*

As Chavín de Huantar rose to prominence in the northern highlands, a separate Early Horizon tradition developed around Lake Titicaca far to the south. The plains landscape of the basin was gradually transformed by ever more intensive agriculture and herding.

*Chiripa* (1400–100 B.C.) is on the southern shore of Lake Titicaca, a fishing and fowling settlement, where farming and herding were integrated into much earlier hunter-gatherer traditions. Chiripa itself remained a small village until about 1000 B.C., when a platform mound was built in the community, then modified many times over the centuries. The platform itself was stone-faced with a sunken square court surrounded by rectangular buildings on the summit.

Between 600 and 100 B.C., the Chiripa platform was enlarged until it measured 55 meters (180 feet) square and 6 meters (20 feet) high. The stone-faced sunken court was 23 meters (75 feet) square and 1.5 meters (5 feet) deep. Carved stone plaques set into the walls depicted serpents, animals, and humans, the earliest appearance of a stone-carving tradition that persisted along the shores of the lake for many centuries. Sixteen rectangular buildings surrounded the court. Many features of the Chiripa shrine, especially the stepped doorways, sunken courts, and nichelike windows, are ancestral to the later Tiwanaku architectural tradition, which used the same devices for its ceremonial architecture (see Chapter 18). The religious beliefs associated with this architecture have been grouped under the Yaya-Mama Religious Tradition, which flourished for many centuries.

*Pukara* (400 B.C.–A.D. 100) 75 kilometers (47 miles) northwest of the lake, was a major center, with a large residential area and an imposing ceremonial complex on a stone-faced terrace, complete with rectangular sunken court and one-room structures on three sides. Pukara's elite lived on nearby terraces, the entire settlement being large enough to be classified as a protocity. Such a dense population could be achieved only by a major investment in agriculture, including many acres of raised fields and large shallow ponds, known as *cochas*, which filled seasonally and where crops were planted at the water's edge as the pond dried up.

Judging from the distribution of Pukara pottery styles, the kingdom's power was confined to the northern Titicaca basin, but ceramics and other artifacts from as far afield as the north coast reflected widespread trade connections. Tiwanaku presided over the southern shores of the lake between 400 B.C. and A.D. 100. There is no evidence that Pukara incorporated its southern neighbor.

## *The Coast: The Paracas Culture (c. 500 B.C.)*

By 1200 B.C., ceramics, woven textiles, and irrigation agriculture spread from the Titicaca region to the south coast, where human populations were much smaller.

The subsequent Paracas culture of the south coast was partially influenced by Chavín culture but developed its own distinctive art styles, reflected mainly in its

**Figure 17.4** An ecstatic shaman depicted on a Paracas textile. (Paracas, Woolen fabric, detail, Peru. National Archaeological Museum, Lima Peru. Copyright Giraudon/Art Resource, NY)

fine, embroidered textiles (Figure 17.4). The term *Paracas* refers both to a distinctive pottery style and also generically to a southerly coastal society of some complexity, best known from a large cemetery on the Paracas Peninsula. Hundreds of well-to-do people were buried in the necropolis, their bodies bound with cord into a flexed or seated position and then covered with textiles and set upright in large, shallow baskets that contained richly adorned garments and other offerings. Basket and mummy were then wrapped in plain cotton cloth to form a large bundle, which was placed in a subterranean crypt next to the bodies of as many as 40 others, presumably relatives. Interestingly, some of the Paracas people had undergone cranial surgery. Their skulls display evidence of trephination, a procedure used to treat tumors by removing portions of the skull or drilling through the cranium. The arid environment has preserved more garments and textiles there than at any other Andean site, revealing superb artistry in alpaca wool and cotton (for Andean textiles, see Box 17.1, p. 478).

Paracas is somewhat of an enigma, for we have no means of assessing the true complexity of this southern coastal society. Judging from the rich adornment of the Paracas burials and their subterranean crypts, some families may have achieved an elite status, as if political power and high status were inherited in some communities, even if elaborately decorated burials are relatively rare.

By 2,000 years ago, a diverse patchwork of Andean kingdoms flourished in both highlands and along the coast. They shared some common religious beliefs and ideologies, reflected in the archaeological record by similarities in art styles, architecture, and artifacts. A complex web of interconnectedness linked coast and highlands, an interconnectedness that became all-important in later centuries, as we see in Chapter 18.

## Summary

The roots of Andean civilization lie in ancient hunter-gatherer societies along the Pacific coast and in the highlands dating to at least 5000 B.C. Coastal civilization is thought by Michael Moseley to have had a strong maritime foundation, for the exceptional marine resources enabled the support of larger-than-average sedentary populations. Ceremonial centers like El Paraíso, with their U-shaped precincts, suggest that a common religious ideology linked much of the northern Andean region between 2000 and 1000 B.C. This Initial period was one of continuous interaction and trade between coast and highlands. The growth of social complexity, new art traditions, and monumental architecture coincided with the appearance of several small kingdoms along the north coast. The culmination of this trend is seen in various local Early Horizon traditions, among them the famous Chavín style, perhaps the manifestation of an important religious cult that spread widely.

## Guide to Further Reading

Michael Moseley, *The Incas and Their Ancestors,* 2nd ed. (New York: Thames and Hudson, 2000) is the definitive synthesis of Andean archaeology. For the origins of civilization, see Moseley, *The Maritime Foundations of Andean Civilization* (Menlo Park, CA: Cummings Publishing, 1975). Jonathan Haas, T. Pozorski, and S. Pozorski, eds., *The Origins and Development of the Andean State* (Cambridge: Cambridge University Press, 1987) contains useful essays. For highland religious traditions, see Christopher Donnan, ed., *Early Ceremonial Architecture in the Andes* (Washington, DC: Dumbarton Oaks, 1985). For Chavín, see Richard Burger, *Chavín and the Origins of Andean Civilization* (New York: Thames and Hudson, 1992). Andean religions, ancient and modern, are superbly described and analyzed by Lawrence Sullivan, *Icanchu's Drum* (New York: Free Press, 1989).

# Chapter 18

# Andean States

## (200 B.C.–A.D. 1534)

Peru, Moche culture, Stirrup spout head vessel, 100 B.C.–500 A.D. (Ceramic, 26 × 17.8cm, Buckingham Fund, 1955.2341 Photo © The Art Institute of Chicago. 

The Early Intermediate Period (200 B.C.–A.D. 600)

North Coast: Moche Civilization (A.D. 100–700)
- *Moche Origins*
- *Public Works*
- *Moche Domains*
- *Warrior-Priests: Royal Burials*
- *Moche Metallurgy*
- *Moche Society*
- *Collapse*

Southern Pole: Nazca (200 B.C.–c. A.D. 700)
- *The Nazca Lines*

The Middle Horizon: The First Highland States (A.D. 600–1000)
- *Tiwanaku (A.D. 200–1000)*
- *Wari (A.D. 500–750)*

The Late Intermediate Period (A.D. 900–1400)
- *Chimor (the Chimú state) (A.D. 1100–1400)*

The Late Horizon: The Inka Empire (A.D. 1476–1534)
- *Origins*
- *Split Inheritance and Conquest*
- *State Organization*
- *Cuzco*
- *An Empire in Trouble*

The Spanish Conquest (A.D. 1532–1534)

*The llama train walks steadily up the steep incline, zigzagging along the rugged mountain face, their drivers urging on the laden beasts with sticks. Each carries an odoriferous load of fish meal, tied in coarse fiber sacks. Their owners are oblivious to the smell, as the llamas walk sure-footedly along the narrow track, dense mist swirling at their feet. Then, suddenly, a cry from the head of the caravan brings everyone to a halt. Cursing, the drivers urge their animals against the hillside. An Inka runner trots around the corner ahead, steadying himself on the bend, but keeping up a stiff pace. He raises a hand as he lopes on, never slacking his speed, his destination the tiny government rest house 2,000 feet down the mountain. The drivers watch him incuriously, for royal dispatches pass up and down the mountain pass every day, regardless of the weather.*

In A.D. 1532, the Inka empire, Tawantinsuyu, controlled the lives of over 6 million people. This extraordinary domain was unique in world history because it included peoples living both at extreme high altitudes and in some of the driest environments on earth. The Inka, like the Aztec of Mesoamerica, created their own imperial propaganda. Their historians taught that civilization was invented by the Inka at Cuzco and spread from there throughout the Andes. They denied that any civilizations existed before their great conquests and proclaimed that in their city civilization began. Inka propagandists wrote history to promote their own self-image, but even they revered the silent ruins of the great city of Tiwanaku on the shore of Lake Titicaca, said to have been built by giants turned into stone by the Inka god Viracocha before he created people. Tiwanaku in the highlands and Chan Chan and Pachacamac on the coast make a mockery of Inka official histories, for powerful states and empires flourished throughout the Andean region while Cuzco itself was still a small village. Chapter 18 tells the story of these early Andean states, which in turn developed from earlier kingdoms described in the previous chapter (Figure 18.1; Table 17.1).

## The Early Intermediate Period (200 B.C.–A.D. 600)

By 200 B.C., Andean civilization was developing at both the northern and southern poles of the region, at a time when populations were rising steadily. Further agricultural expansion required substantial investments by well-organized labor forces, which in turn depended on centralized governments run by a wealthy elite, ruling in the name of the gods. On the coast, the U-shaped shrines and the ideology associated with them vanished, reflected in new, standardized art styles, which recounted origin myths, heroic deeds, and burial themes. Rulers became semigods, supported by creation myths that separated them from everyone else and allowed them to rule by divine right.

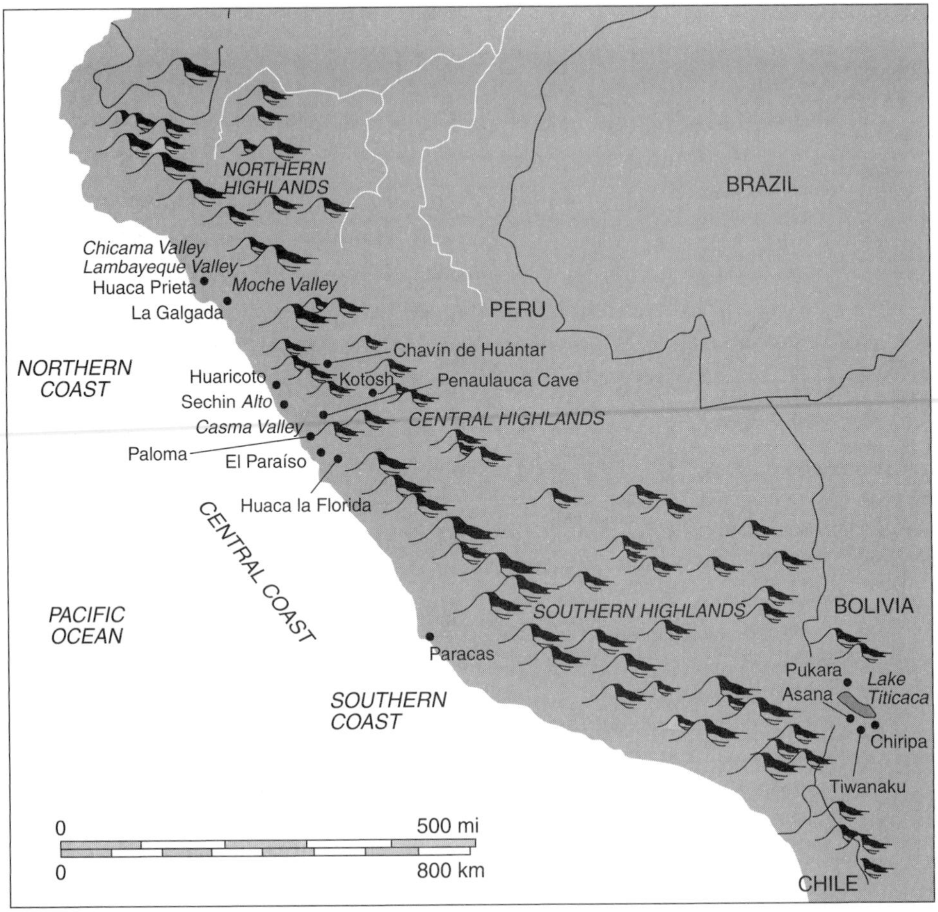


**Figure 18.1** Map of archaeological sites and states described in Chapter 18.

A series of brilliant states flourished on the coast and in the highlands during the Early Intermediate period: Moche on the northern coast, Nazca in the south, and Recuay and Pukara in the highlands, to mention only a few. We can only describe a few of them here.

## North Coast: Moche Civilization (A.D. 100–700)

### *Moche Origins*

By using ceramics from well-preserved north coast burials, archaeologist Rafael Larco Hoyle created a long cultural sequence that linked societies contemporary with Sechin Alto (see Chapter 17) to the appearance of Moche civilization in about A.D. 100. The ceramic sequence masks a complicated process of cultural development, which transformed small kingdoms based on single valleys into states that straddled several watersheds. During the Initial period and the Early Horizon, coastal societies were highly fragmented, even within the confines of single valleys. As populations grew and farming land was taken up, competition for arable territory intensified and the cost of exploiting marginal acreage rose. Conquest was an attractive alternative, reflected in an increase in defensive works along the north coast. An increasingly wealthy and powerful elite organized the construction of large valley-neck irrigation canals, opening up the lower floodplains to both intensive farming and human settlement. The small hamlets and villages of earlier times gave way to a hierarchy of much larger communities, dominated by a single primary center of exceptional size. While commoners lived in simple houses with stone foundations and cane walls, the elite built residences of adobe brick, the same material used to fashion public buildings. Widespread irrigation created the necessary claylike soils that were ideal for making adobe bricks in standardized molds.

The new cultural and political order reflected in adobe architecture came into being during the Gallinazo phase 2,000 years ago, centered on the Virú Valley. After centuries of change, a new emphasis on monumental construction caused Gallinazo builders to fashion *huaca* (shrines) on a grand scale, often huge terraced platforms perched on steep hillsides. The Gallinazo site itself, located in the Virú Valley, was a community of adobe houses scattered over 5 square kilometers (2 square miles). At this time, the Virú Valley may have been the center of a multivalley kingdom, where each watershed had its own hierarchy of nobility and commoners, linked by kin ties.

The people of Cerro Blanco in the lower Moche drainage gained control, by means unknown, over the larger, neighboring Chicama Valley. Little changed as far as architecture, subsistence, or settlement patterns were concerned, but political realities were very different. A new Moche style reflected a new and powerful form of coastal Andean civilization, which appeared around A.D. 100.

## *Public Works*

The Moche was a multivalley state that may have consisted of a series of satellite centers, which ruled over individual valleys but owed allegiance to the great centers of the Moche Valley. The capital was at Cerro Blanco, where two enormous adobe structures, Huaca del Sol and Huaca de la Luna, rose within 500 meters (1,600 feet) of each other. Huaca del Sol's platform measures 340 by 160 meters (1,115 by 525 feet) and stands more than 40 meters (130 feet) high (Figure 18.2). In its original form, this enormous monument was probably cross-shaped and faced north; it was built in four sections, which gave it a stepped effect, the widest step at the bottom and the smallest at the top. The facade was painted in red and other colors. The Spaniards dug into the Huaca in search of treasure and eventually diverted the river to wash out the treasure they believed lay in the tombs within the platforms. The scanty records from their activities suggest that rich finds were made and that the Huaca del Sol was the royal palace and burial ground. Nearby

**Figure 18.2** Moche pyramid at Huaca del Sol.

Huaca de la Luna consisted of three platforms connected and enclosed by high adobe walls. The walls were adorned with rich polychrome murals depicting anthropomorphic and zoomorphic beings, as well as animated artifacts. Some of the motifs were also found on Moche pottery. Michael Moseley theorizes that Huaca del Sol was the imperial palace and mausoleum, while Huaca de la Luna was the place of worship for the major deities of the state. The two huacas reflect powerful, centralized rule, the peak of a hierarchy of lesser settlements built in surrounding coastal valleys.

Huaca del Sol was built in segments, using more than 100 million standard-sized bricks. Each segment was apparently the responsibility of an individual workforce, often delineated by a distinctive maker's mark impressed on the bricks. Construction of the huacas spanned many generations, performed by communities throughout Moche territory as an annual *mit'a* tax, or labor for the state.

Much of this *mit'a* labor also went into the construction of new irrigation schemes near the capital. Much cultivated land lay along the terraced sides of valleys, where soils were better drained and easily planted with wooden digging sticks. The ancient irrigation canals wound along the sides of the valleys, a series of narrow channels approximately 1.2 meters (4 feet) wide, set in loops and S-shaped curves and watering plots approximately 22 meters (70 feet) square.

## *Moche Domains*

In its heyday around A.D. 500, the Moche state held sway over drainages in the Piura region of Ecuador, apparently by creating dozens of subject kingdoms. In the smaller valleys and coastal areas as far south as the Huarmey Valley, the

Moche ruled indirectly, incorporating conquered rulers into their own nobility and ruling through them, an administrative approach used in later centuries by both the Chimú of the coast and the Inka of the highlands. Moche seafaring canoes established a presence on more than 30 offshore islands, as far south as the southern Chincha Islands, where they mined guano as fertilizer, a royal monopoly. Where possible, the Moche extended their ambitious irrigation schemes to link several neighboring valleys; they then constructed lesser copies of their capital as a basis for secure administration of their domains. Traders were in touch with people far to the north and on the highlands and with Nazca on the south coast. Moche was the first state to forge a nation out of hundreds of local coastal groups, which survived for several centuries before the inexorable consequences of a series of strong El Niños brought chaos to the Moche heartland and resulted in the loss of the southern provinces of what had, effectively, become an empire.

## *Warrior-Priests: Royal Burials*

A series of spectacular royal burials have revealed the staggering wealth of Moche's elite. In 1987, tomb robbers broke into the gold-laden sepulcher of an ancient Moche lord deep in the pyramids of Sipán on the north Peruvian coast. Fortunately, archaeologist Walter Alva was early on the scene and excavated the tomb. The burial platform had been rebuilt six times between the first century A.D. and about A.D. 300. Alva has subsequently excavated three royal burials at Sipán, graves awash in gold, silver, and copper. Each Moche lord was caparisoned in his full ceremonial regalia, wearing headdress and backflap, necklaces, and elaborate tunics. One burial chamber contained a plank coffin that held the extended skeleton of a man in his 30s, lying on his back with his arms along his sides (Figure 18.3; Box 18.1). He wore gold nose and ear ornaments, gold and turquoise bead bracelets, and copper sandals. A ceremonial rattle, crescent-shaped knives, scepters, spears, and exotic seashells surrounded the body. Three young women, each about 18 years old, lay at the head and foot of the coffin, and two males in their mid-30s were on either side. A dog, two sacrificial llamas, and hundreds of clay vessels were also in the grave.

The Lords of Sipán are an enigma. Clearly, they were individuals of great importance in Moche society. Archaeologist Christopher Donnan from UCLA has compared the artifacts from the sepulchers with paintings on Moche pots. He believes that the Lords were warrior-priests, men at the pinnacle of Moche's elite, who enjoyed immense political and spiritual power.

In 1998–1999, Christopher Donnan unearthed a further set of royal burials at Dos Cabezas in the lower Lambayeque Valley, those of five unusually tall young men, surrounded by textiles, ceramics, llama skeletons, and fine metalwork. None of them was aged more than 22. Their exceptional stature may be the result of a genetic bone disorder, similar to modern-day Marfan syndrome, which produces people with unusually long legs (Box 18.2).

**Figure 18.3** (a) A mannequin wears the full ceremonial regalia of a lord (warrior priest) of Sipán, designed to glitter brightly in the sun ; (b) artist's reconstruction of Tomb 1 at Sipán, showing the lord in his regalia set in his coffin, also male and female attendants.

(a)

(b)

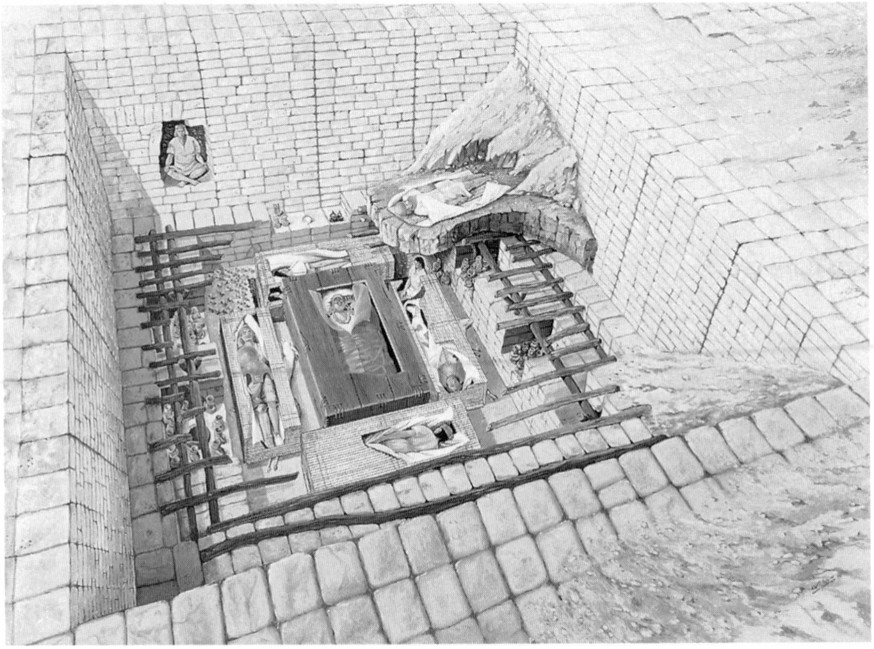

## *Box 18.1 The Lords of Sipán*

Who were the Lords of Sipán? Clearly, they were nobles, but what was their role in society? The Moche had no writing, so there are no written records to identify these wealthy and powerful men. There are clay portraits on ceremonial pots of some Moche nobles, proud, serene men staring into the distance (see chapter opener). In an ingenious and convincing use of indirect evidence, Christopher Donnan has "unrolled" dozens of intricate friezes on Moche vessels in an attempt to decode their society and its religious beliefs. He has found hundreds of scenes in which two men engage in combat, one defeating and capturing the other. The victor strips off his enemy's clothing, bundles up his weapons, and attaches a rope around his neck. He parades his prisoner, forcing him to walk in front of him. All the captives appear in front of an important individual, sometimes at a pyramid. Then their throats are cut and their blood consumed by priests and attendants. The most important participant in the sacrificial ceremonies was a "warrior-priest," wearing a conical helmet with a crescent-shaped headdress, circular ear ornaments, and a crescentlike nose ornament, just like the Lords of Sipán. Donnan is certain the lords were warrior-priests, the men at the pinnacle of the elite, who presided over the most important ceremony in Moche society (Figure 18.4).

The elaborate regalia of the Lords of Sipán varied little from one generation to the next. Nearly every artifact buried with the warrior priests had intense symbolism. For example, the lords wore gold on the right and silver on the left, representing the duality of moon and sun. Depictions of ullucu fruit in gold and silver may reflect their use during human sacrifices; they contain anticoagulants, perhaps used to prevent blood from congealing during the ceremony.

**Figure 18.4** A Moche lord presides over a parade of prisoners who are being sacrificed. A frieze from a painted pot "unrolled" photographically.

## Box 18.2 Moche Burials at Dos Cabezas

Dos Cabezas lies in Peru's lower Jequetepeque Valley, a 32-meter-high (105-foot-high) Moche pyramid close to the river mouth at the Pacific Ocean. Three richly decorated Moche nobles' tombs dating to A.D. 450 to 550 were excavated from the south side of the pyramid between 1997 and 1999. Each contained a small copper statue depicting the deceased, who were remarkable for their exceptional stature. Average Moche males stood between about 4 feet 10 inches and 5 feet 4 inches in height. The Dos Cabezas men towered between 5 feet 9 inches and 6 feet and died between the ages of 18 and 22 years. Biological anthropologists suspect that they may have suffered from a genetic disorder like Marfan syndrome, which causes thin, elongated bones.

The three appear to have died within a few weeks of one another. The most important of the three men lay in Tomb 2, cocooned in clay and wrapped in textiles together with his ceremonial possessions. He was buried with an exquisite ceramic bat, a sacred animal to the Moche, in a headdress adorned with gilded copper bats, and a nose ornament of solid gold also modeled in the form of a bat. Bats were prominent in Moche ritual, usually appearing in scenes of human sacrifice and ritual blood drinking depicted on painted pots. The man wore a copper funerary mask with shell eyes, golden eyebrows and nose ornament, with beardlike bangles. He was buried with numerous clay vessels, gold and silver nose ornaments, and 18 headdresses. He wore a tunic adorned with a cloth human figure with gilded head, hands, and feet. He held chisels used in metalworking and lay with a funerary bundle crammed with war clubs, spear-throwers, and gold plated shields. A young man, also wrapped in textiles, lay beneath him, perhaps a relative. Sacrificial offerings, a llama and a young woman, lay at a slightly higher level. All three tombs boasted of a small compartment nearby which were models of the burial chambers, a feature unlike Dos Cabezas. Burials 1 and 3 were less elaborately decorated, those of men of presumed lesser importance to the individual in Tomb 2. Each lay with a female sacrificial victim and fine clay vessels. Tomb 3 also contained the body of a 9-year-old child.

The excavators believe that the three men were related to one another, but their exact role in early Moche society remains a mystery. Were they warrior-priests, like the later Sipán lords, or was the man in Tomb 1 a metalsmith, a valued skill in Moche society? At this early stage in the research, we do not know.

### *Moche Metallurgy*

The artifacts buried with the Lords of Sipán testify to the skill of Moche metalsmiths. For example, each of a pair of ear ornaments from one tomb carries a warrior that is about the size of a thumb. Moche artisans had developed ways of hammering gold into fine sheets and embossing it to make raised designs. They used the technique of annealing—softening the metal and then hammering it into more elaborate forms—and they joined sheets with fine solder. The craftspeople also used gold as a setting for turquoise and shell ornaments, crafted crowns, circlets, necklaces, pins, and tweezers. Gold was in such short supply in prehistoric times that the metalworkers became expert at depletion gilding, an annealing technique that oxidizes the metal in an alloy of copper and gold to give the finished product a goldlike appearance, even when the gold content is as low as 12 percent by weight. Many of the large gold objects such as animals and plate decorations seized from the Inka by Pizarro's soldiers were in fact made of an elaborate alloy of some gold, silver, and copper.

## *Moche Society*

What little we know about Moche society as a whole comes from undisturbed burials and from museum studies of looted pots. They show that it consisted of farmers and fishermen, as well as skilled artisans and priests, who are depicted on pots with felinelike fangs and wearing puma skin headdresses. A few expert potters created superb modeled vessels with striking portraits of arrogant, handsome men who can only have been the leaders of Moche society. The potters modeled warriors, too, complete with shields and war clubs, well-padded helmets, and colorful cotton uniforms. Moche burials show that some members of society were much richer than others, lying in graves filled with as many as 50 vessels or with weapons or staffs of rank. We do not know exactly how Moche society was organized, but we can assume that the ruler wielded authority over a hierarchical state of warriors, priest-doctors, artisans, and the mass of the agricultural population.

Fortunately, the Moche artists and artisans allow us some more intimate glances at their society than do many civilizations. We see Moche soldiers in battle, charging their opponents with raised clubs. The defenders raise their feather-decked shields in defiance as the battle is fought to the death. The potters modeled drunks befuddled by maize beer and supported by their solicitous friends; women giving birth, with the midwife in attendance; and wives carrying babies on their backs in shawls and in wooden cradles suspended by nets. The women carried out all domestic activities, and the men served as warriors, farmers, and fishermen. We see them on a seal hunt, clubbing young seals on the rocky coast as their prey scurries in every direction. A clay llama strains reluctantly under its load, and a mouse eats a maize cob.

The pots also depict vividly what the Moche people wore. The men worked in short loincloths or cotton breeches and short sleeveless shirts underneath tunics that ended above the knee, fastened around the waist with colorful woven belts. More important people wore large mantles and headdresses made from puma heads or feathers from the highland jungles of Ecuador and Amazonia. Nearly everyone donned some form of headgear: brightly decorated cotton turbans wound around small caps and held in place with fabric chin straps were in common use. A small cloth protected the back of the neck from the burning sun. Moche women dressed in loose tunics that reached the knee and went bareheaded or draped a piece of cloth around their heads. Many men painted their lower legs and feet in bright colors and tattooed or daubed their faces with lines and other motifs. They often wore disk or crescent nose ornaments and cylindrical bar earrings, sometimes modeled in gold. Their necks bore large collars of stone beads or precious metal, and bracelets covered their arms and legs. Many people wore fiber sandals to protect their feet from the hot sand.

### *Collapse*

Like all Andean coastal societies, the Moche lived at the mercy of droughts and El Niños. Michael Moseley believes that a series of natural disasters struck Moche domains in the late sixth century. The first may have been a devastating drought cycle between 564 and 594, identified from the growth rings deep in mountain glaciers between Cuzco and Lake Titicaca. Crop yields in some valleys may have fallen as much as 20 percent. Some time between 650 and 700, a great earthquake struck the Andes, choking rivers with debris from landslides. Silt-laden floodwaters may have blocked irrigation canals, preventing water from reaching nearby fields. The silt flowed into the ocean, was washed ashore, and then blown inland by the prevailing winds to form huge sand dunes. Dense sandstorms may have blanketed entire villages and many acres of irrigated land.

The imperial capital itself was flooded by an El Niño just before A.D. 600, repaired, and then overwhelmed by coastal dunes that buried most of the city except the great huacas under fine sand. The same El Niño devastated the coastal fisheries. Anchovies vanished from inshore waters and torrential rains flooded the arid coastal plains, turning them into swamps and sweeping away entire villages and carefully maintained irrigation schemes. The smooth sides of Huaca del Sol were eroded and cratered by the constant rainfall. At this point, the southern Moche domains broke off from the state. The great lords abandoned Huaca del Sol and moved northward to Pampa Grande in the Lambayeque Valley, more than 50 kilometers (30 miles) from the Pacific and close to major irrigation works. But only half a century later another El Niño descended on the coast with catastrophic effects. Moche civilization collapsed. The houses of the Pampa Grande nobles were burned, perhaps as a result of a commoners' revolt against the harsh demands of *mit'a* taxation.

## Southern Pole: Nazca (200 B.C. – c. A.D. 700)

The south coast, with its smaller drainages and much sparser populations, saw the emergence of the Nazca state, centered on the Ica and Nazca drainages with outliers from the Chincha to Acari valleys. The earliest phases date to about 200 B.C.; the latest manifestations to about A.D. 600, or as much as a century later. At first, Nazca communities lived in "oases," terraced hillsides where surface runoff could be used for irrigation. But sometime after A.D. 500, perhaps in response to drought, the farmers tapped natural aquifers by digging ventilated tunnels, creating tunnel-fed farmlands (which were densely inhabited) out of formerly dry landscape.

Cahuachi, the Nazca capital, was 50 kilometers (31 miles) inland, on the south bank of the Nazca River. It began life as a dispersed farming village but grew to become an important ceremonial center, covering about 150 hectares (370 acres).

Archaeologist Helene Silverman believes Cahuachi was a unique ceremonial center of mounds, cemeteries, and shrines, the smaller ones kin-based. The Great Temple, a stepped platform 20 meters (66 feet) high capping a natural prominence—with a plaza, adobe rooms, and courts at the base—was the largest. With its natural springs, Cahuachi may have been a sacred place, but it was not a city. It was a location where offerings to the ancestors were made: Kin groups congregated at certain times in the sacred calendar for special ceremonies honoring their forebears. Nazca art from the site and other locations emphasizes masked ritual performances by priests and many mythical beings. Silverman and others believe many of the rituals at Cahuachi were connected with rain, water, and fertility. There are signs of human heads as valued trophies, too. Eventually building at Cahuachi virtually ceased as it became a vast cemetery and a place for votive offerings.

## *The Nazca Lines*

The Nazca lines are world-famous markings in the flat desert pampa, which lies between the tributaries of the Rio Nazca. The Pampa de Ingenio is covered with a layer of fine sand and pebbles that overlies thick, white alluvium. By sweeping away the topsoil, the Nazca created a web of white lines—triangles, rectangles, spirals, and zigzags—some mere narrow tracks, others as wide as an airport runway (Figure 18.5). On the ground the lines make no sense, but high above the desert in a helicopter they focus into birds, monkeys, a whale, spiders, and plants. Armed with aerial photographs and even satellite images, astronomer-archaeologists have now pored over the Pampa de Ingenio with all the armory of modern science. Their photographs reveal not only geometric figures but also more than 1,300 kilometers

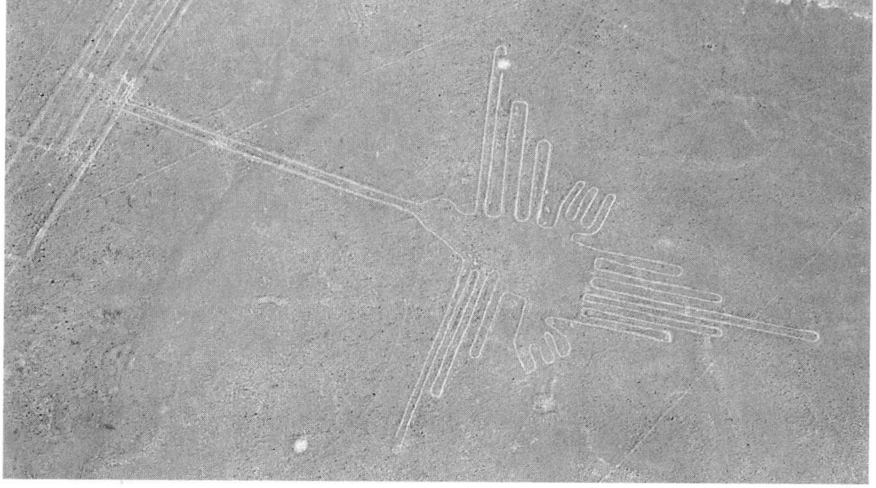

**Figure 18.5** Nazca lines, scratched out on the desert plain in the form of lines, some representing birds and other symbols.

(800 miles) of straight lines, some as much as 20 kilometers (12 miles) long. Some radiate from hills, interconnected by more linear marks, which lead to well-watered areas and may have served as pathways. All the drawings were of transitory importance, for many figures were drawn across earlier ones, as if they were no longer important. Geoglyphs, like those at Nazca, occur elsewhere in the Andes and were a common part of Native American belief, but their precise significance eludes us. Did the lines and figures form part of rituals that connected the living and spiritual worlds of the Nazca? Anthropologist Johan Reinhard has pointed out that mountain gods protect humans, guard their livestock, and control the weather. They are associated with lakes, rivers, and the ocean—the ultimate source of both water and fertility. Reinhard thinks coastal people like the Nazca shared in some of these beliefs, for local mountains figured prominently in rainmaking rituals because they were the source of water for vital irrigation canals. Thus, the Nazca lines were political, social, and religious phenomena that were deeply entrenched in the local world, so much so that those who traversed them became transformed into ritual beings as they arrived at the sacred center—a transformation wrought by dance, elaborate costumes and masks, and shamanistic trance.

## The Middle Horizon: The First Highland States (A.D. 600–1000)

While Moche ruled the north coast of Peru, two highland urban centers, Tiwanaku and Wari, rose to prominence in the south-central Andes. They reached their peak during the so-called Middle Horizon, which lasted from A.D. 600 to 1000.

### *Tiwanaku (A.D. 200–1000)*

Two thousand years ago, two kingdoms dominated the shores of Lake Titicaca: Pukara and Tiwanaku (see Chapter 17). Pukara ruled the northern Titicaca basin at first but faded into comparative obscurity, while its southern neighbor became the center of the first Andean empire.

Tiwanaku lies in the altiplano country at the southern end of the central Andes, where camelid herding was always important. By A.D. 200 Tiwanaku was a major population center. By A.D. 600 Tiwanaku traded extensively around the lake's southern shores. Copper was especially important and probably developed independently of the well-established copper technology on the north coast. Well-made Tiwanaku textiles, pottery, wood carvings, and gold objects have come from well-preserved burials on the coast, hundreds of miles from the altiplano. Llama caravans played an important role in Tiwanaku's coastal trade, carrying wool and all kinds of trade goods, most of them of lightweight construction and especially designed for llama transport. At its height during and after the eighth century, the capital covered more than 400 hectares (1,000 acres) and was able to support as many as 20,000 people because of elaborate, irrigated raised-field systems that covered at least 75 square kilometers (30 square miles). Many thousands more lived in

**Figure 18.6** The "Gateway God" at Tiwanaku.

the surrounding Tiwanaku Valley. Modern experiments have shown that such fields are both frost resistant and highly productive under potatoes, with yields as much as 400 percent higher than dry plots on surrounding hillsides.

Tiwanaku was both an economic and a religious force. The great enclosure and temple of Kalasasaya is dominated by a large earth platform faced with stones and aligned with the cardinal points of the compass. Carved stelae serve as symbols of imperial power. Nearby, a rectangular enclosure is bounded with a row of upright stones and a doorway carved with an anthropomorphic god, believed to be the creator deity, Viracocha (Figure 18.6). A large artificial platform, the Akapana—about 200 meters (650 feet) along the sides and some 15 meters (50 feet) high—dominates the city. This terraced platform had massive, stepped retaining walls, with a sunken court on the summit that was surrounded by priestly residences. During the rains, water would gush out of this court onto the terraces, ending up in a large moat that surrounded the ceremonial precincts. Alan Kolata, who is studying Tiwanaku, believes this precinct was a symbolic island, like the sacred Island of the Sun in nearby Lake Titicaca. This was where Tiwanaku's leaders would appear on ceremonial occasions, dressed, so sculpture tells us, like gods, with elaborate headdresses, or as condors or pumas. There is ample evidence that the Tiwanaku religion revolved around human sacrifice. One recently excavated temple contained the skeleton of a young warrior, perhaps a captive, sacrificed in A.D. 600.

Tiwanaku's striking art style represents a powerful iconography. The motifs include jaguars and eagles, as well as anthropomorphic gods being attended by lesser deities or messengers. The same styles occur over much of the southern Andes.

Tiwanaku carved out an empire in the south-central Andes by a combination of aggressive and tightly controlled trading activity, judicious conquest, and colonization. Many of its institutions endured, albeit in modified form, in Inka imperial rule in later centuries. Tiwanaku's empire was long-lived by Andean standards, enduring two or three centuries after Moche collapsed on the north coast. In the end, Tiwanaku may have succumbed to a severe drought cycle, which persisted over several decades in the eleventh century. Eventually, the central government collapsed, the city's field systems fell into disrepair, and the empire dissolved into its constituent parts.

## *Wari (A.D. 500–750)*

Tiwanaku was by no means unique, for other states of lesser importance flourished in the highlands at the same time. As Moche faltered on the north coast, a new state, Wari, arose in the Ayacucho region of the central Andes. The influence of Tiwanaku can be seen at the capital in the Mantaro Valley, an important ceremonial center, covering several square kilometers, that stands on a hill and is associated with huge stone walls and many dwellings. The Wari art styles show some Pukara influence, especially in anthropomorphic feline, eagle, and serpent beings depicted on ceramic vessels. Like their southern neighbors, the Wari people seem to have revered a Viracocha-like being. By A.D. 800, their domains extended from Moche country in the Lambayeque Valley on the northern coast to south of Nazca territory, down the Moquequa Valley of the south-central Andes and into the highlands south of Cuzco. They were expert traders who probably expanded their domain through conquest, commercial enterprise, and perhaps religious conversion. Storehouses and roads were probably maintained by the state. As with the Inka of later centuries, the state controlled food supplies and labor.

The Cerro Baul site in the Moquequa Valley was a fortified settlement placed by the Wari on an impregnable mesa, with only a single, heavily defended trail giving access to the flat summit, where the inhabitants constructed complexes of rectangular structures, courts, patios, and occasional D-shaped buildings. Cerro Baul is a powerful Wari presence in a foreign valley, perhaps sited there to exploit local sources of copper, lapis lazuli, or obsidian.

Wari was a highly stratified society, organized along kin lines, with a nobility that controlled elaborate irrigation works. Its rulers built and maintained a long canal that linked high-altitude springs and streams with acres of terraced fields on steep, lower slopes. The constantly expanding terrace works supported thousands of people, for they enabled the growing of high-yielding local maize strains.

Wari was expanded by the simple and shrewd expedient of moving its people into unoccupied highland valleys and then building elaborate and well-protected irrigation canals to bring water to new field systems. In each valley, members of the Wari nobility lived among the local people in rectangular administrative centers, thereby forming a string of highland colonies that linked mountain basins from near Cuzco northward for nearly 1,000 kilometers (600 miles). Wari straddled key trade routes across the mountains and down to the Pacific, a strategic location that kept it in touch with Tiwanaku and other major kingdoms. As with the Inka of later centuries, the state controlled food supplies and labor through an anual *mit'a* tax. Wari enjoyed long-standing connections with the Ica and Nazca valleys on the south coast, but it never seized or colonized coastal valleys because its agricultural methods were unsuited to the desert.

Wari itself was abandoned in the eighth century A.D., perhaps as a result of internal revolt, but its art styles persisted on the coast for at least two more centuries. Its aggressive reclamation of mountain slopes for maize farming resulted in rapid population growth and in intense political competition in the highlands. Both Wari and Tiwanaku were turning points in Peruvian prehistory, a stage when small regional states became integrated into much larger political units. This unification may have been achieved by conquest and other coercive means, but the iconography shared by many coastal and highland Peruvians at the time must have been a powerful catalyst for closer political unity. There was constant and often intensive interaction between two poles of Andean civilization in the highlands and lowlands, each with quite different food resources and products. This interaction, long a feature of Andean life, was to intensify in the centuries ahead.

## The Late Intermediate Period (A.D. 900–1400)

As Wari and Tiwanaku collapsed, political power on the highlands fragmented, and the center of development shifted once again to the coast. The decline of Moche in the Lambayeque Valley left somewhat of a vacuum, filled by the Sicán culture after A.D. 700. Sicán, centered on the Lambayeque Valley and remarkable for its magnificent gold work, reached its peak between 900 and 1100. In Sicán society, metals of all kinds served as markers of social status and wealth—and as a prestigious medium of political, social, and religious expression—since access to artifacts and ornaments in different ores was carefully limited according to rank. Sicán lords encouraged intensive metal production, as well as seagoing trade in copper and other metals far to the north along the Ecuadorian coast. At the same time, they supervised massive irrigation works from major centers like Tucume in the Leche Valley. These various cities were sometimes linked by intervalley canals, requiring constant cooperation between lords in neighboring centers. If oral traditions are to be believed, many of them were related to one another and shared common ancestors.

Between 1050 and 1100, a massive El Niño caused widespread flooding and disruption. The royal precincts at Sicán itself were burned as political power shifted west to the El Purgatorio region. In 1375, an expanding Chimú state overthrew Sicán and absorbed its domains into a new empire.

### *Chimor (the Chimú state) (A.D. 1100–1400)*

Chimor was born out of the political chaos that followed the collapse of the Moche capital at Pampa Grande. The Moche Valley had long been densely cultivated, but the Chimú now embarked on more ambitious irrigation schemes: They built large storage reservoirs and terraced hundreds of miles of hillside to control the flow of water down steep slopes. One channel extended nearly 32 kilometers (20 miles) from the Chicama Valley to the new capital, Chan Chan, to supplement local water supplies. The Chimú created thousands of hectares of new fields and used water from great distances to harvest two or three crops a year from plots where only one crop had been possible before. So effective were these irrigation techniques that the Chimú controlled more than 12 river valleys with at least 50,600 cultivable hectares (125,000 acres), all of them farmed with hoes or digging sticks. Today, the local Indians water their maize crops approximately every ten days, and this probably was the practice in Chimú times.

During the thirteenth century, the rulers of Chimor embarked on an ambitious campaign of conquest and expansion, which continued intermittently for two centuries. They soon absorbed the Sicán city-states and the Lambayeque Valley. By 1470, Chimor encompassed over 1,000 kilometers (620 miles) of coastline, two-thirds of all irrigated lands along the Peruvian coast, bringing the northern pole of early Andean civilization under the rule of a single state.

According to Chimor oral traditions, between nine and eleven rulers ruled the kingdom from Chan Chan before Minchancamon, an ambitious conqueror who began fighting the Inka in 1462. Minchancamon and his predecessors governed through a network of hereditary local nobility. His courtiers held specific ranks, such as Blower of the Shell Trumpet; Master of the Litter and Thrones; and Preparer of the Way, the official who scattered powdered shell dust wherever the ruler was about to walk. An archaeologist working at Chan Chan between 1969 and 1970 found a layer of powdered shell dust on a bench in a forecourt, perhaps evidence that the Preparer of the Way had been at work. The various provinces of the kingdom were ruled by loyal local leaders. They enjoyed not only tribute privileges but also rights to crops and land and to agricultural labor by commoners. Perhaps the most privileged members of society were the *oquetlupec*, herb curers paid by the state to look after the sick. This was a hierarchical, highly organized society with strict social classes of nobles and commoners.

The focus of the Chimú state was Chan Chan, a huge complex of walled compounds, which covers nearly 20 square kilometers (8 square miles) near the Pacific at the mouth of the Moche Valley. The central part consists of nine large enclosures laid out in a sort of broken rectangle, which covers 6 square kilometers (2.3 square miles) (Figure 18.7). Each enclosure was erected by *mit'a* labor and probably functioned as the palace for the current ruler of Chan Chan, who built himself new headquarters near those of his predecessors. The adobe walls of these compounds once stood as high as 10 meters (33 feet) and covered areas as large as 200 by 600 meters (670 by 2,000 feet). The walls were not constructed to defend the rulers but to provide privacy and some shelter from the ocean winds. Each enclosure had its own water supply, a burial platform, and lavishly decorated residential rooms roofed with cane frames covered with earth and grass. The same enclosure that served as a palace during life became the ruler's burial place in death, for the Chimú god-kings were buried under platforms once reserved for deities. Some 6,000 *karaka*, nobles, lived in 30 smaller compounds with low walls. More than 26,000 artisans

**Figure 18.7** Chan Chan, with its great enclosures reserved for the elite.

and their families, many of them metalworkers and weavers, lived in tracts of small adobe and reed-mat houses on the western side of the city. Farmers and fishermen lived outside the central precincts.

Chimú rulers soon learned the value of efficient communications. Officially maintained roadways, which connected each valley in their domain with the capital, enabled them to move their armies rapidly from one place to the next. The rural routes were little more than tracks between low adobe walls or widely spaced posts, mostly following centuries-old paths through the fields. In the densely populated valleys, Chimú roads were between 4.5 and 7.5 meters (15 and 25 feet) across. In some places the roadway widened dramatically to 24 meters (80 feet) or more. These were the roads that carried gold ornaments and fine-hammered vessels to Chan Chan and textiles and fine, black-painted vessels throughout the empire. The traveler would occasionally encounter heavily laden llamas carrying goods to market, but most loads were carried on people's backs, for the Chimú never developed the wheeled cart. All revenues and tribute passed along the official roadways, as did newly conquered peoples being resettled in some area far from their original homeland. This draconian resettlement tactic was so successful that the Inka adopted it. The ruler then would install his own appointee in the new lands, in a compound palace that was a smaller version of Chan Chan itself.

The Chimú empire extended far south, at least to Casma and perhaps near modern Lima, but the main focus of civilization was on the northern Peruvian littoral, where large-scale irrigation was a practical reality. Chimú armies fought with powerful neighbors to the south, among them the chief of Pachacamac, who controlled some narrow valleys south of Lima. Pachacamac had long been a venerated shrine and already boasted a terraced temple covering 0.3 hectares (0.75 acres). Later, the Inka built a vast Temple of the Sun at Pachacamac, an irregular trapezoid in a commanding position on a rocky hill.

For all its wide-ranging military activities and material wealth, the Chimú empire was vulnerable to attack from outside. The massive irrigation works of the northern river valleys were easily disrupted by an aggressive conqueror. We know little of the defenses, except for Paramonga in the Fortaleza Valley, a massive terraced structure of rectangular adobes that overlooks the probable southern limits of Chimú territory. The Chimú were vulnerable to prolonged drought, too, for the storage capacity of their great irrigation works was only sufficient to carry them over one or two lean seasons. Moreover, perhaps the irrigated desert soils became too saline for agriculture, so that crop yields fell drastically at a time when population densities were rising sharply. Since the Chimú depended on a highly specialized agricultural system, once that system was disrupted—whether by natural or artificial causes—military conquest and control of the irrigation network were easy. Between 1462 and 1470, Minchancamon fought constantly with Inka armies. Some years later, the Inka prevailed. Chimor became part of Tawantinsuyu, and thousands of Chimú artisans were resettled in Cuzco to serve their new masters.

## The Late Horizon: The Inka Empire (A.D. 1476–1534)

During the Late Horizon, the Andean region was united into a single empire under Inka rule. Tawantinsuyu was ruled from Cuzco in the south-central Andes by a people who, like the Aztec of Mesoamerica, rose from total obscurity with great rapidity.

### *Origins*

The collapse of Tiwanaku and Wari during the late first millennium left a political vacuum in the south-central Andes, filled by many small kingdoms vying for power and control of lucrative trade monopolies. The Inka called these centuries *auca runa*, "the time of the warriors." At the time the Inka were a small-scale farming society, their homeland lying to the northwest of the Titicaca basin in the area around Cuzco. They lived in small villages, organized in kin groups known as *ayllu*; these groups claimed a common ancestry and owned the land in common. Their *ayllu* leaders contributed labor to one another as a means of organizing and distributing resources on a reciprocal basis. The *ayllu* were legitimized in their land ownership and protected by the ancestors.

The later Inka rulers clothed their origins in a glorious panoply of heroic deeds, but the earliest Inka rulers were probably petty war leaders (*sinchi*), elected officials whose success was measured by their victories and booty. Unreliable Inka genealogies speak of at least eight, probably legendary, rulers between 1200 and 1438. But when Viracocha Inka rose to power at the beginning of the fifteenth century, he turned from raiding to permanent conquest and soon presided over a small kingdom centered on Cuzco. Viracocha Inka became the living god, the first in a series of constant religious changes that kept the new kingdom under tight control. At about the same time a new religious cult emerged, that of Inti, a celestial divine ancestor associated with the sun.

### *Split Inheritance and Conquest*

Around 1438, a brilliant warrior named Cusi Inka Yupanqui was crowned Inka. He assumed the name Pachakuti (He Who Remakes the World) and set about transforming the Inka state. He reworked an age-old Andean ancestor cult and the associated law of split inheritance, changing Inka royal life fundamentally. A dead ruler was mummified. His palace, servants, and possessions were still considered his property and were maintained by all his male descendants except his successor, normally one of his sons. The deceased's mummy attended great ceremonies. Those entrusted to look after the king ate and talked with him, just as if his life were still going on. The symbolism was vitally important, for dead rulers were living sons of Inti and visible links with the gods, the very embodiment of the Inka state and of the fertility of nature. Meanwhile split inheritance gave the ascending ruler prestige but few possessions. The new king had to acquire wealth so he could both live in royal splendor and provide for his mummy in the future—and the only wealth in the highland kingdom was taxable labor.

Every adult in Inka country had to render *mit'a* service to the state. This system repaired bridges and roads, cultivated state-owned lands, manned the armies, and carried out public works (Figure 18.8). It was a reciprocal system. The state, or those benefiting from the work, had to feed and entertain those doing it. The split inheritance of the Inka rulers meant that all taxes levied by their predecessors went to them and not to the newcomer. The latter had to develop a new tax base and could do so in only two ways: by levying more labor from existing taxpayers or by conquering new lands. Since the Inka rulers needed land to provide food for those who worked for them and the earlier kings owned most of the land near Cuzco, the only way a new ruler could obtain his own royal estates was by expansion into new territory. The conquest had to be permanent, the conquered territory had to be controlled and taxed, and the ruler's subjects had to be convinced of the value of a policy of long-term conquest.

**Figure 18.8** Intensive use of land by the Inka: terracing in the Urubamba Valley.

The Inka rulers turned into brilliant propagandists, reminding everyone that they were gods and that the welfare of everyone depended on the prosperity of all rulers, past and present, and on constant military conquest. There were initial economic advantages, too, in the form of better protection against famine. Also, the rulers were careful to reward prowess in battle. Nobles were promoted to new posts and awarded insignia that brought their lifestyle ever closer to that of the king. Even a brave commoner could become a member of the secondary nobility. A highly complicated set of benefits, economic incentives, rewards, and justifications fueled and nourished the Inka conquests. Their successful ideology gave them a crucial advantage over their neighbors. Within a decade of Pachakuti's accession they were masters of the southern highlands. In less than a century the tiny kingdom taken over by Pachakuti had become a vast empire.

The topography of mountains and deserts provided refuge for myriad ethnic groups, creating a rich cultural diversity within Tawantinsuyu. This very diversity made conquest relatively easy but consolidation of territorial gains extremely challenging. Even under the all-embracing Inka political umbrella there were no fewer than 80 provinces within the empire. Topa Yupanqui (1471–1493) extended the Inka empire into Ecuador, northern Argentina, parts of Bolivia, and Chile. His armies also conquered the Chimú state, whose water supplies Topa already controlled. Another king, Huanya Capac, ruled for 32 years after Topa Yupanqui and pushed the empire deeper into Ecuador.

## *State Organization*

The Inka rulers developed an efficient administrative system to run their empire, one based firmly on the precedents of earlier societies. Tawantinsuyu was divided into four large provinces known as *suyu* (quarters), each subdivided into smaller provinces, some of them coinciding with older, conquered kingdoms. The conquered peoples in the Inka empire were usually ruled by a leading member of a local family. These hereditary chiefs were a form of secondary, non-Inka nobility who governed a taxpaying population of a hundred people or more, but all the really important government posts were held by Inka nobles. The Inka rulers realized, however, that the essence of efficient government in such varied topography was efficient communications, so the road builders commandeered a vast network of age-old Indian highways from the states they conquered. They linked them in a coordinated system with regular rest houses so that they could move armies, trade goods, and messengers from one end of the kingdom to the other in short order.

The Inkas' passion for organization impinged on everyone's life. Their society was organized into 12 age divisions for the census and for tax assessment, divisions based on both physical changes like puberty and major social events like marriage. The most important stage was adulthood, which lasted as long as one could do a day's work.

All the census and other data of the empire were on knotted strings, *quipu*, which were a complex and sophisticated record-keeping system that seems to have been so efficient that it more than made up for the lack of writing. The word comes from the word "knot" (*Khipu*). Each *quipu* was a length of cord, held horizontally, from which numerous yards of different colors were suspended. Each of these secondary cords supported a descending hierarchy of depended colored strings. The scribe entered the data by using different types of knots. Other information was encoded by cord length, color, and hierarchical position. Unfortunately, the *quipu* code was lost at the Conquest with the disintegration of the royal court, but it was basically an inventory system that reinforced human memory. This, and an efficient road system, enabled the Inka to govern enormous tracts of highland and lowland territory with remarkable, standardized efficiency. The *quipu* was also a powerful instrument for enforcing social conformity, codifying laws, and providing data for the inspectors—who regularly visited each household to check that everyone was engaged in productive work and living in sanitary conditions.

Everything about the Inka lifeway stressed conformity and the need to respect and obey the central government.

## *Cuzco*

Inka political and religious power was centered on major urban complexes like Cuzco, where the four quarters of the empire met. Laid out on a cruciform plan, Cuzco had sufficient water to allow stone-lined channels down the major streets, providing better sanitation than any European city of the time. Two small rivers ran through the city, one of them dividing the great central plaza into two parts. Aucaypata, to the east, was surrounded on three sides by the closely fitted granite walls of the Inkas' palaces and other ceremonial buildings. The Coriancha, the Temple of the Sun, was a few hundred meters south of the central plaza, six one-roomed buildings with gold-covered walls that surrounded a central courtyard. A close-fitting masonry wall 4.5 meters (15 feet) high surrounded the entire complex. The Spaniards described a garden of golden plants, adorned with replicas of maize with silver stems and golden ears in the center of the temple. This lay in front of a room that contained an enormous gold image of the sun inlaid with semiprecious stones.

Inka architects, master builders in stone, had red granite blocks from distant quarries dragged to the capital. Hundreds of stoneworkers dressed the stone by using river cobbles to pound concave depressions in the blocks and then trimming them to ensure a close fit with their neighbors. Inka masonry walls are so perfectly fitted that it is often impossible to drive a thin knife blade through the cracks between neighboring stones (Figure 18.9).

Like all early royal capitals, Cuzco was a major religious and administrative center and also an enormous repository. Rows of identical fieldstone storehouses contained vast inventories of cloaks (some covered with gold and silver disks that

**Figure 18.9** Inka architecture at the fortress of Sacsahuaman, near Cuzco.

gave the effect of chain mail), metal objects, textiles, tropical bird feathers, woolen garments, weapons, and tribute from all corners of Tawantinsuyu. Dozens of outlying and often very inaccessible centers paid tribute to the capital (Figure 18.10).

### *An Empire in Trouble*

The Inka ruler held court in Cuzco, surrounded by plotting factions. One villain was the very institution of split inheritance that fueled Inka military conquest. Every ruler faced increasingly complex governance problems as a result. The need for more and more conquests caused great military, economic, and administrative stress. The logistics of long-distance military campaigns were horrendous, and the soldiers had to be fed from state-owned land, not royal estates. Moreover, although their tactics were well adapted to open country, where their armies were invincible, the rulers eventually had to fight in forests, where they fared badly. Meanwhile the empire had grown so large that communication became a lengthier and lengthier process, compounded by the great diversity of peoples living within the Inka domain. Also, the increasing number of high-ranking nobles devoted to the interests of dead rulers led to chronic factionalism in Cuzco. Under its glittering facade, Tawantinsuyu was becoming a rotten apple. In the end, the Inka empire was overthrown not by Peruvians but by a tiny band of foreigners with firearms, who could exploit the inherent vulnerability of such a hierarchical, conforming society.

## The Spanish Conquest (A.D. 1532–1534)

When Spanish conquistador Francisco Pizarro landed in Peru in 1532, the Inka state was in some political chaos, its people already decimated by smallpox and other diseases introduced by earlier European visitors to Central America. Inka Huanya

**Figure 18.10** Forgotten for 400 years after the Spanish conquest, Macchu Picchu was rediscovered for archaeology by American explorer Hiram Bingham in 1911.

Capac had died in an epidemic in 1525. The empire was plunged into a civil war between his son Huascar and another son, Atahuallpa, half-brother to Huascar. Atahuallpa eventually prevailed. As he moved south from Ecuador to consolidate his territory, he learned that Pizarro had landed in Peru.

The Spaniards had vowed to make Peru part of Spain and were bent on plunder and conquest. Pizarro arrived in the guise of a diplomat, captured Atahuallpa by treachery, ransomed him for a huge quantity of gold, and then brutally murdered him. A year later the Spaniards captured the Inka capital with a tiny army. They took over the state bureaucracy and appointed Manco Inka as puppet ruler. Three years later, Manco Inka turned on his masters in a bloody revolt. Its suppression finally destroyed the greatest of the Andean empires.

## Summary

By 200 B.C., increasingly complex city-states had appeared along the north coast of the Andean region, ruled by a powerful hereditary elite. The Moche state flourished between A.D. 100 and 700, a multivalley polity based on trade and intensive irrigation agriculture supported by taxed labor. The burials of Sipán lords reveal the great power and riches of Moche civilization, based on as-yet-unknown religious beliefs. In the south-central Andes, Tiwanaku and Wari rose to prominence during the first millennium A.D., controlling trade over a wide area of highlands and lowlands. The Chimú state emerged from the chaos of the Moche collapse in A.D. 1100, unifying much of the coast under rulers based at Chan Chan on the north coast. Chimú was absorbed into the Inka empire in 1470, at which point highlands and lowlands were joined in a single political unit. Andean civilization ended with the Spanish conquest of 1532.

## Guide to Further Reading

Michael Moseley, *The Incas and Their Ancestors,* 2nd ed. (New York: Thames and Hudson, 2000) is the major synthesis of Andean archaeology. Up-to-date and authoritative, it includes a comprehensive bibliography. For Moche, see Walter Alva and Christopher Donnan, *Royal Tombs of Sipán* (Los Angeles: Fowler Museum of Cultural History, 1993). This lavishly illustrated book includes a general description of Moche civilization. See also Christopher Donnan and Donna McClelland, eds., *The Burial Theme in Moche Iconography* (Washington, DC: Dumbarton Oaks, 1979). Alan Kolata, *Tiwanaku* (Oxford: Blackwell, 1993) offers an excellent account of this important kingdom; Clark L. Erickson, "Applied Archaeology and Rural Development: Archaeology's Potential Contribution to the Future," *Journal of the Steward Anthropological Society* 20, nos. 1 and 2 (1992): 1–16 describes raised field agriculture on the altiplano. For Wari, see Katherina J. Schreiber, "Conquest and Consolidation: A Comparison of the Wari and Inka Occupations of a Highland Peruvian Valley," *American Antiquity* 52, no. 2 (1987): 266–284, where specialized references will be found. For Chimor and Chan Chan, see Michael Moseley and Kent Day, eds., *Chan Chan: Andean Desert City* (Albuquerque: University of New Mexico Press, 1982). For Nazca, see Anthony Aveni, *Between the Lines: The Mystery of the Ancient Ground Drawings of Ancient Nazca* (Austin: University of Texas Press, 2000). A growing literature surrounds the Inka civilization. The outdated classic is John Rowe, *Inca Culture at the Time of the Spanish Conquest,* Vol. 2: *The Handbook of South American Indians* (Washington, DC: Smithsonian Institution, 1946). See also Geoffrey W. Conrad and Arthur A. Demarest, *Religion and Empire: The Dynamics of Aztec and Inca Expansionism* (Cambridge: Cambridge University Press, 1984), which contains an admirable account of split inheritance and royal ancestor worship. John Hyslop, *The Inca Road System* (Orlando, FL: Academic Press, 1984) and *Inka Settlement Patterns* (Austin: University of Texas Press, 1990) are excellent studies. For governance, see Terence D'Altroy, *Provincial Power in the Inka Empire* (Washington, DC: Smithsonian Institution, 1993).

*Chapter 19*

# Epilogue

Khmer soldiers and war elephants advance to war. Angkor Wat, Cambodia.

Similar but Different
Interconnectedness
Volatility
The Stream of Time

*The absence of romance in my history will, I fear, detract somewhat from its interest; but I shall be content if it is judged useful by those inquirers who desire an exact knowledge of the past as an aid to the interpretation of the future. Thucydides,* **History of the Peloponnesian War** *(431–413 B.C.).*

Spanish conquistador Bernal Diaz del Castillo was the last survivor of Hernán Cortés's motley band of soldier-adventurers. Born in the year Columbus landed in the Indies, Diaz died on his estates in Guatemala in 1581. His life spanned the greater part of the Spanish subjugation of Central and Latin America, but he never became wealthy. Blessed with a graphic memory and a great sense of the dramatic, the aged conquistador bequeathed his family and history a priceless account of the Spanish conquest of Mexico and of Aztec civilization. He wrote his *History of the Conquest of New Spain* while in his 70s and added a preliminary note to it at the age of 84. Diaz was no writer, but his memories of Tenochtitlán and the brilliance of Aztec civilization resonate with a vividness that places the reader by the young soldier's side. Nearly three-quarters of a century later, every detail of the great capital and of a vanished civilization was still etched in an old man's mind. The colors, the costumes, the smells, the bustle of Tenochtitlán's great market, all come down to us across nearly five centuries with an immediacy one can never gain from archaeological sources alone. Diaz wrote of a society headed by a supreme ruler, Moctezuma, who lived in great state and was surrounded by immense wealth. Hundreds of people attended to his personal well-being and administered his government. And high above Tenochtitlán towered the great temple of the sun god, Huitzilopochtli, with its great drum that could be heard 10 kilometers (6 miles) away. The blood-stained shrine of the god symbolized the immense power of the divine forces that controlled the fate of the Aztec world. Aztec civilization was a pyramid, with all political, religious, and economic power centered in one person—Moctezuma, the *tlatoani*, "the Speaker." But this same ruler and his predecessors and equivalents in other societies were often the victims of economic circumstances, presiding as they did over societies based on the efficient collection of tribute and the labor of thousands of commoners.

## Similar but Different

We have told the story of the early civilizations on a deliberately global canvas, trying to give equal coverage to state-organized societies that were widely separated in time and space. This has allowed us to show that all civilizations do not organize the world either today or in the past in the same way as we do. These differing worldviews resonate through the centuries and millennia in many ways. Great public edifices like Maya ceremonial centers or Angkor Wat reproduced the cosmos, the symbolic world, in stone, plaster, and other durable materials. They provided the setting for lavish public ceremonies, which validated the special relationship between the ruler and the spiritual realm and between the ruler and the ruled. Archives of codices, inscriptions, papyri, and clay tablets sometimes illuminate the philosophies and spiritual beliefs of early civilizations. So do distinctive art traditions, like those of the Chavín of the Andes or Classical Greece. The lesson from all these sources is clear: Comparisons except at the most general level between different early civilizations mean little, for the differences between them outweigh the similarities. For example, many early archaeologists compared the pyramids of Egypt with those of the Mesoamericans, arguing for a possible cultural connection between them. But closer examination of both Egyptian and Maya pyramids revealed major architectural differences, quite apart from the fundamentally dissimilar religious beliefs that lay behind their construction.

The popular literature still abounds with stirring accounts of how the ancient Egyptians sailed across the Atlantic and founded Maya civilization; one fantasy sees native copper ore from the shores of Lake Superior as the catalyst for the development of all early civilization. But historical reality is much more complicated. The art and artifacts of the Egyptians bear no resemblance to those of the Maya—as archaeologist John Lloyd Stephens pointed out in the 1840s. Nor has a single Egyptian object ever come to light in an archaeological site anywhere in the Americas. The great traditions of early, preindustrial civilization developed independently from one another, in the Near East and along the Nile River, in East Asia, and in the Americas. They were markedly different from one another in their architecture, artifacts, and technologies; in their social and political institutions; and in their religious beliefs. But they shared one common characteristic: Each of them nurtured a far more complex human society than ever before—a civilization. And all of them allowed denser populations than ever before, supported by intensive agriculture and complex administrative structures but at the price of personal freedom and built-in social inequality.

This process of becoming more complex varied in detail from one culture to another, and (as we pointed out in Chapter 2) it would be rash to invoke a single overarching theory to explain this complex transformation. That it was connected with climate change, with environmental circumscription, with new styles of leadership, and with responses to the need to grow and store food efficiently is obvious. But the processes by which these changes came about varied considerably from one area to the next. In Mesopotamia and Egypt, competition between neighboring leaders for the control of trading networks may have been an important catalyst for greater political and social complexity. In the Maya lowlands, shamanistic powers were a major factor in establishing royal lineages.

The important point is that cultural, political, and social complexity arose in widely separated areas; this complexity was diverse in origin but remarkable in sharing a number of common features:

- Intensive, well-organized agriculture, which supported dense populations but at the cost of great social inequality and sometimes catastrophic environmental degradation
- Strongly centralized political and social organization, which institutionalized social inequality—the right of a tiny minority of the population to command the labor of thousands of farmers, artisans, and slaves
- Stratified social classes with a well-defined nobility, often closely linked by kin ties, at the peak of a pyramidlike society in which upward mobility was difficult to achieve except on the battlefield
- A universal set of religious beliefs, which often supported the notion of the leader as a divine monarch, a living god on earth
- Elaborate public architecture, which usually mirrored the symbolic architecture of the state: for example, Angkor Wat or Teotihuacán or, in their own way, the Parthenon at Athens and the Colosseum at Rome
- A closely organized, centralized bureaucracy, backed by force or the threat of force; this bureaucracy administered the gathering of tribute, a major activity in many preindustrial civilizations
- Some form of record keeping, usually a written script in the hands of powerful officials; power came from literacy
- Some type of communication system by land or water, often road networks or caravan routes, usually administered by the state
- Cities, or lesser but still large administrative centers and agglomerations of population, and a hierarchy of lesser centers positioned strategically across the landscape.

Preindustrial civilizations developed in different parts of the world in remarkably similar ways because, in the absence of fossil fuels, complex societies had to rely on the ability to organize enormous labor forces to accomplish their goals. These goals were such phenomena as large-scale irrigation works (Moche Peru), the Great Wall (Han China), and vast road systems (Imperial Rome); but they could never have been built or have operated efficiently without highly centralized control of the labor to build and maintain them, the crops they yielded, or the armies who guarded and used them. Built-in and accepted social inequality; political and economic mechanisms to ensure social conformity; and sheer, naked force or the threat of it were the foundations of preindustrial civilizations everywhere, simply because no one—whether pharaoh, Chinese leader, or Maya lord—could ever develop other ways of ensuring and controlling the loyalties of those who kept them in power. Ideology and ritual sanctions played their part but were often ineffective in the long term. The institutions, the beliefs, the nature of kingship itself might differ, but the mechanisms of centralization—of control of every aspect of human life—were always basically the same. Such societies endured in one form or another over many centuries in the Near East, Asia, and the Americas, but they were remarkable for their volatility and their penchant for rapid collapse.

## Interconnectedness

We live in a world of global economic systems and instant communication, where market forces in Asia can have radical effects on the economies of North America and Europe, where the health of, say, the computer industry in Sweden is dependent on the abilities of software writers in India. A web of interconnectedness joins us all, large nation and small, vast continent or tiny Pacific island. We are tied together by ever-changing commercial, social, and political links—sharing information, competing for raw materials and in different marketplaces, and occasionally waging war. Historians like Immanuel Wallerstein have long written of the emerging world economic system, which resulted from the European age of discovery between the fifteenth and nineteenth centuries. Anthropologist Eric Wolf has described the many, often subtle, ties that have linked widely separated parts of the world—the industrializing nations of Europe with faraway tribal groups who controlled fur trade outlets, gold deposits, or fertile agricultural land.

But these interconnections are nothing new. Enormous trading networks, albeit on a smaller, less intense scale, developed much earlier in history. Sumerian Ur and Uruk maintained regular trading connections with the Levant, across the Iranian plateau with Afghanistan, and through the Persian Gulf with the Indus Valley. By the time of Christ, China, India, Mesopotamia, and much of the Near East had been part of a large global trading network for many centuries. The network brought Chinese silk to Alexandria and Rome, cheap Indian textiles to the Nile, and precious stones from the Red Sea to the Persian Gulf. Some Mesoamerican cities maintained irregular trading connections with Andean coastal states and, indeed, may have learned from them the art of metallurgy. These interconnections were vital to the survival of early civilizations. The Sumerians obtained their timber and metal ore from their highland neighbors and traded grain for semiprecious stones. The Harappan civilization of the Indus Valley traded such commodities with Agade and other Mesopotamian ports. Along with trade spread the institutions of early civilization. The states of Southeast Asia were based on notions of divine kingship imported along centuries-old trade routes from India. The constant interactions between highland and lowland Andean states led to complete interdependence and, after centuries of increasing competition and elaboration, to the Inka empire.

But everything depended on communication, for without efficient means of transporting bulk goods and of moving armies rapidly to trouble spots, the territory of an individual state will be highly flexible, especially at its borders. Old World civilizations had the benefit of the wheel and draft animals like donkeys, mules, and oxen. The domestication of the horse and the camel revolutionized warfare and caravan trade, while the downwind sailing ship was vital to riverine civilizations, like those of Egypt and Mesopotamia, and later to ocean trade routes. Nevertheless, larger states and empires, like that of the Romans, had constant problems with long-distance communications, despite an extensive road network. It was no coincidence that the Romans used ships as bulk carriers of foodstuffs wherever possible. In the New World, the ancient Americans had few draft animals and few sailing vessels. They relied on the backs of human beings, on llamas (in the Andes only), and on canoes and rafts.

But even with fast-moving horses, chariots, galleys, and sailing boats, communication was a constant problem, even for strong rulers with firm control of their domains. Communication difficulties were compounded as states grew in size and scale. Small city-states were confronted with problems of organization within the city and in a limited territory. Their primary concerns were the regulation of ethnic, ideological, and social conflicts. But the imperial civilizations, with their vast empires, dealt with a much wider world, to the point that communications became a major factor in daily life. The Inka maintained vast road networks with rest houses and teams of runners that linked the Andean highlands and lowlands. The Romans realized that efficient highways were vital if they were to be able to maintain order by the rapid deployment of legions to remote frontiers.

## Volatility

All of these problems led to uncertainty and to constant political and economic flux. Factionalism was a powerful factor in civilizations where power flowed from kin ties and fierce loyalties engendered by birth, distribution of tightly held wealth, and important official positions. Rulers rewarded loyalty with responsibility, often sowing the seeds of restless ambition in the heretofore most loyal provincial governors, priests, and viziers. For instance, despite the seeming linear serenity of pharaonic succession along the Nile, reality was much less comfortable, with constant plotting and maneuvering for position among close and not-so-close claimants to supreme power. Maya lords took enormous pains to legitimize their dynasties, to the extent of manipulating genealogies. Chinese rulers emphasized their close ties to revered and powerful mythic ancestors. But in all cases, rulers' longevity, and thus the longevity of the state, depended on a delicate balancing act: ensuring the loyalty of those who governed the provinces of their domains and collected riches in their name, while at the same time ensuring that tribute, food surpluses, and labor flowed to their courts, contributed by law-abiding subjects who perceived the advantage in supporting the state. Then, as now, supreme power was a powerful elixir. Civilizations enjoyed high prestige among envious neighbors, who sometimes vied to adopt similar trappings and sometimes tried to become the dominant power. But often the balancing act failed, and political chaos ensued until a new ruler rose to prominence.

Nowhere can one discern this more clearly than in Egypt, where the pharaohs were thought to control the bounty of the annual inundation. The collapse of the last Old Kingdom dynasty and the disorders at the end of the Middle Kingdom—which brought the alien Hyksos to Egypt—resulted in large part from cycles of drought, which undermined the myth of the infallible pharaoh and brought local leaders to political prominence. Some civilizations were the authors of their own demise. The Maya collapse in the southern lowlands around A.D. 900 may have resulted from droughts but also from overexploitation of the land and harsh demands from the elite. In this case, the entire apparatus of the state fell apart, cities were abandoned, and the people reverted to village farming. Even the largest preindustrial empires, like that of the Romans, collapsed when the inadequate and overstressed mechanisms of omnipotent, centralized government were no longer able to cope.

Volatile; in a constant state of flux; based on institutionalized social inequality and on force, slavery, and religious institutions that sometimes included human sacrifice—on the face of it, the preindustrial civilizations do not present an attractive portrait of humankind's ability to live in large, complex societies. Their endless cycles of rise and fall occur with such regularity that we are tempted to think of modern industrial civilization in similar cyclical terms. Does, then, the chronicle of preindustrial civilization in these pages—of volatility and ultimately of collapse—presage a similar fate for twenty-first-century civilization?

## The Stream of Time

"Today all that I then saw is overthrown and destroyed; nothing is left standing." The aged Bernal Diaz knew he had witnessed a climactic moment in history, the last spasms of a tradition of indigenous American civilization that extended deep into the remote past. The Aztec and Inka civilizations were the last preindustrial civilizations to become part of an expanding global economy. Their institutions belonged to a now-vanished world of ancient civilization, known to us from incomplete historical documents, sometimes from oral traditions, and above all from archaeological data. Only archaeology provides a scientific basis for understanding the preindustrial civilizations in true chronological and cultural perspective, against the enormous and global time scale of human evolution. Thousands of excavations and field surveys have revealed the astounding diversity of ancient civilizations and documented their constant volatility and their rapid rise and fall in the face of external and internal challenge. But with the Spanish conquest of Mexico and Peru, archaeological sources give way to richer ethnohistorical and documentary sources, which show how the volatility of civilization, that most complex of human societies, has continued into modern times.

By the time of the collapse of Inka civilization in the threat of Francisco Pizarro and his soldiers just under five centuries ago, world history had entered a new phase. At the middle of the sixteenth century, the Asian civilizations of China, Mughal India, and the Ottomans were perhaps the best organized and most powerful. All these civilizations flourished under highly centralized rule, with supreme rulers who insisted on uniformity in religion, commercial activities, and even in warfare. In this sense, they were similar to earlier, volatile preindustrial civilizations. But there was no supreme authority in Europe, where kingdoms and city-states fought one another constantly and vied for commercial superiority. This political and economic free-for-all stimulated military improvements and technological innovations on a scale unimagined in other, more centralized societies.

By 1500 Europe had entered into an upward spiral of economic growth and enhanced military capacity, which in time carried Western nations ahead of all other civilizations on earth. They reached out over the oceans with their long-range sailing vessels, armed with guns, and highly organized military tactics. And over the next five centuries, the unfolding story of civilization became a constant chronicle of rise and fall, of never-ending competition among what Yale University historian Paul Kennedy has called the "Great Powers"—civilizations on a far larger scale than anything seen before. Kennedy points out that like their preindustrial predecessors, these Great Powers were also subject to cycles of rise and fall, often triggered by circumstances beyond their control.

Both the nineteenth and twentieth centuries have seen constant political, economic, and social change. Great Powers competed for power and economic advantage, sometimes resorting to warfare to gain objectives unattainable by diplomacy. In this century, two world wars and uneasy decades of peace have seen bloodshed and genocide on unimaginably brutal scales, far greater than anything committed by Rome or any other early civilization. But just as in much earlier times, the international system is subject to constant changes. The ebb and flow of political and military events and the day-to-day deeds of leaders such as Adolf Hitler of Germany, Mao-tse-tung of China, or John F. Kennedy of the United States cause inevitable changes in the international system. But deeper transformations in the foundations of world power also make their way to the surface, especially in the economic sphere. The rise of Germany and Japan as major economic powers after World War II and the ongoing and rapid transformation of China into a dominant global trading partner are good examples. The competition among global civilizations, Great Powers if you will, often results in lengthy wars, such as those of this century. Productive economic forces have always played a vital role during the wars and after them, when new territorial orders emerge from the bloodshed and agony of battle. But the coming of peace does not mean that change will cease, for the differentiated growth among the Great Powers ensures that they will go on rising and falling relative to one another.

The reality of civilization means that to hold one's own against a rival, one must possess a flourishing economic base. This means a focus not on short-term goals like conquest but on productive investment for long-term growth. Since the earliest times, civilizations, preindustrial and industrial, have grappled with the age-old dilemmas of rise and fall—the shifting pace of productive growth, technological innovation, alterations in the balance of power among competing states, and the ever-rising cost of warfare and conquest. These developments cannot be controlled by one state or a single individual. As the great nineteenth-century German statesman Otto von Bismarck once remarked, all nations (civilizations) are adrift on a "stream of time." They navigate or have navigated on this stream with more or less skill and experience. As the record of the past shows, much depends on the quality of their leaders—on the leadership skills of divine kings, priest-rulers, emperors, and latterly politicians. But they grapple, and have grappled, with the constant verities that have faced the Sumerians, the Egyptians, the Harappans, the Maya, and every other early civilization on earth: the uneven pattern of economic growth, which causes some to become wealthier and stronger than others, and the competitive and sometimes dangerous world beyond their borders. Their leaders have always trodden a fine line between economic growth and the need for self-defense and the constant danger of overstraining their society. All too often, the inexorable stream of time has carried civilization after civilization from power and prosperity to precipitate collapse. The experiences of the world's earliest states do not necessarily mean that early twenty-first-century industrial civilization is in danger. But the record of the past shows that many of the same forces that beset our forebears still lurk as unpredictable rapids on the ever-flowing stream of time.

## Guide to Further Reading

Paul Kennedy, *The Rise and Fall of the Great Powers* (New York: Random House, 1987) offers a telling account of the shifting parameters of global power during the past five centuries. Eric Wolf, *Europe and the People without History* (Berkeley: University of California Press, 1982) and Immanuel Wallerstein, *The Modern World System* (London: Academic Press, 1974, 1980) are essential reading. Stephen K. Sanderson, ed., *Civilizations and World Systems* (Walnut Creek, CA: AltaMira Press, 1995) provides a critique of world systems approaches. Ahsan Jan Qaisir, *The Indian Response to European Technology and Culture A.D. 1498–1707* (New Delhi: Oxford University Press, 1982) offers an excellent account of the reasons why Mughal India adopted some features of European technology and rejected or ignored others.

# References


Birley, Robin. 1994. *Vindolanda's Roman Records.* Rev. ed. Greenhead, England: Roman Army Museum Publications.

Chang, K-C. 1980. *Shang Civilization.* New Haven, CT: Yale University Press.

———. 1986. *The Archaeology of Ancient China.* New Haven, CT: Yale University Press.

Diaz, Bernal. 1963. *The True Story of the Conquest of New Spain.* Trans. J. M. Cohen. Baltimore: Pelican Books.

Dibble, Charles E., and Arthur J. O. Anderson. 1950–1975. *Florentine Codex: General History of the Things of New Spain.* Salt Lake City: University of Utah Press.

Fedder, Robin. 1965. *Egypt: Land of the Valley.* London: Faber and Faber.

Keightley, David N. 1996. "Art, Ancestors, and the Origins of Writing in China." *Representations* 56: 68–95.

Kovak, J. 1989. *The Epic of Gilgamesh.* Palo Alto, CA: Stanford University Press, 1989.

Lattimore, Owen, trans. 1967. *The Odyssey.* New York: Harper & Row.

Layard, Austen Henry. 1849. *Nineveh and Its Remains.* London: John Murray.

———. 1853. *Nineveh and Babylon.* London: John Murray.

Lewis, Naphtali, and Meyer Reinhold, eds. 1990. *Roman Civilization: Selected Readings.* 3rd ed. 2 vols. New York: Columbia University Press.

Lichtheim, Miriam. 1973. *Ancient Egyptian Literature, A Book of Readings.* Vol. 1: *The Old and the Middle Kingdoms.* Berkeley: University of California Press.

———. 1976. *Ancient Egyptian Literature, A Book of Readings.* Vol. 2: *The New Kingdom.* Berkeley: University of California Press.

Linduff, Katheryne, and Yan Ge. 1990. "Sanxingdui: A New Bronze Age Site in Southwest China." *Antiquity* 64: 505–512.

Oates, Joan. 1979. *Babylon.* London: Thames and Hudson.

Prestcott, William. 1843. *The Conquest of Mexico.* New York: Harpers.

Pritchard, James B., ed. 1958. *The Ancient Near East.* Vol. 1: *An Anthology of Texts and Pictures.* Princeton, NJ: Princeton University Press.

Sanders, Nancy K., ed. 1960. *The Epic of Gilgamesh.* Harmondsworth, England: Penguin.

Schele, Linda, and David Freidel. 1990. *A Forest of Kings.* New York: William Morrow.

Schliemann, Heinrich. 1885. *Ilios.* London: John Murray.

# Credits

**Frontmatter** page xvii: Chris Scarre; page xviii: Brian M. Fagan.

**Chapter 1** page 4: Adapted from *World Civilizations: The Global Experience,* vol. 1, by Peter N. Stearns, Michael Adas, and Stuart B. Schwartz © 1996 HarperCollins College Publishers, Inc.; page 13: © Werner Forman/Art Resource, NY; page 15: Victoria and Albert Museum, Searight Collection. Photograph: Photographic Survey, Courtauld Institute of Art; page 20: Courtesy of the Library of Congress.

**Chapter 2** page 50: Nathaniel Issaacs/National Library of South Africa.

**Chapter 3** page 64: © Ronald Sheridan/Ancient Art & Architecture Collection LTD; page 71: Louvre, Paris, France. The Bridgeman Art Library; page 74: Adapted from *Cultural Atlas of Mesopotamia and the Ancient Near East* by Michael Roaf © 1990 Facts on File and *The Archaeology of Mesopotamia* by Seton Lloyd © 1978 Thames & Hudson; page 76: Adapted from *Heartland of Cities* by Robert McC. Adams © 1981 University of Chicago Press; page 77: © Ronald Sheridan/Ancient Art & Architecture Collection Ltd.; page 80: Adapted from "How Many Sumerians per Hectare?—Probing the Anatomy of an Early City," *Cambridge Archaeological Journal,* 4, by Nicholas Postgate, © 1994 McDonald Institute for Archaeological Research; page 83: Adapted from *Cultural Atlas of Mesopotamia and the Ancient Near East* by Michael Roaf © 1990 Facts on File; page 84: Adapted from *The Uruk World System: The Dynamics of Expansion of Early Mesopotamian Civilization* by Guillermo Algaze © 1993 Chicago University Press; page 89: British Museum, London. The Bridgeman Art Library; page 90: Adapted from *Ur of the Chaldes* by Sir Leonard Wooley and P. R. S. Moorey, ed., © 1982 Barnes & Noble; page 98: Adapted from *Cultural Atlas of Mesopotamia and the Ancient Near East* by Michael Roaf © 1990 Facts on File.

**Chapter 4** page 104: O. Louis Mazzatenta/NGS Image Collection; page 117 (left) Pharaonic, 1st dynasty, c. 3100–2890 BC. Nekhen (Hierakonlolis). Greywacke, H-63, W-42cms. The Egyptian Museum, Cairo. © Werner Forman/Art Resource, NY; page 117 (right): Egyptian Museum, Cairo, Egypt. © Erich Lessing/Art Resource, NY; page 118: Adapted from *People of the Earth: An Introduction to World History* by Brian Fagan © 1995 Lindbriar Corporation; page 124: Robert Harding Picture Library Limited; page 127 (top): Will and Deni McIntyre/Photo Researchers, Inc.; page 127 (bottom): Adam Sylvester/Photo Researchers, Inc.; page 128: John Ross/Robert Harding Picture Library Limited; page 137: Hirmer Fotoarchiv, Munich, Germany; page 142 (top): Trans-World Photos/SuperStock, Inc.; page 142 (bottom): Agricultural scene. Wall painting from the tomb of Mennah, scribe of the fields and estate inspector under Pharaoh Thutmosis (18th dynasty). Tomb of Mennah, Deir el-Medina, West Thebes, Thebes. Archaeological Site, Luxor-Thebes, Egypt. © Photograph by Erich Lessing. Art Resource.

**Chapter 5** page 147: © Ronald Sheridan/Ancient Art & Architecture Collection LTD; page 156 (top): Harappa.com; page 156 (bottom): © Ashik Arbani/Ancient Art & Architecture Collection Ltd.; page 157: Greater London Council; page 158: Getty Images, Inc.; page 160: Robert Harding/Robert Harding Picture Library Limited; page 164 (left and right): Professor Gregory L. Possehl.

**Chapter 6** page 170: Wang Lu/China Stock; page 181: Adapted from *Civilizations: Past and Present* by T. Walter Wallbank et al., © 1996 HarperCollins College Publishers, Inc; page 184: Adapted from *Journal of Field Archaeology,* vol. 18 Summer 1991; page 185 (top): Adapted from *China, Korea, and Japan: The Rise of Civilization in East Asia* by G. L. Barnes © 1992 Thames & Hudson; page 185 (bottom): Adapted from *Archaeology of Ancient China* by Kwang-Chi Chang © 1986 Yale University Press; page 186 (top): Adapted from *Archaeology of Ancient China* by Kwang-Chi Chang © 1986 Yale University Press; page 186 (bottom): Adapted from *China, Korea, and Japan: The Rise of Civilization in East Asia* by G. L. Barnes © 1992 Thames & Hudson; page 191: Adapted from *Ancient China: Art and Archaeology* by Jessica Rawson © 1980 British Museum; page 192 (top): Adapted from *Archaeology of Ancient China* by Kwang-Chi Chang © 1986 Yale University Press; page 192 (bottom): Adapted from *China, Korea, and Japan: The Rise of Civilization in East Asia* by G. L. Barnes © 1993 Thames & Hudson.

**Chapter 7** page 200: photo Josephine Powell; page 207: Adapted from *Atlas of Ancient Archaeology* by Jacquelta Hawkes © 1974 Heinemann; page 211: Adapted from *Atlas of Ancient Archaeology* by Jacquelta Hawkes © 1974 Heinemann; page 215: Adapted from *Ancient Civilizations and Ruins of Turkey* by E. Akurgal © 1978 Haset Kirabevi; page 216: Adapted from *Ancient Civilizations and Ruins of Turkey* by E. Akurgal © 1978 Haset Kirabevi; page 217: Bronwyn Douglas/Professor J. Nicholas Postgate.

**Chapter 8** page 225: Chris Scarre; page 226: Adapted from *The Early Alphabet* by John F. Kealy © 1990 British Museum Publications; page 227: Courtesy of Chris Scarre; page 228: Adapted from *The Phoenicians* by D. B. Harden © 1971 Penguin Books; page 229: Mansell Collection/TimePix; page 232: © R. Sheridan/Ancient Art & Architecture Collections Ltd.; page 233: Adapted from *World Civilizations: The Global Experience,* vol. 1, by Peter N. Stearns, Michael Adas, and Stuart B. Schwartz © 1996 HarperCollins College Publishers, Inc.; page 234: Chris Scarre; page 237: © Julian Worker/Ancient Art & Architecture Collection Ltd.; page 238: Adapted from *Babylon* by Joan Oates © 1986 Thames & Hudson; page 241: Maynard Owen Williams/NGS Image Collection.

**Chapter 9** page 246: *The Serpent Goddess of Knossos.* Archaeological Museum, Heraklion, Crete, Greece. © Nimatallah/Art Resource, NY; page 248: Adapted from *Societies and Cultures in World History* by Mark Kishlansky et al. © 1995 HarperCollins College Publishers, Inc.; page 260: National Archaeology Museum, Athens, Greece/Giraudon/Art Resource, NY; page 261: Greek National Tourism Organization; page 263: Adapted from *The Aegean Bronze Age* by Oliver Dickenson © 1994 Cambridge University Press; page 264: Chris Scarre; page 268: Institute of Nautical Archaeology/D. Frey; page 270: Chris Scarre.

**Chapter 10** page 276: Adapted from *Burial and Ancient Society: The Rise of the Greek City-State* by Ian Morris © 1987 Cambridge University Press; page 278: Adapted from *World Civilizations: The Global Experience,* vol. 1, by Peter N. Stearns, Michael Adas, and Stuart B. Schwartz © 1996 HarperCollins College Publishers, Inc.; page 282: Chris Scarre; page 283: Adapted from *Etruscan Italy: An Archaeological History* by Nigel Spivey and Simon Stoddart © 1990 Batsford; page 290 (left): © Ronald Sheridan/Ancient Art & Architecture Collection Ltd.; page 294: George Holton/Photo Researchers, Inc.; page 252 (top): Ancient Art & Architecture Collection; page 252 (bottom): Chris Scarre; page 297: Courtesy of Chris Scarre; page 299: Adapted from Lisa C. Nevett, *House and Society in the Ancient Greek World* reprinted with the permission of Cambridge University Press.

**Chapter 11** page 305: © Ronald Sheridan/Ancient Art & Architecture Collection LTD; page 315: Adapted from *The Roman World,* vol. 2, by John Wacher, ed., © 1987 Routeledge; page 316: Oliver Benn/Getty Images Inc.; page 318: Adapted from *Atlas of the Roman World* by T. J. Cornell and J. Matthews © 1982 Phaidon; page 319: Chris Scarre; page 320: Chris Scarre; page 321: Adapted from *Atlas of the Roman World* by T. J. Cornell and J. Matthews © 1982 Phaidon; page 323: Adapted from *Atlas of Classical Archaeology* by M. Finley, ed., © 1977 Chatto & Windus; page 324: Villa of the Mysteries, Pompeii/A. K. G., Berlin/Superstock; page 325: Adapted from *Roman Imperial Architecture* by J. B. Ward-Perkins © 1981 Penguin Books; page 326 (bottom): Chris Scarre; page 328: Adapted from *Amphorae and the Roman Economy* by D. P. S. Peacock and D. F. Williams © 1986 Longman; page 329: Adapted from *Amphorae and the Roman*

*Economy* by D. P. S. Peacock and D. F. Williams © 1986 Longman; page 331: © The Vindolanda Trust.

**Chapter 12** page 339: © J. Stevens/Ancient Art & Architecture Collection LTD; page 341: Adapted from *World Civilizations: The Global Experience,* vol. 1, by Peter N. Stearns, Michael Adas, and Stuart B. Schwartz © 1996 HarperCollins College Publishers, Inc.; page 346: Professor Stuart Tyson Smith; page 350: Timothy Kendall; page 354: Peter Shinnie; page 358: Werner Forman Archive/Art Resource, NY.

**Chapter 13** page 372: Eliot Elisofon/TimePix; page 373: Greg Davis/TimePix; page 375: www.corbis.com/Michael S. Yamash.

**Chapter 14** page 380: Wang Lu/ChinaStock Photo Library; page 383: Adapted from "Early Urbanization in the Eastern Zhou in China (770–221 B.C.): An Archaeological View," *Antiquity,* by Shen Chen © 1994; page 384: The Ancient Art & Architecture Collection Ltd.; page 387 (top): Adapted from *China, Korea, and Japan: The Rise of Civilization in East Asia* by G. L. Barnes © 1993 Thames & Hudson; page 387 (bottom): Gavin Hellier/Robert Harding Picture Library Limited; page 389: Adapted from *World Civilizations: The Global Experience,* vol. 1, by Peter N. Stearns, Michael Adas, and Stuart B. Schwartz © 1996 HarperCollins College Publishers, Inc.; page 390: Adapted from *Ancient China* by Jessica Rawson © 1980 British Museum; page 391: Wang Lu/ChinaStock; page 394: Adapted from *Han Civilization* by Wang Zhongshu © 1982 Yale University Press; page 396: Jeffrey Newbury; page 401: Courtesy of Chris Scarre.

**Chapter 15** page 406: Rollout photograph© Justin Kerr 1980; page 408: Adapted from *People of the Earth: An Introduction to World History* by Brian Fagan © 1995 Lindbriar Corporation; page 409: Adapted from *People of the Earth: An Introduction to World History* by Brian Fagan © 1995 Lindbriar Corporation; page 413: Boltin Picture Library; page 414: Robert & Linda Mitchell Photography; page 418: Ray Matheny; page 420: Adapted from *The New Archaeology and the Ancient Maya* by Jeremy Sabloff © 1990 Scientific American Library; page 426: Robert Frerck/Odyssey Productions, Inc.; page 431: Robert Frerck/Odyssey Productions, Inc.; page 433: Courtesy of the Carnegie Institution of Washington and The Peabody Museum of Archaeology and Ethnology, Harvard University; page 434: Courtesy of the Carnegie Institution of Washington and The Peabody Museum of Archaeology and Ethnology, Harvard University; page 439: Ulrike Welsch/Photo Researchers, Inc.; page 441: Carnegie Institution of Washington.

**Chapter 16** page 444: Dumbarton Oaks Research Library and Collection, Washington, D.C.; page 446: Adapted from *People of the Earth: An Introduction to World History* by Brian Fagan © 1995 Lindbriar Corporation; page 448: Robert Harding Picture Library Limited; page 451: Robert Frerck/Odyssey Productions, Inc.; page 452: Lesley Newhart; page 458: Lesley Newhart; page 460: Neg./Transparency no. 326597. Courtesy Dept. of Library Services, American Museum of Natural History; page 461: Robert Frerck/Odyssey/Chicago; page 463: Library of Congress; page 465: The Bodleian Library, University of Oxford, MS. Arch. Selden A. I. Folio 60; detail.

**Chapter 17** page 472: Adapted from *People of the Earth: An Introduction to World History* by Brian Fagan © 1995 Lindbriar Corporation; page 473: Adapted from *People of the Earth: An Introduction to World History* by Brian Fagan © 1995 Lindbriar Corporation; page 479: Jeffrey Quilter.

**Chapter 18** page 494: Dumbarton Oaks Research Library and Collection, Washington, D.C.; page 496 (top): Photo by Susan Einstein. Courtesy UCLA Fowler Museum of Cultural History; page 496 (bottom): Painting by Percy Fiestas. Courtesy Bruning Archaeological Museum, Lambayeque; page 501: Robert Frerck/Odyssey/Chicago; page 503: © Hubert Stadler/Corbis; page 507: M. E. Moseley/Anthro-Photo File; page 509: Mark Keller/SuperStock, Inc; page 512: Photo Researchers, Inc.; page 513: Adalberto Rios/Getty Images, Inc./PhotoDisc, Inc.

**Chapter 19** page 515: Bruno Barbey/Magnum Photos, Inc.

# Index

Page references to figures are in *italics.*

## J



## K

## L

## M

## N

## O

## Q

## R

## S

## U



## V

## W



## X



## Y

## Z